AF262883

ATHENA'S SISTERS

Athena's Sisters transforms our understanding of classical Athenian culture and society by approaching its institutions – kinship, slavery, the economy, social organisation – from women's perspectives. It argues that texts on dedications and tombstones set up by women were frequently authored by those women. This significant body of women's writing offers direct insights into their experiences, values, and emotions. With men often absent, women redefined the boundaries of the family in dialogue with patriarchal legal frameworks. Beyond male social and political structures, women defined their identities and relationships through their own institutions. By focusing on women's engagement with other women, rather than their relationships to men, this timely and necessary book reveals the richness and dynamism of women's lives and their remarkable capacity to shape Athenian society and history.

KATHERINE BACKLER began her academic career as an Examination Fellow at All Souls College (2016–22) and was then Career Development Fellow in Ancient History at Trinity College, Oxford (2022–5). She is now Lecturer in Ancient History at the University of Leeds.

ATHENA'S SISTERS

Reclaiming the Women of Classical Athens

KATHERINE BACKLER

University of Leeds

CAMBRIDGE
UNIVERSITY PRESS

Shaftesbury Road, Cambridge CB2 8EA, United Kingdom

One Liberty Plaza, 20th Floor, New York, NY 10006, USA

477 Williamstown Road, Port Melbourne, VIC 3207, Australia

314–321, 3rd Floor, Plot 3, Splendor Forum, Jasola District Centre, New Delhi – 110025, India

103 Penang Road, #05–06/07, Visioncrest Commercial, Singapore 238467

Cambridge University Press is part of Cambridge University Press & Assessment, a department of the University of Cambridge.

We share the University's mission to contribute to society through the pursuit of education, learning and research at the highest international levels of excellence.

www.cambridge.org
Information on this title: www.cambridge.org/9781009672320

DOI: 10.1017/9781009672290

First published 2025

Cover illustration: © Katie Idle

Printed in Great Britain by CPI Group (UK) Ltd, Croydon CR0 4YY

A catalogue record for this publication is available from the British Library

Library of Congress Cataloging-in-Publication Data
NAMES: Backler, Katherine author
TITLE: Athena's sisters : reclaiming the women of classical Athens /
Katherine Alexandra Lauren Backler, Trinity College, Oxford.
DESCRIPTION: United Kingdom ; New York, NY : Cambridge University Press,
2025. | Includes bibliographical references and index
IDENTIFIERS: LCCN 2025019168 (print) | LCCN 2025019169 (ebook) |
ISBN 9781009672320 hardback | ISBN 9781009672306 paperback |
ISBN 9781009672290 ebook
SUBJECTS: LCSH: Women – Greece – Athens – History – To 500 | Sex role – Greece – Athens |
Athens (Greece) – Social conditions | Greece – Civilization – To 146 B.C.
CLASSIFICATION: LCC HQ1134 .B175 2025 (print) | LCC HQ1134 (ebook) |
DDC 305.40938/5–dc23/eng/20250615
LC record available at https://lccn.loc.gov/2025019168
LC ebook record available at https://lccn.loc.gov/2025019169

ISBN 978-1-009-67232-0 Hardback

For Claire Hall,
πιστῆς ἡδείας τε χάριν φιλότητος.

Contents

Figures

Tables

Acknowledgements

Appropriately for a book chiefly concerned with relationships, producing *Athena's Sisters* was far from a solitary exercise. I wrote most of the thesis on which the book is based in company, with my 'writing buddy' Xavier Buxton; at writing sessions organised by Emily Troscianko through the Baillie Gifford Writing Programme; at the Academic Writing Group run by Alice Kelly; and with various friends, particularly Claire Hall. Warmest thanks to all of them.

Equally appropriately, I was fortunate enough to have not one brilliant, supportive, invested, clear-sighted, constructive supervisor, but three: Josephine Crawley Quinn, Teresa Morgan, and Rosalind Thomas. I left every meeting with them energised, excited, and equipped to make dramatic improvements and have continued to benefit from their generosity and encouragement since. At a much earlier stage, my undergraduate tutor in ancient history, John Ma, shaped my thinking and being as an historian, for which I sincerely thank him. My thesis examiners, Peter Thonemann and Lin Foxhall, have been truly remarkable in their generosity with their (very limited) time and (seemingly unlimited) talent. Both read, commented in detail on, and vastly improved drafts at several stages; in between, they answered questions, quelled qualms, and offered devoted support with various other aspects of my work. Peter deserves special thanks for making me a better teacher as well as a better researcher and writer. I am also grateful to the anonymous readers at Cambridge University Press who engaged with my manuscript in careful detail and offered some very constructive suggestions, to my editors Michael Sharp and Katie Idle for being consistently helpful, patient, and encouraging, and to Kathleen Fearn for her meticulous and thoughtful copyediting. Additional thanks to Katie Idle for the beautiful cover art.

I would never have embarked on this project at all had I not been awarded an Examination Fellowship at All Souls College. I am profoundly grateful to the Warden and Fellows for granting me that opportunity, and to the entire college community for their kindness, wit, stories, ideas, and respect for my work, which helped me respect it too. I am indebted to my college advisor, Catherine Morgan, for her generous support and pragmatic advice, and for introducing me to modern Athens, which has been a joy. Most of all I am grateful to the other Examination Fellows. It is such a privilege, and such *fun*, to know them. I am also deeply grateful for the support, encouragement, and good cheer of all my colleagues at Trinity College, particularly Gail Trimble and Rebecca Bullard. Meanwhile, practical help from Sue Walters at All Souls and Alberto Garzoni, Sophie Baptista, Bhadrajee Hewage, and James Green at Trinity have made the whole process much easier.

I am grateful for the warmth and generosity of myriad people who answered questions, shared material, and helped me think better. Among these were Ammouna Alkhalaf, Abigail Allan, Luigi Battezzato, Aneurin Ellis-Evans, Caitlin Clerkin, Emily Clifford, Catherine Conybeare, Jaime Curbera, Bruno Currie, Santanu Das, Peter Davidson, Beate Dignas, Bela Dimova, Olivia Elder, Florence Felsheim, Elizabeth Foley, Constanze Güthenke, Max Harris, Wolfram Hoepfner, Sally Humphreys, Theodora Jim, Eddie Jones, Juliane Kerkhecker, Mark de Kreij, Stephen Lambert, Jessica Lamont, Leah Lazar, Dmitri Levitin, Sian Lewis, Lloyd Llewellyn-Jones, Nino Luraghi, Dan-el Padilla Peralta, Robert Pitt, Christine Plastow, Lucia Prauscello, April Pudsey, John Ritzema, Carrie Sawtell, Hannah Smyth, Jane Stevenson, Claire Taylor, Sally Waite, Marianne Weldon, Frederick Wilmot-Smith, Aleksander Wolicki, and George Woudhuysen. There will also be people I have forgotten but whose contributions remain in the memory of the book.

Particular thanks are due to the librarians at All Souls, Gabrielle Mathews and Gaye Morgan, for helping me find material with patience and good humour, and to Tania Gerousi and Vicki Tzavara at the British School at Athens, for working hard to arrange permits for me. Thanks also to the archaeologists and staff at the Epigraphic Museum, the National Archaeological Museum, the Agora Museum, and the Canellopoulos Museum. Working with the objects in these museums has been one of the greatest privileges of the process. I am also grateful to staff at various museums across the world for providing image permissions, especially to those who granted them free of charge: the Acropolis Museum, Bryn Mawr's Art and Artifacts collections, the Canellopoulos Museum, the Chau Chak Wing Museum, the Getty Museum, the Harvard Art Museum, and the Metropolitan Museum of Art.

All this time, I have been sustained by the prayers and kindness of the Assumption Sisters at Twickenham, whose unconventional lives were an early inspiration for the project; the communities at the Oxford University Catholic Chaplaincy and the Blackfriars 9.30 Mass; and my precious Lectio Divina group. I have been encouraged and supported by wise and helpful friends further along their academic and career paths, particularly Clare Bucknell, Rey Conquer, William Ghosh, and Claire Hall, and by numerous other friends who have brought great joy to my life. I owe enormous thanks to my wonderful, patient, generous *synoikoi*, Elizabeth Crabtree, Maria Czepiel, and Cynthia Liu; it is such a delight to come home to you all. I am grateful to Rebekah Wallace and Cynthia again for lovely patterns of shared work and shared fun, and to Ralph Morley, singularly kind, patient, brilliant, and hilarious, who read through a draft with characteristic generosity and acuity, and who cared about Artemis the reed-seller and Soteris and her *miltos* almost as much as I did. I am especially grateful to my parents, Ann Edes and Gary Backler, who have been fantastically supportive from the very first, in concrete ways (reading and commenting on drafts; helping with seemingly interminable image permissions) and in subtler but more important ones – I am a better writer but also a much better person because of your teaching. Special thanks to my beloved sister Emily, and to Katie and Betsy, who have taught me a great deal, and shaped this book more than they know.

My deepest gratitude is to Claire Hall, my very best friend, who every day is kind, generous, supportive, affectionate, patient, wise, brilliant, and ridiculously funny. My life is immeasurably richer for knowing and loving her, and being known and loved by her in return. And I am grateful first, last, and above all, to God, the great Author.

Author's Note

For ease of reference, I refer to most texts by the name that is most familiar in current anglophone scholarship, whether that be English (*Laws, Frogs*), Latinised Greek (*Ecclesiazusae, Choephori*), or transliterated Greek (*Athenaion politeia, Dyskolos*). I anglicise the names of authors and some gods but transliterate the names of historical personages and literary characters, with one or two exceptions where a transliteration would be obstructive (e.g. Homer's Penelopeia becomes Penelope). I do not pretend at consistency. Key Greek words are transliterated and rendered into lemmata (first person singular, present indicative for verbs; nominative singular for nouns; masculine nominative singular for adjectives) wherever it seemed helpful. When abbreviating authors and texts for reference, I use the *Oxford Classical Dictionary* conventions, except for [Demosthenes] 59 (*Against Neaira*), now attributed to Apollodorus, which I abbreviate as Ap. *Neaira*, and the abbreviations in the List of Abbreviations, which are not included in the *Oxford Classical Dictionary* conventions. For papyrological texts, I use the University of Chicago Library sigla, online at https://papyri.info/docs/checklist. Unless otherwise stated, all dates are BC and all translations my own.

Abbreviations

AB	Austin, C., and G. Bastianini (eds.) (2002). *Posidippi Pellaei quae supersunt omnia* (LED: Milan).
Agora xxi	Lang, M. (1976). *The Athenian Agora* xxi. *Graffiti and Dipinti* (American School of Classical Studies at Athens: Princeton, NJ).
Agora xvii	Bradeen, D. W. (1974). *The Athenian Agora* xvii. *Inscriptions: The Funerary Monuments* (American School of Classical Studies at Athens: Princeton, NJ).
APF	Davies, J. K. (1971). *Athenian Propertied Families 600–300* BC (Clarendon Press: Oxford).
Bergk	Bergk, W. T. (ed.) (1915). *Poetae Lyrici Graeci, 4is. Poetae Melici: Vol. 2* (Teubner: Leipzig).
BM	British Museum, London.
Carey	Carey, C. (ed.) (2007). *Lysiae orationes cum fragmentis*, 2nd ed. (Oxford University Press: Oxford).
CAT	Clairmont, C. W., and A. Conze (eds.) (1993). *Classical Attic Tombstones* (Akanthus: Kilchberg).
CEG (1)	Hansen, P. A. (ed.) (1983). *Carmina epigraphica Graeca saeculorum VIII–V a. Chr. n.* (De Gruyter: Berlin).
CEG (2)	Hansen, P. A. (ed.) (1989). *Carmina epigraphica Graeca saeculi IV a. Chr. n.* (De Gruyter: Berlin).
CIL	*Corpus Inscriptionum Latinarum* (1863–). (Berlin-Brandenburgische Akademie der Wissenschaften: Berlin).
Darmezin 1999	Darmezin, L. (1999). *Les affranchissements par consécration en Béotie et dans le monde grec hellénistique* (Association pour la Diffusionde la Recherche sur l'Antiquité: Nancy).

DGE	Adrados, F. R., and E. Gangutia Elícegui (eds.) (1980–). *Diccionario griego–español* (Consejo Superior de Investigaciones Científicas, Instituto Antonio de Nebrija: Madrid). Online at http://dge .cchs.csic.es/xdge/.
DTA	Wünsch, R. (ed.) (1897). *Defixionum tabellae Atticae* (Reimer: Berlin).
DVC	Dakarēs, S., I. Vokotopoulou, and A. P. Christidēs (eds.) (2013). *Τὰ χρηστήρια ἐλάσματα τῆς Δωδώνης τῶν ἀνασκαφῶν Δ. Ευαγγελίδη* (Η εν Αθήναις Αρχαιολογική Εταιρεία: Athens).
EM	Epigraphic Museum, Athens.
FD	Bourguet, É. et al. (eds.) (1929–). *Fouilles de Delphes,* III*: Épigraphie* (De Boccard: Paris).
FGrH	Jacoby, F. (ed.) (1923–58). *Die Fragmente der griechischen Historiker* (Brill: Berlin and Leiden). https:// scholarlyeditions.brill.com/bnjo.
GE	Clairmont, C. W. (ed.) (1970). *Gravestone and Epigram: Greek Memorials from the Archaic and Classical Period* (Verlag P.V. Zabern: Mainz on Rhine).
I.Délos	Durrbach. F., et al. (eds.) (1926–50). *Inscriptions de Délos* (Académie des inscriptions et belles-lettres: Paris).
I.Eleusis	Clinton, K. (2005). *Eleusis, the Inscriptions on Stone: Documents of the Sanctuary of the Two Goddesses and Public Documents of the Deme, Volume 1A (Text)* (Archaeological Society at Athens: Athens).
IG	*Inscriptiones Graecae* (1903–). (Berlin-Brandenburgische Akademie der Wissenschaften: Berlin).
IGASMG IV	Arena, R. (ed.) (1996). *Iscrizioni greche arcaiche di Sicilia e Magna Grecia, Vol. 4: Inscrizioni delle colonie achee* (Edizioni dell'Orso: Alessandria).
Jensen	Jensen, C. C. (ed.) (1917). *Hyperidis Orationes sex cum ceterarum fragmentis post F. Blass* (Teubner: Leipzig).
Kenyon	Kenyon, F. G. (ed.) (1906). *Hyperidis orationes et fragmenta* (Clarendon Press: Oxford).
Kock	Kock, T. (ed.) (1880–8). *Comicorum Atticorum Fragmenta* (Teubner: Leipzig).

LGPN	*Lexicon of Greek Personal Names* (1987–) (Clarendon Press: Oxford). Updated online at https://www.lgpn.ox.ac.uk.
LGPN ii	Osborne, M. J., and S. G. Byrne (eds.) (1994). *Lexicon of Greek Personal Names, vol.* ii *(Attica)* (Clarendon Press: Oxford). Updated online at https://athnames.org/.
Lindos ii	Blinkenberg, C., and K. F. Kinch (eds.) (1941). *Lindos: Fouilles et recherches, Vol.* ii. *Inscriptions* (De Gruyter: Berlin).
LSCG	Sokolowski, F. (1969). *Lois sacrées des cités grecques* (E. de Boccard: Paris).
LSJ	Liddell, H. G., and R. Scott (1996). *Greek–English Lexicon*, 9th ed., revised by H. S. Jones (Clarendon Press: Oxford).
Mette	Mette, H. J. (ed.) (1982–5). 'Euripides: die Bruchstücke', *Lustrum*, 23/4 (1982); 25 (1983): 5–14; 27 (1985): 23–6.
NAM	National Archaeological Museum, Athens (often NM in other publications).
Nauck	Nauck, A. (ed.) (1880). *Tragicorum Graecorum Fragmenta*^{2} (Teubner: Leipzig), reprinted in 1964 with a supplement by B. Snell (Olms Verlag: Hildesheim).
OR	Osborne, R., and P. J. Rhodes (eds.) (2017). *Greek Historical Inscriptions, 478–404* BC (Oxford University Press: Oxford).
Pendrick	Pendrick, G. J. (ed.) (2002). *Antiphon the Sophist: The Fragments* (Cambridge University Press: Cambridge).
RA	*Revue Archéologique*; specifically J. Frel (1968). 'Quelque sculpteurs attiques au Musée du Louvre', *Revue Archéologique*, 1 (Études de sculpture antique offertes à Jean Charbonneaux, 1): 155–60.
RO	Rhodes, P. J., and R. Osborne (eds.) (2003, rev. 2007). *Greek Historical Inscriptions, 404–323* BC (Oxford University Press: Oxford).
SEG	*Supplementum Epigraphicum Graecum* (1923–) (Gieben: Amsterdam).
SEMA	Bardanē, V. N., and G. K. Papadopoulou (eds.) (2006). *Συμπλήρωμα των επιτύμβιων μνημείων της*

Ἀττικῆς (Ἡ ἐν Ἀθήναις Ἀρχαιολογικὴ Ἑταιρεία: Athens).

SGD — Jordan, D. R. (1985). 'A Survey of Greek Defixiones Not Included in the Special Corpora', *Greek, Roman, and Byzantine Studies*, 26: 151–97.

SGDI — Bechtel, F., H. Collitz, R. C. Meister, and A. Bezzenberger (eds.) (1884–1915). *Sammlung der griechischen Dialekt-Inschriften* (Vandenhoeck & Ruprecht: Göttingen).

Voigt — Voigt, E.-M. (ed.) (1971). *Sappho et Alcaeus: Fragmenta* (Polak & van Gennep: Amsterdam).

Introduction

A Girl in the Girl-Goddess' City

In around 434, as work was being finished on the Parthenon, temple of the Maiden Goddess, a baby girl was born in Kollytos, an urban neighbourhood south-west of the Akropolis on which Athens' dazzling new temple stood. We will call her *Diognete*. (Figure I.1 offers an idealised image of the early years of an Athenian girl.) In *Diognete*'s toddlerhood, Sparta invaded Attica, heralding the outbreak of the Peloponnesian War in 431. Athens' leading political and military strategist, Perikles, persuaded the Athenians to evacuate the countryside and bring its inhabitants into the city, its port Peiraeus, and the narrow strip of land within the defensive Long Walls that linked the two. The consequent overcrowding massively worsened the devastating plague that struck the following year.[1]

This little girl was her parents' only surviving child. Under a system formalised by the early sixth-century lawgiver Solon to prevent the disintegration of family estates, girls without brothers became *epiklēroi*, a term which broadly means 'girls attached to the estate'. An *epiklēros* was legally required to be married to her nearest available paternal relative, her father's brother having first claim,[2] so that she could give birth to a son or sons in that marriage to inherit her father's estate, since her father could not pass it directly to a son of his own.[3] Accordingly, in about 419, assuming she first married at fourteen, *Diognete* was married to her paternal uncle, Diodotos, a wealthy shipping

---

[1] I have calculated *Diognete*'s approximate birth year by counting backwards, with *APF* 3885 (p. 151), from her first husband's death in 409 when her eldest son was about ten, and assuming she first married at fourteen, the normal age of marriage for *epiklēroi* ([Arist.] *Ath. pol.* 56.7; Lys. 32.4, 8). *Epiklēroi* or not, Athenian girls from propertied families like *Diognete*'s were married from fourteen or fifteen; others were married from their late teens: Ingalls 2001. For the evacuation and the plague, see Thuc. 2.13–17, 47–54. For the house in Kollytos, see Lys. 32.14.
[2] Harrison 1968: 23.   [3] For bibliography on the *epiklēros*, see Cudjoe 2010: 191, fn. 423.

I

Figure I.1 Attic red-figure *khous* (plural *khoes*, small pots often given to children on the Dionysiac festival day of the same name, which was part of the Anthesteria festival), c. 420. The pot shows a female toddler playing with a dog. Athens, National Archaeological Museum NAM A1322 © Hellenic Ministry of Culture.

investor in his thirties who lived in Peiraieus.[4] Even for girls who were not *epiklēroi*, marriage to one's uncle was common in classical Attica, at least among propertied families.[5] *Diognete* and Diodotos had three surviving children, two boys and a girl. In summer 409, after they had been married for about ten years, Diodotos was called up as a hoplite, a heavily armed citizen infantryman, to serve with the general Thrasyllos in his campaign in the East Aegean during the Ionian War.[6] *Diognete* never saw him again.

Diognete was not this woman's real name. We do not know her real name, because in classical Athens it was considered disrespectful for men

---

[4] [Arist.] *Ath. pol.* 56.7; Lys. 32.4, 8. See fn. 1 for likely age at first marriage.

[5] See e.g. Dem. 44.10 (paternal uncle); 59.2 (maternal uncle); 41.3 (maternal uncle and father's adoptive son); 59.22 (maternal uncle, a metic: see Kapparis 1999 *ad loc.*), noted by Carey 1989: 166, 212.

[6] Lys. 32.4–5; Xen. *Hell.* 1.2. The Ionian War, characterised by naval warfare around the Ionian coast and islands, is also referred to as the Dekeleian War, after the Spartan occupation of Dekeleia in northern Attica.

publicly to refer to women by name. When speaking about living women of citizen status (i.e. women born to two married Athenian parents), men typically used a periphrasis, identifying the woman by her relationship to a named male relative:[7] 'daughter/wife/sister of [man's name]'. This has caused problems for writing histories of women. In this book, I offer a new solution. Rather than referring to historical women whose names are suppressed or lost by their relationship to a man (as the sources and most scholars do), or by a number (as in one study of Athenian widows),[8] I assign them names of their own. These are most likely not the names they held in life, but historically plausible 'imagined' names, which stand in for the names they once had and used themselves. Though Athenian conventions mean we rarely learn the names of women known to us only through lawsuits, in comedy women address each other by name and typically refer to themselves and other women by name even when addressing men.[9] Women had their own names inscribed on public or semi-public dedications; their names were published in sanctuary inventories of dedicators;[10] dead women were named on their tombstones.[11] Where the name of one of the women I discuss has been lost or suppressed, I have chosen her a name from those attested in the *Lexicon of Greek Personal Names* (*LGPN*) for fifth- and fourth-century Attica. There is not enough evidence to speak confidently about 'naming patterns' for women as we do for men,[12] but girls were often given names of female relatives (particularly paternal grandmothers, but also mothers), or names based on those of the men in the family.[13] Therefore, where possible, a woman's assigned name is based on that of a known natal relative. Assigned names are given in italics to distinguish them from cases where a woman's name is known from the evidence.[14]

---

[7] Oratory: Schaps 1977; comedy: Sommerstein 2009.

[8] Hunter 1989. Gagarin 2001 calls *Diognete* '"D's daughter" or "D. d." (Didi) for short' (p. 162), which does not adequately counter the text's androcentricism.

[9] Sommerstein 2009; Willi 2003: 186–7 and Dickey 1996: 245–6 discuss women's use of affectionate terms, particularly for each other. At Ar. *Eccl.* 41–51, women identify some women with mononyms (as at *Lys.* 321–3) and some by the names of male relatives without the women's names; this is possibly because a man's name would need to be given in order to make a joke about him, but the name of a real public figure's wife would not have been said on-stage, if Aristophanes even knew it.

[10] This complicates the assertion that 'respectable' women could only be referred to by name if absolutely necessary, or dead.

[11] The convention was therefore less extreme than in modern Afghanistan (even before its recapture by the Taliban): see e.g. Esfandiari 2017, Joya 2017, Mashal 2017.

[12] On which see Humphreys 2018: 271, 276–84.   [13] Humphreys 2018: 271–3, 285–7.

[14] Compare Boehringer *et al.* 2015 for the Eurykleia database of named ancient women, and names as a tool for making ancient women visible; see also Arist. *Poet.* 1451b on names, 'particular people', and plausibility.

My decision to 'name' the women in this book dispenses with awkward, androcentric periphrases but also establishes each woman as a subject of study in her own right, with an identity distinct from her male relatives. It is partly inspired by feminist biblical scholar Jo Cheryl Exum's analysis of the narrative of the woman in Judges 19, whom the men of Gibeah gang-rape to death before her husband dismembers her body.[15] Exum calls this woman 'Bathsheber', explaining, 'Both naming the woman and making her the focus of our inquiry are interpretive moves that restore her to the subject position the androcentric narrative destroys'.[16] This 'naming' is both an ethical decision and an analytical tool which unifies and personalises as subjects the women I discuss and opens the sources' androcentric assumptions and priorities to question. It also makes an epistemic and historiographical point. As in journalistic writing where the author announces that 'names have been changed', assigning to real women names that were not their real names exposes the limitations and value of attempts to write their history. This self-declaredly imaginative choice acknowledges the tension between reality, uncertainty, and bounds of possibility, while also acknowledging the personhood of the women discussed. The choice forms the starting point of this book's reclaiming and reimagining of the women of classical Attica and how they shaped the society, culture, and history of Athens.

A Separation and a Loss

Diognete's husband, called up for war and expecting a long absence, brought together his wife *Diognete* and his brother, Diogeiton, *Diognete*'s father. He left *Diognete* some cash: twenty Attic minae and thirty Cyzecine staters (electrum coins from the east of Athens' empire). The sum was worth about 920 *drakhmai*, enough to buy ten yoke of oxen or five enslaved human beings.[17] He also provided her with copies of various important documents, probably including his will and an account of his loans and

---

[15] Exum 2016: 140–1, following Bal 1988a, Bal 1988b.

[16] Compare Fuentes 2016: 3, in her study of enslaved women in eighteenth-century Bridgetown, Barbados, who are 'fragmented' in and by the archival record, discussed at my p. 22: '[My] chapters are titled after the women who are named in the [archival] fragments I explore when possible, in order to contest their fragmentation and to challenge the impetus of colonial authorities to objectify enslaved people in the records by generic namings such as "Negro" or "slave".' I have made a similar decision about my chapter titles.

[17] Evidence for classical Attic purchasing power is not very reliable, but it seems that 20 minae (200 *drakhmai*) was more than enough to buy four oxen or an enslaved adult at this time: see e.g. RO 172 C58–9 (oxen) and A 34–49 (enslaved people; cf. Dem. 41.8, from a later date, for an enslaved person valued at two minae). Cyzecine electrum staters were worth about 24 *drakhmai* each, so 720 *drakhmai*: Eddy 1970. I am grateful to Leah Lazar for discussing this with me.

investments.[18] Knowing full well the dangers of war – disease-ridden camps as well as battle – he gave Diogeiton the original documents and told him that 'if something should happen' – a typical Greek euphemism – Diogeiton was to arrange for the marriage of their daughter and the remarriage of *Diognete*, giving them each a dowry of a talent (6,000 *drakhmai*). Diogeiton should also give *Diognete* the contents of the bedroom – presumably some of the best furniture and fabrics, and any jewellery.[19] With that, Diodotos departed. He was killed at Ephesos in 409, along with about 400 other Athenian hoplites.[20]

In classical Attica, varying degrees of male absence shaped women's lives. Near-constant warfare across much of the fifth and fourth centuries took large numbers of men away from home for seasonal campaigns, or even longer. Lysias 32 and Demosthenes 57, discussed in Chapter 1, offer glimpses into individual women's experiences of separation during the Ionian/Dekeleian War. [Demosthenes] 50.60–1 describes a mother- and daughter-in-law struggling with illness, crop failures, and debt during the householder's absence on trierarchic service in 362/1. In *Lysistrata*, spousal separation defines the female experience of war for women across Greece. We have little evidence for women's experiences of such separation from their own perspectives. By contrast, women's letters from Egypt addressed to husbands absent on military service vividly express their emotions. One woman, Dionysia, writing in 127 BC (*P.Bad.* 4.48), says she has been 'extraordinarily anxious' (ἠγωνίακα … οὐχ ὡς ἔτυχεν) because she has not heard from her husband; she tells him to take care of himself. Her postscript, however, furiously expresses her sense of abandonment: 'above all, I bid you remember how you left me behind alone like the dogs' (παρὰ πάντα δέ σοι ἐντέλλομ⟨α⟩ι μνησῆναι, ὥς με ἐνκα⟨τα⟩λέλοιπας μόνην ὡς τοὺς κύνας).[21]

On a smaller scale, some women knew temporary spousal absence for economic reasons. Menander's *Samia* begins with the return of two men, both with families, from a months-long business trip. Their absence is necessary to the plot, but a business trip must have been a ready explanation. Some rich Athenian men lived with their families in the *asty* but periodically spent time at rural landholdings, leaving their wives intermittently living singly. Lysias 1 concerns such a household (§§11–13, 20), where the husband spends stretches of time (διὰ χρόνου, §12) in the country.

---

[18] Lys. 32.7.
[19] Lys. 32.6; cf. Dem. 27.10. For fabrics as liquid wealth, see Wagner-Hasel and Nosch 2019.
[20] Xen. *Hell.* 1.2.9.   [21] Bagnall and Cribiore 2006: 107–8.

Menander dramatises similar situations.[22] Other families lived in the countryside while the male householder or his sons visited the *asty* or Peiraieus or resided there longer-term.[23] In the narrative of Lysias 1, the husband's absence facilitates the wife's relationship with her lover and his mother. Lack of surveillance may not have been the only factor here: a married woman with an absent husband would have turned to others for practical and emotional support. Other sources attest to the possibility of separation for 'affective' reasons: disputes or abandonment.[24] Discounting situations of medium- or long-term absence, norms of gender segregation meant most women spent more time with other women, particularly those of their household, than with their husbands.

Like *Diognete*, many women and girls lost husbands and fathers altogether. Demographic studies and model life tables suggest that across the ancient Mediterranean, earlier female than male average age at first marriage led to higher levels of widowhood than widowerhood,[25] despite skeletal evidence for shorter female life expectancy, attributable to the dangers of childbearing and possibly to gendered undernourishment.[26] Athenian girls from propertied families were married from fourteen or fifteen; others were married from their late teens.[27] By contrast, men rarely married before thirty and often married considerably later.[28] Male deaths on campaign (probably more often from poor living conditions than battle injuries), particularly during the Peloponnesian War,[29] but also wars against Sparta, Thebes, and Athens' Eastern Aegean and Hellespontine allies across the first half of the fourth century,[30] would have exacerbated widowhood levels, including by reducing opportunities for widows to be

---

[22] For example, *Sam.* 38, *Pk.* 364–5.

[23] As in [Dem.] 47 (§§53, 62). Cox 2002b is a helpful survey of split residence.

[24] Isae. 6.21; many of Menander's comedies (*Epitrepontes*, *Samia*, *Perikeiromene*, *Dyskolos*) feature temporary spousal separation as a result of disputes, aggression, or accusations of adultery.

[25] Gallant 1991: 17–22.

[26] Skeletal evidence for shorter female life expectancy attributable to gendered undernourishment: Taylor 2017: 130–1, citing Lagia 2014, Lagia 2015, and Bisel 1990; cf. Demand 1994: 7–8. Obstetric risks, especially malaria consequent on the suppression of cell-mediated immunity during pregnancy: Demand 1994: 71–86. The extent of gendered exposure of infants is more controversial: Golden 1981, Patterson 1985, Brulé 1992, Brulé 2009, and Golden 2015: 75–6, 81 argue for the prevalence of exposing infant girls; Patterson 1985: 119–21 and Ingalls 2002 argue against. Sneed 2021's argument against the assumption that disabled babies were normatively exposed also merits mention. See also Chapter 2, fn. 119.

[27] Ingalls 2001.   [28] Humphreys 2018: 155–61.   [29] Akrigg 2019: 160–3.

[30] The 'Hundred Years War' of Ma 2024: 160–1. Note the example of Astyphilos in Isaeus 9.14, who is said to have fought at Corinth (probably in the Corinthian War of 395–386), then at Thessaly, perhaps as a mercenary for Jason of Pherai or in a conflict under the aristocratic Aleudai or Skopadai houses (Wyse 1904: 635 *ad loc.*), then 'throughout the Theban War' of 378–371, before dying in an expedition to Mytilene, possibly in 369/8 (Wyse 1904: 627), though he is not said to have married.

remarried.[31] Though younger widows might be remarried, this would not have been immediate; for many it would not have been possible at all.[32] *Lysistrata*, produced in 411 following the mass absence and eventual death of perhaps 10,000 or more citizen men on the Sicilian Expedition of 415–413,[33] suggests that wartime losses meant some women were never married (ll. 592–7). Lysias 12.21 claims that, in 404/3, the Thirty 'prevented the daughters of many citizens from being given in marriage' (πολλῶν … θυγατέρας μελλούσας ἐκδίδοσθαι ἐκώλυσαν); commentators infer that this was because confiscation of their fathers' property deprived them of dowries.[34] Though some girls were married without dowries, this was seemingly rare.[35] If we infer from Lysias that individuals' loss of property could lead to lifelong singleness for daughters, the widespread decrease in individual fortunes that came with the loss of Athens' empire in the late fifth century may have left significant numbers of women dowerless and perhaps unmarriageable – though social expectations around dowries may have changed in response.

The effect of Diodotos' absence and later death on *Diognete* was complicated by the fact that Diogeiton allegedly concealed Diodotos' death from *Diognete* for some time. He also took the duplicates on a pretext, leaving her without legal documentation of the property to which she and her children were entitled. When he finally told the family, they performed what death ritual they could, given that Diodotos and those who died with him were buried by comrades in Notion on the west coast of modern Turkey, just north-east of the island of Samos.[36] As the widow, *Diognete* would have played a significant role in the funeral, though she would not have been able to lay out his body.[37] Chryssanthi Papadopoulou has

---

[31] Cudjoe 2010: 17–23.

[32] Thuc. 2.45.2 (Perikles' exhortation of widows to silence in his 430/1 funeral oration), read politically (as by e.g. Hardwick 1993 and Bosworth 2000: 2–3), treats war widows as a significant socio-political force. Hardwick argues that the exhortation was addressed primarily towards widows of the cavalrymen killed in 431, but Bosworth contextualises the oration within the wider losses of the early years of war and plague, which produced widows across the social spectrum.

[33] Hansen 1988: 14 16.

[34] For example, Jebb 1888 and Edwards 1999 *ad loc*. Lysias' fragmentary *On the Daughter of Antiphon* concerns the marriage of the daughter of a man killed by the Thirty, who became an *epiklēros*. The speech may have come from an *epidikasia*, the legal procedure for determining who was the closest relative and therefore had the first claim to the daughter's hand in marriage and the estate it came with. Evidently, with property attached, this daughter of a victim of the Thirty was an attractive marriage prospect. See Lys. frg. 25a Carey (= Plutarch, *Lives of the Ten Orators* 833a), discussed by Kapparis 2021: 26–9.

[35] Harrison 1968: 48–9, with fn. 1; Ingalls 2002: 250, with fn. 17.

[36] Lys. 32.6 (cf. Carey 1989 *ad loc*.); Xen. *Hell*. 1.2.11.

[37] See Isae. 8.22 and 6.39–41 for the cultural expectation that widows should be able to tend their husbands' corpses.

suggested that the Adonia festival, in which women held and mourned dolls of Adonis, a man beloved of Aphrodite who died young in a hunting accident, helped women cope with deaths of loved ones whose bodies were not recovered.[38] Diogeiton erected Diodotos' funerary monument.[39]

After Diodotos' death, *Diognete* and her children continued to live in the house in Peiraieus for a year, because all their provisions had been left there.[40] When the provisions began to run out, Diogeiton sent the children to the *asty*, the city proper, to live with him, his second wife, and his children by her. By this point, then, *Diognete* had lost her mother. At the same time (c. 408), Diogeiton remarried *Diognete* to a man named Hegemon at a reduced dowry, apparently keeping the rest for himself.[41] As *Diognete* had already given birth to sons to inherit her father's estate, she was no longer bound to be married to a relative as an *epiklēros*.

Perhaps seven years later, Diogeiton married off *Diognete*'s daughter.[42] Shortly afterwards, when the eldest son turned eighteen (c. 401), Diogeiton allegedly threw him and his brother out of the house penniless, claiming all their inheritance had been spent.[43] Horrified and destitute, the boys went straight to their mother.[44] They brought her to their sister's husband, her son-in-law, and begged him to help them. *Diognete*, too, implored him to hold a meeting of her social circle – which had significant overlap with Diogeiton's, given that her natal extended family and first marital extended family were one and the same because of the institution of the epiklerate – to hold Diogeiton to account.

Drawing Social Circles

Who might have been in *Diognete*'s social circle, which came together to support her? Classical Attica had a rich language for relationships and relatedness, which did not always distinguish between what we might think of as two distinct senses of 'relationship'. The first is the formal sense, a circumstance which results in a perceived connection between two

---

[38] In 'Dancing Fear Away: Basic Human Fears and Athenian Religious Rituals', a paper given at the Greek Archaeology Group & Prehistoric and Early Greece Graduate Seminar at the University of Oxford, 16 May 2019. For the dolls and the mourning, see Plut. *Vit. Nic.* 13.10–11 and *Vit. Alc.* 18.4–5.

[39] Lys. 32.21.   [40] Lys. 32.8.   [41] Lys. 32.8.

[42] Towards the end of Diogeiton's eight-year guardianship of the children: Lys. 32.20.

[43] Lys. 32. 9, 16, 17, and possibly 14, with Moore 1982.

[44] Lys. 32.10. Compare, at the bottom of the social spectrum, the enslaved boy Lesis, who wrote the lead letter Agora Inv. IL 1702 (Jordan 2000, Harris 2004, Harvey 2007). He too sought help from his estranged mother and a male associate of hers. Lesis' estrangement was a consequence of slavery, not remarriage.

people: a woman who marries a man has the relationship of 'sister-in-law' to his siblings, which may or may not engender an affective relationship. Which circumstances are perceived to result in a connection, and how that connection and its development are understood, depend on the society or community and its own social structures. To take a simple example, the relationship 'fellow deme member' is peculiarly Attic.[45] Those circumstances need not be permanent or even lasting (as in, for example, a commercial relationship consisting in a single sale). The second sense of 'relationship', and the one most important to this book, is the affective sense: the existence of persisting emotions in one person regarding another, and persistent (even if infrequent) interactions between them. Of course, these meanings shade into each other: in an economy in which trade is predominantly face to face, a woman's commercial relationship with a buyer – that is, the fact of their coming into contact through an economic exchange – is likely, over repeated interactions, to develop into an affective relationship with her, whether that relationship is characterised by trust, mistrust, affection, fear, contempt, gratitude, or anything else.

A common word for kin or relatives was *philoi*, literally, 'dear ones' – this is one of the words used for the circle of people who came to support *Diognete*.[46] Being related to someone normatively made them an ally; correspondingly, affection was understood as a constituent component of relatedness.[47] This is nicely illustrated by a late fifth-century comment of Antiphon the Sophist on the difficulty of divorcing a wife and in so doing, τοὺς φίλους ἐχθροὺς ποιῆσαι, 'making friends/relatives (*philoi*) into enemies' (frg. 49 Pendrick). Anthropologist Janet Carsten proposes using the term 'relatedness' rather than 'kinship', partly 'to signal an openness to indigenous [in this case, classical Attic] idioms of being related rather than a reliance on pre-given definitions', and partly 'to suspend a particular set of assumptions about what is entailed by the terms social and biological'.[48]

Though in some contexts Athenians were very invested in demarcating who was and who was not kin, in other contexts, one's *philoi* were one's social circle, one's allies, without sharp distinction. As well as denoting 'kin', the word *philos* (in its various iterations, including feminine and

---

[45] See Osborne 1985b: 41–2 for Athenian men's identification with other members of the same deme; by contrast (p. 183), 'women do not even belong to demes, they are located more precisely by the demotic of their father and then their husband but in their own right they are residents in settlements whose political status is irrelevant: thus it is that Lysistrata refers to Kalonike at the opening of the *Lysistrata* as ἥ γ' ἐμὴ κωμῆτις (line 5), one who lives in the same village, rather than as one who lives in the same deme'.

[46] LSJ *s.v.* φίλος, 1a, b; cf. 11c.   [47] See pp. 104–115.

[48] Carsten 2000: 4; see also Carsten 2004 and Sahlins 2013.

plural) sometimes has the sense 'friend', a person with whom one has a positive affective relationship, but not a kinship relationship. In such cases, the word is sometimes paired with *epitēdeios*, literally 'serviceable', here with something like the sense of 'supportive', a supporter. It was *Diognete's philoi* and *epitēdeioi* who gathered to help her. 'Friendship' is not a transparent, cross-cultural category. In this book, I use the term 'friendship' for relationships in which particular, established, reciprocal affection subsists between two people, neither of whom is fully dependent on or subordinate to the other. (This nevertheless allows for differences of social status, and even for a level of dependence or deference.) Such relationships are understood and experienced differently across cultures; Chapter 5 discusses how they were understood and experienced by women in classical Attica. It argues that Athenians saw affection, trust (often associated with the sharing of private concerns), mutual support, and voluntary sharing of time and space (typically visiting one another) as the defining characteristics of 'friendship'. Understood in these terms, there might be overlap between kinship and friendship – which Greek idiom easily accommodates. Indeed, perhaps for women in particular, one's closest affective relationship might be with, for example, a particular cousin or sister-in-law. This example illustrates how formal and affective relationships could interact but were not mutually determining: a woman could not choose her relatives, but she could choose her friends among them. On the other hand, this book suggests that some of the most important relationships in women's lives were not friendships: women were emotionally enmeshed with the enslaved women in their homes, but the violent hierarchy of such relationships precludes the term 'friendship'. Differently, though women's affectionate relationships with their pre-adult children were of great importance, I would not call them 'friendships'.

There is a significant scholarly history of studying the complex dynamics of classical Athenian society through the relationships or 'associations' that constituted it, but these studies generally think in terms of men's relationships. How might we see Athens afresh through the eyes of its women and through the relationships they formed and shaped?

Athens Afresh: A Methodology

The history of studying Athenian society through relationships and 'associations' arguably starts with Aristotle.[49] More recently, Stephen Lambert's work

---

[49] Arist. *Eth. Eud.* 1241b (7.9.3) and *Eth. Nic.* 1160a (8.9.4–6); see Jones 1999: 27–33.

on Attic phratries and their subgroups and David Whitehead's on the demes demonstrate the large-scale social networks of which Athenian men – and to a lesser degree, and more indirectly, Athenian women – were a part.[50] Robin Osborne has shed light on the role of the deme in men's relationships to the land of Attica, to other Athenians, and to the workings of Athenian democracy. Osborne uncovers the social strategies of men – their choices (partly but not wholly determined by social status) about whether to form links through marriage with kin or demesmen; how they interacted with and used kin and neighbours (e.g. for labour or political purposes);[51] and how interpersonal and community relationships and attitudes were sometimes a more significant determinant of community membership than legal status.[52] Relevant too is Nicholas Jones' work on Attic 'associations', which argues that groups below the level of the *dēmos* offered, in their flexibility, opportunities for non-citizen involvement, and for bringing together those with shared backgrounds or interests, 'alternatives' to democratic social organisation. This work has been developed by Paulin Ismard, who shows how individual and community identities were shaped by overlapping memberships of organised groups. However, Ismard bases his analysis in associations constituted not just by a sense of solidarity but also by organisational structures (officers, formal decision-making processes and documents, collective goods, regular cult practice), criteria unsuited to assessment of women's sociality in this period. Similarly, Jones excludes 'groups of women' from his study of associations because they have not, in his view, produced an epigraphic record.[53]

All these works focus overwhelmingly on the relationships and sociality of men, and predominantly citizen men. However, a recent wave of studies in Attic social history is re-examining marginalised groups with a focus on how the relationships which helped constitute their social identities materially shaped their lives. Particularly notable here is the work of Kostas Vlassopoulos and Claire Taylor.[54] This book does something

---

[50] Lambert 1993, with pp. 178–89 on the question of women and girls' relationship to the phratry; Whitehead 1986, with pp. 7–81 on the question of women's relationship to the deme.

[51] Osborne 1985b especially pp. 127–53, e.g. pp. 145–6 for cooperation between male neighbours in agricultural labour; see also p. 67 for a demesman seemingly getting a fellow demesman who was on the *boulē* to lay the groundwork for an assembly motion he wanted passed.

[52] Osborne's case study here (pp. 148–51) is that of Euxitheos in Demosthenes 57, whose mother Nikarete is central to my Chapter 1. Osborne argues that what is at stake in this case is deme politics: is Euxitheos accepted as a member of his deme or not, given that he does not live in the deme and has few connections there? In other words, Osborne's argument is that recognition as a member of a deme was not just about descent (i.e. legal status as an Athenian).

[53] Jones 1999: 5–6.

[54] Especially Vlassopoulos 2011, Taylor 2011c, Taylor 2015b, Taylor 2017, and Taylor and Vlassopoulos 2015. Also relevant is Kennedy 2014, on immigrant women in Attica.

similar but for women specifically. As such, it focuses not on formal organisations like demes and phratries, with which women were more or less closely associated but which were not structured by or around women, nor on associations defined by shared property or evidenced by decree-making. Rather, it focuses on women's own networks, micro-communities, and informal interpersonal relationships. Interestingly, Aristotle's discussion of the formal and informal 'associations' (*koinōniai*) that make up the macro-association of the *polis* understands 'association' (*koinōnia*) and 'affection', sometimes translated as 'friendship' (*philia*), as closely connected. Those who share in an association (which might be, for example, a shared sea voyage or military campaign) call each other *philoi*, 'friends'.[55] The book also takes a more fine-grained approach, looking at the emotional constituents of women's relationships and how they shaped the lives of their participants, as well as the communities of which they were a part.

Given the relative paucity of sources from pre-classical Attica, and the associated risk of overemphasising certain evidence because of its lack of contemporaries or being able to offer only limited conclusions, this book takes the turn of the fifth century as its approximate starting point, with the turn of the third as its approximate end point. One political change midway through the fifth century which had particular significance for women was the 'Periklean Citizenship Law' of 451/0, which stipulated that only children born to an Athenian father *and mother* qualified for citizen status ([Arist.] *Ath. pol.* 26.4).[56] This stipulation incorporated women into the legal definition and conferral of citizen status. Previously, citizen status was inherited solely from the father and so was open to children of Athenian fathers and non-Athenian mothers. Leaving aside the politically oriented question of 'female citizenship', discussed later (p. 26), the law shaped the social position of citizen-status Athenian women by assigning new importance to the roles and identities of citizen-status wives and mothers,[57] and correspondingly lessened the status – and reshaped the landscape of possibilities for – non-Athenian women. Probably because of the demographic and social shocks of the Peloponnesian War and the

---

[55] Arist. *Eth. Nic.* 1159b–1160a (8.9).

[56] An earlier change of great significance for women was the Solonic laws on the family, particularly the formalisation of *engyē* (betrothal), *ankhisteia* (degrees of kinship), and the epiklerate, and the restriction of legitimacy and inheritance to children born of monogamous marriage by *engyē*, on which see pp. 340–1 and Lape 2002. Solon's sumptuary laws would also have had an effect on richer, higher-status women.

[57] See e.g. Osborne 1997.

plague of the early 430s, the law had lapsed by the late fifth century, but it was reinstated in 403.[58]

The body of sources for classical Attica is sufficiently large and diverse to allow one to draw out a relatively full and balanced picture of many women's lives,[59] but sufficiently limited to render such drawing out necessary and valuable. The later fifth and fourth centuries offer a wider range of epigraphy, including smaller-scale religious dedications by women and curse tablets aimed against women; these, combined with portrayals in Aristophanic comedy of women of middling and low socio-economic status, allow us to say more about the lives of more ordinary Attic women. Pre-and post-classical evidence appears in this book as comparanda rather than crucial sources and need not bear so much weight.

The book looks at the shaping of women's relationships, by those women and by their circumstances. It also looks at the *portrayal* of women and their relationships, in antiquity, modernity, and by women themselves. Figure I.2, a painting on a fifth-century white-ground funerary *lekythos*, offers an image of the project of this book. The *lekythos* shows a woman garlanding a grave *stēlē*, which depicts a seated woman looking at herself in a mirror. We have a woman viewed through her own eyes and the eyes of one who loved her. This book takes a holistic view of women's relationships, considering their quality (what did these relationships look like?), their dynamics (how did they form, change, and interact with other relationships?), and their shaping effect on society (what role did they play in relation to other social institutions and phenomena?). Better recognition and understanding of the possibilities for women's relationships adds depth, nuance, and colour to our understanding of household, marital, and wider kinship relations, and of the dynamics of Attic society.

Most of the women discussed in this book were of citizen status, the daughters of two married Athenian parents; some were metics (registered immigrants). It is not always possible to tell. Although status distinctions are clearly drawn for some women in some sources (legal speeches where it matters for the case; plays where it matters for the plot; many gravestones), for other women – sometimes in those same sources – there is no clear distinction; it may not have mattered much in some contexts.[60] Women frequently identified themselves without explicit reference to socio-legal status: for example, making dedications in their own names, without a husband's name (which would indicate married status), or paternal or spousal demotic

---

[58] See e.g. Dem. 57.30.   [59] Compare Humphreys 2018: 2 on evidence for Athenian kinship.
[60] Compare Vlassopoulos 2007, Sawtell 2018, esp. pp. 18–19.

Figure I.2 Attic white-ground funerary *lekythos* showing a woman garlanding
a grave *stēlē*, which depicts a seated woman looking at herself in a mirror: a woman
looking at an image of another woman, who looks at an image of herself. Attributed
to the Tymbos painter, fifth century, Paris, Louvre MNB 3059
© Musée du Louvre, Dist. GrandPalaisRmn/Daniel Lebée/Carine Déambrosis.

(which would indicate citizen status). Some of their important relationships
paid little regard to socio-legal status, most notably relationships with those
identified as 'neighbours', an identification based primarily on physical proximity mediated by domestic architecture, which crossed status boundaries.[61]
In their religious practice, women were sometimes heavily invested in policing
status distinctions and, in other contexts, strikingly relaxed about them.
Chapter 3 discusses relationships between enslaving and enslaved women,
a sharper distinction. Though this book focuses on free women, whose

---

[61] See Chapter 5 ('Good Neighbours Become Good Friends') on relationships between neighbours.
On the place of neighbours within 'relatedness' in other cultures, see e.g. Stafford 2000 and Watson
1982 on China and Carsten 1995 and Carsten 1997 on Malays in Pulau Langkawi; on the role of the
house in neighbour relationships, see Carsten and Hugh-Jones 1995.

experiences and perspectives are more accessible in the sources, and who had more agency in shaping and portraying their relationships, across the book we also get glimpses of enslaved women negotiating their own positions and relationships, despite extreme constraints.

Through its study of women and their relationships, this book shows that women's formal and circumstantial relationships did not necessarily commit them to fixed roles or social behaviours defined for them by men – or assumed for them by modern scholars. Rather, they provided a framework within which women could develop and shape their affective relationships (their emotional connections to other people, as opposed to their social positions in relation to others) and negotiate their own roles. There has been an historic tendency to overread the double meaning of the Greek word *gynē* ('woman' and 'wife')[62] and understand the social position of the adult woman in classical Attica – usually assumed to be of citizen status – as primarily consisting in wifehood. In fact, the self-presentation and relationships of both married and single women were diverse, expansive, and malleable by the women themselves. Affective relationships might overlap with other types of relationship (kin relationship, working relationship, shared membership of a household, shared link to a deme), but women gave these relationships new shapes and meanings. The book demonstrates the potential breadth of women's networks, affiliations, and relationships; how they were formed and changed across women's lives, and how they cross-cut other social groupings and divisions. In the manner of Juliet du Boulay's *Portrait of a Greek Mountain Village*, it offers a holistic portrayal of a society and the relationships of its members 'largely through the world of the women'.[63]

This book argues for the fruitfulness of looking at Attica from personal, interpersonal, and experiential perspectives,[64] rather than from the perspective of legal, socio-economic, and political institutions and statuses. It shows that the latter considerations were not always of great significance in people's lives, interactions, and self-descriptions. As the story of *Diognete* shows, women lived through and between different marital statuses, and women's experiences of spousal separation, particularly in war, could be almost indistinguishable from experiences of widowhood. This was particularly true where poor communications left women unaware of whether their husbands were alive, captured, or dead. Further, some women's ability to maintain relationships across different households meant that

---

[62] See Patterson 1991: 58 on the term.

[63] Du Boulay 1974: vii; cf. Ardener 1972's 'problem of women' (fn. 98 in this chapter).

[64] On the question of 'personhood' and the 'person', 'individuality' and the 'individual' see pp. 20–21 for an anthropological perspective and pp. 17–18 for an historical perspective.

their networks were not necessarily contingent on their marital status,[65] and that relationships initially derivative of a marriage (e.g. relationships with a husband's relatives or friends) could last into widowhood or subsequent marriages. These findings illustrate more generally the potential diversity and persistence of classical Attic social networks.

The relationships explored in this book resist traditional scholarly frameworks for understanding Attic women: 'citizen/metic', 'wife', '*oikos*' (both in the senses of 'household' and of 'family line': the term's polyvalence is discussed in Chapter 2.1, pp. 106–8). This resistance is visible in the continuation of women's relationships with members of *oikoi* of which they themselves were no longer a part; relationships and joint action by women (and men) of different socio-legal status; women's experiences of husbandlessness within marriage, or as wives to sequential husbands; women's ability to persuade men from outside their households or immediate kin to take on roles proper to close kin, like sepulchral commemoration, and to persuade men to take into their households children from other households and descent groups and act as father to them.

These insights into women's relationships speak to a wider anthropological conversation, beyond the ancient world, on kinship, gender, and the functioning of households and families. The book's distinctive contribution to kinship studies is its provision of a fuller picture of Attic kinship or 'relatedness' based not just on descent and marriage but also on 'everyday' processes and experiences: cohabitation, cooperation, commensality, mutual affection, shared religious practice. As Carsten and others have argued, formalist approaches to kinship have 'omitted not only some of the crucial experiential dimensions of kinship, including its emotional aspects, but also its creative and dynamic potential'.[66] Through these experiential, processual elements of Attic kinship, women played a significant role in 'kin-creation', well beyond the kin-creation role within which scholars have tended to see them, as links between men through marriage.[67]

This book illustrates the interaction between legally recognised and informal kinship structures, both of which women could manipulate. It demonstrates the flexibility of kinship structures in the face of demographic challenges, through which bereaved women ensured care for their fatherless

---

[65] *Contra* e.g. Sommerstein 2007: 184 who imagines an entirely distinct 'world of wives' and 'world of maidens'.

[66] Carsten 2000: 14.

[67] Stafford 2000 is an illuminating comparison for understanding the role of women within Chinese kinship, traditionally understood as exclusively patrilineal, with women having 'power only as disruptive outsiders' (p. 38).

children by prevailing on natal families and second husbands. Its study of Athenian society through women's relationships also offers other new insights. It illuminates the emotional mechanics of a slave society on a domestic scale. It shows how women built up intimacy with and power over the girls and women they kept in slavery through a combination of care, (violent) 'education', and forced cooperation and used these relationships to negotiate their own positions in their households and marriages. It argues that monetisation of female domestic labour could threaten gender construction within the household, and that income-generating labour gave women alternative ways of negotiating relationships and constructing social roles. It describes relationships and interactions between inhabitants of tenement houses, which could be home to social units less conventional than nuclear or extended families, including single women, enslaved mothers and their children, and informal partnerships between enslaved and freed people. More generally, its methods provide encouragement and example to social historians of marginalised groups in other times and places.

Hidden Stories

Diognete's life story, as I told it at the beginning of this book, was never recorded as such. After *Diognete's philoi* and *epitēdeioi*, presumably at her son-in-law's encouragement, had compelled Diogeiton to undergo a scrutiny into his handling of the boys' finances, they came together as a group, including *Diognete*, for the meeting she had requested. Private arbitration failed, and *Diognete's* son-in-law eventually helped the eldest son take Diogeiton to court for defrauding them of their estate. I have reconstructed *Diognete's* life from a legal speech, Lysias 32, written for the trial.

The speech, written by the speechwriter Lysias for delivery by *Diognete's* son-in-law, mainly concerns her sons. At the end of the narrative portion of the speech, *Diognete's* life story, such as it is, cuts off – we do not even know the outcome of the case. In ancient narratives and modern ancient history writing, biography – continuous narrative of an individual's life – is traditionally reserved for male subjects.[68] While historians ancient and modern concede that men progress through lives of which they are the subjects, women in many ancient narratives appear as bit parts in men's lives. Modern scholarship has not often tried to reassemble the bits into portrayals (necessarily partial, shadowy)

---

[68] The male, disabled speaker of Lysias 24 rather sarcastically observes, 'I am almost grateful, Council Members, to my accuser for bringing about this court case for me. Previously I had no opportunity to give a story of my life (τοῦ βίου λόγον), but now, because of him, I have got one' (§1).

of individuals with their own identities. In these texts, as Exum writes of women in biblical narratives, 'the "stories" of women … are parts of the more cohesive stories of their fathers, husbands, and sons – fragments of the "larger story" that … scholarship has traditionally taken as *the* story'.[69]

The launch of Routledge's 'Women of the Ancient World' biographical series in 2006, and Oxford University Press' series 'Women in Antiquity' in 2010, part of wider academic interest in 'life-writing',[70] has begun to change this. As Rebecca Flemming has noted: 'Late republican and late antique women dominate the catalogue overall, with some empresses and exotic leaders in between, and alongside a smaller set of Hellenistic royalty.'[71] Flemming perceptively observes that biography that depends heavily on the subject's environment and relationships – 'the networked, relational and situated, rather than misleadingly individualised, life' – 'more accurately represents the essentially social nature of the self' but 'has some particular pitfalls for women', whose 'relationality and collectivity are often taken for granted, socially and epistemically prioritised, with agency, intersectionality and individuality paying the price'.[72] Feminist biographical writing can 'challenge overgeneralised accounts of social systems, including those relating to sex and gender, through the focus on the specificities and contingencies of a single life' and assert, as sociologist Liz Stanley puts it, the 'indomitable uniqueness of people who share social structural similarities'.[73] However, when only certain kinds of prominent women have their lives written up, as is the tendency for biographies of ancient women in particular, 'individuality threatens to become the prerogative of the rich and famous'.[74] Perhaps consequently, these biographies tend to evaluate women through the lens of power – were they powerful or powerless, and what kind of power did they exercise?[75]

Flemming's discussion of biographies of women raises the question of agency, another framework that scholars are increasingly using to approach ancient women,[76] and more useful and widely applicable than 'power'. A recent volume on *Female Agency in the Ancient World* attempts to mediate

---

[69] Exum 2016: xxii.
[70] Centres for life-writing were established at the University of Sussex in 1999, King's College London in 2007, and the University of Oxford in 2011; the *European Journal of Life-Writing* launched in 2012; the *Journal of Modern Life Writing Studies* in 2013. A surprising forerunner in the biographical movement is John Davies' 1971 reference work *Athenian Propertied Families*, which includes several miniature biographies of women.
[71] Flemming 2023: 1.   [72] Flemming 2023: 3.
[73] Stanley 1992: 242, quoted by Flemming 2023: 3.   [74] Flemming 2023: 3.
[75] Flemming 2023: 3.
[76] Notably Gilles *et al.* 2024a, Cenerini and Rohr Vio 2016, Boehringer and Sebillotte Cuchet 2013, but for a fuller bibliography see Gilles *et al.* 2024b: 1, fn. 1.

between 'relationality' and 'agency', rightly acknowledging that 'all social agents … were and are relational … and that therefore, agency was and is relational'. Its chapters 'consider women as social agents … embedded and integrated in various cultural systems, even under conditions of oppression, by providing contextualized examples of women acting on their varying degrees of agency'.[77] However, in deliberately avoiding 'cases of individuals with exceptional access to power', the authors 'focus primarily on instances where agency and action may have been accessible to groups or categories of women'. My book, in working to 'restore women to the subject position', as Exum puts it, addresses the lives of women who were neither powerful nor ultra-rich and does not frame the description or examination of their lives in terms of power. Further, my methodology allows for the study of agency and action not just for 'groups or categories' of Attic women, but also for individual women, including 'ordinary' individuals like the women who worked in Attica's shops and markets.

Reconstructing women's biographies is one method of gynocentric history writing. It is the method I use in the first chapter of this book, which compares this reconstruction of *Diognete*'s life story with that of another woman, Nikarete, to demonstrate how factors including age, wealth, and social status shaped these and other women's relationships and their experiences of marriage, separation, and widowhood. (Nikarete, unlike *Diognete*, was for some of her life poor and without reliable family connections.) The biographical approach allows us to view women diachronically across the duration of their lives and to see ancient women's lives as wholes; it illuminates patterns not visible when focusing on particular transitional moments like marriage. By paying attention to the particular, distinct experiences of the two women in the first chapter, rather than treating them as data points within the category 'widows', I demonstrate that for these two women, the experience of widowhood differed relatively little from some of their experiences of wifehood. This strategy is part of the gynocentric, inductive methodology used in this book to identify, describe, and assess women's relationships and networks, and so to build a picture of women's interpersonal lives in classical Athens, and to show how these women shaped classical Athenian society and sociality.[78]

---

[77] Gilles *et al.* 2024b: 1.

[78] Strathern 1988, esp. 3–21, problematises the assumption that it is universally possible to speak of 'individuals shaping society', as if in every culture it were possible to think in terms of 'individuals' as distinct from a 'society' on which they act. The thinking of classical Greek authors like Aristotle about concepts such as the *polis* and *koinōnia* (cf. p. 12) suggests this is less of a problem for classical Athens than for Melanesia, which Strathern is describing, but it remains the case that our concepts

The methodology is gynocentric in two main aspects. One of these aspects is that it rigorously evaluates the possibility of female agency in source creation and gives particular attention to sources which may have been generated or actively influenced by women, for example, dedications made by women and sepulchral monuments where women appear as commemorators. The authors of *Agency in the Ancient World* worry that the 'scarcity of women's voices in ancient writing makes it difficult to ascertain ancient Mediterranean women's capacities in terms of agency, because these capacities are generally related to the individual's internal knowledge, experience, and conception of their own needs, desires, and rights, which are usually best expressed by the individual themselves'.[79] They write of classical Greece as 'experiencing a particular dearth of genuine women's self-expression'. In this book, I argue that the self-expression of classical Attic women is more accessible than is usually assumed, and that such expressions do offer us glimpses of some women's experience and conception of their own desires, intentions, and actions.

The other, prior, aspect of my gynocentric methodology is that it focuses on women, employing a personal and interpersonal approach which begins from *particular* or 'individual' women rather than 'categories' of women and focuses on relationships between particular women rather than on groups, often using extended case studies. This focus on particular women and the relationships between them complements and sometimes corrects existing scholarship focused on women's 'status'. This book's search for particular or 'individual' women necessitates a few words on the related concepts of selfhood and identity. Classical Attic women likely conceived of selfhood and identity differently from how most readers of this book understand the same concepts. Anthropologists including Marilyn Strathern and Juliet du Boulay, through extensive interviewing and observation, have offered analyses of different models of selfhood, identity, and individuality in their communities of study.[80] Strathern's account of the persons of Melanesia has been particularly influential: 'Far from being regarded as unique entities, Melanesian persons are as dividually as they are individually conceived … persons are frequently constructed as the plural and composite site of the relationships that produced them.'[81] The political theorist Chantal Mouffe, thinking in more general terms, argues that any social agent is 'constituted by

---

of 'individuals', 'shaping', and 'society' are modern and not necessarily straightforwardly shared by the people this book discusses.

[79] Gilles *et al.* 2024b: 2–3.

[80] Du Boulay 1974: 73–81, esp. 74–5, 77, 79–81, Strathern 1988, esp. 12–15; cf. Sahlins 2013: 1–2, 19–53.

[81] Strathern 1988: 13.

an ensemble of "subject positions"', whose identity is 'contingent and pre-carious, temporarily fixed at the intersection of those subject positions and dependent on specific forms of identification'; an agent is not a 'unified, homogenous entity' but a 'plurality'.[82] To attempt a theory of selfhood or identity for the women of classical Attica is beyond the scope of this book. Where this book refers to a woman's 'identity', it refers to her sense of her social position in relation to others, her sense of the role she is occupying: worshipper, mother, relative, earner. Its discussion of 'self-presentation', 'self-portrayal', and 'self-writing' do not assume equivalence between our construction of the self and classical Attic construction(s). In any case, this book concerns not 'individuals' alone but relationships between them.

The most straightforward employment of my methodological focus on particular women is visible in the biographies of Chapter 1. However, biography is not always an appropriate tool. Roy Gibson, analysing ancient letter collections, argues against the modern impulse to present or read them 'biographically'.[83] He shows that ancient editors preferred to arrange collections by addressee, to illustrate the quality of the writer's relationships with various types of person, or thematically, to illustrate the 'constituent aspects' rather than the 'evolving story' of a life.[84] It is rarely possible to tell the 'evolving story' of the life of an Attic woman.[85] Detailed portrayal of its 'constituent aspects', as often as possible through her own depiction of those aspects, though necessarily inferring them from others' depictions too, may be more successful. Other chapters, therefore, take briefer mentions of aspects of, or moments in, particular women's lives from various sources (a litigant's explanatory note about the relationship between his mother and his opponents' mother; a record of sanctuary officials' purchase of twenty-eight cloth caps from a woman named Thettale)[86] and draw insights from them through sustained analysis, supported by comparative and contextual information from contemporary sources. Working outwards from these brief mentions of women – which is to put those women at the centre of the analysis – is what allows me to extend my focus beyond a narrow elite while still approaching 'ordinary' women as individuals.

This method of rereading familiar source material to centre peripheral groups is indebted to Jo Cheryl Exum's *Fragmented Women: Feminist (Sub)versions of Biblical Narratives* (itself building on Mieke Bal's work

---

[82] Mouffe 1995: 33, quoted by Gilles *et al.* 2024b: 9; cf. Arist. *Poet.* 1451a.   [83] Gibson 2012.
[84] Gibson 2012: 75–6.
[85] Note, however, Kennedy 2014: 76–83 on Aspasia, Elpinike, and Koisyra.
[86] Dem. 55.23–4, pp. 256–71, 323–4; *I.Eleusis* 177.70–1, pp. 228–9.

on gendered fragmentation, coherence, and narrative), which applies this method to women in the Hebrew Bible as a literary rather than an historical exercise.[87] Also helpful, from modern history, has been Marisa Fuentes' *Dispossessed Lives: Enslaved Women, Violence, and the Archive*, a study of enslaved women in eighteenth-century Bridgetown, Barbados, which focuses on the fragmenting, objectifying, reductive processes through which they became visible in historical archives.[88] Fuentes, describing her approach to fragmentary archival records of enslaved women in Bridgetown, shows that 'changing the perspective of a document's author to that of an enslaved subject, questioning the archives' veracity and filling out minuscule fragmentary mentions or the absence of evidence with spatial and historical context [shift] our historical interpretation . . . to the enslaved viewpoint'.[89] Though most of the women in this book did not suffer the violence of slavery, they did suffer the fragmentation of an historical record rarely interested in their experiences and perspectives. We may approach this record as Fuentes approaches Bridgetown's: changing the perspective to that of the women it describes (or omits); questioning its veracity; paying attention to gaps and absences; filling out minuscule fragmentary mentions with spatial and historical context.

Nathan Sowry argues for a similar methodology in his study of a planned insurrection by Bengali sepoys and Javanese aristocrats against British colonial authority in Java in 1815. While many voices in British colonial archives survive 'only as fragments, faint traces, or muffled in reported speech', Sowry shows how 'reading records against the grain to recover voices of the marginalized' can 'produce a plurality of voices'.[90] He draws inspiration from anthropologist Ann Laura Stoler's process of 'upside-down reading', reading against 'the priorities and perceptions of those who wrote [colonial records]', which can, as archival scholar Jeanette Bastian puts it, 'reveal the lives, the cultures, the feelings of those appropriated within them'.[91] Like Fuentes, Sowry emphasises the importance of 'combining contextual information [from outside the archival records] with a reading against the grain'. He also advocates for reading against the grain by 'matching' colonial sources with Bengali and Javanese ones, as in this book I bring male-authored literary sources into contact with female-authored epigraphic sources.

This kind of reading 'against the grain' is possible for 'archival' records like sanctuary accounts, in which women briefly came into contact with

---

[87] Exum 2016, Bal 1988a, Bal 1988b.   [88] Fuentes 2016.   [89] Fuentes 2016: 4.   [90] Sowry 2012.
[91] Stoler 1985 and Bastian 2005: 28, quoted in Sowry 2012.

Athenian bureaucracy. It is also possible for brief mentions of women in other sources, like forensic oratory. Here, I read 'against the grain' by picking apart brief textual references to women's experiences, emotions, positions, and connections, interrogating their language and their operation within the source to uncover implications and assumptions which shed light on the quality and dynamics of women's affective relationships. (Though not all my evidence is textual, the source emphasis and analysis in this book are more philological than archaeological. This reflects my interest in women's articulation of their relationships,[92] and more pragmatically, my training in philology and epigraphy, through which I make my distinctive contribution to the collective effort of writing women's history.) Chapter 2, for example, discusses an account of how a man brought his wife's son to live with him 'and [the boy's] mother' (Isae. 7.7). A close reading of the passage alerts us to the likelihood that the tension in the text between the speaker's emphasis on the man's initiative and his description of that man's actions arises from the speaker's failure to repress the role of the boy's mother in the decision.

Drawing useful inferences from these readings entails paying attention to how the sources are inflected by genre, context, and authorial intent, and tempering the inferences accordingly. It entails evaluating the plausibility of inferences based on their correspondence or otherwise with inferences from other evidence, including evidence of different types (the inductive approach). It involves asking of inferences, 'If this were true, what would also have to be true? If it were not true, what are the other possibilities and explanations, and what is the balance of probability between them?' For example, Chapter 5 discusses the claim in Lysias 31.20–1 that a woman was forced by her son's untrustworthiness to entrust her burial to an unrelated man. I evaluate this claim by attending to the purpose of the speech (an excoriation of the son) and its generic limitations (to be viable in a legal context, no claim may be easily falsifiable by an opponent, though it may be – and is perhaps likely to be – exaggerated), and considering other possible explanations. Finally, by adducing further instances from the epigraphic record as well as forensic oratory of burial by remoter kin or non-relatives, along with evidence for women's relationships with remoter male relatives and unrelated men, I am able to infer from this and other sources that women could and did turn to men as well as women outside their close family for support and could even call on them to perform roles proper to immediate kin.

---

[92] Though it is also possible to find women's articulation of their relationships in material culture: see e.g. Foxhall 2011, 2012 and Quercia and Foxhall 2014.

The method of rereading familiar source material to centre peripheral groups finds more radical expression in Saidiya Hartman's *Wayward Lives, Beautiful Experiments*, which uses archival materials ('all of which present [the women in question] as a problem') to write the previously 'unthought', 'nearly unimaginable' history of young black women in twentieth-century North America, 'girls deemed unfit for history and destined to be minor figures'. Hartman uses the words of the young women she describes when possible; this book likewise gives particular attention to sources likely shaped by women.[93]

Methods and Models

We have already seen some of the benefits of this gynocentric methodology; we ought also to consider potential problems with it. The methodology employed in this book is inductive: it draws conclusions out of the evidence available rather than making and testing hypotheses. Like all methods, the inductive method has limitations. It necessarily emphasises what the sources choose to show, which risks excluding, or leaving undiscovered, what sources do *not* show. This is a particular problem for a history of women in a society which valued the concealment of aspects of women's lives (names, sexual and reproductive health, family disputes, daily activities).[94] Classical Athens is also a society from which a large proportion of our sources are authored by men, who are less well placed to inform us about certain aspects of women's lives, particularly given strong norms of gender segregation.

Moses Finley argued that because of the problems presented by the evidence (or lack thereof) for the ancient world, it is essential to use models. By 'model', he means 'a simplified structuring of reality which presents supposedly significant relationships in a generalised form',[95] Max Weber's 'ideal types'. The historian's task, according to Weber and Finley, is then to determine the extent to which the model does or does not match reality in particular cases.

---

[93] Hartman 2019: xv–xvii.

[94] Names: Schaps 1977, Sommerstein 2009; sexual and reproductive health: e.g. Eur. *Hipp.* 273–6; family disputes: see pp. 48–9, on apologies in the preliminaries of forensic speeches; daily activities: e.g. Lys. 3.6, though this ought not to be taken at face value; see also Llewellyn-Jones 2003 on women's veiling in ancient Greece.

[95] Finley 1985; problems with documents: pp. 11–13, 33–46; problems with statistics, including demography: pp. 27–31, 43–4; definition of 'model', pp. 60–1; cf. Weber's 'ideal types' (Weber 1982 [1922]: 191, English translation: Weber, Shils, and Finch 1949: 90), quoted by Finley 1985: 61.

In the 1980s, John Gould and Roger Just attempted to use Athenian law, along with descriptions of women's behaviour, and the characterisation of women in comedy, tragedy, and myth more generally, to construct a model of the 'social position' of Athenian women.[96] Though their emphasis on law offers an impression of a system and therefore of the possibility of a systemic account, there remains the problem that what we know of Athenian law we know through its partial, often misleading quotation and application in forensic oratory, where each law was interpreted afresh by litigants and jurors in each case.[97] Neither scholar attempts to understand women's lives from women's own perspectives:

> Either . . . we know what men said about women and how they represented them, or we know very little about them at all . . . we can claim to be determining only what Athenian men thought about women, and how rules and regulations constructed by men sought to define and locate women within a male conception of society.[98]

By contrast, Lin Foxhall's 'The Law and the Lady' and discussions in Sally Humphrey's *Kinship in Ancient Athens* use forensic oratory to attempt to uncover how women negotiated Athens' legal system and what these negotiations might reveal about the realities of their lives and their own attitudes and priorities.[99] This is the approach I take to Athenian law in this book. More recently, Konstantinos Kapparis has argued that women had much more access to Athens' legal system than has been assumed. He offers a systematic account of women's access to and interaction with the Athenian legal system, rightly understood as broader and more diverse than the jury courts, opening new avenues for study.[100]

---

[96] Gould 1980; Just 1989. Gould's and Just's work on women's legal position was preceded by Schaps 1979, on women's economic rights. More recently Cudjoe 2010 has addressed the socio-legal position of widows specifically. Foxhall 1989 Cox 1998, and Johnstone 2003 take more anthropological approaches to women's property rights.

[97] Todd 1993: 60 2.

[98] Just 1989: 1, paraphrasing Gould 1980: 38–9; Ardener 1972, in another context, calls this 'the problem of women'.

[99] Foxhall 1996; Humphreys 2018, e.g. pp. 216, 258.

[100] Despite its overall usefulness, in my view the book is over-optimistic about the degree of access and agency women had to and in the legal sphere, and sometimes anachronistic in the terms of its evaluation. For example, I do not think that the Athenians thought in terms of – never mind enshrined for women – 'fundamental rights such as their right to . . . sexual and personal autonomy . . . and the right to a happy and prosperous family life' (p. 225; cf. Kapparis 2019: 30–6, 46–9, 96–101), nor do I find it 'almost unbelievable that an adult free woman in Athens could not actually choose a husband or get herself married, no matter how old, rich, or accomplished she was' (p. 228).

While work on women's relation to the law continues, recent years have seen growing interest in women's political status. Josine Blok, partly anticipated by Cynthia Patterson and Edward Cohen,[101] frames citizenship in terms of participation and argues that women were full citizens of Athens as men were, insofar as they were fully members of the *polis* community (she cites, among other things, the Athenian concept of citizenship by descent, which included women, and certain citizenship vocabulary that included women), but that women exercised their citizenship in *polis* religion, while men exercised theirs in the assembly, law courts, and military.[102] There is value in paying close attention to the terms in which Athenians (and not only Athenian philosophers) understood citizenship and political participation, and how it differs from our understandings – though in my opinion sources like Aristophanes (not just Aristotle) suggest that the ability to participate in *government* was more central to the Athenian conception of citizenship than this argument claims. Certainly women's citizen status granted them important social and legal privileges denied to metics, enslaved people, and non-Athenians and gave them a stake in the *polis* as a socio-political entity as well as a sense of self-value. Nevertheless, we should be wary of the implications of an argument verging on 'equal but different', which risks attributing to women a level of power that they did not have and deflecting attention from real inequalities in Athens' and other socio-political systems. In this book, I use the term 'citizen-status women' rather than 'citizen women' to acknowledge that this status conferred some but not all the benefits of 'citizenship'.[103]

This book is not primarily concerned with women's political or socio-legal status, but with their relationships and their experiences of those relationships, in which, as the book shows, status was a shaping but not always a defining factor. In this, the book is closer in approach to the 'ancient anthropology' of Sally Humphreys,[104] Lin Foxhall, and others, following their emphasis on interpersonal behaviour.[105] In its efforts to access the complex range of women's experiences and the way they dealt with these experiences as agents, it is also part of wider advances in gynocentric, experience-focused approaches to ancient social history. It builds on the work of Claire Taylor, Angelos Chaniotis, Esther Eidinow

---

[101] Blok 2017, Patterson 1994: 199–203, Cohen 2000: 30–8; cf. also Blok 2009.
[102] Blok 2017: 100–46, descent; pp. 147–86, vocabulary; pp. 200–48, religion. For more recent work in this line, see e.g. Campa 2022.
[103] For a dedicated discussion of this problem, see Sebillotte Cuchet 2017.
[104] Compare Humphreys 2018: 1.   [105] Especially Foxhall 1998a.

and others on the social, interpersonal, and emotional contexts and functions of epigraphy;[106] Josine Blok's and Lisa Nevett's use of comparative anthropology and archaeology to reimagine women's experiences of the built environment of Athens;[107] Chryssanthi Papadopoulou's phenomenological readings of the Arkteia and Adonia, which illustrate the possibility of reconstructing women's emotions and experiences from ancient evidence;[108] and Lin Foxhall's and Alessandro Quercia's work on the role of matrilineally inherited loom weights in Southern Italian-Greek women's relationships with their mothers, daughters, and selves.[109]

Comparisons and Contradictions

Another way in which some ancient historians have attempted to use models to understand aspects of a society which are not shown in the surviving evidence is through 'comparative history'. The comparative method has been prominent in the study of women in ancient Greece because of the source problems this chapter has outlined. Particularly significant has been David Cohen's work on seclusion and segregation, in which he examines the insistence on female seclusion in classical Athenian literary evidence in light of similar insistence in modern anthropologists' interviews with people from various twentieth-century Mediterranean communities. As historians cannot, these anthropologists contextualised their subjects' statements with field observations that women in fact did *not* live in seclusion but maintained it as an ideal by a combination of self-segregation, careful observance of socially acceptable compromises (e.g. moving around in public only at quiet hours, or in company, or veiled and not making eye contact), and polite fictions ("'We are here in the house and we have nothing to do with anyone; we just stay in the house and see our neighbours'", to which Cohen asks, 'How did the neighbours get there?').[110] Cohen is able to assemble from classical Attic literature a 'considerable body of evidence indicat[ing] that Athenian women participated in a wide range of activities which regularly took them out of their houses', 'little bits of evidence about the details of women's lives' which scholars had tended to ignore, having 'already reached conclusions based upon the grand ideological statements' about

---

[106] For example, Taylor 2011a, Chaniotis 2012, Eidinow 2007, Eidinow and Taylor 2010.
[107] Nevett 2011, Blok 2001.
[108] Arkteia: Papadopoulou 2015; Adonia: 'Dancing Fear Away' (see fn. 38).
[109] Foxhall 2011, Foxhall 2012, Quercia and Foxhall 2014.
[110] Cohen 1989: 11, citing Williams 1968: 76–7.

seclusion. With the help of the comparative evidence, he reinterprets these 'little bits' in line with 'a typical Mediterranean pattern' in which 'separation is not the same as seclusion or isolation'.[111] Blok, working along the same lines with similar evidence, has proposed a more developed 'choreography' of Athenian women's speech and movement.[112]

In a 2014 essay, Kostas Vlassopoulos addressed the important question of *which* comparisons ancient historians could soundly use to draw historical conclusions: one cannot, he argues, simply choose two societies which have some similar features and extrapolate from one to the other.[113] This brings us to the ongoing debate about 'Mediterraneanism', the thesis that a large collection of societies located around the Mediterranean Sea, perhaps particularly before the hyperconnected twenty-first century, broadly share certain cultural features because of a long shared past of close interconnection and of shared, culturally defining, geo-climatic situations.[114] This thesis has been particularly influential in the study of gender in ancient Greece, and therefore, despite my desire to reserve judgement on it, it is very much in the background of some of the comparisons used in this book. More recently, Lisa Nevett and Lloyd Llewellyn-Jones have argued for the anthropological comparability of some modern Islamic societies (sometimes in preference to modern 'Mediterranean' societies, though of course there is overlap) with classical Athenian society.[115]

Increasingly and somewhat regretfully I am of the view that in most cases using evidence from one culture to fill in 'gaps' in the evidence for another based on certain perceived similarities between those cultures is not a reliable way of doing history. One problem with the comparative method is the risk of a kind of confirmation bias: the historian notices, and encourages her audience to notice, points of correspondence (or of conflict), but can never comprehensively account for every aspect of the societies compared (even assuming that these 'aspects' were identifiable or commensurable).[116] This results in a distorted, decontextualised picture. Unfortunately, avoiding (or attempting to avoid) the pitfalls of comparativism leaves one without evidence from other contexts to test one's hypotheses against. However, I do think cross-cultural comparisons can help us to imagine in more detail

---

[111] Cohen 1989: 7–9.   [112] Blok 2001.   [113] Vlassopoulos 2014.

[114] See, centrally, Horden and Purcell 2000, esp. Parts One and Five, itself inspired by Braudel 1972: 14; Blok 2001 defending 'Mediterranean' as a term and methodology, p. 96 with fn. 5, citing especially Cohen 1991: 38, 40; she argues that differences between Mediterranean societies are 'variations on a theme' (pp. 98–9).

[115] Nevett 1994: 104–7 (and later Nevett 2011: 581–2, 588–9), followed by Llewellyn-Jones 2003: 11–14. For a sustained defence of the comparative method in anthropology, see Strathern 1988.

[116] A problem articulated and discussed in detail by Strathern 1988.

phenomena which we already have enough culturally specific evidence to attest to in the culture being studied. These comparisons can 'fill out' a picture rather than 'filling in' a gap. For example, evidence from fourth-century Attic fragmentary comedy suggests that free women controlled enslaved people's access to food in their households; contemporary evidence from Xenophon suggests that free women had the power to reward or punish enslaved people in their households. It is a reasonable assumption based on this evidence that women could use access to food to reward or punish enslaved people. Comparative evidence, in the form of a Greek papyrus letter from third-century Egypt, offers us an instance where a woman does precisely this, rewarding an enslaved girl for her 'faultless' work by requesting that she be given an extra ration of food (*SB* 22.15276).[117] To use comparative evidence in this way is not to infer anything new from data from another culture, but to suggest a plausible way in which a phenomenon already observed might play out.

Qualities and Quantities

Other scholars have used quantitative models to counteract a different limitation of the inductive method: that it is qualitative, without much quantitative guidance. The scenarios constructed through the inductive method are socially possible, but it can be hard to evaluate whether they were rare or common. One of the few possibilities for quantitative assessment lies in the field of demography.[118] Without population data, one can make estimates about populations by extrapolating from model life tables. Model life tables construct the mortality patterns one might expect in a population for which detailed data is missing and have been used by ancient historians since the 1960s to reconstruct historical populations, though their usefulness is disputed.[119] Such hypothetical constructions, combined with a hypothesised population growth rate (assuming it is

---

[117] See discussion on pp. 166 7.

[118] Ancient historians have also used quantitative methods in other contexts, notably in modelling the distribution of wealth and income: see e.g. Ober 2010 (drawing on modelling of economic growth by Ian Morris), Kron 2011, and Taylor 2017: 69–114.

[119] See Frullini 2021: 114–15 for a recent, brief discussion of model life tables and their use, and, more fully, Akrigg 2019: 9–37 outlining their various problems and their key advantage – that there is nothing better available; see also Hin 2013: 102–24. For criticism of the use of model life tables in ancient history, see e.g. Engels 1984 and Earnshaw-Brown 2009. Currently most ancient historians use the 'Princeton' or 'Coale–Demeny' tables (Coale, Demeny, and Vaughan 1983), well discussed by Akrigg 2019: 16–33 in relation to classical Attica. Hin 2013: 110–24 argues that newer tables, using better data from populations with low life expectancy in Chile and sub-Saharan Africa, are more useful.

constant, and the population is closed, i.e. unaffected by migration), allow one to deduce, for example, total fertility rates and life expectancy by age and sex. This could in turn allow one, perhaps, to reconstruct certain features of typical women's lives, like rates of widowhood and single motherhood, and the predominance of pregnancy and childbirth in women's lives. Various model life tables are available; some are better than others; none is a perfect fit for classical Attica; one's choice of model makes more difference for some questions than for others. While some ancient societies have left demographic data in the form of census returns, calculations for classical Attica are generally made on the basis of comments in ancient texts about military musters and assumptions around the number of citizens – in other words, data and assumptions about men. Demographers then make educated guesses about the sex structure of the population (i.e. whether mortality patterns and age distribution looked more or less the same for both sexes or not). Assumptions about the age and sex structure of the metic and enslaved populations are even more tenuous.

On the basis of most plausible models for Athenian mortality, life expectancy at birth must have been between about twenty and about thirty. A population with an overall life expectancy persistently below twenty would have collapsed; overall life expectancy over thirty is unlikely given ancient standards of medical care and likely prevailing disease regimes. Whether or not more precise estimates are possible or wise, for any plausible model within this range, maintaining the population would have required every woman to bear, on average, five or six children in order to counteract high infant and juvenile mortality – itself a devastating toll on those children's relatives, as attested by numerous grave monuments for children and by portrayals in tragedy of the heartbreak of parental and sibling grief. These five or six births would represent an even greater number of pregnancies, since model life tables begin from live births and do not account for miscarriages and stillbirths. Of course, not all women would have managed six births. Therefore, unless the population was contracting, many women would have borne eight or more children – and experienced even more pregnancies – over the space of around twenty-five years, assuming a norm of first marriage by around eighteen (often younger)[120] and menopause at around forty-five.

In the most recent study of Athenian demography, Ben Akrigg argues that across much of the classical period the population was in fact increasing, possibly at a rate as high as 1.5–2.5 per cent between about 480 and 431,

---

[120] Ingalls 2001.

before massively contracting in the final decades of the fifth century and then slowly recovering across the fourth century.[121] Though populations do not necessarily need increased fertility to recover from losses, only later mortality or more immigration, any dramatic increase probably did entail increased fertility, so it is possible that across the mid fifth century women were experiencing even more pregnancies and giving birth to even more children. It must therefore be true that a huge proportion of the life of a woman in classical Athens was spent pregnant, postpartum, breastfeeding, or grieving a child, usually while caring for other young children. This would have been the context in which she experienced most of her adult relationships, and in which those relationships were shaped.

A paradox in scholarship on classical Attic women is that the implications of this predominance of childbearing (and -rearing) in women's lives are rarely fully worked out,[122] and yet the predominance of childbearing in women's lives is translated, explicitly or implicitly, into the assumption that women's entire social role and life experience was of wifehood and motherhood (sometimes with a side note on priestesses and other religious roles, though these too are often read through the lens of potential motherhood).[123] In fact, as this book shows, women played and shaped a variety of social roles, including, for example, as neighbours, companions, employees, employers, as well as mothers, sisters, grandmothers, aunts, in-laws. They also had varied life experiences, including – often within the same lifetime – periods of wifehood, widowhood, and marital separation, but also economic participation beyond the domestic economy. These experiences would have been shaped by fertility. A childbearing woman's experience of 'neighbourhood' would have differed from a postmenopausal woman's experience. It would have differed, for example, in her likely degree of mobility and hence in the spatial distance across which she could maintain a relationship with a 'neighbour', and therefore which and how many 'neighbours' she had relationships with; it would have differed in the locations – her home, another's home, at local fountains or shrines – in which she developed those relationships; it would have differed in the conversations and shared activities through which she developed them.

---

[121] Akrigg 2019: 139–70. Other important demographic work on Athens includes Osborne 1985b: 43–4, Patterson 1981: 42, Hansen 1988.

[122] Demand 1994 is an exception.

[123] One extreme example discussed in this book is Avramidou 2015's attempt to read all Akropolis dedications by women as related to childbearing and -rearing.

Experiences of the demands of motherhood might themselves have been a basis for relationships between women. Caring for the children of other women – of sisters, sisters-in-law, cousins, neighbours – and having other women care for one's own children likely increased the sense of affinity between women (see Chapter 2). Relatedly, the need for support in birthing and caring for a large number of children would have increased women's interdependence on other women. In a study of the friendships of women in twentieth-century Hatzi, Crete, where gender relations in some ways resemble those of classical Attica,[124] anthropologist Robinette Kennedy found that women's friendships were 'based primarily upon the expression of the participant's personal feelings and secrets',[125] which they were less able to share with others, including their husbands. These included feelings and secrets about their children. One woman said of her best friend: 'She comforted me, because I had so many children and so much trouble with them. I needed comforting, and she was a great comfort to me.'[126] However, fertility and motherhood were not the only shaping factor in women's relationships and roles and should not necessarily be used as the 'lens' through which other roles are viewed.

In any case, models too have their limitations. There is little secure that can be said about classical Athenian demography with reference to women. Akrigg himself largely ignores women in his book.[127] Given the limitations of the evidence, my book does not offer any new demographic modelling. However, though it is not always possible to use models to assess the commonness of certain scenarios, part of my argument is that by noting and assessing certain possible scenarios which seem not to fit expected norms, we can see for the first time the diversity of Attic women's lives and the ways in which it was possible for women to shape the society in which they lived. This sheds light on elements of women's lives beyond marriage and motherhood; these other elements may well have been less prominent

---

[124] Compare e.g. Cohen 1991: 59, fn. 104, 59–60, 69–70; Foxhall 1998a: 55, fn. 13.

[125] Kennedy 1986: 131.   [126] Kennedy 1986: 130; see further discussion on my pp. 332–3.

[127] Akrigg estimates the size and age structure of the category 'citizens' by applying various models to data about political participation and military musters (data about men) and appending four pages on the question of sex structure, which conclude that, contrary to the assumptions of some other scholars, there is little reason to think that the Athenian population structure differed significantly by sex (Akrigg 2019: 33–7). Akrigg defines the category 'non-citizens' as 'metics and slaves' but does not discuss the sex structure of the enslaved population – there is little if any secure evidence to discuss. Akrigg 2019: 138 offers a paragraph on the possible sex structure of Attica's metic population; Kennedy 2014: 14–16 offers more discussion, noting the work of Vestergaard 2000: 87–8 on the proportion of tombs for non-Athenians in Athens which commemorate women (14 per cent in the fifth century and 34 per cent in the fourth) – not necessarily a reliable indicator of population structure.

in women's lives than, for example, their maternity but are nevertheless necessary to the whole picture. My methodological focus on the experiences of *particular women* (rather than on norms or representations) offers a much fuller picture of elements of women's lives which have long been neglected or simplified.

Women as Sources

Although an inductive method does emphasise the features that sources choose to show, one important and unique element of this book is its emphasis on portrayals of women and their relationships by the women themselves. Its emphasis on what women like Melinna (who made an inscribed dedication to Athena discussing her work, childrearing, and relationship with the deity, Chapter 4) and Euthylla (who set up an inscribed monument to her companion Biote describing their relationship, Chapter 5) chose to show – things not usually visible in other evidence – gives us a new view of women in classical Athens.

What did these women choose to show, and how? A useful concept for considering women's own portrayals of their lives and relationships is the Foucauldian concept of 'self-writing'.[128] For Michel Foucault, 'self-writing' is writing as 'a certain way of manifesting oneself to oneself and to others [which] makes the writer "present" to the one to whom he addresses it . . . present with a kind of immediate, almost physical presence'. Women in classical Attica did not write narratives of their lives ('autobiographies'). However, they did write about themselves, 'in various ways and for various reasons that often do not conform to our modern assumptions about the nature of the self and the act of writing about it', as Gur Zak puts it in his discussion of 'self-writing' through antiquity and the later Middle Ages.[129]

For example, women used inscribed dedications to the gods to describe their own religious experiences and to claim authority from them. In the mid fourth century, a woman named Meneia dedicated a marble *stēlē* to Athena and had it inscribed 'Meneia dedicated (this) to Athena, having seen a vision, the excellence of the god' (Ἀθηνάαι Μένεια ἀνέθηκεν | ὄψιν ἰδοῦσα ἀρετὴν τῆς θεοῦ, *IG* ΙΙ² 4326). More famous is Xenokrateia's dedication and foundation of a cult for the river-god Kephisos, 'because of instruction (i.e. from the god[s])' (*didaskalias*, *IG* Ι³ 987 with *IG* ΙΙ² 4547).[130] A woman making an inscribed dedication would physically come to the sanctuary to give it to the

---

[128] Foucault 1983. See also Zak 2012, esp. 485–6; Conybeare 2025. [129] Zak 2012: 485–6.
[130] See Blok 2018: 18–20; as she notes, other scholars have interpreted this word differently.

gods, interacting with temple officials and with those who accompanied her. Through her dedication, however, which would forever proclaim her name and her act of worship, renewing the offering on the lips of those who saw the inscription and read it aloud, she continued to be present and to interact with visitors and previous and future dedicators, as well as physically returning to make offerings and show the dedication to others.[131] This is Foucauldian self-writing as 'a certain way of manifesting oneself to oneself and to others [which] makes the writer "present" to the one to whom he addresses it'. Through inscribed monuments, women wrote their experiences, their desires, their ideas, their affections, their relationships, themselves into their built environment. The framework of self-writing invites us to attend to the elements of self these women chose, within the (often considerable) constraints of their cultural circumstances, to commit to writing.

Assertions that we have no classical Attic texts authored by women ignore epigraphic texts or deny any female authorship role in any epigraphic text which makes a statement on behalf of a woman.[132] Scholars are often insufficiently explicit about their assumptions concerning the authorship of formal inscriptions like dedications or epitaphs.[133] Some inscriptions were most likely commissioned by women who had significant input into the product;[134] some may have been composed by women. If there is a strong argument for female authorship of a significant number of

---

[131] Compare Herodas' *Mime* 4, with Day 2010: 69–73.

[132] It also misses traces of female oral composition in surviving texts: cf. Karanika 2014.

[133] For example, Tsagalis 2008 does not discuss the authorship of the epigrams he treats; nor does Kaczko 2016, except to discuss the attribution of *IG* I³ 501 to Simonides (p. 7). Discussion of the dedicator's choice of words at p. 49 (I³ 601) could imply either composition or commission. The suggestion of Raubitschek 1949: 431 that 'the composing of the dedicatory inscriptions (metrical and prose) was presumably done by the artists [i.e. sculptors] or their stone-cutters' seems unlikely given the difference in required skill sets, though some sculptors may have had a repertoire of simple options; Raubitschek cites Friedländer and Hoffleit 1987 and O'Neill 1942, but O'Neill does not discuss inscribed epigrams, while Friedländer and Hoffleit sometimes imply composition by the dedicator (e.g. p. 13, on e.g. *IG* I³ 1206; p. 25 on I³ 865), and at least once explicitly attribute the epigram to the dedicator (p. 26 on I³ 633, a potter), without explanation. A rare exception is Jacqmin 2015: 1.2.7, who asserts that women's inscribed dedications are 'one of the few direct testimonies women are unequivocally recognised as having authored'. If this recognition is unequivocal (which I think is optimistic), its implications have not been fully appreciated. The problem is much more fully addressed by Hunter 2022: 9–21, who writes in his discussion of sepulchral inscriptions (p. 10):

> The text of the inscription might already have been agreed with the deceased before his/her death (or indeed the deceased might have composed the verses to be inscribed), or would be composed by a member of the deceased's family … or a friend of the deceased, or the stonemason would either put the family in touch with a professional composer … or offer them 'ready-made' verse-patterns which could easily be adapted to individual circumstances.

[134] See e.g. Keesling 2005: 414 on *IG* I³ 683, a case study of a female dedicator's control over the inscribed text of her commission, in this case its lettering.

inscriptions – which may require a richer, more nuanced understanding of authorship – we find ourselves with myriad women's testimonies from the ancient world, offering valuable insights into women's perspectives in a discursive world from which the remnants are overwhelmingly male.[135]

In order to address this question, we have to consider whose agency is at play in the creation of an inscription, and how. The creation of an inscribed object has various strands. One strand is the creation of the object (whether a sculpture and its base, a *stēlē*, or, differently, the wall of a building, or a loom weight, or a naturally occurring rock, any of which might host a graffito). Another strand is the act of inscribing, done either by a person acting on behalf of another in a paid or an 'official' capacity, or done without an intermediary, as in the case of graffiti. Another strand again is control over the inscribed text.

The nature and exerciser of this control depend on the type of inscription.[136] For example, who determined the description of dedicator and dedication in sanctuary inventories – the dedicator or an official?[137] At the opposite end of the scale of formality is graffiti, where, though it was of course possible for one person to inscribe, say, a verse of poetry composed by another, many instances are direct records of, for example, the inscriber's own name – and presence at that place, or interaction with that object.[138] In a different category again are sepulchral and dedicatory inscriptions. Some were commissioned by known epigrammatists,[139] but one would not need to commission someone to produce a text for a sepulchral monument which gave only the name of the dead

---

[135] Compare Bagnall and Cribiore 2006: 60 for a cautionary note on 'women's voices' in the context of women's letters from ancient Egypt. For discussion of composition possibilities and levels of authorly influence in this context, see Bagnall and Cribiore 2006: 6–8 and 59–67. I am more sympathetic to Richlin's hope to locate 'the subaltern's speech' (Richlin 1993: 293, cited at Bagnall and Cribiore 2006: 6) than they. For reflections on the voices of ancient Greek women, see Lardinois and McClure 2001: 3–11, and Karanika 2014: 1–20, esp. 15–17.

[136] On the authorship of the texts of Athenian decrees, see Osborne 1999: 341–58. I am grateful to Eddie Jones for discussing this with me, along with the questions around inventories.

[137] For the literary construction of temple inventories, see Kirk 2021: 110–52; Kirk does not explicitly engage with the question of authorship but thinks overall in term of the 'creation' of cumulative *lists* (rather than entries) by officials (pp. 125, 140). See, however, Kirk 2021: 145, based on Meyer 2010 (Kirk does not refer to specific pages in Meyer, but note e.g. Meyer 2010: 61, 66–7), for *phialai* with inscriptions individualised (by the dedicants?) being converted, by standardised formatting, from 'a more irregular assortment of discrete commemorative objects [into] a neat and orderly list that privileges the new collective rather than the individual'. The fourth-century inscription *IG* II² 120 comprises a decree mandating an enslaved public servant, Eukles, to make a record of the contents of the Khalkotheke (the treasury of bronze dedications on the Akropolis) and the record he was mandated to make. The decree is very prescriptive in how it requires Eukles to record the dedications (by type, with weights). The names of dedicants are not recorded.

[138] On the significance of name graffiti in Attica, see e.g. Taylor 2011a and Taylor 2015a.

[139] Famous examples include the epitaph on the Spartan dead at Thermopylai (*Palatine Anthology* 7.249) and the epitaph for Archedike (Thuc. 6.59.3 with Arist. *Rhet.* 1367b31), both attributed to

person, or a dedicatory inscription reading something like Ἱμέρα Ἀθαναίαι ἀνέθεκε, 'Himera dedicated (me) to Athena' (*IG* i³ 571, on a bronze wine jug from the Akropolis). A reasonable degree of variation even in very simple formulae in dedicatory inscriptions (compare the multiple different ways women describe their dedications of first-fruits in Chapter 4, 'Athena the Worker') tells against heavy intervention by temple officials. As is characteristic of epigraphic texts from this period, the 'author' typically uses the third rather than the first person, which tends to be reserved for the dedicated object rather than the dedicator, or, in the case of sepulchral commemoration, the person commemorated rather than the commemorator.[140]

Female agency is traceable in most categories of inscription.[141] There was a Greek epigraphic tradition of 'love-names', or better, '*kalos*-names', inscriptions which declare one person to be beautiful (*kalos*) to a named or implicit admirer, presumably the writer.[142] In the handful of instances of *kalos*-names where the admirer is a woman, we may venture to assume that these are women's articulations of their own desire – though other inter-pretations are possible. Among such instances are an inscribed *lekanē* (bowl) from c. 475–450. On the inside, we find Πυθόδορος καλό[ς], 'Pythodoros is beautiful'. On the underside: Ἀλ⟨λ⟩καῖος καλὸς | τὸ δοκεῖ Μέλιτι, probably 'likewise, Melis thinks Alkaios is beautiful'.[143] Μελίς is a woman's name (though the much less common Μέλις is a man's); Mabel Lang, who published the inscription, thinks the form here is 'most prob-ably feminine'.[144] Similarly, women seem to have participated in the practice of inscribing one's own name, which Claire Taylor has understood in terms of self-memorialisation and connectivity.[145] One such name

---

Simonides, and Ion's epigrams on the Spartan victory dedications from Aigospotamoi at Delphi (*FD* 1:50, 1:51).

[140] This causes some problems for literary approaches to 'the authorial voice' which think in terms of the poetic 'I'. Bowman 2019 writes: 'Women may have of course authored many of the surviving unattributed epigrams. Female authorship of unattributed epigrams whose speaker (mourner or dedicator) is female cannot however be assumed; when authorship of an epigram is known, the author and speaker are rarely the same'; she cites Tueller 2008: 52–3. However, most of the epigrams in this book that I propose women had a hand in authoring (notably *IG* ii² 4334 and i³ 1295 bis = *CEG* (1) 97) have no identifiable 'speaker' ('I') but 'speak' in the third person; *IG* ii² 7873 is a trickier case: see p. 258.

[141] For women elsewhere in Greek history authoring texts of decrees, see Wolicki 2021: 191–2.

[142] See e.g. Ar. *Ach.* 142–4 and *Vesp.* 98–9, where the graffitist is the admirer.

[143] Lang 1976 (*Agora* xxi C 19); or 'I tell you, Melis thinks Alkaios is beautiful' (*SEG* 42:75, Laurent Dubois) or 'Alkaios is beautiful. Who thinks so? Melis' (*SEG* 66:95, Angelos Matthaiou). An inscription on the outside reads μὲ φέρε, 'don't carry me (off)' (see Steiner 2002: 358) or perhaps 'bring me (to him?)'.

[144] Lang 1976: 11; Steiner 2002: 359 refers to this as a 'preserved expression of a female opinion.'

[145] See fn. 138.

inscription, on a rock in Agrizela, Laureion, is the female name Antidike, probably carved in the sixth or fifth century (Ἀντιδίκε, *IG* ι³ 1409 bis).

When women gave their own names in inscriptions, as when female characters in comedies spoke their own names aloud, they did so in various forms. A woman might use her name alone, a mononym. This was the norm in dedicatory inscriptions in the early fifth century, but still common in the late fourth. It was the predominant form in the mid fourth-century inventories of women's clothing dedications at Brauron.[146] It was occasionally used on tombstones. Where a mononym is used, a woman's legal status (citizen-status, metic, even enslaved; married or not) is not identifiable other than sometimes from contextual clues and may not always have been at issue.[147] However, freeborn women's names were often supplemented by the father's name (patronymic); less often, the husband's; rarer still, a brother's. (When used as parts of or substitutes for women's names, I refer to fathers', husbands', and brothers' names collectively as 'andronymics', 'names from men'.)[148] For citizen-status women, particularly on fourth-century gravestones, the andronymic was mostly supplemented by the man's demotic (his deme membership, in which his citizenship consisted). One woman in Aristophanes gives her full, three-part name – Krytilla, daughter of Antitheos of Gargettos (*Thesm.* 898); shorter forms usually sufficed. A citizen-status woman's legal status was founded on her descent from a citizen man and a citizen-status woman and further verified by her legitimate marriage to a citizen man: her *kyrios'* demotic indicated her citizen status. (A *kyrios* was a woman's legal guardian and representative. All citizen-status girls and women had a *kyrios*, usually her father, her husband if married, or, failing those, another male relative – the word means 'having authority'.)[149] Women were not members of demes in the way men were – their names were not inscribed on deme registers, for example[150] – but the deme of a woman's *kyrios* was an important site of her social and civic identity, consisting most visibly in participation in religious

---

[146] Of the 121 naming phrases for clothing dedicants collected in Cleland 2005 for 349/8 and 336/5, 90 (74 per cent) are mononyms.

[147] Compare Vlassopoulos 2007, Vlassopoulos 2010; Sawtell 2018, esp. pp. 18–19.

[148] Sometimes the man's name is given in the genitive without the specifying term *thugatēr* (daughter) or *gynē* (wife); these are probably but not certainly patronymics, on analogy with men's names: Humphreys 1980: 116, fn. 47. In commemorative contexts, the formulation of a woman's name may depend on other names on the monument or in the *peribolos* (Heine Nielsen *et al.* 1989: 415–16 and Oliver 2000: 67 show this for demotics).

[149] See Harrison 1968: 30–2, Schaps 1979: 48–60, Just 1989: 26–39, and, for helpfully nuanced pictures, Hunter 1994: 9–29, Foxhall 1989, and Johnstone 2003: 267–71.

[150] Kapparis 1999: 193; Kennedy 2014: 97–8.

activities with the other 'wives of the demesmen' (αἱ γυναῖκες αἱ τῶν δημοτῶν, as in Isae. 8.19–20; the phrase neatly illustrates that for women, deme membership was meaningful but indirect). Accordingly, demotics were not applied to women in their own right, though occasionally versions ending in -θεν (from) were.[151] Metics, men and women, were sometimes identified on their tombstones with a toponymic (adjective based on place of origin). Those who appeared as contractors or dedicators in fourth-century sanctuary accounts or inventories were identified as '[Name], living in [deme]'.[152] Occasionally, women of various statuses identified themselves or were identified by occupation. Here, as with mononyms, legal status is not apparent and may not much have mattered. More rarely, women seemingly suppressed their own names:[153] 9 of the 121 women identifiable in the clothing inventories from Brauron described themselves with an andronymic but without their own name, a form we would expect from men speaking but not women dedicating. Perhaps these women (or their *kyrioi*?) were particularly conservative.

Dedicatory and sepulchral inscriptions offer some of the richest examples of 'women's epigraphy' from classical Attica and provided women with an opportunity to communicate about themselves. To what extent are inscribed texts on dedications or sepulchral monuments erected by women 'women's inscriptions', 'female-authored texts'? There are two related elements here: commissioning and authorship. Commissioning an inscribed dedication or sepulchral monument entails a degree of control over the object and the text; in this way, commissioning and authorship are linked. Questions around commissioning include access to and control over resources, and ability – or

---

[151] For example, *IG* I³ 1136 (5th-c. sepulchral monument); II² 6285, 6897 (4th-c. sepulchral monuments), respectively Μαραθονόθεν, Ἰκαριόθεν, and Μυρρινοντόθεν, where the standard demotics are Μαραθώνιος, Ἰκαριεύς, and Μυρρινούσιος; cf. Humphreys 1980: 116, fn. 47. *IG* II² 1523.20 = 1524.193–4 (4th-c. sanctuary inventory) is more unusual: Φρεαρ for the demotic that for a man would be Φρεάρριος. Because it is abbreviated, the inflected ending is lost, and we do not know whether the cutter had in mind a feminine form, *Φρεάρρια, or would have applied the masculine form to the woman. I thank Aleksander Wolicki for discussing this with me. Linders 1972: 7–8, n. 5, on *IG* II² 1523.20, cites eight instances of demotics applied to women, mostly around the fourth century, with prepositional forms (ἐκ + deme name) or uninflected -θεν forms, including those just noted. Bradeen 1974: 49 notes feminine demotics (not -θεν forms) in four or five sepulchral inscriptions from the first century and later (*IG* II² 6780, 6781, 6810, *Agora* XVII 117; *IG* II² 6255 is undated). Whitehead 1990 compiles a list of attested demotics; some already end in -θεν, in which case the difference is not visible.

[152] Sawtell 2018: 72. Metics were registered in a deme by the fourth century (Kennedy 2014: 12–13) and probably by the end of the fifth century (e.g. *IG* I³ 476, *SEG* 50:69).

[153] Nicknames, particularly common for women, were a different type of suppression (Humphreys 2018: 267, though she does not make clear her distinguishing criteria for a nickname rather than a name). Confusion over women's names could be exploited against them: Isae. 3.30–4, with Wyse 1904 *ad loc.*; Ap. *Neaira* 50, 121, with Kapparis 1999 *ad* §50.

in Senian terms, 'competence'[154] – to operate within and navigate the context of monumental dedication or commemoration. These questions have received attention from Blok, who uses the dedication of Xenokrateia (*IG* I³ 987 with II² 4547) as a case study for Athenian women's competence (required abilities, resources, knowledge) in various spheres.[155] The dedication, Blok argues, shows that Xenokrateia, and 'many' other Athenian women,[156] had the religious knowledge and licence to make dedications and even found cults, using the appropriate religious language and in accordance with the relevant religious laws and conventions. Xenokrateia, and at least some other women, had financial resources and the ability to spend them on religious dedications. And, Blok argues, she had the ability to compose hexameters.[157]

One major aspect of the question of women's financial competence is the law cited in Isaeus 10.10 in relation to whether a child could make a will. The speaker says, παιδὸς … οὐκ ἔξεστι διαθήκην γενέσθαι· ὁ γὰρ νόμος διαρρήδην κωλύει παιδὶ μὴ ἐξεῖναι συμβάλλειν μηδὲ γυναικὶ πέρα μεδίμνου κριθῶν, 'it is not possible that a child could have a will, for the law forbids a child or a woman to make a contract (*symballein*) above the value of a *medimnos* of barley'. A *medimnos* of barley, worth about three *drakhmai* (three days' wages for a skilled labourer, or about six to nine days' subsistence wages) was probably enough to feed a small family for five or six days.[158] Scholars have struggled to reconcile this with attested instances in which women *did* make large financial transactions. Some argue that the law as applied to women had long ago fallen into disuse;[159] others, that the law de facto forbade women to make large transactions without the mediation, supervision, or at least permission of her *kyrios*, which may have been tacitly assumed in most cases.[160]

It seems unlikely that the law was a *totally* dead letter, given the joke made about it in Aristophanes' *Ecclesiazusae* (c. 390), where, under the topsy-turvy women's government, a man is being forced to have sex with

---

[154] See Taylor 2017: 19–22, following Amartya Sen.

[155] Blok 2018; see also Dillon, Eidinow, and Maurizio 2017 for competence-based approaches to ancient women within the sphere of religion.

[156] Blok 2018: 20.

[157] Blok 2018: 21–4 also argues that Xenokrateia had a literacy level high enough to read other dedications and imitate their language in her own; I think this possible, but not certain (or necessary for composition; see pp. 40–41).

[158] Kuenen-Janssens 1941: 202–6.   [159] For example, Hunter 1994: 19–29.

[160] See e.g. Kuenen-Janssens 1941 for various interpretations of the law; her view is that *kyrioi* tacitly gave permission in most cases (pp. 210–12).

an old woman before he has sex with the young woman he wants. Trying to escape the obligation, he asks, 'what if one of the men from my deme or circle of friends came to claim me as a free man (i.e. ransom me, or buy my freedom)?', to which the old woman replies, ἀλλ᾽ οὐ κύριος / ὑπὲρ μέδιμνόν ἐστ᾽ ἀνὴρ οὐδεὶς ἔτι, 'no; no man any longer has authority to dispose of (*kyrios . . . est[i]*) more than a *medimnos*' (ll. 1023–5).[161] That the law was a sufficiently familiar referent to joke about and could be paraphrased (at least one of the two citations of the law by Isaeus and Aristophanes must be a paraphrase) suggests it was not entirely obsolete. Various intersecting factors probably determined the application of the law. Perhaps it applied strictly to *contracts* (evidently including wills).[162] If the law did require the mediation (or, less onerously, permission – but demonstrated how?) of a *kyrios* or a man acting in a similar capacity, this would have kept some women from making large transactions; others might have been able to get by with persuasion (either of their *kyrios* or of the other party to the transaction).[163] Most likely there was a cultural norm, shaped by this law, against women dealing independently with large amounts of money, which some women were occasionally able to negotiate ways around.

The second major question about competence here is the question of whether some women could compose metrical inscriptions of the kind we sometimes find on women's dedications and on sepulchral monuments erected by women. The balance of evidence here tilts in favour: ancient Greek women were steeped in poetic culture, in the form of funerary laments, wedding songs (*epithalamioi*), hymns, work-songs, and lullabies.[164] The ability of women to compose as well as perform funerary laments is now well accepted; the relationship of laments to the epigrams found on sepulchral monuments is complex but demonstrable. Similar links have been made between hymns and the composition of dedicatory epigrams. The hypothesis that dedicators and commemorators, female and

---

[161] As Sommerstein 1998 *ad loc.* notes (followed by Blok 2018: 27, fn. 106), the line is strictly inconsistent with the abolition of private property earlier in the play (590–602).

[162] Compare Blok 2018: 26. [163] Compare Johnstone 2003.

[164] Lamentation: McClure 1999: 40–7, Blok 2001: 104–7. Influence of lament on Sappho's compositions: Lardinois 2001: 80–8. Comparative studies of modern Greek laments focusing on composition: Caraveli-Chaves 1980, Alexiou 1974: 131–206. Relationship between lament and sepulchral epigram: Hunter 2022: 7–8. Link between hymns and the composition of dedicatory epigrams: Day 1994. Links between women's work, work-songs, and poetic composition: Karanika 2014. In Euripides' *Hypsipyle*, Hypsipyle considers the songs she knows for relieving the monotony of textile work to be inspired by the Muses (frg. 752f Nauck, ll. 9–11). She also sings lullabies. In *Ion*, even the enslaved women are exposed to mythical stories told (in song?) during textile work (ll. 194–200). Women's facility with oral and even literate composition: Blok 2018: 21–4. Likely female composition of oracles: Maurizio 2017, esp. p. 100.

male, sometimes or often composed metrical inscriptions assumes facility with poetry and composition. It does not assume literacy.

It is necessary for the question of female authorship to ask what constitutes authorship of an inscribed text. Choice of words is partly determined by other choices necessarily made by the commissioner. In the case of a brief, formulaic inscription like Λύσιλλα ἀπαρχὲν Ἀθεναίαι ('Lysilla, first-fruits for Athena', *IG* I³ 547, c. 500–475), the words reflect the dedicator's decision of what to dedicate (or what kind of dedication to make – here, a first-fruits dedication) and to whom (here, Athena). The dedicator would probably know the conventions for what to say and how from experience.[165] In such an inscription, it was likely also the dedicator who chose how to describe herself: Lysilla uses a mononym, but other dedicators add a patronymic or another descriptive phrase (e.g. an occupational term). To take another example, for the inscription, Σμικύθε πλύντρια δεκάτεν ἀνέθεκεν ('Smikythe the launderer dedicated a tenth', *IG* I³ 794, c. 490–480), Smikythe almost certainly provided three of the four words: her identity as dedicator, and the form in which she wanted it expressed, i.e. Σμικύθε πλύντρια; and the nature of the dedication, a *dekatē* (an offering of a tenth, as opposed to another kind of dedication).[166]

Such details would also determine some of the words of inscriptions in verse. If a dedicator or commemorator commissioned an epigram, she would have to give the epigrammatist key details to incorporate, in which case the commission would still reflect the sentiments and some word choices of the commissioner. In other words, she collaborated in its authorship.[167] Alternatively, the dedicator or commemorator herself composed the text. Joseph Day, imagining the reading context of a man's inscribed statuette dedicated in Thebes in 700–675, suggests that 'even if the artist alone knew how to write the inscription, the dedicator, having memorized *the text that he perhaps composed*, could recite it from memory to others in front of the statuette' (my emphasis).[168]

Another way to approach the question of women's agency in inscribed dedications and (to a lesser extent) sepulchral monuments is to think about the cultural relevance of the agent in the specific context of the monument. The act (of, say, dedicating or commemorating, which is both material and symbolic, and where both the inscription and the object together 'do' the act) is often attributed to one or more agents in the text, and usually who

---

[165] Blok 2018: 20–4. [166] For *dekatē* offerings, see pp. 198–200.

[167] Compare Dover 1968: 148–74 for a discussion of this question as applied to the composition of forensic speeches.

[168] Day 2010: 43.

the agent is matters. If someone dedicates something to the gods, it matters that the gods (and secondarily, other worshippers and viewers) know who she is. (The agent seems to matter less ubiquitously in sepulchral commemoration.) Therefore the words on the object are in some meaningful sense hers insofar as she is the one thanking the gods or commemorating the person. Even on the most minimalist interpretation, even if she has paid someone else to write the words, the words are in some sense hers and communicate what she wants to communicate. And on the basis of evidence for women's competence in composition, I suggest that on the 'spectrum' of authorship, many women's inscriptions are closer to 'total authorship' than 'commission'.

In view of all this, it is likely that many if not most inscribed texts which make statements on behalf of women (usually in the third person) were to some degree authored by women. Even if a woman gave directions to someone else about what information to include or emphasise in the text and left the composition to them, that text still reflects her perceptions of what was important. We should take such texts seriously as sources for women's perspectives.

Women making dedications often present themselves as doing so as individuals, beginning their inscriptions with their names. Though these self-presentations can be formulaic, they did allow for expressions of individuality: in choice of dedicated object, choice of dedicatee, type of dedication, form of dedicator's name, and sometimes more. Longer inscriptions sometimes convey a great deal of individualised detail, which may tell us about the dedicator's circumstances, intentions, priorities, and relationships. Melinna, for example, dedicated a proportion of her earnings to Athena Ergane (*IG* II^2 4334, pp. 208–16). She had her dedication inscribed with an explanation of her circumstances and rationale, attributing her earnings – by which she says she raised her children, probably without husbandly support – to her skilled handiwork, 'righteous courage', and Athena's favour: a self-portrait.

Sepulchral epigrams, where used, tend to be individualised with personal details (names and relationships), and sometimes with a fuller description of the dead person or the grief of the commemorator or others left behind. These do not tell us just about generalised societal values (though this is important, not least insofar as such values shaped individuals' behaviours and indeed circumstances); they may also tell us specific things about the individuals they mention. Though the sentiments they express may be partial and the terms of expression broadly conventional, the use of conventional forms of expression does not make the sentiments expressed less real[169] – and the circumstances occasionally described in the epigrams are informative about those they commemorate and those who commissioned them. Even simple inscriptions – the names of the dead only – point to the realities of an individual's life: joint commemorations may attest to enduring relationships between those commemorated, or at least between the commemorated and a common commemorator; group commemorations sometimes allow us to infer whether the women named married into or out of their fathers' demes or give partial sketches of a woman's kinship network. Where women appear as commemorators, even allowing for the possibility that they acted through intermediaries who had some degree of control over the monument, they make statements about relationships that were important to them.

Women as Subjects

It is now evident that fifth- and fourth-century ('classical') Attica is a field of investigation where ample evidence about women's relationships exists alongside a prevailing scholarly assumption of a paucity. Many ancient historians assume that the experiences of women in classical Attica are almost inaccessible. The view of David Pritchard, writing in 2014,[170] is fairly typical, despite considerable work by feminist historians:

> Women and their pastimes were prominent subjects in this state's literature and in the pictures on its painted pottery, while comedies and tragedies regularly had articulate and forthright female characters. But none of this gives us access to the ways in which women conceived of their own lives; for they were – as the late John Gould explained so well – 'the product of men and addressed to men in a male dominated world'.[171] What is more, we lack any works from democratic Athens by female writers to counter this persistently male perspective.

There are factual inaccuracies here. Not all painted pots were 'addressed to men', and it is possible that not all were the product of men.[172] Further, some epigraphic evidence arguably constitutes 'works … by female writers', giving 'access to the ways in which women conceived of their

---

[169] Compare Foxhall 1998a: 57.   [170] Pritchard 2014: 174.   [171] Gould 1980: 36.

[172] Pots 'addressed to women': Sutton 1992: 22–32; Bérard 1989: 89, with Keuls 1985: 118 *contra*. Women as viewers, intended or not: Petersen 1997; Rabinowitz 2002: 109. See Lewis 1998–9: 71–4 for problems with assuming an 'addressee'. The 'Caputi *hydria*' (attrib. Leningrad Painter, Banca Intesa private collection, Vicenza, no. 278; Beazley *ARV* 571.73) shows a woman working at the far end of a pottery workshop (Kehrberg 1982, Venit 1988). Williams 2009: 308–9 lists several possible women potters and painters, but all of these readings are contested; see my pp. 172–3 for an example.

own lives'. It is true that the major literary sources,[173] and a good deal of iconography, are male-authored and androcentric. However, through readings which are alive to the perspective and strategy of the male, androcentric author, but which centre women, one can establish windows of possibility and hold them against each other in order to produce the most plausible picture.

Some scholars hold that we can only ever speak in terms of *representations* of women.[174] I reject this pessimistic principle. Without 'assum[ing] that literary texts offer an unmediated reflection of ancient realities', as Leslie Kurke puts it, we can approach them as a refraction of ancient realities through the lens of the authors' perspectives, interests, and agendas, while also considering how representations shaped realities. Marilyn Skinner's approach is more constructive: 'Real women, like other muted groups, are not to be found so much in the explicit text of the historical record as in its gaps and silences – a circumstance that requires the application of research methods based largely upon controlled inference.'[175] 'Controlled inference' deals in gaps, silences, distortions, and refractions, but also in expressions.

Skinner's metaphor of 'silence' and 'mutedness' for the experiences and perspectives of women in the historical record is pervasive, visible in titles like *Making Silence Speak* and 'The Most Silent Women of Greece and Rome', and in statements in books on women like 'To give silence a voice is the main task I undertake in this book.'[176] Amy Richlin draws attention to another silence, not in sources but scholarship. Critiquing Foucault's *History of Sexuality*, Richlin writes, 'when I read these books I sense not consciousness but silence, a failure to ask where women's subjectivity was'.[177] The twenty-first century has seen some productive discussions of women's self-perception in classical Attica,[178] but scholarly silence, 'failure to ask', still pervades. This book makes efforts to correct this failure.

The book is divided into five chapters, each named after women who feature prominently within them. Chapter 1 demonstrates women's

---

[173] Traditionally, inscribed archaic and classical epigrams, some of which offer women's voices, have (unhelpfully) been viewed as sub-literary: Baumbach, Petrovic, and Petrovic 2010: 1–19, esp. 3–8.

[174] For example, Pelling 2000: 190 (cf. 210); Kurke 1997: 107; see also the discussion of Gould 1980 and Just 1989 on my p. 25.

[175] Skinner 1987: 3.

[176] Lardinois and McClure 2001; Scheidel 1995, Scheidel 1996; Karanika 2014: 1.

[177] Richlin 1992: xiv; cf. Zweig 1992: 147–9, Petersen 1997: 35–6.

[178] For example, Quercia and Foxhall 2014: 70–9 (women's expressions of community through marking loom weights); Taylor 2017: 133–48 (poor women's awareness of their value); Blok 2018: 16–20 (the self-perception of Xenokrateia).

capacity to build and draw on relationships through and against the vicissitudes of their lives, particularly transitions between marriages and households. Chapter 2 elucidates women's role in kin formation, often understood too narrowly as solely descent- and marriage-based. Chapter 3 argues that women used relationships with enslaved people to confirm or challenge their other roles and relationships within the household. Chapter 4 shows how income-generating work expanded women's networks, gave them opportunities publicly to present themselves independently of kin relationships, and enabled them to redefine their roles within their households. Chapter 5 shows how women formed, used, and defined relationships with those outside their kinship circles.

CHAPTER I

Diognete and Nikarete
Women's Networks through Women's Lives

We begin with two women in Attica: *Diognete*, whom we met in the Introduction to this book, and Nikarete, who lived around the same time as *Diognete* and whose life was in some ways similar but in others, very different. By following these two women through their complicated, challenging, interesting lives, we see a new side to the social world of classical Athens.

As this chapter progresses, the life stories of *Diognete* and Nikarete form a starting point for a new evaluation of the relationships and networks of classical Attic women. The diachrony of a 'biographical' approach (following individual women through their progressing lives, rather than considering 'snapshots' of their lives at moments when they occupied one status or another) makes new contributions to the understanding of women's social networks. In particular, it reveals that at least some women accumulated rather than replaced interpersonal relationships as they moved between households. In doing so, they were able to build, maintain, and exploit diverse networks, which included natal kin, affines (relatives by marriage; 'in-laws'), former affines, and non-kin.

The first section of the chapter offers us biographies of *Diognete* and Nikarete, two women from the late fifth and early fourth centuries, reconstructed from legal speeches written for cases chiefly concerning their sons. Analysis of these biographies, individually and then in parallel, demonstrates how factors including age, wealth, and social status shaped these women's relationships and their experiences of marriage, separation, and widowhood. These analyses illuminate themes developed later in the book: male absence and death; women's perspectives on and role in 'making' kinship; the supportive function of women's relationships with non-relatives; opportunities afforded by remunerated work for women to expand their networks. They show that the lives of women in classical Attica could follow complex routes, and that women's changing social positions, varied living situations, and new and changed relationships

46

materially affected their experiences from one stage to the next. The analyses question the traditional scholarly emphasis on a single transition between girlhood in the natal home and womanhood in the marital home. Without denying the potential for great trauma in such a transition, audible in women's poetry,[1] they offer new insights into potential mitigating factors. Their emphasis on experience rather than socio-legal status reveals the potential similarity between experiences of widowhood and of spousal separation during marriage, undergone by many Attic women amid the campaigns of the classical period. This reveals the unhelpful narrowness and false dichotomisation of the category 'widow'.

The next section brings more women into the picture. Their stories develop an important theme arising from the biographies in the first section: women's ability to construct and maintain networks spanning the households in which they had lived. This analysis demonstrates that this ability was not an isolated phenomenon and illustrates further permutations of women's marital experiences and social networks. The chapter then identifies cases in which remarried women maintained relationships – and sometimes residence – with children from former marriages, and relationships with former husbands. Though scholars have shown that many women maintained relationships with their natal families after marriage and played an important role in linking their natal and marital households,[2] this chapter for the first time draws out some women's ability to maintain relationships with former marital families after remarriage, a factor sometimes lost in discussions of marital status and relationships that lack a diachronic perspective.[3] Finally, the chapter shows that women's cumulative networks are visible on certain sepulchral monuments, which commemorate women alongside individuals from both their natal and marital families, and in even wider familial contexts.

This chapter argues that a woman's social identity was not exclusively tied to her immediate circumstances, much less was it solely derivative of that of her *kyrios* at any given time, but could be rich and cumulative, reflecting a lifetime of experiences and relationships.

---

[1] For example, Sappho frg. 94 Voigt, Erinna *Distaff*.

[2] For example, Cox 1988, Demand 1994: 2, Foxhall 1998a: 63, Foley 2003: 129–30, Taylor 2011c: 705–6.

[3] For example, Menekles (Isae. 2, discussed pp. 82–6) is sometimes identified as the brother-in-law of the speaker at the time of his adoption; in fact, he had divorced the speaker's sister (e.g. Cox 1988: 387, Cox 1998: 75, but correctly on p. 127; Humphreys 2018: 85, though noting the divorce; Rubinstein 1993: 21 has it correctly).

Two Women in Attica

We begin with the story of *Diognete*, drawn from Lysias 32, the prosecution of a guardian for fraudulently mismanaging the estate of the orphans in his care, and the story of Nikarete, drawn from Demosthenes 57, an appeal against the denial of a man's citizenship. These speeches centre around questions of kinship and citizen identity (itself based on certain kinds of kinship, because citizen status in Athens was determined by parentage), spheres in which androcentric sources are more likely to incorporate discussions of women. Neither woman's life fits the 'girlhood, wifehood, death' model once assumed to be the near-universal pattern of ancient female life. Both depart from that model in superficially similar ways: both were married twice, with children in both marriages; both lived without husbands for a period during their marriages because their husbands were campaigning in the Ionian War; both were widowed. In other ways, they differ even from each other quite dramatically. These two initial case studies make clear the unhelpfulness of imagining women as a collection of demographic types (unmarried girl, wife, widow), or women's lives as an inevitable sequence of clearly defined stages. Rather, they show that women shifted between porous socio-legal categories, and that a variety of factors – age, wealth, family, geography, politics – could determine and complicate the course of a woman's life.

Speeches from legal disputes, like the ones which conceal the stories of *Diognete* and Nikarete, are particularly valuable for the glimpses they offer of some of the messier realities of Attic women's lives and relationships. Using forensic oratory as a source mitigates the risks of an inductive approach: these speeches definitionally revealed to the public matters which would otherwise be concealed, by discussion before a large body of judges – and spectators[4] – who might then talk about them with their families.[5] Where those speeches became part of the oratorical canon, this also made these matters accessible to historians. Many speakers in these trials begin with an apology for bringing 'private' matters – that is, matters concerning the *oikos* (the family and its property) which might bring shame upon its members – to public attention. In Lysias 32, *Diognete*'s son-in-law begins by saying,

εἰ μὲν μὴ μεγάλα ἦν τὰ διαφέροντα, ὦ ἄνδρες δικασταί, οὐκ ἄν ποτε εἰς ὑμᾶς εἰσελθεῖν τούτους εἴασα, νομίζων αἴσχιστον εἶναι πρὸς τοὺς οἰκείους διαφέρεσθαι . . . (1)

---

[4] See Glazebrook 2022: 11–13.   [5] See e.g. Ap. *Neaira* 110–11.

> If this were not a major disagreement, gentlemen of the jury, I would never have allowed these men [my brothers-in-law, *Diognete*'s sons] to come before you [i.e. bring this case to court], because I consider it highly shameful (*aiskhistos*) to have a dispute with one's kinsmen (*oikeioi*).

Such apologies also address the failure to maintain *oikos* solidarity; like *Diognete*'s son-in-law, speakers bringing a case against a relative typically apologise for doing so.

Similarly, the speaker of Lysias 3 speaks of his great anguish at having to reveal before a court things he would rather hide:

> μάλιστα δ' ἀγανακτῶ, ὦ βουλή, ὅτι περὶ τῶν πραγμάτων εἰπεῖν ἀναγκασθήσομαι πρὸς ὑμᾶς, ὑπὲρ ὧν ἐγὼ αἰσχυνόμενος, εἰ μέλλοιεν πολλοί μοι συνείσεσθαι, ἠνεσχόμην ἀδικούμενος. ἐπειδὴ δὲ Σίμων με εἰς τοιαύτην ἀνάγκην κατέστησεν, οὐδὲν ἀποκρυψάμενος ἅπαντα διηγήσομαι πρὸς ὑμᾶς τὰ πεπραγμένα. (3)

> What especially causes me anguish, gentlemen of the council, is that I shall be compelled to speak to you about matters in which I put up with being wronged because I was ashamed (*aiskhynomenos*) at the thought that many people might share my knowledge of them. But since [my opponent] Simon has brought me to this state of compulsion, I will hide nothing and tell you everything that happened.

The shameful thought of publicising the events, he claims, initially led him to conceal them; now, he is compelled to 'hide nothing and tell everything'.[6]

Beyond drawing out women's life stories from the carefully constructed narratives these speeches offer, I also use the speeches to learn more about women's relationships and social worlds more generally. I read the speeches looking for indications of women's relationships and the changes that occurred in them, noting in particular to whom the women mentioned are implicitly or explicitly linked; their reported or inferable movements between households; and the emotional quality of their relationships, where this is attributed to them by the speaker or inferable from their reported actions. To answer the question of how women's relationships intersected with other relationships and social structures, I ask pertinent

---

[6] See also e.g. Isaeus 6.17, 'it is perhaps unpleasant for Phanostratos, gentlemen, to make visible/bring out into the open (*phaneras kathestanai*) the misfortunes of Euktemon, but I am compelled to say a few things so that, knowing the truth, you might more easily give a just verdict' (ἴσως μέν ἐστιν ἀηδὲς Φανοστράτῳ, ὦ ἄνδρες, τὰς Εὐκτήμονος συμφορὰς φανερὰς καθεστάναι· ὀλίγα δ' ἀναγκαῖον ῥηθῆναι, ἵν' ὑμεῖς τὴν ἀλήθειαν εἰδότες ῥᾷον τὰ δίκαια ψηφίσησθε).

questions: first, where are women's relationships a source of potential friction because of their 'misalignment' with other relationships evident in the speech? Two important examples are Lysias 32.11–12, where *Diognete* is said to have brought together her *philoi* and *epitēdeioi* (her social circle: kin, friends) to bring pressure on her father, and Demosthenes 55.23–4, where the speaker's mother is on intimate terms (*khraomai*) with his opponent's mother (pp. 268–9). Second, where are women's relationships treated as differing from generally held social expectations? Examples include Lysias 1.20, where a woman's going to the temple with another woman (her alleged lover's mother) for the Thesmophoria is portrayed as highly transgressive (pp. 316–9); Lysias 31.20–1, where a woman asks someone other than her son to arrange her burial (pp. 306–8 and 319–22); Isaeus 2.19, where the speaker suggests that a woman would be more likely to engineer the adoption of one of her sons than of her brother (pp. 82–6 and 147–9). In all these cases, it is in the speaker's interest to portray the relationship as unusual; we must evaluate them within the context of the speaker's agenda and the bounds of possibility suggested by other evidence.

Women who appear in the narratives of forensic speeches correspond in most cases to real women (though even here there are possible exceptions).[7] However, the words and actions attributed to them are shaped by the requirements of the speaker's argument, which may include the requirement to make a real individual conform to a 'type' for a more compelling story. These words and actions suggest the parameters within which certain women were expected to behave, in order that they might be plausible to a jury of Athenian men. Even here, better understanding of ideals allows us to make controlled inferences about likely realities. Cohen has illustrated the way in which ideals and ideology shape behaviour, including by shaping discourse about that behaviour: often, even if people seem not to behave in line with a cultural ideal, they transgress it only in certain limited, tacitly acceptable ways and remain committed to the ideal in principle, reframing their actions in discussion to bring them into line with it.[8] Nevertheless, the actions described or implicit in legal speeches are moderated to some extent by the realities of the case: some are affirmed – often in carefully limiting phrases – by witnesses; some are

---

[7] Isae. 6, Isae. 8, and [Dem.] 43 all involve disputes over whether or not a particular woman existed (see p. 74), and sometimes there is reason to suspect that certain convenient minor figures, like the woman in Lys. 1.15–17, who supposedly informed the speaker of his wife's adultery and her lover's other affairs, may be inventions to serve the narrative.

[8] Cohen 1989, Cohen 1991.

uncontested; some are inferable from other aspects or accepted events of the dispute; some are unlikely to be complete fabrications because of the susceptibility of such fabrications to disproof by opponents. Women's formal relationships are often noted as contextual information; they only tend to become central issues in cases concerning inheritance or citizenship. We may sometimes infer affective relationships based on reported behaviours; these too must be evaluated for plausibility, considering why the speaker reports such behaviours. It is here where the greatest possibilities for drawing out individuality lie.

Diognete, *Lysias 32*

Lysias 32, which contains the story of *Diognete*,[9] was probably delivered in 400.[10] The speech is part of the prosecution of *Diognete*'s father Diogeiton on a charge of mismanaging the estate of his orphaned wards. *Diognete* was married to her father Diogeiton's brother, Diodotos. When Diodotos was called up on campaign, the couple were separated, and before long, Diodotos died, leaving *Diognete* a widow.

When Diodotos died, Diogeiton became guardian of the children and their estate. The daughter's inheritance from the estate consisted in a dowry, besides which she was not entitled to inherit further.[11] When the eldest son came of age, the boys claimed that the amount Diogeiton had handed over to them was considerably less than what their father had left them. The eldest son, with the support of his brother-in-law, prosecuted Diogeiton for mismanaging their estate, accusing him of concealing his debts to them and making illegitimate or unreasonable claims about his expenditure on them. At the trial, the eldest son would have spoken briefly first. His speech was followed by the speech we know as Lysias 32, delivered by their sister's husband, acting as *synēgoros* (co-speaker, a role which could be fulfilled by a relative or friend in a legal system which would not countenance professional legal representation).[12] Much (though not all) of Diogeiton's alleged fraud is substantiated by witness testimony – indeed, Diogeiton admitted to some of it (§20)[13] – but the details of the narrative are not. The speaker aims to portray Diogeiton as deceitful, harsh, self-interested, and devoid of family loyalty. He brings *Diognete* most clearly into view towards the end of his narrative, where she castigates Diogeiton

---

[9] For the family, see *APF* no. 3885 (pp. 151–4).   [10] Compare Carey 1989: 204.
[11] Harrison 1968: 132.
[12] Carey 1989: 206. On *synēgoria*: Todd 1993: 94–5, and, much more fully, Rubinstein 2000.
[13] §§18, 27; cf. Carey 1989: 206.

at a family meeting. Here, the speaker portrays her as modest, courageous, and full of righteous anger; elsewhere in the speech, we see little of her character. As Christopher Carey puts it: 'For jury sympathy no detail was needed.'[14]

Between Wifehood and Widowhood
Attention to certain elements of *Diognete's* story and the speech in which it is concealed offers new insights into women's potential life experiences, which undermine the assumed sharp distinction between wifehood and widowhood. In the speech, *Diognete's* son-in-law tells the story as follows:

> [4] Diodotos and Diogeiton, gentlemen of the jury, were brothers who had the same mother and the same father. They had divided up their movable property but held their real estate in common. When Diodotos had made a lot of money in shipping, Diogeiton persuaded him to marry his daughter – his only daughter – and two sons and a daughter were born to him. [5] Some time later, when Diodotos was called up to serve as a hoplite with Thrasyllos, he summoned his wife, who was his niece, and her father, who was his in-law and his brother, and the grandfather and uncle of his little children, thinking that because of these family ties, it was his [Diogeiton's] job more than anyone's to act justly in regard to his [Diodotos'] children, and gave him his will and 5 talents of silver as a deposit. [6] He also produced an account of his shipping loans – 7 talents and 40 minae . . . and 2,000 [*drakhmai*] invested in the Chersonese [probably the Thracian Chersonese, now the Gallipoli Peninsula]. He charged him, if anything should happen to him [Diodotos], to give his wife a dowry of a talent and to give her the things in the bedroom [i.e. the furniture, textiles, and jewellery],[15] and to give his daughter a dowry of a talent. And he also left his wife 20 minae and 30 Cyzecine staters. [7] When he had done this, and left duplicates in the house, he left to campaign with Thrasyllos.
>
> When he died at Ephesos, for a while Diogeiton concealed from his daughter the death of her husband and took the sealed documents he [Diodotos] had left, claiming that he needed these documents to recover the shipping debts. [8] But when he eventually revealed the death to them and they had done the customary things, for the first year they lived in Peiraieus, because all the provisions had been left there. But when they were running out, he sent the children up to the city and married off their mother, giving her a dowry of 5,000 *drakhmai*, 1,000 less than what her husband gave her.

---

[14] Carey 1989: 211; cf. 207.   [15] Compare Isae. 2.9.

Though Diodotos made arrangements for his wife's remarriage in the event of his death, he is not said to have made direct arrangements for her care during his absence.[16] Rather, he left her personally with a large sum of cash, distinct from the dowry and possessions he charged Diogeiton to give her in the event of his death.[17] His leaving duplicate copies of financial documents in the house indicates that he expected her to continue living there while he was gone. Apparently, he hoped to provide her with the legal security (and independence, of a sort) of having the necessary documentation to hand in the event of a dispute and money for emergencies.[18] He expected her to remarry if he died, but these interim arrangements suggest that he expected her to live more or less independently – with some enslaved members of the household – during his absence. (Later in the speech, when the speaker reckons up the money Diogeiton claims to have spent on the children, it is assumed that the children have had a *paidagōgos*, an enslaved man to accompany the boys to school and back, and a *therapaina*, an enslaved maid, for the eight years since Diodotos' death.)[19] *Diognete*'s eldest son was younger than ten, so in no position of authority.[20] This apparent independence contrasts with the scenario described in Xenophon's *Memorabilia* 2.7, where women whose *kyrioi* had left home (in this case following the counter-oligarchic revolution of 403) went to stay with a male relative, Aristarkhos. In this context of civil war (*stasis*), the women were particularly vulnerable to violence and would have needed the physical protection of Aristarkhos and his home; democratic counter-revolutionaries were seizing land, and their own homes may have been destroyed or rendered inaccessible (2.7.2). *Diognete* did not face such immediate danger, and Diodotos' wealth meant that, for a time, she did not need to rely on Diogeiton for support but could live off the provisions in the house.

Where the various people lived at various times is unclear. However, the comment about the provisions, and certain other details, suggest that though Diogeiton and Diodotos held their real estate in common, Diodotos, *Diognete*, and their children lived in Peiraieus, given Diodotos' work in

---

[16] Compare Cohn-Haft 1995: 7, with fn. 28.   [17] Lys. 32.6; cf. Adams 1905 *ad loc*.

[18] We might have expected *Diognete* to spend some of this during her separation and widowhood, but the speaker has her claim to have given the undiminished sum to Diogeiton after Diodotos' death (§15). After Diodotos' death, Diogeiton became liable for the children's needs, even while they lived in Peiraieus (cf. §9, with Carey 1989 *ad loc.*, and §20).

[19] Lys. 32.28.

[20] Compare Hunter 1989: 298–300 for widows as de facto heads of household during their sons' minority, but *Diognete* was not (yet) a widow. Taylor 2017: 146–7 suggests that metronymics on tombstones may attest to woman-headed households; see my pp. 122–3.

shipping, while Diogeiton, his first and later second wife, and his children by her, lived in the city, where *Diognete*'s children went to live after they could no longer live in Peiraieus.[21] The speaker's implicit logic when he says that 'for the first year they lived in Peiraieus, because all the provisions had been left there, but when they were running out, he sent the children to the city' (§8) is that the depletion of provisions necessitated the departure of the children and their mother. This detail also suggests that Peiraieus was not Diogeiton's ordinary residence: otherwise, either he would have continued to buy provisions, or his departure would also be mentioned here. If Diogeiton customarily lived in the city, the point about provisions becomes a necessary explanation as to why the children did not go to live there as soon as they learned of the death of their father. That they could only live there until provisions ran out suggests they were without a breadwinner, though Diogeiton should have been administering from the orphans' estate some money for their daily needs.[22]

That Diogeiton is said to have 'sent up' (ἀναπέμπει, §8) the boys to the city after the year in Peiraieus, however, implies that Diogeiton had been living in Peiraeus with them and continued to live there without them.[23] But if he had always lived with the children, the speaker might have mentioned this in §5 as another form of intimacy which bound Diogeiton to take care of the children;[24] conversely, if he had sent the boys to someone else at this stage, we would expect the speaker to imply a failure of care. Diogeiton was apparently living with the boys (in Kollytos?) when the eldest turned eighteen (see §§9–10); the Peiraieus house was apparently vacated when provisions ran out. The comment that Diogeiton 'took' (λαμβάνει, §7) on a pretext the documents left in the house (οἴκοι) suggests that Diogeiton came to the Peiraieus house from another property and removed the documents. No pretext would have been necessary if he had not removed them from the house. Finally, in the sentences from §8 quoted on p. 52, Diognete and her children are the indirect objects of the first verb ('he told them', αὐτοῖς), making them (a plural excluding Diogeiton) the most natural subject of the plural verbs that immediately follow ('they did the customary things', ἐποίησαν; 'they lived in Peiraieus', διῃτῶντο), without

---

[21] Compare Carey 1989 *ad* §4: 'Since the only reason given for living in the Piraeus for the first year after Diodotos' death is the presence of provisions there (§8) this is unlikely to be the paternal home. The house in Kollytos (§14) is a more plausible candidate.'

[22] Lys. 32.9, Dem. 27.36, [Arist.] *Ath. pol.* 56.7; Harrison 1968: 104.

[23] Had he not been living in Peiraeus with them, we might expect *komizō*, used in Isae. 7.7 for bringing a fatherless child to live with one; had he moved from Peiraeus with them, we might expect a phrase like 'went with', along the lines of Isae. 9.27: ἦλθε καὶ αὐτὸν ἐκεῖνον ἔχουσα μικρὸν ὄντα.

[24] Compare pp. 104–14 for the role of cohabitation in constructing and recognising kinship.

any explicit change in subject to indicate that Diogeiton is included. 'He sent up' (ἀναπέμπει) most likely points to a scenario in which Diogeiton came to Peiraieus when the provisions were running out and from there organised *Diognete*'s remarriage, the departure of the children, and perhaps the leasing of the house, then returned to the city after the children had gone ahead of him. The details about duplicates and provisions respectively tell against the alternative possibilities that he came to live with them once Diodotos left or after he had told them about the death.

In sum, there is a strong possibility that during *Diognete*'s separation and first year of widowhood, she lived in her husband's house in Peiraieus with her young children and without an adult male citizen. On Diodotos' death, *Diognete* fell under the *kyrieia* (legal guardianship) of her father Diogeiton but apparently lived apart from him; this is presented as the practical thing to do. *Diognete* had a level of independence, limited by her dependence on the provisions and by Diogeiton's alleged theft of her financial documents. This is particularly significant given the delay between her widowing and her remarriage,[25] and the consequent similarity between her life during separation and in the year after her widowing.

Second, we consider the accusation that Diogeiton concealed Diodotos' death from *Diognete*, by which he evaded his responsibility to provide for the children and exercised psychological control over his daughter. It would be interesting to know whether the witnesses confirmed this.[26] On a level between the real and the symbolic, his alleged deception provides an image of the similarity between separation and widowhood: there was a period when *Diognete* did not know the difference herself.

Even without deception, limited communications led to similar uncertainty for other women whose husbands had left on campaigns. One woman in the first half of the fourth century had to consult the oracle at Dodona to ask if her husband was dead, and whether she and her children should 'carry out the customary rites' (*t[elesousi] ta nomima*; cf. *epoiēsan ta nomizomena*, Lys. 32.8). She had presumably been waiting uncertainly for some time before she asked.

> ἦ τέθνακε Ἀρισώνυμος [καὶ ὡς τεθ]-
> νακότι τοὶ παῖδες καὶ ἁ γυνὰ τ[ελέσουσι][27]
> τὰ νόμιμα ὡς τεθνακότι; (DVC, no. 2980)

---

[25] Contrast Dem. 27.13.   [26] So too Carey 1989: 211–12.
[27] Dakarēs, Vokotopoulou, and Christidēs 2013 restore τ[ελεῖν], which is less likely; I thank Peter Thonemann for discussing this with me.

Has Aristonymos died, and as for a dead person his children and his wife should do the customary rites for him as for a dead person?

These situations find an iconographic parallel in 'departure scenes' commonly painted on Attic pots, which show men leaving their families to fight.[28] Where a woman appears in such a scene, it is rarely clear whether she is supposed to be the departing warrior's mother or wife. Contextual evidence (pairings with an aged man; the predominance of images with labelled figures showing Hektor leaving his parents over images showing Hektor leaving Andromakhe) suggests she is most often supposed to be his mother.[29] Nevertheless, the painter sometimes adds a wife (as in Figure 1.1). Pots with 'departure scenes' depict the moment of a man's departure into battle but could be used in funerary contexts where the image doubled as illustrating his departure into death. The younger woman portrayed is simultaneously a separated wife and a widow.

Figure 1.1 Drawing of design on Attic red-figure amphora, c. 460, Oxford, Ashmolean Museum ANFortnum.C.196, c. 460. Drawing by Zadia Green, from Lewis 2002: 41, fig. 1.22, courtesy of Sian Lewis.

---

[28] On which see Lissarrague 1989: 44–50 and Lissarrague 1990: 43–69.

[29] Lewis 2002: 39–42, Lissarrague 1990: 43–69. Bérard and Durand 1989 argue that images on painted pots are in conversation with one another and may only fully be understood in such terms; certainly knowledge of the repertoire of 'departure scenes' is helpful here, but it is possible to draw significant connections between images on pots and textual reflections or refractions of women's experiences even without comparison to a large body of related iconography.

Kinship Ties and Social Strategies

Close, gender-aware analysis of the relationships and their presentation in Lysias 32 revises our understanding of the operation of kinship in classical Attica and offers new insights into different strategies of relationship-building. The obligations conferred by kinship are a central theme of the speech. The speaker tells how Diodotos, preparing to go on campaign,

> καλέσας τὴν ἑαυτοῦ γυναῖκα, ἀδελφιδῆν οὖσαν, καὶ τὸν ἐκείνης μὲν πατέρα, αὑτοῦ δὲ κηδεστὴν καὶ ἀδελφὸν ὁμοπάτριον, πάππον δὲ τῶν παιδίων καὶ θεῖον, ἡγούμενος διὰ ταύτας τὰς ἀναγκαιότητας οὐδενὶ μᾶλλον προσήκειν δικαίῳ περὶ τοὺς αὑτοῦ παῖδας γενέσθαι ... (§5)

> called together his wife, who was his niece, and her father, who was his father-in-law and homopatric brother, and the grandfather of the little children and their uncle, thinking that because of these kinship ties there was no one better suited to deal justly with his children ...

In the speech Lysias gives her, *Diognete* repeats the same catalogue of connections, insisting that they confer a religious obligation on Diogeiton to look after his children (§12–13). The speaker returns to the theme later (§19).

The strategy of 'doubling' kinship ties (e.g. making one's brother one's son- or father-in-law) is also visible in cases that do not involve *epiklēroi*. In Demosthenes 27, Demosthenes' father made his fraternal nephew and sororal nephew guardians of his son and estate and for good measure married them to his widow and daughter respectively in his will, making Demosthenes' paternal cousins his stepfather and brother-in-law. Demosthenes explains: ἡγούμενος, καὶ τούτους ἔτ' οἰκειοτέρους εἴ μοι ποιήσειεν, οὐκ ἂν χεῖρόν μ' ἐπιτροπευθῆναι ταύτης τῆς οἰκειότητος προσγενομένης, 'he thought that if he made these men even more closely connected to me by family ties (*et' oikeioteroi*), I would be taken care of better because of the additional family connection (*oikeiotēs*)', §§4–5. A vain hope: Demosthenes' guardians defrauded him.

In Demosthenes 41, Polyeuktos, who had two daughters but no biological sons, adopted his wife *Philokrateia*'s brother Leokrates, making him his son as well as his brother-in-law (his daughters were therefore not *epiklēroi*, as their father now had a son and heir). Similarly, in Isaeus 7.9, a man is said to have adopted his half-sister; in Isaeus 8.40, a man adopts his wife's son from a previous marriage.[30] Polyeuktos then went further and

---

[30] Osborne 1985b: 128, pointing to a full list of adoptions attested in the orators in Gernet 1920: 139–41. For a comprehensive treatment of adoption in fourth-century Athens, see Rubinstein 1993.

married his younger daughter Kleiokrateia[31] to Leokrates, so that the man was now also his son-in-law (§3). Again, there are comparanda: we also hear of a man who married his half-sister (Dem. 57.20)[32] and of a pair of families from the deme of Myrrhinous in which the two brothers from one family married two sisters from the other (i.e. the second brother married his sister-in-law).[33] However, despite these close, overlapping ties, Polyeuktos later divorced Kleiokrateia from Leokrates after quarrelling with him and married her to another man, Spoudias (§4). This seems not to have affected Leokrates' relationship with his sister *Philokrateia*: he was probably one of the brothers who acted as witnesses to her lending Spoudias 1,800 *drakhmai* (§8–9).[34]

Louis Cohn-Haft suggests that such 'complicated interconnections that dazzle the modern observer … appear to have been everyday occurrences in Classical Athens'. He implies that they were a strategy to stabilise marriages: 'Marriage in Athens joined two families as well as two individuals, and the man who would divorce a wife, even for a dazzling improvement in his circumstances, would need to consider carefully his potential advantage as against the almost certain enmity of the family he was rejecting.'[35] Antiphon the Sophist commented in the later fifth century:

χαλεπαὶ μὲν ἐκπομπαί, τοὺς φίλους ἐχθροὺς ποιῆσαι, ἴσα φρονοῦντας ἴσα πνέοντας, ἀξιώσαντα καὶ ἀξιωθέντα. (Frg. 49 Pendrick.)

Divorce [literally, 'sending away (a wife)'] is difficult: to make friends/ relatives (*philoi*) into enemies, those who thought the same [things as he], breathed the same [air as he], after deeming them worthy and after being deemed worthy [by them].[36]

---

[31] Name known from *SEG* 17:83: Shear 1937: 341.

[32] Compare Osborne 1985b: 150, noting that this 'reduces the extent of family on the paternal side'; this downside to the strategy is discussed at pp. 60–1.

[33] Osborne 1985b: 133; another man from the family married the daughter of one of these two marriages. Osborne notes that two family members were *manteis* (seers); the family's important religious role may have motivated their endogamy.

[34] Compare Cox 1988: 387. The same may not have been true for Kleiokrateia's relationships: *SEG* 17:83, the base of a statue by Praxiteles, has Kleiokrateia's name as dedicant on the right hand side, and a blank space on the left; possibly it had been intended as a joint dedication but the other dedicator later pulled out. Shear 1937: 341 wonders whether this space on the left had been planned for the name of the elder daughter and then left blank as a result of the dispute. The dedication is for Demeter and Kore, so the other intended dedicant, if there was one, would probably have been a woman; if it had not been Kleiokrateia's sister, it might have been her mother *Philokrateia* (a mother-and-daughter dedication to the Mother and Daughter?). In such a large transaction as the loan (1,800 *drakhmai* could buy several plots of land: cf. RO 172 C 80–99), *Philokrateia*'s brothers presumably acted as her *kyrioi*.

[35] Cohn-Haft 1995: 8, 13. Foxhall 1998a: 61 suggests that men used analogous strategies to stabilise their friendships.

[36] I thank Peter Thonemann for drawing my attention to this fragment.

Cohn-Haft concludes that 'the deterrent of family enmity' suggests that 'divorce was relatively infrequent and marriage a fundamentally stable institution'. The examples of *Diognete*, Demosthenes, and Kleiokrateia, however, all illustrate failures of this strategy. The doubled connections between Diogeiton and Diodotos could not save *Diognete*'s marriage from Diodotos' early death – a much greater threat to the stability of marriage than divorce – nor did they prevent the breakdown of trust and development of enmity. Anxiety to shore up family connections by multiplying them might be evidence not of the stability of marriages and families but of the opposite.

A second illuminating element of the family ties theme in Lysias 32 is the implication of a particularly close tie between a grandfather and his daughter's children, who are denoted by the term *thygatridē* (daughter's daughter, §3) or *thygatridous* (daughter's son, §§16, 24, 27). Given classical Attica's gendered disparity in average age at first marriage, it was much likelier for a grandparent–grandchild relationship (particularly a grand*father*–grandchild relationship) to exist through one's daughter than one's son. (The father of Mantitheos in [Dem.] 40.12 apparently persuaded his son to marry young so that he might survive to see his grandchildren.) We have some touching evidence for grandparents' relationships with their daughters' children. The late fifth-century grave *stēlē* of Ampharete celebrates her relationship with her daughter's child.[37] The mid fourth-century epitaph of Philokydis says that her daughter Eukleia was taken in by Philokydis' parents when she died[38] – the arrangement Diodotos intended.[39]

One could argue that the word *thygatridous* implies an inferior class of grandson: the daughter's son, who would, unless his mother were an *epiklēros*, grow up in another household and inherit from another man, as opposed to the son's son, *huidous*,[40] who would ideally grow up in what had been his grandfather's household and ultimately inherit from him. While *Diognete was* an *epiklēros* – which helped motivate the double

---

[37] *IG* II² 10650, Athens, Archaeological Museum of Kerameikos, P695/I221; pp. 121–2.

[38] *SEMA* 2516; Cranbrook Academy of Art, Bloomfield Hills, Michigan, 1938.27, late second quarter of fourth century, unknown provenance. Compare Clairmont 1970: 169–70, appendix 2, and plate 37; Pomeroy 1997: 130–31.

[39] Some fourth-century epitaphs celebrate women as grandmothers without discussing the grandparental relationship in detail: *IG* II² 5673 (discussed on pp. 91–3), 6288, 11998. For the important role of maternal grandparents, see pp. 119–21, Foxhall 1994: 95–6, and Golden 2015: 115–18; for the importance of maternal grandfathers and uncles in Greek society more generally, see Hdt. 3.50, Isae. 8.15 with Griffith-Williams 2013 *ad loc.*, and Bremmer 1983.

[40] *Huidē*, son's daughter, does not appear until the first century AD.

kinship ties – the speaker of Lysias 32 is not concerned with the boys'
inheritance status with regard to Diogeiton, which is not at issue in the
speech, but with the obligations consequent on Diogeiton's kinship with
them. The speaker's consistent preference for the term *thygatridous* (§§16,
24, 27) over the term *adelphidous* (nephew) to emphasise (rather than
minimise) the family tie, paralleled by the choice to emphasise
Diogeiton's status as grandfather over his status as uncle (e.g. §3) therefore
suggests that the relationship between a grandfather and his daughter's
sons was privileged over the relationship between paternal uncle and
nephew.

The potential value for *women* of relationships through one's daughter is
illustrated by another aspect of the case: *Diognete* fought her sons' case
through her daughter's husband. This would have been particularly
important for *Diognete* as an *epiklēros*, a status which bound her tightly
to her natal family. It was only through her daughter (who, having
brothers, could be married outside the descent line), and through her
own second marriage to Hegemon (also outside the descent line, permissible because *Diognete* had already had sons with her paternal uncle to
inherit Diogeiton's estate), that *Diognete* had allies not immediately related
to Diogeiton. That she had two such allies may have been crucial: Kapparis
suggests that her new husband Hegemon, her first recourse, seems to have
been unwilling to get involved.[41] Nikarete, whom we will meet in the next
section, was similarly able to recruit the husband (and son) of her daughter
from her first marriage for legal support, this time as witnesses rather than
advocates. Chapter 2 ('Bringing People In'), discusses women's use of kin
networks for help from the opposite perspective, considering the role of
maternal rather than filial kin.

Third, given that, from a legal perspective, the power to appoint
guardians, adopt, and contract marriages was men's, we may refer to the
'doubling' of family connections as a male 'social strategy'.[42] The logic
behind it (ἡγούμενος ..., Lys. 32.5, Dem. 27.5) is attributed to and
appealed to by men. This book concerns the 'social strategies' of women.
One such strategy, born of compulsion, was to diversify rather than
consolidate relationships, developing support systems which branched
across households and kin groups (including families not connected to

---

[41] Kapparis 2021: 48.
[42] Compare Osborne 1985b: 135–7 on marriage as a 'strategy' of (male) 'actors', though he notes the
'parental' calculation implied by Xen. *Oec.* 7.10–11. In fn. 28 (printed on p. 246), he adds 'This is not
to deny the considerable informal rôle of women'; in Chapter 2, I make the footnote into the main
text.

the woman by birth or marriage) so that if one relationship failed or did not suffice, they could rely on another, rather than attempting to prevent relationship failure or weakness by overlaying ties, which had the potential to shrink the pool of allies.[43] This is the strategy employed by *Diognete* in Lysias 32, and by Nikarete in the next section of this chapter.

How Much Agency?

According to the speaker of Lysias 32, when Diogeiton turned *Diognete*'s sons out of his house, they went first to *Diognete* and brought her to the speaker (their sister's husband, *Diognete*'s son-in-law), begging him to help them. She 'implored and entreated' him to assemble 'her father and her *philoi*' for a meeting (ἡ μήτηρ αὐτῶν ἠντεβόλει με καὶ ἱκέτευε συναγαγεῖν αὐτῆς τὸν πατέρα καὶ τοὺς φίλους, §11). The son-in-law spoke first to *Diognete*'s second husband Hegemon, then to τοὺς ἄλλους ἐπιτηδείους (§12), 'the other friends (*epitēdeioi*)' – of *Diognete*? Of her sons? Of the family?[44] Humphreys suggests that at least some of them, who later served as witnesses in the court case, 'may have been kin of [*Diognete*'s] son-in-law, and perhaps of [her] second husband, rather than of Diogeiton himself'.[45] As discussed in the Introduction, *philoi* and *epitēdeioi* are capacious terms which could include kin and non-kin. *Diognete*'s group of *philoi* and *epitēdeioi* can constructively be compared with the various men – some kin, some not – who testified for Nikarete. As we will see, hers is an interesting illustration of the potential extent and diversity of women's networks.

Though it is not entirely clear, this meeting may have been the private arbitration mentioned at the beginning of the speech (ἔπεισα τοῖς φίλοις ἐπιτρέψαι δίαιταν, 'I persuaded [both parties] to submit the matter to the arbitration of their *philoi*', §2), which was ultimately unsuccessful. Private arbitration, the attempt to settle a dispute by the judgement of a mutually agreed-upon third party, was an important element of the Athenian legal system to some degree accessible to women.[46] Its likely prevalence and importance is masked by the fact that our chief sources for Athens' legal

---

[43] As was the case in Nikarete's family: as Osborne 1985b: 150 notes, 'the family endogamy whereby [Euxitheos'] grandfather married a half-sister reduces the extent of family on the paternal side.'

[44] Compare pp. 321–2.   [45] Humphreys 2018: 235–6.

[46] Kapparis 2021: 2–3. Kapparis frames arbitration as the 'second tier' of the Athenian legal system, after the magistrates ('the first tier') and before the courts, but note that *private* (as opposed to public) arbitration would *precede*, not follow, a potential appeal to a magistrate. For pre-trial legal processes, see Todd 1993: 123–9. For arbitration more generally, see Roebuck 2001. For discussion of some of the legal aspects of this scene, see Kapparis 2021: 47–51, though he may overstate *Diognete*'s role; see p. 64. Humphreys 2018: 213 discusses this meeting under the heading 'Mediation'.

system, the extant forensic speeches (themselves a tiny fraction of all the speeches delivered in Athens' courts)[47] all derive from disputes where arbitration had failed or not been attempted. For women, and others who did not serve as jurors, arbitration was probably the primary context for engagement with Athens' legal system. The best-known depiction of an arbitration is the scene which gives its name to Menander's *Epitrepontes* ('People Submitting a Dispute to Arbitration'). Significantly, the dispute in *Epitrepontes* is between an enslaved couple[48] and another enslaved man, who choose a citizen to arbitrate. In this case, the woman in the couple does not speak, largely because of the conventional limit of three speaking actors per scene.[49] However, she is present at the arbitration: at ll. 302–3, her husband Syros asks her to pass him the baby, whom she is said at ll. 267–9 to be holding. When Daos, the other party, describes the beginning of the dispute, he says: μετὰ τῆς γυναικὸς περιτυχών μοι νῦν, ἄφνω / τὰ τότε συνεκτεθέντα τούτῳ … / … ἀξιοῖ / ἀπολαμβάνειν, 'And now [Syros] turns up with his wife (*meta tēs gunaikos*) and out of nowhere is suddenly asking to have back the things that were left with this [baby] back then' (ll. 275–8). The enslaved woman is represented as a participant in the dispute and the search for a resolution.[50]

As far as the speaker of Lysias 32 tells it, *Diognete* was not in a position to instigate such a meeting or arbitration independently but could persuade male allies – beginning with her son-in-law – to do so on her behalf and was able to play an active part, speaking (§§12–17) and presenting evidence (§14–15). The speaker reproduces her supposed speech, in which she castigates Diogeiton for his treatment of her children. If this was an arbitration, it was unsuccessful: those present left in silence (§18) rather than coming to an agreement; at §2 the speaker says that the arbitration failed because Diogeiton refused to be persuaded by his *philoi*. Whether or not these were the same meeting, the arbitration evidently failed, and the

---

[47] Carugati 2019: 78 estimates 0.025%.

[48] Compare ll. 376–80 with 407–8; the couple are enslaved but permitted to live outside of their enslaver's household, keeping some of their earnings but paying him a proportion (*apophora*); they are also able to have an informal partnership. See Kamen 2013: 19–31 for this category of enslaved people.

[49] This explains why the woman is unable to speak even when asked a direct question by her husband at ll. 382–3.

[50] For women taking more active roles in legal disputes outside of the jury courts, see Ap. *Neaira* 45–7, where Neaira speaks at an arbitration concerning her own status, and [Dem.] 40.10–11, where Plangon (a woman of citizen status) swears an oath at an arbitration (cf. Kapparis 2021: 109–10, though his view of the outcome of Neaira's arbitration is very rosy; contrast my p. 160); see also Lysias 23.9–11, where a woman lodges a claim of ownership over a man named Pankleon, whose status is disputed.

case came to court. This marks the end of the narrative portion of Lysias 32; the remaining extant chapters of the partially preserved speech detail Diogeiton's financial abuses and stress their betrayal of the ideal and convention of trust between relatives.

The readings of *Diognete*'s role in this case by Lin Foxhall and later, Michael Gagarin, differ significantly from mine. Foxhall contrasts the presentation of *Diognete*'s behaviour in Lysias 32 both with what she constructs as *Diognete*'s actual behaviour and with her reconstructions of the behaviour of Kleoboule, the mother of Demosthenes, from Demosthenes 27 and 28.[51] Foxhall plausibly argues that when Kleoboule's husband died, though he had arranged in his will that she should marry her nephew Aphobos, she refused and so retained economic control of her dead husband's household – though Aphobos did take the dowry, for which Demosthenes sued when he came of age.[52] Foxhall suggests that *Diognete*, by contrast, 'forfeited any authority she might have been able to claim to her father', accepting a smaller dowry than she was owed because 'she had neither the courage nor the wits, nor perhaps the resources of Kleoboule'.[53] She believes *Diognete*'s 'supposedly courageous defiance against this unjust authority' to be 'a fabrication', pointing out that 'it was the speaker who organized the gathering of relatives' and that the account of the meeting 'makes it sound very staged, almost as if she had been given a script by the children of her first marriage and her son-in-law'. Instead, Foxhall hypothesises that the remarriages of *Diognete* and Diogeiton, and the birth of children in both second marriages, rendered the boys 'effectively surplus to the households to which they were most closely related'. Gagarin follows Foxhall's interpretation: 'Since [*Diognete*] had remarried and was raising a new family, it seems unlikely that she took as much initiative in the matter as the speaker represents.' He suggests that 'Lysias may give her such an extended voice precisely in order to compensate for her lack of more substantive action on behalf of her orphaned children'.[54]

Sally Humphreys' view is closer to mine:

> A woman who felt herself wronged might . . . have to wait some time before she could mobilize a man to champion her cause; but Attic women could be tenacious . . . Diogeiton's daughter had to wait until her own daughter was married in order to find, in her son-in-law, an ally willing to help her sons claim their rights.[55]

[51] Kleoboule's name is known from [Plut.] *Mor.* 844a = *X orat.* 8, *Demosthenes*.
[52] Foxhall 1996: 144–7.   [53] Foxhall 1996: 149.   [54] Gagarin 2001: 170, 176.
[55] Humphreys 2018: 213.

Konstantinos Kapparis goes further: 'even though on the surface it is a dispute between men – her son-in-law has sued her father on behalf of her young sons – she stands at the centre of this dispute and in all but name she is the true prosecutor of her father'.[56] This, I think, is to overstate her role and later veers into distortion, where Kapparis states that *Diognete*:

> is not represented by her second husband, who was her *kyrios* at the time when she enacted litigation against her father for the inheritance of her children … Instead, she is represented by her son-in-law. This case makes clear that the law did not insist that her *kyrios* ought to represent her. She could choose another man if she wished, without further ado.[57]

Though Kapparis is right about the flexibility of *kyrieia*, discussed more fully later in this chapter, this may have been less a matter of 'choice' and 'wish' than necessity, and in any case, the speaker is representing not *Diognete* but her son (§§1–2).[58]

Foxhall and Gagarin are right that the speech Lysias gives *Diognete* is unlikely to bear much relation to what she actually said,[59] but there are reasons to think that she did take the kind of initiative the speaker suggests. Foxhall emphasises that 'it was the speaker who organized the gathering of relatives'. However, as the speaker presents it, *Diognete* suggested the meeting and which men to bring, an important element of organisation. She would have known who her father's friends were better than his granddaughter's husband, whose role was rather to go and speak to them (§11–12). There is no compelling reason to believe that he emphasised *Diognete*'s role at the expense of his own rather than vice versa, particularly given that he casts her in a highly feminine role, performing a lament for her sons, entreating and supplicating the speaker – the typical way Attic men describe women's attempts to influence them[60] – and saying she was not accustomed to speak among men (§11).[61] Gagarin rightly shows that this is a version of a common forensic trope, but it is a specifically gendered version. The speaker could have cut *Diognete* entirely and just have had the brothers go to their brother-in-law. Either he puts her in because she did have an important role (we note the detail that the children brought *to her* their uncle's mislaid accounts book when they found it, §14 – incidentally, this

---

[56] Kapparis 2021: 12, set out more fully at 47–51.
[57] Kapparis 2021, fn. 24 to p. 116, printed on p. 123.
[58] Probably just the eldest, though he speaks as if it were both: Carey 1989: 206.
[59] Foxhall 1996: 149; Gagarin 2001: 170; Kapparis 2021: 48–50 concedes this.
[60] Johnstone 2003: 270–1.   [61] Gagarin 2001: 164.

implies that she had functional literacy and numeracy),[62] though he may still have exaggerated it, or he invents or exaggerates her role because the image of the brave widow fighting for her sons is potent. This is possible, but not necessary: for example, *Diognete*'s complaint that her sons were thrown out ἐν τριβωνίοις, ἀνυποδήτους ('in worn-out clothes, without shoes', §16) is similar to the accusation in Isaeus 5.11 that another allegedly abusive guardian sent off his fatherless charge wearing ἐμβάδας καὶ τρίβωνα ('flimsy felt shoes and a worn-out cloak'), but Isaeus does not attribute the accusation to the young man's widowed mother. Demosthenes chooses not to present his widowed mother Kleoboule as fighting on his behalf, though she may well have been. The speaker claims that Diogeiton concealed the full extent of the financial abuse until the last moment, when friends compelled him to submit his claims to scrutiny (§§20–5) – though *Diognete* was aware of some of it (§§14, 25). Foxhall implies this concealment was fabricated by the speaker to exculpate *Diognete*, but the simpler explanation – that Diogeiton concealed the abuse to protect himself from prosecution – is just as likely.

Both Foxhall and Gagarin assume that once a woman had remarried she would be less interested in her children from a former marriage, a view first articulated by Athena in Homer's *Odyssey*, where it forms part of a discourse about female fickleness which sits in tension with the portrayal of Penelope. Athena warns Telemakhos not to stay too long away from his mother, in case she remarries in his absence:

> οἶσθα γὰρ οἷος θυμὸς ἐνὶ στήθεσσι γυναικός·
> κείνου βούλεται οἶκον ὀφέλλειν ὅς κεν ὀπυίῃ,
> παίδων δὲ προτέρων καὶ κουριδίοιο φίλοιο
> οὐκέτι μέμνηται τεθνηκότος οὐδὲ μεταλλᾷ. (15.20–3)

You know what the spirit in the breast of a woman is like: she wants to benefit the household (*oikos*) of whatever man should marry her, and when her dear husband dies, she does not remember him or the children of her former marriage [literally, 'her earlier/former children'], and does not ask after them.

In Euripides' *Electra*, the title character makes a similar claim, describing how after her father Agamemnon's death, her mother Klytaimnestra, τεκοῦσα δ' ἄλλους παῖδας Αἰγίσθῳ πάρα / πάρεργ' Ὀρέστην κἀμὲ ποιεῖται δόμων, 'having given birth to other children with Aigisthos, treats Orestes and me as superfluous to the house' (62–3).[63]

---

[62] Kapparis 2021: 50 compares *Philokrateia* (Dem. 41) and Kleoboule (Dem. 27–31), who also have facility with household accounts.

[63] Contrast Humphreys 2018: 216, quoted on p. 81 in fn. 121.

The final section of this chapter tells against this assumption. It illustrates cases of women maintaining connections to the households of their former husbands, including one woman who seemingly had her new husband take in her child by her previous husband who was being financially abused by his guardian. These comparative cases newly demonstrate the potential importance and persistence of remarried women's relationships with their children from earlier marriages, a phenomenon not much considered in existing studies of the Attic family.

Nikarete, Demosthenes 57

Diognete's story makes an interesting comparison with the story of Nikarete, whom we meet in Demosthenes 57.[64] Demosthenes 57 is an appeal by a man named Euxitheos against the decision of his deme, Halimous, to strike him from its register of members, and therefore from the citizen body. A review of the citizen roll in the mid fourth century, carried out on the deme level, had found that he was not descended from an Athenian father and mother and therefore was not a citizen. One who appealed against such a decision and lost could be sold into slavery, the penalty for non-citizens posing as citizens. The deme's decision also posed a threat to Euxitheos' mother Nikarete, by exposing her to the charge of being an unregistered metic (immigrant). All non-citizen residents of Attica had to register with an Athenian guarantor (*prostatēs*) and pay the metic tax (*metoikion*), but Nikarete, considering herself of citizen status, would not have done this. The punishment for being an unregistered metic was also sale into slavery.[65]

Euxitheos argues that both his parents were Athenian, and that Euboulides, the demarch (chief deme official) of Halimous making the case against him, is motivated by personal enmity. He says that Euboulides' case is based on his father's accent and his mother's lowly employment. He counters that his father acquired his accent after he was captured in war and enslaved outside Attica, and his mother was compelled into such work by poverty. The review of citizens probably took place in 346/5; this speech was probably delivered the following year, 345/4. Because it is so crucial for Euxitheos to prove that he is the child of two Athenian parents, he does, exceptionally and only once, at almost the very end of his speech (§68), give his mother's name in full – Nikarete, daughter of Damostratos of Melite.

---

[64] Compare *APF* no. 3126 B (pp. 93–5) and Lacey 1980. Osborne 1985b: 148–51 discusses this case from a different perspective.
[65] Compare Kennedy 2014: 97–101.

Nikarete was born to Damostratos of Melite, a city deme, and his second wife Khairestrate some time before 420, in the devastating years of the plague and Arkhidamian War (§37).[66] She had an older full-brother, Timokrates, and a much older half-brother and half-sister. Damostratos died before Nikarete married, which was probably around age fifteen: it was Timokrates who married her to her first husband, Protomakhos (§40). With Protomakhos, she had a daughter, whom he later married to a man from Kholargos, a deme a few miles north of Athens (§40). Protomakhos then divorced Nikarete to marry an *epikleros*, with whom he later had sons (§§41, 43).[67] When he divorced her, Protomakhos persuaded his acquaintance (γνώριμος) Thoukritos of Halimous, a coastal deme about four miles from Athens, just south of Peiraieus, to take Nikarete as his wife. Again, her brother Timokrates gave her in marriage. This was probably in about 410–407,[68] when she was somewhere between sixteen and twenty; Thoukritos was presumably at least thirty. Nikarete had two children with Thoukritos before he went away on military service with Thrasyboulos,[69] and she became a wet nurse:

μετὰ δὲ ταῦτα χρόνῳ ὕστερον παιδίων αὐτῇ δυοῖν ἤδη γεγενημένων, καὶ τοῦ μὲν πατρὸς στρατευομένου καὶ ἀποδημοῦντος μετὰ Θρασυβούλου, αὐτὴ δ' οὖσ' ἐν ἀπορίαις, ἠναγκάσθη τὸν Κλεινίαν τὸν τοῦ Κλειδίκου τιτθεῦσαι. (§42)

Some time after [her marriage to Thoukritos], when by now she had two children [with him], and my father was away on military service with Thrasyboulos, and she was struggling financially, she was compelled to become nurse to Kleinias, the son of Kleidikos.[70]

Nikarete may have moved into Kleidikos' house to nurse Kleinias, bringing her children with her, the youngest of whom she must still have been breastfeeding, unless she had lost a baby. However, a line of Menander

---

[66] *APF* no. 3126 B (p. 94) has 420 as a *terminus ante quem* for Nikarete's birth based on §42. Lacey 1980: 59 dates her second marriage – by which time she had had a child with her first husband – to 410–405, based on the assumption that 'the disasters afflicting the city' (§45) refer to 405–403, and closely connecting them with her separation, a dating accepted here but not insisted on. *APF* no. 3126 B (p. 94) puts the second marriage c. 395, followed by Phelan 2016: 200, who thinks 'the disasters' refer to the 390s (p. 185; cf. 165, fn. 129).

[67] Following Lacey 1980; Phelan 2016 *ad* §43 (pp. 206–7) argues that Nikarete and Protomakhos had, as well as their daughter, other children who died in childhood.

[68] Lacey 1980: 59 thinks a few years later, but Thoukritos was taken prisoner in the Dekeleian War (§18), ending 404, having previously had two surviving children with Nikarete: it cannot have been much later.

[69] Lacey 1980: 58–9 thinks this was Thrasyboulos of Steiria; Phelan 2016: 203–4, adopting the later dating, thinks Thrasyboulos of Kollytos, on his campaign of 387.

[70] For the possibility of a link between Kleidikos' family and Alkibiades', see *APF* no. 600, III–IV (pp. 12–15).

suggests she might have brought him into her own home to nurse, continuing to live there with her children. In Menander's play *Samia*, Khrysis, who has been nursing her neighbour Plangon's baby after the loss of her own, says that she could not bear to '[let] a nurse [raise] this child in some tenement-house (*synoikia*)' (τοῦτο τίτθην ἐν συνοικίᾳ τινὶ . . ., ll. 84–5). She does not imagine the nurse coming to live with her or with Plangon, though the circumstances of the plot complicate the evidence: Plangon is unmarried, and the baby is being kept secret. Wet-nursing contracts from first-century Graeco-Roman Egypt frequently stipulate that the nurse care for the child in her own home and bring her to the hirer for regular inspection,[71] but these babies were foundlings raised in slavery by the hirers, rather than biological children of a hiring family in which the mother could not breastfeed. Hippocrates, Galen, and Soranus; wet-nursing contracts; and stable isotope evidence from classical-period skeletons in the Greek colony of Apollonia Pontike (modern Sozopol, Bulgaria), which had close cultural and political relations with Athens in the fifth century, all attest to a norm of exclusive breastfeeding until about six months, followed by progressive weaning usually completed between the ages of two and three.[72] Nikarete and her children would have lived with Kleinias, in her house or his, for some time.

Meanwhile, Nikarete's husband Thoukritos, away on campaign, was taken prisoner, sold into slavery, sent to Leukas (modern Lefkada), and ransomed. He eventually made his way back to Attica but was probably gone ten or fifteen years (§§18–19, 42).[73] Like Penelope, Nikarete did not remarry but was reunified with Thoukritos after his eventual return, when Nikarete was probably between thirty and thirty-five. The couple had three more children. Four of their five children predeceased their father (§28), who was dead by 346. The widowed Nikarete was again compelled to earn, this time selling *tainiai* with her surviving son Euxitheos (§§31, 34–5). *Tainiai* were woollen bands produced by tablet-weaving (a technique performed with pierced, hand-held, wooden or bone tablets instead of a loom) which could be worn around the head at festivals, symposia, and sacrifices; tied around monuments; or affixed to larger textiles as borders. Foxhall suggests that *tainia* production is strongly associated with singleness in women: unlike a warp-weighted loom, which would usually have been operated by at least two women,[74] a weaving tablet could be operated

---

[71] For example, *BGU* 4.1106 and 1107, Alexandria, 13 BC. On nurses in Attica, see Kennedy 2014: 133–6, Taylor 2017: 135–41.
[72] Kwok and Keenleyside 2015.   [73] Lacey 1980: 59.
[74] As depicted on the Amasis *lekythos*, New York, Metropolitan Museum of Art 31.11.10, c. 550–530.

alone and was therefore a better option for a woman who did not live with a sister- or mother-in-law.[75] Nikarete and Euxitheos were still selling *tainiai* at the time of the speech.

Working and Networking

Euboulides apparently used Nikarete's work as evidence that she was not a citizen-status woman but a metic or enslaved woman. Euxitheos responds:

> ὡς γὰρ ἔγωγ᾽ ἀκούω, πολλαὶ καὶ τιτθαὶ καὶ ἔριθοι καὶ τρυγήτριαι γεγόνασ᾽ ὑπὸ τῶν τῆς πόλεως κατ᾽ ἐκείνους τοὺς χρόνους συμφορῶν ἀσταὶ γυναῖκες, πολλαὶ δ᾽ ἐκ πενήτων πλούσιαι νῦν. (§45)

> From what I have heard, many women became nurses and woolworkers and grape-harvesters because of the misfortunes of the city at that time – citizen-status women – and many women who were poor are now rich.

'The misfortunes of the city' probably refers to the devastating Dekeleian War (also called the Ionian War), which ended in 404 with siege, starvation, and *stasis*. Euxitheos suggests that the financial consequences for households, many of which lost their breadwinner temporarily or permanently, compelled citizen-status women to do paid work they would not otherwise have done. In Nikarete's family alone, her half-brother Amytheon died on the Sicilian Expedition in 415–413 (§38); her husband was taken prisoner during the Dekeleian War of 415–404 (§18); later, in 388, her nephew Ktesibios was killed on Thrasyboulos' expedition to Thrace (§38). Attic legal speeches are littered with dead soldiers and their widows, as was the wider Attic population in the fifth and fourth centuries. Euxitheos' analysis finds support in Xenophon's *Memorabilia* 2.7, which describes how women whose menfolk had fled to Peiraieus to escape the *stasis* of 403 became *erithoi*, woolworkers. Like Nikarete while she was wet-nursing, they were not widows but women separated from their husbands and *kyrioi* by conflict.

Claire Taylor evaluates Nikarete's nursing in a relatively positive light. She argues for the existence of inter-household networks developed by wet-nursing, which connected those who required wet-nursing services with those who could provide them. These were probably primarily networks of women.[76] Some plots in Menander hint at this possibility. When Plangon

---

[75] Pers. comm.

[76] Taylor 2017: 136, 138–9. We might also see wet-nursing contracts from the Hellenistic period as evidence of wet nurses negotiating their role and value.

in *Samia* needs someone to help her nurse her child, her next-door neighbour, who has just lost her own baby, steps in. That they happen to live next door to each other has a lot to do with staging requirements, but similar connections among slightly more distant neighbours are easily imaginable. (Cynthia Patterson hypothesises a similar 'feminine network' connecting mothers who felt they could not keep their babies with women who wanted a baby but could not have one;[77] again, in Menander's *Perikeiromene*, a woman finds two exposed babies, rears the girl herself, and gives the boy 'to a rich woman . . . who wanted/needed/lacked a baby': τὸ δ' ἕτερον / [γυναικὶ] δοῦναι πλουσίᾳ . . . / . . . δεομένῃ παιδίου, ll. 121–3.) Taylor argues that such networks 'allowed women like Nikarete to ameliorate their immediate poverty, but also to negotiate their own social roles by challenging the discourse which devalued this activity'. Nursing enabled Nikarete to support her family until Thoukritos finally returned, though she might also have received help from Thoukritos' brothers.[78] Euxitheos insists on his and Nikarete's present poverty but says his opponents claim he is rich (§52), which may suggest *tainia*-selling was fairly profitable;[79] he also implies that the work women took on during these crises lifted many out of poverty and even into wealth.

The social connection Nikarete made by her nursing lasted well beyond her employment and continued to benefit her and her family: her charge Kleinias and his family served as witnesses for her and her son (Dem. 57.44).[80] Though wet-nursing was stereotypically associated with enslaved women and metics, it was also done by citizen-status women, and not only in military or political crises.[81] Euxitheos claims that though his mother was a nurse 'when the city was in hard times, and everyone was faring badly' (ὅθ' ἡ πόλις ἠτύχει καὶ πάντες κακῶς ἔπραττον), 'even now [i.e. in better times], you will find many citizen-status women (*astai*) working as nurses' (καὶ . . . νῦν ἀστὰς γυναῖκας πολλὰς εὑρήσετε τιτθευούσας, §35). A citizen-status nurse appears without comment in Aristophanes' *Thesmophoriazusae*. One of the women celebrating the Thesmophoria, a festival celebrated only by married citizen-status women, is identified as the nurse (*titthē*) of another woman (ll. 608–9). Some commentators have identified her as enslaved,[82] but this goes against a core principle of the festival,[83] already articulated in the play (ll. 293–4). Her employer is married to the politician Kleonymos (l. 605),[84] so this might be an oblique

---

[77] Patterson 1985: 116.   [78] Compare Lacey 1980: 59.   [79] Taylor 2017: 120.
[80] Compare Taylor 2017: 139.   [81] Compare Kennedy 2014: 133–6.
[82] For example, Austin and Olson 2004 *ad loc.*   [83] See e.g. Parker 2005: 270–1, 275–6.
[84] See Austin and Olson 2004 *ad loc.*

joke about, say, his dependence on others, or disregard for religious requirements, but this seems unlikely. Taylor argues for a counter-discourse on paid work which emphasises the value of wet nurses, against the discourse of shame and 'last resort' in which Euxitheos' speech primarily participates. This counter-discourse is most evident in literary portrayals of enslaved nurses as figures of trust, and in monuments celebrating nurses.[85]

Clearly there were prejudices against wet nurses: we recall Khrysis' horror that Plangon's baby might be raised by a nurse in a tenement-house. Part of her horror may be at poor living conditions in tenement-houses; Khrysis associates wet-nursing with poverty and ill health.[86] Equally clearly, some families who employed nurses valued them and articulated this publicly on sepulchral monuments. Taylor's argument arises out of consideration of the evidence from the perspective of the Attic working poor. Consideration of the evidence from women's perspectives leads us to the same conclusion (of course, there is much overlap). A sepulchral monument set up for a metic nurse, Melitta, by or on behalf of her charge Hippostrate, proclaims not just Hippostrate's affection for her nurse (ζῶσαν σ' ἐφίλουν, τίτθη, 'nurse, I loved you while you lived') but also her respect for her (νῦν σ' ἔτι τιμῶ … καὶ τιμήσω σε ἄχρι ἂν ζῶ … σοὶ τιμαί, τίτθη, παρὰ Φερσεφόνει Πλούτωνί τε κεῖνται, 'even now I honour you … and I shall honour you as long as I live … there are honours laid up for you, nurse, with Persephone and Plouton', *IG* II² 7873).[87] This testifies against attempts to resolve the tension between negative and positive portrayals of wet nurses by arguing that hired wet nurses were held in suspicion but enslaved wet nurses in honour.[88] Also significant is the emphasis on the persistence of the relationship between nurse and charge, lasting even beyond death (νῦν … ἔτι, 'even now'; ἄχρι ἂν ζῶ, 'as long as I live'). Kleinias too was willing to help Nikarete and her family long after she had ceased nursing him. Respect for wet nurses was not felt only by women. Kleinias and his male relatives voluntarily testified on behalf of Nikarete; a man named Diogeitos erected a grave *stēlē* to commemorate 'the nurse of Diogeitos' children, a most just (*dikaiotatē*) woman from the Peloponnese, Malikha of Kythera' (*IG* II² 9112).[89] If the

---

[85] Taylor 2017: 136–40, Kennedy 2014: 133–6; for monuments for enslaved nurses, see my pp. 188–91.
[86] Compare Sommerstein 2013 *ad loc*. For tenement-houses, see pp. 276–9.
[87] This monument is discussed more fully at pp. 257–8.
[88] For example, Sommerstein 2013 *ad* Men. *Sam*. 85–6.   [89] Kennedy 2014: 133–4.

child's mother had died, it would have been the father who lived to be grateful to the nurse.

Taylor rightly comments that women with husbands at home were less likely to participate in this kind of network, which connected women to other households and enabled them to support themselves and their families.[90] Nikarete's period of separation compelled her to do things she would not have been required to do had she still been living with her husband, but under this compulsion she created a new economic and social role for herself.

Parallel Lives

For both *Diognete* and Nikarete, wartime separation changed their lives. For the poorer woman, the change was more dramatic. She took up paid work and possibly moved home. While *Diognete* was supplied with provisions enough to support herself, three children, and two enslaved people for over a year, and at least in theory had the support of a rich father, Nikarete would have earned little as a nurse. We have no evidence for wet nurses' wages in classical Attica, but Walter Scheidel estimates that in Roman Egypt they earned about a third of a male worker's annual pay.[91] We cannot rule out the possibility that *Diognete* worked for money during her husband's absence or after his death and that the speaker refrains from mentioning it, but given her wealth and access to resources it is unlikely. Nikarete's work exposed her to real risk: it called her citizen status into question, which contributed to Halimous' denial of her son's citizenship and threatened her in turn. Kapparis, commenting on the effects of mass male absence and death during the Peloponnesian War, notes that 'the higher the percentage of women working outside the house and trying to stand on their own two feet in a competitive world, the higher was their chance of having a brush with the law'.[92] He is thinking of disputes with customers (discussed in Chapter 4, 'Women in Retail') rather than challenges to citizenship, but the point remains relevant. The pairing starkly illustrates how different experiences of singleness could be across the spectrum of wealth. Nevertheless, as we have seen, Nikarete's nursing had advantages, not least the expansion of her network.

For both women, temporary separation was followed, immediately or later, by widowhood. Here, age differentiated their experiences, as well as

---

[90] Taylor 2017: 139–40. [91] Taylor 2017: 188, n. 92, citing Scheidel 2010: 433–4.
[92] Kapparis 2021: 194–7; quotation p. 194.

wealth. *Diognete* was widowed within about ten years of her first marriage, after having three children; she was probably about twenty-five. Nikarete was probably under twenty when she married her second husband and between thirty and thirty-five when he returned from Leukas. She subsequently had three more children. When Thoukritos died, she might have been forty or older. *Diognete*'s relative youth, along with her substantial, if reduced, dowry, meant she was married again about a year after Diodotos' death. She remarried as an older, more experienced woman, which could have reduced the gendered power imbalance in her new marriage. This may partially explain her apparent confidence in organising men and taking on male authority figures.[93] Though age may have advantaged Nikarete in her second marriage, it disadvantaged her in widowhood, interacting with other factors. Nikarete did not remarry after her second husband's death and was again compelled to work for money. While *Diognete*'s father was still alive to arrange her second marriage and look after her children, however badly, Nikarete's father had died in her childhood. Her brother seems not to have supported her; by the time of her widowhood, he may also have died. By the end of her second marriage, Nikarete, older, poor, and with a dependent child, was probably not a viable marriage prospect.

Both women, however, drew on connections from former marriages for legal support. *Diognete*'s new husband formed part of her network of male supporters, but most important was the husband of her daughter by her first husband. (Kapparis notes that *Diognete* 'seems [to have] turned to her new husband, Hegemon' first, 'but reading between the lines it seems that he did not want to get involved in this bitter family feud between Diogeiton and his daughter and grandchildren'; after him, 'the determined mother then turned to her son-in-law'.)[94] When Nikarete's son by her second husband was threatened with loss of citizenship, the sons of her first husband Protomakhos *by his subsequent wife* testified to her citizen status (§§40, 43).[95] Possibly Euxitheos had built a relationship with them based on his father's relationship with their father (cf. γνώριμος, §41), but Thoukritos had been absent for most of Euxitheos' childhood and had since died. As their relationship to Euxitheos was even remoter than their relationship to Nikarete, it seems likelier that she was the primary contact: though they had not even been born when Protomakhos divorced her, she

---

93 Compare p. 77.   94 Kapparis 2021: 48.
95 Compare Lacey 1980: 58, Phelan 2016: 209 *ad loc.*, *contra APF* p. 94.

apparently had enough of a relationship with them to contact them and persuade them to testify.

Proving a woman's citizen status was difficult. Citizen men were registered as members of their demes and phratries (phratries were groups of citizens with hereditary membership; unlike the demes, they were not an administrative division of Attica). Metics – men and women – were registered in their demes of residence. Citizen-status women were not registered anywhere. Women's marriages were among the only events in citizen-status women's lives which had legal significance and rendered women other than legally invisible.[96] The difficulty becomes particularly clear in certain speeches written for inheritance disputes. Isaeus 8 responds to the speaker's opponent's claim that the man whose inheritance was disputed, Kiron, 'never had a daughter at all' (§1). In [Demosthenes] 43, the opponents denied that Polemon had a sister, Phylomakhe. In Isaeus 6, the speaker claims his opponents have invented the woman they claim is their mother, Kallippe. As Rebecca Futo Kennedy puts it, 'speakers … deny the existence of a woman … based on a lack of witnesses to testify and verify that they had lived'.[97] Disputes over a woman's existence are a more extreme example of women's precarity than disputes over a woman's status, like Demosthenes 57 (citizen or metic?), Isaeus 3 (married or not?), and Apollodorus' *Against Neaira* (pretending citizen status or not?). Having had two marriages effectively doubled a woman's legal visibility.

The starkest example of this is Kiron's daughter (*Klearete*) in Isaeus 8. In response to his opponent's insistence on her non-existence, the speaker stressed that *Klearete* was δὶς ἐκδοθεῖσαν, δὶς ἐγγυηθεῖσαν ('twice given in marriage, twice betrothed by *engyē*', §29). *Engyē*, betrothal of a woman in the presence of witnesses 'for the ploughing of legitimate children', was only performed for legitimately born citizen-status women.[98] The occasion of the wedding (*gamos*) provided further opportunity to affirm a woman's existence and the legitimacy of the marriage before the couple's relatives and social circle, as the speaker makes clear when he cites as evidence for *Klearete*'s legitimacy that her second husband hosted a wedding celebration (*gamous hestiaō*) when he married her, inviting friends and relatives, and gave a *gamēlia* for his fellow phratry members (§18). The *gamēlia* was a feast given by newly married men for their phratry; it served for the social recognition of the marriage and the bride, who was introduced to the husband's phratrymen on the occasion.[99]

---

[96] Compare Kennedy 2014: 98; Scafuro 1994: 157–8, 62–4, 67–8.   [97] Kennedy 2014: 98.
[98] Patterson 1991: 49–52.   [99] Lambert 1993: 182–3; Humphreys 2018: 581.

Phratries played a crucial role in policing the legitimacy of marriages and children.[100] Though women could not strictly be *members* of phratries, and were not inscribed on phratry lists, the introduction of a married woman to her husband's phratry served as served as a guarantee of her citizen status and the legitimacy of her marriage, at which her husband's phratrymen 'effectively accepted her as capable of bearing children whom they could subsequently receive as phratry members and citizens'.[101] Litigants in disputes on citizenship and legitimacy often cite the provision of a *gamēlia* – or the conspicuous absence of such provision – as evidence for the legitimacy or otherwise of a marriage and therefore its offspring.[102] The *gamēlia* either followed or was combined with the *gamos*: poorer Athenians whose social circles largely overlapped with their phratries might combine the feasts to economise; richer Athenians who did not live near their phratry centres might make the most of the opportunity to display their wealth and generosity and feast relatives, neighbours, and other associates at the *gamos* before returning to the phratry centre to give a *gamēlia*.[103]

Nikarete's two marriages meant Euxitheos could call as witnesses to his mother's citizen status the sons of her first husband by his subsequent wife; the witnesses of her *engyē* to her second husband; the phratrymen present at her second husband's *gamēlia* for her; the husband of her daughter from her first marriage (i.e. the husband of Euxitheos' half-sister); and that daughter's son (§41). Her two marriages increased her legal visibility and, as with *Diognete*, the number and diversity of men who could act for her. The man Nikarete nursed in his infancy and his family also served as witnesses (§44): though Nikarete's employment made her more vulnerable to legal attacks, the connections it brought her provided an additional defence. Among their other witnesses were phratrymen from the same phratry as Nikarete's relatives and 'demesmen' (§40). As Osborne points out, these must have been members of Nikarete's natal deme, Melite, not her marital deme and Euxitheos' deme, Halimous, which had rejected

---

[100] See e.g. Lambert 1993: 35–8, though Jones 1999: 198 suspects that this was mostly done by demes rather than phratries: because of Attic settlement patterns and the proximity of deme members to each other, they were better able to police infidelity, he argues. He also points out that litigants tend more often to appeal to demesmen on questions of descent, wills, and adoption (cf. Whitehead 1986: 227–8). See Lambert 1993: 170 on the oath at the phratry introduction, that the boy was born of a legally married citizen woman, and (if the child was being introduced by his father and not another male relative) was the introducer's son.

[101] Lambert 1993: 182–3. See my pp. 301–8 for women at phratry celebrations.

[102] Isae. 3.76, 79, 8.18, 20; Dem. 57.43, 69.   [103] Humphreys 2018: 309–10.

him.[104] In other words, they were Nikarete's network more than Euxitheos', or at least, they were Euxitheos' network through Nikarete. Osborne argues that Euxitheos was rejected by his deme because he neither lived there nor had many connections there: his 'most powerful family ties . . . are outside the deme'.[105] For our purposes, what is significant is that Nikarete retained links to her father and brother's deme and phratry and could prevail on their members to support her and her son.

The additional set of relatives to which twice-married women could turn constituted a significant legal and social advantage given the relative stricture of women's social circles. Steven Johnstone shows that while men had two ways of controlling property – through personal relationships built on trust, and through anonymous 'surveillance' by the citizen body – women could only do so by cultivating trust in their relationship with their *kyrios*.[106] This required them to instrumentalise their personal relationships and constantly to engage in building trust. Johnstone focuses on the instrumentalisation of a woman's relationship with her *kyrios* but acknowledges that if she wanted to take action *against* her *kyrios*, she would also need to cultivate and exploit a relationship with a man from her natal family.[107] Johnstone concludes, though, that 'unlike men who might trust a range of other men, a woman had to rely on only one man, her *kyrios*'.[108] Johnstone's broader argument is very useful, but *Diognete* and Nikarete were among a number of women who were able to exploit relationships with men beyond their husbands and their natal family. Foxhall is closer to the mark in arguing that Athenian legal speeches 'suggest that *kyrieia* is a much fuzzier, less formalized institution than social and legal historians have generally thought' and that 'women often had several potential *kyrioi* and could sometimes play one off against another'.[109] However, Foxhall's calculations about which potential *kyrioi* were more likely to be more enthusiastic supporters of their female relatives depending on degree of kinship and other competing ties over-emphasise the importance of *kyrieia*. In the stories of *Diognete* and Nikarete, we see women mobilising networks of men to work together. *Kyrieia* is not at issue because the men are not representatives but supporters.

In either situation, more male connections meant women had more options. (In modern Saudi Arabia, which also has a system of male

---

[104] Osborne 1985b: 149.   [105] Osborne 1985b: 149.   [106] Johnstone 2003.
[107] Johnstone 2003: 268–9.
[108] Johnstone 2003: 270, though one of his examples is a metic woman (without a *kyrios*) instrumentalising multiple acquaintances (pp. 270–1, on Dem. 25.56–7).
[109] Foxhall 1996: 150.

guardianship based on kinship, having more male connections also affords more options.)[110] Menander's fourth-century comedy *Dyskolos* offers another suggestion of the additional possibilities available for twice-married women with connections from their first marriage: a remarried widow is able to leave her aggressive husband because her now-adult son from her first marriage can take her in (ll. 13–29). The additional connections from *Diognete*'s first marriage placed her in a stronger position in her second; the additional connections from Nikarete's two marriages placed her in a stronger position in her widowhood. These connections were important to both women, but particularly Nikarete, whose freedom was at stake.

This parallel analysis of *Diognete* and Nikarete's lives and networks offers new insight into women's varied experiences of separation and widowhood, and into the effects of second marriages on individuals and their relationships to others and to the *polis*. The prevalence of second marriage has long been recognised;[111] its effects are less frequently discussed. Hunter makes some comments on the second marriages of widows, including that they did not seem to require a higher dowry to make them more attractive. Brulé points out that 'the psychological conditions in which [remarried widows and divorcées] found themselves no longer had much to do with those of the first wedding of a *parthenos*'. Humphreys writes that 'a woman in her second marriage, who had dealt with two husbands and sets of affines and had renewed contact with her own kin, on a more mature footing, at the time when her first husband died or divorced her, was quite capable of taking an active role in family business' – as this chapter's readings demonstrate.[112]

Persistent Relationships

In the previous section, we saw how a comparison of two women's progressing lives reveals how women could build up networks across households over time. Building networks across households had social and emotional as well as legal advantages; it is these which form the focus of the remainder of this chapter. This section explores this phenomenon in the lives of other women known from forensic oratory, beginning with cases in which women were able to bring children from former marriages

---

[110] See e.g. Human Rights Watch 2016: 24–6.   [111] For example, Thompson 1972; Isager 1981–2.
[112] Hunter 1989: 296; Brulé 2003: 184–5; Humphreys 2018: 223. Osborne 1985b: 130 notes, from a male perspective, comparative evidence for different factors in choosing a second spouse than a first, citing Mair 1971: 44, 81.

Table 1.1 *Some Attic vocabulary for making distinctions between different kinds of family relationship*

Term	Part of Speech	Meaning
γαμετή	noun or adjective	a *married* wife as opposed to another kind of female partner
μητρυιά	noun	stepmother
ποιητός	adjective	adoptive, as opposed to γεννητός, born (to describe a child) or γόνῳ, by birth (to describe a father)
πρόγονος	noun or adjective	child from a first marriage, among other meanings
ὁμομήτριος	adjective	having the same mother
ὁμοπάτριος	adjective	having the same father

into their new households, then turning to cases of women maintaining relationships with men who had divorced them. Finally, the chapter turns to attestation of women's cumulative networks in sepulchral monuments, some of which commemorate women alongside individuals from both their natal and marital families, and in even wider familial contexts.

Children from Former Marriages: Hierokleia *and* Apollodora

Given high rates of remarriage, 'blended' families (in which not all the children have the same mother and father but are half- or stepsiblings) were quite common. Classical Attic Greek had no word for such a family. However, it did have an extensive vocabulary for making distinctions between different kinds of relationship within a family (see examples in Table 1.1).

The twice-married *Klearete*, whom we encountered on p. 74, was herself brought up alongside the children of her father's second marriage (Isae. 8.7). *Diognete*'s children lived with their uncle-grandfather and the children he had with his second wife. These children were not their half-siblings but their *mother's* half-siblings; they were cousins. Other examples abound.

Many classical authors mention the proverbial hostility found within such blended families. The speaker of Isaeus 12 (probably delivered in 344/3)[113] generalises that 'stepmothers and the daughters of a former marriage very often tend to be hostile to each other' (εἰώθασι δέ πως ὡς ἐπὶ τὸ πολὺ διαφέρεσθαι ἀλλήλαις αἵ τε μητρυιαὶ καὶ αἱ πρόγονοι, §5). This

---

[113] Wyse 1904: 714–16.

belief was articulated about a century earlier by Euripides' Alkestis (the eponymous play was first performed in 438), who at her death fears her daughter's potential stepmother might sabotage her marriage prospects (*Alc.* 314–26). Similarly, in Euripides' fragmentary *Aegeus*, one character comments that 'a woman is naturally somewhat hostile to the children of a previous marriage when she is the second wife of their father' (πέφυκε γάρ πως παισὶ πολέμιον γυνὴ / τοῖς πρόσθεν ἡ ζυγεῖσα δευτέρα πατρί, frg. 4 Nauck). In Euripides' fragmentary *Dictys*, one character asks a man whether, since he has children already, he really wants to have 'new' children (καινοὺς ... παῖδας, i.e. children with a second wife), and so bring about 'great hatred' (ἔχθραν μεγίστην) between the children from the two marriages (frg. 338 Nauck).

However, Daniel Ogden's claim that 'the suggestion that one set of half-siblings might help and support one another ... flies directly into the teeth of the inevitable hatred between amphimetric siblings [siblings with different mothers] in the Greek world'[114] is untrue. The comment from Isaeus 12 on the tendency to hostility between stepmothers and step-daughters comes from a speech in which a man is defending his father's son from his second marriage – there seems to be no hatred between these amphimetric brothers. He also says that his full-sisters are supportive of their amphimetric brother and have 'allowed' (ἐπέτρεψαν) their hus-bands to give evidence in his favour. We saw in the last chapter that the amphimetric brothers of Nikarete's son Euxitheos (his father's sons by his second wife) were willing to defend him in the same way (Dem. 57.43).[115] The relative commonness of blended families in Attic oratory, including positive portrayals, suggests social tolerance of such arrange-ments. Blended families could bring continuity to women's lives and reduce the potential trauma of transition between families and house-holds. The diversity of maternal experiences in classical Attica included relationships with children from former marriages. However, these rela-tionships rarely feature in studies of Attic motherhood. We may consider two case studies.

The sister of Hierokles of Iphistiadai in Isaeus 9 (*Hierokleia*) was married to Euthykrates of Araphen (Iphistiadai is in the northern part of the Attic plain, Araphen on the east coast).[116] *Hierokleia* and Euthykrates had a son,

---

[114] Ogden 1996: 195; cf. 19–21, 189–99.
[115] Compare Dem. 57.20, a marriage between amphimetric siblings.
[116] *APF* no. 7252; this means *Hierokleia*'s brother-in-law Thoudippos of Araphen was the proposer of the tribute reassessment decree (RO 153) and the son-in-law of the notorious politician Kleon. Compare Humphreys 2018: 217–19 on this case.

Astyphilos, and a daughter. Euthykrates was later allegedly killed by his brother Thoudippos in a quarrel over a division of land (§17). By the time of her husband's death, *Hierokleia*'s father was also dead; when she returned home it was to Hierokles (§27). He married her to Theophrastos (deme unknown). *Hierokleia* brought her young children from her first marriage with her into this marriage; the speaker, more interested in the relationships between men in the case, says that she brought her son, Astyphilos (§27), but we infer that her daughter, the younger child, came too. When *Hierokleia* had a son with Theophrastos, the two boys from her two marriages were apparently educated together (§28).

Hierokleia's new husband Theophrastos may have been the guardian of her children from her first marriage: he is said to have planted and cultivated the children's paternal plot of land and then returned the boy Astyphilos' property to him when he came of age (§§28–9).[117] However, he is never explicitly said to have been their guardian. It was permissible to lease an orphan's estate even if one was not the guardian – possibly Theophrastos was not the guardian but merely the lessee. That the children came to live with Theophrastos does not necessarily mean he must have been their guardian,[118] as we will see from the next story, that of *Apollodora*.

In Isaeus 9, the speaker, *Hierokleia*'s second son, attempts to assert his right to his now-dead half-brother Astyphilos' property. He is keen to portray a positive relationship not just between himself and Astyphilos but between his father Theophrastos and Astyphilos, in order to present an image of family closeness and connectedness supporting his (in fact dubious) claim to the inheritance. Part of this image is his claim that Theophrastos had arranged the marriage of Astyphilos' sister, *Hierokleia*'s daughter, 'to Astyphilos' satisfaction' (τῷ Ἀστυφίλῳ ἐξήρκει, §29). At the time, Astyphilos had recently come of age and was his sister's nearest male kinsman, which probably made him her *kyrios* and responsible for her marriage. That Astyphilos seems to have entrusted this responsibility to his stepfather not only suggests Astyphilos' respect for and trust in Theophrastos but also positions Theophrastos as the girl's father and *kyrios*, rather than as her stepfather, further eliding biological and legal distinctions within the stepfamily. Again, if Theophrastos *was* the girl's guardian, this is less interesting; arranging her marriage might have been his duty rather than Astyphilos'. But if Theophrastos was not the legal guardian, and the story is true, it suggests a remarkable degree of

---

[117] See Griffith-Williams 2013: 183–5; Wyse 1904: 642, citing Schulthess 1886: 69, 118.
[118] *Contra* Griffith-Williams 2013: 183–4.

integration. In any case, though *Hierokleia* was passed from her father to Euthykrates, from Euthykrates to Hierokles, and from Hierokles to Theophrastos, the constant across three households was her children, who travelled with her.

Isaeus 7 features a woman (*Apollodora*) whose husband, Thrasyllos of Leukonion, died in the Sicilian Expedition (§5), like Nikarete's half-brother and at least 10,000 other Athenian men.[119] *Apollodora*'s son Apollodoros fell under the charge of his paternal uncle Eupolis, who apparently defrauded him as Diogeiton had defrauded his wards. *Apollodora*'s new husband Arkhedamos allegedly 'saw that [Apollodoros] was being deprived of all his money, and brought him up while he was a boy, having brought him to live with him and his mother' (ὁρῶν αὐτὸν πάντων ἀποστερούμενον τῶν χρημάτων, ἔτρεφέ τε αὐτὸν παῖδα ὄνθ', ὡς ἑαυτὸν[120] καὶ τὴν μητέρα κομισάμενος, §7). *Apollodora* and Arkhedamos later had a daughter together, *Arkhedike* (§9). In the next chapter, I argue that the speaker's phrasing points to *Apollodora*'s persuading Arkhedamos to take in her son. That Arkhedamos 'saw' (ὁρῶν) what was happening to Apollodoros suggests that there was still some contact between mother and son, as in the case of *Diognete* in Lysias 32, whose sons knew where to find her even after seven years' separation. Perhaps Arkhedamos and *Apollodora* lived near Eupolis? Like *Diognete*, *Apollodora* was able to enlist the help of a male relative – Arkhedamos – on behalf of her child against his guardian. Separation did not necessarily entail total severance of contact. In *Apollodora*'s case, even separation was not final.

The stories of *Hierokleia* and *Apollodora* bear out the more complex picture of motherhood and second marriage first suggested in those of *Diognete* and Nikarete. The claim that children from first marriages would be 'surplus' to the households of remarried women with new children may misunderstand the role of the 'household' in the way women thought about and experienced their relationships, particularly their relationships with their children.[121]

---

[119] *APF* no. 1395. The location of Leukonion is not known. For Sicilian Expedition mortality, see Hansen 1988: 14–16.

[120] ὡς ἑαυτὸν Sauppe: ὡς αὐτοῦ; see pp. 124–5.

[121] Compare Humphreys 2018: 216: 'The Diokles case [Isae. 8, discussed on my p. 147] ... indicates ... that a woman with sons by one husband might sacrifice to them the interests of her daughters by another husband. It is likely enough that a woman tended to think of her children as a single group, in which sons had a right to take precedence over daughters even when they had different fathers.'

Husbands from Former Marriages: Epistheneia *and Phano*

Hierokleia and *Apollodora* were able to maintain relationships – and even residence – with the children born in their first marriages even after they had been remarried and gone to live with their new husbands. Some women maintained links to their former husbands after the end of the marriage; this section examines two such cases.

Isaeus 2 contains the story of *Epistheneia*, the younger daughter of Eponymos of Akharnai (northern Attica).[122] *Epistheneia* was married to a man named Menekles, whose first wife had recently died. Her brother, the speaker of Isaeus 2, describes their father as a close friend of Menekles:

[3] Ἐπώνυμος γὰρ ὁ Ἀχαρνεύς, ὁ πατὴρ ὁ ἡμέτερος, ὦ ἄνδρες, φίλος ἦν καὶ ἐπιτήδειος Μενεκλεῖ, καὶ ἐχρῆτο οἰκείως· ἦμεν δὲ αὐτῷ παῖδες τέτταρες ἡμεῖς, δύο μὲν ὑεῖς, δύο δὲ θυγατέρες. τελευτήσαντος δὲ τοῦ πατρὸς ἐκδίδομεν ἡμεῖς τὴν πρεσβυτέραν ἀδελφήν, ἐπειδὴ εἶχεν ὥραν, Λευκολόφῳ, προῖκα ἐπιδόντες εἴκοσι μνᾶς. [4] καὶ ἀπ' ἐκείνου τοῦ χρόνου τετάρτῳ ἔτει ἢ πέμπτῳ ὕστερον ἥ τε ἀδελφὴ ἡμῖν ἡ νεωτέρα σχεδὸν ἡλικίαν εἶχεν ἀνδρὶ συνοικεῖν, καὶ τῷ Μενεκλεῖ ἡ γυνὴ τελευτᾷ ἣν εἶχε πρότερον. ἐπειδὴ οὖν ἐκείνη τὰ νομιζόμενα ἐποίησεν ὁ Μενεκλῆς, ᾔτει τὴν ἀδελφὴν ἡμᾶς, ὑπομιμνήσκων τήν τε φιλίαν τὴν τοῦ πατρὸς καὶ ἑαυτοῦ, καὶ ὡς πρὸς ἡμᾶς αὐτοὺς ἦν διακείμενος. [5] καὶ ἡμεῖς εἰδότες ὅτι καὶ ὁ πατὴρ οὐδενὶ ἂν ἔδωκεν ἥδιον ἢ ἐκείνῳ, δίδομεν αὐτῷ, οὐκ ἄπροικον, ὡς οὗτος λέγει ἑκάστοτε, ἀλλὰ τὴν ἴσην προῖκα ἐπιδόντες ἥνπερ καὶ τῇ πρεσβυτέρᾳ ἀδελφῇ ἐπέδομεν· καὶ ἐκ τοῦ τρόπου τούτου, πρότερον ὄντες αὐτοῦ φίλοι, κατέστημεν οἰκεῖοι.

[3] Gentlemen, Eponymos of Akharnai, our father, was a friend and ally (*philos ... kai epitēdeios*) of Menekles, and was on close terms with him (*khraomai oikeiōs*). [Our father] had us four children, two sons and two daughters. After our father died, we gave our elder sister in marriage, when she was old enough, to Leukolophos, with a dowry of twenty minae. [4] And four or five years after that, our younger sister was almost of marriageable age, and the first wife of Menekles died. When Menekles had performed the customary rites for her, he asked for our sister in marriage, reminding us of the friendship (*philia*) between our father and himself, and of the fact that he was well disposed to us. [5] And we, knowing that our father would have given her to no one with greater pleasure, gave her to him, not without a dowry, as [our opponents] say every time, but with the same dowry as we gave with our elder

---

sister. And in this way, having formerly been friends (*philoi*), we became kin (*oikeioi*).

Epistheneia's father is said to have been a close friend of Menekles (*philos . . . kai epitēdeios . . . kai ekhrēto oikeiōs*, §3); there was *philia* between them (§4). The marriage, *Epistheneia*'s brother says, transformed him and his brother from Menekles' *philoi* (here 'friends') into his *oikeioi* (here 'family'). According to *Epistheneia*'s brother, a few years after the marriage, believing himself infertile and wanting to give *Epistheneia* a chance to have children, Menekles divorced *Epistheneia*, supposedly with her and her brothers' reluctant agreement. She was remarried to Eleios of Sphettos (central Attica). The childless Menekles then sought to adopt a son and could find no one *oikeioteros* ('closer', 'more part of the family') than his former wife's brothers:

> εὕρισκεν οὖν οὐδένα ἄλλον οἰκειότερον ὄνθ' ἡμῶν ἑαυτῷ. λόγους οὖν πρὸς ἡμᾶς ἐποιεῖτο, καὶ ἔφη δοκεῖν αὐτῷ καλῶς ἔχειν, ἐπειδὴ οὕτως αὐτῷ ἡ τύχη συνέβη ὥστε ἐκ τῆς ἀδελφῆς τῆς ἡμετέρας παῖδας αὐτῷ μὴ γενέσθαι, ἐκ ταύτης τῆς οἰκίας υἱὸν αὐτῷ ποιήσασθαι, ὅθεν καὶ φύσει παῖδας ἐβουλήθη ἂν αὐτῷ γενέσθαι. (§11)

> So he found no one closer (*oikeioteros*) to him than us. Therefore he had a conversation with us, and said that he thought it a good thing, since chance had meant that children were not born to him by our sister, that he should adopt a son for himself from the family (*oikia*) from which he would have wanted to have children naturally.

The use of *oikeioteros* (from *oikeios*, 'close', 'related', 'part of the family') here is striking.[123] Despite the use of *oikeios* language earlier in the speech, these men were not strictly Menekles' kin, either by birth or, any longer, by marriage. The speaker cleverly uses the language of kinship for those who are not formally kin in order to legitimise their legally becoming kin by adoption. The circumstances described in the speech – Menekles' approach to the brothers to seek an adoption – suggest a continuing relationship between *Epistheneia*'s brothers and her former husband, mediated either symbolically or actively by *Epistheneia*, even though she was now married to someone else. When her marriage to Menekles ended, the ties created by it did not.

That *Epistheneia* was no longer married to Menekles but to Eleios at the time Menekles adopted her brother is frequently overlooked.[124] Analyses that rely on the incorrect identification of *Epistheneia*'s brother as

---

[123] See p. 106 on the term.   [124] Compare fn. 3.

Menekles' brother-in-law at the time of the adoption are misleading and mask women's potential to maintain relationships with former husbands and former marital households.

Epistheneia's brother's speech is a response to his opponents' claim that Menekles chose to adopt him *gynaiki peithomenos* ('at the persuasion of a woman', §§1, 19–20, 25, 38), which would have rendered the will invalid.[125] Partly in order to counter this argument, the speaker emphasises the friendship between his father and Menekles, out of which Menekles' friendship with him and his brother developed. However, his opponents evidently argued that if Menekles' regard for anyone had led to the adoption, it was his regard for *Epistheneia*. Tantalisingly, the speaker claims that most of his opponent's speech concerned her: we have the text that plays down her role rather than playing it up. The speaker counters his opponent's argument as follows:

> ὅτι δὲ οὐ παρανοῶν οὐδὲ γυναικὶ πειθόμενος ὁ Μενεκλῆς ἐποιήσατο, ἀλλ᾽ εὖ φρονῶν, ἐνθένδε ἐστὶν ὑμῖν ῥᾴδιον ἐπιγνῶναι. πρῶτον μὲν γὰρ ἡ ἀδελφή, περὶ ἧς οὗτος τὸν πλεῖστον τοῦ λόγου πεποίηται, ὡς ἐκείνη πεισθεὶς ἐμὲ ἐποιήσατο, πολλῷ πρότερον ἦν ἐκδεδομένη ἢ τὴν ποίησιν γενέσθαι, ὥστ᾽ εἴ γ᾽ ἐκείνῃ πεισθεὶς τὸν υἱὸν ἐποιεῖτο, τῶν ἐκείνης παίδων τὸν ἕτερον ἐποιήσατ᾽ ἄν· δύο γάρ εἰσιν αὐτῇ. (§19)

> That Menekles did not adopt in a state of insanity or at the persuasion of a woman, but in his right mind, you can easily observe from the following. First, our sister, with whom most of [my opponent's] speech is concerned (περὶ ἧς οὗτος τὸν πλεῖστον τοῦ λόγου πεποίηται), [in which he argues] that he adopted me at her instigation, had been [re]married long before the adoption took place, so if he *had* adopted a son at her instigation, he would have adopted one of her sons – she has two.

The speaker's argument is not that a woman could not have influenced the adoption choice of a man she had once been married to, or that the length of time in her second marriage would have decreased her influence over him, but that if she *had* influenced him, she would have encouraged him to choose differently.

Though we have lost the opponent's speech, we have several speeches accusing women of persuading men to adopt their sons.[126] Perhaps the speaker's argument that this is what *Epistheneia* was likelier to have done was intended to recall such cases. The speaker implies that on (re)marrying, a woman's loyalty would naturally move away from her

---

[125] [Dem.] 46.14, 16; Hyp. 3.18; [Arist.] *Ath. pol.* 35; Isae. 2.1, 19, 20, 25, 38; cf. Lys. frg. 283 Carey.
[126] Isae. 6.19–24; [Dem.] 40.10–11; Ap. *Neaira* 51, 55–6; perhaps Isae. 3. See Chapter 2.

natal family and towards her new marital family and her sons within that family – compare the assumption of Foxhall, Gagarin, and Homer's Athena – or that sons trump brothers more generally.[127] Later in this chapter (pp. 91–7) we encounter several cases of married women commemorated with their natal families – often their brothers – as well as or even instead of their husbands. These instances, along with considerable evidence for supportive sibling ties between living, married adults,[128] further challenge the assumption of changing loyalties.

There were also practical reasons for *Epistheneia* to propose the adoption of her brother rather than one of her sons, if she did indeed propose it. The speaker stresses that one key motivator in Menekles' choice to adopt was his need for care in old age (§§10, 12, 25). *Epistheneia*'s sons may have been too young to be helpful; perhaps her brother was a surer horse to back. He would also have benefited more. *Epistheneia*'s sons were growing up in the security of their parents' marriage, due an inheritance from their father Eleios. Her brother, by contrast, may have had no living male kin other than his brother, a mercenary who would have spent much of his life abroad on campaign, and his brother-in-law Eleios (§3).[129] In his speech, *Epistheneia*'s brother (naturally) portrays his relationship with *Epistheneia* as respectful and even affectionate (§8); perhaps she was acting out of returned affection, or simply to promote her natal family, to which she still felt loyalty.

Understandably, scholarly discussions of supportive relationships between adult siblings primarily cite instances of support provided by brothers to sisters.[130] Such support finds its archetype on the tragic stage in the figure of Orestes, on whom his sister Elektra pins her hopes.[131] Newly

---

[127] The sentiment of Sophocles' Antigone, ll. 905–14 (late 440s), that a brother is owed more honour than a son or husband, may be pressed into service as evidence either way, at face value, or as provocatively counterintuitive and situation-specific: Antigone's parents are dead, so she can never have another brother.

[128] Cox 1988a, Cox 1998: 105–29; Golden 2015: 103–12; Lewis 2002: 181–3.

[129] Both brothers were mercenaries for a time (§6), §14 implies the speaker later adopted a settled lifestyle while his brother continued to travel.

[130] Exceptions include Cox 1988a: 380, noting two instances of sisters (with their husbands) defending brothers against challenges to their citizenship (Dem. 57.43, 68, and Isae. 12.5, both also discussed in this chapter), and Humphreys 1986: 76–9 and Cox 1988a: 386–9 on supportive relationships between men and their sister's husbands; these were presumably mediated by the sisters. Note Humphreys 1986: 77 on the sister's role in Lysias 13. Griffith-Williams 2013: 56–7 comments on *Arkhedike*'s allowing her bereaved, elderly half-brother Apollodoros to adopt her son (see pp. 148 and 155–6) that 'it would, in any event, have been natural for Apollodoros to turn to his sister for help in his distress'.

[131] For example, Soph. *El.* 303–4, where he is described as 'stopper of these [troubles]' and, at l. 454, 'helper'; similarly Aesch. *Choe.* 212–37; the dynamic is slightly different in Euripides' *Electra*.

setting Isaeus 2 within the pattern of women's mediation in men's kin relationships argued for in this chapter and the next allows us to consider *Epistheneia*'s story as an instance of support given in the opposite direction, from a sister to a brother.

Apollodorus' *Against Neaira* tells how a divorcée, Phano, nursed her former husband Phrastor when he became ill, together with Neaira, who was either her mother or her stepmother:

> [50] The daughter of this woman Neaira, whom she brought with her as a little baby when she came [to live with Stephanos] – at the time they called [the baby] Strybele, but now they call her Phano – this man Stephanos gave her to an Athenian husband, Phrastor of Aigilia, as if the girl were his own daughter. He gave a thirty-minae dowry with her. When she came to the house of Phrastor, a working man who had carefully scraped together his livelihood, she did not know how to adjust to Phrastor's way of living but strove for her mother's habits and the uninhibited lifestyle of her mother's house – I suppose because she had been brought up in that kind of permissiveness. [51] Phrastor, seeing that she was not a decent woman, and that she was unwilling to listen to him, and also by this point having learnt for certain that she was not Stephanos' daughter but Neaira's, and that he had been deceived from the start when she was betrothed to him and he took her as the daughter of Stephanos, not by Neaira but by a citizen-status woman who had been Stephanos' wife before he lived with Neaira, was angry at all this and considered himself insulted and cheated. He threw out the woman (*anthrōpos*, derogatory) after he had lived with her for about a year – she was pregnant – and he did not return the dowry . . .
>
> [55] Not long after Phrastor had dismissed the daughter of Neaira, he became ill and was in an utterly dreadful condition and reached a state of total helplessness. He had a long-standing disagreement with his relatives and felt anger and hatred towards them, and he was also childless. He was beguiled in his weakness by the care he received from Neaira and her daughter: they went to visit him [56] in his weakness when there was no one to tend to his sickness, bringing him what he needed for his illness and keeping watch over him – of course, you yourselves know how valuable a woman is in times of illness, being there for a person who is suffering – and in the end he was persuaded to take back the baby to whom the daughter of this woman Neaira had given birth after Phrastor had sent her away pregnant . . . and to make him his son.

This episode is part of a narrative told to illustrate Apollodorus' claim that Phano's mother was the metic Neaira, and that Neaira was illegally pretending to be the citizen-status wife of her Athenian partner Stephanos. Marriage between Athenians and metics was illegal at this point, as was pretending to be of citizen status. According to Apollodorus' narrative, Stephanos and Neaira had attempted to pass Phano off as being of citizen status, marrying her to the citizen Phrastor as if she were the daughter of married citizen parents – a crime under Athenian law.

Konstantinos Kapparis convincingly argues that despite Apollodorus' claims to the contrary, Phano was in fact not Neaira's daughter, but the daughter of Neaira's citizen partner Stephanos by an earlier, citizen-status wife, as Stephanos is said to have claimed.[132] It is impossible to know for certain. If Kapparis is right, Neaira's relationship with Phano led Neaira to care for a man who had strictly not been her son-in-law even during his marriage to Phano and was now 'merely' Neaira's partner's child's ex-husband.[133] Whatever Phano's parentage, the story suggests a flexible attitude to kinship and the obligations and behaviours it entailed.

Apollodorus has his own reasons for narrating this episode. He claims that Phano and Neaira took advantage of Phrastor during his illness to persuade him to acknowledge as legitimately born the son Phano had given birth to after Phrastor divorced her. Phano's divorce had not been amicable: Phrastor had divorced her while she was pregnant because he found her behaviour and character disagreeable. Apollodorus also claims Phrastor suspected Phano of not being of citizen status (§§50–1). This last part may be Apollodorus' recasting of the incident.[134] Possibly Phrastor's own social position was precarious: Apollodorus' description of him as ἄνδρα ἐργάτην καὶ ἀκριβῶς τὸν βίον συνειλεγμένον ('a working man who had carefully scraped together his livelihood', §55) suggests he was from a family of less wealth and lower standing than the other men involved in the case. This could have made him wary of the social repercussions of a marriage to a woman whose status was suspect – as well as making him manipulable by Apollodorus. In any case, despite the disagreement and divorce, Phano and Neaira allegedly cared for Phrastor in his illness. Apollodorus chooses to describe an incident which initially portrays Neaira and Phano, whom he is at pains to slander and discredit, in a very positive light (this is why he must attribute their actions to manipulation and deceit). That he tells a story that might be taken to reflect well on his opponents somewhat increases the likelihood of its truthfulness. Affective ties formed by marriage did not necessarily end when the marriage itself ended.

---

[132] Kapparis 1999: 31–43.   [133] See pp. 134–5 on Neaira's relationship with Phano.
[134] Kapparis 1999: 34–6.

Lifelong Connections in Stone

Contemporary sepulchral monuments are an illuminating complement to forensic evidence for women's cumulative connections and their persistence over time. Images on sepulchral reliefs are often very similar to one another. Commemorated women, like men, are often shown clasping hands with someone left behind, sometimes in the presence of others. These can usually be assumed to be close relatives, and are sometimes labelled by name, allowing us to infer particular relationships from, for example, a shared patronymic. As we will see in Chapter 3 (pp. 167–70 and 182–4), other commemorated women (like some men) are shown with enslaved people, although as on pots, their identification is rarely certain. In these images, women's relationships – almost always family relationships – are of paramount importance. Because of this book's emphasis on the potential variety and richness of women's social lives, it focuses on unusual examples of sepulchral iconography as well as typical ones: women commemorating or commemorated by employers, clients, patrons, friends, enslaved people, enslavers. Though the commemoration of these relationships in death was rare, this book argues that their existence in life was not.

Women commemorated on grave monuments certainly correspond to real women who once lived. However, accessing those women is not straightforward. When depicted in reliefs, they are often presented as idealised 'types' (e.g. mother with infant). These types usually tell us some basic information about the individual they represent: it is unlikely that a 'woman and infant' relief would be chosen to commemorate an unmarried girl, so at the very least such an image suggests the woman it commemorates was a mother and had at some point been married. One 'woman and infant' image in Chapter 2 (Figure 2.2), is explicitly said to represent a woman and her grandchild;[135] here and in other instances, where a relief has an associated inscription we get a fuller picture of the individual's relationships, and occasionally of the qualities attributed to her by her commemorators. The figures depicted in reliefs do not always straightforwardly 'map on' to the individuals named in the associated inscription, which cautions against overconfident inferences of (formal or affective) relationships from reliefs alone. However, in some rare cases idealised images are 'individualised' with details specific to the person they commemorate, which may be understood by reference to the

---

[135] *IG* II² 10650, Kerameikos P695/I221; pp. 121–2.

associated inscriptions: the relief of the enslaved nurse Pyraikhme in Chapter 3 shows her with wine cups which may represent her inclusion in family celebrations of the Dionysiac Anthesteria festival;[136] the relief of the doctor and midwife Phanostrate in Chapter 4 shows her with another woman and, less typically, four children, who may represent children she delivered and cared for.[137]

Some monuments set the dead person within the context of her relationships to survivors. A woman named Polyxena, for example, who died c. 380–360, is said to have left a grieving husband, mother, and father (πένθος κοριδίωι τε πόσει καὶ μητρὶ λιπῦσα / καὶ πατρὶ τῶι φύσαντι Πολυξένη ἐνθάδε κεῖται, *IG* 11² 12495; 'Polyxena lies here; she left grief to her wedded husband and her mother and the father who begot her').[138] The associated relief fills out the picture of her connections by portraying her with a son and an enslaved woman. Other commemorators implicitly set the dead person within the context of her relationships to the dead by commemorating her alongside dead relatives, inscribing her name alongside others' on a monument or erecting her monument alongside others' in the *peribolos* (family tomb enclosure) of her natal or marital family.[139] The contexts of living and dead come to overlap: monuments could be adapted over time, so a relief which had been erected to portray a dead woman clasping hands with a bereaved relative might later serve to commemorate that relative too. Though we cannot straightforwardly infer affective relationships in life from shared commemoration in death, the choice by a surviving relative to bury and commemorate one person with another (or a number of others), a choice which may have reflected wishes expressed by that person while alive,[140] attests at least to a perceived relationship between them, and a desire publicly to represent that connection. Certain sepulchral representations of dead women's connections to the living and the dead demonstrate that women were able to maintain relationships across multiple households through to the end of their lives.

Polyxena's epitaph suggests that she maintained a good relationship with her parents as well as her husband and also, since it includes all of them, that the survivors had good relationships with each other. Other women are commemorated in their natal family context (alongside dead

---

[136] NAM 3935 = *SEG* 21:1064; p. 189.   [137] NAM 993 = *IG* 11² 6873; pp. 252–6.
[138] Clairmont and Conze 1993 no. 2.850.
[139] For *periboloi*, see Garland 1982 and Marchiandi 2011.
[140] Compare *IG* 11² 7711: a man's burial with his mother, motivated by affection.

siblings or parents, or by still-living siblings or parents) without reference to a marital relationship. Some would have been girls or women who had never been married; others, divorcées or widows who had returned to their natal families; others still, married women whose parents asserted themselves in the commemoration process to the exclusion of the husband, because of closer relationships, family tensions, greater resources, or higher social standing.[141] Philokydis, who died c. 355–350, is one example. The inscription on her monument reads:

> Τιμαγόρας θύγατερ καὶ Ἀριστοκλέους Φιλοκύδι,
> χαῖρε· ποθεῖ σὲ Εὐκλεία ἥν ἔλιπες προγόνοις.

> Daughter of Timagora and Aristokles, Philokydis,
> farewell. Eukleia, whom you left to her grandparents, misses you.[142]

Though the mention of her daughter, Eukleia, strongly suggests that Philokydis had been married, there is no mention of a husband. Rather, the emphasis is on Philokydis' relationship to her parents, and particularly her mother: she is described first as her *mother's* daughter, which may represent her parents' desire to emphasise the bond between the two women. Given that Eukleia was 'left to her grandparents', Philokydis was likely a widow.

The *stēlē* for Phylonoe (c. 380–370; modern Pyskhiko, north-east of the *asty*) is similar.[143] Like Philokydis, she was presumably at some point married: her relief shows her handing a baby to another woman.[144] Her epitaph describes her as Φυλονόη ... θυγάτηρ ⌣ ⌣ — ⌣ |/σώφρων, εὐσύνετος, πᾶσαν ἔχο[υσ᾽ ἀρετήν] ('Phylonoe, daughter of [name lost], prudent, intelligent, possessing every [virtue]'). As with Philokydis, Phylonoe's husband is not depicted or mentioned; Phylonoe is identified in the context of her natal family (θυγάτηρ ⌣ ⌣ — ⌣, most likely a patronymic).[145] Pomeroy makes some suggestions: 'Was Phylonoë a new bride whose claims on her father's (*sic*) affections were stronger than her claims on her husband's? Did the latter predecease her, divorce her when she was pregnant, or simply refuse to pay for the monument?'[146] Any of these are possible, but it might simply have been that Phylonoe's parents

---

[141] Thonemann's (2022: 25–71) systematic study of sepulchral monuments in rural Graeco-Roman Anatolia allows for firmer conclusions in a different context about commemoration patterns and the motivations behind them.

[142] *SEMA* 2516; see fn. 38 for the monument.

[143] Athens, NAM 3790; *IG* II² 12963; Clairmont and Conze 1993, no. 2.780.

[144] See Margariti 2016: 87–8 on the relief.   [145] Though see pp. 122–3 for metronymics.

[146] Pomeroy 1997: 130. Compare the character Pamphile in Menander's *Epitrepontes*, abandoned by her husband after she gives birth to a child conceived before their marriage (in fact conceived when he raped her, though neither knew the other's identity) and supported by her father.

Figure 1.2 Grave monument of Philostrate and Melino, c. 350, Athens, Epigraphic Museum EM 8888, Epigraphic Museum, Athens. © Hellenic Ministry of Culture/ Hellenic Organization of Cultural Resources Development (H.O.C.RE.D.). Photograph by author.

were more emotionally or financially invested in her commemoration, and therefore chose to foreground the parental rather than the marital relationship.[147]

The monument for two sisters named Melino and -ostrate (the beginning of her name is lost) is more explicit about their relationship (*IG* ɪɪ² 5673, EM 8888, c. 350, Peiraieus; Figure 1.2).[148] Here, I reproduce the text visible to me, a more conservative reading than Kirchner's in *Inscriptiones Graecae* and underline the text recorded by Ludwig Ross and Kyriakos Pittakis but no longer visible on the stone.[149] We will call the other sister *Philostrate*.[150]

καὶ ζῶσαι πλούτου πατρικοῦ μέρος
εἶχον ὁμοίως, / τὴν αὐτῶν φιλίαν κạὶ
χρήματα ταῦτ᾽ ἐνόμιζον. /

[οὐδ]ένα λυπήσασα τέκνων δ᾽ ἐπιδοῦσ-
[α ἔτι] παῖδας / τῆς κοινῆς μοίρας πᾶσ-
[ιν ἔχει] τὸ μέρος. /

---

[147] For the emotional investment of one relative trumping another relative's claim to bury a person, compare Isae. 8.21–2, where the widow's emotional investment trumps the grandson's.

[148] *CEG* (2) 541. [149] Ross 1837: 692–3, 710–11 (no. 9); see also Pittakis 1839: 277, no. 311.

[150] Because of the *philia* between her and her sister.

– – οστράτη, <u>Μελινώ</u>
– – νος Ἀναφλυστ[ίου]

> While they were alive, they had an equal portion of
>   their father's wealth;[151] they considered their affec-
>   tion (*philia*) and wealth the same.
> She caused grief to no one, but having even seen chil-
>   dren's children, she has a portion of the fate that is
>   shared by everyone.[152]
> —ostrate, Melino,
> [daughter(s)][153] of —on of Anaphlystos.

The couplets were inscribed at the same time. Georg Kaibel suggests that the sister praised in the second couplet died first (presumably she is therefore *Philostrate*, named first), and that her sister (presumably Melino) set up the monument for her before later being buried in it herself. He suggests that Melino had the couplet referring to both of them inscribed before and in preparation for her own death, at the time she commemorated *Philostrate*.[154]

The sisters were almost certainly *epiklēroi*. This gave them particular importance in their family and likely motivated the emphasis on their inheritance. Possibly their sense of their own significance, in combination with some level of access to or influence over financial resources, led to the erection of such a detailed monument, into which Melino must have had input. The striking phrase τὴν αὐτῶν φιλίαν ϙαὶ | χρήματα ταῦτ' ἐνόμιζον ('they considered their love/affection (*philia*) and wealth the same') seems to mean 'they valued their relationship as much as their money'. Though *Philostrate* was evidently at some point married, the sisters apparently maintained a strong relationship with each other throughout their long lives. By the joint commemoration and the reference to their paternal inheritance, Melino uses the monument to set herself and her sister within the context of the natal family whose estate they had carried. She advertises not just their wealth, but

---

[151] Peek 1960: 281 has it that they held their inheritance portion *in common* ('die Schwestern ihren Anteil am väterlich Reichtum als gemeinsamen Besitz behandelt'); this stretches ὁμοίως. Κοινόω and κοινός are the usual ways of describing inherited property held in common (Lys. 32.4, [Dem.] 47.34).
[152] For the connection drawn between the inheritance portion and the 'portion' of death, see Tsagalis 2008: 139–40.
[153] The genitive alone could equally have conveyed 'daughter of' when only *Philostrate*'s name was on the monument, and 'daughters of' when Melino's name was added.
[154] Kaibel 1878, no. 81 (pp. 26–7).

their love for each other. The monuments of Philokydis, Phylonoe, and Melino and *Philostrate* demonstrate that though women might move into new households, relationships, and social roles, this did not necessarily entail the severance or even the demotion of their earlier relationships.

Even where sepulchral inscriptions do not explicitly link joint commemoration to shared affection, we may cautiously infer from joint commemoration the existence of a relationship during the lifetime of those commemorated. Most fourth-century sepulchral monuments commemorate the dead singly, in spousal pairs, or as nuclear families. However, those which bring together larger numbers of people confirm inferences from oratory, newly developed in this chapter, that women were able to make and maintain connections that bridged households and families.

Humphreys' survey of about 600 monuments for fourth-century Athenians found that over half (336) commemorated one person; 88 commemorated spouses; at least 91 commemorated nuclear families; 12 commemorated sibling pairs; 37 were larger groupings.[155] She later acknowledged that group commemoration was commoner than the survey suggests: stones commemorating only one or two people were frequently erected in family *periboloi*, allowing for group commemoration of a family across several stones commemorating individuals or subgroups.[156] The survey's examples of groups commemorated on the same stone therefore serve not as an exhaustive list of instances of group commemoration but as illustrations of possible kinship combinations in any kind of group commemoration, including groups commemorated across several stones within the same *peribolos*. For example, the existence of stones commemorating sibling pairs suggests the possibility that a stone which only names one person could once have stood next to the stone for that person's sibling to form a joint commemoration across two stones. Without precise findspots, *peribolos* groupings are hard to reconstruct; group commemorations on individual stones therefore offer a valuable starting point for the study of group commemorations in general.

---

[155] Humphreys 1980: 116–31.
[156] Humphreys 2018: 362, citing Bergemann 1997; for fuller treatment of *periboloi*, see Garland 1982 and Marchiandi 2011.

Four stones in the survey commemorate women with *both* their spouse and their brother(s), and sometimes also brothers' spouses. Humphreys points out that such cases:

> show one partner in a marriage being separated in burial from his or her family of origin in order that the other partner can maintain both the close bond of siblingship and the marriage tie. Of course it is more common for a woman to be buried with the family of her husband than for a man to be buried with the kin of his wife, but the latter situation does occur.[157]

I referred earlier to the importance and longevity of the sibling bond, and I have shown that women were sometimes able to maintain links with their natal families once they became part of new, marital families. Commemorative groupings of women with brothers *and* spouses show that the importance of women's relationships across families could be recognised, publicised, and celebrated by a woman's commemorating relatives. The tension between membership of multiple families was not always insurmountable.

The four sibling-and-spouse monuments in Humphreys' survey include a monument for Demokleia, her brother, and her husband (*IG* 11² 5479, fourth century, from Sepolia, about two miles north of the ancient city walls), and a monument for Arkhippe, her brother, and each of their spouses (*IG* 11² 6216, mid fourth century).[158] On both stones, all the names were carved by the same hand, strongly suggesting simultaneous commemoration. We infer that both Demokleia and Arkhippe maintained links with their natal families not just beyond their marriages and departures from their natal households but to the ends of their lives: they were presumably commemorated by surviving members of those families. They were able to do this without estranging their affines; the presence of their husbands' names on their monuments suggests their affines allowed the men to be buried with their wives rather than their siblings or parents. For Arkhippe, maintaining a relationship with her brother most likely entailed forming a relationship with his wife Nikoptoleme, commemorated with them on the stone, further expanding her network.

The third example is a Pentelic marble monument from the second half of the fourth century (*IG* 11² 5712), found in the *agora* (Figures 1.3 and 1.4). It incorporated a sculpted relief of a pot; the lip and the curls of its handle survive, at the bottom left of the fragment. This pot may have been a *loutrophoros* (a water container for ritual washing, particularly for

---

[157] Humphreys 1980: 117.   [158] EM 10504.

Figure 1.3 (left) Photograph of Khairestrate's monument, second half of fourth century, Athens, Agora I 501 (Bradeen 1974, no. 81 (p. 43), pl. 8), Ephorate of Antiquities of Athens City, Ancient Agora, ASCSA: Agora Excavations. © Hellenic Ministry of Culture and Sports/Hellenic Organization of Cultural Resources Development (H.O.C.RE.D.).

Figure 1.4 (right) Drawing PD 2119-c of Khairestrate's monument by James Oliver (Oliver and Dow 1935, no. 28 (p. 65)). American School of Classical Studies at Athens: Agora Excavations.

weddings),[159] which in a sepulchral context usually indicates that the commemorated person died unmarried.[160] The monument commemorates the son of Khairephanes of Atene, whose own name is lost, with Thrasylokhos(?) son of Xenokles of Euonymon, and Khairestrate daughter of Khairephanes of Atene. Khairestrate was the first man's sister;[161] Thrasylokhos would have been her husband.[162]

Like Demokleia and Arkhippe, Khairestrate was commemorated with both her brother and her husband. It is even possible that the link she made between the two men meant that they were commemorated together as brothers-in-law even before her name was added to the monument. Before the monument was broken up for building material, it was copied by Ludwig Ross, Alexandros Rangavis, and Stephanos Koumanoudes, on whom we rely for much of the reading below. Letters visible to them but since lost are underlined, with Donald Bradeen's hypothesised corrections in triangular brackets.[163]

---

[159] Grossman 2013: 159 calls it an '*amphora loutrophoros*'; Bradeen 1974: 43 (*Agora* XVII 81) a '*hydria*'; Humphreys 2018: 819, fn. 19, an 'unidentifiable vase'.

[160] Dem. 44.18; cf. Humphreys 2018: 368–72.

[161] Less likely, the first man had the same name as his father, and Khairestrate was his daughter, not sister. This would require that the pot shape made no reference to his marital status.

[162] For this family, see *APF* no. 11221, and Humphreys 2018: 819, fn. 19.

[163] Ross and Meier 1846: 62, no. 55; Rangavis 1842, no. 1391; Koumanoudes 1871, no. 275. See Bradeen 1974: 43 for discussion of the restorations; I follow his judgements, except for his iota subscript under the eta of θυγάτηρ, presumably a misprint.

[—] Χαιρεφάνου[ς]
Ἀ[τ]η[ν]ε̣ύς
[Θρασ]ύ⟨λ⟩[ο]χ[ο]ς Ξενοκλέ[ο]υς
[Ε]ὐ̣[ω]ν̣[υ]μεύς
[Χ]αιρε[στρ]ά⟨τ⟩[η] Χαιρεφάνους
Ἀτηνέως θυγάτηρ

The names were carved in different hands, at different times: James Oliver posits that each name was inscribed by a different hand (presumably when each individual died), Peter Thonemann that one hand inscribed the first name, and a second inscribed the other two.[164] The monument was originally erected for the son of Khairephanes, who probably died unmarried. Thrasylokhos and then Khairestrate were added later, either at the same time or as each died. This meant Thrasylokhos was commemorated alongside his brother-in-law, with Khairestrate linking the two of them. *If* the names were all inscribed at different times, as each person died, then Thrasylokhos was commemorated directly with his brother-in-law even before his wife had died and motivated his inclusion on the monument. We compare the way in which the formal and affective relationship *Epistheneia* constituted and constructed between her brother and her sometime-husband Menekles led to the two men being linked by a kinship tie (adoption) which was legally independent of her, after her own legally recognised kinship tie (marriage) to Menekles had ceased, though perhaps not her affective connection. The distinctions between legally recognised and affective kinship seem to have mattered little in this case. On the *agora* monument, Khairestrate's brother and husband may for a period have shared the family link of joint commemoration independently of Khairestrate, not yet commemorated on the stone. If Thrasylokhos' and Khairestrate's names were added at the *same* time, the inscribing of Thrasylokhos' name next to that of the son of Khairephanes, not next to Khairestrate's, may paradoxically reflect the commemorator's prioritisation of men, or of relationships between men, over the relationship between siblings – even though it was the sibling relationship that led to the joint commemoration and brought the men into an affinal relationship.

The fourth siblings-and-spouses monument, a mid fourth-century Hymettian marble *stēlē* from Patision (about two miles north of the city, but a mile east of Sepolia), commemorates the sons and daughter of Hierokleides of Aphidna, north-eastern Attica (*IG* ii² 5753; only the

---

[164] Oliver and Dow 1935: 66 (no. 28); Thonemann pers. comm.

endings of the siblings' names are preserved). These siblings are commemorated with three women and one man with other patronymics:[165]

> — — νος Ἱεροκλείδου Ἀφιδναῖος.
> — — ξις Ταυρίσκου Ἀμφιτροπῆθεν.
> [— — μ]αχος Ἱεροκλείδου Ἀφιδναῖος.
> — — πιόδωρος Χαριδήμου Φλυεύς.
> — — στράτη Ἱεροκλείδου Ἀφιδναίου.
> — — ατεια Τιμάνδρου Ἀχερδουσίου.
> — — εια Φρασίου Ὄαθεν.

Listed beneath one brother (— — νος) is a daughter of Tauriskos of Amphitrope (southern Attica), perhaps his wife; listed above the sister (— — στράτη; we will call her *Polystrate*)[166] is a son of Kharidemos of Phlya, presumably her husband. What was their relationship to the two women, daughters of men from Akherdous (location unknown) and Oa (central Attica) respectively, whose names were later added below? One of these women may have been the wife of the other brother ([— — μ]αχος), and the other, a second wife of one of the brothers. If so, we would have *Polystrate* commemorated with her two brothers, her husband, and two or even three sisters-in-law. There are various other possibilities for reconstructing the relationships between them. Possibly the juxtapositions among the first five names indicate, for example, order of death rather than spousal relationships. Possibly the two women added at the bottom had married into the next generation of the family, making them *Polystrate*'s daughters-in-law or nephews' wives.

The inscription is 'rather unusual in scope for a tombstone' but 'can hardly be a dedication'.[167] Without necessarily assuming affective relationships in life from juxtapositions in death,[168] we may still see this monument as an illustration of the numerous potential links within women's kin networks – to their brothers and their marital families, to their husbands and their husbands' natal families, to their children and their children's marital families[169] – and the ways in which the dynamics of those relationships, the relative importance of those links, shifted or persisted over time.

Though questions over possible reconstructions leave some details uncertain, all these monuments illustrate women's potential to retain strong relationships with their natal families until the very ends of their

---

[165] I thank Peter Thonemann for discussing this stone with me.
[166] Because of the large number of relatives with whom she is commemorated.
[167] Humphreys 2018: 371, fn. 43.
[168] Though note *IG* II² 7711 for joint burial and commemoration reflecting the commemorated person's wish.
[169] Compare also Humphreys 1980: 119 on *IG* II² 5374, 5376, 5378 and 5379.

lives. Traces of these connections are also visible in much smaller items in the archaeological record. Foxhall has shown how Greek (and non-Greek) women in Southern Italy personalised their loom weights by, for example, impressing personal items like hairpins or engraved seals into the clay weights during their production, and then passed them from mother to daughter as way of maintaining emotional and relational ties even after separation by marriage.[170] A girl entering a new marital home, where she would spend much of her time producing textiles with her mother- and perhaps sisters-in-law, would bring with her loom weights she had used to make textiles with her mother and sisters in her natal home, while her sisters took matching ones to their new homes.[171]

Though equivalent detailed studies of impressed loom weights and women's networks have not yet been done for Attica, the existence of Attic loom weights marked in this way may suggest that Attic women employed similar strategies. Many loom weights impressed with seals have been found at the Pnyx and Kerameikos, including at least one apparent instance of loom weights impressed with the same seal – showing a seated woman, probably Penelope – found at both sites, perhaps belonging to two women from the same family.[172] Connections through marriage, or through multiple marriages, added to and intertwined with rather than replaced these first relationships.

Lifelong Connections on Stage

These monumental attestations of lifelong relationships between siblings confirm assumptions articulated in Attic tragedy that sibling relationships could last a lifetime. Attic tragedies are typically set in the heroic past, but they thematise questions that were of contemporary interest. Athenians had some expectation that mythistoric tragic characters perceived the world in the way they themselves did, and those characters seem broadly to hold and behave in accordance with the attitudes of their fifth-century Athenian authors and audiences. What is more, Jasper Griffin has shown that the 'acute suffering, extreme situations, and agonizing decisions' which appear on the Athenian tragic stage 'are intimately linked to events in real, recent, and contemporary life'; these situations resonated because

---

[170] Foxhall 2011, Foxhall 2012: 199–205, Quercia and Foxhall 2014.
[171] For the transition between textile work in the natal home and the marital home, see Foxhall 2012: 194–9.
[172] Knigge 2005, no. 128, inv. 5689l, p. 127, from Building Z1 (circa 430s), with Davidson, Thompson, and Thompson 1943, no. 142, p. 93, fig. 39, p. 92 (fifth century: p. 79).

they could and did happen in the real world.[173] Griffin draws parallels between events on the tragic stage and stories told in the historians; there are similar parallels to be drawn with stories told in the orators.[174] Tragedy, like much forensic oratory, is strikingly concerned with family and household dynamics and the potentially disastrous consequences of domestic relationship breakdown.

Sophocles' fragmentary play *Tereus* relies for its plot on the assumption that sisters separated by marriage would maintain a relationship.[175] As often in tragedy, the scenario of *Tereus* is an extreme version of something probably familiar. In the play, the marriage of Prokne sees her leave her childhood home and her sister Philomele in Athens to become the wife of the king of Thrace – beyond the boundaries of the Graecophone world. Though few if any real girls in classical Athens would be sent to Thrace on marriage, girls do seem to have been married outside of their natal demes more often than not. A few girls were even married to Athenians who lived on Lemnos, an island in the north-west Aegean which for most of the classical period was an Athenian cleruchy, something like an 'Athenian overseas territory', occupied by Athenians who retained their Athenian citizenship but lived mostly on Lemnos and owned land there. A fragmentary legal speech, Hyperides' *Against Timandros*, tells the story of one girl who, at about seven years old, was taken from her brothers and sisters in Attica to be brought up on Lemnos, probably to be married to her guardian (she was an orphan) or one of his relatives.[176] Though many girls were married within their deme or to men in nearby demes, others endured more dramatic separations.

According to a second- or third-century hypothesis (plot summary) of Sophocles' *Tereus*, after Prokne's marriage and move to Thrace, 'when time went by and Prokne wanted to see her sister, she asked Tereus to travel to Athens to bring [Philomele to visit her]' (χρόνου … διελθόντος καὶ | βουλομένης τῆς Πρόκνης θεά|σασθαι τὴν ἀδελφήν, ἠξίωσε τὸν | Τηρέα πορεύσασθαι εἰς Ἀθήνας | ἄξειν, *P.Oxy.* 3013, ll. 8–12).[177] Tereus did indeed go to Athens, but while Philomele was in his care, he raped her and cut out her tongue (ἐγλωσσοτόμη[σε], l. 19) 'so that she could not tell her sister' (μὴ τῇ ἀ[δελφη μηνύσῃ], l. 18 – a reconstruction, but a convincing one). When Tereus and Philomele reached Thrace, Philomele told her sister what had happened 'through weaving' (δι' ὕφο[υς ἐμήνυσε], l. 23),

---

[173] Griffin 2007: 189.   [174] Wilson 1996: 311–21; Backler 2022: 470–1.

[175] I am grateful to Lindsay Coo for discussing this play with me.

[176] For the text, see Tchernetska *et al.* 2007. On the separation, see Backler 2022: 469–78.

[177] Parsons 1974: 46–50. On sisterhood in the play, see Coo 2013, Coo 2020.

depicting or spelling out what had happened by weaving it into a textile. Prokne, overcome with a desire to avenge her sister – and, the hypothesis strikingly tells us, by jealousy – kills the son she had with Tereus and tricks Tereus into eating him (ll. 24–30). Prokne, separated from her sister by marriage, misses her, prevails on her husband to arrange a visit, and, when her husband rapes her sister, 'destroys both her mother–child and wife–husband familial bonds in order to avenge her sister'.[178]

Fragments that survive from the play itself suggest that sororal grief at separation was a key theme. Prokne says, probably to a chorus of Thracian women, that she envies them for never having experienced a foreign land (frg. 584 Nauck). Our longest fragment seems to be from another speech by Prokne. In the lost beginning of the speech, she has evidently been describing her happy childhood with her sister Philomele – 'but now, separated (from her?), I am nothing' (νῦν δ' οὐδέν εἰμι χωρίς, frg. 583 Nauck, l. 1). This, she says, is the universal female experience. 'Young girls live the sweetest life of all mortals' in their fathers' homes, until they reach 'adolescence and understanding' and are 'sold away from our parents and family gods, some to foreign men, some to barbarians, some to joyless homes, some to homes where we are threatened'. To make matters worse, she says, newly married girls are expected to think all this is something lovely, to be spoken well of (ll. 1–12). Though citizen-status Athenian girls in the mid fifth century were not literally being married to 'foreign men', they might be married to men whom they had scarcely met and who perhaps lived at a distance from the girls' homes, who may have seemed very foreign. However, despite its emphasis on separation, the plot of *Tereus* also shows how women could find strategies to maintain relationships with sisters from whom they were separated by marriage, and how they retained loyalties to them throughout their lives.

In the Hyperides fragment, meanwhile, the speaker alleges that the girl raised in Lemnos entirely lost touch with her siblings, 'so that [in adulthood] the sisters could not recognise each other when they saw each other in the street or the sanctuary, not having seen each other for thirteen years' (ὥστε τὰς μὲν ἀδελφὰς ἀλλήλας μὴ ἀναγνῶν(αι) μήτε ἐν ὁδῶι ἐν ἱερῶι ἰδούσας, πλεόνων γ(ὰρ) ἐτῶν ἢ τριῶν καὶ δέκα οὐχ ἑωράκασιν ἑαυτάς, *Against Timandros* ll. 42–5). In the fragment as it survives, this is portrayed as 'brutal' (ἀσελγές, l. 32), 'an injustice deserving of death' (θανάτου ἄξια ἠδικηκεν, ll. 19–20). Clearly the speaker was confident that the jurors would share the expectation that even after

---

[178] Coo 2020: 49.

marriage, it was normal and indeed right that sisters should maintain some kind of relationship with each other.

Conclusion

Attic women could be strikingly mobile, often not simply moving from a childhood home into a marital home, but moving back again and then out to another home. Despite these moves, women were sometimes able to maintain and draw on relationships from previous *oikoi* and further afield. Chapter 5 explores some of the ways in which they might have nurtured these links, depending on the nature of the connections and the distances between the *oikoi* of which they had been part. The potential for women to maintain links to natal families after marriage is already recognised; this chapter has illustrated the possibility of maintaining links with former marital families after remarriage. The chapter demonstrates that women were not socially defined by or confined to their marital relationship, or even their household or near kin, but connected to a number of other people, widening their networks as they moved through their lives. Through these networks they were able to give and receive help, and not always to or from immediate family. This chapter has focused on connections with relatives. I develop the theme of women's extra-familial relationships and networks later, but already in Nikarete's story we see that women formed connections with women and men to whom they were not related, and that these people became part of their help networks. Women were able to activate ties developed at earlier stages in their lives to help them, or to help them to help others, in their current stage.

The study of women in classical Attica is benefited by an approach which centres them as individual subjects of their own progressing lives. Women's lives did not necessarily take a linear route through straightforward social categories; their marriages were not static, and not always stable. A woman's experiences and relationships in one life stage might materially affect the next; such effects merit further discussion than they have so far received. The next chapter develops and broadens the picture I have begun to sketch of women's interpersonal relationships, showing how women shaped families and households to meet their needs and the needs of others – including people beyond their kin.

CHAPTER 2

Hipparkhe and *Piste*
Women Shaping Kinship

The stories of *Apollodora*, *Hierokleia*, and *Epistheneia* in the previous chapter attest to women's ability not just to maintain and exploit connections with former families, but also to help determine who became part of a household or descent group by persuading men to take in people for whom they felt affection, obligation, or need. This chapter sets these instances within a wider picture of female influence over kinship. The chapter offers a new argument that, despite patrivirilocal patterns of residence (where a wife tended to move into her husband's father's home on marriage) and the patrilineal structure of inheritance, the desires and pre-existing relationships of women were a significant shaping force in family and household composition. This enabled some women to remain close to their children by former husbands, alleviate loneliness, and ensure the care of people who mattered to them.

The first part of the chapter advances a new analysis of fourth-century thought on the nature and origin of affective relations between kin, and on the construction of kinship more generally. This analysis demonstrates the multiformity and malleability of classical Attic kinship, to contextualise the arguments that follow. This multiformity and malleability made space for women to manipulate patriarchal-patrilineal kinship structures, for example, by influencing men's decisions in the highly patriarchal, patrilineal sphere of adoption. It also made space for alternative, non-patrilineal structures, modes, and expressions of kinship: for example, matrilocal residence and the commemoration of individuals and families from female perspectives which do not reflect androcentric socio-legal conventions. The Attic family was constructed not just by the daily experience of shared living, or by legal recognition and transmission of names, identities, and property, but also by postmortem commemoration. As such, this section assesses the possibility for women to use commemorative practices to shape perceptions of kinship relations and to assert affective relationships within their kinship networks.

The next section of the chapter considers how women's kinship-making worked in practice, counteracting patriarchal and patrilineal constructions of kinship. It starts by demonstrating the importance of maternal kin as caregivers in a demographic context where high mortality, and a dramatic gendered discrepancy in average age at first marriage, left a large minority of children fatherless and without paternal relatives. The chapter goes on to offer new readings of forensic speeches, illuminated by Old and New Comedy, which demonstrate that women could influence household membership to ensure that people they cared about – including non-kin – were cared for. The effects of this influence were particularly valuable to women who lacked the support of *kyrioi*, either because of their metic status or because of adverse circumstances. This section brings to light cases in which women persuaded their husbands to foster their children from former marriages; cases of women voluntarily caring for other people's children; and cases of women encouraging their husbands to take in vulnerable adults. Moving from informal to formal arrangements, the chapter then discusses the potential for women to influence the legal inclusion of individuals into the descent group, nominally a male prerogative. It argues that men's discussions both of suppositious children and of illegal adoptions may reflect anxieties about this potential. This analysis sheds new light on the spectre of suppositious children which haunts so much classical literature, presenting it for the first time not just as the product of anxiety about female sexuality but also of anxiety about women's influence over household composition and kinship.

The third section of the chapter offers detailed analyses of two speeches of Isaeus in which these two phenomena – women's influence over informal care arrangements and over formal adoptions – intersect and are explored from a variety of angles, differently portrayed and evaluated by the speakers.

Overall, this chapter offers a new account of Attic kinship and a new synthesis of phenomena which have previously been approached separately and from different angles, allowing for fuller understanding through fuller contextualisation. It approaches changes to household composition not from a demographic perspective but from an affective perspective, considering the potential influence of individuals, including women. It emphasises the challenges posed to a patriarchal vision of the household by the prominent role of maternal kin in childrearing. It considers fears of suppositious children as connected to fears of illegal adoptions. A gynocentric approach which emphasises the role of women in all these phenomena allows us to draw new connections between them, illuminate new aspects, and draw new conclusions.

Relationships, Relatedness

The late twentieth and early twenty-first century have seen a shift towards new anthropological understandings of kinship, developed through the work of David Schneider, Marilyn Strathern, Janet Carsten, Marshall Sahlins, and others.[1] What Carsten describes as the 'reinvention of kinship' recognises that 'the boundaries between the biological and the social which . . . have been so crucial to the study of kinship are in many cases distinctly blurred, if they are visible at all'.[2] Oppositions between 'biological' and 'social' dimensions of kinship, or between 'real' and 'fictive' kin, are oversimple and do not necessarily reflect the ways in which kinship is actually conceived of in different cultural contexts. Aspects of biology (biogenetic substance, procreation, 'blood ties') have different and sometimes varying meanings in different contexts and are differently related to (combined with, reflected in, mutually constituted in, distinguished from) behaviour. Feminist scholarship has led to greater emphasis on *processual* understandings of kinship – how kinship is *made*, often through 'everyday' domestic processes like care and feeding, predominantly done by women.[3] It is through this new frame that this book addresses classical Attic kinship and the place of women within it. Attention to women's role in kinship gives us a fuller understanding of kinship itself, and particularly of kinship cultures with strong patriarchal and patrilineal aspects: naming conventions, inheritance and property law, and certain residence patterns.

What Kinship Is

'You all know what kinship is' (τὴν ... τοῦ γένους οἰκειότητα πάντες ἐπιστάμενοι τυγχάνετε), one Athenian tells a jury (Isae. 1.41). Unlike a will, he continues, it cannot be falsified. The corpus of Isaeus, who seems to have specialised in disputed inheritances, is an interesting testing ground for Athenian ideas about kinship. Many of Isaeus' cases require him to persuade the jury that his client was a closer relative to the dead man than his opponent – but in what did Athenian jurors believe family relatedness (*hē tou genous oikeiotēs*, as Isaeus has it) consisted? In Isaeus, family relatedness, or kinship, is characterised and constituted by a combination of *genos* ('descent', although the word is not easily pinned

---

[1] See Carsten 2000: 1–36 for a summary. Particularly important works include Schneider 1968, Schneider 1984, Strathern 1992, Carsten 2004, and Sahlins 2013.
[2] Carsten 2000: 1–36; quotation from p. 4.   [3] Carsten 2000: 35–6.

down), experience (nurturance, cohabitation, religious practice), and affection. These components are not straightforwardly separable.

As well as the term *oikeiotēs*, 'relatedness', here specified as family- or kin-closeness (*hē tou genous oikeiotēs*), another key Attic term for kinship was *ankhisteia. Ankhisteia* refers to nearness of kinship. Under Solon, *ankhisteia* was systematised according to a scheme based on genealogical position and prioritising paternal over maternal kin, but the term continued to be used predominantly as an abstract noun, 'kin-closeness'.[4]

In Isaeus 1, Kleonymos' nephews position themselves as his closest relatives, and therefore rightful heirs, by portraying themselves as his quasisons.[5] They establish the closeness of their relationship to Kleonymos according to descent, law, and affection.

> ἡμεῖς δὲ γένει μὲν ἐγγυτάτω προσήκοντες, χρώμενοι δὲ ἐκείνῳ πάντων οἰκειότατα, δεδωκότων δ' ἡμῖν καὶ τῶν νόμων κατὰ τὴν ἀγχιστείαν καὶ αὐτοῦ τοῦ Κλεωνύμου διὰ τὴν φιλίαν τὴν ὑπάρχουσαν αὐτῷ (§4)

> We were most closely related to him by descent (*genos*), and were on terms of closest intimacy (*khraomai . . . oikeiotata*) to him than anyone; the laws have assigned [his property] to us according to degree of kin-closeness (*ankhisteia*), as has Kleonymos himself through his affection [for us].

And again,

> εἴ τε γὰρ διὰ τὴν τοῦ γένους ἀγχιστείαν δεῖ γενέσθαι τινὰς κληρονόμους, ἡμεῖς ἐγγυτέρω γένει προσήκομεν· εἴ τε διὰ τὴν φιλίαν τὴν ὑπάρχουσαν, ἴσασιν αὐτὸν ἅπαντες ἡμῖν οἰκειότερον διακείμενον. (§37; cf. §§19, 21, 45)

> For if those who inherit are to be determined on the grounds of kin-closeness by descent (*hē tou genous ankhisteia*), we are most closely related by descent (*genos*), and if on the grounds of the presence of affection (*philia*), everyone knows that he was closer (*oikeioteros*) to us.[6]

---

[4] This was the system used to rank potential heirs in cases of intestate succession, as well as the right/ obligation to marry an *epiklēros*. It prioritised (1) homopatric brothers and their descendants; (2) homopatric sisters and their descendants; (3) paternal uncles, and their children and grandchildren; (4) paternal aunts, their children and grandchildren; (4a) paternal great-uncles, their children and grandchildren; (4b) paternal great-aunts, their children and grandchildren – though these two categories are uncertain), (5–8) the corresponding relations from the mother's side (as set out in Harrison 1968: 143–6). See Todd 1993: 217–21; Humphreys 2018: 37–45, with fn. 90, p. 37, on the usage of the noun in ancient texts and modern scholarship; compare her pp. 12–18 on the different conception of kinship in Draco's homicide law.

[5] Compare Humphreys 2018: 228–30 on this case, and Gherchanoc 2012: 84–5 on its discussion of kinship: 'these ties [of *syngeneia, philia* and *oikeiotēs*], and the affection this uncle showed them throughout his life . . . justify the inheritance' ('ces liens et l'affection que leur a portée cet oncle tout au long de sa vie . . . justifient l'héritage').

[6] Compare H. Lambert 2000 on the combination of affection and substance in Rajasthani relatedness.

Elsewhere the speaker leaves descent aside and focuses on experience and attitudes, using the adverb *oikeiōs* ('closely', 'like a relative') with various verbs of being and living:

> [18] [Our opponents] base the strength of their case on the will, saying that Kleonymos sent for the magistrate not because he wished to revoke it but to revise it and confirm that the legacy belonged to them. Now, you consider whether it is more likely that Kleonymos wanted to cancel the will he had made in anger now that he was close (*oikeiōs ekhō*) to us, or whether he was looking to deprive us even more decisively of his property. [19] Other men who have wronged close relatives (*oikeioi*) in anger later repent of it; [our opponents] present [Kleonymos] instead as wanting, at the time when he felt closest (*oikeiotata diakeimai*) to us, to shore up the will he had made in anger . . .
>
> [30] [When he made the will], he was at odds with Deinias, who was our guardian, and was not yet close (*khraomai*) to us, and was well intentioned towards all [my opponents], but [when he died] he had become at odds with some of them, but was closest (*khraomai oikeiotata*) of all to us . . . [34] As far as I'm concerned, they've said everything they could to you to denounce the will and the deceased, in so far as they have made clear that the will was not correct or satisfactory to the man who made it, whom they accuse of such insanity that they say he cared more about those who were at odds with him than those who were close to him (*hoi oikeiōs khrōmenoi*), and that he left all his property to people he didn't speak to when he was alive, while deeming those who had been on closest terms (*hoi oikeiotata khrōmenoi*) with him as unworthy of the smallest part of his estate. Which of you, then, could vote such a will as valid . . . ?

The closeness connoted by the adverb *oikeiōs* is the closeness of the household as an economic unit (*oikos*), the physical home (*oikia*), the small-scale kin unit based around a couple who live together (*synoikeō*) in marriage,[7] and what is private to oneself (*oikeios*). We may therefore translate *khraomai oikeiōs* as 'to live as family'. This translation is supported by the speech, where the relationship of *oikeiotēs* is glossed as and demonstrated by the nephews' living in Kleonymos' *oikia* (§§12, 28), and his caring for them (*therapeuō*), providing for them, educating them, and keeping their property safe (§§1, 12, 28): the tasks of a parent.

Given the prominence of its cognates in the vocabulary of relatedness, the term *oikos* merits some discussion. *Oikos* can have the sense of 'home' or 'household', a built space occupied by a group of people linked by kinship of various kinds (as we have seen, their living together helped

---

7 Compare Patterson 1991: 48–9, 58–9 on *synoikeō*; Patterson argues for the marital relationship as created *processually*. See further Gherchanoc 2012: 23–34.

constitute this kinship) or by enslavement (enslaved people kept within the home were often termed *oiketai*), which functioned as an economic (and ideological and political) unit. The spatial, social, economic, and other meanings are variously salient in different contexts. As has been demonstrated by other ancient historians and is brought out in new ways in this book, membership of an *oikos* in this sense was dynamic: it changed with time, with vicissitudes in the lives of particular members or of the group, and in response to personal motivations. Domestic space and, among women in particular, domestic work were often shared by those who were not long-term members of the *oikos*. Some of these people would have been kin; others were connected to *oikos* members by different ties of relatedness (mutual affection; living nearby). Tellingly, the word *philos* (masculine) or *philē* (feminine), literally 'dear one', often appears in these contexts, denoting those in one's close circle without sharply distinguishing between 'kin' and 'non-kin'.[8]

In Attic law, *oikos* also refers to an estate to be passed down (ideally) along a patriline. In this sense, it incorporates not just the physical house(s) to be passed from one member to the next along patrilineal principles, but also all the associated property (including some household members: those held in slavery). A boy raised by his mother and stepfather would be heir to his biological father's *oikos* (in the legal sense) while living as part of the physical, social, and economic *oikos* ('household') presided over by his stepfather. Relatedly, *oikos* can refer to the descent group, incorporating any adoptees, eligible to inherit this estate.[9]

Certain metaphorical uses demonstrate the perceived relationship between these various meanings.[10] The speaker of Isaeus 2, the adoptive son of Menekles, claims that by challenging his adoption, his opponent is seeking 'to render deserted [Menekles'] *oikos*' (τὸν οἶκον αὐτοῦ ἐξερημώσων, Isae. 2.35; cf. 7.31). He means that his opponent would undo Menekles' efforts to pass on his property and continue his patriline by adopting an heir. The speaker stresses that he named his own son after Menekles, ἵνα μὴ ἀνώνυμος ὁ οἶκος αὐτοῦ

---

[8] On such terminology, see pp. 9–10.

[9] In Isaeus 10, for example, the speaker repeatedly asserts that his opponent has been adopted into another *oikos* (descent group) which renders him ineligible to inherit the *oikos* (estate) of his biological father: §§8, 17, 26.

[10] Other languages share this close association between house and kinship (Carsten 2004: 39–40, 46). The Nuer of South Sudan call lineage *thok mac*, the hearth, or *thok dwiel*, the entrance to the hut (Evans-Pritchard 1940: 195). Similarly, in north-western Amazonia, the word for the Tukanoan longhouse, *maloca*, can be used for both the house and its people; the *maloca* is also sometimes described as a woman's body, with a head, womb, and vagina (Carsten and Hugh-Jones 1995: 233). Compare my p. 318 on the analogy between the house and the wife's body in Lysias 1.

γένηται, 'so that his *oikos* might not be nameless' (§36).[11] The metaphor of 'desertion' or 'emptiness' illustrates the speaker's simultaneous perception of the *oikos* as a descent line and as a normatively inhabited *space*, a perception he expects the jurors to share. This privileged role of domestic space in creating and conceiving kinship is common to many cultures, as anthropologists have shown.[12] Carsten has shown that, among the Malay of the Langkawi archipelago, 'relatedness is created both by ties of procreation and through everyday acts of feeding and living together in the house … Here the small acts of hospitality and feeding, together with longer-term sharing of food and living space which fostering and marriage involve, create kinship where it did not previously exist.' 'Women and houses' are therefore 'central' to the process of creating relatedness.[13]

Complex interrelations between ideas about descent, bodily substance, experience, and affection such as those articulated by Kleonymos' nephews in Isaeus 1 are also evident in other fourth-century accounts of kinship. Aristotle, in a philosophical discussion of various kinds of *philia*, affection (e.g. between family, friends, fellow citizens, fellow members of a tribe, colleagues), seems to claim that affection between kin (*hē syngenikē [philia]*) has its basis in shared substance (*NE* 1161b). He writes:

> καὶ ἡ συγγενικὴ δὲ φαίνεται πολυειδὴς εἶναι, ἠρτῆσθαι δὲ πᾶσα ἐκ τῆς πατρικῆς· οἱ γονεῖς μὲν γὰρ στέργουσι τὰ τέκνα ὡς ἑαυτῶν τι ὄντα, τὰ δὲ τέκνα τοὺς γονεῖς ὡς ἀπ' ἐκείνων τι ὄντα. γονεῖς μὲν οὖν τέκνα φιλοῦσιν ὡς ἑαυτούς … τέκνα δὲ γονεῖς ὡς ἀπ' ἐκείνων πεφυκότα, ἀδελφοὶ δ' ἀλλήλους τῷ ἐκ τῶν αὐτῶν πεφυκέναι·

Affection between kin seems to be of many different kinds, but it is all dependent on (ἠρτῆσθαι) parental affection: for parents love their children because the children are something of themselves (ὡς ἑαυτῶν τι ὄντα), but children love their parents because they are something of them (ὡς ἀπ' ἐκείνων τι ὄντα) … Parents love their children as themselves, children love their parents as having been produced by them, and brothers love each other as having been produced by the same [parents].

[11] Compare du Boulay's (1974: 21) explanation of the connections between house and family in a twentieth-century Greek village, where 'it is with the house and land … and those who live in the house … that responsibilities both to the living and the dead are connected; and … in the individual lives of the children born to the house the continuity of the family [is] ensured, and "the name is heard again" (ἀκούγεται τὸ ὄνομα πάλι)'.

[12] 'The very qualitative density of experiences in the houses we inhabit leads many people around the world … to assert that kinship is made in houses through the intimate sharing of space, food, and nurturance that goes on within domestic space' (Carsten 2000: 35). See especially Carsten and Hugh-Jones 1995.

[13] Carsten 2000: 18, citing Carsten 1995 and Carsten 1997.

Sahlins argues that:

> Anchored as it may be in concepts of birth and descent, Aristotle's discussion of kinship at once goes beyond and encompasses relations of procreation in larger meanings of mutual belonging that could just as well accommodate the various performative modes of relatedness. Or so I read the possibilities of his sense of kinship as 'the same entity in discrete subjects'.[14]

Though it is evident that different cultures have different understandings of the relationship between kinship and biology (encompassing procreation, gestation and birth, biological substance, and other material realities which operate as concepts in a great variety of ways),[15] I am not sure Aristotle's conception of kinship is quite so flexible as Sahlins imagines. Aristotle's 'same entity in discrete subjects', his 'being of [the other, where in fact, 'the other' is always and only the parent]' is biological: parents are 'close' (*oikeios*) to their children, he explains, because the children have come from and belong to their bodies, like a tooth or hair (1161b2). Sahlins, however, following Robert McKinley, proposes that such biological expression in fact 'comprise rather a "folk biology" that itself expresses the larger principles of kinship order, including (one presumes) the relations of marriage, filiation, and descent'.[16] In any case, Aristotle does add a social element to his analysis, claiming that *philia* between brothers is much *increased* (though not generated) by their shared upbringing and similar age (μέγα δὲ πρὸς φιλίαν καὶ τὸ σύντροφον καὶ τὸ καθ' ἡλικίαν). He cites the saying οἱ συνήθεις ἑταῖροι ('familiarity breeds friendship', or, more literally, 'those who spend time in each other's company [become] friends', 1161b4).

Aristotle's view was not universal in the fourth century. The orator Hyperides, in a fragmentary prosecution of the guardian of four orphans (*Against Timandros*),[17] does offer a more constructivist view. The speaker condemns the guardian for separating the siblings, which he presents as destroying their relationship: as adults, the two sisters did not recognise each other. He explains:

---

[14] Sahlins 2013: 20.

[15] Perhaps the most striking example in classical Greek thought is the argument advanced in Aeschylus' *Eumenides* 658–61 that a mother is no relation (ξένη, a stranger, foreigner) to her child; only the father is its parent (contrast ll. 605–8).

[16] Sahlins 2013: 72–4, following McKinley 2001, McKinley 1981.

[17] See Tchernetska *et al.* 2007 for the text.

αἱ ... | εὔνοιαι τοῖς ἀνθρώποις εἰσὶ διὰ τὴν συνήθει|αν καὶ τὸ συντρόφους
αὐτοὺς εἶναι μᾶλλον ἢ δι|ὰ τὰς συγγενείας (ll. 35–8)

Affectionate feelings between people exist because of shared lives (*synetheia*)
and shared upbringing (*to syntrophous ... einai*), rather than because of
shared descent (*syngeneia*).[18]

In this speech, unlike in Aristotle, 'sharedness' between siblings is therefore
not dependent on the children's relationship to the parents. Hyperides
argues that fathers separated from their children in infancy would not be
fond of their children, and children brought up by people other than their
parents would not be fond of their parents (ll. 38–42). More gnomically,
a fragment of Menander asserts that πατὴρ ὁ θρέψας κοὐχ ὁ γεννήσας
πατήρ, 'a father is the one who raises (a child), not the father who sired it'
(frg. 647 Jaekel).[19]

The indices of family relationships articulated in Isaeus 1, discussed at the
beginning of this chapter, appear elsewhere in Isaeus. In Isaeus 2, which
concerns an adoptive relationship and so cannot appeal to biology, the speaker
claims that in looking to adopt to remedy his childlessness, his adoptive father
Menekles sought 'someone who in [Menekles'] lifetime would care for him in
old age, and after his death would bury him, and thereafter would perform the
customary rites for him' (ὅς τις ζῶντά γηροτροφήσοι καὶ τελευτήσαντα
θάψοι αὐτὸν καὶ εἰς τὸν ἔπειτα χρόνον τὰ νομιζόμενα αὐτῷ ποιήσοι, §10).
The speaker asserts that he fulfilled his duty as a son by doing all these things,
along with his wife (§§18, 36). The importance of mutual obligation in
the construction of kinship is reflected in the widespread Greek usage of the
substantive adjective *anankaios* for 'kinsperson'; the primary meaning of the
adjective has to do with the bonds of necessity.

Significantly, the behaviour of the speaker's wife *Philonis* (the daughter
of Philonides, §18) helps create the speaker's sonship of Menekles. The
speaker explains:

κἀκεῖνός τε τὴν πρόνοιαν εἶχεν ὥσπερ εἰκός ἐστι πατέρα περὶ ὑέος ἔχειν,
ἐγὼ τὸν αὐτὸν τρόπον ὥσπερ γόνῳ ὄντα πατέρα ἐμαυτοῦ ἐθεράπευόν τε
καὶ ᾐσχυνόμην, καὶ ἐγὼ καὶ ἡ γυνὴ ἡ ἐμή ... (§18)

---

[18] Compare Sahlins 2013: 73: 'the most general acceptation of parent–child and sibling terms is not
biological but sociological: they describe domestic and familial relationships of co-existence, the full
mutuality of being in quotidian social practice'. An example from modern Britain is an NSPCC
factsheet drawing attention to the fact that in the stipulation of the Children Act (1989) that siblings
in care be accommodated together wherever possible and appropriate, 'the term "sibling" is not
legally defined. It can include step-siblings, half-siblings, or unrelated children who have been
brought up together' (NSPCC 2010).

[19] See Keuls 1973 for a reading of *Samia* as having this idea as its central theme.

> He was attentive to me as a father would naturally be attentive to his son,
> and in the same way, I took care of and respected him as though he were my
> father by birth – both I and my wife . . .

He repeats the point later:

> ἐγὼ . . . ὁ ποιητὸς ἐκεῖνόν τε ζῶντα ἐθεράπευον, καὶ αὐτὸς καὶ ἐμὴ γυνή . . .
> καὶ τελευτήσαντα ἔθαψα. (§36)

> I, his adopted son, took care of him when he was alive – both I myself and
> my wife – and when he died, I buried him.

Caring (*therapeuō*) for the sick and elderly was predominantly the task of
women,[20] which, along with caring for children, would have dominated
much of most women's adult lives, as well as the childhoods of girls with
younger siblings. Though *Philonis* drops out of the picture in the speaker's
elaborate account of the burial, caring for the corpse and lamenting at the
funeral were also the province of women, so her contribution would have
been central here too.

In Isaeus 8, part of the proof of the legitimacy of Kiron's daughter
(*Klearete*) by his first wife (i.e., of their relatedness) is that Kiron brought
her up with his second family: ἐκείνην τε ἔτρεφε παρὰ τῇ γυναικὶ καὶ μετὰ
τῶν ἐξ ἐκείνης παίδων ('he brought her up (*etrephe*, from *trephō*) with his
[second] wife and alongside his children by that wife', §7). As in the case of
Philonis and Menekles, presumably most of the actual nurture (*trophē*,
cognate with *trephō*) was done by the women of the household, free and
enslaved. The importance of cohabitation is stressed again when *Klearete* is
described as being *trephomenēn endon*[21] ('brought up inside [Kiron's
home]', §14).[22] The centrality of shared residence to the construction of
family relationships is illustrated by inversion in the story of Euktemon and
Alke in Isaeus 6.21, where the horror of the married man's relationship with
another woman is first his eating at her home, and then leaving the home of
his wife and children to live with her.[23]

Helpful for understanding the interaction between the apparently patrilineal nature of kinship by descent, including adoption – typically, as in
Menekles' case, the adoption of adult men as heirs within a patrilineal

---

[20] Compare Ap. *Neaira* 56, discussed at pp. 86–7, and Xen. *Mem.* 2.2.10; see Demand 1994: 23.
[21] ἔνδον is Reiske's widely accepted correction for εἶδον.
[22] Compare Isae. 1.12, 18, 28; 6.21; 8.7, 14; 9.27, 30.
[23] Compare Carsten 2004: 40–1 on the Malay, for whom eating together in the same house is central to
    kinship: 'The motives of people who habitually go elsewhere to eat are viewed with suspicion. As
    I was repeatedly told, houses never have more than one hearth.'

inheritance system – and the central role of women in 'making' such kinship, beyond their potential role in procreation (not directly at issue in cases of adoption), is the work of Charles Stafford on Chinese kinship. Stafford, following James Watson, argues that anthropologists working on China have tended to overprivilege descent-based kinship, which is highly patrilineal, and to draw a false distinction between the study of Chinese 'kinship' (understood in terms of formal descent groups) and the Chinese 'family' (understood as 'the informal business of everyday family life').[24] These tendencies, which Stafford diagnoses as resulting partly from the use of a formalist definition of kinship and of historical sources which take a male-dominated view of kinship rather than of participant-observation fieldwork, among other factors, have led to an impression of Chinese kinship as rigidly patrilineal and 'of women who have power only as disruptive outsiders'.[25] In fact, he argues, Chinese kinship also has processual and creative aspects, including the 'cycle of *yang*', reciprocal care between (mainly) parents and children, and the 'cycle of *laiwang*', reciprocity between friends, neighbours, and acquaintances, which like *yang* often involves eating together, sharing responsibilities, and transfers of money. Women are central to *yang* and *laiwang* processes and thus play a crucial role in kinship. There are instructive parallels with Attica, where patrilineal descent was central to formal definitions of kinship, particularly after Solon, and many of our sources portray women as 'disruptive outsiders'. However, as we have seen and will continue to see throughout this book, Attic women played a central role in kinship and other kinds of relatedness.

Another recurring theme in discussions of kinship is shared participation in religious rites: the speakers of Isaeus 8, for example, cite as proof of their descent from their supposed grandfather Kiron that he included them in every sacrifice he made, took them to the Dionysia and to other public spectacles, and invited them to celebrate all the festivals at his house (§§15–16). In particular, he included them at sacrifices to Zeus Ktesios, protector of home and property, from which he zealously excluded those outside his family, and 'prayed that we be given health and good possessions, as he naturally would, being our grandfather' (ηὔχετο ἡμῖν ὑγίειαν διδόναι καὶ κτῆσιν ἀγαθήν, ὥσπερ εἰκὸς ὄντα πάππον). Brenda Griffith-Williams comments on this passage: 'Shared sacrifices in fourth-century Athens were

---

[24] Stafford 2000 (quotation from p. 37), following Watson 1986; see also Watson 1982. Both identify the (in many other ways valuable) formalist approach of Maurice Freedman as influential on this false distinction, for which see especially Freedman 1979: 240–1.

[25] Stafford 2000: 38, 47–9.

a means of creating and cementing bonds of intimacy both within family units and in wider social groups.'[26] The phenomenon is discussed by Robert Parker, who points to votive reliefs depicting family groups, including children, approaching shrines.[27] Some dedicatory inscriptions mention the dedicator's children and grandchildren, including a mid fourth-century dedication by a man named Autophilos 'and his children and his children's children' (καὶ οἱ παῖδες καὶ παῖδες παίδ[ων], *IG* ιι² 4327) – who are, in this case, three sons, and three grandsons by three different daughters, though the daughters are not themselves included.[28] Autophilos, like Kiron, included his daughters' sons in his religious offerings.

Other speakers similarly claim inclusion in ritual as evidence of kinship, or cite opponents' failure to attend sacrifices with supposed relatives or intended adopters as betraying a lack of relationship.[29] In Demosthenes 57.54, Euxitheos pairs his relatives' inclusion of him in the phratry, a central locus of kinship recognition, with their inclusion of him in other religious practice: παιδίον ὄντα μ' εὐθέως ἦγον εἰς τοὺς φράτερας, εἰς Ἀπόλλωνος πατρῴου ἦγον, εἰς τἄλλ' ἱερά, 'when I was a little child, they immediately took me to the phratrymen, took me to the sanctuary of Ancestral Apollo [who presided over phratries], and to the other sanctuaries'.[30]

In Isaeus 9, the speaker asserts his claim to his homometric half-brother Astyphilos' estate over the claim of Astyphilos' alleged adoptive son, who, besides his adoption, was arguably closer to Astyphilos under the patrilineal terms of Solonic *ankhisteia*, being his paternal cousin.[31] The speaker treats his opponent's descent claim as void and focuses on disputing his adoption. However, he also describes the kindnesses of his own father Theophrastos to Astyphilos, who was his stepson, and his own relationship with Astyphilos as his half-brother: he and Astyphilos were brought up by the same man, lived in the same house, were educated together, were taken to religious rites together (§§27–30), and Astyphilos was fond of him

---

[26] Griffith-Williams 2013: 122 *ad loc*.; see also Gherchanoc 2012: 81–6 on family definition through religious rites, with particular reference to Isaeus 8 on p. 84: 'being associated with collective celebrations . . . in the domain of the *oikos* . . . defines the circle of family members and characterises bonds of intimacy and familiarity' ('être associé à des célébrations collectives . . . dans le domain de l'oikos . . . définit le cercle des membres de la famille et caractérise des liens d'intimité, de familiarité').

[27] Parker 2005: 37–59, cited by Griffith-Williams 2013: 122.

[28] Parker 2005: 37–59, with fn. 8, cited by Griffith-Williams 2013: 122.

[29] Isae. 1.31; 8.15–16; 9.21, 30; also Lys. 1.20, pp. 316–9; cf. Ar. *Lys.* 1128–31.

[30] See further Golden 2015: 26–8 on the inclusion of children in family religious practice.

[31] The opponent's claim was compromised by the alleged adoption of his paternal grandfather into another family.

(ἠσπάζετό με, §30). None of this counted in law, but he must have felt it would count to the jurors.

William Wyse characterises the speaker's argument as a 'moral claim' based on reciprocity: that he ought to be the beneficiary of Astyphilos' estate because of his father's beneficence to Astyphilos.[32] This reading fits the speaker's assertion that even if he were no relation (*mēden prosēkō*, §27), it would be 'more just' (*dikaioteros*) for him to inherit than his opponent, and explains the stress on his father's kindnesses. It accounts less well for the stress on the boys' shared upbringing. Rather, the speaker is appealing to other elements of kinship, given the weakness of his legal claim based on the link through his mother. His emphasis on his father's role in bringing up Astyphilos, and on the boys' shared education, presents them as if they were homopatric as well as homometric brothers. He sums up: καὶ διὰ τὸ ἀδελφὸν εἶναι καὶ διὰ τὴν ἄλλην οἰκειότητα πολὺ μᾶλλον προσήκειν ἐμοὶ ἢ τῷ Κλέωνος ὑεῖ, 'both because I am [Astyphilos'] brother and because of our other family-closeness (*hē allē oikeiotēs*), he is much more closely related (*poly mallon prosēkō*) to me than to Kleon's son' (§31). The speaker claims the close relationship of being Astyphilos' brother (*adelphos*) – the explanatory qualifier *homomētrios* (homometric) is never used again after the first sentence – *and* 'another kind of relatedness' (*hē allē oikeiotēs*), the relatedness of growing up in the same home, being raised by the same people, and being educated together. That too, he asserts, is a closer relationship than Kleon's son's. As we shall see, there was scope for women to facilitate 'another kind of relatedness', by influencing who lived and received care in the household.

Besides – or perhaps as part of – their role in creating kinship, women also had an important role in attesting to or guaranteeing kinship. Where kinship had to be argued for in court, women were sometimes presented as authorities. Men cited women's knowledge in their testimonies, as women could not give evidence in jury courts themselves. The speaker of Isaeus 12, part of a dispute over a man's parentage (and so citizenship), caps off male relatives' depositions with the testimony of the man's mother, to be given as an oath in a sanctuary (§9). Her testimony is presented as supremely authoritative, trumping the men's: 'who is better placed to know this than she herself?' (τίνα προσῆκε μᾶλλον αὐτῆς ἐκείνης τοῦτο εἰδέναι;). The father's ability to recognise (*gignōskō*) his son is '[next-]best after his mother' (μετὰ τὴν τούτου μητέρα ἄριστα). The speaker of Isaeus 8 adduces female knowledge or recognition of *Klearete*'s legitimacy in

---

[32] Wyse 1904: 626.

parallel to men's behaviour demonstrating it, saying her legitimacy is evident ἐξ ὧν ὁ πατὴρ ἡμῶν ἔπραξε καὶ ἐξ ὧν αἱ γυναῖκες αἱ τῶν δημοτῶν περὶ αὐτῆς ἐγίγνωσκον, 'from what our father did and from what the wives of the demesmen knew/thought/recognised/decided (*gignōskō*) about her' (§18).[33] This same female recognition may be implicit in the demesmen's deposition in [Demosthenes] 43 that Phylomakhe was νομιζομένην, 'considered' – by their wives? – to be the full-sister of Polemon (§35). Another witness cites the 'frequent' (πολλάκις) statements of his mother to the same effect (§36). Outside of forensic oratory, a young man in a fragment of Menander begs his mother to *stop* talking on and on about his family's kinship links (*to genos*) and tombstones and 'counting up' ancestors.[34] Women were keepers of family knowledge and history.[35]

Women, Death, Commemoration, and Relationships

As the mention of tombstones in this Menander fragment illustrates, one particularly important sphere for defining relationships was death ritual and commemoration.[36] This was particularly true among the wealthy, where the inheritance of large amounts of property depended on the articulation of competing kinship claims. As we have seen, in Isaeus 2.36, the speaker, trying to demonstrate the validity of his adoption, stresses that he buried his adoptive father, performed all the funerary rites for him – surely along with his wife *Philonis* – and erected a fine monument, for which the deme praised him. Deme discussion of burials and commemoration evidently formed part of the social affirmation and validation of family relationships. The speaker's mention of the monument points towards the importance specifically of commemoration for articulating (and retroactively constructing) kinship. Sepulchral monuments often positioned the dead person in relationship to family members. Though some inscriptions gave only the name of the deceased, most also gave a patronymic, identifying family membership on a basic but important level. Longer inscriptions might describe relationships in more detail. Sepulchral reliefs often show the dead person with kin, frequently clasping

---

[33] See pp. 310–11.   [34] Frg. 533 Kock.   [35] Foxhall 1994: 94–6; Foxhall 2012.

[36] For example, Isae. 2.36; 4.19; 6.39–41, 51; 9.4, 34. Compare Humphreys 1980: 98–9: 'the heirs or next-of-kin had a statutory obligation to bury the dead … the consequence among the well-to-do was that a man who intended to put in a claim to an estate tried also to take charge of the deceased owner's funeral'; likewise Osborne 1985b: 139: 'Participation in the funerary rites of a man constituted an important way of both showing and claiming kinship, and hence a stake in the inheritance.' Osborne cites (fn. 38, p. 247) various examples of competition over burial (Isae. 8.21f, 3.8f, [Dem.] 43.65, 54.32, Lys. frg. 64) and payment for memorials.

hands to signify the relationship between the dead person and their relative, who was often the commemorator. This hand-clasping gesture is conventionally called *dexiōsis*. Particularly in the fourth century, funerary monuments sometimes commemorated family pairs or groups rather than individuals, on the same stone or, in the case of some elite families, as part of a network of stones within a family *peribolos*, demonstrating relationships implicitly by juxtaposition.[37]

The sphere of death ritual and commemoration – both monumental and otherwise – was also one in which women played a central role and had the opportunity to articulate their perspectives. The role of funerary lament and death ritual as a privileged sphere for women's voices, visibility, and action has long been recognised and productively analysed. Particularly relevant is the importance of funerary lament as a vehicle through which women articulated, positioned, and defined the relationships of the dead person and of themselves.[38] However, lament was not the only element of women's privileged role in burial that enabled them to negotiate and define family relationships.

As well as leading the laments, it was the task of women to care for the dead (washing, dressing, laying out), and women traditionally dominated funerary processions. Particularly after the passing of legislation to prevent the involvement of large numbers of women in death ritual, felt to be dangerously politically potent,[39] these roles were defined by the woman's relationship to the dead person. A Solonic law quoted by [Demosthenes] stipulated that the only women allowed to enter the house of a dead person (presumably to tend to the body) or to participate in the funeral procession were those over sixty or those who were second cousins of the dead person or closer.[40] To mourn – which was predominantly the role of women – was

---

[37] Commemoration does not always correspond to burial: occasionally a person might be buried in one place and commemorated in another, but this was most common for deaths on campaign (as, for example, *Diognete's* husband: see pp. 7–8).

[38] Compare Caraveli-Chaves 1980: 141 on women's laments in Dzermiathes, Crete: 'Binary oppositions [in the laments] do not involve only the living and the dead … they expand to involve various configurations of human characters and … create a microcosm of complex interaction … Depending on who the dead person is, different types and categories of human relationships are reiterated'; p. 153: 'The "I" and "You" [in the lament], far from being merely juxtaposed against each other, serve to build, affirm, or influence vital relationships.' Papadopoulos 1951: 189–90 records the lament of a modern Pontus widow which enumerates her dead husband's relationships to her, his mother, children, and brothers, and her relationships to her grandchildren and mother-in-law (quoted by Alexiou 1974: 176). The best examples in ancient Greek literature are at Hom. *Il.* 24.719–76.

[39] Note also the political implications of women's involvement in death ritual in Sophocles' *Antigone* and in plays which thematise Elektra's obsequies and lamentations for her father (Aeschylus' *Choephori*, Sophocles' *Electra*, Euripides' *Electra*).

[40] [Dem.] 43.62, discussed at pp. 297–8.

to assert one's kinship to the dead person. One speaker in an inheritance case complained that when a man died abroad in Ake (modern Acre, Israel), large numbers of supposed ἀλλότριοί – non-relatives – publicly mourned in order to support their inheritance claims: 'Who didn't cut their hair when two talents [of the dead man's wealth] arrived from Ake? Who didn't wear a black shawl?' (Isae. 4.7).

Women could use non-monumental burial and commemorative practices (burying a body, visiting and decorating a grave, offering libations) to assert kinship. White-ground *lekythoi*, often used for liquid offerings to the dead, were frequently decorated with images of women garlanding or preparing to garland grave monuments with *tainiai*, woollen bands, and *stephanoi*, leafy garlands (see, for example, Figure 2.1).[41] There are two instances in Isaeus where women compete with other relations to carry out burials (6.39–41; 8.22–3). These competitions bear on the competition

Figure 2.1 Attic white-ground funerary *lekythos* showing a grave *stēlē* decorated with *tainiai*; a woman brings *lekythoi*, *stephanoi*, and *tainiai*, c. 475–450, Paris, Louvre CA 1640. © Musée du Louvre, Dist. GrandPalaisRmn/Hervé Lewandowski.

---

[41] See also NAM 1929, Athens, a white-ground *lekythos* showing women preparing grave-offerings including *lekythoi*, *stephanoi*, and *tainiai*, printed in Kurtz 1975, pl. 20. For the production and use of *tainiai*, see pp. 68–9.

between men to be recognised as heir; the woman who buries is understood as a kind of proxy for the man who will inherit. This, the speaker of Isaeus 6 implies, is why his opponents attempted to prevent Euktemon's wife and daughters burying him; this is why the speaker of Isaeus 8 stresses his impeccable and witnessed reasons – the desires of the widow – for allowing Kiron to be buried from a house other than his own. Women's moral claim to bury a close male relative (cf. οἷον εἰκός, 'as was right', Isae. 6.41), and their potential influence associated with that claim played a significant part in demonstrating and defining family relationships, which interacted with the actions of men. The possibility that women might use such practices to differentiate among formal relations those with whom they had particularly strong affective relations, even counter to the expectations and attitudes of other kin, is explored and thematised in Attic tragedy: Sophocles' Antigone insists on the equal burial and commemoration of her brothers against her uncle's orders, and Elektra in Aeschylus' *Choephori* (to some extent echoed in Sophocles' *Electra*) visits and offers libations at her father's grave, which is otherwise unvisited and receives no offerings, including from her father's widow. These concerns may reflect the possibility and potency of such behaviour in real life.

Further, some women were able to 'steer resources into commemoration', as Humphreys puts it.[42] When commemorative inscriptions speak for female commemorators, likelier than not they are women's commissions, if not women's compositions. As I have argued, sepulchral inscriptions, alongside dedicatory inscriptions, were one of the few arenas where Attic women could publicly articulate their perspectives, describing their emotions and situations, within the limitations of genre and circumstance: an opportunity for self-writing. As inscribed dedications by women reflect the opportunity for some 'publicity' of women's voices and action within the sphere of religious worship, inscribed commemorations by women reflect their opportunity for 'publicity' within the sphere of death ritual, which makes them visible to us today.

The existence of a variety of ways of conceiving of and constructing kinship in classical Attica opened up possibilities for women to shape and express relatedness. The analyses in the following section newly demonstrate how women's affections and behaviour were operative in the construction of kinship, by influencing men's adoption decisions, but also by providing care and determining access to care through cohabitation.

---

[42] Humphreys 2018: 368, with fn. 31. To her examples, add *IG* I³ 1206, and some of the monuments discussed in this book.

Patriarchal and patrilineal elements of kinship interacted (sometimes uneasily) with the behaviour and experiences of women, and with cultural conventions which held women as authorities on certain kinship matters – though exercise of this authority was circumscribed by women's inability to give direct evidence in jury courts.

Bringing People In

Women Call on Their Natal Family

One more obvious instance of female influence over household composition is the role of maternal kin in childcare. In times of husbandly absence or death, women often turned to their natal families rather than their affines (or former affines) for support. We saw in Chapter 1 how this mitigated female alienation at marriage; it also meant that maternal kin played a huge role in the care of fatherless children, who were many in classical Attica. Walter Scheidel has drawn attention to the fact that estimated mortality rates in the ancient world, combined with gendered discrepancy in average age at first marriage, particularly pronounced in classical Attica, rendered about a third of all children fatherless before they turned fifteen.[43] (Scheidel's figures are based on simulations run by Richard Saller, which follow different possibilities depending on assumed average ages at first marriage for women and for men, and assumed life expectancies: none of his parameters would ideally fit Athenian marriage patterns even if we were sure we were using the likeliest model and the right life expectancies, but his range leads to fatherlessness rates at age fifteen between 28 and 37 per cent.) In most of these cases, the child would also have lost her paternal grandfather and paternal uncles, who might have served as guardians, though in some cases a child might have been looked after by adult brothers.[44] This would frequently have forced alternative arrangements: the mother's family might step in to support the mother if she was still alive, or take on her role if she too had died.[45] Scheidel's tables and charts show only paternal relatives. Because of the gendered disparity in average age at first marriage, which saw women married and having children much younger than men, it was likelier that

---

[43] Scheidel 2009: 31–5.　　[44] Scheidel 2009: 36–40.

[45] Golden 2009: 49–51; Cox 1988: 381; Hübner and Ratzan 2009: 26–7, including on the role of extended family in the HIV/AIDS orphan crisis in East and Southern Africa as a comparandum. If illegitimate babies were not exposed, they may also have been cared for by maternal kin; cf. the case of Plangon's probably illegitimate children, who were apparently raised by her brothers (Dem. 39.23–4, 28, with Humphreys 1989), and Patterson 1985: 115–16.

a fatherless child's maternal male kin might be alive to look after her even if her paternal male kin were not.[46]

The orators record many cases of children cared for by maternal relatives.[47] The unmarried male speaker of Lysias 3 mentions that his widowed sister and her fatherless daughters live with him (§§6–7): the girls live with their mother in their maternal uncle's house. Andocides mentions that his father Leogoras brought up his (Leogoras') sister's son Kharmides (Andocides 1.48);[48] that is, Kharmides was raised by his maternal uncle. Attempts to reconstruct the vaguely described family relationships of Isaeus 1 suggest that Isaeus' orphaned clients were initially under the guardianship of their father's brother Deinias. Their *residence* during this period is not clear: fatherless children with surviving but not-yet-remarried mothers were typically raised by those mothers in the house of their dead father, on a daily allowance distributed by their guardian out of the child's patrimony.[49] After Deinias' death, however, the children were taken in and raised by their maternal uncle Kleonymos (§§4, 9–12). In neither Andocides 1 nor Isaeus 1 is the mother mentioned. In Lysias 19, when the widow of Phaidros, who died sometime before 393, was widowed again on the execution of her second husband Aristophanes c. 389, she and her three children were taken in by her father, their maternal grandfather. On his death, she and the children, still young, were taken in by her brother, the children's maternal uncle (§§8–9, 32–3; note how often she and later her children moved households during their lifetimes).[50] We infer from Demosthenes 39 that Plangon's sons, after her husband or partner divorced her or distanced himself from her, were brought up among her family; they are said to have danced in the boys' chorus of her family's tribe, not their father's (§§23–4, 28).[51] Outside of oratory, in Xenophon's *Memorabilia* 2.7.2, Aristarkhos reports that he is temporarily caring for his 'sisters, nieces, and female cousins' (ἀδελφαί τε καὶ ἀδελφιδαῖ καὶ ἀνεψιαί) whose menfolk have fled the *asty* because of political conflict. If, as in Lysias 3, some of

---

[46] Golden 2009: 50, table 3.1, shows figures for Rome assuming female average age at first marriage (AAFM) at twenty and male AAFM at thirty; table 3.2, for female AAFM at fifteen and male AAFM at twenty-five; both less disparate than Attica's likely pattern of female AAFM at fifteen and male at thirty. Saller 1994: 52, 8; see 45–6 for his demographic assumptions, justified on pp. 12–42.

[47] Compare Chapter 1, fn. 39 for the importance of maternal relatives.

[48] With *APF*, no. 828 VI A.   [49] Hübner and Ratzan 2009: 14–15, with fn. 52.

[50] *APF*, no. 5951 C.

[51] For Plangon's obscure marital status, see Humphreys 1989. For other kinds of support by maternal relatives, note Ap. *Neaira* 7–8, 12 for the intervention of a maternal uncle to ensure the financial security of his sister's children, including a dowry for the daughter.

Aristarkhos' nieces are his sisters' daughters (as opposed to his brothers'), this is another instance of care by maternal kin.[52]

A child's maternal grandparents, particularly her maternal grandmother, were considerably likelier to be alive during her childhood than her paternal grandparents.[53] Chapter 1 inferred from the mid fourth-century epitaph of Philokydis that her daughter Eukleia was cared for by her maternal grandparents after her (widowed?) mother died (*IG* 11² 12963, NAM 3790). The young man in the relief who appears to be Philokydis' brother, Eukleia's uncle, may still have been living with his parents; perhaps he cared for his niece after they died.

The late fifth-century grave *stēlē* of Ampharete celebrates her relationship with her daughter's child (Figure 2.2):[54]

Ἀμφαρέτη
τέκνον ἐμῆς θυγατρὸς τόδ᾽ ἔχω φίλον, ὅμπερ ὅτε αὐγάς : / ὄμμασιν ἠ-
ελίο ζῶντες ἐδερκόμεθα, / ἔχον ἐμοῖς γόνασιν καὶ νῦν φθίμενον φθιμένη ᾽χω.

Ampharete
I hold this dear child of my daughter, whom when we were alive and looked upon the rays of the sun with our eyes, I held on my knees, and now, dead, I hold [her], dead.

The baby's sex is not identifiable from the epitaph or relief, though Pomeroy argues that because baby boys are typically shown naked, this swaddled baby is probably a girl. We cannot securely infer from the omission of any reference to the infant's father here that he was not around to care for her, as we did for Eukleia's father, though it may have been the case. We can, however, infer from the statement that Ampharete held her grandchild while they were both alive that she had played some role in caring for her. Possibly Ampharete's daughter had died in or shortly after childbirth; or she survived both her mother and her baby and commissioned the *stēlē* to commemorate them.[55]

In death as in life, families were not always constructed patrilineally. Ampharete and her daughter's child were buried together in testament to Ampharete's affectionate relationship with her grandchild rather than in

---

[52] Men. *Dys.* 384–7 implies the commonness of an aunt (τηθίς) being involved in a child's upbringing, but this may be a mother's or father's sister, and it is not clear whether he is imagining a scenario in which the child has lost a parent.

[53] Compare pp. 59–60 for the apparent priority of the relationship between a child and her maternal grandfather over her relationship with her paternal uncle.

[54] *IG* 11² 10650, Kerameikos P695/I221. Compare Pomeroy 1997: 131–2.

[55] Compare Humphreys 2018: 394.

Figure 2.2 Grave *stēlē* of Ampharete and her grandchild, late fifth century, Athens,
Archaeological Museum of Kerameikos P695/I221. © Hellenic Ministry of
Culture.

accordance with patrilineal family structure. Taylor argues that sepulchral
inscriptions in which the commemorated person is identified by
a metronymic – of which we have about twelve examples from classical
Attica – may indicate woman-headed households.[56] Among Taylor's sample, four stones give distinctly non-Athenian names; the rest give names
common among Athenians. She writes: 'It is possible that some of these
families were citizens themselves, with absent husbands or fathers … On
the other hand, if these are non-Athenian families this might provide
evidence of naming practices being used as strategies of integration.'
Pomeroy argues that metronymics are unlikely to indicate illegitimacy,
'for surely such a status would not be announced on a tombstone'; she also
points out further monuments which give neither patronymic nor

---

[56] Taylor 2017: 146–7; lists in fns. 136–7, to which add *IG* II² 12210a, with Pomeroy 1997: 131.

metronymic (including Ampharete's).[57] For Athenian families, one might expect the social premium of citizen status (and the low legal visibility of women and their names) strongly to incentivise patronymics in sepulchral inscriptions. In some cases, stones without patronymics may once have stood in a context which made the dead person's family and citizen lineage apparent.[58] In other cases, they may have commemorated metics (or in rare cases, enslaved people). In others, it is possible that asserting citizen status at death mattered less than, say, asserting an emotional bond between the dead person and her commemorator. To a long-widowed woman whose daughter had recently died, describing her as the daughter of a man she had scarcely known may have made less sense than describing her as the daughter of the woman who had brought her up and was now burying her.

Women Prevail on Their New Husbands

Women's siblings and parents were only part of the story. More remarkable is the phenomenon mentioned in Chapter 1, 'Persistent Relationships', of women prevailing on their new husbands to take in their children by a former husband. Here, the element of persuasion and influence is more salient. In default of a spouse, a woman's natal family were obliged to care for her, and by extension her children. A new husband was not legally obliged to care for his wife's children by another man, particularly when more regular options were technically available.[59]

In Chapter 1 ('Persistent Relationships'), I suggested that Isaeus' description of Arkhedamos' fostering Apollodoros (7.7) points to an intervention by Apollodoros' mother *Apollodora*, Arkhedamos' new wife. When *Apollodora's* first husband Thrasyllos died, leaving her son fatherless, Apollodoros came under the guardianship (*epitropeia*) of his paternal uncle Eupolis, who allegedly exploited him financially. The speaker, Arkhedamos' grandson, also called Thrasyllos, narrates:

---

[57] Pomeroy 1997: 131.   [58] Compare Introduction, fn. 148.

[59] See also Golden 2009: 51–3 on stepfathers in antiquity, noting the cross-cultural propensity among stepfathers for violence against stepchildren. Hübner and Ratzan 2009: 13 point out that unlike in the ancient Near East and Rome, ancient Greece seems not to have understood care of fatherless children as a *religious* responsibility, which is not necessarily to say that it was not considered a moral responsibility. *Harming* fatherless children was an offence against Zeus: Hes. *Op.* 330–4; the scholiast adds that Zeus was the protector of orphans (Plut. frg. 46 Sandbach (not 40 as in Golden 2009) = schol. Hes. *Op.* 327–34). For foster children in the Hellenistic period and beyond, see Corbier 1999; Ricl 2009; Golden 2009: 47, citing Nielsen 1999; and Thonemann 2022: 194–215.

Ἀρχέδαμος . . . ὁ πάππος οὑμός, ἐξ οὗ τὴν μητέρα ἔσχε τὴν Ἀπολλοδώρου, τήθην δὲ ἐμήν, ὁρῶν αὐτὸν πάντων ἀποστερούμενον τῶν χρημάτων, ἔτρεφέ τε αὐτὸν παῖδα ὄνθ᾽, ὡς ἑαυτὸν καὶ τὴν μητέρα κομισάμενος . . . (§7)

Arkhedamos, my grandfather, from the time when he married Apollodoros' mother, my grandmother, seeing that [Apollodoros] was being deprived of all his money [by his guardian], brought him up while he was a boy, since he had brought him to live with him and with his mother.

This was not a formal adoption: Arkhedamos did not make Apollodoros his heir. Indeed, he helped Apollodoros sue Eupolis for his inheritance from his natal father when he came of age. Eupolis remained Apollodoros' guardian, but Arkhedamos became his stepfather. It is in the speaker's interests to de-emphasise the role of *Apollodora* and emphasise the role of his grandfather Arkhedamos, since his overall strategy is to construct a history of mutual affection and obligation – and thus a history of kinship – between Arkhedamos and his descendants and Apollodoros, whose estate he is trying to claim. *Apollodora*, her affections, and influence, are not relevant to his narrative; in fact, they would detract from it. Nevertheless, her role is quietly apparent in the text. Arkhedamos saw (ὁρῶν) Apollodoros' mistreatment 'from the time when he married Apollodoros' mother' and 'brought him to live with him and his mother'. The first phrase connects *Apollodora* with Arkhedamos' noticing (he would not have 'seen' it unless she directed his attention); the second connects her with Arkhedamos' taking Apollodoros in.

Nineteenth-century scholars of Isaeus had trouble with the phrase, ὡς ἑαυτὸν καὶ τὴν μητέρα κομισάμενος, here translated 'since he had brought him to live with him and with his mother'. The twelfth-century codex which provides our text reads ὡς αὑτοῦ instead of ὡς ἑαυτόν, and some readers understood κομίζομαι (from which κομισάμενος) to mean 'marry'. This rendered 'he raised him as his own, having married his mother', repetitive after ἐξ οὗ τὴν μητέρα ἔσχε τὴν Ἀπολλοδῶρου ('from the time when he married Apollodoros' mother'). Georg Schömann implicitly justified the repetition by giving the phrase a causative sense: 'Archidamus . . . who had married Apollodorus' mother . . . took [Apollodorus] because he saw his guardian depriving him of all he had, and raised him through the duration of his childhood as his only son, since ('da'), besides, he had his mother for a wife.'[60] Later, however, he argued for the emendation of ὡς αὑτοῦ to ὡς ἑαυτόν, pointing out that Isaeus had better ways of expressing 'as his own',

---

[60] Schömann 1830: 132.

and rejected the understanding of κομίζομαι as 'marry'.[61] He offered what is now the accepted reading: 'since he took the boy into his own home, to himself and [the boy's] mother' (*quum in domum suam, ad se matremque puerum recepisset*), explaining, 'evidently the boy had earlier been brought up in his guardian's house, but since he was treated very badly by him, Archedamus took care of him, meaning to restore him to himself and to his mother'.

Emil Albrecht still found 'the repeated mention of the mother … quite cumbersome' ('recht lästig').[62] He also thought the speaker would not have mentioned the time delay between marriage and fostering implicit in Schömann's translation, as it 'weakened the speaker's point' where he is 'seeking to make clear [Arkhedamos'] great and long-lasting interest in [Apollodoros]'. 'The most natural thing', Albrecht writes, would have been for Arkhedamos to take Apollodoros 'immediately' on marrying his mother. The interpretation proposed in this chapter is that *Apollodora*, after her marriage to Arkhedamos, and having built up trust with him,[63] drew his attention to Eupolis' alleged depredation of Apollodoros' estate as it gradually became apparent (note the present rather than aorist aspect of ὁρῶν and ἀποστερούμενον)[64] and prevailed on Arkhedamos to take Apollodoros in. This is more satisfactory than the interpretation that Arkhedamos himself identified the diminution of the estate of the son of the woman he was not yet married to (was he likely to have known about it?) and took him in on marrying her.

Wyse recognised *Apollodora*'s importance in the events, though he did not imagine any active role on her part. He comments: 'Archedamus was touched by the forlorn lot of the orphan child *deprived of maternal care* and left in the power of an unjust guardian, and "fetched him to his own home – *and to his mother*"' (my emphases, though Wyse's dash is emphatic).[65] Schömann was right to reject his earlier misunderstanding which *explicitly* rendered Arkhedamos' marital link to *Apollodora* as a partial cause of the fostering, but also right in his apparent sense that *Apollodora*'s relationship to Arkhedamos played more than an incidental role. Albrecht was right to note a tension between the speaker's desire to emphasise Arkhedamos' initiative in the decision and the facts of the

---

[61] Schömann 1831: 361 *ad loc.*   [62] Albrecht 1883: 364–5.

[63] Compare Johnstone 2003: 267–81 for the need for women to build up trust with their *kyrioi*.

[64] Griffith-Williams 2013 *ad loc.* thinks the present aspect 'indicates that Arkhedamos did not just take action after Apollodoros had been deprived of his property, but intervened while Eupolis's allegedly criminal activity was still going on', also true.

[65] Wyse 1904 *ad loc.*

decision as the speaker reports them. The new reading advanced by this chapter holds that this tension arises from the importance of *Apollodora* in the decision, which the speaker cannot entirely repress: *Apollodora* drew Arkhedamos' attention to Apollodoros' plight and persuaded him to bring him 'to live with his mother'. The speaker's words here may echo the words she had used to persuade him.

As noted, there are analogies with the situation of *Hierokleia* in Isaeus 9. *Hierokleia* had two children with her first husband Euthykrates before he was allegedly killed by his brother Thoudippos; she brought them into her new marriage to Theophrastos. If the allegation was true, it constituted a pragmatic reason for disregarding the children's paternal uncle Thoudippos as a potential guardian. There is also a possibility that Euthykrates had appointed Theophrastos as the children's guardian. If not, we do not know whether Theophrastos accepted these two children as necessarily concomitant on his marriage to their mother, or whether she (or her brother on her behalf) persuaded him to take them in, as *Apollodora* persuaded Arkhedamos. That Apollodoros, unlike *Hierokleia*'s children, was not initially 'part of the bargain' of marriage, integral or negotiated, may have made *Apollodora*'s success unlikelier, but succeed she did. As in Isaeus 7, the arrangement which saw *Hierokleia*'s children living with their mother's new husband may have been entirely informal: if he was not their guardian, the children had no legal relationship to the head of the household in which they lived; even if he was, it was not a kin relationship as recognised in law. In Kapparis' interpretation of Apollodorus' *Against Neaira*, discussed later, these roles are inverted: the metic Neaira, moving in with her citizen partner who had recently lost or divorced his wife, may have cared for his four children as her own.[66]

These source texts, Isaeus 7 and 9, are inheritance cases: legal battles – usually between men – over kin relationships in the framework of the *oikos*, both as heritable estate and as patrilineal descent group eligible to inherit that estate. The legal concept of the *oikos* is central to the genre. However, they demonstrate the misalignment between this legal conception of the *oikos* and the *oikos* as household – a conception which probably had much more relevance in the daily lives of classical Athenians, particularly women and children, than its legal correspondent. (As we saw in the last chapter, even in this more informal sense the *oikos* did not necessarily define women's social horizons: women could have strong connections with – and in some cases a degree of influence over – more than one household.)

---

[66] See pp. 134–5.

In Isaeus 7, Apollodoros lived in Arkhedamos' *oikia* (house) and on a day-to-day basis was part of his *oikos* ('household' as economic and residential unit): the verb *etrephe* ('reared', 'brought up') implies that he was fed and clothed out of Arkhedamos' resources. (His *epitropos* Eupolis ought to have dispensed to him an allowance out of his father's estate – a different sense of *oikos* – but he allegedly withheld at least some of this: §§6–7.) Legally, however, he remained part of the *oikos* (descent group) of his dead father, whose demotic and *oikos* (property, estate), administered by his paternal uncle, he would inherit when he came of age. This was also true of Astyphilos (and his sister) in Isaeus 9, and of any Athenian child with a stepfather – a large proportion. The commonness of a child growing up as part of one household and inheriting from another illustrates this misalignment and opens the possibility that the *oikos* that was so central to Athenian legal and political thought – the patrilineal descent group which replicated itself generation after generation – was not so central to the experiences and affections of many women and children, or to the complex reality of Attic kinship.

Dedications made by mothers on behalf of their children add a new angle to this picture. Across the fifth and fourth centuries, a number of women made dedications 'on behalf of their children' or 'on behalf of their children and themselves'.[67] Most of these women, like their slightly fewer male counterparts who did the same, make no reference to a spouse.[68] Some may have been single mothers – widowed, divorced, or even never-married – and their prayers, particularly to kourotrophic deities,[69] were for help in raising their children without fathers. Others, however, may have been married but felt that, in this instance, their care for their children was between them and the god, and not much to do with their marriages. Dedications made by a woman 'on behalf of her children and herself', e.g. *IG* i³ 857 and ii² 4883, are particularly striking in their exclusion of a husband.[70] Evidently women could act semi-publicly as mothers without

---

[67] Compare Parker 2005: 438–9.

[68] *IG* ii² 4588, 4593, 4613, 4671, 4883; Bingen 1971: 149, no. 1; *SEG* 26:267, with restoration by Parker 2005: 439, fn. 83 (primarily to kourotrophic deities including Herakles and Artemis, where the deity is known); also *IG* i³ 857 (a *dekatē* to Athena; see p. 205). Men: *IG* ii² 4400, 4412, 4429 (all to Asklepios). The exception is *IG* ii² 4403 (to Asklepios), by a couple. *IG* ii² 4688 is a second century example. Compare *IG* ix 2, 575 = *SEG* 35:590b, fifth-century Larisa, Thessaly, a woman's dedication to 'Enodia of the City' on behalf of her child, accompanied by a man's prayer – her husband's? I thank Peter Thonemann for drawing my attention to this inscription.

[69] *IG* ii² 4588, Demeter and Kore; 4613, Herakles; 4671, Agdistis and Attis; *SEG* 26:267 (with restoration by Parker 2005: 439, fn. 83) to Artemis Mounikhia.

[70] We know of men making dedications on behalf of their wives, but not vice versa: cf. Chapter 4, fn. 228.

making much – or anything – of their wifehood. Despite the traditional image of the family as oriented around the patriline, or of the household as a unified group of interrelated residents represented by a patriarch, women's relationships with their children were in some contexts separable from their relationships with their children's fathers.

Women Care for Others' Children

Seemingly women could persuade their husbands to take in their children by other men. Did they ever take in children who were not their own? Menander's *Samia* provides an interesting but questionably realistic case study. In the play, an unnamed Athenian mother and her daughter Plangon befriend Khrysis, the Samian *pallakē* (long-term partner, cf. l. 508) of their next-door neighbour Demeas. Demeas' adoptive son, Moschion, raped and impregnated Plangon; she gave birth while their fathers were travelling abroad. The three women are so close that Khrysis, who must have had a baby and lost the child, breastfeeds Plangon's infant son and looks after him in the house where she lives. Plangon regularly visits to take her turn breastfeeding.[71] The arrangement was established while Demeas and Plangon's father Nikeratos were away, and with the complicity of the enslaved people in Demeas' household.[72] The shared breastfeeding is central to the plot (the men begin to discover the situation when Demeas sees Khrysis breastfeeding the child, then Nikeratos sees Plangon doing the same), rather than being an incidental and unremarkable detail. This gives us cause to question its realism, but the dearth of evidence in antiquity and modernity for 'cross-nursing' makes this hard to evaluate.

Unlike most of the women mentioned in forensic speeches, characters in Attic comedy, though 'individualised' to a greater or lesser degree by the author's characterisation, were of course not real women, nor – with one or two possible exceptions[73] – were they based on particular, real women. Often these characters are 'types' supposed to represent stereotyped ideas of 'categories' of women (unmarried girl, wife, old woman, shopkeeper). Their words and behaviours can be used as (exaggerated, simplified) illustrations of how contemporary society generally agreed that women in these 'categories' spoke and behaved. From such portrayals, one can draw out suggested parameters for women's actions and relationships – as well as

---

[71] Lines 55–6, 57–8 (with Sommerstein 2013 *ad loc.*), 84–5, 535–6.

[72] For other portrayals of such complicity, particularly in secrets around sexuality and parentage, see pp. 177–82.

[73] See e.g. Lewis 1955, Thonemann 2020.

a sense of the anxieties besetting, at least, Athenian men, which likely both reflected and constrained women's agency and behaviour. Given that much humour relies on incongruity between the normal and the absurd, historians working from comedy must deduce what is supposed to register as normal (which might offer an image of day-to-day life and assumptions), and what as absurd. Additional sources, ancient and comparative, control our inferences, but again this is the business of probabilities.

It can be difficult to identify the humour in New Comedy, which leaves us on shaky ground attempting to identify norms. Aristophanes' *Lysistrata* packs its first punchline in line 3. Menander's *Samia* begins with a man explaining that he was adopted and generously raised; his adoptive father fell in love with a *hetaira*; she befriended the neighbour and her daughter; the women held a religious celebration while the speaker was away; he returned, watched, and raped the neighbour's daughter; he is ashamed to face her father and ask to marry her. How much of this, if any, is supposed to be funny? How much commonplace? How much implausible, but acceptable in suspended disbelief for the plot's sake? Likewise for the shared breastfeeding – comically absurd? Or a norm on which the plot can rest?

'Cross-nursing', also called 'cross-feeding', describes informal, shared (and sometimes reciprocal) breastfeeding between social equals, typically within the context of an existing affective relationship and done as a favour, a kindness, or an act of support. All this distinguishes it from wet-nursing, which is typically a more formal, paid arrangement.[74] In classical Athens and elsewhere in antiquity, the exploitation of enslaved women for breastfeeding complicates this distinction (it was not paid, nor would there have been a formal 'contract'); it is probably more usefully excluded rather than included from this working definition of cross-nursing. The question of whether Khrysis and Plangon are 'social equals' is also not straightforward, but the situation in the *Samia* is not one of wet-nursing and fits within the scope of 'cross-nursing'.

Despite considerable new scholarly attention to breastfeeding and wet-nursing in antiquity, there has been almost no discussion of cross-nursing, particularly in ancient Greece.[75] Some Roman sepulchral monuments

---

[74] Thorley 2008: 89.

[75] On breastfeeding and wet-nursing, a large number of unpublished presentations by April Pudsey; a special section of *Illinois Classical Studies* (Vol. 42, No. 1, Spring 2017); and most recently, Constantinou 2023. Compare Yee 2009 for an ancient Near Eastern perspective. Marshall 2017, in the *Illinois Classical Studies* volume, briefly mentions cross-nursing, though only to say that the ancient Greeks avoided it. He discusses the situation in *Samia* but does not call it cross-nursing and thinks that the question of who is nursing the baby is left open.

commemorate a *conlact(an)eus* (m.) or *conlactia* (f.), 'co-nursling', a person nursed by the same woman as the commemorator (e.g. *CIL* 6.27119, 11.6345, 13.2104), but it is not clear whether these were people nursed by the same wet nurse, siblings fostered in babyhood, or something else. Plutarch mentions that Licinia, Cato the Elder's first wife, nursed the children of the women she kept in slavery as well as her son in the hope that their being nursed together (*syntrophia*) would engender in the enslaved children goodwill (*eunoia*) towards her son (*Vit. Cato Mai.* 20.3; note the perceived relationship between biological substance and affect here).[76] Though this is not wet-nursing, it does not easily fit the model of 'cross-nursing' either. Otherwise, we hear very little of the phenomenon. However, in classical Attica, a culture with broad social acceptance of wet-nursing, (probably) high fertility,[77] a norm of at least partial breastfeeding for up to two years, residence patterns that brought together extended family but segregated space use by gender, and the possibility of sharing childcare with neighbours, it was likely that a lactating woman might temporarily entrust her baby to the care of a neighbour, friend, or cohabiting or nearby relative who was also lactating and could feed the baby if necessary. She might also have exploited a postpartum enslaved mother in her household for the same purpose.[78] In households where a baby could not be fed by her mother, but which could not afford to hire a wet nurse, informal arrangements between neighbours, friends, or relatives might have been a lifeline.

The very few scholarly studies of cross-nursing include one from 2017 which found that nearly a third of Rio de Janeiro mothers interviewed (204 of 695) had either breastfed another woman's child or had their child breastfed by another woman; it was particularly common among adolescent mothers and mothers not in formal employment.[79] Of these 204 cases, in 115 the mothers were related; in 52, the mothers were friends or neighbours. The most commonly cited motivation was that the baby was occasionally cared for by the other mother. Other studies in Brazil had similar results.[80] The authors hypothesise that cultural acceptance of cross-nursing in Brazil may be due to the prevalence of wet-nursing in the country in the nineteenth

---

[76] I thank April Pudsey for drawing these to my attention.

[77] Fertility in antiquity: Caldwell 2004; Roman fertility: Frier 1994; link between nutrition and fertility: Frisch 1978 and Menken, Trussell, and Watkins 1981. Isotopic analysis suggests that classical Attic nutrition was good by ancient standards (Taylor 2017: 17, citing Lagia 2014 and Lagia 2015).

[78] Compare Arist. *Thesm.* 565–6 for the 'convenience' of an enslaved woman giving birth around the same time as her enslaver, though here the convenience is that the enslaver can swap her female baby for the enslaved woman's male baby.

[79] Von Seehausen, de Oliveira, and Boccolini 2017.

[80] Nogueira 2008/9, Boccolini, Carvalho, and de Oliveira 2012, cited by von Seehausen, de Oliveira, and Boccolini 2017: 1678, fns. 18 and 19; cf. von Seehausen *et al.* 2017.

century.[81] A study of forty-three Australian women who had cross-fed in the period between 1978 and 2008 used a very different sample (self-selected, middle-class, and with high levels of interest in breastfeeding: they were found through internet birth and breastfeeding forums) from a cultural context where this was not the norm[82] (in contrast to some contemporary Aboriginal Australian communities, where it was).[83] It found similar patterns in cross-nursing mothers' motivations and relationships. The most common motivation was again convenience, for example, when one mother was caring for the other's child, combined with mothers' desires that their children be fed breast milk rather than animal or formula milk.[84] In 45.3 per cent of cases, the women were sisters or sisters-in-law; in 34 per cent, they were friends; one was the child's grandmother.[85] In twentieth-century Farimabougou, Mali, cross-nursing between relatives (most commonly by maternal grandmothers, in a culture with, like Attica, early female average age at first marriage) was 'routine'. By contrast, cross-nursing between friends was avoided except in emergencies, because taboos on intermarriage between 'milk-siblings' would limit the child's marriage prospects[86] – apparently not a limitation in classical Attica.[87] A number of Australian and North American women interviewed said that cross-nursing had brought them into closer relationships with the women with whom they shared infant feeding.[88]

Were shared childcare arrangements more widespread than male-authored sources let on? One fourth-century source from either Teos or Tenos in the Eastern Aegean offers a woman's perspective. This is Erinna's *Distaff*, a fragmentary hexameter poem which narrates the speaker's relationship with her friend Baukis, which began in their childhood.

---

[81] Von Seehausen, de Oliveira, and Boccolini 2017: 1674.

[82] Thorley 2009. This study defined cross-nursing very widely, including mothers who had expressed breast milk for another mother to bottle-feed to her child, and a non-lactating woman who had put another woman's baby to her breast to soothe it. For the sense of cultural taboo among the women, see Thorley 2009: 14–16.

[83] Thorley 2008: 89, with fns. 80–1.   [84] Thorley 2009: 13.

[85] Thorley 2009: 12. A second grandmother gave her daughter's baby her non-lactating breast to soothe the child.

[86] Dettwyler 1988: 179–80; cf. Thorley 2009: 11.

[87] Athenian law did forbid the marriage of homometric (but not homopatric) siblings (Harrison 1968: 22–3); Spartan law was supposedly the opposite way round. There is no indication that this was because of a 'milk-sibling' taboo; Humphreys 2018: 82–3 suggests it was to prevent the transfer of estates from paternal to maternal kin.

[88] Krantz and Kupper 1981: 717; Thorley 2009: 13, note b. Von Seehausen, de Oliveira, and Boccolini 2017: 1677 suggest that higher prevalence of cross-nursing among adolescents was due to the stability of their friendships, characterised by time spent together, sharing of experiences, trust, and mutual support in pregnancy and motherhood; cross-nursing in this group was 'possibly experienced as a practice of social interaction and mutual help'. This is appealing but not demonstrated by the study.

The relevant lines describe childhood memories, left behind when Baukis married:

δαγύ[δ]ων τε χ[(-)   -]ίδες ἐν θαλάμοισι
νύμ[φ]αι.[-   -]έες· ἅ τε πὸτ ὄρθρον
μάτηρ αε[-   (-)] οισιν ἐρείθοις
τήνας ἦλθ[- . . .

ἀκίνα δ᾽ ἐς [λ]έχος[τ]όκα πάντ᾽ ἐλέλασο
ἄσσ᾽ ἔτι νηπιασα( ) τ.[-   ]ματρὸς ἄκουσας
Βαυκὶ φίλα . . .

. . . of dolls . . . nymphs/brides in upstairs rooms . . . but when towards
   dawn, mother [singing?] with . . . wool-workers,
then [. . . came/went] . . .
. . . but when you went to the bed [of a husband?], then you forgot
what you had heard as a child . . . [from/of your/my] mother,
dear Baukis . . .

Martin West reads and reconstructs the lines as follows:

δαγύ[δ]ων τε χ[οροὶ καὶ ἑταιρ]ίδες ἐν θαλάμοισι
νύμ[φ]αι, ν[υκτί τε κοῖται ἀκαδ]έες, ἅ τε ποτ᾽ὄρθρον
μάτηρ ἀε[ίδοισ᾽, ὄχ᾽ἁμᾶι λιπό]δουσιν ἐρίθοις
τήνας ἦλθ[ομες ἔργα . . .]

(21–4)

ἀκίνα δ᾽ἐς [λ]έχος [ἀνδρὸς ἔβας, τ]όκα πάντ᾽ἐλέλασο
ἄσσ᾽ἔτι νηπία εἶτα τ᾽ἐ[μᾶς ἐν(ὶ)] ματρὸς ἄκουσας,
Βαῦκι φίλα . . .

(28–30)[89]

. . . choruses of dolls, our nymph-friends in upstairs rooms, lay forgotten at
night, and towards dawn, my mother, singing; with her and gap-toothed(?)[90]
wool-workers we went to work . . .

   But when you went to a husband's bed, you forgot all the things you
heard in your infancy and then in my mother's house, dear Baukis . . .

---

[89] West 1977: 105–6, 8.

[90] See Liston 2012: 134 for shallow grooves on front teeth 'consistently seen on the teeth of women but not men' in skeletal evidence, most likely a result of girls and women biting on wool in the spinning process. Similarly, Jane Masséglia and Lana Williams found that female skeletons in a 100-strong cache of skeletons from a third-century Roman tomb in Anatolia consistently showed damage to teeth; considering the heavily gendered funerary iconography of the region, which typically shows women with spinning and weaving paraphernalia (Masséglia 2013), they hypothesise that the tooth damage is a result of biting on wool (pers. comm.). However, the damage discussed by Liston consists in shallow grooves on teeth, not the loss of teeth resulting in gaps.

This is one of a number of interpretations. The gist of lines 21–3 is broadly agreed on, though West admits that whatever adjective describes the *erithoi* (wool-workers; the word is typically used for wool-workers who gained an income) is very unusual; his suggestion λιπόδουσιν (gap-toothed) is tentative. That Baukis' early childhood is discussed at the beginning of line 28 is uncontroversial; West's dissent concerns the reading of the letters, but his alternative has broadly the same meaning. More controversial is West's argument (followed by Camillo Neri) that the mother of line 29 is Erinna's, not Baukis', which he makes on the basis (in my view plausible) that the mother of l. 23 must be Erinna's,[91] and a transition would be 'awkward'. According to West's interpretation, 'Baucis came at a certain age to live with Erinna, whether as an orphan or as the child of one of the ἔριθοι' mentioned in line 23.[92] The suggestion of overnight stays and perhaps shared work may imply a child rearing arrangement more substantial than occasional supervised play. Whether or not we entirely subscribe to West's reading, even a conservative reading strongly suggests an element of shared childcare, with the young girls playing in each other's company and interacting with Erinna's mother in the early morning. In the Eastern Aegean and Attica, as in many societies,[93] mothers living nearby took turns looking after each other's children.

The myth of Hypsipyle, dramatised by Euripides in an eponymous tragedy some time between 412 and 405,[94] sees an enslaved Hypsipyle caring for Opheltes, the baby son of Lykourgos, king of Nemea, and his wife Eurydike.[95] Unlike most other enslaved nurses who appear in Attic tragedy, Hypsipyle is of noble birth, which is central to the myth – she is the daughter of the king of Lemnos, whom she saved from the Lemnian women's massacre of all the Lemnian men, forcing her to flee Lemnos,

---

[91] Neri 2003: 327 notes that μάτηρ without a pronoun or personal adjective is 'used by Theocritus (4.9) affectionately to designate "Mother", (i.e. the mother of the speaker … necessarily Erinna [here])'. Like West 1977: 108, Neri notes that Erinna's mother certainly played a role in the poem: an allusion to *Distaff* in *Anth. Pal.* 9.190.5 tells how fear of (her own) mother kept Erinna at her distaff. However, Maas' reconstruction of line 29 as ἄσσ' ἔτι νηπιάσα[σα] τ[εᾶς παρά] ματρὸς ἄκουσας (Maas 1934: 208), taking the mother here and earlier in the poem to be Baukis', is widely accepted. West 1977: 108 explains the problems with it; Neri also holds that the traces suggest τ'[ ]ματρὸς rather than τε[ᾶς] ματρὸς and point towards Erinna's mother. The view of Page 1942: 487, fn. b, that in line 23 the girls are *playing* mother, has very little support.

[92] West 1977: 108.

[93] E.g. Cutileiro 1971: 137 mentions supervising neighbours' children's play as a common favour exchanged among poor neighbours in Vila Velha, Portugal.

[94] Compare Σ Ar. *Ran.* 53.   [95] For discussion of Hypsipyle's nursing, see Marshall 2017: 194–5.

whereupon she was enslaved (frg. 759a Nauck, ll. 72–88). Her ambivalent status is highlighted when Amphiarios, seeing her for the first time, addresses her as εἴτε δούλη τοῖσδ' ἐφέστηκας δόμ[οις]/εἴτ' οὐχὶ δοῦλον σῶμ' ἔχουσ[α], '[you] standing in this house, whether you are a slave or do not have a slave's body'. Hypsipyle's own sons by the Argonaut Jason were raised by someone else in Colchis and then educated by Orpheus in Thrace (frg. 759a, ll. 90–102). Hypsipyle's affection for Opheltes is illustrated through a number of scenes in which she is shown holding and even singing to the baby (frgs. 752d Nauck, ll. 2–3; 752f Nauck, ll. 2–14). She speaks of the friendly care (εὐ-/ωποῖς ... θεραπείαις) with which she nurtures him (frg. 752f, ll. 6–7) and describes him as her 'nursling' (τιθήνημα), whom she 'fed and loved in my own arms in every way except that I did not give birth to him' (frg. 757 Nauck, ll. 42–4). We are given to understand that she breastfed him.[96] (She seems still to have been breast-feeding her own babies when she left Lemnos: frg. 759a, l. 94.) Disaster strikes when Hypsipyle agrees to show the seer Amphiarios, one of the Seven against Thebes, a spring to provide water for a sacrifice on behalf of the army; Hypsipyle takes the baby with her to the spring, and he is attacked and killed by a snake. Hypsipyle is struck with grief and horror, particularly when Eurydike, the child's mother, accuses her of deliberately killing the child on whom she doted (frg. 757, ll. 40–4, 67–8). Though on one level the circumstances are deeply connected to the myth – the seer, the Seven, the establishment of the Nemean Games in honour of the child – they are in other ways easily recognisable as the material of daily life. A woman might well keep a child in her care with her in the course of her daily activities, like going to a spring for water, and the child would be at risk of injury – far more often fatal than today. The horror of such a situation would have an additional, complicating layer if the child were not her own, as may have been the case in a society where childcare was frequently shared.

In *Against Neaira*, Apollodorus may unwittingly provide us with a portrayal of a woman raising the children her partner Stephanos had with his former wife. Apollodorus claims that these children are the metic Neaira's, and so not of citizen status as Stephanos and Neaira claim. Kapparis offers a potential explanation: when Neaira moved in with her partner Stephanos, 'she became a mother figure' to his young sons and daughters and 'treated them as her own children'.[97] He continues: 'The ties between [Neaira] and the children of Stephanos were misunderstood by

---

[96] See Marshall 2017: 194–5 on the apparent dramatic licence here.   [97] Kapparis 1999: 42–3.

the community and this . . . gave rise to the rumours that she was their biological mother, and that Stephanos had fraudulently presented his offspring from a concubine as citizens', the accusation Apollodorus makes in his speech. Stepmothering must have been commonplace in Attica, though it is scarcely visible in the sources, excepting what Mark Golden calls 'the abundant and often bloodstained traces of stepmothers in the mythic imagination' (e.g. Hera and Herakles, Phaidra and Hippolytos).[98] In this case, more unusually, Neaira was Stephanos' long-term partner rather than his second wife.

Despite Apollodorus' hostility to the family, he portrays Neaira maintaining a close and supportive relationship with Stephanos' daughter Phano in particular, helping her care for her former husband Phrastor when he becomes ill (§§55–6). As we have seen, caring – for children or for the sick – could be a constituent of kinship.[99] For *Philonis*, discussed earlier in this chapter (pp. 110–11), her own care for her husband's adoptive father Menekles was part of what made her husband Menekles' son. In the case of Neaira and Phano, their care for Phrastor 'made' kinship in a different way: as the (hostile) Apollodorus tells it, Neaira and Phano's care for Phrastor persuaded him to recognise and affirm his legitimate paternity of Phano's child. Though Apollodorus describes this cynically, it is also possible to understand the women's care for Phrastor as reaffirming their family relationship to him and leading to his re-evaluation of his relationship to his child with Phano. If so, Neaira's care, like *Philonis'*, helped to form a kinship relationship in which she was not a direct participant: Phrastor and his son, Menekles and *Philonis'* husband.

Women Persuade Their Husbands to Take in Needy Adults

Women may also have been able to influence the acceptance of needy, non-related adults into the household. In [Demosthenes] 47, we learn of a family who took in a widowed freedwoman (*Piste*),[100] who before her freedom and subsequent marriage had been enslaved by the householder's father. After *Piste*'s later murder by intruders, the Exegetes (traditional interpreters of sacred and customary law) told the householder he had no

---

[98] Golden 2009: 51–3; cf. also Watson 1995. Mary Renault's novel *The Last of the Wine* (Renault 1956), set in late fifth-century Athens, features an affectionate (though conflict-generating) relationship between a young man and his stepmother.

[99] Compare Xen. *Mem.* 2.2 where a mother's care for her child is part of the network of mutual obligations which binds kin to each other.

[100] Because the speaker describes her as *pistē*, 'trustworthy', §55.

legal remedy for her murder, because she was neither related to nor enslaved by him: οὐ γάρ ἐστιν ἐν γένει σοι ἡ ἄνθρωπος, οὐδὲ θεράπαινα ('the woman [derogatory] is not in your family, nor is she your slave-woman', §70).[101] This implies he was under no particular legal obligations to her in life either, once she became free. Rather, he and his wife (*Hipparkhe*)[102] reportedly took her in out of affection and a sense of moral obligation. Again, *Hipparkhe* may have exercised some influence. The speaker describes the situation at the time of a break-in:

[55] ἔτυχεν ἡ γυνή μου μετὰ τῶν παιδίων ἀριστῶσα ἐν τῇ αὐλῇ, καὶ μετ᾽ αὐτῆς τιτθή τις ἐμὴ γενομένη πρεσβυτέρα, ἄνθρωπος εὔνους καὶ πιστὴ καὶ ἀφειμένη ἐλευθέρα ὑπὸ τοῦ πατρὸς τοῦ ἐμοῦ. συνῴκησεν δὲ ἀνδρί, ἐπειδὴ ἀφείθη ἐλευθέρα· ὡς δὲ οὗτος ἀπέθανεν καὶ αὐτὴ γραῦς ἦν καὶ οὐκ ἦν αὐτὴν ὁ θρέψων, ἐπανῆκεν ὡς ἐμέ. [56] ἀναγκαῖον οὖν ἦν μὴ περιιδεῖν ἐνδεεῖς ὄντας μήτε τιτθὴν γενομένην μήτε παιδαγωγόν· ἅμα δὲ καὶ τριηραρχῶν ἐξέπλεον, ὥστε καὶ τῇ γυναικὶ βουλομένῃ ἦν τοιαύτην οἰκουρὸν μετ᾽ αὐτῆς με καταλιπεῖν.

[55] My wife happened to be having lunch with the children in the courtyard, and with her was an elderly woman who had been my nurse, a kind and faithful (*eunous kai pistē*) person, who had been set free by my father. After she was set free, she lived with her husband; but when he died and she was an old woman and there was no one to look after her, she came back to me. [56] I could not let my former nurse or my *paidagōgos* go in need; and at the same time, I was about to set sail as trierarch, so my wife wanted me to leave such a woman to look after the house with her.

The speaker's house plays home to (and is expected to continue to play home to during his impending absence)[103] his wife, his children, enslaved women (§56; enslaved men worked the land he owned, §§52–3), and one or two formerly enslaved people, *Piste* and the *paidagōgos*, whom he says he had taken in out of a combination of his own goodwill and, in *Piste*'s case, *Hipparkhe*'s desire for company and support during her husband's absence. *Hipparkhe*'s (real or believable) desire may have been for the company of this particular woman, whom she may have already known. The sense of

---

[101] Compare Kennedy 2014: 102–3.

[102] Because she lived near the Hippodrome by the Ilissos: §53, with Scafuro 2011: 317, fn. 70.

[103] Scafuro 2011: 318, fn. 7 notes that at §§49–50, the speaker is expecting to 'send off' (ἀποστέλλω) the trireme he is to fund as trierarch in the charge of the general Alkimakhos – apparently without the speaker on it. In §51, the trireme is indeed sent off while the speaker remains in the city. Scafuro suggests that 'the chronology may have been distorted to create sympathy for the trierarch about to abandon his wife for public service'. The speaker had *already* served as trierarch on an expedition which took him from home (§45); it may have been in anticipation of this earlier absence that *Hipparkhe* initially wanted *Piste*'s company and support.

τοιαύτην ('this sort of woman') is presumably that *Piste* was kind and trustworthy (*eunous kai pistē*); the speaker implies that *Hipparkhe* shared his assessment. He stresses his own motivation of moral obligation but also suggests *Hipparkhe*'s own, distinct motivations, and her influence: he claims that she *wanted* (βουλομένῃ) such a woman to manage the *oikos* with her.

The speaker had evidently remained in contact with *Piste* after she had left his home, through which *Hipparkhe* may also have got to know her. In this nexus of relationships, *Piste*'s primary affective ties would have been to the speaker, whom she had nursed, and to the speaker's father, who had esteemed her enough to free her. Whether merely for the sake of the case or in actuality, the speaker was dissatisfied by the Exegetes' ruling and went to his friends (*philoi*) for a second opinion (§§71–2). Perhaps his frustration stemmed in part from the law's non recognition of his relationship to *Piste*, despite his having explained to them about her affection (*eunoia*) towards the family, and her residence in the family home (τὴν εὔνοιαν τῆς ἀνθρώπου, καὶ ὡς εἶχον αὐτὴν ἐν τῇ οἰκίᾳ, §68). He also arranged for her medical care (§67) – though only after trying to make one of his opponents do it (§62). Foxhall suggests that *Hipparkhe* may have resented *Piste*'s presence in the house as an intrusion: 'From the wife's point of view such a person might be perceived as keeping an overly watchful eye on her and the children rather than looking after them, as almost a mother-in-law substitute.'[104] Alternatively, *Hipparkhe* may have valued her support, as the speaker suggests, and considered her *eunous kai pistē* as he did. *Piste* was later brutally beaten to death by intruders in her attempt to safeguard a cup (§§56–9). The text implies that this cup was part of the σκευή (utensils, furniture) which *Hipparkhe* insisted was reckoned as part of her dowry (§§56–7), and not eligible for confiscation by the intruders if her husband had defaulted on his obligations as they claimed. We might infer from this that *Piste*'s kindness and loyalty did not extend only to her former charge but also to *Hipparkhe*, but the ownership of the cup is not clear, and this may be a colourful detail to portray the intruders as gratuitously rapacious. If *Hipparkhe* did indeed want *Piste* to rejoin the household, it is possible she was motivated by mutual goodwill and trust, as well as pragmatism. We cannot know. Whatever the affective nature of the relationship, it is striking that a relationship between a freedwoman and an Athenian should so closely resemble kinship.

---

[104] Foxhall 1998a: 65.

Hellenistic inscriptions from Boiotia, Delphi, and elsewhere attest to a practice whereby men and women consecrated or sold an enslaved household member to a god or hero. The terms of sale could stipulate that the 'sold' person continue to live and serve in slavery in her enslaver's home (an arrangement conventionally called *paramonē*), but legally belong to the god.[105] This meant she could not be seized as part of her enslaver's property by creditors or heirs. Lene Rubinstein has argued that sellers sometimes used these contracts to ensure care for themselves or relatives in difficult circumstances, particularly women without a male protector.[106] For example, in late third-century Koroneia, Boiotia, two siblings named Paramona and Philoxenos consecrated the enslaved Homolois, and all her children, to Herakles Kharops, stipulating that Homolois 'be free' but 'remain with Paramona as long as Paramona lives', that she should 'look after (θρέ⟨ψ⟩[ι]) Paramona and perform all the customary rites when she is dead'.[107] (This was not true freedom but effectively a continuation of enslavement under a different legal form.) We infer that Paramona was a widow; otherwise, these tasks would have fallen to her husband, and we would expect him to have been involved in the consecration. Rubinstein suggests that this sale was part of a strategy to ensure that if Philoxenos died before Paramona, Paramona would still be cared for. Among the witnesses were Philoxenos' sons Olympikhos and Euboulos; in theory, these nephews should have cared for Paramona in the event of her brother's death, but Paramona and Philoxenos evidently wanted to take an additional precaution. Perhaps the nephews lived at a distance and could not be relied upon to look after her. Rubinstein suggests that families in the classical period could have used similar strategies. The situation in [Demosthenes] 47 did not involve a contract, but there are similarities: the woman lived in the household of her former enslaver and provided support to a free woman living there without a husband. The key difference is that women sold to the gods supported free women from a position of slavery, while *Piste* did so from a position of freedom – though still under the constraints of dependency on and obligation to her former enslavers. As elsewhere in this book, we see how valuable the support of other women (whether violently extracted within the context of slavery or given within a less exploitative, more mutual context) could be to women who were temporarily or permanently husbandless.

To consider the situation from *Piste*'s point of view: after her husband's death, 'there was no one to look after her' (οὐκ ἦν αὐτὴν ὁ θρέψων, §55).

---

105 Sosin 2015.   106 Rubinstein 2021: 473–6.   107 Darmezin 1999, no. 127.

One of the consequences of enslavement, not easily undone by emancipation, was estrangement from one's natal family and community.[108] What of her marital family – children, in-laws? If she had married another freedman, he too was probably estranged from his family. Her children, if she had any, might have been dead or otherwise unable to look after her. Unlike the citizen-status Nikarete in Demosthenes 57, whose former employer was one of many people she could call on for support, *Piste* could *only* call on her former enslavers. The speaker of [Demosthenes] 47 focuses on *Piste* because she will be the victim of his opponents' attacks later in the speech; the former *paidagōgos* is mentioned incidentally in the middle of the discussion of *Piste* with no introduction, explanation, or further acknowledgement. Indeed, his inclusion is so incongruous that the situation implied is not quite clear. Perhaps he too was a freed person who needed care in old age and was taken in by his former enslaver, but Adele Scafuro suggests he had married the former nurse when they both gained their freedom, making him *Piste*'s husband who had since died; the speaker might be 'referring to his care over his [the former *paidagōgos*'] household over the length of his adulthood'.[109] This elision of explanation would not be out of place in a speech characterised by sentence structure that Scafuro describes as 'unclear and confusing to the reader and probably to the ancient listener as well'.[110] Otherwise, his casual inclusion may suggest it was not unusual for formerly enslaved people to return to the homes of their former enslavers in old age; or the phrase might have a gnomic sense – 'one shouldn't let one's nurse or *paidagōgos* go in need'; or, closer to the Greek imperfect, ἀναγκαῖον … ἦν, 'there was [the customary] obligation not to let a nurse or *paidagōgos* go in need' – syntactically unusual, but plausible as an ethic, and consistent with the speaker's actions.[111] Some formerly enslaved people apparently never left their enslavers' homes: the old woman who lives with Demeas in *Samia*, initially an enslaved nurse, then an enslaved maid, then free, still lives in her former enslaver's house (ll. 236–8).[112]

---

[108] But see Hunt 2015 for the possibility of some enslaved people retaining a sense of ethnic identity and community.

[109] Scafuro 2011: 318, fn. 72.   [110] Scafuro 2011: 298.

[111] I thank Peter Thonemann for this suggestion.

[112] Many households in tragedy (Euripides' *Hippolytus* and *Medea*, Aeschylus' *Choephori*) include an enslaved former nurse whose charges have reached adulthood. Presumably, where possible, such women continued to do other work than nursing (as Eurykleia in the *Odyssey*), but in tragedy they are portrayed as companions to the household's women. These women remain enslaved; it is to be expected that they remain in their enslaver's house.

Back in *Samia*, Nikeratos' wife reciprocates Khrysis' care of her grandson: when Demeas throws Khrysis out, the next-door neighbour Nikeratos takes her in on the understanding that his wife, Khrysis' friend, will look after her: πρὸς τὴν γυναῖκα δεῦρ' ἀκολούθει τὴν ἐμήν ('Follow me in here, to my wife', l. 418). In the next scene, his wife has been urging him to confront Demeas and ensure justice for Khrysis: he leaves his house calling back inside, παρατενεῖς, γύναι. βαδίζω νῦν ἐκείνῳ προσβαλῶν ('Wife, you wear me out [i.e. with your urging]! I'm going right now to challenge him', l. 421).[113] Similarly, in Menander's *Perikeiromene*, seemingly set in Corinth but performed to an Athenian audience, a Corinthian mercenary assaults Glykera, his *pallakē* (long-term partner). Doris, the woman Glykera keeps in slavery, apparently asks the married, citizen-status woman who lives next door, Myrrhine, to take Glykera in, and she does (ll. 184–5, 262–4).[114] Myrrhine's husband is away in the country (ll. 364–5); she seems to take the decision on her own (cf. ll. 274, 400–3). Daos, the man she keeps in slavery, comments, ἐπαινῶ διαφόρως κεκτημένην· / εἴσω πρὸς ἡμᾶς εἰσάγει τὴν μείρακα. / τοῦτ' ἔστι μήτηρ, ('I praise Mistress highly; she is taking this young woman into our house. There's a mother!' ll. 242–4). Daos understands Myrrhine's care for Glykera as maternal. We may read these comedic scenarios alongside [Demosthenes] 47. In this speech, *Piste* and her story are mentioned incidentally and would not have been mentioned at all had she not been violently and fatally attacked by the intruders. But without the episode, we might assume the *Samia* scenario where Nikeratos' wife takes in Khrysis to be an unrealistic fabrication of comedy. Reading from *Samia* to Demosthenes, we note that in *Samia*, the citizen-status woman is motivated by affection for the metic woman; this may also have been a factor in [Demosthenes] 47.[115]

---

[113] Compare Johnstone 2003 and Blok 2001: 103–4 for women's use of emotional pressure to influence their husbands.

[114] The citizenship status of the couple in *Perikeiromene* is less clear. The play is set in Corinth; the male partner is a mercenary, so not fully socially integrated even if he is Corinthian-born. His *pallakē* Glykera is of unknown status; she initially lives with her partner in an informal arrangement, but at the end, when the identity of her (wealthy, Corinthian) father is revealed, she is formally married to him.

[115] For a much later, chilling comparandum, note *O.Lips.Copt.* 24 (probably from Egyptian Thebes, c. 600 AD), a letter from a priest or monk (Mark) to a woman named Elisabeth and her husband Papnoute, who are sheltering a 'young girl' who has fled her husband (see Cromwell 2019: 326). The Coptic term *sheere shem*, 'young girl', is usually used of children and suggests she was a very young bride. Mark threatens the couple with excommunication if they do not tell her to return to her husband and be obedient. Had Elisabeth persuaded her husband to take the girl in? Mark addresses both her and her husband.

Historians now recognise that household composition in Attica varied throughout the course of a family's life[116] and give some consideration to how experiences of household living might change with the people present inside the home.[117] However, demographic studies of household composition rarely offer detailed consideration of non-demographic factors. These case studies newly illustrate how individuals' circumstances, choices, and inclinations could shape household composition, and that women played an important role in determining who came in. Our sources imply that men's compassion could be aroused or accompanied by women's persuasion, arising from women's own motivations (reunion with children; desire for company and support; friendship; compassion). In Isaeus 7, the persuasion I hypothesise is disguised; its motivation of compassion is attributed to the husband and praised. In [Demosthenes] 47, the woman's motivation is acknowledged and presented as sensible, but the act of persuasion – if there was one – is left implicit. Only in the comedy is the woman's persuasion more explicit, where it may contribute to an intendedly comic portrayal of the fierce Nikeratos as 'hen-pecked'. Nevertheless, her motivations are endorsed by the plot: Khrysis, whom she aims to shield, is innocent of Demeas' accusations.

Women Influence Inclusion into the Legally Recognised Family

So far this chapter has focused on evidence for female influence over the composition of 'households', understanding 'households' as people bound by shared living space and common consumption of household resources on a day-to-day basis, as well as emotional ties. We have seen how 'experiential' or 'processual' construction of the household differed from the legal construction of the patrilineal inheritance group, and not just in the latter's exclusion of enslaved people and any formerly enslaved residents. As both of these constructions are different aspects of kinship or 'relatedness', implicit accounts of women influencing their husbands informally to care for particular children or adults may productively be considered alongside explicit accusations in forensic oratory, comedy, and other genres of women coercing or tricking men into formally becoming fathers of particular children or adults. This of course was not just a legal 'form' but entailed providing for the newly 'fathered'

---

[116] Discussed most comprehensively by Gallant 1991: 11–33.

[117] For example, Demand 1994: 15–17; Foxhall 1994: 93, 9; Taylor 2011c: 705; cf. Hübner 2013: 141–51, 54–5.

person, whether in one's will or also, in the same way as in informal arrangements, on a day-to-day basis.

Classical Attic texts are full of jokes about and accusations of women introducing supposititious babies and tricking their husbands into believing them to be their own and raising them.[118] Chapter 3 ('Intimacy and Power') argues that the prominent role of enslaved women in some of these insinuations reflects some men's anxieties about the (forced) intimacy and collaboration between enslaved women and the women who kept them in slavery in their homes. The frequency of stories of supposititious children in the context of a society with great social stigma against unmarried mothers, enormous social pressure on women (and indeed, couples) to have children, ideally including boys, high foetal and infant mortality (one Euripidean character speaks as though burying one's children were as inevitable as dying oneself),[119] and little remedy for infertility raises the question of whether they represent more than mere fantasy.[120] However, amid frequent male absence, women's deceptions about the origins of their pregnancies and babies are more likely to have concerned paternity than maternity.

Meanwhile, a number of legal speeches for inheritance disputes accuse women of coercing men into recognising their sons by other men or, in one case, adopting a brother. In Athenian law, adoption reflected and

---

[118] Austin and Olson 2004 *ad* Ar. *Thesm.* 339–41 and 407–9 collect further references: ll. 502–17, 565–6 (though note that the enslaved woman's baby boy 'swapped' for her enslaver's baby girl may also be the husband's); elsewhere in Old Comedy: Teleclides fr. 44. 1–2; Tragedy: Eur. *Alc.* 637–9, *Phoen.* 28–31; history: Hdt. 5.41.2; Oratory: Dem. 21.149; New Comedy and Roman comedy: Men. Ὑποβολιμαῖος; Epinicus Ὑποβαλλόμεναι; Ter. *And.* 506–15. Satyros *P.Oxy.* ix. 1176 fr. 39 col. vii. 10–11 includes ὑποβολὰς παιδίων ('substitution of babies') in a list of themes New Comedy derived from Euripides; Plaut. *Capt.* 1031 and Ter. *Eun.* 39 list it as a hackneyed motif. Patterson 1985: 116 adds Ar. *Nub.* 530–1. *Thesm.* 690–755 and *Lys.* 742–55, respectively a pretend baby and pretend pregnancy, should be added too. Isae. 8.36, feigned pregnancies and feigned miscarriages, is a different but related suspicion: see p. 157. Humphreys 2018: 296, fn. 9 suggests potential sources of such suspicions.

[119] Amphiarios in the fragmentary *Hypsipyle*: ἔφυ μὲν οὐδεὶς ὅστις οὐ πονεῖ βροτῶν· / θάπτει τε τέκνα χἄτερα κτᾶναι νέα, / αὐτός τε θνῄσκει· καὶ τάδ' ἄχθονται βροτοί …, 'No mortal has ever existed who does not suffer: a person buries children and gets new ones, and dies himself, and mortals grieve these things …' (frg. 757 Nauck, ll. 121–4). Note his explicit acknowledgement of the grief caused by infant death, despite its frequency; cf. Golden 2015: 70–4.

[120] Compare the suggestion of Patterson 1985: 116 of 'a "feminine network' which could place an unwanted infant in the hands of a woman wanting to be a mother' (see my p. 70). The extent and motivation of the practice of exposing babies is controversial and difficult to determine: see Introduction, fn. 26 (mostly on the exposure of baby girls). Exposure did not necessarily equate to infanticide either in intent or outcome: babies might have been taken in by families who wanted a child, as often in the literature, or, far less happily, raised in slavery, as was common in Roman Egypt – cf. Ap. *Neaira* 18 for the acquisition of μικρὰ παιδία, 'very little children', to be trained for prostitution.

contributed to a highly patriarchal, patrilineal conception of the family. One of its most important purposes was to secure an heir for the patrilineal *oikos*: a man could only adopt if he had no living legitimate sons; if he had living legitimate daughters, he had to marry his adopted son to one of them.[121] Given this purpose, adoptees were usually (though not always) adult men,[122] and while adoptees' relationship to their natal father was legally severed, their relationship to their natal mother remained (Isae. 7.24–5). Even more strikingly, female influence over post-mortem adoptions was explicitly outlawed in classical Attica. Wills made 'at the persuasion of a woman' (*gunaiki peithomenos*) were invalid; the speaker's opponent in Isaeus 2 extends this invalidation to *inter vivos* adoptions, an extension the speaker does not dispute. Humphreys rightly notes this as 'an interesting indication of the extent to which adoption and wills had become identified in Athenian minds'.[123] Speakers wanting to dispute the validity of adoptions and their associated inheritance rights sometimes presented scenarios of female pressure on men as part of their arguments. Though accusations about suppositious children and accusations about illicit adoptions are distinct types, we may see them as constituent parts of a matrix of images of women shaping kinship *as it was legally recognised*, involving formal membership of the citizen family, which entailed the right to inherit and, for men, to be a full member of the deme and *polis*. A third element of this matrix, between stories of women pretending to a husband that another woman's child was their own, and accusations of women coercing a man to adopt someone of the woman's choosing, were accusations of women coercing a man to recognise her child by another man as his.

Fears of bringing up another man's child in a resource-scarce society may have been felt across the socio-economic spectrum, though as we saw in Chapter 1 ('Persistent Relationships'), the orators offer some examples of willing stepfathers, and there are portrayals in drama of both poor and rich couples jointly, knowingly, and willingly taking in children not their own.[124] Fears of being disinherited by the adoption of another adult or the recognition of another child, however, would primarily have concerned propertied Athenians. These fears manifest themselves in the inheritance disputes of the rich, where adoption often entailed inheritance of a large estate.

---

[121] See further Harrison 1968: 84–9.   [122] Exceptions include Isae. 7.9 and Isae. 11.8 and 41.

[123] Humphreys 2018: 237.

[124] For example, the enslaved couple Syros and his wife in Menander's *Epitrepontes*, and the royal couple Merope and Polybos in Sophocles' *Oedipus Rex*.

Accusations about illicit adoptions and suppositious children are most often accusations of women persuading husbands or citizen partners to adopt or recognise their children by other men. Some cases concern metic women accused of trying to achieve citizenship for their children (e.g. Alke, Isae. 6.19–24); others concern citizen-status women whose children are alleged to be illegitimate, and so not entitled to inherit (e.g. Plangon, [Dem.] 40.10–11). The vague accusations in Isaeus 3 against Nikodemos' sister, the mother of Phile (who was also called Kleitarete), fall into the same pattern. We shall call the woman *Nikodike*. The speaker claims *Nikodike* was a *hetaira* and not properly married to Phile's father Pyrrhos, rendering Phile illegitimate (he nowhere alleges that *Nikodike* was not Athenian, so it is highly likely she was of citizen status). The speaker does not directly accuse *Nikodike* of persuading Pyrrhos to adopt Phile, because he is trying to sustain a claim that Phile was not recognised as Pyrrhos' legitimate daughter, but at §15 he changes tack and seems to imply *Nikodike* was infertile (οὐδ' ἐξ ἑνὸς ἄλλου φαίνεται τεκοῦσα, 'she manifestly never bore a child to any other man'), obliquely suggesting that Phile was a suppositious child, born to another woman and passed off as *Nikodike*'s.[125] We see in this peculiarity the close conceptual relationship between suppositious children and illegal, woman-influenced adoption.

More unusual is the accusation Apollodorus makes against Phano in *Against Neaira*: he accuses Phano of persuading her former husband Phrastor, in collusion with Neaira, to 'adopt' (or formally recognise as his legitimate son) the child he had conceived with her (Phano). Phrastor had supposedly discovered that the marriage was void because Phano was not of citizen status, rendering the child illegitimate – but still his own (§§51, 55–61). According to Apollodorus, Phrastor, ill and fearing for his survival, without an heir and at odds with the rest of his family (and therefore unwilling to adopt another relative), was 'beguiled (ψυχαγωγούμενος) in his weakness by Neaira and her daughter', who 'visited him in his illness when there was no one else to look after him, bringing him what he needed and keeping watch over him'; 'he was in the end persuaded (ἐπείσθε δή) . . . to take back the child and make him his son'. Here the speaker uses the phrase ποιήσασθαι υἱὸν αὐτοῦ ('make him his son', §§56–7, 63), a phrase used both for adoption and, Kapparis explains, for 'acknowledgement of the legitimacy of a child whose parentage and legitimacy had been initially questioned, and restoration of this child to his/her rightful position within the *oikos*'.[126] No verbal distinction is made between adopting a person accepted to be the biological child of someone else and formally

---

[125] Compare Wyse 1904 *ad loc.*   [126] Kapparis 1999 *ad loc.*, citing Rudhardt 1962: 52–6.

recognising one's own allegedly illegitimate child, though adopting an illegitimate child was illegal.[127]

Phrastor then presented the child to his phratry and *genos* (§§59–60). As Stephen Lambert puts it, 'a large proportion of our evidence for the activity of the phratries demonstrates a concern with the affirmation, maintenance, and control of kinship ties and the principle of descent'.[128] ('Kinship ties' should be understood here to include ties of adoption; by 'principle of descent', Lambert refers to the principle that an Athenian citizen had to be the child of an Athenian father, and, after the Periklean Citizenship Law, an Athenian mother.) Phratry membership, which entailed public acknowledgement that the member was the legitimate son of two legitimately married Athenian parents, was important for a boy's capacity both to inherit and, in adulthood, to become a fully fledged citizen.[129] (Despite this, because of settlement patterns which saw many and perhaps most Athenians living or at least owning land in their deme, and the clustering of residences within demes, demes rather than phratries might have been better placed to police legitimacy. In 'such matters as the entry of strangers into houses, the movement of women, and the observation of pregnancies', Jones writes, 'secrecy or deception will have been difficult under the cramped circumstances evidently prevailing in such tiny, closely clustered hamlets'.[130] Indeed, in the orators, speakers are likelier to appeal to the testimony of demesmen rather than phratrymen on questions of descent, wills, and adoption.)[131] *Genē* (singular: *genos*) were subgroups of phratries, of which membership was also hereditary. Acceptance into (or rejection by) a *genos* seems to have resulted in automatic acceptance into (or rejection by) the phratry of which the *genos* was a subgroup.[132]

However, according to Apollodorus, in this case members of Phrastor's *genos*, the Byrtidai, voted not to admit the boy, and Phrastor brought a case against them for refusing him. In Apollodorus' account, it is very strongly

---

[127] Lape 2002: 122.   [128] Lambert 1993: 35.

[129] Phratry membership and inheritance: Lambert 1993: 38–40; phratry membership and citizenship: Lambert 1993: 25–57, Jones 1999: 199, though note the qualifications of e.g. Kapparis 1999: 278–80 on the (significant) exception of the descendants of those granted citizenship en masse, particularly the Plataians and the Samians (also covered by Lambert).

[130] Jones 1999: 198.   [131] Jones 1999: 198; Whitehead 1986: 227–8.

[132] Philochorus *FGrH* 328, F35a: τοὺς δὲ φράτορας ἐπάναγκες δέχεσθαι καὶ τοὺς ὀργεῶνας, καὶ τοὺς ὁμογάλακτας, οὓς γεννήτας καλοῦμεν, 'and/but the phratries were compelled to accept both the *orgeōnes* and the *homogalaktai*, whom [nowadays] we call *gennētai* [members of *genē*]'. See Lambert 1993: 46–9, and, on this case specifically, p. 68; compare Isaeus 7.15–17, though (as is evident from a careful reading of the passage), admission procedures varied between phratries. Legitimate sons of ethnic Athenians were *always* presented to the phratry (sometimes via a phratry subgroup); whether girls were sometimes presented to some groups is contested; see Chapter 5, fn. 128.

implied that Phrastor failed to get the child admitted, though Kapparis has argued that Apollodorus' account is designed to mask the child's eventual successful admission.[133] The point for our purposes is that it is Phano *and her mother* who are said to have persuaded him to accept the child and at least try (perhaps successfully) to have him publicly acknowledged as his son by the *genos* and phratry.

Andocides makes a similar accusation against Khrysilla, a citizen-status woman who had at one point been married to Iskhomakhos.[134] Andocides alleges she had become the mistress of Kallias (who was married to her daughter, *Khrysanthe*)[135] and given birth to his illegitimate son (Andoc. 1.124). According to the story, Khrysilla's (male) *relatives* (οἱ προσήκοντες τῇ γυναικί, §126; compare Neaira's role in the Phano story) presented the boy for admission to the phratry at the Apatouria, a role usually performed by the father unless he was dead, and told him to begin the sacrifice.[136] (Evidently Khrysilla's family were part of the same phratry as Kallias.) Kallias asked who the child's father was, to which they replied, 'Kallias, son of Hipponikos'; 'But that's me,' he said. 'Yes', they said, 'and he is your child.' At this, he took hold of the altar and swore that the only child he had ever had was Hipponikos, who had been born to his first wife, the daughter of Glaukon. His supposed child with Khrysilla was presumably not admitted.

In the case of Khrysilla and Kallias' supposed child, Khrysilla's relatives' influence in the phratry,[137] perhaps combined with the potential difficulty of the phratry in precisely establishing the circumstances of a child's birth, apparently gave them reason to hope that they could get the boy admitted, which they were willing to do for the boy's and for Khrysilla's sake. Though this opens up the possibility that women might indirectly exercise influence within phratries, or at least that their interests might be represented there, on this occasion Khrysilla's relatives did not succeed.[138] However, Andocides goes on to claim that when the child was older, Kallias fell in love with Khrysilla again (ἀνηράσθη, §127) and – implicitly under her influence, though Andocides does not spell it out – successfully introduced the young man to his *genos* as his legitimate son by her, despite

---

[133] Kapparis 1999: 278–80.   [134] Compare Humphreys 2018: 215.   [135] Named for her mother.

[136] He seems to have been phratry priest or phratriarch: cf. Lambert 1993: 68–71.

[137] Of course, they were also *Khrysanthe*'s relatives. *Khrysanthe* had apparently run away from Kallias by this point (§125), probably to her father Iskhomakhos' house, though he may have died in the interim.

[138] It is difficult and perhaps in this case not meaningful to try to differentiate the interests of the women and the interests of their family.

some initial opposition. Andocides here presents acceptance by a *genos* as 'a back door to automatic acceptance into the phratry that had, at Kallias' own instigation, earlier rejected the child'.[139] Lambert, following Antony Andrewes, suggests that Khrysilla's relatives had access to the phratry but not the *genos*, which could explain why they did not themselves try the route through the *genos* and instead made the risky attempt to get the boy admitted on the phratry level.[140] This lurid story, some of which – but how much? – was confirmed by witnesses (§127), is told to slander Kallias and cast doubt on his son's legitimacy. Though it cannot be taken at face value, it is another illustration of the power attributed to women – often acting through their networks – over family membership. The situation in some ways resembles that presented in Demosthenes 39.3–5 and [Demosthenes] 40.8–11, where Plangon, either the former wife or the citizen-status partner of Mantias, who had apparently rekindled her relationship with him, publicly swore that her sons Mantitheos (also called Boiotos) and Pamphilos were his. Her oath effectively compelled him to register them with his phratry, which he did successfully.

Differently, in Isaeus 8.40, we find a man said to have adopted his wife's son by a previous husband. The claim is made to criticise the son, Diokles, as having defrauded his homometric half-sisters (his mother's daughters by her second husband) who would otherwise have carried the estate as *epiklēroi*. The speaker claims that Diokles 'made himself the adoptive son of [the girls'] father, though the man had made no will on the matter' (αὐτὸν τῷ πατρὶ αὐτῶν εἰσποιήσας, οὐδεμίαν ἐκείνου περὶ τούτων ποιησαμένου διαθήκην). Again, it is possible – perhaps likely – that Diokles' mother had some influence here. Humphreys writes that the case 'indicates . . . that a woman with sons by one husband might sacrifice to them the interests of her daughters by another husband. It is likely enough that a woman tended to think of her children as a single group, in which sons had a right to take precedence over daughters even when they had different fathers.'[141] As Humphreys points out, the arrangement certainly favoured her, 'since it allowed her to stay on in a wealthy home with her son as *kyrios*'.[142]

All these cases concern the women's children. In Chapter 1 ('Persistent Relationships') however, we saw how *Epistheneia* was accused of persuading her former husband to adopt her brother (Isae. 2). Demosthenes 41.3 mentions that Polyeuktos adopted his wife's brother Leokrates, then

---

[139] Lambert 1993: 68–71; quotation from p. 70.   [140] Lambert 1993: 70; Andrewes 1961: 6.
[141] Humphreys 2018: 216.   [142] Humphreys 2018: 206.

married his younger daughter Kleiokrateia to him. Possibly his wife (*Philokrateia*) influenced his decision, wanting the man charged with looking after her husband (and her) in old age and death to be someone she trusted. She may also have wanted to keep Kleiokrateia close and married to someone she (*Philokrateia*) knew and liked. However, potential intervention on *Philokrateia*'s part is not implied, nor is it levelled as an accusation against her. This adoption was apparently not contested but is presented as a straightforward fact (ὁ Πολύευκτος, ἐπειδὴ οὐκ ἦσαν αὐτῷ παῖδες ἄρρενες, ποιεῖται Λεωκράτη τὸν ἀδελφὸν τῆς ἑαυτοῦ γυναικός, 'Polyeuktos, since he had no male children, adopted Leokrates, the brother of his own wife'). Humphreys suggests that the speaker of Isaeus 7, adopted by Apollodoros, the homometric half-brother of his mother (*Arkhedike*), 'may … have had to contend with claims that a woman's influence [*Arkhedike*'s] was responsible'.[143] If there were such claims, he does not address them head-on. Indeed, he almost courts them by describing how Apollodoros, who 'respected her immensely' (ἦν περὶ πλείστου πάντων ἐποιεῖτο, §14), 'wanted' (ἠξίωσέ) to adopt *Arkhedike*'s son, so 'asked' (ᾔτησε) her whether he could. The speaker would not have wanted to give his opponents ammunition. Evidently he believed this framing, which emphasised Apollodoros' desire (ἠξίωσέ) and agency (ᾔτησε) instead of *Arkhedike*'s, would not raise or fuel suspicions. His comment on Apollodoros' esteem of *Arkhedike* somewhat undermines it.

Humphreys, who like me groups cases like Alke's, Phano's, and Khrysilla's with allegations about women's illicit influence over adoptions, argues that 'a distinction should be made between accusations of undue influence directed at *hetairai* and those aimed at respectable women of citizen descent', with a 'strong sexual component' in the former absent from the latter ('there is no suggestion that a wife might influence her husband's decision by such means'). This distinction is not so straightforward. After Alke, Humphreys cites 'Apollodoros' account of Phrastor's relations with the *hetaira* Neaira and her daughter' in *Neaira* 55–8. However, though elsewhere in the speech Apollodorus portrays Neaira as influential through her sexuality (e.g. §§30–2), the accusation he makes against her and Phano here concerns their exploitation of his dependence on them for care during his illness to persuade him to adopt. Though Phano had been married to Phrastor as a woman of citizen status, Apollodorus presents her as a *hetaira* – but chooses not to suggest that her influence over Phrastor had a sexual component. (Apollodorus'

---

[143] Humphreys 2018: 231; cf. her p. 216, fn. 80.

wider accusation against Neaira herself, a metic, is less direct. He alleges that her citizen partner Stephanos offered to introduce her children by other men to his phratry as his own, and to marry her alleged daughter Phano to a citizen husband as his own, out of affection for Neaira (e.g. *Neaira* 13, 38, 49). He portrays Stephanos as the initiator of the plan, and Neaira as a willing participant – for which he is prosecuting her. He does not portray her as having deceived or manipulated Stephanos, as Alke, Plangon, Phano, and *Epistheneia* are portrayed as deceiving or manipulating their respective partners or former partners.) Humphreys' other example is equally ambiguous: Khrysilla, whom Andocides accepts was of citizen status but accuses of behaving like a *hetaira*. Khrysilla falls through the middle of Humphreys' distinction between *hetairai* and 'respectable women of citizen descent'. Humphreys writes that Andocides 'handle[s her] … with some restraint'. However, he *does* imply a sexual component to her influence by associating Kallias' recognition of the young man with his falling back in love with her (ἀνηράσθη, §127). We do not know whether there was a sexual component to the allegations made against *Epistheneia* by the opponent of the speaker of Isaeus 2. In these cases, the 'respectable woman of citizen descent' is not a clear category but becomes part of a pattern of accusations made against women of various statuses and of unclear status: the point is that all these women were perceived as potentially influential over the processes by which men asserted and confirmed paternity.

Instances of women persuading husbands and other men to adopt their children or brothers, newly collated, contextualised, and parsed here, parallel instances of women persuading husbands to care for children or adults for whom they felt affection or obligation. Adoption was another means of ensuring care and security for a person – with the enormous added benefit of enfranchisement if an adopter could be made to adopt a non-citizen.

Evaluating Women's Influence

Two speeches of Isaeus, analysed anew with a view to their presentation of female influence over household and family composition, and how this influence is differently portrayed and evaluated by the speakers, offer more detail on Athenians' ambivalent attitudes towards such influence.

Case Study 1: Isaeus 6

In Isaeus 6, influence over informal care arrangements in a household *and* influence over formal adoption into a family are attributed to the same woman, Alke. Isaeus 6 concerns the estate of Euktemon. Euktemon had initially been married to the daughter of Meixiades of Kephisia (*Ergo*).[144] Euktemon and *Ergo* had two daughters (*Korallion* and *Khairestrate*)[145] and three sons. Euktemon lived into his late nineties; only his daughters and their children (a daughter of *Korallion* and two sons of *Khairestrate*) survived him. Euktemon's last surviving son by *Ergo*, Philoktemon, predeceased him by at least ten years. Among the claimants to Euktemon's estate were two young men, represented by their guardians, who professed to be the sons of a second wife of Euktemon, Kallippe. Euktemon had enrolled the eldest in his phratry as his son, so Euktemon was publicly recognised as the young man's father. One counter-claimant was Khairestratos, the son of *Khairestrate*, Euktemon's daughter by *Ergo*. Khairestratos claimed Philoktemon had adopted him, effectively rendering Euktemon Khairestratos' paternal grandfather (as well as his maternal grandfather, which he was already, but which counted for less in Athenian law).[146] This would have put Khairestratos in a good position to inherit had it not been for Euktemon's alleged sons by Kallippe.[147]

The speaker, a friend of Khairestratos, argued that his opponents had invented Kallippe entirely and were in fact the sons of a once-enslaved, prostituted woman named Alke, either by her earlier freedman partner or by one of the men who paid her enslaver to use her sexually. The speaker contends that Euktemon began a relationship with Alke, who took advantage of him in his old age and persuaded him to introduce her sons to his

---

[144] Based on the name of her second son, Ergamenes (§10). Second sons were often named after maternal relatives, typically the maternal grandfather, though Ergamenes' maternal grandfather was called Meixiades; possibly Ergamenes was a name in his mother's family.

[145] *Korallion* because she had only a surviving daughter (*korē*); *Khairestrate* based on the name of her son.

[146] Relationships through the maternal line still had legal force after adoption: Isae. 7.25.

[147] See Humphreys 2018: 193 for epigraphic evidence for the outcome. There was also at least one other claim: if the two young men were not accepted as heirs and had Khairestratos not been adopted, Euktemon would have been survived only by his two daughters, who would then have been *epiklēroi* and entitled to half of the estate each. According to the speaker, the guardian of one of the young men, Androkles, who was Euktemon's relative (συγγενής, §55), *also* claimed the hand of *Korallion*'s daughter as an *epiklēros*, and, on her behalf, half of the estate accordingly (§46; πέμπτου μέρους, 'a fifth part', is widely agreed to be corrupt). It is hard to understand how Androkles could have made this claim *as well as* the claim on behalf of Kallippe/Alke's sons – as the speaker points out, both claims could not simultaneously be valid, as a woman only became an *epiklēros* if her father had no male heirs.

phratry as his own, so that they would be able to inherit from him not just his estate but also Athenian citizenship.

Elements of this account are decidedly unflattering to Khairestratos' grandfather – deserting his wife of his own volition for a prostituted woman, much to his wife's and their children's distress (§21) – which increases the likelihood of there being some truth in them. Other elements are harder to evaluate. The speaker produces witnesses to what he has said (§26), but it is unclear how much of his story they confirmed. He brings forward relatives to affirm that they had never heard of Euktemon's having married a second wife (§11), but their exact relation to the family is not given, unless they gave it in their witness statements. His claim that many of the jurors know Alke (§19) suggestively supports the credibility of his story and, by alluding to Alke's sexual availability, casts further doubt over the paternity of her alleged sons. It does not in fact mean that many jurors *did* know her, much less paid for sex with her – no juror was likely to volunteer his ignorance. In any case, Isaeus 6 is a valuable case study in how influence over kinship, in various senses, is attributed to a woman, and in how that influence is portrayed.

The speaker claims Alke twice persuaded or coerced men into assuming a paternal role over her children, once informally and once formally. Each claim serves his strategy differently. According to the speaker's account, Euktemon had a freedwoman who ran a tenement-house in Peiraieus and pimped prostitutes (§19). This woman bought Alke, who was prostituted from the tenement-house for many years. The speaker says:

> διαιτωμένη δὲ αὐτῇ ἐν τῇ συνοικίᾳ συνῆν ἄνθρωπος ἀπελεύθερος, Δίων ὄνομα αὐτῷ, ἐξ οὗ ἔφη ἐκείνη τούτους γεγονέναι· καὶ ἔθρεψεν αὐτοὺς ὁ Δίων ὡς ὄντας ἑαυτοῦ. (§20)

> A freedman named Dion was with (*synēn*, from *syneimi*) her while she was living in the tenement-house, by whom she claimed she had had these boys; and he brought them up as if they were his own.

The phrase διαιτωμένη δὲ αὐτῇ ἐν τῇ συνοικίᾳ ('while she was living in the tenement-house') suggests Alke was still an enslaved prostitute at this point. If so, her sons would have been born into slavery, and this would be a rare representation of a family of enslaved people in classical Attica.[148]

---

[148] Wyse 1904 *ad loc.* thinks ἔθρεψεν αὐτοὺς ὁ Δίων implies Alke was now free, 'otherwise the children would have been her owner's property'; but Dion could still have had a hand in raising them even if in law they were owned by Euktemon's freedwoman. Compare the family of the enslaved child Lesis (Agora Inv. IL 1702; see Introduction, fn. 44); he writes to his mother – an enslaved woman or

Apparently Dion, her freedman partner – perhaps a tenant in the tenement-house, or a man who bought sex there? – helped bring up her sons (possibly their sons), and they lived as a family. The speaker describes the relationship with the verb *syneimi*. In non-technical contexts *syneimi* could mean 'live together as husband and wife' (e.g. Hdt. 4.9, Soph. *El.* 276, 611), but in Athenian legal discourse such a meaning is typically reserved for the term *synoikeō*. *Syneimi* came to mean 'have sex with' (Ap. *Neaira* 33, Arist. *Pol.* 1262a33) and was also used of animals (Arist. *HA* 540a13). The verb delegitimises Alke, her relationships, and her children. The speaker also implies that the children's father(s) were unknown, among the men who paid Euktemon's freedwoman for sex with Alke. He says Alke 'claimed' the children were fathered by Dion, and that Dion brought them up 'as if' they were his, which insinuates they were not. If true, this would be akin to the situation of *Apollodora*, whose second husband fostered ('raised', *etrephe*, Isae. 7.7) her son by another man without formally adopting him, though she did not claim the boy was his. Dion might have celebrated an *amphidromia* and *dekatē* for the boys, rites to welcome and acknowledge new babies. However, as a freedman, there was no procedure for adopting them (he could not have introduced them to a deme or phratry for civic recognition as his) and no point in it (they could not inherit citizenship or property from him).

According to the speaker, Dion later fled to Sikyon to avoid prosecution for an unrelated misdemeanour,[149] and Euktemon put Alke in charge of another of his tenement-houses, this time in the Kerameikos. By this point she may have been freed; Euktemon's Peiraieus tenement-house/brothel was run by one of his freedwomen, and the speaker says that Alke ceased to be prostituted after a certain age; perhaps then she gained her freedom.

The speaker claims Alke successfully induced Euktemon to recognise and publicly legitimate through the phratry one of her sons as *his* son born of a legitimate marriage to an Athenian woman. This would entitle the boy and his future descendants to inherit from Euktemon, and to be Athenian citizens:

> ὁ Εὐκτήμων . . . τὰ πολλὰ διέτριβεν ἐν τῇ συνοικίᾳ, ἐνίοτε δὲ καὶ ἐσιτεῖτο μετὰ τῆς ἀνθρώπου, καταλιπὼν καὶ τὴν γυναῖκα καὶ τοὺς παῖδας καὶ τὴν οἰκίαν ἣν ᾤκει. χαλεπῶς δὲ φερούσης τῆς γυναικὸς καὶ τῶν ὑέων οὐχ ὅπως ἐπαύσατο, ἀλλὰ τελευτῶν παντελῶς διῃτᾶτο ἐκεῖ, καὶ οὕτω διετέθη εἶθ'

---

a freedwoman – and to a man named Xenokles, who may have been her enslaver, *prostatēs*, partner, or friend. See Schmitz 2012 on families of enslaved people.

[149] See Wyse 1904 *ad loc.* for discussion of the phrase ζημίαν εἰργασμένος.

ὑπὸ φαρμάκων εἴθ᾽ ὑπὸ νόσου εἴθ᾽ ὑπ᾽ ἄλλου τινός, ὥστε ἐπείσθη ὑπ᾽ αὐτῆς τὸν πρεσβύτερον τοῖν παίδοιν εἰσαγαγεῖν εἰς τοὺς φράτορας ἐπὶ τῷ αὑτοῦ ὀνόματι. (§21)

> Euktemon began to spend most of his time at the tenement-house, and sometimes he even ate with the woman (*anthrōpos*, derogatory), leaving his wife and his children and the home (*oikia*) where he lived. Though his wife and his sons scarcely bore it,[150] not only did he not stop but in the end he lived there entirely and was reduced to such a condition either by drugs or by illness or by something else that he was persuaded by her (Alke) to introduce the elder of her two sons to his phratry under his name.

The speaker constructs this as a rivalry between two households: Euktemon left his wife and children and the home where he lived and started dining – and eventually living 'entirely' – with another woman in another home. The speaker's emphasis on *Ergo* in this passage – left at home, trying to stop him from leaving – sets up the relationship with Alke as a corrupt pastiche of a marriage, as he sets up the uncertainties and alleged deceptions around the children's parentage as a corrupt pastiche of a family.[151] That the process begins with shared domestic space and food and culminates in phratry admission nicely illustrates the spectrum of kin-making activity and women's potential role in it: women directly participate in the 'informal' but significant processes of shared living that mutually constitute kinship, along with more formal, patriarchal, and patrilineal processes like the public recognition of a kinship tie by a phratry, where women's role is presented as one of persuasion and often corruption. The insinuation that Alke drugged Euktemon evokes the wording of an inheritance law which stipulated that a man could only dispose of property by will if he had no legitimate sons and 'if he is not deluded, either by old age or by drugs or by illness, or persuaded by a woman' (ἂν μὴ μανιῶν ἢ γήρως ἢ φαρμάκων ἢ νόσου ἕνεκα, ἢ γυναικὶ πειθόμενος, [Dem.] 46.14). It also develops the caricature of Alke as a dangerous woman: not just a 'whore' but also a 'witch'.[152]

As in the case of Phano and Khrysilla's sons, the phratry is again important here – and its structural weaknesses, or, more positively, flexibility, allow for manipulation, where women sometimes play an indirect role. The speaker claims that Euktemon's son by *Ergo*, Philoktemon,

---

[150] The phrase could have the sense of 'it hurt them' or 'they tried to stop him' (or both).

[151] Compare pp. 316–9 on the relationship between *Thesmonike* and *Eratokleia* in Lysias 1 as a corrupt pastiche of a mother- and daughter-in-law relationship.

[152] Compare Eidinow 2018: 312–27 for the forensic figure of the 'dangerous woman' and Glazebrook 2022: 43–62 for Alke specifically.

necessarily also a member of his father's phratry, refused to admit the boy; the other phratrymen followed suit. His father retaliated by threatening that he would betroth himself to a sister of a man named Demokrates of Aphidna, recognise any children born of her, and make them part of his *oikos* (both his household and, crucially, those eligible to inherit his property, §22), unless Philoktemon consented to his recognition of 'Alke's son'. Philoktemon's relatives advised him to consent, 'because they knew Euktemon could have no more sons at his age, but that sons would appear in some other way (φανήσοιντο δ' ἄλλῳ τινὶ τρόπῳ) causing even greater quarrels' (§23). The vague but potent threat of sons 'appearing' in 'some other way' and being falsely legitimised sees a man, Euktemon, using female fertility and the unprovability of paternity against his son, allegedly to please Alke. The speaker has Euktemon conjure up a picture of an *oikos* based on women's lies, full of false sons by uncertain parents, riven with legal disputes, and beset by gossip and scandal.

After this mediation, Philoktemon allegedly agreed, on condition that the boy would have only a nominal share of the inheritance. Humphreys convincingly suggests that the rest of the phratry would have agreed to admit the boy in the face of the united front of the wealthy, influential father and son, and their supporting relatives.[153] The speaker presented some of these phratrymen to testify. He claimed that 'all the relatives, and the phratrymen, and many of the demesmen' knew Euktemon's three sons and two daughters and 'their mother, the daughter of Meixiades of Kephisia [our *Ergo*], whom Euktemon married' (τὴν μητέρα αὐτῶν, ἣν ἔγημεν ὁ Εὐκτήμων, Μειξιάδου Κηφισιῶς θυγατέρα, §10), but that 'no one' knew of Euktemon marrying a second wife who then gave birth to the claimants. He apparently produced witnesses, probably including at least one representative from each group (relatives, phratrymen, demesmen).

The reference to *Ergo*'s marriage in this context may allude to Euktemon's *gamēlia* for *Ergo*. That the phratrymen (and others) 'knew' (ἴσασι) the girls too may imply the daughters' as well as the sons' presentation to the phratry,[154] though it might as well or instead mean that the men the girls married, Khaireas (*Korallion*'s husband) and Phanostratos (*Khairestrate*'s husband), were fellow phratrymen of Euktemon and had formally introduced their wives to the same phratry at their own *gamēliai*. Phanostratos was at least a fellow demesman of Euktemon,[155] who had

---

[153] Humphreys 2018: 189.   [154] Compare Chapter 5, fn. 128.

[155] His homonymous grandson, Phanostratos of Kephisia, appears in Dem. 54.7–8; cf. Humphreys 2018: 828 with fn. 47.

himself married within his deme, Kephisia. The family resemblance between the name of *Khairestrate*'s son, Khairestratos, and the name of *Korallion*'s husband, Khaireas, may suggest that the girls' husbands were related. Alternatively, the phratrymen may have known *Ergo* and Euktemon's daughters on a more informal, social basis. Perhaps the women were members of an orgeonic group, a religious subgroup of the phratry in which women had greater involvement. Or perhaps the phratrymen knew them as companions of their own daughters, or as presences on the periphery of the phratry festival of the Apatouria.[156] A boy had to be introduced to a phratry as the son of *two married Athenian parents*, so Euktemon must have presented the young claimant as being his son by an Athenian wife – Kallippe? *Ergo*? Another woman? Given that the phratry *did* accept the boy, it is hard to see whom they implicitly accepted as his mother. The testimony of the phratrymen cited early in the speech may have consisted in positive assertions that they knew *Ergo* and her children, leaving denial of knowledge of a second wife to the demesmen. Perhaps, cowed into submission by a reluctantly united Philoktemon, Euktemon, and their relatives, it did not much matter. In any case, the speech illustrates a complex interplay of anxieties, flexibilities, and possibilities around women and kinship.

Case Study 2: Isaeus 7

Isaeus 7 offers three different perspectives of women's roles in influencing household and family composition. First, as we have seen, the speaker Thrasyllos tells how Arkhedamos took in his wife *Apollodora*'s son from her first marriage, Apollodoros; I have argued that *Apollodora* was influential in this, though Thrasyllos suppresses her role. Later, Apollodoros adopted a son, after his biological son died:

> ἐπὶ τοῖς παροῦσιν ἀθυμήσας καὶ τὴν ἡλικίαν τὴν ἑαυτοῦ καταμεμψάμενος οὐκ ἐπελάθετο ὑφ᾽ ὧν καὶ ἐξ ἀρχῆς εὖ πεπονθὼς ἦν, ἀλλ᾽ ἐλθὼν ὡς τὴν ἐμὴν μητέρα ἑαυτοῦ δὲ ἀδελφήν, ἣν περὶ πλείστου πάντων ἐποιεῖτο, λαβεῖν ἠξίωσέ με ὑὸν καὶ ᾔτησε καὶ ἔτυχεν. (§14)

> Disheartened at his circumstances and made uneasy by his own age, he did not forget that he had been kindly treated by [Arkhedamos' family] from the very beginning, so he came to my mother, his own sister, whom he respected most of all, wanting to take me as his son, asked, and was successful.

---

[156] See pp. 301–8 for women at phratry celebrations.

The speaker's father is not portrayed as having any part in the discussion, nor is any *epitropos*, which may mean this woman (*Arkhedike*) was a widow, living with her adult son.[157] It is not clear whether the mother's permission for her son to be adopted was required formally, informally, or not at all, nor how this would have differed if the would-be adoptee had a living father or *epitropos*. Brenda Griffith-Williams comments: 'Presumably Thrasyllos's natural father was dead by this time, otherwise Apollodoros would have sought his permission for the adoption. The extent of the mother's authority is unclear; as Thrasyllos presents the story, Apollodoros sought and obtained her permission, but he could probably have proceeded even without her agreement.'[158] Later, in another context, Thrasyllos points out that adoption does not sever the legal relationship between a man and his mother (μητρὸς . . . οὐδείς ἐστιν ἐκποίητος, ἀλλ' ὁμοίως ὑπάρχει τὴν αὐτὴν εἶναι μητέρα, §25),[159] which may suggest there was no legal requirement for her permission. Nevertheless, the speaker portrays Apollodoros as needing to ask *Arkhedike* whether he could adopt her son, even if that requirement was moral rather than legal.

The third perspective comes in Thrasyllos' criticism of his female cousins for not giving their sons to their childless brother to adopt (ἐκείνῳ δ' οὐκ εἰσποιούσας[160] ὄντων αὐταῖς παίδων, 'they did not adopt out their sons to him, though they had sons', §31), such that his *oikos* was 'shamefully and shockingly desolate'.[161] He contrasts the women's apparent disregard for the continuation of their brother's *oikos* (family line) with their willing inheritance of his estate. He mentions their husbands only in the context of the estate and its management, placing the failure to render sons for adoption squarely with the sisters. Thrasyllos is making a point about family disloyalty and distrust: the women have been disloyal to their brother, so their cousin cannot trust them. Their husbands, related only by marriage, are not relevant to his picture. Besides, it is one of these women – not her husband – who is legally his opponent, though her husband represents her. Still, Thrasyllos again portrays adoption – from which

---

[157] For *Arkhedike*'s obscure marital history and status, see Wyse 1904: 557, *ad* Isae. 7.9.5, 6, *APF* no. 1395 (p. 44), Humphreys 2018: 77, fn. 11.

[158] Griffith-Williams 2013 *ad loc.*   [159] See discussion by Griffith-Williams 2013 *ad loc.*

[160] I have found no other instance of this verb with this meaning having women as the subject.

[161] Compare Isae. 2.35, with pp. 107–8. Griffith-Williams 2013 *ad loc.* points out that 'neither of the sisters could realistically have been expected to provide a son for Apollodoros Eupolidos by posthumous adoption unless she and her husband had another son who could remain in his father's *oikos*. Isaios does not make it clear whether this was the case.'

female influence was legally excluded – as something in women's power to grant or withhold.

In sum, Thrasyllos twice presents women as 'gatekeepers' of adoption, once permitting the adoption of their sons, once preventing it (he is conveniently vague about whether they were asked and refused or simply did not offer). However, in the informal matter of Apollodoros' fostering, he downplays the woman's role, attributing the initiative to her husband though the reported circumstances suggest it was hers. Unsurprisingly, he portrays women as agents when to do so will suit his case. He is keen to portray a close, positive relationship between Apollodoros and his own mother and maternal grandfather, so he uses the adoption to illustrate her positive relationship with Apollodoros. He is keen to portray a distant, negative relationship between Apollodoros and his cousins, so he attributes the failure to establish a positive relationship through adoption to those cousins. Nevertheless, a picture emerges of women able to facilitate or refuse men's adoption choices and to influence their decisions about household composition.

A coda: one of the strangest accusations of this type is the allegation in Isaeus 8 that the sister of Diokles, as part of a plot with her brother to retain control of her husband Kiron's estate after he died, repeatedly feigned pregnancies to prevent him adopting a son as his heir (§36). The proposed scheme is convoluted; perhaps the speaker is twisting a series of genuine miscarriages into his argument that Diokles was trying to manipulate Kiron out of his property (cf. §37). However, it brings together a number of this chapter's themes: men's belief that women could influence men's ability and choices in adoption; men's portrayal of women and their fertility as weapons in disputes (cf. Isae. 6.22–3); men's fear of women's potential to deceive men about their pregnancies (visible in stories about supposititious children); and men's suspicion that women's loyalty to their brothers might override their loyalty to their husbands, detectable in Isaeus 2 but visible at its most extreme in Lysias' claim that Hipponikos divorced his wife because her brother came into Hipponikos' house 'not as her brother but as her husband' (14.28).

Conclusion

This chapter newly brings together various sources which suggest the ability of women to use informal mechanisms – chiefly persuasion, which male-authored sources, depending on their strategies, sometimes elide and sometimes portray as coercion – to affect who became part of a household or descent group, not only to benefit themselves but also to ensure care for people they loved. Analysis of these sources offers a new challenge to the supposed rigidity and potency of patriarchal and patrilineal family structures and procedures and illustrates the part women could play in a more malleable reality. It demonstrates the instability of the family, especially in the face of male absence and death, and the ways in which women responded to, counteracted, and occasionally exploited that instability. Male accusations against women of illegally influencing men's adoption choices, like accusations of introducing suppositious children into the household and family, may stem from male unease about women's ability to shape kinship, and from the uncomfortable tension between women's privileged knowledge about kinship – a woman knows her child's maternity but her husband cannot be certain of its paternity – and the patriarchal, patrilineal structuring of family law. In later chapters, we shall see how women used the behavioural language of kinship, particularly burial and commemoration, to express other kinds of relatedness.

Thesmonike and *Praxagora*
Relationships between Enslaving and Enslaved Women

In the first two chapters of this book, we saw how women could shape kinship, influencing who became part of the descent group and the household. This chapter explores how women shaped their relationships with the enslaved members of their households. It argues that though these relationships could challenge marital and family relationships, often they reinforced the dominant ideology of the household and the free woman's place in it.

Enslaved women, men, and children were an integral part of most free women's lives and social environments. From the impression given by comedy and oratory, most families kept at least one person in slavery.[1] Free women across the socio-economic spectrum were expected to do at least some work inside the home, particularly textile production,[2] and in doing so they would have collaborated with the household's enslaved workers. Free women in households that could not afford to keep people in slavery would have come into contact through their work with those kept in slavery by others.[3] Sharing space and tasks had the potential to create intimacy between free women and those they kept in slavery,[4] but the stark power imbalance between them complicated or counteracted this intimacy.

---

[1] See Akrigg 2019: 94–8 for the relative reliability of this impression, and pp. 90–120 on the likely size of the enslaved population.

[2] Xen. *Oec.* 10–11 suggests that even women in households with many enslaved workers were expected to join in some of the work themselves.

[3] Compare Golden 2011: 135–7. For comparable observations about free Athenian children, cf. Golden 2015: 123–4.

[4] Compare Davies 1994: 9: 'their shared tasks within the house must often have created friendships, fellow-feeling and intimacy' – though 'friendship' implies an equality not possible in relationships between enslaver and enslaved and sanitises a more complex reality. Davies is closer to the mark with her analysis of the grave *stēlē* of Ameinokleia (figure 3.1 in this book), where Ameinokleia's hand on the head of the enslaved girl fastening her sandal 'creates an aura of intimacy while at the same time reinforcing the status difference between them' (p. 8); see this chapter, p. 168. Cf. also Foxhall 1998a: 64–5.

I refer to women who kept others in slavery in their homes as 'enslavers', as I do for men. The level of agency a woman had in keeping the enslaved people in her home in a condition of slavery is difficult to assess. Some forensic speeches attest to women's ownership of enslaved people. The dowry of Arkhippe, married to the freedman Phormion by her first husband Pasion in his will, included *therapainai*, enslaved maids ([Dem.] 45.28). We know of a woman lodging a claim of ownership over a man named Pankleon with the polemarch, the official responsible for affairs concerning non-Athenians (Lys. 23.10–13).[5] Pankleon's status was disputed: the woman asserted that he belonged to her; another man, Nikomedes, that he belonged to him. Pankleon himself claimed to be a free Plataian. The arbitration to settle the status of Neaira stipulated that she was (at least nominally) free and under her own legal and economic authority (ἐλευθέραν . . . καὶ αὐτὴν αὑτῆς κυρίαν), though she was compelled to live and implicitly have sex with (*syneimi*) the two men who had disputed her status on alternate days. She had to return the possessions she had brought with her when she escaped from the house of one of the men, who had abused her, but was allowed to keep 'the clothes and the gold jewellery and the maids, which had been bought for [her] specifically' (ἱματίων καὶ χρυσίων καὶ θεραπαινῶν, ἃ αὐτῇ τῇ ἀνθρώπῳ ἠγοράσθη, Ap. *Neaira* 46). These girls' names were Thraitta ('Thracian') and Kokkaline (§35); they seem to have travelled with Neaira from Athens to Megara and back again. Though a woman would have been able to liberate an enslaved person who was legally hers, I do not know any classical-period instances of women doing so, and it is unlikely that she could herself liberate a person who was legally the property of her husband or father, or even that she could liberate a person who was legally part of her dowry, should she have wanted to.[6] However, as this chapter shows, women actively participated in the violent, dehumanising treatment which maintained the status quo of slavery; they were part of the continuous process of enslavement.

Mark Golden suggests that enslavers often felt great trust towards enslaved male *paidagōgoi* in particular, in part because of 'their role as a stable and familiar element in households often assailed by divorce, disease and death'.[7] Some of these enslaved men would have remained in

---

[5] That the speaker refers to her as a *gynē*, not an *anthrōpos*, suggests she was of citizen status, though she may have been a metic.

[6] For the extent to which women had control over dowries and other property, see e.g. Foxhall 1989: 32–9, Johnstone 2003: 267–71.

[7] Golden 2011: 141; this also applied to enslaved nurses.

the home even when their male enslavers periodically departed on campaigns or other ventures. However, literary and iconographic sources which discuss relationships between free women and those they kept in slavery focus predominantly on their interactions with enslaved women. This may be because although enslaved people were in some ways less rigidly gendered than their enslavers, at least in the domestic sphere – a phenomenon which both resulted from and contributed to the ideological claim that they were less than fully human – they were not ungendered.[8] Textile production and care of young children would likelier have been assigned to enslaved women and girls, and their female enslavers would have shared those tasks with them. Partly because of this gendered division of labour, free men in comedy and tragedy are more often shown interacting with enslaved men, and free women with enslaved women. This chapter focuses on free women's relationships with the *women* they kept in slavery. It offers a new account of the emotional dynamics of these relationships, analysing in detail aspects and evidence mostly noted only briefly in scholarship. It considers women's role in shaping these relationships and thereby shaping their own social positions and their other relationships. The significance of these relationships in women's lives is disproportionate to the little space given them in treatments of Attic women.

The first section of this chapter takes two literary sources as a jumping-off point. The first is the account of the relationship between a free woman and an enslaved woman in Lysias 1. The second is the instructions in Xenophon's *Oeconomicus* which Iskhomakhos gives to his wife (very probably the woman named Khrysilla discussed in the previous chapter)[9] on her responsibilities regarding the enslaved members of the household. The chapter demonstrates how women used enslaved household members to construct their positions as citizen-status wives by establishing and maintaining a hierarchy of labour, sexuality, and dignity.

While the rest of the book finds women living and acting in ways which resisted dominant discourses on wifehood and the *oikos* (here in its sense of 'household'), the evidence for citizen-status women's relationships with enslaved women suggests that here their behaviour was more aligned with men's thinking on social status and the *oikos*. Most likely this reflects citizen-status women's alignment with citizen men as the dominant social

---

[8] Thalmann 1998: 25, 33 and Rabinowitz 1998: 58, citing Arist. *Pol.* 1252b1–9 with Spelman 1988: 14, 41–3, 52–4; gendered division of labour: Biezunska-Malowist and Malowist 1989: 18–19, cited by Rabinowitz 1998: 58. Cf. Saller 1998: 87–8 on 'ungendered' slaves in the Roman household.

[9] See p. 146; cf. *APF* no. 7826 XI B–XIV (pp. 264–8); Pomeroy 1994: 261–4.

group against the subaltern group constituted by enslaved people, but it may reflect merely the poverty of our evidence. While much of the information on women's behaviour and relationships elsewhere in this book is inferred from brief statements and clauses which are secondary to the interests of the male speaker, the two most detailed sources explored in this chapter (Lysias 1, Xenophon's *Oeconomicus*) are centrally concerned with the ideology of the *oikos* and the place of the citizen-status wife in it. There are fewer female-authored sources to develop the picture.

More of a challenge to the status quo is implied by the trope found across comedy, tragedy, forensic oratory, and iconography of free women colluding with enslaved women, particularly in the male householder's absence. This chapter analyses the trope and argues that it is a distorted reflection of a reality of close (though forced) interaction and cooperation in the context of profoundly unequal power relations.

The second section of this chapter discusses portrayals of enslaved women in the sepulchral iconography of their enslavers. These too express and reflect a complex interaction between intimacy and hierarchy, where enslaved people are pointedly included in 'family groups', portrayed in intimate relationships with their enslavers, but generally kept at a distance, despite their proximity, by differentiated clothing, stance, or action. The chapter then addresses the commemoration of enslaved women themselves, discussing monuments seemingly erected for enslaved nurses by their enslavers. It argues that the iconography here emphasises inclusion rather than distinction. These nurses, while implicitly acknowledged in the inscriptions as enslaved, are depicted as 'part of the family'.

Together, our sources suggest that free Athenian women's relationships with the girls and women they kept in slavery were characterised by an uneasy forced intimacy which was exploited by the enslaving women and loomed large in their emotional landscapes.

Intimacy and Power

The account given by the speaker Euphiletos in Lysias 1 of the relationship between his wife (*Thesmonike*)[10] and the enslaved woman or girl in their home (*Praxagora*)[11] serves as a case study for the complex forced intimacy between enslaver and enslaved. The speech, composed in the early fourth century, forms part of a homicide trial: Euphiletos admits he killed the

---

[10] Because of her celebration of the Thesmophoria (§20).   [11] Because she acts in the *agora* (§8).

victim, Eratosthenes, but claims he killed him in the act of adultery, justifiable under the law.

Euphiletos introduces *Praxagora* as τὴν θεράπαιναν τὴν εἰς τὴν ἀγορὰν βαδίζουσαν, 'the slave-attendant who goes to the *agora*' (§8). This phrase establishes Euphiletos as a man who abides by status and gender ideals, using an enslaved girl to run errands outside the home, particularly in the busy *agora*,[12] in order to keep his wife 'uncorrupted' in the home. In reality, as Deborah Kamen and Mark Golden point out, *Praxagora* probably had a large number of obligations indoors and outdoors, particularly if she was the only enslaved person in the household.[13] Conversely, various activities would have brought *Thesmonike* out of the house,[14] possibly even to the *agora*. Euphiletos means the jury to understand that Eratosthenes' alleged adultery with *Thesmonike* was an act of corruption, not an inevitable consequence of the 'loose' lifestyle other speakers ascribe to women already 'corrupt'. (The speaker of Isaeus 3, from a mid fourth-century inheritance dispute, uses *Nikodike*'s interactions with other men as evidence that she cannot have been a *gynē engyētē*, a legally married wife, or literally, a wife married by *engyē*, §§11, 13.)

Euphiletos' phrase also explains how the alleged adulterer Eratosthenes was able to 'access' such a 'respectably secluded' wife: by using a go-between who went outside the house.[15] As Euphiletos tells it, Eratosthenes, having seen *Thesmonike* at a funeral, 'looked out for the slave-attendant who goes to the *agora*, and bringing messages [to *Thesmonike*, through the enslaved girl], destroyed her', ἐπιτηρῶν γὰρ τὴν θεράπαιναν τὴν εἰς τὴν ἀγορὰν βαδίζουσαν καὶ λόγους προσφέρων ἀπώλεσεν αὐτήν (Lys. 1.8). Euphiletos reinforces these impressions later in the narrative by repeating his own description of *Praxagora* in the mouth of a woman (probably also enslaved) from another household. He has the woman describe *Praxagora* as τὴν θεράπαιναν τὴν εἰς ἀγορὰν βαδίζουσαν καὶ διακονοῦσαν ὑμῖν ('the slave-attendant who goes to the *agora* and waits on you', §16).

From *Praxagora*'s perspective, this particular kind of forced work might have afforded her opportunities to meet and develop her own relationships outside the *oikos*, whether with shopkeepers or stallholders, free or enslaved,[16] or with enslaved people from other households engaged in tasks like her own. Though some enslaved people in Attica would have been Greeks enslaved in

---

[12] Where 'men and women mingled more than formal morality would allow' (Blok 2001: 111).

[13] Golden 2011: 140; Kamen 2013: 11. Carey 1989: 70 thinks there were at least two enslaved girls in the household, distinguishing the girl mentioned here and at §11 from the one mentioned at §12.

[14] Cohen 1989, esp. pp. 9–13.   [15] Compare Eur. *Hipp.* 645–50, discussed at p. 178.

[16] For enslaved women (and men) selling in the markets of the fourth-century city and Peiraieus, see RO 25.30–2.

war,[17] most were non-Greek, the victims of war, piracy, or kidnap, from all over the Mediterranean. In Athens, there were particularly large numbers of Thracians, Phrygians, Syrians, Lydians, and Paphlagonians, along with Carians, Illyrians, Phoenicians, Colchians, and others.[18] The *agora* is likely to have been one of the most multiethnic spaces in Attica, and *Praxagora* may briefly have been able to meet compatriots – or other enslaved or freed people of any ethnicity.[19] A free woman in Aristophanes' *Lysistrata* complains of being 'jostled by slave-women' (δούλαισιν ὠστιζομένη, ll. 329–30) when she goes to collect water from the local spring, suggesting that other such errands might have offered similar opportunities for socialising.

Praxagora's work buying supplies would also have brought her into particular closeness and collaboration with her enslaver *Thesmonike*. Though among the wealthy, it was typically men who shopped, accompanied by an enslaved person to carry the bags and pay,[20] the wife was (ideally and probably in reality) in charge of maintaining household supplies. In Xenophon's mid fourth-century Socratic text on household management, *Oeconomicus*, the character Iskhomakhos describes to Sokrates how he told his wife Khrysilla:

> τά τε εἰσφερόμενα ἀποδεκτέον καὶ ἃ μὲν ἂν αὐτῶν δέῃ δαπανᾶν σοὶ διανεμητέον, ἃ δ' ἂν περιττεύειν δέῃ, προνοητέον καὶ φυλακτέον ὅπως μὴ ἡ εἰς τὸν ἐνιαυτὸν κειμένη δαπάνη εἰς τὸν μῆνα δαπανᾶται. (7.36)

> you must receive what is brought in, and whatever of that needs to be spent, you must spend it, and whatever must be kept in reserve, you must take care of, and must be careful that the expenditure set for the year is not spent in a month.[21]

Similarly, in Aristophanes' *Lysistrata* (first performed 411) the women argue that they should have control of the city's finances on the grounds that they manage household finances (ll. 493–5; cf. *Thesm.* 418–19). In Euripides' fragmentary *Melanippe Captive*, a woman (probably the title character?) defends women against male criticism by saying that they manage households and keep imported goods safe within the house (frg. 660 Mette, ll. 9–11).

---

[17] See Gaca 2010 and Gaca 2010–1 on the (specifically gendered) nature of conquest enslavement.

[18] See e.g. Forsdyke 2012: 27–9 and, more fully, Hunt 2015 on ethnic identity and community among enslaved people in Athens. See Vlassopoulos 2010 on the names of real and fictional enslaved people and their relationship to ethnicity. A late fifth-century document recording the sale of several enslaved people identified by ethnicity gives a sense of the potential diversity: OR 172 A 34–9.

[19] Hunt 2015: 148.   [20] Compare e.g. Men. *Sam.* 189–92.

[21] In a household with many enslaved workers, the woman might share this task with an enslaved housekeeper (*tamia*): Xen. *Oec.* 7.41, 9.10–13.

Control of household supplies seemingly entailed control of enslaved members' diets, which brought enslaved people into the intimacy of direct dependence on their female enslavers. Two Middle Comic poets writing in the first half of the fourth century, Antiphanes and Epicrates (one seemingly borrowing lines *verbatim* from the other), have enslaved men articulate their resentment at:

> ὁρᾶν τε κείμενα
> ἄμητας ἡμιβρῶτας ὀρνίθειά τε,
> ὧν οὐδὲ λειφθέντων θέμις δούλῳ φαγεῖν,
> ὡς φασιν αἱ γυναῖκες.[22]

seeing half-eaten milk cakes and bird-meat lying around, leftovers which a slave isn't allowed to eat – that's what the women (*hai gynaikes*) command.

It is 'the women' (probably referring to the various free women in the house, not just the *kyrios*' wife; less likely, to wives in general) who determine what, or whether, the enslaved people eat. As the poets present it, this control was expressed verbally in face-to-face interactions, as well as more indirectly in food allocation.

Along with his instructions about management of resources, Xenophon's Iskhomakhos tells Khrysilla:

> [7.37] ἐν μέντοι τῶν σοὶ προσηκόντων, ἔφην ἐγώ, ἐπιμελημάτων ἴσως ἀχαριστότερον δόξει εἶναι, ὅτι, ὃς ἂν κάμνῃ τῶν οἰκετῶν, τούτων σοι ἐπιμελητέον πάντων ὅπως θεραπεύηται.[23] νὴ Δί', ἔφη ἡ γυνή, ἐπιχαριτώτατον μὲν οὖν, ἂν μέλλωσί γε οἱ καλῶς θεραπευθέντες χάριν εἴσεσθαι καὶ εὐνούστεροι ἢ πρόσθεν ἔσεσθαι ... [41] ἄλλαι δέ τοι, ἔφην ἐγώ, ἴδιαι ἐπιμέλειαι, ὦ γύναι, ἡδεῖαί σοι γίγνονται, ὁπόταν ἀνεπιστήμονα ταλασίας λαβοῦσα ἐπιστήμονα ποιήσῃς καὶ διπλασίου σοι ἀξία γένηται, καὶ ὁπόταν ἀνεπιστήμονα ταμιείας καὶ διακονίας παραλαβοῦσα ἐπιστήμονα καὶ πιστὴν καὶ διακονικὴν ποιησαμένη παντὸς ἀξίαν ἔχῃς, καὶ ὁπόταν τοὺς μὲν σώφρονάς τε καὶ ὠφελίμους τῷ σῷ οἴκῳ ἐξῇ σοι εὖ ποιῆσαι, ἐὰν δέ τις πονηρὸς φαίνηται, ἐξῇ σοι κολάσαι.

[37] 'But one of these tasks of yours', I said, 'will perhaps seem rather thankless: if any one of these slaves (*oiketai*) is ill, it will be your job to see that they are cared for.'

---

[22] Antiphanes frg. 89 and Epicrates frg. 5, quoted in Ath. *Deip.* 6.262c–d. Cf. Men. *Peri.* 544–6, where an enslaved man is reported to have eaten food laid out for his enslavers.

[23] Compare Ap. *Neaira* 56. Xen. *Mem.* 2.10.2 implies that care for enslaved people who were sick was the male householder's job, but the verb used is *epimeleomai*, not *therapeuō*, and may have the sense of 'arrange care for' rather than 'nurse'; he was also responsible for calling a doctor.

'God no', said my wife, 'it will be so gratifying, at least if, having been well looked after, they will feel a sense of affectionate obligation (*kharis*),[24] and be better-disposed to me than before … '

[41] 'But your other personal tasks, my wife, will be pleasant for you – when you take someone (the forms used here are feminine) who does not know about wool-work and teach her it, and she becomes worth twice as much to you; and when you take in hand someone (f.) who does not know about housekeeping and service, and you teach her and make her trustworthy and serviceable, and you have a slave (f.) worth any amount; and when you are able to treat well those (masculine plural, which may include male and female) who are sensible and useful to your household (*tōi sōi oikōi*), and if anyone (masculine, allowing for male or female) turns out to be worthless, you are able to punish them.'

This combination of tasks (nursing, training, rewarding, punishing) creates, instantiates, and reinforces the complex interplay of intimacy and power in the relationship between free and enslaved. Xenophon portrays Iskhomakhos and Khrysilla as being aware of this process. Nursing enslaved household members who are sick makes them grateful (increasing intimacy) and more loyal (increasing the enslaver's power). Teaching an enslaved girl makes her trustworthy (increasing both intimacy and power: 'trustworthy' presumably entails 'unlikely to engage in resistance', and the enslaver may derive additional power from being cast in the role of 'teacher' as well as 'mistress'). Though Khrysilla exercises her power to 'reward' and punish over enslaved men and women, it is the enslaved women she is envisioned teaching, given that they will be doing tasks she herself knows how to do. It is unlikely that a girl or woman from any culture from which Athens enslaved people would 'not know about wool-work', unless she was very young. More likely, enslaved girls and women were violently deprived of their own skills and techniques and taught the skills and techniques of their enslavers. This teaching would have led to particular intimacy with (and particular power over) the women.

A third-century papyrus letter from Philadelphia, Egypt, which a woman named Khoirine wrote to a man called Zenon about an enslaved girl (*paidiskē*), whom she does not name (*SB* 22.15276), gives a sense of how this might have worked. The girl has been made to weave for her enslavers, and Khoirine has evidently found her, in Iskhomakhos' terms, 'useful to her household': οὐ[κ . . .] ἔχω πῶς ἐπιτειμήσω αὐτῆ⟨ι⟩, 'I cannot fault her at all' (l. 5). To 'reward' her, Khoirine asks Zenon whether he would

---

[24] On the term *kharis*, see p. 231.

consider τῆς παιδίσκης ἢ ὀψώνιον δοθῆναι ἢ εἴρια, 'that the slave-girl be given *opsōnion* (either a food ration, payment, or allowance), or wool', since she is 'naked' (γυμνή, l. 4).[25] (Iskhomakhos too gives enslaved people better or worse clothes to 'reward' or punish, Xen. *Oec.* 13.10.) Khoirine, through Zenon, has power over the enslaved girl's basic needs, which she can see met as a 'reward'.

As Xenophon portrays it, it is partly through Khrysilla's power over her slaves (*oiketai*) that the *oikos* (household) becomes *her oikos* (*tōi sōi oikōi*); this the only place in the text where it is described as such. This accounts for the chilling statement that her ability to punish 'worthless' slaves will be 'pleasant' to her: being able violently to establish and enforce the household hierarchy further secures her own position towards the top. Relatedly, her status as 'wife' derives partly from her place in the hierarchy above those she keeps in slavery. (We recall how Euphiletos' description of *Praxagora* as τὴν θεράπαιναν τὴν εἰς τὴν ἀγορὰν βαδίζουσαν helped secure his portrayal of *Thesmonike* as 'wife'.) This hierarchy has a sexual dimension. Iskhomakhos tells Khrysilla she will be more attractive to him if she behaves *despotikōs* (like a mistress) instead of *doulikōs* (like a slave). Behaving *despotikōs* involves, among other things, instructing and supervising enslaved workers (§10.10).

A visual expression of this interaction between intimacy and power, and the construction of the wife through her subjection of the enslaved, is found on the grave *naiskos* of Hegeso (NAM 3624, *IG* I[3] 1289), erected at the end of the fifth century in a Kerameikos *peribolos*.[26] The relief shows a standing woman in a *sakkos* (snood) and *khitōn kheiridōtos* (long-sleeved *khitōn*) holding a box for a larger seated woman in a *khitōn* (tunic) and *himation* (shawl), which veils her head. The seated woman takes an item from the box, presumably a necklace that was originally painted on but has now worn off. Both women look at the box rather than each other, but this means their heads incline towards one another. The box, which they both touch, forms a point of contact. They are very close together: though Hegeso's feet rest on a footstool, the tip of her left foot touches the enslaved woman's right foot; their other legs (not visible to the viewer) could be touching. The inscription reads Ἡγησώ Προξένο, 'Hegeso, [daughter] of Proxenos'. Identifying enslaved people in art is notoriously difficult and can become circular ('enslaved women tend to wear *x*, or do *y*, and therefore because this woman is wearing *x* or doing *y* she must be

---

[25] Less likely, the adjective could apply to Khoirine or another woman.

[26] For this *peribolos* and the evidence it offers for Hegeso's kinship relations, see Marchiandi 2011: 302–5.

enslaved'). Here we assume that the standing woman is enslaved because of the combination of her smallness relative to the seated woman, and her action, holding a box for someone else.[27] Hegeso is the seated woman whom the *naiskos* commemorates.

Why has Hegeso's commemorator chosen to portray her with an enslaved woman? John Oakley suggests that because it was so common among Athenian households to keep people in slavery, the portrayal of an enslaved person did not convey high status but 'a household working in harmony'.[28] This sits uneasily with what is portrayed in Hegeso's relief: an enslaved woman holding a box of jewellery for another woman to admire, a scene of wealth and leisure rather than productivity – unless it is supposed to suggest a household so productive and harmoniously run that there is wealth and time to spare for jewellery and its admiration. That this woman is employed in adorning her enslaver is surely intended to convey (and thus increase) the status of the enslaver. She is an index of Hegeso's wealth and status as much as is the jewellery in the box she holds. However, it also reflects the reality that the two women's lives were closely connected; in life as in death, they shared a scene.

The relief on the *naiskos* for –ine, the daughter of Demokleos (–ινη Δημοκλέος, NAM 4006, *SEMA* 1702; we may supplement, for example, *Myrrhine*) is similar to Hegeso's, though the commemorated woman stands. She is almost twice the height of the figure holding a box.[29] A similarly close dynamic, with more emphasis on power, is visible on the fourth-century grave *stēlē* of Ameinokleia, daughter of Andromenes (NAM Γ718, *IG* I² 1082, Peiraieus; Figure 3.1).[30] Ameinokleia is shown with two other female figures. One stands opposite, holding a box. She is as tall as Ameinokleia and wears a *himation* but has cropped hair where Ameinokleia is veiled. She may be either enslaved or a mourning relative. Kneeling in front of Ameinokleia, in a *sakkos* and *khitōn kheiridōtos*, is a girl who puts on Ameinokleia's shoe for her, certainly enslaved. Ameinokleia steadies herself by resting her hand on the girl's head in a gesture that suggests both domination and reliance. The girl touches Ameinokleia's feet and Ameinokleia touches her head; she does not look at her.

---

[27] Others, following Barker 1924, adduce her *khitōn kheiridōtos* (sleeved *khitōn*) as evidence that she is enslaved. *Khitōnes kheiridōtoi* were worn by free as well as enslaved women (Miller 1997: 156–65, Lee 2015: 121–2, 5–6), but they may still have been used as a 'shorthand' in art.

[28] Oakley 2000: 237.

[29] Compare Wrenhaven 2012: 103–4. Contrast e.g. NAM 950 and 951, sepulchral *hydria* for (probably) three siblings, where the seated figures are proportionate to the standing figures. It is difficult to tell whether the smallness of enslaved people in art symbolises lower status or represents enslaved children: Lewis 2002: 28–35.

[30] Compare Davies 1994: 9; see *IG* I³, Fasc. 2, p. 974, for date.

Figure 3.1 Grave *stēlē* of Ameinokleia, fourth century, Athens, National Archaeological Museum, NAM Γ718. © Hellenic Ministry of Culture.

The enslaved women in all three reliefs are depicted as properly fed and decently dressed. Sian Lewis, writing about painted pots which show 'a lack of careful distinction' between enslaved and free women, suggests that

> perhaps ... viewers were being protected from the reality of slavery ... As the pottery moves away from realistic representation, the images begin to sidestep the reality of slavery, of the dirty, ill-fed girls who waited on most women, and to depict instead graceful young women handing fans and jewellery to aristocratic mistresses.[31]

---

[31] Lewis 2002: 140–1.

But visitors to the Kerameikos knew of and enacted the reality of slavery in their homes and lives. Perhaps the artists (and commissioners) were not sidestepping or protecting viewers from this reality so much as responding to commissioners' desires to portray these relationships as less exploitative than they were, offering instead a fantasy of a more dignified relationship. The women commemorated may well have shared this fantasy during their lifetimes.

Though the monuments of Hegeso, *Myrrhine*, and Ameinokleia name them with their fathers, they portray them with enslaved women. As in Xenophon, women's position in their household derived from their status as legitimately born and married daughters of Athenian citizens but was enacted and made visible in their power relations with those they kept in slavery.

Sex

Back in Xenophon's *Oeconomicus*, Iskhomakhos goes on to comment – probably not to Khrysilla, but to Sokrates, in his retelling of the conversation – ὄψις δέ, ὁπόταν ἀνταγωνίζηται διακόνῳ καθαρωτέρα οὖσα πρεπόντως τε μᾶλλον ἠμφιεσμένη, κινητικὸν γίγνεται ἄλλως τε καὶ ὁπόταν τὸ ἑκοῦσαν χαρίζεσθαι προσῇ ἀντὶ τοῦ ἀναγκαζομένην ὑπηρετεῖν, 'the sight [of one's wife], when compared to a slave, is a turn-on, because she is purer and more fittingly clothed – and it's a turn-on especially on those occasions when you also get willing gratification, rather than [a slave's?] forced service' (10.12).[32]

How did men's sexual exploitation of enslaved women and girls in their households affect their wives' relationships with their husbands and with the enslaved women and girls? In *Oeconomicus*, Iskhomakhos sees Khrysilla and the enslaved women of his household as competing objects of his sexual interest, though 'competing' only as ideas: he recognises that the enslaved women do not desire his sexual attention – and Khrysilla does only sometimes. That said, some enslaved women forced into sex with their enslavers may have used the sexual relationship as a survival strategy, a possibility to which I return.[33] Iskhomakhos' response to Khrysilla's question about how to be

---

[32] 'Forced service' could refer to the wife, but in the context of the comparison it is likelier that he is referring to a hypothesised enslaved woman. Though the noun διάκονος may refer either to an enslaved man or woman, the participle ἀναγκαζομένην (compelled), like the adjective ἑκοῦσαν (willing), is feminine.

[33] Compare Marshall 2013: 188–96, primarily concerned with sex slaves rather than domestic slaves used for sex, but the arguments still apply (and cf. p. 178: 'Not all younger slave women will have been intended primarily for sex, but given that they were without rights, the possibility always exists for them to be used in this way').

beautiful (§10.9) begins with a command to be more like a mistress than a slave. As we have seen, *Oeconomicus* is concerned with establishing an ideology of the household which involves a clearly defined hierarchy of citizen-status wife over slave. The wife's superiority has a sexual component. Her greater sexual appeal to her husband is understood as partly innate (perhaps implicit in καθαρωτέρα, 'purer') and partly established through behaviour.

Lysias 1 offers another angle on this question through Euphiletos' account of an exchange he supposedly had with *Thesmonike* in which she seemed to joke about his abuse of *Praxagora*. As part of what Euphiletos claims he later learned was a ruse co-organised by *Thesmonike* and *Praxagora*, *Praxagora* supposedly provoked the baby so *Thesmonike* would have a reason to be downstairs with her supposed lover Eratosthenes while Euphiletos remained upstairs (§11). According to Euphiletos' account, when he sent *Thesmonike* away to nurse the baby, she initially refused 'as if glad to see me home after so long' (§12). When he got angry, she said he was only sending her away so as to have a chance to take sexual advantage of *Praxagora*: ἵνα σύ γε ἔφη πειρᾷς ἐνταῦθα τὴν παιδίσκην· καὶ πρότερον δὲ μεθύων εἷλκες αὐτήν '"yes, so that you can have a try there at the slave-girl (*paidiskē*)!"[34] she said. "You've dragged her [about? to bed?] before, when you've been drunk."' Euphiletos' abuse of *Praxagora* seems to have been habitual. Translations by Walter Lamb and Stephen Todd respectively render καὶ πρότερον δὲ μεθύων εἷλκες αὐτήν as 'Once before, too, when you were drunk, you pulled her about', and 'You made a grab at her once before when you were drunk'.[35] However, the verb εἷλκες is imperfect, not aorist, suggesting repeated action in the past; and πρότερον, as distinct from πότε, does not mean 'once'. Golden has it better with 'you used to maul her before when you were drunk'.[36] Another possibility is that the imperfect is conative, rendering 'you were drunkenly trying to grab her earlier',[37] but it is not clear why Euphiletos should be drunk on this occasion. He says he responded with a laugh, and *Thesmonike* locked him in the bedroom, 'pretending it [the locking] was a joke' (προσποιουμένη παίζειν, §13). This suggests we are to imagine *Thesmonike* making the accusation light-heartedly.

Euphiletos means this scene to sound candid and realistic. It gives us an unusually intimate (even if fictionalised) perspective of a marital relationship: a husband's expectation that his wife would greet her long-absent spouse with

---

[34] The term can connote sexual availability; cf. Whitehead 2009: 141.
[35] Lamb 1957: 9, Todd 2000: 18.   [36] Golden 2011: 149.
[37] I thank Bruno Currie for this suggestion.

great attention and increased sexual interest; a husband who gets angry with his wife for letting their child cry; a wife who might play practical jokes on her husband; a wife's casual references to her husband's sexual abuse of the girl they keep in slavery. The language Euphiletos gives *Thesmonike* acknowledges his violence: ἕλκω is not a colloquial verb for sex but is used specifically for sexual violence.[38] The closest comparandum is Lysias 3.12, where a man who (sexually) 'desires' (ἐπιθυμέω) a Plataian teenager allegedly begins or tries, with three accomplices, to 'drag' him (εἷλκον, imperfect), apparently as a prelude to sexual assault.[39] According to the logic of what Euphiletos reports was his initial understanding of the interaction, *Thesmonike* tried to prevent him abusing *Praxagora*, but playfully rather than earnestly. Euphiletos seems to consider his behaviour less than exemplary (it is something he does when drunk, μεθύων) but not shameful: he recounts these details to the jury without a disclaimer. So far as Euphiletos sees it or portrays himself as seeing it, his occasional sexual use of *Praxagora* is an indiscretion rather than an offence, and an insulting irritation to his wife, hence his desire to do it out of her sight.[40] Euphiletos does not expect the abuse to turn the jury against him; he may even expect a little sympathy for his vice.[41]

The Chorus of Aristophanes' *Peace* (first performed 421), composed of Greek men of various city-states, strikes a similar note when it lists among the joys of life 'kissing the [female] Thracian [slave] while one's wife is having a wash': ἥδομαί γ' ἥδομαι … τὴν Θρᾷτταν κυνῶν/τῆς γυναικὸς λουμένης (ll. 1127, 1138–9). Again, sexual use of one's slave, portrayed here as fairly 'tame', is done out of view of one's wife, but something many men can relate to. Similar too in its sympathies is the interior of a red-figure *kylix* (drinking cup) by Δορις (traditionally 'Douris' and assumed to be male, but possibly a woman, Δορίς/Doris). The cup was painted in about 480 and is now at the Museum of Fine Arts in Boston (Figure 3.2). The cup shows two figures: a bearded man penetrating a short-haired woman who supports herself stiffly against a stool.[42] The grand furniture (lion's-paw stool; elaborately carved

---

[38] Compare *DGE s.v.*, A.II.1, 'dragging, forcing or harassing in the sexual sense' ('arrastrar, forzar *en el sent[ido] sexual de* acosar'), citing this passage, Lys. 3.12, and others.

[39] Compare also Dem. 21.221, of physical but non-sexual violence.

[40] Compare Carey 1989 *ad loc.*; Ar. *Pax* 1138–9 (below); Dem. 59.22; contrast [Andoc.] 4.14.

[41] Compare Carey 1989 *ad loc.*: 'The alleged act involves no illegality, but is not for that reason commendable in a society which prized restraint. The tacit admission of a little weakness helps avoid the implausibility of too much virtue.'

[42] Some early red-figure pots (e.g. Pedeius painter cup, Paris, Louvre, G 13; Brygos painter cup, c. 490, Florence 3921) show groups of men raping and beating women whose short hair strongly suggests they are enslaved, but the imagined scenario in these scenes is probably of enslaved prostitutes hired for an occasion, rather than a group of men abusing enslaved household members. Compare Wrenhaven 2012: 71.

Figure 3.2 Attic red-figure *kylix* by 'Douris', c. 480, Boston, Museum of Fine Arts
1970.233. Gift of Landon T. Clay. Photograph
© 2025, Museum of Fine Arts, Boston.

klinē topped with a fat, striped cushion) suggests the *andrōn* in a home (the
'men's room', used for entertaining), rather than a brothel. The woman does
not have the attractive clothes and hair we might expect of a *hetaira*; she is
probably a woman kept in slavery in the household. An inscription across the
top reads *hε παῖς καλε* ('the (slave-)girl is pretty'); an inscription issuing from
the man's mouth reads *hεκε hεσυχος* ('keep still' or 'be quiet'), which Robert
Sutton characterises as 'a peremptory command that captures well the
master's voice'.[43] The woman attempts to resist; the man suppresses her
resistance. That the image is at the bottom of the cup, visible to the drinker
only when it had been drained, fits the tone of *Thesmonikē*'s reported words
and Aristophanes' Chorus: male sexual abuse of enslaved women is treated as
an open secret, an amusing indiscretion. The male drinker, finishing his
drink, is confronted with his vice, but the painter sympathises with him:
after all, 'the slave-girl *is* pretty'.[44]

A red-figure *pyxis* (cosmetics box) in the British Museum, from about
430–425, depicts a household full of women (Figure 3.3).[45] A large door
emphasises their interiority; the viewer is allowed privileged access into the

---

[43] Sutton 1992: 11.
[44] If the painter *was* a woman, this might suggest that her sympathies were more strongly determined
by socio-legal status than gender. I am grateful to Abigail Allan for discussing Δορις with me.
[45] BM 1874,0512.1.

Figure 3.3 Drawing of design on Attic red-figure *pyxis* showing preparations for
a wedding, c. 430–425, London, British Museum BM 1874,0512.1.
© Ivy Close Images/Alamy Stock Photo.

women's space.[46] Unlike on superficially similar *pyxides* from a few decades
earlier, showing groups of women in the house engaged in textile production
and childcare,[47] these women are not working but dressing and adorning
themselves. In the room are two *lebētes gamikoi*, pots to hold water for the
bridal bath, one of which depicts a bridal procession; this suggests that they
are preparing for a wedding.[48] The women on the *pyxis* – excepting one – are
dressed for a special occasion, with jewellery and headbands. They are also –
excepting one – given names, painted beside their figures as labels. The scene
is idealised and aestheticised. It forms part of a pattern in later fifth-century
Attic pot-painting which saw the appearance of nuptial imagery seemingly
intended for a female audience,[49] and a wider move in pot-painting and
grave sculpture from the Peloponnesian War and afterwards towards intimate images of families, which perhaps reflected a decreasing aesthetic interest
in labour and the prioritisation and celebration of family relationships amid
the sufferings and losses of the plague and war.

Among these seven women is a woman a third of the size of the others
and without a name label, bent down to tie or untie one woman's shoe.
Unlike the others, who have long, curly hair, loose or done up with
headbands, she has a short, straight, unadorned bob. There are many
women in the scene, but she is distinctly differentiated by her smallness.
Yet her action brings her into close physical contact with the woman whose
shoe she ties. The appearance of enslaved women alongside free women in

---

[46] Pots granting the (male) viewer 'privileged access to the private world of women': Llewellyn-Jones
2003: 87–91; door as symbol: pp. 195–7; 'women's space' not a designated room but the space in the
house to which visiting men were not admitted, because of the presence of women there: Nevett
1995; door as visual barrier to this space: p. 372.

[47] For example, red-figure *pyxis*, New York, Metropolitan Museum of Art 06.1117, c. 460, drawing at Lewis
2002: 65, fig. 2.3; red-figure *pyxis*, Athens, NAM TE 1623, c. 470, drawing at Lewis 2002: 81, fig. 2.25.

[48] Lewis 2002: 184–5, with 135, cautions against reading all 'getting ready' scenes as 'wedding preparation' scenes, but the *lebētes gamikoi* here, and the magic wheel for drawing a lover, make this
reading securer.

[49] Sutton 1992: 14–24.

attractive scenes on pots made for and used by women suggests that women liked to look at such scenes. Perhaps the emphatic smallness and subjection of the enslaved woman tying her enslaver's shoe, so plain next to her 'more becomingly dressed' enslaver (cf. πρεπόντως … μᾶλλον ἠμφιεσμένη, Xen. *Oec.* 10.12), assuaged the user's fear of being supplanted in affections or respect. This may have been particularly important in a wedding scene, where the nubility of the bride and her transition into the status of wife, with both its sexual and managerial elements, was at stake.

The sexual element of women's competition for status in the household was explored in fifth-century tragedy and dithyramb. Aeschylus' *Agamemnon*, first performed in 458, portrays the 'competition' between Klytaimestra and Kasandra; Sophocles' *Trachiniae*, first performed somewhere in the mid-fifth century,[50] portrays a similar 'competition' between Deianeira and Iole; Bacchylides' *Dithyramb* 3 (= Ode 16), roughly contemporary,[51] takes the same theme. The mythological exempla, and their dramatisation on the fifth-century stage, suggest anxiety about such competition and its potential to disrupt household stability by engendering conflict between members on whose collaboration the household depended, and blurring the distinctions on which the ideology of the slaveholding society relied.

In *Trachiniae*, Herakles is said to be bringing Iole home 'not as a slave' (οὐδ᾽ ὥστε δούλην, l. 367); this expression makes clear the threat she poses to Deianeira. Deianeira says that Herakles has had sex with a number of women during their marriage, and that she has been kind to them; she intends to be kind to Iole too, largely out of pity (ll. 459–67). Her pity is a specific response to Iole's peculiar mythical predicament of involuntary culpability for her city's destruction, ll. 463–7; wives' pity for enslaved women is not visible elsewhere in our sources. It is possible to read pity for *Praxagora* in the language Euphiletos puts in *Thesmonike*'s mouth, but he has her follow it with a joke. The unmarried daughter in Menander's *Dyskolos* worries for her elderly enslaved nurse who has dropped a bucket down a well; she fears her violent father 'will beat [the nurse] to death' (ἀπολεῖ κακ[ῶς πάνυ] / παίων ἐκείνην, ll. 195–6), but the relationship dynamics here are different, without 'competition'. Despite her pity, Deianeira is jealous: she will be 'sharing her marriage' (κοινωνοῦσα τῶν αὐτῶν γάμων, l. 546), and in the competition between 'wives', she will lose because she is ageing and becoming less attractive (ll. 536–51).

In Attica after 451, a man partnered with a woman not of citizen status could not have citizen-status children with her, but this may not have been much of

---

[50] Hoey 1979.   [51] Compare Davies 2017: xxxii–xxxiii.

a deterrent against forming such partnerships, particularly for men who already had healthy, grown-up children. Stephanos in *Against Neaira* (delivered c. 340) was the partner of a formerly enslaved woman, probably having previously been married to a citizen-status woman. Isaeus 6 (delivered 364) tells the story of Alke, kept in slavery by the freedwoman of Euktemon, in one of Euktemon's properties (though not his marital home). When Alke was freed (either by Euktemon or the freedwoman – the exact legal arrangement is perhaps deliberately unclear), Euktemon abandoned his wife for her, raising the spectre of social disruption consequent on transgression of the enslaver–enslaved hierarchy in a similar way to the fifth-century tragedies.

Cathy Gaca has argued that contrary to the prevailing scholarly view, freeborn Greek men were not entitled to sexual use of the enslaved women and girls in their homes. Rather, she argues, male sexual entitlement to enslaved women was the rule only on military campaigns, and for married men to exercise such entitlement in a domestic context was an insult to their wives not primarily insofar as it provoked sexual jealousy but insofar as it constituted a transgression of married women's prerogative to control sexual access to enslaved household members, which was part of their role as household managers, and 'an unacceptable carryover of martial rape norms from the army camp to their homes'.[52] Gaca's contribution is a valuable reminder that many enslaved women and girls in Greece were either war-captives themselves or the daughters of war-captives, which must have shaped the dynamics of domestic slavery. Her argument that women's managerial responsibility over enslaved household members, particularly enslaved women and girls – a responsibility discussed in this chapter – extended to control over sexual access to those women and girls is in some ways persuasive. However, I think she underplays the possible contradictions between men's normative sexual behaviour and actual sexual behaviour, which might be socially tolerated or even broadly accepted even if it was not how they were 'supposed' to operate.

Perhaps it is misleading to say that men were 'entitled' to sexual use of enslaved women in their homes; hence the concealment – cheerfully discussed – supposedly practised by Euphiletos and the *Peace* Chorus. However (as is evident in the various examples in Gaca's chapter), such (ab)use did take place and, I argue, does seem to have been to some degree *socially* expected and tolerated, even if it was unacceptable to the men's wives and their male relatives. Examples abound in many cultures of sexual behaviour which is simultaneously 'not acceptable' and yet broadly socially accepted. Gaca's argument that the perceived threat to the wife's status constituted by such sexual activity was

---

[52] Gaca 2021; quotation from p. 42.

in part about usurping her prerogative to manage sexual access to enslaved women and girls is interesting and worth consideration, but the way the threat is talked about in many sources (e.g. Deianeira's fear of having to 'share her marriage', Iskhomakhos' sexual comparisons between his wife and the enslaved girls in his household) emphasise the element of sexual jealousy and fear of displacement rather than disregarded authority.[53] However, a man's (transgressive) sexual (ab)use of an enslaved woman in his household *would* likely have threatened his wife's authority by revealing his lack of respect for her to the enslaved woman and to other enslaved household members under the wife's management, possibly shifting their loyalties and priorities.[54]

Nevertheless, Gaca's argument as framed in the conclusion to her chapter, though different in emphasis, seems essentially correct and important: that though 'as the master's delegated overseer, the mistress of the house' was supposed to have control over its enslaved members and their sexuality, 'to her recurrent anger and fury she found herself having to fight to stop the master' from disregarding her position and her wishes. This male behaviour, Gaca argues, was driven by 'ravaging warfare with its acquired tastes of exceedingly licentious sexual violence'.[55]

For enslaved women, particularly those kept specifically as sex slaves as Neaira and Alke had been, cultivating a relationship with one's rapist could be a survival strategy. It might lead to a greater level of freedom, as for Alke, or merely a lower level of suffering. Antiphon 1 mentions an enslaved woman (*Phile*) who had become her enslaver Philoneos' *pallakē* (informal sexual partner).[56] When Philoneos tired of *Phile*, he intended to consign her to a brothel, where she would be raped by any man who paid. As the speaker tells it, in her desperation to escape, *Phile* gave Philoneos what she thought was a love potion to win him back and regain her position in his household. In fact it was poison. This killed him; she was tortured and executed.

Collusion, Collaboration, Coercion

Despite these tensions over sexuality, Euphiletos presents *Praxagora* as having a close relationship with *Thesmonike*, taking messages for her

---

[53] Unlike Gaca, I do not think it is straightforwardly possible to read a sense of usurped authority into, for example, the 'anger' Homer says Laertes' wife Antikleia would have felt if he had had sex with the enslaved Eurykleia, *Od.* 1.428–33.

[54] Compare Olson 2013: 69–72 on Aristophanes' *Knights*' image of shifting power dynamics and loyalties between (here) enslaved men and their male enslaver in a case where one enslaved man has become particularly influential with the enslaver.

[55] Gaca 2021: 62.   [56] See p. 279 with fn. 59 for *Phile*'s name.

(§§8, 20), playing her part in supposed ruses to facilitate her affair (§§11, 20), and even being willing to undergo torture to protect her (§§18–19). Euphiletos says that he told *Praxagora* he knew about *Thesmonike*'s affair and said he would forgive *Praxagora* if she told him everything, but if she did not, he would whip her and send her to a life of hard labour in a mill (§18).[57] According to Euphiletos, *Praxagora* 'at first denied it, and said I could do what I wanted, because she knew nothing' (τὸ μὲν πρῶτον ἔξαρνος ἦν, καὶ ποιεῖν ἐκέλευεν ὅ τι βούλομαι· οὐδὲν γὰρ εἰδέναι, §19). Whether or not this is true, Euphiletos seemingly believed a jury could imagine an enslaved woman risking torture and a lifetime of hard labour to defend her enslaver.[58] He uses *Praxagora*'s loyalty to *Thesmonike* to suggest a threat to his authority and to the social order. Only when Euphiletos makes clear to *Praxagora* that he knows some of the details does she beg for mercy and tell him the rest, including how she took messages from Eratosthenes to *Thesmonike* and sneaked him into the house.

This account is part of a strong association in Attic literature and art between citizen-status women and enslaved women which manifests as collusion to deceive the free women's husbands, in order to have affairs or introduce suppositious children – extra-marital sex and illegitimate children naturally being strongly associated in the Athenian (male?) mind.[59] The deception around the baby in Menander's *Samia*, illegitimate and being passed off as someone else's, involves collusion between free and enslaved women: the secret is kept from the male householders Demeas and Nikeratos by their children (the baby's citizen-status parents), Nikeratos' wife, Demeas' metic partner Khrysis, and an enslaved woman and a freedwoman in Demeas' house (ll. 231–61). The scenario presented in Lysias 1 bears certain resemblances to the plot of Euripides' *Hippolytus* (first performed 428), where Phaidra's enslaved nurse attempts (unsuccessfully) to act as a go-between between Phaidra and the object of her affections, Hippolytos. The horrified Hippolytos suggests the extreme solution that free women not be allowed contact with enslaved people, because they can carry women's plots outside the house (ll. 645–50). Aristophanes makes a joke of the same stereotype in *Thesmophoriazusae* (produced 411), where he has the women's herald pronounce a curse on, among others:

---

[57] Apparently a common threat: Eurip. *Cyc.* 240, [Dem.] 45.33.
[58] My reading of *Praxagora*'s actions differs significantly in emphasis from that of Lewis 2002: 141.
[59] Compare Golden 2011: 137, citing Ar. *Pax* 674–8, *Thesm.* 564–5, and Dem. 21.149 (note that only *Thesmophoriazusae* says that the suppositious child was born to an enslaved woman).

δούλη τινὸς
προαγωγὸς οὖσ᾽ ἐνετρύλλισεν τῷ δεσπότῃ
ἢ πεμπομένη τις ἀγγελίας ψευδεῖς φέρει . . .   (340–2)

> anyone's slave-woman who, acting as a go-between, whispers in her master's ear, or, sent out [for information], brings back false news.

Praxagora's supposed revelations of τὰς εἰσόδους οἷς τρόποις προσίοιτο ('the means by which she used to get him inside', §20), including the crying baby ruse, recall the kaleidoscope of images of female ingenuity in deceiving their husbands presented by Euripides' disguised male in-law in Aristophanes' *Thesmophoriazusae* (ll. 466–519).

Another possible element of this picture of collaboration consists in a potential second enslaved–enslaver pair in Euphiletos' story. Euphiletos claims he learnt about the affair from τις πρεσβῦτις ἄνθρωπος, ὑπὸ γυναικὸς ὑποπεμφθεῖσα ἣν ἐκεῖνος ἐμοίχευεν, 'an old female (*anthrōpos*, with a feminine adjective), sent by a woman (*gynē*) with whom [Eratosthenes] was having an affair' (§15; cf. 16). Where *anthrōpos* is used instead of *gynē* it tends to have a derogatory sense and is often used for enslaved women or for women of low social status, like freed prostitutes.[60] In *Thesmophoriazusae*, Euripides' in-law, pretending to be a woman confessing to the common crimes of womankind, says that women steal the meat from Apatouria sacrifices and give it to the women who arrange their extramarital affairs (ταῖς μαστροποῖς, ll. 558–9). This joke derives its particular irony from the fact that the sacrifices at the Apatouria served to affirm the legitimacy of the children they were offered for. We might also consider the old woman (γραῦς) who finds and sneaks in the suppositious baby in *Thesmophoriazusae* (ll. 502–16), whose status and relationship to the would-be mother are unclear. Were these women enslaved by the women using them, or were they local specialists – or simply 'gossips'?[61] The evidence for a trope of wives' collaboration with enslaved women suggests that the imaginations of Athenian men were not haunted so much by an underclass of meddling women but by a fear of enslaved members of their own households going behind their backs with their wives.[62]

---

[60] Compare *DGE s.v.* ἄνθρωπος III, IV. Enslaved women: Antiph. 1.17, Isoc. 18.52. Freed prostitutes: Men. *Sam.* 348, Isae. 6.20. The term is occasionally used for citizen-status women, e.g. Ar. *Lys.* 936.

[61] For women and 'gossip' in classical Athens, see Hunter 1990 and Hunter 1994; for a study of women using inscribed texts to manage gossip surrounding their households and families in second and third century AD western Asia Minor, see Gordon 2016.

[62] Petrova 2019 offers a contrasting perspective from Augustan literature.

Figure 3.4 Attic red-figure *skyphos* showing a storeroom, mid fifth century, Malibu, Getty Villa 86.AE.265. Digital image courtesy of the Getty's Open Content Program.

Some Athenian men feared collusion between the free and enslaved women of their households for other purposes. One mid fifth-century red-figure *skyphos* (wine cup) at the Getty Villa in Malibu carries an image of a storeroom (Figure 3.4). On the other side, however, is an enslaved girl (small, short-haired) looking on while a woman in a striped *peplos*, presumably her enslaver, drinks deeply from a *skyphos* (Figure 3.5).[63] The girl carries a full wineskin on her head and a jug in her hand. The woman in the *peplos*, whose body tilts forward, seems to be moving away from or towards the storeroom.

The *skyphos* was presumably designed primarily for use by men, though it would have been free or enslaved women who handled it as they washed it up and put it away afterwards. The image fits into a tradition of jokes and comments across archaic and classical Greek literature about women stealing from food stores[64] and female drunkenness.[65] The contrast between the woman illicitly drinking contrasts sharply with the tidy storeroom with items hung in place, a visual shorthand for an excellent wife. Xenophon dedicates an entire chapter of *Oeconomicus* to Iskhomakhos' lecture to his

[63] Getty 86.AE.265.
[64] Collected by West 1978 *ad* Hes. *Op.* 373–4, including: Hes. *Op.* 704, Hes. *Theog.* 594ff., Sem. 7.6, 24, 46–7, Ar. *Thesm.* 418–22, 556–7, 812–13., *Eccl.* 14–15.
[65] For example, Sommerstein 2013 *ad* Men. *Sam.* 302–3.

Figure 3.5 The other side of the *skyphos*, showing a woman drinking as a girl looks on. Malibu, Getty Villa 86.AE.265. Digital image courtesy of the Getty's Open Content Program.

wife on the importance of a tidy storeroom (§8), and a female character in Euripides' *Melanippe Captive* says that it is the particular role and skill of a woman or wife to keep a household εὐπινής, clean and tidy (frg. 660 Mette, ll. 10–11). This contrast echoes Semonides of Amorgos' seventh-century warning that the man who thinks he has an excellent wife is in fact deluded (Sem. 7.108–11). Someone holding the *skyphos* who looked first at the storeroom side of the *skyphos* and then turned the cup round to reveal the thieving woman would experience a similar 'shock' to the one experienced by the listener of Semonides 7 between lines 108 and 109: ἥτις δέ τοι μάλιστα σωφρονεῖν δοκεῖ, / αὕτη μέγιστα τυγχάνει λωβωμένη, 'But I tell you, the woman who seems most self-controlled, she is the most outrageous.' A viewer looking first at the woman and then at the storeroom might enjoy seeing through the delusion of the husband described next: κεχηνότος γὰρ ἀνδρός, οἱ δὲ γείτονες / χαίρουσ' ὁρῶντες καὶ τόν, ὡς ἁμαρτάνει, 'while the husband gapes [like an idiot who does not realise?], the neighbours enjoy seeing that he too is mistaken' (ll. 110–11). But the artist's point about women stealing from storerooms and drinking wine could have been made without the inclusion of the enslaved girl. Her presence adds a dimension: not only is your wife 'stealing', the cup tells the drinker, but the enslaved girl is in on it too.

Men's fears of collusion reflected a reality of forced close collaboration. Our evidence offers a picture of an uneasy forced intimacy between free women and the enslaved members of their households, particularly enslaved women, with whom they shared much of their work, space, and lives. For enslaved women, cultivating the trust of female enslavers, even at the cost of the trust of male enslavers, may have been the better strategy, given that the women spent more time with them and determined things like food allocation. Aristophanes' claim that women gave meat from the Apatouria sacrifices to the women who arranged affairs for them is self-consciously outrageous, but as we saw with Khoirine (*SB* 22.15276), women could 'reward' enslaved, underfed girls and women with extra food.

'Part of the Family'?

Enslaved Women in Sepulchral Iconography

As we have seen, commemoration was an arena for the retroactive portrayal and positioning of relationships that had existed in life by those left behind. It was ordinarily the task of close family, and, particularly after about 430, sepulchral reliefs took an increasing interest in intimate family relationships. Such reliefs portray idealised representations of real families, which give us insight into the kind of relationships the commemorators imagined or wanted to suggest they and the dead had in life. Where did enslaved people fit into these relationships? Does the physical inclusion of enslaved household members in sepulchral iconography represent the commemorators' perception of their membership of the family, or do they appear merely as indices of their enslavers' status?

The grave reliefs of Hegeso, *Myrrhine*, and Ameinokleia show the women being served by enslaved girls. Enslaved women also appear in sepulchral compositions for citizen-status women which include children. There is little reason to think that the enslaved women are 'symbolic' any more than the other people shown, whom we assume represent real relatives.[66] Kelly Wrenhaven understands family scenes including enslaved people as instances of 'infant care' as a 'type of assistance' shown by enslaved people on sepulchral reliefs, analogous to the box-holding we saw in the *naiskos* of Hegeso. But a child is not a box; rather, she is a participant in a nexus of interpersonal relationships which artists explored and represented.[67] Hegeso's box illustrated her status by depicting her wealth and illustrated the status of the woman she

---

[66] See Humphreys 2018: 363–73 on how monuments and their makers met families' requirements, with a convincing argument at pp. 371–2 against suggestions of 'off-the-peg' monuments.

[67] Marchiandi 2011 also argues that children depicted on the grave monuments of adults 'embody the last generation of the *oikos* and, therefore, the hopes and expectations of survival in the future of

enslaved by depicting her enforced service. The children in these scenes illustrate their mothers' status as wives and mothers, and perhaps their enslaved carers' status as enslaved carers, but they are also persons in affective relationships with the other persons in the scene.

Katia Margariti argues that in scenes which show more than two figures and an infant, 'the iconography focused foremost on the relationship between the dead woman and the adult members of her family, while the female holding the infant occupies a less prominent position'.[68] One example is a grave *naiskos* from the Louvre (c. 340–325, Figure 3.6, *RA* (1968, 1) 157), which Wrenhaven describes as 'a crowded family scene'.[69]

A seated woman labelled 'Aristonike' clasps hands with a smaller woman labelled 'Bako' opposite her, who pulls at the *himation* around her shoulders.[70] Between them is a boy knee-high to the seated woman, who tugs at the standing woman's sleeve. He is labelled 'Sokrat[e]s' and from his action must be the son of one of the two. Behind these three labelled figures are two more women, about Bako's height. One, on the far right, holds an infant; the other, in the centre, holds a box and lifts her other hand to her cheek in mourning. The latter figure, looking towards Aristonike and Bako, but also out at the viewer, and grieving, seems to guide the viewer's response to the relief. The two women unlabelled and in the background probably represent enslaved women. Though they are not named, and do not interact as Bako, Sokrates, and Aristonike do, they *are* included. The 'crowdedness' is a product of their deliberate inclusion.

An Attic red-figure *hydria* from about 440–430, now at Harvard (Figure 3.7), offers a different image. *Hydriai* were for carrying and storing water, but this one has a hole pierced in the bottom: it was intended for funerary use, and was apparently found in a grave in Vari on the west coast of Attica, near the deme of Anagyrous.[71] The image on the *hydria* shows a seated woman handing a baby boy to a standing woman. On the left is a loom; on the right, a beardless young man in a *himation*, with a staff. The

---

those who preceded them' (p. 71), 'but also the fulfilment of the social obligation to reproduce, to guarantee the survival of the *polis*' (p. 77).

[68] Margariti 2016: 90.   [69] Wrenhaven 2012: 103.

[70] The 'veil-gesture': see Llewellyn-Jones 2003: 91–110.

[71] The archaeologist and collector David Moore Robinson described the *hydria* as 'from a cemetery near Vari in Attica; purchased in Western Europe' (Robinson 1937: 31), which suggests that the information was given to him by the dealer. Robinson seems to have preferred objects with known findspots, which may mean that the information is true or that dealers knew that giving an object a findspot made it more valuable to him. Beazley 1938 raises doubts about the Vari findspots of two other pots in Robinson's collection, but not explicitly about this one. I am grateful to Caitlin Chien Clerkin at the Harvard Art Museums for discussing this with me.

Figure 3.6 Grave *stēlē* of Bako, Aristonike, and Sokrates, c. 340–325, Paris, Louvre
MND 909/MA 3113. © Musée du Louvre, Dist. GrandPalaisRmn/Hervé
Lewandowski.

baby reaches to the woman who takes him, yet she looks at the seated
woman, who tilts her face up to meet her gaze, suggesting a relationship
between the two. The women partake in one cooperative movement, their
arms forming a gently curving line; the baby's reach is higher up, towards
the receiving woman's breast, not her arms. The artist seems less interested
in the standing woman's relationship with the child than her relationship
with the seated woman.

It is difficult to 'read' female relationships from painted pots.[72]
Relationships and intimacy are sometimes suggested by physical touch,
shared gazes,[73] exchanged objects,[74] or the overall 'shape' of the

[72] Compare the methodology of Lewis 2002: 1–13.　　[73] Rabinowitz 2002.
[74] Blundell and Rabinowitz 2008: 126–8.

Figure 3.7 Attic red-figure *hydria*, c. 440–430, Cambridge, MA, Harvard Art Museums/Arthur M. Sackler Museum 1960.342, bequest of David M. Robinson.

iconography bringing figures into closer relation.[75] Ironically, given the relative paucity of female voices in our sources, scenes of women conversing are common on pots.[76] However, we cannot usually infer the nature of the relationships between individuals depicted (friendship? Kinship? What kind of kin relation?).[77] Painters may not have been interested in such specifics. Lewis points out the agelessness of adult women on pots, which 'removes [depictions] from any consideration of the roles played by women throughout their lives – as daughters, sisters, wives, mothers and grandmothers'.[78] On the other hand, as this book shows, women moved into and out of different roles through their lives, often quite quickly, and perhaps the 'unmarkedness' of women's relational statuses on pots reflected this lack of fixity. Perhaps different viewers filled the interpretative gap differently: different women might have imagined the same scene to show sisters, in-laws, or friends.[79] Some 80 per cent of surviving Greek pots come from graves – mostly graves in

---

[75] See also Blundell and Rabinowitz 2008 for the question of whether group 'adornment scenes' suggest women's community.
[76] Lewis 2002: 4.   [77] Lewis 2002: 35–6, 8.   [78] Lewis 2002: 13.   [79] Petersen 1997.

Italy, an important export destination,[80] though the Harvard *hydria* is said to have come from a grave in Attica. If Athenians selected these pots as grave goods, as in this case, women or men may have chosen depictions of female interactions to commemorate a woman's role as a companion to other women within or beyond her family, a role not typically high-lighted in sepulchral epigrams.[81]

As well as women's social roles (daughter, sister, wife, mother, grand-mother, friend), women's socio-legal statuses (citizen-status, metic, enslaved, wife, widow) are often indiscernible on pots, which Lewis notes is in sharp contrast to the emphasis written sources place on such statuses.[82] Some written sources, however, suggest it was not always possible to distinguish status based on appearance;[83] this book argues that socio-legal status was less of a determining factor in women's experiences and relationships than is often assumed. Images on pots may reflect this or merely remind us of it.

Scholars differ on the identification of the women on the Harvard *hydria*. Sutton argues that the woman handing over the baby is probably intended to represent the wife and mother, because of her central position and because she is seated, as most women in apparent husband–wife pairings are.[84] He suggests the standing woman 'could be either a relative or a nurse, whether free or slave', though 'other interpretations are possible'; for example, the standing woman could be the child's mother and the seated woman his grandmother (we recall Ampharete's relief in Chapter 2, Figure 2.2), 'or even a very honoured wetnurse'.

Margaret Miller understands the standing woman as the mother and does not posit an identity for the seated woman.[85] Miller's interest is in the standing woman's *khitōniskos kheiridōtos*, a thigh-length *khitōn* with fitted sleeves. *Khitōniskoi kheiridōtoi* were inspired by sleeved Persian clothes but made in Attica; they appear on pots from about 450. Art historians trad-itionally associate them with enslaved women; women in sleeves on late fifth- and fourth-century grave reliefs (including Hegeso's and Aristonike's) seem from other attributes to be enslaved. However, there are four dedica-tions of sleeved *khitōnes* (ankle-length) or *khitōniskoi* (thigh-length) to Artemis at Brauron, which strongly suggests they were also worn by citizen-status women.[86] It may be that iconography conservatively associated the foreignness of sleeves with enslaved women even after they began to be

<hr>

[80] Spivey 1991: 149–50.
[81] Exceptions include *IG* 1^3 1295 bis and 1329 (pp. 327–31) and 11^2 5673 (pp. 91–3).
[82] Lewis 2002: 7–8. [83] Vlassopoulos 2007: 33–5. [84] Sutton 2004: 340. [85] Miller 1997: 158.
[86] *IG* 11^2 1514.6, 1523.9–10 (recorded again at 1524.182–3), 1523.22–3 (recorded slightly differently at 1524.196–7), 1529.10, cited by Miller 1997: 157.

Figure 3.8 Detail from Attic red-figure *lebēs gamikos*, c. 430, Athens, National Archaeological Museum NAM A1250. © Hellenic Ministry of Culture.

adopted by women of citizen status. Miller describes the *khitōniskos kheiridōtos* on the Harvard *hydria* as the 'least elaborate example' in Attic art. Its simplicity may suggest the wearer is enslaved rather than highly fashionable. Its crenellated borders recall a patterned Thracian garment called the *zeira*[87] (though again, the style appears on clothes dedicated at Brauron).[88] Thracians represented a large proportion of Attica's enslaved population and were a popular choice for nurses;[89] perhaps this is the association the painter draws.[90] This funerary *hydria* may acknowledge that a dead mother would leave her child to be cared for by an enslaved nurse,[91] but the difficulty in identifying the women's roles and statuses is partly a product of the dignified portrayal of the standing woman, which minimises the distinction between the two.

The intimacy of the women's shared gaze recalls a husband–wife–child composition on a contemporary Attic red-figure *lebēs gamikos* (Figure 3.8).[92] Sutton writes: 'Representing the physical bond between its parents and the future of the *oikos*, the child reaches with one arm to steady itself on its mother's breast and extends the other arm toward its father, reinforcing the link of their reciprocal glance'.[93] He associates this glance with the 'nuptial glance' of a groom towards his bride in painted depictions of weddings on Attic pots, which she sometimes returns.[94] In a 'family composition' like the Harvard *hydria*, we would expect such eye contact between husband and

---

[87] Lee 2015: 122, 4–5, though note Beazley 1937: 268 *contra*.
[88] *IG* ii² 1514.25–6, 45–7, 1517 B 135–6.   [89] Kosmopoulou 2001: 286.
[90] Schulze 1998: 22–3 (no. A v 9).
[91] Compare Margariti 2016 and Cohen 2011: 466–7 for the motif on *stēlai*.
[92] Athens, NAM 1250, manner of the Naples Painter.   [93] Sutton 2004: 338.
[94] Compare Sutton 1997–8.

wife rather than between wife and another woman in the household – yet a woman may have been likelier to form an intimacy with a woman she shared her space and time with than with her husband, even if that was a compromised intimacy with a woman she kept in slavery.[95] Identifications on pots are never certain, but there is no reason we should base an identification on an assumption of non-intimacy between enslaved and free women, rather than using it as potential evidence for (real, imagined, or aspirational) intimacy.[96] Again, in images like this relationships seem more important than status distinctions.

Memorials for Enslaved Women

Memorials for enslaved people constitute more persuasive evidence for the understanding of *certain* enslaved household members as 'part of the family', and perhaps for relationships of less dramatic inequality. Enslavers were responsible for burying those they had kept in slavery, but this duty did not extend to erection of a monument, much less one in marble. However, it seems that some enslavers did commemorate individuals they had kept in slavery, not just with inscribed stones but with sepulchral reliefs, in iconographic styles similar to monuments for citizens. The only such monuments we can be reasonably sure belonged to enslaved people are labelled as belonging to *paidagōgoi* and, more commonly, *titthai*, nurses.[97] Not all monuments for nurses were for enslaved nurses,[98] but those which identify the dead person only as *titthē*, without even a name, almost certainly were.[99] Those which describe the dead woman with her name and the description *titthē khrēstē*, 'a good nurse', where 'good' has the sense of 'useful', were probably also for enslaved women: in Attic sepulchral contexts, the adjective *khrēstos* is strongly (though not definitively) associated with enslaved people.[100] Simple memorials for women whose patronymics are not given may memorialise enslaved women,[101] but it is likelier that they were for free

---

[95] See Rabinowitz 2002 for female–female intimacy on Attic pots.

[96] Compare Lewis 2002: 141 on pots as potentially aspirational for enslaved people. Enslaving women might also aspire to intimacy with the women with whom they spent so much of their lives: cf. my pp. 169–70. See Lewis 1998–9 for enslaved people as viewers and users of pots.

[97] For the respect and affection a woman might feel for her nurse, see *IG* II² 7873 (p. 71) – though this nurse was a metic employed by the family, not enslaved by them.

[98] For example, the monuments for Melitta and Malikha (*IG* II² 7873, 9112: pp. 71, 257–8).

[99] NAM 1027 = *IG* II² 12813; NAM 2076 = *IG* II² 12814; NAM 1020 = *IG* II² 12815; Agora I 6508 = Bradeen 1974: 186 (*Agora* XVII 1048).

[100] Wrenhaven 2012: 97–9; Sawtell 2018: 73.

[101] For example, EM 10241 = *IG* I³ 1328 and EM 10246 = *IG* I³ 1307 bis.

women and originally belonged in *stēlē* groupings where other stones made their family relationships clear.[102]

Reliefs for enslaved nurses present them as their enslavers' peers, often in similar dress and clasping hands with their commemorating enslavers. They suggest that those enslavers felt towards them something well beyond a sense of legal obligation. It is relevant that the role of nurse is a quasi-mothering role. In Aeschylus' *Choephori*, first performed in 458, Klytaimestra, Orestes' biological mother, and Kilissa, his enslaved wet nurse, both claim a privileged relationship with Orestes because of having breastfed him (ll. 759–60; 896–8). This maternal role may have contributed to the mitigation of status distinctions within the household, and the sense that a memorial of a more 'familial' type was appropriate. The iconography of memorials for enslaved nurses differs little from that of memorials for free nurses.[103]

A grave *stēlē* from Kato Petralona inscribed *Pyraikhmē tittē khrēstē* ('Pyraikhme, a good nurse') shows a seated, short-haired woman holding a *skyphos* in her lap, with a *khous* (small wine cup) at her feet.[104] Semni Karouzou and Erika Simon suggest that Pyraikhme's cups represent drinking cups from the Anthesteria.[105] This was an important Attic festival celebrated in families, in which enslaved household members were allowed to participate: the cups symbolise her inclusion in the family. A different image of inclusion is offered by the grave *lekythos* of Theoxene from the Mesogeia (inland, rural Attica), carved in about 350.[106] Theoxene, described as *Theoxenē titthē khrēstē* ('Theoxene, a good nurse'), veiled with a *himation* like a citizen-status woman, clasps hands with a bearded man – her enslaver? her former charge?[107] – also in a *himation*.[108] The hand-clasping gesture (*dexiōsis*), common in sepulchral depictions of the dead and their relatives, but also used in reliefs depicting treaties, is an image of a familial rather than hierarchical relationship, whether or not that reflected reality.[109]

---

[102] I thank Carrie Sawtell for discussing this with me.

[103] Compare the descriptions at Kosmopoulou 2001: 306–11.

[104] NAM 3935 = *SEG* 21:1064; *tittē* is a variant spelling of *titthē*.

[105] Karouzou 1957: 311–23; Simon 1963: 9–10.

[106] NAM 1845 = *IG* 11² 11647. The description at Kosmopoulou 2001: 306–7 actually describes another *lekythos*.

[107] Cf. [Dem.] 47.55–6.

[108] The man *could* be her husband, but this is unlikely for a woman described as '*khrēstē*'.

[109] Further *stēlai* depicting (probably) enslaved nurses with adult men: EM 4983 = *IG* 11² 12559, c. 360 ('Sunete, *tithē khrēstē*', where *tithē* is a variant spelling of *titthē*); NAM 2076 = *IG* 11² 12814, c. 350 ('*teitthē*', another variant spelling); NAM 1020 = *IG* 11² 12815, 340–30 ('*titthē khrēstē*').

Figure 3.9 Relief on Khoirine's monument, c. 350–325, Athens, National Archaeological Museum NAM Γ1021. © Hellenic Ministry of Culture. Photograph by author.

The nurse Khoirinē (*Khoirinē titthē, stēlē* from Patissia, c. 350–325) is shown with a man and a woman, clasping hands with the woman rather than the man (Figure 3.9).[110] Khoirine sits on a stool with her feet on a footstool, looking up at the woman whose hand she clasps; the nurse and the other woman – her former charge? – are similarly dressed, both in *khitōnes* and veiled in their *himatia*. An older man (possibly the standing woman's husband, or her father, who acquired Khoirine to nurse her) stands in the background, looking at Khoirine. Through the hand-clasping, it is Khoirine's relationship with the woman that is emphasised, perhaps because the nurse's relationship with her charge was – either really or normatively – stronger than that with the enslaver at the head of the household. Possibly Khoirine's memorial was the woman's initiative but the man's inclusion signifies his financial contribution to the memorial, or more straightforwardly, the fact that Khoirine was felt to be 'part of the family', rather than important solely to her charge.[111]

---

[110]　NAM 1021 = *IG* 11² 13065.

[111]　The relationship portrayed on a contemporary *stēlē* from the Agora (Agora 1 6508), though damaged, is more unambiguously that of nurse and charge: the unnamed nurse (*titthē khrēstē*) apparently clasps hands with a young girl.

Though the slave systems of classical Attica and the antebellum American South were too different to draw straightforward comparisons, an episode in Harriet Jacobs' *Incidents in the Life of a Slave Girl*, the nineteenth-century autobiography of a formerly enslaved woman, warns us against over-optimism in our reading of these monuments. Jacobs scathingly tells the story of the funeral of her enslaved aunt Nancy, who died prematurely after losing eight babies, largely because of overwork and the appalling living conditions forced on her by her enslaver, Mrs Flint. When Nancy died, Mrs Flint had intended to have her buried in the family plot but was encouraged to consult Nancy's mother, who wanted Nancy to be buried with her own family. Mrs Flint, with her husband, joined Nancy's funeral procession and wept. Jacobs comments: 'Northern travellers . . . might have described this tribute of respect to the humble dead as . . . a touching proof of the attachment between slaveholders and their servants; and tender-hearted Mrs. Flint would have confirmed this impression, with a handkerchief at her eyes. *We* could have told them a different story.'[112]

Conclusion

The literary texts at the centre of the analysis in the section 'Intimacy and Power' are highly concerned with the ideology of the household as understood by men, and their discussion of the relationships between enslaved women and the women who kept them in slavery – women whose wifehood is of paramount importance to the texts – is central to the construction and upholding of this ideology. The suggestion in Xenophon that a woman secured her position in the *oikos* as a wife through subjugation of the household's enslaved workers – echoed in the monuments of Hegeso, *Myrrhine*, and Ameinokleia in the following section – aligns more closely with male thinking on women's social position than the other relationships in this book. The more counter-hegemonic suggestion of the Harvard *hydria*, that relationships between enslaving and enslaved women might take emotional precedence over relationships with kin, rests on uncertain identification in an image which may also have been produced by a man.

Perhaps because of this source bias, according to which descriptions of free women's relationships with enslaved women mostly come from texts highly invested in the ideology of the *oikos*, most of our evidence about these relationships, and therefore most of this chapter, concerns relationships

---

[112] Jacobs 2015 [1861]: 136–7.

between married women and the enslaved people who legally belonged to their husbands – relationships largely developed during husbands' daily absences from the home. We get only a few glimpses of how these relationships worked for other women, or of whether an enslaved person might remain with the same free woman across different households.[113] Lysias 32 implies that *Diognete*'s sons' *paidagōgos* and her daughter's *therapaina*, who probably also served *Diognete*, lived with the family during her year of widowhood in the Peiraieus, though they then went to live with the children in the *asty* (§28, with §§8 and 20). After this, *Diognete* was presumably served by a woman her new husband kept in slavery. By contrast, Pasion gave his wife Arkhippe two enslaved women in his will to remain with her in her marriage to Phormion ([Dem.] 45.28). Similarly, Phrynion gave Neaira two enslaved girls, Thraitta and Kokkaline, as a gift. When Neaira escaped the abusive Phrynion to go to Megara, she took the girls with her; when she moved back to Attica with Stephanos, they came too (Ap. *Neaira* 35, 42, 46). Neaira was later confirmed at an arbitration to be free and legally independent (αὐτὴ αὐτῆς κυρία, §46);[114] Thraitta and Kokkaline were judged to be legally hers.[115] Tragedies including Euripides' *Hippolytus* and *Medea* show mythological women who have moved into new territories on marriage but bring with them their enslaved childhood nurses. In *Hippolytus* in particular, the confidence between Phaidra and her nurse is presented as a threat to her marriage and household. More intriguing are the Hellenistic *paramonē* contracts discussed in Chapter 2 (p. 138), by which single women in particular secured care from enslaved people without legally possessing them.

This chapter, like those which precede and follow it, demonstrates the ability of women – free women and, to a lesser extent, enslaved women – to shape their relationships and experiences, though it seems that in relationships between free and enslaved women, the circumscriptions of the dominant discourse on wifehood and family were more limiting. Many free Attic women spent much if not most of their time in the company of those they enslaved, working and raising their children alongside them, which gave rise to close (though for the enslaved parties, forced) relationships. These relationships were characterised by a complex interplay of intimacy and hierarchy. Citizen-status women depended on enslaved

---

[113] Foxhall 1998a: 64 believes that 'when a wealthy woman married, [she brought] her personal domestic slaves with her to her new household'.

[114] Kennedy 2014: 2, 105, 114.

[115] In Menander's *Samia*, Demeas seems to give Khrysis (who is in a similar legal position to Neaira) an elderly enslaved woman when he expels her from his house (l. 373, with Sommerstein 2013 on l. 302).

household members not just for their labour and skills but also indirectly to establish their position within their households and society. Enslaved household members, by contrast, were forced to depend on the women who enslaved them for food and care.

This asymmetrical co-dependence was further complicated by free men's sexual access both to their wives and to those they kept in slavery, which resulted in tensions between spouses and between free and enslaved women in the same household. The trope of free women's nefarious collusion with enslaved women to achieve purposes misogynistically attributed to women is a distorted reflection of a reality of close (though again, for enslaved women, forced) cooperation. It also reflects the intimate access enslaved people had to their enslavers' relationships, bodies (for physical care), and homes.

The intimate part enslaved women played in family life is reflected in family death, or at least in its commemoration, where enslaved members of the household are presented, with more or less enthusiasm, as members of the family. Attributes which might differentiate enslaved from enslaver are sometimes hard to read. In turn, it is hard to tell whether this difficulty is because as modern viewers we are unaware of certain iconographic connotations that would have been instantly comprehensible to the ancient viewer, or because differentiation was not particularly important in the context of a death, where commemorators were more interested in affective than hierarchical relationships. Exceptionally, some enslaved nurses, who had a quasi-maternal role in life, were depicted in death as if they had been free family members. Together, our sources suggest that free women depended not just practically but also emotionally on the women they kept in slavery.

CHAPTER 4

Melinna and Phanostrate
How Women's Work Shaped Women's Relationships

Previous chapters have argued that the classical Attic family was relatively unstable, and that women's social experiences transcended, competed with, and shaped family structures. This chapter, through a new consideration of women's work-related dedications, alongside new readings of literary texts which draw out the relationship between women's work and social roles, demonstrates the role of women's remunerated work (work either for wages or for profit) within these dynamics. It suggests that the instability of the family sometimes brought women into remunerated work. It shows how remunerated work could challenge family relationships, by giving women a new axis and language of self-evaluation, offering them a different understanding of their role in and contribution to their household and society, and bringing them into contact with a wider range of people, enabling them to form relationships – economic, collaborative, affectionate, inimical – beyond their kin and neighbourhoods, which could compete with kinship ties.

For reasons of space, this chapter does not cover agricultural work, though historians have recognised the sociality of shared tasks and emotional experiences like threshing and harvesting.[1] Nor does it cover prostitution, distortingly overemphasised in scholarship on women's work.[2] The legal status of prostituted women in our sources is often unclear, but it seems that the majority, prostituted in *porneia* (brothels) and *oikēmata* (cubicles), were enslaved.[3] Enslaved prostitutes were not in any straightforward sense economic agents 'selling' (themselves, their bodies, body parts, time, acts), but girls and women enduring serial rape for the enrichment of their

---

[1] McHugh 2019; cf. the literary analyses of Karanika 2014 of grape-harvesting songs (pp. 115–27), threshing songs (153–9), and harvesting songs (201–8). On women's agricultural work more generally: Scheidel 1995, Scheidel 1996, Brock 1994: 342–4.

[2] Kennedy 2014: 123–61; Taylor 2024: 5–12.

[3] Compare Marshall 2013: 175–6. The descriptions of Davidson 1997: 78–92 are vague about this but anecdotally indicate the predominance of slavery.

enslavers.[4] Of course, this does not mean they were without agency or sociality. Indeed, a few enslaved prostitutes were able, initially by cultivating relationships with the men who paid to rape them and then by shaping these relationships into something less immediately violent, to obtain freedom.[5] We get an account of such a process in Apollodorus' *Against Neaira*; it is also the implied back story of several plays of Menander, including *Samia*. Such trajectories were probably rare; most girls and women enslaved in Athens' sex industry probably died enslaved and exercised what agency they had in less obvious ways, choosing between compliance in the hopes of increasing their chances of safety or better treatment, or small but significant acts of resistance (Aristophanes' *Wasps* includes a joke about an enslaved, prostituted woman who talks back to a man who demands a particular sexual position, ll. 500–2). Even free women in prostitution could be subject to slave-like conditions which further complicates the assessment of such prostitution as 'remunerated work'. Free prostitutes (*meretrices*) in Plautine comedies which draw inspiration from Menander are sometimes prostituted under compulsion by older female relatives in a situation analogous to debt bondage, from which they cannot free themselves.[6] Elements of the story of Neaira illustrate that even supposedly free, high-earning prostitutes could be controlled by the men who used them such that their condition was akin to slavery (Ap. *Neaira* 29–35).[7] Further, like Neaira (and perhaps the Samian Khrysis portrayed in Menander's *Samia*), most immigrant women in prostitution were probably sex-trafficking survivors. The trauma and dislocation this entailed left women in a state of high dependence which severely diminished their freedom.[8] Demeas in *Samia*, a man who himself uses *hetairai*, coldly describes how they 'drink strong wine' (to cope?) 'until they die, or they starve, if they don't do it readily and quickly' (πίνουσ' ἄκρατον ἄχρι ἂν ἀποθάνωσιν, ἢ / πεινῶσιν, ἂν μὴ τοῦθ' ἑτοίμως καὶ ταχύ / ποῶσιν, 394–6). Grouping women's experiences of sexual violence with other women's experiences of income-generating work risks false equivalence.

In Chapter 1, we saw how Nikarete (Dem. 57), separated from her husband and then widowed, worked as a wet nurse and sold *tainiai*. Euxitheos claimed Nikarete was not unusual: 'many women became nurses (*titthai*) and woolworkers (*erithoi*) and grape-harvesters (*trygētriai*) because of the troubles affecting the city at that time – citizen-status women – and

---

[4] Compare Marshall 2013: 175–6, 188–96; cf. Glazebrook 2022: 19–20, though I think her view on the modern sex industry and those involved in it is understates the predominance of enslavement, coercion, and violence.

[5] Compare Marshall 2013: 188–96. [6] Foxhall 2013: 176–7. [7] See also Foxhall 2013: 101–3.

[8] Marshall 2013: 194; cf. e.g. Men. *Sam.* 390–8.

many women who were poor are now rich' (Dem. 57.45). Producing textiles and harvesting crops would have been among the normal tasks of many women. However, the context here, where the roles are given names, presented as new for those engaging in them, grouped with the waged role *titthai* and linked to financial gain, shows that Euxitheos is making a claim about women newly taking on paid roles or adapting existing roles in order to monetise them: selling textiles produced or harvesting another house-hold's grapes for pay. Euxitheos suggests that the number of women making such changes was a result of 'the troubles affecting the city', which left many women without male breadwinners. He probably refers to the period between 415 and 403, which saw the Sicilian Expedition, Dekeleian War, first oligarchic coup and first democratic restoration, second oligarchic coup, rule of the Thirty, and *stasis*. Among those who began working to earn money after (temporarily) losing male breadwinners in the *stasis* were the women of Aristarkhos' family, described in Xenophon's *Memorabilia* 2.7; when their menfolk fled to Peiraieus, they became *erithoi* (wage-earning textile-workers). In *Thesmophoriazusae* (produced 411), Aristophanes por-trays a woman compelled to sell garlands to support her children following the death of her husband, perhaps in the Kypros campaign of 451 or 450 (ll. 443–58),[9] but with contemporary resonance for an audience reeling from the massive losses of the Sicilian Expedition.

Though the exceptionally destructive events of the late fifth century may have led to an unusually steep increase in the number of women working to earn, Attic women knew high levels of spousal death and absence regardless of political or military events. The demographics of classical Attica may have made female breadwinners common. Husbandlessness and female work were strongly associated among citizen-status women like Nikarete and Aristarkhos' relatives as they appear in literature, and perhaps among metics: the metic tax (*metoikion*) was levied at twelve *drakhmai* per year for men and for households headed by men; women not under the charge of male relatives were taxed six *drakhmai* a year.[10] Women living in house-holds with men did not pay tax in their own name. Of course, some married women whose husbands were not absent also did remunerated

---

[9] Sommerstein 1994 *ad loc.*

[10] Kennedy 2014: 2. Kapparis 2019: 90–1 argues that women who were not of Athenian citizen status but were part of Athenian *oikoi*, as Athenian men's informal partners (like Khrysis in Menander's *Samia*), or non-citizen-status relatives (illegitimate daughters or half-sisters) did not need to register independently as metics and pay the *metoikion*, because the *metoikion* was paid by the head of the household, and only by non-Athenian households; see Kapparis 2021: 33 for the potential dangers of this loophole for non-Athenian women when their relationships broke down.

work, alongside their husbands or in separate roles.[11] Excepting the garland seller, the familial circumstances of the many earning women in Aristophanes, mostly of citizen status,[12] do not merit mention by the poet. Though it may have been a matter of family pride for women not to earn, not all families could afford this pride – a tension discussed by Sokrates and Aristarkhos in Xenophon.[13]

This chapter begins with working women's portrayals of themselves, considering publicly visible dedications whose dedicators identified and represented themselves as earners. This is the first sustained consideration of these dedications as expressions of working women's attitudes to their employment. Most of these women describe themselves in terms other than their relationships to men. Two women use occupational nouns to describe themselves (*plyntria*, launderer, *IG* 1³ 794; *artopōl[is]*, bread seller, *IG* 1³ 546). Occupational terms are also used to describe women (and men) in the *phialai* inscriptions, records of one specific type of religious dedication,[14] and in comedy and oratory. Such designations need not have represented the full range of the person's economic activity: a woman who sold sesame seeds and could be described as a sesame seller (*sēsamopōlis*) might also have earned money by occasionally selling surplus products generated in the ordinary course of domestic vegetable-growing and animal husbandry, as well as contributing to her household economy with unremunerated tasks (cooking, cleaning, childcare). Occupational terms do, however, represent the occupation most salient in that context: the occupation by which a person chose to describe herself, or the role in which the speaker or writer encountered and interacted with her.

There follows an examination of the social lives of the many women who participated in the commercial textile economy, an extended case study of one area of remunerated work which emphasises the situatedness of women within commercial networks. It also asks a new question: how did women's remunerated labour affect interpersonal dynamics within a household? A new reading of the story of Aristarkhos' relatives, focusing on language around emotions and value, furnishes a partial answer.

The chapter goes on to demonstrate the commercial relationships entailed by women's involvement in the larger-scale supply chains of the sanctuary of Eleusis and the Akropolis Erekhtheion, and to consider

---

[11] Compare Brock 1994: 344, arguing against the assumption that women's labour was a response to crises.

[12] The innkeepers at *Frogs* 549–78 are metics; see p. 238.

[13] Compare Cohen 1989: 11–13 for how this conflict could be managed.

[14] See discussion at pp. 218–22.

women's interactions with clients and colleagues in public markets and semi-public shops. Curse tablets aimed at women retailers develop the 'social picture' of the networks women formed through remunerated work. These form a counterpart to joint dedications made by colleagues. Both show women situated and acting as workers within commercial networks rather than as family members in kinship networks.

The chapter concludes with two monuments for the midwife and doctor Phanostrate, which portray her as intimately connected with her clients' families. These monuments attest to the possibility that the emotional force of relationships arising from remunerated work could compete with, take on the character of, and even displace kin relationships.

Athena the Worker

Since at least the 1990s, historians have recognised that many women in classical Attica, including citizen-status women, earned money through work, despite the impression from classical literature that earning women were stigmatised, and that earning, citizen-status women were few.[15] Most recently and thoroughly, Claire Taylor has drawn attention to the ambivalence of these sources and to an 'alternative discourse' which valued female work. Using Amartya Sen's terminology, Taylor shows the transformative effect paid work could have on expanding women's 'capabilities' (what a person can do or be with the resources available to her), particularly by enabling them to develop and draw on interpersonal relationships.[16] Contributing voices to this discourse of value which Taylor does not address in her analysis are those of women themselves,[17] some of whom made dedications portraying themselves as earners. This chapter brings these voices into the discussion for the first time.[18]

Dedications of Working Women

Most of these dedications form part of a group of late archaic and early classical inscribed dedications from the Akropolis marked with the terms *dekatē* and *aparkhē*, respectively meaning 'tenth' and something like

---

[15] For example, Brock 1994, Labarre 1998.
[16] Taylor 2017: 135–47, with pp. 19–22 on Sen's 'capability' approach.
[17] She mentions the dedications briefly (p. 146) as evidence for women's prosperity through work.
[18] Jacqmin 2015's section on first-offerings (pp. 7–8) does not make a case for, or bring out, their significance as self-presentations of earners.

'preliminary offering from the whole'.[19] I argue here that at least some, perhaps most, *dekatai* and *aparkhai* made by women on the Akropolis represented proportions of work profits rather than of dowries, as is sometimes assumed. Following Claire Jacqmin's discussion of women's dedications as instances of self-presentation to the god and the community, I assess what inscribed first-offerings tell us about the role of remunerated work in women's self-presentation and relationships. While Jacqmin focuses on dedications which do not refer to men, my analysis brings together both dedicatory inscriptions which refer only to the dedicator's relationship with the god, and dedicatory inscriptions which also indicate human relationships, to show how remunerated work interacted with women's relationships and allowed women to position themselves within them.

Inscribed *dekatai* and *aparkhai* were one expression of the practice of offering a proportion of something to the gods as a 'first offering'.[20] Inscribed first-offering dedications (as opposed to, say, first-offerings at meals, or as cult fees) are strongly associated with earnings from work or, less frequently, other successes. Dedicators of first-offerings who describe themselves or their dedications in any detail often identify themselves by an occupational term or identify their dedications as proportions of work income (e.g. *IG* 1³ 628, Νέαρχος ἀνέθεκεν [hο κεραμε]|ὺς ἔργον ἀπαρχὲν τ̣ἀθ[εναίαι], 'Nearkhos [the pott]er dedicated (this) to Ath[ene] as a proportion of his works').[21]

Catherine Keesling argues that *aparkhē*, unlike *dekatē*, specifically refers to a first-offering from inheritance, citing Herodotus 1.92.2, in fact the only Herodotean instance in which the word is associated with inherited wealth.[22] This leads her to assume that women's *aparkhai* are proportions of dowries, which Athenian girls received out of their father's property. However, Theodora Jim's study of first-offerings shows that both *aparkhē* and *dekatē* dedications were typically made from profits of successful enterprises: work, trade voyages or sales of agricultural produce (which we would understand as 'work earnings', though our categories may not map on to theirs), and so on.[23]

---

[19] Jim 2014: 36–8.   [20] Jim 2014.   [21] See fn. 23.

[22] Keesling 2003b: 6–10, repeated at Keesling 2005: 398 (where she acknowledges that inheritance was not the only occasion for dedicating *aparkhai*); she is followed by Jacqmin 2015: 6. The other Herodotean uses are 4.71.4 (Scythian kings buried with *aparkhai* from their possessions) and 4.88.1 (architect of Darius' boat-bridge dedicates *aparkhai* from the reward he received from Darius for completing the bridge, i.e. earnings from work). In a second-century BC Egyptian papyrus, the word refers to a tax on inheritance (*UPZ* 11 162.7.10).

[23] First-offerings described as proportions of work earnings: Attica: *IG* 1² 730, 1³ 608 (supplemented), 628, 695, 766, 828, 11² 4320 (supplemented), 4334, 4587. Elsewhere: *I.Délos* 1417.A. 11.102–3, *IG* IX 1, 131, *IG* XI 4, 1248, *IGASMG* IV 15, *Lindos* 11 2 B 9–14, *SEG* 26:451, 28.838, 34.1189, Segre 1952 no. 100.

Less often, inscribed first-offerings are described as being 'of possessions', 'of wealth', or 'of silver'. Whether these represent proportions of profits from unmentioned enterprises or proportions of existing (as opposed to newly acquired) wealth is not clear; the distinction is somewhat artificial. First-offerings could be made on a range of occasions; inheritance was apparently one, but by no means predominant. Women may have dedicated first-offerings of dowries, but the practice is not attested.

One hundred and forty-five surviving Attic dedications describe themselves as first-offerings.[24] Most were marble or bronze and presumably required expenditure of accumulated savings, though people likely also dedicated less expensive items that have not survived.[25] (We know that women made dedications – though not specifically first-offerings – of wooden items at the sanctuary of Artemis at Brauron, for example, as well as dedications of gold, bronze, ivory, horn, and textiles.)[26] Of these self-described first-offerings, sixteen were made by women (see Appendix).[27] One identifies herself as a launderer (*plyntria*, *IG* i³ 794), implying that her *dekatē* was a proportion of income from washing clothes and other fabrics. One seems to have made her *dekatē* in the sanctuary of Athena Ergane, patron of craftspeople (*IG* ii² 4889). A third, also to Ergane, explicitly states that her *dekatē* came from possessions earned from working with her hands (*IG* ii² 4334). The others are less explicit, but given the overall pattern of first-offering dedications, it makes more sense to interpret them as proportions of work earnings than dowries, including the *aparkhai* (*IG* i³ 547, 615, 934). Evidently these women could afford monumental dedications. We

---

IG vii 37, Hicks 1891: 263–4, no. 49, and *Lindos* ii 88 and 291, are described as plunder 'earned' by soldiers or captains. Dedicator identified by occupation: Attica: *IG* i³ 616, 628, 633, 794, 824, 905. Elsewhere: *IGASMG* iv 15 (with Jim 2014: 145), *Lindos* ii 88, 291, *SEG* 28:838. First-offerings from unspecified wealth: Attica: *IG* i³ 647, 698, 730, 779, *IG* ii² 3846, 4904; cf. Isae. 5.42. Elsewhere: *SEG* 60:1130.14–15 (by a woman, first century AD). Other first-offerings: Attica: *IG* i³ 542 (athletic victory: Jim 2014: 150); *IG* ii² 2939 (crowning by *thiasos*). Elsewhere: *IGASMG* iv 2 (athletic victory); *SEG* 22:509 (manumission). Jim 2014: 142 suggests that *IG* i³ 800 and 735, mentioning *dekatē khorioō* (a tenth of the land), may be proportions either of farmers' produce or of the value of land acquired or sold. References assembled from Jim 2014: 130–75. On the terms: Jim 2014: 36–8 (*aparkhē*); pp. 47-8 (*dekatē*); 52–5 (difference between terms).

[24] Jim 2014: 131.   [25] Compare Jim 2014: 158–61, 172.

[26] IG ii² 1517.212, with Linders 1972: 46 *ad loc.*

[27] *IG* i³ 536, 540, 547, 548 bis, 565, 574, 615, 644 (a woman dedicating with a man), 767, 794, 814, 857 (reconstructed: δ[εκάτην]), 921, 934, *IG* ii² 4334, 4889. The name in *IG* i Suppl. 373,²⁰ '[Al]kippe ([Ἀλ]κίππη) dedicated a *dekatē*', is now read as 'Lysippos' (Λυ]σίππω, with ω for the genitive ending -ου, *IG* i³ 838). The missing text in *IG* i³ 700 (two women dedicating together) may have included the word *dekatē* or *aparkhē*.

recall Euxitheos' claim that many women who took up remunerated work became rich (πολλαὶ … πλούσιαι νῦν, Dem. 57.45).[28]

Most of these sixteen first-offerings from women are dated between 525 and 470; two are fourth-century. Survivals of inscribed first-offerings initially follow the chronological distribution of other inscribed dedications by Attic women, with a heyday between about 525 and about 475 and a dramatic trough across the rest of the fifth century.[29] There are no surviving women's dedications from 440 to 400, though sanctuary inventories for this period record women's dedications of metal and fabric alongside men's; women's dedications represent between a third and a half.[30] We do not know how many were themselves inscribed, and with what text. In the fourth century, women again made inscribed dedications in stone, to other gods as well as Athena. Only two of about forty-five are marked as first-offerings.

Matt Dillon argues that women (but not men) stopped making publicly visible dedications on the Akropolis after around 450 and instead made dedications inside the Parthenon and Erekhtheion after their completion in 432 and 406 respectively, which were kept in treasuries and recorded on publicly exposed inventories.[31] Dillon understands this transition as part of a cultural shift in which 'women and their piety to the gods become much less public'. Jacqmin, however, notes the possibility that dedications in the treasuries may have been exposed to the public.[32] She sees the transition to 'indoor' rather than 'outdoor' dedications as part of a longer, less straightforwardly gendered process of 'civic redefinition' bookended by the Kleisthenic reforms in the late sixth century and the Periklean Citizenship Law of 451, after which 'the family and the individual retreated into the inside of the temples to leave the "public space" to the community'. From a practical standpoint, the Akropolis would now have been crowded with dedications, another contributor to the shift. Catherine Keesling also suggests a trend away from inscribed stone offerings towards expensive metal dedications like gold crowns, which were kept inside temples.[33] To some extent, public inventories emphasised the collective dedicatory practice and collective identity of the community, as opposed to the wealth and prestige of the individual. They made *individual* women

---

[28] Compare Taylor 2017: 140: women's work was a means 'by which households made ends meet and perhaps also prospered'; see also her pp. 120, 146–7.

[29] Counting relevant inscriptions from those collected by McClees 1920: 45–6, with additions from Jacqmin 2015, twenty-three inscribed dedications by women in Attica between 525 and 440 survive; fifteen are marked as first-offerings.

[30] Kron 1996: 165, cited by Jacqmin 2015: fn. 31. [31] Dillon 2002: 17–18. [32] Jacqmin 2015: 4.

[33] Keesling 2003b: 61, also noting a move towards dedications at other sanctuaries, not just the Akropolis.

and their piety less visible, burying their names and dedications in *stoiche-don* (grid-form) lists designed to be cumulatively impressive rather than easily legible. Men had other spheres (politics, athletics, battle) in which to become visible and known; women had fewer. Unlike the dedication of monumental inscribed stone and bronze, which afforded a few women the ability to describe themselves to their communities, the inventorying process transferred the power of description to temple officials, who recorded the dedicator's name – though she might have chosen the naming formula[34] – and a simple description of the dedication.

The Dedications and Their Dedicators

As is typical of fifth-century female dedicators, women who dedicated first-offerings almost always described themselves without reference to other family members, using mononyms.[35] If these dedications were from work earnings, they are instances of women publicly describing themselves to their worshipping community and to other viewers, either explicitly or implicitly, as workers and earners.[36]

One such dedication is a marble pedestal base which once supported a marble basin, dedicated by a launderer named Smikythe in about 490–480. She had it inscribed: Σμικύθε πλύντρια δεκάτεν ἀνέθεκεν ('Smikythe the launderer dedicated a tenth', *IG* I³ 794). Smikythe identi-fies herself not by her position within a family, as a man's wife or daughter, but by her occupation. Her choice to dedicate a basin (rather than, say, a statue) may be part of her self-representation as a washer; one fuller also dedicated a marble basin as an *aparkhē*.[37] Jim notes that Smikythe's

---

[34] Compare Humphreys 2018: 388. Some dedications in the Brauron catalogues are described as ἄγραφος or ἀνεπίγραφος, which implies a norm of some kind of textual label.

[35] Jacqmin 2015's study of women's dedications on the archaic Akropolis takes as its corpus fourteen dedications in which the dedicator describes herself without a patronymic. Where Jacqmin empha-sises the individualism of these women's dedications and their equivalence to men's dedications, Avramidou 2015 argues that women made dedications on the Akropolis in their capacity as mothers, specifically mothers of citizens – but some of her readings are difficult to sustain; see p. 208. Counting from McClees 1920, in the fourth century, twenty-three out of about forty-two women dedicators of inscribed stone offerings refer to themselves without an andronymic, though seven of these say they are dedicating on behalf of their children or depict themselves with other family members. Fifteen use andronymics (*contra* Dillon 2002: 15, who says andronymics are the norm); in the other cases, the name form is unclear.

[36] For women's dedications as attestations of women's agency, competence, and awareness of their own position in relation to their society and to the deity, all constitutive of identity, see Blok 2018: 3–5.

[37] *IG* I³ 616. However, another fuller dedicated a marble column (*IG* I³ 905), while a man of unknown profession (Jim 2014: 136–7), dedicated seven marble basins as *aparkhai*. Kron 1996: 162–3 concep-tually separates the basin from Smikythe's work.

Figure 4.1 Miniature bronze shield dedicated by Phrygia, c. 500, Athens, Acropolis Museum NAM X6837. © Acropolis Museum, 2025. Photo: Socratis Mavrommatis.

dedication represents 'extraordinary expenditure for a washerwoman': either the profession was more lucrative than we might expect, or Smikythe saved for a long time, or both.[38]

Phrygia the bread seller dedicated a miniature bronze shield (about 10 cm in diameter) decorated with a gorgon's head (*gorgoneion*) in c. 500 (*IG* I³ 546, Figure 4.1). She did not mark it as a *dekatē* or *aparkhē* but did explicitly dedicate it in her capacity as a wage-earner by identifying herself with an occupation: Φρυγία ... hε ἀρτόπολ[ις] ('Phrygia the bread seller'). Her name suggests that she had been trafficked into slavery in Attica from Phrygia in Asia Minor.[39] By the classical period, Phrygians constituted a large proportion of the enslaved population of Attica,[40] and there was even a place in the deme of Athmonon, a little less than 7.5 miles from Athens, called 'Phrygia', perhaps

---

[38] Jim 2014: 171–4, noting Vickers 1985: 125, fn. 162.

[39] See Vlassopoulos 2010 and Vlassopoulos 2015 for the significance of names given to enslaved people in Attica, esp. Vlassopoulos 2015: 106–9 arguing that enslaved people with 'ethnic' names are likelier to have been taken into captivity from their birthplace rather than born into slavery.

[40] Vlassopoulos 2010 finds that 'Manes', a name the Athenians thought common in Phrygia and therefore often gave to Phrygians they had enslaved (Strabo 7.3.12), was the commonest name for an enslaved person in Attica (see esp. pp. 117–18). Lauffer 1979: 124–8 estimates that about a third of the enslaved mine workers at Laureion were Phrygian.

after its inhabitants (Thuc. 2.22.2; compare modern 'Chinatown').[41] Even in the late archaic period, Phrygia may have known other Phrygians in Attica.[42] Possibly she had since been freed; if so, it is interesting that she seems to have kept her name.[43] In either case, she seems to have adopted at least some Greek religious beliefs and practices and managed to put aside enough money from her work to make this dedication to Athena. Where Smikythe's choice of item may allude to the identity of the dedicator, Phrygia's alludes to the identity of the recipient, Athena, whose *aegis* usually featured a *gorgoneion*. Later, colossal statues of Athena on the Akropolis incorporated a *gorgoneion*, though not on her shield.

Phrygia had the shield inscribed: Φρυγία ∶ ἀνέθεκέ με τ̣ἀθεναίαι | hε ἀρτόπολ[ις] ('Phrygia dedicated me to Athena, (Phrygia) the bread seller'). Where such a simple dedicatory formula is used, small variations are noticeable. Smikythe expressed her occupation as a launderer as an integral part of her identity: Σμικύθε πλύντρια, where the noun is attributive. Phrygia had the words Φρυγία ∶ ἀνέθεκέ με τ̣ἀθεναίαι inscribed round the rim of the shield, then added hε ἀρτόπολ[ις] above, a predicative noun giving additional information. Did the cutter run out of space, or did Phrygia have these words added as an afterthought or clarification? The difference may reflect the differing role of the women's occupations in their self-presentation and self-perception.

Other dedicators do not mention occupations. However, those who chose to identify their dedications as first-offerings, implicitly of earnings, publicly identified themselves as earners by doing so. Between about 525 and about 475, nine or ten further women dedicated first-offerings without an andronymic:[44] Glyke (*IG* I³ 536), Meleso (I³ 540), Lysilla (I³ 547), Glyke (I³ 548 bis), Kapanis (I³ 565), [S]mikythe (I³ 574), Ergokleia (I³ 615), Empedia (I³ 767), Kal(l)is (I³ 814), Kal(l)ikrite (I³ 921). They dedicated marble columns and basins, bronze discs, statues, pots, and mirrors. The columns and statues would have been commissioned for the purpose of dedication and paid for out of the proportion of earnings set aside. The pots and mirrors may have been items the dedicators already owned, symbolically rather than precisely equated with the proportion to be

---

[41] See Hornblower 1991 *ad loc.*

[42] See Hunt 2015 and Forsdyke 2012: 27–9 on the possibility of enslaved people retaining a sense of ethnic identity and building ethnic communities in Attica.

[43] See Vlassopoulos 2015: 113–19 on the possibility of enslaved people choosing names for themselves or changing their names on gaining their freedom.

[44] Compare Jacqmin 2015: 5–6.

dedicated.[45] Marble basins and bronze pots were probably too valuable to have been used in work.[46]

Like their male contemporaries, almost all the dedicators use the same formula, with minor variations like word order inversions: Name + ἀνέθεκεν ('dedicated') + δεκάτεν/ἀπαρχέν ('a *dekatē/aparkhē*') + Ἀθεναίαι ('to Athena', sometimes with the definite article).[47] A possible later addition, with a longer inscription, is a Pentelic marble statue (only the base survives) from 470–450 (*IG* 1³ 857):

[Μ]ικύθη μ' ἀνέ[θηκεν]
[Ἀθ]ηναίηι τό[δ' ἄγαλμα] /
[εὐξ]αμένη δ[εκάτην]
[καὶ] ὑπὲρ πα[ίδων]
[κ]αὶ ἑαυτῆ[ς].

Εὔφρων [ἐπο]-
[ί]ησεν

Mikythe(?) dedicated me, this [statue], to Athena, as a [tenth], having made a prayer-vow, on behalf both of her children and of herself.
     Euphron made this.

The possible delta is not enough securely to identify this as a *dekatē*, but if the reconstruction is correct,[48] this may be the dedication of a working mother. Mikythe tells us she had prayed and vowed to make a dedication if her prayer were answered ([εὐξ]αμένη). She made the dedication 'on behalf both of her children and of herself', because she hoped Athena's favour would extend over them all, but perhaps also because they had all worked for or benefited from the income of which this represented a tenth. She does not mention the children's father. Instead, the inscription attests to a different relationship: a working relationship with Euphron, the sculptor Mikythe commissioned.

Evidently some women were able to dispose of considerable sums, which they apparently earned themselves. Smikythe the launderer and Phrygia the bread seller did so in ways which explicitly presented them as workers

---

[45] Snodgrass 1989–90: 291–2 distinguishes between commissioned ('converted') dedications, and already-owned ('raw') dedications. For women's dedications of pre-worn clothes at Brauron, see Cleland 2005: 9, 91.

[46] On the possibility and problems of dedicating 'tools', see Jim 2014: 145–8.

[47] All *dekatai* apart from *IG* 1³ 547, 615, and 934, which are *aparkhai*. *IG* 1³ 548 bis does not specify a dedicatee but may be a pair with 536; 921 'speaks' with a first-person pronoun: Καλ(λ)ικρίτε μ' ἀνέθεκεν, 'Kallikrite dedicated me'. Ἀθηναία is a variant spelling of Ἀθήνη.

[48] Jim 2014: 157, fn. 80 accepts the restoration.

Figure 4.2 Brass mirror handle with inscription, dedicated by Glyke, fifth century, Athens, Paul and Alexandra Canellopoulos Museum X 724.
© Paul and Alexandra Canellopoulos Museum. Photo: G. Vdokakis.

and earners; the others did so implicitly by marking their dedications as first-offerings.

Phrygia, Ergokleia, who dedicated a marble pillar (*IG* i³ 615), and Glyke, who dedicated a bronze mirror (*IG* i³ 548 bis, Figure 4.2) all pick out their names with triple interpuncts (⋮).[49] Apparently, they hoped to draw attention to their names: the attention of Athena, but also of potential human readers, wanting to increase the likelihood that those who saw their dedications would note and discuss the dedicators. That dedicators expected their dedications and themselves to be noticed and talked about is illustrated by the inscription on the base of a bronze statue from about 490–480:

πᾶσιν ἴσ' ἀνθρόποι|[ς] hυποκ|ρίνομαι, hόστις ἐ[ρ|ο]τᾶι· /
hός μ' ἀνέθεκ' ἀνδ|ρõν· "Ἀντι|φάνες δεκάτεν." (*IG* i³ 533)

To every person who asks which man dedicated me, this [dedication/ inscription] will say the same thing: 'Antiphanes, [as] a tenth.'

The inscription's economical response to the imagined questioners supports recent scholarly hypotheses about 'partial reading' of inscriptions, and the ways in which the arrangement of inscribed texts encourages readers to pick out essential information.[50] The response illustrates what the dedicator felt was essential: the dedicator's name and the type or purpose of the dedication – in Antiphanes' case, a *dekatē*. Phrygia, Ergokleia, and Glyke intended and expected those who saw their dedications to read their names aloud and talk about them in public as women who worked and earned.

Almost all the women who dedicated first-offerings named themselves and the god only (Mikythe mentions but does not name her children), but

---

[49] Interpuncts were often used to guide the reader, encouraging partial reading that pulled out the name of the dedicator: Keesling 2003a: 42–4; cf. Butz 2010: 20, 60–2.

[50] Day 2010: 39–40; cf. Keesling 2003a.

two also gave the names of a father and husband respectively. Their dedications attest to their human relationships as well as their relationship with Athena. Kallisto, identifying herself as [Καλ]λιστὸ Ναυκύδος θυγ[άτερ] ('Kallisto, daughter of Naukydes'), dedicated a marble basin to Athena around 480–470 as an ἀπαρχή (*IG* i³ 934). Much later, in the first half of the fourth century, another Kallisto dedicated a Pentelic marble statue (only the base survives) as a *dekatē* near the supposed site of the sanctuary of Athena Ergane, Athena the worker, patron of crafts (including and especially textile work) and craftspeople. This may suggest it was a proportion of earnings from craftwork, most likely textile manufacture. She had it inscribed: [Καλ]λιστώ [ἀνέ]θηκεν δεκάτην Σιβυρτίο γυνή, 'Kallisto dedicated a tenth, wife of Sibyrtios' (*IG* ii² 4889). By the fourth century, it was much commoner for women to use andronymics in dedicatory inscriptions, though many still used mononyms. We have too few inscribed women's dedications from the mid and late fifth century to know when this trend began; to my knowledge, Kallisto, daughter of Naukydes, who dedicated the basin around 480–470, was the first in Attica. If the statue base of Kallisto, wife of Sibyrtios, represented a *dekatē* of earnings as opposed to other wealth or income, she was apparently a married woman disposing of her income, simultaneously holding and publicising the roles of 'worker' and 'wife'.

What was the status of the women who made these dedications? Native Athenians or immigrants?[51] Married, never-married, widowed? There is no reason to assume they all belong in the same socio-legal category. Humphreys suggests they were all widows,[52] which is unnecessary; Kallisto wife of Sibyrtios, though late in the distribution, was probably not. The label for Glyke's mirror at the Canellopoulos Museum states that it is προφανώς ανάθημα εταίρας ('obviously the dedication of a *hetaira*'). This is not obvious at all. It is not clear whether the inference is drawn from her name, 'Sweetie', in fact very common in Attica, including among citizen-status women,[53] or from the mirror, which the curators perhaps take as a 'tool of her trade', but other women owned and used mirrors. The Beazley archive records myriad fifth-century Attic pots decorated with women holding mirrors, which tells against a link with *hetairai*.[54] Amalia

---

[51] The legal status of 'metic' was probably not defined until later than most of these dedications were made, perhaps the 460s: Kennedy 2014: 12–14.

[52] Humphreys 2018: 412.

[53] *LGPN* ii *s.v.* Γλύκη; see Taylor 2020 on the problem of reading certain names (including names beginning with Glyk-) as '*hetaira* names'.

[54] Note also Bérard and Durand 1989: 33 on the mirror in Attic pots as a signifier of female domestic space.

Avramidou attempts to read as many as possible of the forty Akropolis dedications (not just first-offerings) made by women between 530 and 450 as 'maternal dedications'.[55] She argues that bronze vessels like those dedicated by Kapanis and Smikythe, and marble basins like those dedicated by Smikythe the launderer and Kallisto, daughter of Naukydes, may have been associated with postpartum purification, 'an appropriate gift to Athena and other family gods for granting a safe delivery of a future citizen, and at the same time, [a signal of] the end of pollution after birth'.[56] The dedicators' explicit description of some of these dedications as proportions of income, which Avramidou acknowledges,[57] tells against this hypothesis.

When a woman made a dedication, she interacted both immediately, and transcendentally and continually with the worshipping (and touristic) community.[58] In making a dedication, she literally appeared at the sanctuary, interacting with family, friends, enslaved people from her household and from the temple, and temple officials. Afterwards, she continued to be present there and to interact with visitors and previous and future dedicators through her dedication, as well as physically returning to sacrifice and show others the dedication.[59] A dedication was a public statement to her community of who she was within that community. Women's earnings gave them the opportunity to describe themselves to the public; some chose to describe themselves as workers.

A Case Study: Melinna

In the second half of the fourth century, a woman named Melinna dedicated a Hymettian marble altar or statue base on the Akropolis as an *aparkhē* to Athena Ergane. This might be considered along with the earlier fourth-century statue base of Kallisto, wife of Sibyrtios, associated with Athena Ergane's Akropolis sanctuary, which may also draw a link between the dedication's recipient and its nature as a share of income from remunerated labour. Melinna had the dedication inscribed with the following epigram (*IG* II² 4334, EM 8804, Figure 4.3):[60]

---

[55] Avramidou 2015.

[56] Avramidou 2015: 19, but note that these dedications pre-date the Periklean Citizenship Law: in this period, any woman could be the mother of an Athenian citizen, provided the child's father was Athenian.

[57] Avramidou 2015: 7.

[58] Compare Jacqmin 2015: 3: 'This written utterance [the inscription] allows these women to dialogue with the rest of the community, reaffirming on each occasion [of reading] her place in the heart of the city.'

[59] Compare Herodas' *Mime* 4, with Day 2010: 69–73.

[60] The catalogue number in *IG* II² is erroneously given as 8004.

Figure 4.3 Melinna's dedication, second half of fourth century, Athens, Epigraphic Museum EM 8804. © Hellenic Ministry of Culture/Hellenic Organization of Cultural Resources Development (H.O.C.RE.D.). Photograph by author.

χερσί τε καὶ τέχ[ν]αις ἔργων
τόλμαις τε δικαίαις /
θρεψαμένη τέκνων γεν[εὰ]ν
ἀνέθηκε Μέλιννα /
σοὶ τήνδε μνήμην, θεὰ Ἐργάνη,
ὧν ἐπόνησεν /
μοῖραν ἀπαρξαμένη κτεάνων,
τιμῶσα χάριν σήν.

With her hands and the skills of her work, and with righteous daring, Melinna raised a generation of children, and (having done so) dedicated to you, goddess Ergane, this memorial, offering as first-fruits a share of the possessions for which she laboured, in honour of your favour.

Melinna's epigram foregrounds her work. She begins with the hands and skills she used in her work; she identifies her dedication as the product of her toil (*eponēsen*, from *ponos*); she dedicates it to Ergane, goddess of craftwork. She then sets her work and moral character in the context of her motherhood: though her skill and effort earned her possessions, from which she made her dedication, she first points out that that skill and effort enabled her to raise her children. This is the primary achievement she celebrates. The assertion that she raised them by her work (*erga*) suggests she was a single mother. Her situation recalls a much earlier working mother – the first single working mother in Western literature – described by Homer, who sings of how the battle lines of the Greeks and Trojans were evenly strained,

> . . . ὥς τε τάλαντα γυνὴ χερνῆτις ἀληθής,
> ἥ τε σταθμὸν ἔχουσα καὶ εἴριον ἀμφὶς ἀνέλκει
> ἰσάζουσ᾽, ἵνα παισὶν ἀεικέα μισθὸν ἄρηται.   (*Il.* 12.433–5)

> as a woman, a careful woman who earns by the work of her hands, holding a pair of scales, draws up the weight and the wool equally on both sides, keeping them evenly balanced, to gain a pitiful (even 'shameful') wage for her children.

Melinna's poem, however, has none of this pathos. Melinna articulates values of *tekhnē* (technical skill), *tolma* (courage, daring, or endurance), *dikaiosynē* (justice or righteousness), *ponos* (toil or labour), and *timē* (honour) for the gods. The language of *tekhnē* and *ponos* is found in other first-offerings,[61] but *tolma* and *dikaiosynē* are more intriguing. *Tolma*, 'endurance', 'courage', 'daring', even 'guts', may refer to Melinna's persistence in work and childrearing, perhaps working long hours or enduring the gossip that circulated about women who worked for pay,[62] and women raising children without husbands, common though both circumstances were. Packard Humanities Institute's Greek epigraphy database has this as the sole attestation of the stem *tolm-* in Attic inscriptions before the second century BC, except in names.[63] The noun does not appear in any known Attic inscription of any period; the verb *tolmaō* is most common in late antique curses against grave desecrators. *Tolma* is, however, common in Greek tragedy, where it often has the negative sense of 'audacity'. While it is sometimes used of dignified courage, including of women,[64] it more often describes men and women doing or plotting shocking, transgressive things (murder, violence, adultery).[65] In the case of women, such 'audacity' is implicitly also transgressive of gendered expectations of female shame. It is striking that a woman should use it of childrearing; clearly she felt that

---

[61] Jim 2014: 150, fn. 58.

[62] Inferable from Dem. 57.30–6 and Xen. *Mem.* 2.7.6, discussed at pp. 213–4.

[63] The one possible exception is a reconstruction, ἐὰ-|[ν δέ τις τολμᾶι ἀδικεν], in *IG* 11² 111, a decree of 363/2.

[64] For example, Eur. *Alc.* 741, *Heracl.* 555.

[65] Of men, e.g. Aesch. *Choe.* 1029, Eur. *Hipp.* 937, Soph. *Aj.* 46, 1004, *OT* 125; of women, e.g. Aesch. *Choe.* 996; Eur. *Andr.* 837, *Hec.* 1123, *Hipp.* 414, *Med.* 394, 859, Soph. *Trach.* 582–3. The cognate poetic verb *τλάω is used similarly: its frequent occurrences in Aesch. *Ag.*, for example, cover the murders by Agamemnon and Klytaimestra and the adultery of Helen, as well as courageous endurance of suffering.

what she had achieved was remarkable. Possibly what we have here is a woman combatively reappropriating a gendered term, asserting that her courage, though transgressing gendered expectations, was *dikaios* – 'righteous', 'legitimate', 'proper'.

Dikaios and its cognates appear frequently in fourth-century Attic decrees and honorific inscriptions, mostly describing the required or rewarded conduct of officials or benefactors,[66] though one Diopeithes son of Strombikhos set up a dedication on the Akropolis in honour of another man, possibly his paternal uncle, as a 'memorial of his *dikaiosynē*' ([μνῆ]μα δικαιοσύνης, *IG* 11² 4881 + *SEG* 30:174, early fourth century).[67] *Dikaios* is also used of the dead, male and female, in fourth-century Attic sepulchral inscriptions.[68] Even if the quality was conceived of as primarily civic (though this may reflect the biases of Attic epigraphic culture), it was also used to praise private conduct. Melinna may have been participating in the language of honorific and sepulchral inscriptions, visible around the *asty*.[69]

Dikaios can have the sense of 'god-sanctioned', 'socially acceptable, normative', or 'legal'.[70] The third sense is probably not relevant here. Evidently Melinna did believe her *tolma* – persistence or courage at her work? – was god-sanctioned: she says she has been shown favour by Ergane. A hexameter song composed in the fifth century but imagined to have been sung by Homer for some potters is in part a cletic prayer to Athena for her protection over their production process:

δεῦρ' ἄγ' Ἀθηναίη, καὶ ὑπέρσχεθε χεῖρα καμίνου,
εὖ δὲ μελανθεῖεν κότυλοι καὶ πάντα κάναστρα,
φρυχθῆναί τε καλῶς καὶ τιμῆς ὦνον ἀρέσθαι,
πολλὰ μὲν εἰν ἀγορῆι πωλεύμενα, πολλὰ δ' ἀγυιαῖς,
πολλὰ δὲ κερδῆναι . . .   ([Hdt.] *Vit. Hom.* 32 = [Hes.] frg. 302 West, ll. 2–6)

Come, Athena, and hold your hand over the kiln!
May the *kotyloi* (cups) and all the *kanastra* (dishes) turn a good black,
may they be well fired and fetch the price asked,
many being sold in the marketplace and many on the roads,
and bring in much money . . .   (Trans. Marjorie Milne, adapted)[71]

---

[66] For example, *IG* 11² 143, 204, 217, 223, 1149.   [67] Humphreys 2018: 410, Ma 2013: 203, fn. 15.

[68] Men: *IG* 11² 7268, 13098, 12034 (an enslaved man?), and others. Women: *IG* 11² 9112, 12749, 12244a + 13123 = *SEG* 30:280; later, *IG* 11² 12141.

[69] Blok 2018: 23–4 suggests Xenokrateia, who uses the word *didaskalia* in her dedicatory inscription (*IG* 1³ 987), was influenced by 'the visibility of the verb *didasko* . . . on choregic monuments'.

[70] Compare *DGE s.v.*   [71] In Noble 1966: 106–7.

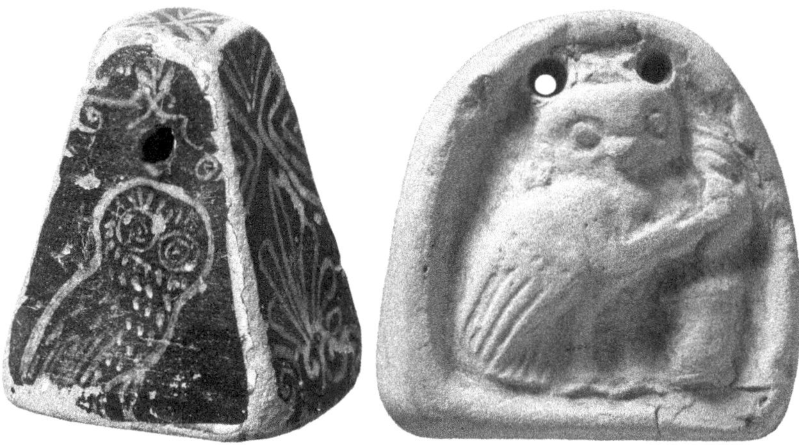

Figure 4.4 Loom weight from the slopes of the Akropolis, decorated with an owl, fifth century. Athens, Acropolis Museum GL I.2758. © Acropolis Museum, 2025. Photo: Vangelis Tsiamis.
Figure 4.5 Loom weight(?) from Taras (modern Taranto, southern Italy) showing an owl spinning wool, late fourth or third century. Bryn Mawr, Bryn Mawr College, Special Collections, Accession No. T. 182. Gift of Cornelius C. Vermeule.

Given Melinna's emphasis on the skill of her hands, among other factors, the work she discusses in her dedication was most likely textile production, though it could have been ceramics, or some other form of artisanship. We may imagine her making a similar prayer over her work, vowing to make a dedication if her prayer was fulfilled. A fifth-century loom weight from the slopes of the Akropolis decorated with an owl, Athena's bird, may suggest women's sense of Athena's involvement in their textile work (Figure 4.4). (What may be a loom weight from Taras, a Greek *polis* in southern Italy, even shows an owl carrying out an earlier stage of textile production: spinning, Figure 4.5.)[72] Some Attic women stamped their loom weights, or had them stamped, with seals engraved with images of Athena.[73] As we saw in Chapter 1, Greek women sometimes 'personalised' loom weights with seals; impressions of cosmetic and personal items like hairpins, earrings, tweezers and gaming pieces; or incised letters or symbols.[74] 'Personalised' loom weights could

[72] Though see Ferrari and Ridgway 1979: 291, arguing that this is not a loom weight but perhaps a pendant.
[73] From the Pnyx: Davidson, Thompson, and Thompson 1943, no. 134, p. 92, with fig. 39; from Building Z in the Kerameikos: Knigge 2005, no. 74, p. 118; no. 128 (inv. 5689r), p. 127; no. 509 (inv. 5093u), p. 180; no. 599 (inv. 5028), p. 190; no. 600 (inv. 5030), p. 191.
[74] Foxhall 2011, Foxhall 2012, Quercia and Foxhall 2014.

become markers of family or even ethnic identity, passed down from mother to daughter. Seals used by wealthier women in Attica had a variety of designs – lotuses, palmettes, chariots with galloping horses, dancers, Penelope[75] – and likely had a variety of significances to their owners. The popularity of impressing loom weights with an engraving of Athena, usually showing the goddess in a long garment with a spear and shield, may indicate the owners' pride in belonging to Athena's city, but also perhaps their sense of the goddess' intimate involvement in the tools and processes of weaving. For Melinna, her subsequent success in her work was thanks to Ergane's favour (*kharis*) over it.

Alternatively or additionally, Melinna used *dikaios* to mean 'socially acceptable', affirming the dignity and respectability of her work and perhaps distinguishing it from 'shameful' means of earning. In Xenophon's *Memorabilia*, the figure of Aristarkhos says that ἐλεύθεροι, freeborn people, cannot be made to work like 'bought foreigners' (i.e., enslaved people), implicitly because it would be socially inappropriate and shameful (2.7.6). Sokrates attempts to persuade him by reframing work as an absolute virtue, whatever the worker's status. Instead of speaking in terms of status, he reframes leisure as τὴν μὲν ἀργίαν καὶ τὴν ἀμέλειαν ('idleness and indolence') and labour as τὴν δ᾽ ἐργασίαν καὶ τὴν ἐπιμέλειαν ('industry and carefulness'), which he evaluates as χρήσιμα ('useful', 'good', 2.7.7). In Demosthenes 57, Euxitheos takes a similar line against Euboulides' attempts to shame him and his mother for working. He pointedly reminds Euboulides that he is beholden to 'another law, about idleness' (καὶ ἕτερος περὶ τῆς ἀργίας νόμος), which he ought to remember when he slanders Euxitheos and his mother, who – and now the verb has become one of dignity – work (ἡμᾶς τοὺς ἐργαζομένους, Dem. 57.32). Back in Xenophon, Sokrates adds a more conservative line of argument:

> εἰ μὲν τοίνυν αἰσχρόν τι ἔμελλον ἐργάσασθαι, θάνατον ἀντ᾽ αὐτοῦ προαιρετέον ἦν· νῦν δὲ ἃ μὲν δοκεῖ κάλλιστα καὶ πρεπωδέστατα γυναικὶ εἶναι ἐπίστανται . . . (Xen. *Mem.* 2.7.10)

> Now, if they were going to do some shameful (*aiskhros*) work, death would be preferable to that; but as it is, the work they understand [i.e. textile production, the work Sokrates is proposing] is the most honourable and fitting for a woman . . .

Sokrates argues that working is not inherently shameful for freeborn women. Rather, certain types of work are shameful, and others are the

---

[75] See examples in Davidson, Thompson, and Thompson 1943: 80–94 with figs. 34 and 39 (pp. 83 and 92 respectively), Knigge 2005, index *s.v. Webgewichte mit Stempel.*

opposite. By 'shameful' work, he may be referring to prostitution.[76] Other types of work sometimes understood as 'shameful' in elite discourses include work for hire, which some orators framed as incompatible with citizenship status,[77] or work in public (Euboulides apparently emphasised the fact that Nikarete's work in the *agora* rendered her φανερὰν πᾶσιν, 'visible to everyone', Dem. 57.34), but it is not clear whether Xenophon's Sokrates would have rejected these attitudes too. Sokrates has previously pointed out (2.7.8) that textile production is the type of work these women learned in early life (2.7.8; cf. *Oec.* 7.6), with the intention of using it. He erases the ideological distinction made – even if only as an ideal – between domestically oriented textile work and income-generating textile work, making it seem not undignified and inappropriate, but virtuous, normative, and socially appropriate: *dikaios*.[78]

Euxitheos engages with these contradictions and asserts the respectability of Nikarete's work in similar terms. He says that given her poverty, her wet-nursing was ἴσως καὶ ἀναγκαῖα καὶ ἁρμόττοντα ('perhaps both necessary and appropriate', Dem. 57.42). Evidently Nikarete judged the work necessary in order to support herself and, like Melinna, raise her children. Euxitheos implies that the very necessity of the work rendered it appropriate – probably a perspective Nikarete shared. Euxitheos and Nikarete might also have judged paid wet-nursing 'appropriate' in the sense that Xenophon's Sokrates judged textile production 'most fitting' (πρεπωδέστατα) for women: childcare, like textile production, was a normative unpaid occupation of women. As noted in Chapter 1, Taylor convincingly argues for an 'alternative discourse' around wet-nursing, particularly among women, which valued nurses and their work. She bases her argument on increasingly idealised images of nurses in fourth-century terracotta figurines, literary depictions of nurses as knowledgeable household authority figures and confidantes, and affectionate, respectful commemorations of nurses on gravestones (cf. pp. 69–72). Nikarete, whose work enabled her family to survive and even to flourish, may have

---

[76] Despite the claims of Cohen 2015: 36–69 and others that prostitution was considered shameful only insofar as it constituted 'work for hire', or that 'sitting in a brothel was no more despicable to the elite than working in the agora' (Glazebrook 2011: 35), it is clear from passages like Ap. *Neaira* 107–34 and Isae. 13–15, and from prevailing Athenian attitudes to women, their bodies, and their sexuality, that prostitution in any form was predominantly considered inherently and particularly shameful.

[77] Kennedy 2014: 124–5.

[78] Aristarkhos draws a sharp ethical and status distinction between weaving for household use and weaving for sale, for which distinction see Kennedy 2014: 123–5; contrast Lewis 2002: 62–3. The sale of surplus textiles may in fact have been common.

judged it not just 'fitting' (ἁρμόττοντα/πρεπωδέστα) but 'very honourable' (κάλλιστα, Xen. *Mem.* 2.7.10). Euxitheos tells the jury not to scorn the poor, particularly τοὺς ἐργάζεσθαι καὶ ζῆν ἐκ τοῦ δικαίου προαιρουμένους ('those who choose to work and to live by decent (*dikaios*) means', §36). Melinna judged her work *dikaios*; Euxitheos judged Nikarete's work likewise, a judgement she likely shared.

Attempting to recover women's perspectives from Demosthenes and Xenophon requires us to 'read against the grain', but Melinna's epigram directly expresses her perspective. Such an unusual poem is unlikely to have been a 'ready-made' composition into which a poet simply inserted Melinna's name, adjusting for metre, and adapted a few details. If Melinna commissioned it, she presumably gave the poet specifics, and the epigram closely reflects the sentiments she wanted to express. Alternatively, the entire composition is her own. In ancient Greek literature, weaving in particular – which may have been how Melinna made her income – is strongly associated with poetic composition.[79] The use of song as a mnemonic for weaving patterns, attested in twentieth-century Greece and Afghanistan, suggests this is more than a metaphor.[80] This poem is a rare record of a woman's own attitudes to her work.

As well as asserting the dignity and respectability of her work, Melinna collapses the distinction sometimes assumed between remunerated work and mothering. She describes herself as having raised a generation of children (θρεψαμένη τέκνων γεν[εά]ν) with her hands and by the skills of her work (χερσί τε καὶ τέχ[ν]αις ἔργων). That she is referring to remunerated labour (not just the manual, skilled work of childcare) is evident from the reference later in the epigram to the 'possessions for which she laboured' (ὧν ἐπόνησεν / … κτεάνων). Her remunerated craftwork was part of her work of bringing up her children.

Melinna's choice of Ergane as a dedicatee for an *aparkhē* of work income, along with Kallisto's *dekatē* (*IG* ii² 4889), probably dedicated in Ergane's sanctuary, should alert us to the possibility that other women's dedications to Ergane may be connected to income-generating craftwork rather than domestically oriented textile production, as might otherwise be assumed. Ergane was patron of both. The Khalkeia, her joint festival with Hephaistos, patron of metalwork, seems to have been celebrated mainly by paid craftworkers, but every fourth year was

---

[79] For example, Snyder 1981. [80] Tuck 2006; see Karanika 2014: xi for Greece.

the day on which the *arrhēphoroi*, two or four well-born girls chosen to help weave the Panathenaic *peplos*, set up the warp for the task.[81] The record in the Erekhtheion building accounts of 1,000 *drakhmai* for a sacrifice by the Erekhtheion builders and artisans probably made at the Khalkeia around the time of the building's completion is another instance of her worship by those who earned money through craftwork.[82] With this in mind, we may reconsider two further fourth-century women's dedications – not first-offerings – to Ergane. The first woman, whose name is lost, dedicated a pillar, on which she described herself as 'daughter of [name also lost] of Akharnai' (– – – (15) – – – | [Ἀ]χαρνέος θυγάτη[ρ] | Ἀθηναίαι Ἐργάνει | ἀνέθεκεν, *IG* ι² 561).[83] The second dedicated a statue, of which the Hymettian marble base survives; she described herself as 'Hedyle, [daughter/wife] of Euphron' (['Η]δ[ύ]λη Εὔφρο[νος – – –] | [Ἀθ]ηνᾶι Ἐργά[νηι ἀνέθηκεν],' *IG* ιι² 4328).[84] Hedyle and the woman from Akharnai may have been invoking Ergane's care over the domestic textile production on which they spent so many hours and in which much of their esteem by self and others resided, or they may have been *arrhēphoroi*. But considering their dedications alongside those of Melinna and perhaps Kallisto, we should be open to the possibility that they dedicated in their capacity as earning craftswomen, making statements of their trust in Ergane's care over their work, and of their own pride in it.

Much earlier, around 560–550 BC, someone dedicated a painted clay tablet (*pinax*) on the Akropolis, which shows a woman in an elaborately decorated *peplos* (Acropolis 2525, Figure 4.6). She is bent over a table with arms extended, apparently hard at work. Four lengths of material hang on the wall, possibly *tainiai* or skeins of yarn tied at the ends. Behind her sits a smaller female figure, painted white to indicate nudity.[85] She may hold an object but seems not be engaged in the work; she is probably a child playing while her mother works. The child's presence casts the woman as a mother, yet the work of her mothering is not direct childcare but some kind of production. Possibly it is tablet-weaving, a technique used to produce small textiles like *tainiai*; unlike loom-weaving, tablet-weaving could be stopped and started as necessary if there were children needing

---

[81] Parker 2005: 266, 409, 464–5.
[82] *IG* ι³ 477.7–8, supplemented by Parker 2005: 464 as X ν[ν εἰς θυσίαν τοῖς Χα]-|λκείοις τῆι Ἀθηναίαι, with Lambert and Morgan 2016: 5–10.
[83] EM 6305, Raubitschek 1949: 89; cf. *IG* ι³, Fasc. 2, p. 972.   [84] EM 8751.
[85] Avramidou 2015: 11.

Figure 4.6 Attic black-figure *pinax* showing a woman at work with a girl behind her, c. 560–550, Athens, Acropolis Museum 2525. © Acropolis Museum, 2025. Photo: Vangelis Tsiamis.

attention.[86] The Acropolis Museum's label describes her as a 'Woman in household occupation' (Γυναίκα σε οικιακή ασχολία), but she could well be producing textiles for sale. Schulze judges it certain ('*sicher*') that 'the *tainiai* hanging on the wall refer to the woman's occupation (*Tätigkeit*)'.[87] This is not certain, but it is possible, given the number of *tainiai* (if that is what they are) and the fact that they are not in use. Schulze, describing the scene as 'unique in Attic painting', proposes that the *pinax* is 'entirely a commissioned work, made to the exact specifications of a dedicator [feminine], whose occupation (*Beruf*) is represented on the *pinax*'. He suggests that, like Smikythe's basin, the dedication is 'a testimony to women's employment (*Berufstätigkeit*)'. Avramidou, commenting on the identification of the *pinax* as a 'craftsman's (*sic*) offering', points out that the image 'would be appropriate for a dedication made by a mother

---

[86] Lin Foxhall's suggestion (pers. comm.); though Foley 2003: 118 suggests she is weaving, Foxhall, following Nixon 1999, points out the impossibility of weaving on a loom with small children around: weaving (and also the prior processes of planning a design and setting up the loom) requires total concentration and is not easily interruptible. This explains the absence of loom-weaving scenes that include children. In any case, the image does not show a conventional loom: small frame looms in Greek art are always shown vertical (Clark 1983; examples include a later fifth-century red-figure lid, NAM BS58, Athens). For tablet-weaving, cf. pp. 68–9. Schulze 2004: 38 describes her as 'busy spreading out or kneading a white mass, woollen material or dough'; given the skeins or *tainiai* on the wall, wool at some stage of processing seems likeliest of the two. Graef and Langlotz 1909 (no. 2525) think she is washing clothes.

[87] Schulze 2004.

running a business: not only does she offer her gratitude to Athena ... for helping her sustain a living but at the same time she publicizes her skillful work'.[88] The possibility that she is working to earn deserves serious consideration.

A better understanding of the relationship between first-offerings and remunerated work, and between the worship of Ergane and remunerated work, allows us to reread certain dedications by women as testimony to their work, their attitudes to that work, and its place in their self-perception and self-presentation. The overall impression given by this collection of dedications is that women's roles as earners could stand independently of or integrally to their roles as family members.

Inside the Textile Industry

Edward Harris has argued that upscaling and monetising domestic work was a common economic strategy in classical Attica.[89] There is strong literary and epigraphic evidence for the practice of monetised textile production in particular.[90] Small-scale production of textiles for sale had the potential to shape household relationships by redefining women's contributions to the household economy, enabling women-headed households to survive and even thrive, and compelling and enabling women to form commercial relationships with buyers and retailers outside their households and families.

Producers, Retailers, and Buyers of Textiles

Textile production for profit is best attested among metics. Fifty-three woolworkers, *talasiourgoi*,[91] are attested in the so-called *phialai* inscriptions,

---

[88] Avramidou 2015: 11–12. She later rejects this interpretation as part of her rereading of women's Akropolis dedications as primarily concerned with motherhood, suggesting instead that the *pinax* is a woman's thank-offering to Athena for her weaving ability as part of the household management skills she will pass on to her daughter, doing double service to 'advertize' for this 'promising bride'. Given the emphasised childishness of the girl, this latter element is unlikely. As a second alternative, she suggests that the *pinax* may be connected to the ritual role of weaving Athena's Panathenaic *peplos*, assigned to young girls. This is hard to connect with what is depicted.

[89] Harris 2002; Harris 2014; see Tsakirgis 2016 for archaeological evidence.

[90] Tsakirgis 2016 argues that weaving surplus for sale was more likely among wealthy families who could afford the necessary resources, but among the women we encounter in this chapter were those who spun or combed rather than wove, which could be done on a small scale. Cf. Taylor 2017: 132, fn. 67.

[91] Rosivach 1989: 365–8 argues that the term *talasiourgos* denoted a 'housewife'; this is rightly rejected by Wrenhaven 2009: 370, who in turn argues that the term denoted a prostitute, rightly rejected by Kennedy 2014: 126, 131–3.

an inventory of dedications of silver *phialai* (offering dishes) which lists dedicators with their name, often an occupational designation, and their place of residence. The dedications have traditionally been understood as marking manumissions. More recently, Elizabeth Meyer has convincingly but controversially interpreted them as marking unsuccessful prosecutions of metics for failure to pay the metic tax or to register a *prostatēs*.[92] Even on the traditional interpretation, if most formerly enslaved people who had a designated occupation continued in that occupation after liberation in order to support themselves, the inscriptions still record metic professions, but of newly rather than historically free metics: formerly enslaved people who remained in Attica assumed metic status.

Meyer counts 413 surviving entries in the inventories, 156 male, 116 female, and 141 of unidentifiable gender. In these 413 entries, 160 occupational designations are preserved, of which 53 are *talasiourgoi*, 'wool-workers'.[93] *Talasiourgoi* account for over 80 per cent of the women listed with an occupational term.[94] By my own count based on Meyer's edition, there are probably 122 female entries (the larger number accounts partly from an assumption that all *talasiourgoi* are women, and that this can therefore be used to reconstruct gender, as well as from some more confident readings), though among this total I count only 48 *talasiourgoi*. The occupations of the women and girls attested or probably attested in the inscriptions are given in Table 4.1.

Talasia strictly refers to an amount of wool weighed out for a project and, from there, to the tasks involved in processing such wool (deworming, washing, beating, combing, spinning); weaving came after this (see Figure 4.7 for illustrations of some of these phases). *Talasiourgoi* may have carried out all or most of these tasks.[95] Guy Labarre shows that most lived and worked in Peiraieus or in four *asty* demes: Melite, Kollytos, Kydathenaion, and Skambonidai. Others lived just outside the walls in Keiriadiai or Alopeke. By my readings and reckonings, of the forty-eight *talasiourgoi* probably attested in the inscriptions (the term *talasiourgos* must sometimes be reconstructed), the residence of nineteen is securely

---

[92] Meyer 2010. For a lucid, up-to-date summary of the debate, see Hewitt 2023: 61–9.

[93] Meyer 2010: 14–15.

[94] Labarre 1998: 793, following Rosivach 1989: 365; see Meyer 2010: 15, fn. 19 on the gender of the *talasiourgoi*.

[95] Labarre 1998: 791–2. Labarre includes both carding and combing in his list of processes, but Lin Foxhall (pers. comm.) notes that, in general, Greeks combed wool but did not card it, carding being unnecessary for spinning on a drop spindle.

Table 4.1 *Occupations of women and girls in the* phialai *inscriptions, listed by frequency and then alphabetically, followed by non-occupational entries*

Occupation	Translation	Women/girls for whom occupation is reconstructed	Women/girls for whom occupation is securely or very probably attested	Probable total of women and girls listed with this occupation	% of all women and girls	% of known occupations attested for adult women
ταλασιουργός	textile worker	6	42	48	39.3%	76.2%
καπηλίς	tavern-keeper	1	2	3	2.5%	4.8%
σησαμόπωλις	sesame seller	1	1	2	1.6%	3.2%
τίτθη	nurse		2	2	1.6%	3.2%
ἀκέστρια	seamstress		1	1	0.8%	1.6%
αὐλήτρια	flautist		1	1	0.8%	1.6%
νευρορράφος	stitcher (or shoemaker)	1		1	0.8%	1.6%
κιθαρῳδός	lyre-player		1	1	0.8%	1.6%
λιβανωτόπωλις	frankincense seller		1	1	0.8%	1.6%
μελιτόπωλις	honey seller	1		1	0.8%	1.6%
πσ⟨η⟩κ⟨ἰ⟩στρι (ψηκτρία?)	groom?	1		1	0.8%	1.6%
ταπε- (ταπιδυφάντις?)	carpet maker?	1		1	0.8%	1.6%
παιδίον	infant		6	6	4.9%	
Lost or not given			53	53	43.4%	
Total given occupations (not including children)				63	51.6%	
Total adult women				116	95.1%	
Grand total				122		

Figure 4.7 Stages of textile production as depicted on an Attic black-figure *lekythos* attributed to the Amasis painter, c. 550–530, New York, Metropolitan Museum of Art 31.11.10. Fletcher Fund, 1931. From left to right (not the order in which the processes were carried out): spinning; drawing washed, raw wool into rovings, loose rolls of fibre which would then be spun into threads; weaving on a warp-weighted loom; weighing out allotments of wool for projects; making rovings; folding finished textiles. Here as in most depictions, women work in pairs or small groups at most textile production tasks, for efficiency and company.

attested; residence can be reconstructed with some confidence for nine more (see Table 4.2). Of these twenty-eight, twenty-three probably lived in or near the *asty*, with probably four more in Peiraieus;[96] one, Rhodia, lived in Thorikos, and another, Okimon, (remarkably) lived in 'Hephai-', perhaps Hephaistia on the Athenian cleruchy of Lemnos. In this, the *talasiourgoi* follow the distribution of the other metics who dedicated *phialai*, who mostly lived in Peiraeus or in and around the *asty*.[97]

Labarre demonstrates considerable demand for textiles for the fleet at Peiraieus: naval catalogues roughly contemporary with the *phialai* inscriptions attest to the need for sails, foresails, and fabric awnings to protect crew from weather and missiles.[98] The repeated rebuilding of the navy (notably after the losses of the Sicilian Expedition in 413; under Konon in the late 390s; and from 378 at the rise of the Second Athenian Confederacy) would have kept producers busy. In 357/6, during the Social War, there was such a shortage of linen sailcloth in Peiraieus that a decree was passed compelling incoming trierarchs to recover it from outgoing trierarchs ([Dem.] 47.20). Labarre also suggests that the large population of Athens 'represented a large-scale market' for textile products and concludes that the tension between time-consuming textile production techniques and high demand for textile products necessitated that production be 'plentiful and dispersed'. 'Dispersion' is also suggested by literary sources,

---

[96] Compare Labarre 1998: 796–7.   [97] Meyer 2010: 14.

[98] Labarre 1998: 799–800. Catalogues: *IG* ii² 1604–32; see references to παραρρύματα λευκά (white – i.e. linen? – awnings); παραρρύματα τρίχινα (hair awnings); κατάβλημα (cloth tarpaulin); ὑπόβλημα (undersheet? bedding?); ἱστία (sails), etc., in 1609, 1613, 1620, 1621, 1622, 1624, 1625, and 1631.

Table 4.2 *Residence of* talasiourgoi *in the* phialai *inscriptions*

Residence	Location	*Talasiourgoi* definitely resident	*Talasiourgoi* probably resident	*Talasiourgoi* probably or definitely resident
Melite	*asty*	6	3	9
Kydathenaion	*asty*	1	5 (either Kydathenaion or Kydantidai, in the Mesogeia)	6
Peiraieus	port	3	1	4
Alopeke	just outside *asty*	2		2
Keiriadai	just outside asty	2		2
Ankyle	just outside asty	1		1
Kollytos	asty	1		1
Skambonidai	asty	1		1
Thorikos	mining district	1		1
Hephaistia?	Lemnos?	1		1
Total in or near asty		14	7	21

which depict citizen-status and metic women producing textiles at home to sell. In many cases this would not have been 'full-time' work: textile production was one of many tasks by which women contributed to their households; selling surplus textiles could generate extra income.[99] High demand for textiles may have brought large numbers of women into the industry; Euxitheos' mention of *erithoi* in Demosthenes 57.45 suggests that meeting that demand could provide ready money for women even in times of crisis.

One could sell (or buy) 'finished' textile products, but also part-worked materials for their production. There is a variety of occupational terms associated with different stages and types of textile production;[100] attention to these stages sheds light on specialisation within the industry and offers glimpses of the networks to which this work gave women access. As well as *talasiourgoi*, the *phialai* inscriptions attest to an *eriopōlēs* (seller of unspun wool; a metic *eriopōlēs* is also attested in an honorific inscription of 401/ 0),[101] two *stuppeiopōlai* (sellers of unspun flax, hemp, tow, or oakum), a *porphyrobapheus* (purple-dyer, who presumably bought in materials, dyed them purple, and sold the finished products) – all male – and a female *akestria* (seamstress, producing clothes by sewing material together). The orator and logographer Hyperides wrote a defence speech for woman called Mika in which he mentioned that she (or possibly someone else discussed in the speech) hired cushion- or mattress-weavers (ἐμισθώσατο τυλυφάντας, Hyp. frg. 125 Jensen).[102] Mika was probably a metic given that her name is preserved in the speech title (we would expect a periphrasis for a woman of citizen status); that she could afford a famous logographer may suggest that she ran a successful textile business. A fifth-century mime by Sophron of Syracuse and a fourth-century comedy by Antiphanes were titled *Akestriai* and *Akestria* respectively. A fourth-century *stēlē*, discussed at pp. 226–7, names a *himatiopōlis* (woman seller of *himatia*, IG 11² 11254), which is also the subtitle of a third-century comedy by Apollodorus of Karystos (frg. 30). These attested occupations allow us to situate *talasiourgoi* within supply chains: *talasiourgoi* were presumably supplied by *eriopōlai* and *stuppeiopōlai*, and in turn supplied *akestriai*, dyers, and *himatiopōlides*. In a premodern economy like Attica's, these were not just supply chains

---

[99] Compare Lewis 2002: 62–3.

[100] Compare Labarre 1998: 796; on the stages of textile production themselves, see Spantidaki 2016.

[101] *IG* 11² 10+2403, with *SEG* 12:84 and 44:34. Alternatively, but less likely, the word in the *phialai* inscription is *erioplytēs*, wool-washer.

[102] = Pollux 7.191. There is no particular reason to think Mika was a *hetaira*, *contra* Kapparis 2021: 67–8.

but chains of economic – and in some cases affective – relationships: sellers would have interacted with buyers.

Literature may offer glimpses of these supply chains. Crates the Cynic, writing across the later fourth and earlier third centuries, mentions a poor married couple combing wool together:[103]

> καὶ μὴν Μίκκυλον εἰσεῖδον . . .
> τῶν ἐρίων ξαίνοντα, γυναῖκά τε συγξαίνουσαν,
> τὸν λιμὸν φεύγοντας ἐν αἰνῇ δηιοτῆτι.
>
> I saw even Mikkylos . . .
> combing wool, and his wife combing with him,
> in a terrible battle to escape famine.

The internal context suggests they were combing this wool for sale. We do not know to what rhetorical use Crates put the description when he composed it, but Plutarch quotes the lines approvingly as an example of using every means possible to earn money rather than stoop to borrowing (*Mor.* 830d). In praising Mikkylos and his wife, Plutarch, like Xenophon's Sokrates, sets himself against an elite culture which opposed work in favour of leisure at all costs. Though Plato often uses a hypothetical male weaver as an example,[104] the description of a married couple doing textile work together in their home is unusual. The point is that they are so desperate that the man is willing to take on the work his wife does in order to help her; in their desperation, the couple dispenses with gendered norms.

Perhaps Mikkylos and his wife could be described as *eriopōlai*, or perhaps they sold small amounts of their combed wool to *eriopōlai* who sold wool on a larger scale. Xenophon's Aristarkhos is said to have bought so much wool for his female relatives to spin and weave for sale that he had to take out a loan (*Mem.* 2.7.12). In the large household of Xenophon's *Oeconomicus*, one of the wife's tasks is to apportion wool to enslaved women in the household for spinning, a task she learned in her childhood home (7.6). Her own textile labour is in the later (more prestigious?) stages of production, namely weaving and storing garments (7.21, 25; 10.10, 11).[105]

---

[103] Fragment 6 Bergk, quoted in Plut. *Mor.* 830c (*That one should not borrow*, Περὶ τοῦ μὴ δεῖν δανείζεσθαι).

[104] *Phd.* 87b–c; *Grg.* 490d, 517e; *Resp.* 369d, 374b (cf. Acton 2015: 160); there is less evidence for men in other stages of textile production, except fulling. For gender and wool-working in the Hellenistic and imperial periods, see Labarre and Le Dinahet 1996.

[105] Note the (enslaved?) old woman described as εἰροκόμος, who 'worked' (ἤσκειν) wool *for* Helen, *Iliad* 3.386–9. This (preparatory?) 'work' may have been combing, spinning, or both. High-ranking women do not comb wool in the Homeric epics (the verb ξαίνω only appears of enslaved women, *Od.* 22.423), but both high-ranking and enslaved women spin and weave.

Women in smaller households who did not have enslaved workers or time to comb and spin as much wool as they needed might have bought thread for weaving which had already been combed and spun in other households. This division of labour across households, along with the variety of occupational terms, attests to the potential for specialisation within the textile industry: a woman's circumstances or talents might have lent themselves to a particular production stage in which she then developed expertise and efficiency.[106]

A figure in Aristophanes' *Frogs* offers another hint at the lives and work of women in these early stages of textile production. In the play, the character Aeschylus mocks the character Euripides' pride in composing plays about οἰκεῖα πράγματ[α] ... οἷς χρώμεθ', οἷς ξύνεσμεν ('homely things, which we're familiar with, which we know well', l. 959) by composing a pseudo-Euripidean monody about a woman whose housemate has stolen her cockerel.[107] She describes what she was doing at the time of the theft:

ἐγὼ δ' ἁ τάλαινα προσέχουσ' ἔτυχον
ἐμαυτῆς ἔργοισι,
λίνου μεστὸν ἄτρακτον
εἰειειειλίσσουσα χεροῖν
κλωστῆρα ποιοῦσ', ὅπως
κνεφαῖος εἰς ἀγορὰν
φέρουσ' ἀποδοίμαν.   (1346–51)

I, ah, poor wretch, was just busy
with my work,
wi-i-i-inding with my hands
a spindle full of flax
to make a skein, so that
I could take it to the *agora*
while it was still dark, to sell.

Sommerstein comments, 'the singer's concern to get to the Agora before dawn suggests that she will be selling her yarn to a stallholder rather than

---

[106] *Contra* Acton 2015, who seems to argue that specialisation was the norm in most Attic industries, but that textile work was not specialised (p. 160); he also suggests that 'everyday wear was hard to differentiate' and understands textile production as 'undifferentiated craft' (p. 163), which is hard to reconcile with this evidence for specialisation or with the astounding variety of materials and styles of clothing dedicated at Brauron and described in detail by its cataloguers, including with terms denoting quality (see e.g. Cleland 2005).

[107] This woman spins at home and then takes her skeins to the market to sell; contrast the garland seller in Ar. *Thesm.* 443–58 who seems to make the garlands in the market where she sells them.

direct to the public: if she arrives too late, other suppliers will have got in first and the stalls will all be fully stocked for the day'.[108] This is probably overreading: markets in modern Mediterranean villages are generally already lively before dawn;[109] it could equally signal her industriousness, her anxiety to make the sale, her desire to get a good 'pitch' in the *agora*, or her need to attend to many other demands on her time. However, it is still possible that a woman working on this small scale sold her skeins to a stallholder supplied by a number of spinners. If she went every day to the same stallholder, or one of a few, they would have built up a relationship, probably with expectations of reliability.

Menander uses the phrase εἰς ἀγορὰν ὑφαίνειν ('weave for the *agora*'), which is glossed in the Suda as τὸ εἰς τὴν ἀγορὰν ἐκφέρειν τὰ ὑφαινόμενα, 'taking what one has woven out to the *agora*' (frg. 962 Kock; Suda *s.v.*). The gloss suggests that the woman who produced the item would herself take it to the *agora*, like the *Frogs* flax-spinner, though perhaps a man would ideally go if there was one. The emphasis on *taking* the weaving (ἐκφέρειν, cf. φέρουσ[α], *Frogs* 1351), rather than selling it, may suggest the weaver sold her work to a retailer who retailed it to the public, rather than operating a stall herself.[110] Lin Foxhall suggests that, in other cases, women who produced surplus textiles in their homes may have arranged for retailers or their agents to come discreetly to the house to buy them (or men may have arranged this on their behalf).[111] This allowed women and their families to avoid the criticism that could attach to women who worked in the *agora* and may also have offered the women who made the textiles the opportunity to assert the value of their skills and time and to negotiate their prices. Perhaps this was how Aristarkhos' female relatives, who spun and wove the wool he bought into clothing (Xen. *Mem.* 2.7.5), made their sales.

Some textile retailers too were women. A fourth-century Pentelic marble funerary *stēlē* commemorates Ἐλεφαντὶς : ἱματιόπωλις, ('Elephantis the *himation* seller', *IG* ii² 11254). As with the early fifth-century launderer Smikythe and bread seller Phrygia, Elephantis is described by name and occupation, without reference to a male relative. She may have worked at the ἱματιόπωλις ἀγορά (clothes market) Pollux mentions (8.78).[112] The choice of inscription suggests she had built up a commercial reputation in which she and her commemorator took pride. It was probably lucrative

---

[108] Sommerstein 1996 *ad loc.*   [109] I thank Lin Foxhall for this observation.
[110] Contrast the Byzantine bread-seller at Ar. *Vesp.* 235–9, who made and retailed her own bread.
[111] Pers. comm.   [112] Compare Ar. *Plut.* 982–5.

work: a *himation* (cloak) might cost between sixteen and twenty *drakhmai*[113] – well above the '*medimnos* of barley' limit discussed in the Introduction to this book.[114]

Where were these women's *kyrioi*, if they had them? (Metics had *prostatai* rather than *kyrioi*, whose role was primarily to represent them in court if necessary.) Xenophon's Sokrates tells Aristarkhos (acting informally as *kyrios* while his relatives' *kyrioi* are in Peiraeus) to respond to his female relatives' criticism that he does no work by saying that, like the dog who, by keeping thieves and wolves at bay, allows the sheep to feed (νέμεσθαι) in peace, Aristarkhos is ἀντὶ κυνὸς … φύλαξ καὶ ἐπιμελητής, 'a guard, in place of a [guard-]dog, and an *epimelētēs* (person in charge)', who enables the women 'to live and work unharmed by anyone, safely and pleasantly' (οὐδ' ὑφ' ἑνὸς ἀδικούμεναι ἀσφαλῶς τε καὶ ἡδέως ἐργαζόμεναι ζῶσιν, 2.7.13–14). Labarre comments: 'Therefore, men must often have played a supervisory role ('*un rôle de contremaître*') in production and have controlled commercial relations with the outside world. That must have been the case for Elephantis the cloak-seller, whose commercial activity was certainly supervised by her *kyrios*.'[115]

This is an over-technical reading. Aristarkhos *is* described as an *epimelētēs*, which has the sense of 'person in charge' and is often used of officials.[116] However, though the word is not used in domestic contexts, the role Sokrates describes is a domestic, familial role rather than a commercial one: *protection* (rather than supervision or management in the 'factory foreman' sense) is the ideologically conventional (unpaid) role of the *kyrios*, a word which also means 'person in charge'. Xenophon also uses the word *kēdemōn* (2.7.12), which has the sense of 'having charge', but with specific focus on protection.[117] Aristarkhos is compared to a guard dog who keeps sheep safe, not a herding dog who gives them directions. If he were taking an active commercial role, the women would have had no grounds for complaint. (This implies that any role he had in negotiating sales was minimal.) The women's ideologically conventional role as wives and daughters has been monetised, but the man's role has not successfully made the transition.[118]

---

[113] Ar. *Eccl.* 408–13, 16 *drakhmai* (c. 393-1); *Plut* 982–3, 20 *drakhmai* (388); *IG* ii² 1672.102-103, 18 *drakhmai* 3 *oboloi* (329/8).

[114] See pp. 39–40.   [115] Labarre 1998: 800–1.   [116] LSJ *s.v.* ἐπιμελητής.

[117] The word is closely linked to kinship at Ar. *Vesp.* 731, where it is paired with *syngenēs*, 'kinsman'; in the same play, the action of a sheepdog is described with the verb ἐφίσταμαι, 'to be stood over' (l. 955).

[118] Compare Taylor 2017: 129: 'By the end of the anecdote Aristarchos is himself cast in the role of dependant, not the women … He has to reassert his masculinity by becoming a guard-dog, not merely to protect but in order to have a role within his family at all.'

Labarre's extrapolation sits uneasily with the evidence that in many cases women themselves sold what they produced without the intervention of a *kyrios* or equivalent. This would have been simple necessity in the case of women who headed their own households like the *Frogs* flax-spinner. However, it was probably also the case for working women in male-headed households where necessity outweighed the societal ideal of male supervision and commercial representation – for example, when the man was engaged in another occupation outside the home. Men may have 'controlled commercial relations with the outside world' in cases where retailers came to producers' households to negotiate and make purchases, but this seems not to have been the rule.

We have one example of a metic household in which a woman produced textiles while her husband worked outside the home: a *talasiourgos* from the *phialai* inscriptions, named Malthake and working in Keiriadai. Recorded alongside her, in the same deme and freed or escaping prosecution by the same man, are a man named Attas and three children, Plangon, Moskhon, and Aristonike (*SEG* 18:36 B 112–22).[119] Attas was likely Malthake's husband; at any rate, he was an adult man in her household. His occupation was not that of supervisor or textile seller, but pulse seller (*ospriopōlēs*).[120] He worked selling pulses, presumably in the *agora* (Keiriadai was just outside the city walls), and she worked producing textiles, presumably at home unsupervised.

The division and dispersion of monetised textile work brought women into supply chains and networks, and so into relationships; regular suppliers and regular buyers would over time form relationships of familiarity and trust. Particularly for women without an involved *kyrios* figure, selling home-produced textiles could expand their networks and reduce their isolation, as well as increasing their independence by allowing them to support themselves financially. The potential scale of these networks is illustrated by the example of Thettale, recorded as having sold *piloi* (fulled cloth caps) to the overseers and treasurers of the sanctuary of Demeter and Kore at Eleusis in 329/8, to be worn by enslaved men engaged in building

---

[119] Each child is designated *paidion*, 'small child'.

[120] There were female pulse sellers (*ospriopōlis*, Σ Ar. *Plut.* 427), but Malthake was not one. This undermines the argument of Rosivach 1989: 358 that 'women without an occupation of their own could be identified by the same occupation as their mate (*sic*), when this was appropriate (e.g. *kapēlos/kapēlis, sēsamopōlēs/sēsamopōlis*); and when it was not appropriate because of her mate's profession (e.g. *chalkeus, grammateus*) the woman was simply called *talasiourgos*, since woolworking was typically the work of women, especially married ones'. Why describe someone as a sesame seller if she did not sell sesame?

work there (*I.Eleusis* 177.70–1).[121] Her name ('Thessalian') suggests she came from Thessaly, either as an enslaved woman named by her seller or buyer, or a free immigrant whose nickname stuck. In 329/8, she was probably either free or freed, given that the transaction is in her name – unless she was an enslaved worker who lived apart from her enslaver and paid him or her some of her proceeds.[122] That this and similar sanctuary purchases from women are in the seller's name, implying direct purchase from her without a middle*man*, is further testimony against Labarre's hypothesis that women's *kyrioi* 'controlled commercial relations with the outside world'.

Piloi were probably made from woollen cloth thickened by soaking it in water and beating it, which causes barbs on the wool fibres to hook together; this process is called 'fulling' or 'waulking'.[123] This could probably have been done in an ordinary house, and the felt dried on the roof. There was plenty of demand in Attica for tough, waterproof, fulled cloth from travellers, fishers, and shepherds, who wore *piloi* to protect them from the weather, and perhaps the Athenian cavalry, who may sometimes have worn mantles based on the Thracian fulled cloth *zeira*.[124] In selling *piloi* to the Eleusinian officials, who may have commissioned her, Thettale formed a professional relationship with them – perhaps she was paid by Nikophilos of Alopeke, *tamias* (treasurer) in 329/8 – but also formed part of a huge, diverse operation encompassing 167 craftspeople, vendors, and workers in the two years recorded by the surviving accounts.[125]

Production At Home and Household Relationships

How did monetisation of domestic textile production affect household dynamics? Xenophon's Sokrates assures Aristarkhos that productive labour will improve interpersonal relations in his household:

νῦν μέν, ὡς ἐγῷμαι, οὔτε σὺ ἐκείνας φιλεῖς οὔτ᾽ ἐκεῖναι σέ, σὺ μὲν ἡγούμενος αὐτὰς ἐπιζημίους εἶναι σεαυτῷ, ἐκεῖναι δὲ σὲ ὁρῶσαι ἀχθόμενον ἐφ᾽ ἑαυταῖς· ἐκ δὲ τούτων κίνδυνος μείζω τε ἀπέχθειαν γίγνευθαι καὶ τὴν προγεγονυῖαν

---

[121] = *IG* II² 1672.70–1. [122] Compare Chapter 1, fn. 48 for such people.
[123] Fulling/waulking differs from felting, which uses hot water and an alkali. It would have been difficult to sustain a consistent supply of hot water in Greek houses or workspaces, which rarely had fixed hearths, let alone furnaces of the sort attested in buildings where felt was made in Roman Pompeii (for which buildings see Moeller 1976, Dickmann 2011 66–71, Dickmann 2013; note the wall-painting in the Casa Dei Postumii of a woman behind a table who may be selling felt shoes: Dickmann 2013: 219, fig. 13.15).
[124] Lee 2015: 124–5. [125] See Clinton 2008: 190–4.

χάριν μειοῦσθαι. ἐὰν δὲ προστατήσῃς ὅπως ἐνεργοὶ ὦσι, σὺ μὲν ἐκείνας
φιλήσεις, ὁρῶν ὠφελίμους σεαυτῷ οὔσας, ἐκεῖναι δὲ σὲ ἀγαπήσουσιν,
αἰσθόμεναι χαίροντά σε αὐταῖς, τῶν δὲ προγεγονυιῶν εὐεργεσιῶν ἥδιον
μεμνημένοι τὴν ἀπ' ἐκείνων χάριν αὐξήσετε, καὶ ἐκ τούτων φιλικώτερόν τε
καὶ οἰκειότερον ἀλλήλοις ἕξετε. (Xen. *Mem.* 2.7.9)

> As things are, I imagine, you do not love (*phileō*) them nor they you, because
> you think them burdensome to you and they see that you are troubled
> because of them; in these circumstances there is a danger that [their?]
> resentment will increase and [their?] sense of affectionate obligation (*kharis*)
> diminish. But if you take charge (*prostateō*) so that they work, you will love
> (*phileō*) them, seeing that they are beneficial/useful (*ōphelimos*) to you, and
> they will feel affection (*agapaō*) for you, seeing that you are happy because of
> them, and having (masculine plural, including both Aristarkhos and the
> women) fonder memories of past kindnesses, your (pl.) sense of affectionate
> obligation will increase because of them, and in these circumstances, you
> (pl.) will be dearer and closer (*oikeioteros*) to one another.

Sokrates primarily imagines the women's feelings as responses to
Aristarkhos' feelings about them: they do not love him because they
recognise he is bothered by them; they will love him because they will
recognise that he is pleased by them. This may be an 'other-focused'
articulation of what is today understood as 'self-esteem'. While today
one might say that the women's capacity for positive relationships
improves because of their increased self-esteem, deriving from an appreci-
ation of the value of their work (an explanation focused on the self),
Sokrates says that the women will love Aristarkhos more because they
will recognise that they make him happy because of their usefulness to him
(an other-focused explanation – or just an androcentric one).[126] More
focused on the women's experiences of themselves is Sokrates' earlier
comment that work one knows how to do is pleasurable: πάντες ... ἃ
ἐπίστανται ῥᾷστά τε καὶ τάχιστα καὶ κάλλιστα καὶ ἥδιστα ἐργάζονται,
'everyone works easiest, quickest, best, and with most enjoyment at work
that they know how to do'. This implies an understanding that they might
derive happiness from their recognition of their own abilities and skill,
from the fact that they can do the work very well, as well as without the

---

[126] Compare Gilligan 1982's 'care perspective' of moral development and particularly of women's
moral agency, summarised by Gilles *et al.* 2024b: 6–7: 'The care perspective stipulated that the self
is predominantly occupied with and concerned for others rather than focused on one's autonomy;
therefore, one's decision making was heavily influenced by one's caring relations ... a person's
identity and agency were shaped by their connection to their social context and relationships with
others.'

frustration of doing something slow, difficult, or shoddy.[127] Sokrates also predicts an increase of *kharis*, an intrinsically reciprocal feeling which combines the ideas expressed by the English words 'favour' and 'gratitude': mutual goodwill engendered by reciprocal obligation.[128]

Broadly, Sokrates' expectations are proved correct:

> ἱλαραὶ δὲ ἀντὶ σκυθρωπῶν ἦσαν· καὶ ἀντὶ ὑφορωμένων ἑαυτοὺς ἡδέως ἀλλήλους ἑώρων, καὶ αἱ μὲν ὡς κηδεμόνα ἐφίλουν, ὁ δὲ ὡς ὠφελίμους ἠγάπα. (2.7.12)

> And the women were cheerful instead of sullen; instead of eyeing [m. pl., including Aristarkhos and the women] each other with suspicion, they looked on each other fondly, and the women loved (*phileō*) him as a guardian, and he felt affection (*agapaō*) for them because they were useful.

However, Aristarkhos reports that the women now criticise him (αἰτιῶνται) because he is the only one in the household (μόνον τῶν ἐν τῇ οἰκίᾳ) who is idle (ἀργὸν ἐσθίειν, literally 'eats idle'). Their objection is that he consumes resources without producing them, a striking inversion of a misogynistic strain in Greek thought which characterises *women* as consumers of the products of men's labour.[129] The women are presented as having become economically aware: they recognise their economic contribution and note and object to the absence of such a contribution from Aristarkhos. They have a new way of understanding and evaluating their household, which upsets its traditional dynamics. Though Aristarkhos has traditional authority as the male householder, the women derive a new kind of authority from their monetised economic contribution in the non-traditional (or at least non-conventional for the elite) monetised household. Aristarkhos lacks this kind of authority, which enables them to criticise him.[130] Sokrates must attempt to reframe

---

[127] Neither Sokrates nor Aristarkhos mentions the enslaved workers of the household (cf. 2.7.2) and the effect of the changes on their emotions and relationships.

[128] Thuc. 2.40.4 neatly illustrates the dual sense of the word: 'We have also always been unusual as regards doing good: for we acquire our friends not by receiving favours but by doing favours. The one who does the favour (*kharis*) is a firmer friend, so as through [continued] kindness to retain the gratitude (*kharis*, understood) owed him by the one for whom he did it; but the one who owes a favour is more indifferent, knowing that he will not be returning the kindness as a favour, but as an obligation.'

[129] For the traditional conception, see Ma 2024: 505 on West 1978 *ad* Hes. *Op.* 373–4 (cf. my Chapter 3, fn. 64).

[130] Compare Blok 2001: 96–7 for women undermining male authority even in a traditional context by reminding the men of their dependence on them.

Aristarkhos' traditional role in the economic terms newly adopted by the women in order to counter their criticisms.[131]

What of the household arrangements of other textile producers discussed in this chapter? The woman in *Frogs* seemingly works alone. Crates' Mikkylos and his wife work together at the same task; the expression ξαίνοντα ... συγξαίνουσαν suggests unity. This is the unity of shared struggle and fear of hunger, but also shared and equal work, not the ideal articulated in Xenophon's *Oeconomicus*, where husband and wife have distinct spheres of work, presented as complementary and equal but in fact hierarchised under the husband's direction. Malthake and Attas' relationship differently challenged societal ideals. They were engaged in different occupations in different places, both contributing to household income. I have suggested that such arrangements undermined the ideal of male guardianship, even in non-citizen households where the formal institution of *kyrieia* did not technically apply.[132]

We saw how Melinna articulated an expanded vision of motherhood which framed her work as part of her childrearing. Malthake's work and her mothering would have interacted in various ways. Because textile production could be done at home, unlike Attas' work as a pulse seller, probably done from a market stall or home-adjoining shop, Malthake might have been able to look after Plangon, Moskhon, and Aristonike while she worked;[133] we recall the *pinax* showing the woman at work with her daughter playing nearby. This might have been an advantage of earning through home-based textile work. In place of an occupational designation, each of Malthake's children is described as *paidion* (little child). This implies they were too young to earn in their own right, which must have been quite young: wages are attested for *paides* (children) in documents from the first and second centuries AD.[134] However, in most families children would have been expected to carry out domestic tasks, and older children may have been more helpful than the girl on the *pinax*. Foxhall argues, partly based on comparative ethnographical evidence from western Mongolia and the Sirwa

---

[131] Note, however, that Sokrates' reframing subtly recasts the women as *consumers* rather than producers: Aristarkhos' reframed relationship to them is like that of the guard dog who allows the sheep to *feed* (νέμεσθαι) in peace (see p. 227).

[132] Metic women were expected to conform to Athenian gender norms: Kennedy 2014: 26–67, esp. 56–8. The *metoikion* implicitly understood metic women in male-headed households to be economically dependent on the head of household; see my p. 196.

[133] Weaving while caring for children under five would have been nearly impossible (cf. fn. 86); other types of textile work might have been less of a problem, or Plangon, Moskhon, and Aristonike might have been older.

[134] Scheidel 2010: 435.

mountains in Morocco, that girls in ancient Greece were gradually inducted into textile work in their childhood homes by observation and imitation; they likely begun by cleaning and combing wool for spinning, then learning to spin themselves, before eventually moving on to more physically and technically challenging tasks like weaving on a warp-weighted loom, which they would perfect under the tutelage of in-laws in their marital homes.[135] Child domestic labour could be monetised like female domestic labour; Malthake, Plangon, and Aristonike might have worked together like Mikkylos and his wife.

Together, these case studies suggest that the monetisation of women's domestic work had the potential to shift and reframe interpersonal relations and power dynamics within the household in women's favour.

Women in Retail

Women Workers in Supply Chains

The accounts of the overseers and treasurers of the Eleusinian sanctuary of Demeter and Kore for 329/8 (*IG* 11² 1672 = *I.Eleusis* 177), along with the Erekhtheion building accounts for 405/4 (*IG* 11² 1654, now *SEG* 50:69),[136] record purchases from Thettale the cap-seller and three other women. Unlike Thettale, who sold fulled cloth caps she probably produced herself in her home or workshop, the others sold building and decorating materials, which they apparently brought or bought in from elsewhere. The accounts offer a picture of their commercial activities and interactions, and their place in trade and social networks.

The Eleusis accounts from 329/8 (*I.Eleusis* 177) and 336/5 or 333/2 (*I.Eleusis* 159) record purchases from and employment of at least 167 people – citizens, metics, enslaved – sometimes directly liaising with each other (visible in transactions between sellers and *tamiai*, or haulage by one person of a product bought from another). Two or three were women. In 329/8, the sanctuary officials, or agents acting on their behalf, purchased reeds (*kalamides*) from a woman named Artemis (l. 64). These would be laid across roof beams and then overlaid with mud to form a supporting layer for the roof tiles of sanctuary buildings. They bought caps (*piloi*) from Thettale (ll. 70–1), and, a few months later, red ochre (*miltos*), probably

---

[135] Foxhall 2012: 194–9. Bela Dimova points out (pers. comm.) that children have smaller fingers and
often sharper eyesight than adults, which may have been an advantage in textile work.
[136] Following S. Lambert 2000.

Figure 4.8 Detail from the Eleusis accounts of 329/8 (*IG* 11² 1672), Athens, Epigraphic
Museum EM 10051–10048. The middle row reads παρὰ Σωτηρίδος Ἀπρο [*vacat*].
© Hellenic Ministry of Culture/Hellenic Organization of Cultural Resources
Development (H.O.C.RE.D.). Photograph by author.

from a woman named Soteris (l. 184; the entry is uncertain). A female
supplier named Satyra appears in the Erekhtheion building accounts for
405/4,[137] providing what may have been pitch for repairing the temple. In
each case, the buyers are recorded as making purchases directly from the
woman, rather than from a male relative or colleague on her behalf. If such
men were present, they were not managing the women's businesses. This
leaves open the question of whether the records mask commercial contributions from other women by entering them under the name of a *kyrios*.
Satyra seems to have been described as ἐ Σκ[αμβω(νίδαις) οἰκ(όσης)] (living
in Skambonidai), suggesting she was a metic; otherwise, the women's socio-
legal statuses are not readily apparent and were presumably not at issue.

   Kevin Clinton understands Ἀρτέμιδος (l. 64) as the genitive not of
Ἄρτεμις, as other readers do,[138] but of Ἀρτεμίδας,[139] a name not attested
in ancient Greece. He assumes Ἀρτέμιδος is a cutter's error for Ἄρτεμιδα,
which would be the genitive of Ἀρτεμίδας if it existed. He draws an analogy
based on l. 246, where Soteris appears: παρὰ Σωτηρίδος Ἀπρο (Figure 4.8),
commenting: 'The name and the demotic of the supplier make no sense.
Soteris is a woman's name, and no demotic begins with Apro-.'[140]
Clinton's second objection is reasonable; his first is not. He continues:
'The stonecutter here realized he had made a mistake after carving
ΣΩΤΗΡΙΔΟΣ instead of ΣΩΤΕΡΙΔΑ, the genitive of Σωτηρίδας; he then
added the correct alpha, either intending to erase the letters ΟΣ or not to
paint them in. An apparent descendant of Σωτηρίδας Προ(σπάλτιος)
appears in ephebic documents of the second century AD' – some five
centuries later. *LGPN* 11 is agnostic, not listing this instance under either

<hr>

[137] I thank Stephen Lambert for drawing Satyra to my attention and discussing her with me.
[138] Including *LGPN* 11, *s.v.* Ἄρτεμις; Brock 1994: 338, n. 12; Kennedy 2014: 127; n. 26 (printed on
       p. 155).
[139] Clinton 2008: 203 *ad loc.*; likewise pp. 189, 191.
[140] Clinton 2008: 217 *ad* 177.246 (= *IG* 11² 1672.184).

'Soteridas' or 'Soteris'. 'Soteridas' is only attested in Attica for the second and third centuries AD. By contrast, there are eight fifth- and fourth-century women named Soteris in *LGPN* II; two were metics. It does seem from the unintelligible string AΠPO and the ensuing vacant spaces in the inscription that something went awry for the cutter, but Clinton's solution is unconvincing and certainly does not warrant extension to Artemis; the error need only have been in carving the next word. The scholarly tendency to misread women's names in the epigraphic record as men's names – of which several examples are given in this book – masks the range of women's activity and both stems from and feeds misguided assumptions.[141]

Artemis operated from Peiraieus (ἐκ Πειραῶς).[142] The reeds she sold the sanctuary in 329/8 were worth fifty *drakhmai*, more than a month and a half's wages for a skilled labourer. Reeds grow in marshy areas;[143] it is unlikely that Artemis gathered these quantities in Peiraieus, a densely built seaport. Possibly she gathered them elsewhere but transported them to Peiraieus, where there may have been more demand, or bought up reeds gathered by other people – probably including women, who would have gathered reeds to produce basketry and other items. This would have required established commercial relationships with reed gatherers and possibly shippers, as well as buyers.

In the sixth prytany, officials bought five *statēres* (about 500 g) of *miltos* from Soteris for two *drakhmai* and three *oboloi*, a per-*statēr* price of three *oboloi* (probably just under the '*medimnos* of barley' limit). *Miltos*, or ruddle, was a red ochre found in silver, gold, and copper mines, used as a pigment, among other things.[144] Clinton comments that the purchase 'appears to be for an operation that followed not long after the bricklaying, i.e. imparting color to the stucco or plaster'.[145] This was probably from the nearby island of Keos: in the mid fourth century, various Kean towns had

---

[141] As well as Artemis and Soteris here, among the other examples discussed in this book are Euarkhis, dedicator of a *dekatē*, whose name is frequently assumed to be male, including on the museum label on her dedication at the Acropolis Museum, Athens (p. 249); Phanostrate the doctor, whose name was previously misread as Phanostrato[s] (p. 254), and another Soteris, who participated in a group dedication at the cave of Pan at Vari (p. 289); again, her name was previously misread as a man's name.

[142] Clinton 2008: 190 understands entries with ἐκ (as opposed to ἐν [deme] οἰκῶν, the typical designation for a metic) to denote place of workshop or warehouse, because two vendors appear both with their deme or deme of residence, and with ἐκ + workshop/warehouse location. Workshops and warehouses could be places of sale (*IG* II² 1013.9).

[143] Reeds grew abundantly in the marshland of the northern Boiotian basin, but also in and near other lakes and rivers (Thphr. *HP* 4.11).

[144] Thphr. *Lap.* 51–4; Photos-Jones *et al.* 2018.

[145] Clinton 2008: 217 *ad* 177.246 (= *IG* II² 1672.184).

passed decrees strictly enforcing an Athenian monopoly on Kean *miltos* (RO 40 = *IG* II² 1128),[146] which was held to be the best.[147] The decree from the town of Koresia stipulates that Kean producers (not shippers, who were more likely to be Athenian) had to pay a 2 per cent export tax.[148] Another possibility is that the *miltos* came from the Laureion silver mines.[149] Evangelos Kakavoyannis suggests that the families who lived at the Laureion *ergastēria* (ore-processing workshops) bred pack animals there for transporting ore (and, one might add, *miltos*).[150] Soteris must have had links to mines in Laureion or Keos – possibly she was Kean herself, though she could have been Athenian – and to shippers or haulers. At least two men also supplied *miltos* to the sanctuary (ll. 12–13, 69–70).[151] One sold twenty-five *statēres* at the higher per-unit price of 3½ *oboloi* (ll. 12–13); the officials paid a man named Diokleidas, probably a Megarian (ll. 15–16, cf. l. 95), to transport it. These purchases give us an impression of the complexity and diversity of Attic supply networks, and of Soteris' commercial competition.

Satyra appears in the Erekhtheion building accounts for 405/4, the year of its completion. Lambert's text suggests she was a metic living and working in Skambonidai, just north of the Akropolis (ἐ Σκ[αμβω(νίδαις) οἰκ(όσης) – –], *SEG* 50:69.42). Satyra supplied something of unknown nature and value ἐς τὴν ἀλει[. Possibly this was pitch: for comparison, the Eleusinion officials bought two earthenware jars of pitch (πίττης κεράμια) in the first prytany of 329/8 and five more later to coat (ἀλεῖψαι) the wood of a wall and the roof beams and doors of the Eleusinion (*I.Eleusis* 177.13–14, 170–1).[152] The cost of pitch at Eleusis in the late fourth century ranged between 10 and 12½ *drakhmai* per jar,[153] and the size of purchases between two and five jars.

---

[146]	For the politics of the decrees, see Lazar 2024: 249–51.

[147]	Thphr. *Lap.* 52; cf. Caley and Richards 1956: 179 on the desirability of importing high-quality *miltos* even if cheaper but lower-quality *miltos* were available domestically, despite the scepticism of Rhodes and Osborne 2003: 208.

[148]	Compare Lambert 2018c, n. 4.

[149]	Compare Plin. *HN* 33.158–60; Vitr. *De arch.* 7.7.1; Rhodes and Osborne 2003: 208.

[150]	Kakavoyannis 2001: 376.

[151]	Rhodes and Osborne 2003: 208 state that only one supplier is named in this inscription: in fact there were three, Pamphilos, Artemon, and Soteris.

[152]	Compare l. 180, payment for a pitcher (τῶι ἀλείψαντι, but payment is also recorded τοῖς πιττοκοποῦσιν ('for pitch-smearers') in the previous line – an earlier stage in the process?), and l. 69, pitch for other buildings; cf. *IG* II² 1673.20–2. Pitching at the Asklepieion at Epidauros in the fourth century: *IG* IV² 1.102, ll. 245–6, 255–6, 277–8. The verb used at the sanctuary on Delos in 200 and 179 BC is χρῖσαι (*I.Délos* 372.84–5, 442.A.188), a similar idea. See further Clinton 2008: 197 and Meiggs 1982: 467–8.

[153]	Following Clinton's reading Δ[Δ]Π in l. 14 instead of Kirchoff's ΔΗ, which would bring the cost of a *keramion* of pitch down to six *drakhmai* (Clinton 2008: 197, with reference to Clinton 2005: 190, 202, *ad* ll. 14).

Given that the set of entries in which Satyra appears follows apparent references to the Akropolis fire of 406 (l. 28; cf. Xen. *Hell.* 1.6.1), Lambert comments that 'the overall impression [of this part of the accounts] is of post-fire repair and/or finishing work'; it was apparently a one-off purchase. Satyra, who worked very near to the Erekhtheion, may have been the nearest supplier; transporting the pitch would not have been a problem.

The choice of the officials at such prestigious sanctuaries to purchase from these women implies that each had acquired a commercial reputation, reflecting a number of positive commercial interactions. Their appearance in the accounts attests to their dealings with the sanctuary officials and their indirect connection to others in the supply chain. Though Artemis, Thettale, Soteris, and Satyra are vastly outnumbered by male suppliers in the extant records, their entries show how women's work was part of the fabric of Attica.

Women Workers in Public

Aristophanic comedy portrays women trading on a small scale from stalls and shops rather than workshops and warehouses. Female traders outnumber male in Aristophanes,[154] perhaps because women were more likely to be involved in small-scale marketplace trade, particularly of foodstuffs, which formed a familiar backdrop to the civic life in which Aristophanes is interested, as opposed to the more specialised trade of building materials with which the sanctuary accounts are concerned. Nevertheless, like the accounts, Aristophanes' plays, with other literary sources, suggest the diversity of trading women's contacts. Women in and around the *agora* of the *asty*, the one or two further *agorai* in Peiraieus, and other markets across Attica,[155] worked alongside and traded with men and women; citizens, metics, and enslaved people; rich and poor.

The impression given by Aristophanes is that women retailers tended to work as individuals, though we have some evidence for women retailers working alongside family members, which was probably common.[156]

---

[154] The exception is the *Knights* sausage seller (*allantopōlēs*). In *Acharnians*, Dikaiopolis trades in the *agora* with a Megarian and a Boiotian (ll. 719–970), but the scene is quasi-allegorical, and atypical in various ways: Dikaiopolis is usually a farmer; the Megarian is selling his daughters out of starvation; the Boiotian buys an informer as one would buy pottery.

[155] Peiraieus *agora(i)*: Hoepfner *et al.* 1994: 43, with map, fig. 14; cf. Paus. 1.1.3 (second century AD); other markets: Blok 2001: 98. Osborne 1985b: 34–5 suggests there may have been as many as five *agorai* in the deme of Sounion.

[156] Humphreys' chapter on economic cooperation between kin (Humphreys 2018: 171–84) focuses almost exclusively on men's occupations and business ventures, except when discussing family

Nikarete seemingly sold *tainiai* in the *agora* alongside her son.[157] A fourth-century Attic curse tablet, *DTA* 87, curses the work (*ergasia*) of a series of tavern-keepers, including 'Kallias, the tavern-keeper from the neighbourhood, and his wife Thraitta', which implies they kept the tavern together.[158] Mania, the other woman tavern-keeper cursed in *DTA* 87, apparently worked alone (l. 8). Another Attic curse tablet, dated between the mid fourth and second centuries,[159] curses [Δι]ονύσιον | τὸν κρανοποιὸν καὶ τὴν | γυναῖκα αὐτοῦ Ἀρτέμείν | τὴν χρυσωτρίαν καὶ τὴν [o]ἰ-|[κ]ίαν αὐτῶν καὶ τὴν [ἐ]ργα-|σίαν, 'Dionysios the helmet-maker and his wife Artemis the gilder, and their household and their work' (*DTA* 69.1–6). The *phialai* inscriptions record two couples who worked together. Consecutive dedications were made by sesame sellers named Soteris and Midas, living in Melite and freed by or acquitted of a charge brought by the same man (*IG* ıı² 156.22–30). It is likely that they worked as a wife-and-husband (or sister-and-brother?) team in the *agora*. Similarly, a set of dedications by perfume sellers, Habrosyne and Hermon, and a *paidion*, all living in Peiraieus, suggests a family business, including a number of household members (*SEG* 25:180.29–37). Aristophanes only once indicates the marital status of a retailer: the oft-cited garland weaver in *Thesmophoriazusae* (ll. 443–58), who says that her husband's death left her with five little children to look after, ἀγὼ μόλις / στεφανηπλοκοῦσ' ἔβοσκον ἐν ταῖς μυρρίναις, 'whom I just about manage to feed by weaving [and selling] garlands (*stephanoi*) in the myrtle market'. Women without husbands might have been disproportionately represented among female retailers, but we do not know. More unusual combinations of colleagues were also possible. The inn in Aristophanes' *Frogs* 549–78 is run by two metic women who have different *prostatai*, which suggests that they are not sisters or liberated from the same enslaver. Though the situation is fictional, it is striking that an Athenian audience could imagine a joint venture by unrelated women.

How did the diverse social world of retail affect the women who worked in it? Aristophanes' garland seller leaves the Thesmophoria to

---

relations in the *phialai* inscriptions (she refers to the dedicators as slaves, but even if the records are of manumissions, by the time of the dedications the dedicators were free).

[157] In Dem. 57.31 and 35, Euxitheos speaks of the *tainiai*-selling in the first person plural, but at §34 he says that his opponent's charge is that his *mother* is a *tainiai* seller. Probably both sold *tainiai*, but it was only cited against Nikarete; less likely, only Nikarete sold *tainiai*, and Euxitheos uses the first person plural to talk about his family as a unit. Compare *P.Lond.* 7.1976, third-century Egypt, for a widow(?) working in a shop with her daughter.

[158] Compare *DTA* 69.   [159] Gager 1992: 157.

return to the myrtle market to fulfil a commission (στεφάνους συνθηματιαίους, 'agreed-upon garlands', l. 458) for twenty men. Her husbandlessness, rather than isolating her, has brought her into contact – and into contracts, however informal – with other men. Konstantinos Kapparis also notes the geographic range her work may have necessitated: 'her domain extends far beyond her doorstep to the hillsides and mountains of Attica where she collects the material for her wreaths, and to the marketplace and the whole network of clients where she can sell her product'[160] – though it is also possible that she had access to a small plot where she grew the plants she needed or bought them from someone else. In *Lysistrata*'s portrayal of the highly militarised *asty* of the Dekeleian War[161] (413–404; the play was produced in 411), armed men shop in the *agora*, frequenting the stalls of pot sellers, herb sellers, and fish sellers (ll. 556–64). An aristocratic cavalryman buys porridge from an old woman; a Thracian mercenary intimidates a woman fig seller in order to steal some figs.[162] The description is a comic exaggeration – the cavalryman uses his helmet as a porridge pot – but gives an impression of a diverse human environment, even if some of its variety as described here is attributable to unusual circumstances. The *agorai* in Peiraieus, the Greek world's most important port, peopled by over ten per cent of Attica's metics[163] and large numbers of foreign traders and visitors, would have been even more diverse.

Kostas Vlassopoulos argues that the shared experiences and interactions of different sorts of people in the *agora* had a democratising effect, blurring status distinctions and opening to non-citizens certain privileges and protections of citizenship, including participation in political discussion, which he argues emboldened women.[164] Which women? Blok argues, based on suggestions from classical texts, alongside observations from conservative twentieth-century communities in southern France, Spain, Thessaloniki, Crete, and Algeria, that 'respectable' women might only have used public spaces when men were not occupying them, and 'only if [the women] have a distinct and socially accepted purpose, when it is the right time to do so, and if they can behave in such a way – for instance, by being in the company of other women, children, or male kin – so as to prevent

---

[160] Kapparis 2021: 6–7.   [161] Compare Thuc. 7.28.1–2, 8.69.1.

[162] In 413, Thracian mercenaries in Athenian pay massacred women and children at Mykalessos in Boiotia (Thuc. 7.27.1–2, 29); this might have informed these lines.

[163] If the metics recorded in the *phialai* inscriptions are representative: Meyer 2010: 14.

[164] Vlassopoulos 2007. For a comic portrayal of a highly politically aware female grocer and prostitute (separate women), see Ar. *Vesp.* 488–503, discussed by Vlassopoulos on p. 45.

the neighbors' gossip'.[165] However, she concedes that in the 'bustle' of a busy marketplace like the *agora*, 'men and women mingled more than formal morality would allow'.[166] Even without accepting particular correspondence between classical Attic and modern 'Mediterranean' social norms, anthropological descriptions of gender segregation by time and conventions for mitigating non-segregation suggest possible strategies by which similar values may have been upheld in Attica. Women who could might have avoided the *agora*;[167] women stallholders could not, and Aristophanes shows them working without other women or male kin, selling to male non-relatives. (They are never shown or mentioned selling to other women, which might support Blok's theory, though the description of shopping soldiers in *Lysistrata* comes from a woman who saw them (ἐγὼ … εἶδον, 561); she was either shopping or a stallholder herself: cf. ll 456–60.)[168] Women stallholders' necessary interactions with unrelated men in the predominantly male-occupied *agora* accounts in part for contemporary questions about the respectability of such work[169] and left them at risk of damage to their reputation or social standing as a result of others' talk. In Demosthenes 57, Euxitheos cites a law that ἔνοχον εἶναι τῇ κακηγορίᾳ τὸν τὴν ἐργασίαν τὴν ἐν τῇ ἀγορᾷ ἢ τῶν πολιτῶν ἢ τῶν πολιτίδων ὀνειδίζοντά τινι ('one who uses a male or female citizen's work in the *agora* as a reproach against them shall be held liable for slander', §30). The law's existence, and the context of its deployment here, where Euxitheos has lost his citizenship partly because of insinuations based on his mother's work, suggest stigmatisation was prevalent and potentially dangerous.

Around the *agora* were shops and workshops which also served as places to socialise. Vlassopoulos argues that these, too, were diversely populated spaces where status distinctions were blurred. However, those who stopped to talk in shops were probably predominantly men;[170] women who lingered among chatting men would attract unwelcome attention and criticism.[171] Nevertheless, some women *kept* shops and taverns. These women would have known regulars well and been privy to considerable

---

[165] Blok 2001; quotation p. 109; differences between these communities as 'variations on a theme', pp. 98–9; defending 'Mediterranean' as a term and a methodology, p. 96 with fn. 5, citing especially Cohen 1991: 38, 40.

[166] Blok 2001: 111. [167] Compare Lys. 1.8, with p. 163. [168] Blok 2001: 111, fn. 67.

[169] Compare Blok 2001: 111, fn. 67. [170] Lewis 1995, Gottesman 2014: 59–60.

[171] Compare Chowdhry 1994: 1–2 on twentieth-century rural Haryana, India: '[Women] are noticeably visible in the streets, walking along purposefully, not loitering or hanging about … avoiding the bazaars and places of male gathering.'

amounts of the men's talk,[172] which they might discuss with female friends at home.[173] Women who kept shops and taverns would have had unusually close involvement in male social networks and been particularly well informed.

As the *Lysistrata* scene with the mercenary suggests (and Vlassopoulos concedes),[174] women stallholders' and shopkeepers' interactions with buyers were often negative. In Aristophanes' *Wealth*, Khremylos and Blepsidemos mistake Poverty, personified as a woman, for an innkeeper or porridge seller on the grounds that she yelled at them even though they had not done her any harm (ll. 426–8; they then wonder whether she is the neighbourhood tavern-keeper, l. 435). The implication that people were accustomed to harm (ἀδικέω) innkeepers or porridge sellers fits with Aristophanes' frequent portrayals of theft from women vendors (*Wasps* 235–9, 1388–1408; *Frogs* 549–78), and the Athenian's statement in Plato's *Laws* that because of their supposed greed, those involved in tavern-keeping, trade, or innkeeping were subject to degrading verbal abuse (11.918d). As Roger Brock notes, Old Comedy strongly associates abusive language and shouting with women vendors themselves.[175] The portrayed frequency of theft from and aggression against female traders may account for their portrayed assertiveness as much as the democratising mingling proposed by Vlassopoulos.

Lysistrate's 'army' of older women (cf. ll. 176–9), called upon to attack the men, consists in hybrid female traders, σπερμαγοραιολεκιθολαχανοπώλιδες (women who sell seeds, porridge, and vegetables in the *agora*) and σκοροδοπανδοκευτριαρτοπώλιδες (women who sell garlic, keep inns, and sell bread, ll. 456–60). The connection between their age and work is not clear. Perhaps older women were felt to be particularly fearless, as retailers were: the army comprises the toughest of the tough. Framed negatively, this is the interaction of misogynistic stereotypes about female assertiveness: women with the authority and confidence of age might be more assertive;[176] women who traded in public would have to be assertive; this assertiveness was framed as aggression; an 'army' of women would therefore best be portrayed as elderly traders. One curse tablet from the later part of the fourth century, found in a Kerameikos grave, curses Μυρτάλη | γραῦς καπηλίς, 'Myrtale, the old woman tavern-keeper/retailer' (*SGD* 11, ll.

---

[172] Compare Lewis 1995: 435–6 on 'regulars'.

[173] Compare Vlassopoulos 2007: 43 on Praxagora in Ar. *Eccl.* 241–7, who picks up men's talk on the Pnyx from her temporary home there.

[174] Vlassopoulos 2007: 43–4.   [175] Brock 1994: 344, also 339, n. 17.

[176] For the authority of older women, see Pratt 2000 and Foxhall 1994: 93–4.

7–8)[177] – an historical example of an older woman in retail who had evidently bothered the curser. Possibly retail was particularly associated with older women, who were more likely to be without male breadwinners and so obliged to undertake income-generating work to support themselves. Or perhaps this band of Aristophanic women, already presented as ridiculous for being armed and occupying the Akropolis, are made more ridiculous by being presented as old.[178]

Some Aristophanic retailers initiate legal retaliation. When the metic innkeepers in *Frogs* recognise in Dionysos the customer who refused to pay for his food and threatened them, they send for their *prostatai* (legal guardians and representatives), who will summon him to court (ll. 549–78).[179] In *Wasps*, the drunken Philokleon knocks to the ground loaves of a bread seller named Myrtia (ll. 1388–414). Myrtia swears Philokleon will not get away with destroying 'the wares of Myrtia, the daughter of Ankylion and Sostrate' (ll. 1393–8). She asserts her legal protections as a citizen-status woman by emphasising her family relationships, an element of identity usually de-emphasised in the context of work. She formally summons him before the *agoranomoi*, the officials who regulated the *agora*, for damage done to her stock. She calls a male citizen as witness to the summons (προσκαλοῦμαί σ[ε] … / πρὸς τοὺς ἀγορανόμους βλάβης τῶν φορτίων, / κλητῆρ' ἔχουσα Χαιρεφῶντα τουτονί, 'I summon you [Philokleon] before the *agoranomoi* for damage to my wares, with Khairephon here as my witness', ll. 1406–8). Sommerstein notes that this is 'our sole (but sufficient) evidence that it was possible for a woman to serve a summons'.[180] Kapparis argues that women compelled to earn money through work after losing male providers, particularly in the near-constant warfare of the classical period, were likelier to become involved in one way or another with the Athenian legal system:

---

[177] Full text at Eidinow 2007: 411–12. For taverns and tavern-keepers, see Davidson 1997: 53–60. I mostly translate *kapēlis* as 'tavern-keeper', with emphasis on selling drinks (the word can simply mean 'retailer'), and *pandokeutria* as 'innkeeper', with emphasis on overnight guests (the word literally means 'welcomer of all'). The distinction is often unclear and may have been unimportant, but it is notable and perhaps significant that many *kapēlides* (feminine) and *kapēloi* (masculine) are victims of curse tablets, but to my knowledge, no *pandokeutriai*.

[178] Older women are mocked elsewhere in Aristophanes, e.g. esp. *Eccl.* 877–1111.

[179] The women's *prostatai* turn out to be the prominent political figures Kleon and Hyperbolos respectively, which is almost certainly a joke about the men's enthusiasm for prosecutions (cf. Sommerstein 1996 *ad loc.*). Kapparis 2021: 8 reads the significance of Kleon and Hyperbolos differently.

[180] Sommerstein 1983 *ad loc.*; contrast *P.Bad.* 4.48, from second-century Egypt.

> the larger the exposure of women to the world of the outdoors, the marketplace, the business centres and practices of an open economy like that of classical Athens, the greater the danger and the need for direct encounters with the legal system of the city . . . to defend their property and business interests, or to fend off attacks by enemies upon their person, family, or property.[181]

The Aristophanic examples attest to the legal options open to women who needed to defend themselves and their livelihoods; Kapparis also points out the potential liabilities.[182]

Myrtia's emphasis on her citizen status in response to Philokleon's actions undermines Vlassopoulos' argument that status distinctions mattered little in the *agora*. While we frequently find, in Aristophanes at least, women 'asserting their rights',[183] which Vlassopoulos attributes to the blurring of status distinctions which emboldened women to speak up for themselves, Aristophanic women 'asserting their rights' do so by distinguishing themselves from those who lack those rights, usually enslaved people, who could be mistreated with relative impunity (e.g. *Wasps* 1393–8; *Lysistrata* 379, 435–6, 463–5, all cited by Vlassopoulos).[184] Certainly women in the *agora* and the shops and inns around it would be exposed to a greater variety of people and a wider range of discussion, including political discussion, which may have awakened them to the privileges of their free or citizen status. It is also true that status distinctions *could* be unclear in Attica, perhaps particularly in the *agora*.[185] Nevertheless, the Aristophanic passages suggest that when that unclarity became a threat to women, they would make the distinction clear.

Connections through Work

Women Workers in Conflict

Connections women formed through their work could be potent and even threatening. The social and informational networks of retailers, particularly shop- and tavern-keepers, gave women significant social influence. This is suggested by efforts to use curse tablets magically to 'bind' (constrict, hinder) working women to reduce the impact of their work, talk, and relationships.[186]

---

[181] Kapparis 2021: 7.   [182] Kapparis 2021: 205–6 with Rubinstein 2018 on summary fines.
[183] Vlassopoulos 2007: 43.   [184] Vlassopoulos 2007: 43–4.   [185] Vlassopoulos 2007: 34–5.
[186] For a recent, comprehensive account of the development of curse tablets and binding spells as a social and religious practice, see Lamont 2023, with pp. 134–87 on Athenian curse practice specifically.

Around fifty curse tablets which number women among their victims survive from classical Attica.[187] Three curse *kapēlides*, women who kept shops or taverns; tavern-keeping, by men and women, is the occupation most often mentioned in curses.[188] One curses an older tavern-keeper named Myrtale along with men of various statuses and occupations (*SGD* 11, ll. 7–8; see pp. 241–2). It targets 'their tongue and mind and soul and body and their actions/work (*erga*) and mind and mental faculties and thinking and their planning/intention (*bou[l]ēn*)', which suggests a perceived conspiracy between the victims. The curser believed Myrtale was cooperatively planning something as part of a group of mixed sex and status.

A longer curse, found in Patisia and dating from the classical or Hellenistic period (*DTA* 68), curses upwards of twenty victims, each with their 'workshop and everything in the workshop' (τὸ ἐργαστήριον καὶ τὰ ἐν τῶι ἐργαστηρίωι ἄπαντα, l. a.7). Some of the workshops were run by women; one, Lyde, is cursed twice (ll. a.5, b.10), which suggests the curser's preoccupation with her – was she particularly influential? Other victims include Phileas the miller (l. a.1), a male tavern-keeper whose name is lost (l. a.12), Areskousa the go-between or 'procuress' (τὴμ μαστρ[ο]π[όν], l. a.15), and two female tavern-keepers, Parthenion and Anyta (ll. a.5 and b.6).

Perhaps the most informative of the three is *DTA* 87:

Side A:

καταδῶ Καλλίαν : τὸν κάπηλον τὸν ἐγ γειτόνων καὶ τὴν γυναῖκα αὐτοῦ
Θρᾶιτταν : καὶ τὸ καπηλεῖον τὸ φαλακροῦ καὶ τὸ Ἀνθεμίωνος καπηλεῖον
τὸ πλησίον ΔΑ . ΟΗ
καὶ Φίλωνα τὸν κάπηλον· τούτων πάντων καταδῶ ψυχὴν ἐργασίαν
χεῖρας πόδας : τὰ καπηλεῖα αὐτῶν.
καταδῶ Σωσιμένην τ[ὸν] ἀδελφόν : καὶ Κάρπον τὸν οἰκότην αὐτοῦ τὸν   5
σινδο[νο]πώλην καὶ Γλύκανθιν ἣν καλοῦσι Μαλθάκην : καὶ Ἀγάθωνα τ[ὸ]
ν κάπηλον
[τ]ὸν Σωσιμένους οἰκότην : τούτων πάντων καταδῶ : ψυχὴν ἐργασία
[ν β]ίον χεῖρας πόδας.
καταδῶ Κίττον τὸν γείτονα τὸν καναβιο(υ)ργὸν καὶ τέχνην τὴν Κίττου
καὶ ἐργασίαν καὶ ψυχὴν καὶ νο(ῦ)ν καὶ γλῶτταν τὴν Κίττου.
καταδῶ Μανίαν τὴν κάπηλιν τὴν ἐπὶ κρήν⟨η⟩ι καὶ τὸ καπηλεῖον τὸ
Ἀρίστανδρος   10
Ἐλευσινίου καὶ ἐργασίαν αὐτοῖς καὶ νο(ῦ)ν.

---

[187] At least forty among the tablets assembled by Eidinow 2007: 352–454, to which Lamont 2023: 134–87 adds about seven.

[188] Gager 1992: 163, Eidinow 2007: 196.

ψυχὴν χεῖρας γλῶτταν πόδας νο(ῦ)ν : τούτους πάντας καταδῶ ἐμ
μνήμασι ΑΣΦΑΡ̣ΑΓΙΑΙ
κ   πρὸς τὸν κάτοχον Ἑρμῆν

Side B:

τοὺς Ἀριστάνδρου οἰκέτας

I bind Kallias the tavern-keeper from the neighbourhood, and his wife Thraitta, and the tavern of the bald man, and the tavern of Anthemion nearby ... and Philon the tavern-keeper. Of all these people, I bind soul, work, hands, feet, their taverns. I bind Sosimines his brother and Karpos his slave, the fabric-seller, and Glykanthis whom they call Malthake, and Agathon the tavern-keeper, who is the slave of Sosimines. Of all these I bind soul, work, life, hands, feet. I bind Kittos the [my? Sosimenes'?] neighbour, the maker of wooden frames [or of ropes?] and Kittos' craft and work, and soul and mind and the tongue of Kittos. I bind Mania the tavern-keeper by the spring, and the tavern of Aristandros of Eleusis and their work and mind. Soul, hands, tongue, feet, mind. All of them I bind in the ... grave in the presence of Hermes the Binder.

[I bind] the slaves of Aristandros. (Trans. Esther Eidinow, with adjustments.)[189]

The fact that most victims are in the same occupation, combined with the fact that the curser binds the victims' 'work' (*ergasia*) may suggest they were motivated by commercial competition. Alternatively, they had personal grudges against various neighbours and wanted to damage their businesses both in vengeance and as a means of reducing whatever damage they felt had been done to them. Perhaps they believed the tavern-keepers were cheating them: Aristophanes' Blepsidemos in *Wealth* complains of being cheated by the (female) neighbourhood tavern-keeper (ἡ καπηλὶς ἡκ τῶν γειτόνων, l. 435–6; cf. τὸν κάπηλον τὸν ἐγ γειτόνων here) with false measures. Similarly, the Woman Herald in *Thesmophoriazusae* asks the gods to curse τις κάπηλος ἢ καπηλὶς τοῦ χοῶς / ἢ τῶν κοτυλῶν τὸ νόμισμα διαλυμαίνεται, 'any male or female tavern-keeper who falsifies the legal measures of the *khous* and *kotylai*' (ll. 347–8). The slander and insults levelled at tavern-keepers (Pl. *Leg.* 11.918d) may sometimes have escalated into binding spells. Or perhaps the curser was or believed themselves to be the subject of tavern gossip, hence the binding of Mania and Aristandros'

---

[189] Eidinow 2007: 375–6 translates τούτων πάντων, l. 3, as 'of all these men', but it must include Thraitta.

tongues (l. 10).[190] One Aristophanic fragment describes someone (or something?) as ἐν κωμήτισι καπηλοῖς ἐπίχαρτον, 'a source of spiteful joy among the neighbourhood women who keep taverns' (frg. 274 Kock). Perhaps this someone was the subject of gleeful gossip, expressed and fostered at the taverns where people talk, or was easy to trick into paying full price for less than a full *kotylē*.

The victims are situated within the context of their neighbourhood with its familiar landmarks, like the spring (l. 8), and within a network of relationships. Thraitta, whose name ('Thracian') suggests she was either enslaved or a freedwoman, was connected to Kallias by marriage. Perhaps the two were an enslaved couple in an informal union who gave their enslavers a proportion of their earnings, like Syros and his wife in Menander's *Epitrepontes*; or they had married after gaining their freedom, like *Piste* in [Demosthenes] 47 and her husband; or this was a mixed union, perhaps like Alke and Dion in Isaeus 6. Sosimenes was connected to Philon by kinship; Agathon was connected to Sosimenes by enslavement; Kittos was connected to Sosimenes and his household – or the curser? – by proximity, and so on. Given that everyone else in the second group of victims is connected to Sosimenes, it seems likely that Glykanthis/ Malthake was too: perhaps this was an informal romantic or sexual relationship. A picture emerges of a thickly linked community in which work relationships compounded and intersected with kinship, household, and neighbourly relationships. The connection between neighbourhoods and taverns here and in Aristophanes suggests that taverns functioned as neighbourhood social hubs.[191]

Another curse describing women by occupation was inscribed into a lead tablet found about two miles north-west of the *agora*, probably in a sanctuary of Zeus Melikhios, dated to 345–335 (NAM 14470).[192] The tablet lists almost 100 victims, by far the most of any surviving curse tablet. Based on the list's length, format, and patterns of association, Humphreys has argued that though the curser was provoked by a specific incident, as they wrote they began simply to list everyone they disliked. Between any two

---

[190] Eidinow 2007: 197–9 warns against assuming that all curses identifying victims by occupation are commercially motivated; she gives *DTA* 87 as an example, noting that Kittos may have been the curser's neighbour, which may itself have been a source of enmity. However, Venticinque 2022 takes a similar approach to mine, understanding 'commercial curses' as evidence for 'support networks tied to a household, a neighbourhood, or . . . profession, and the qualities used to sustain those relationships' (p. 71); targeting those networks would make a commercial curse more effective.

[191] Compare Davidson 1997: 55, 60.

[192] Also referred to as NM 14470; republished as Jordan and Curbera 2008.

persons listed on a curse tablet was at most one degree of separation: the curser. A tablet like NAM 14470, which curses a huge range of people including wealthy and politically prominent citizens, female and male prostitutes, and workers in the grain industry, 'does suggest', Gottesman writes, 'that relationships between citizens, metics, and slaves, were quite prevalent indeed'.[193] Their attestation on curse tablets used against perceived plots shows that such relationships could be cooperative or adversarial.

Nine women are cursed in NAM 14470: Isokrite (named near the beginning and near the end,[194] each time next to different names); Satyra the *alphitopōlis* (barley seller); Kallistrate; Phainippe; Themistia; and four *laikastriai*, Kleinis, Skylla, Sophronis, and Arkhis. *Laikastria* seems to mean 'a woman who performs oral sex on men' and is probably used here as an 'occupational designation' – prostitute – rather than an insult,[195] though of course, as with all the victims, the curser viewed them with hostility.

A woman named Kallistrate was cursed in another tablet from about 350 (*DTA* 57.3).[196] If this was the same Kallistrate, her being cursed twice would suggest she was particularly influential, though the name was very common in the fourth century. Isokrite, mentioned twice in NAM 14470, may have been prominent in the curser's mind. Her name is otherwise unattested in Attica. David Jordan and Jaime Curbera suggest that the women named without further qualification 'may have been related to some of the men cursed' and, we might add, thought able to influence them: binding curses were supposed to prevent or hinder action.

As well as Satyra the *alphitopōlis*, the tablet curses four individuals identified as *akhyreus*, probably 'chaff seller'. Chaff was used as animal food, as fuel, and as a temper in mud-brick.[197] The tablet also describes three individuals with the term *paltos*, which Humphreys suggests is connected to *palē* ('fine, sieved flour', possibly from *pallō*, 'to shake' and so perhaps 'to sieve'): they may have processed cereals.[198] Humphreys situates the curser 'in a milieu of sycophants, or at least of men who resorted readily to litigation', who probably had enemies across social classes.[199] 'They would have an interest in picking up gossip from prostitutes, while the targets involved in the grain trade could have been

---

[193] Gottesman 2014: 57.

[194] Assuming Jordan and Curbera's hypothesised writing order, according to which the curser eventually began writing vertically between the columns.

[195] Humphreys 2010: 86; cf. Jordan and Curbera 2008: 144.

[196] See Wilhelm 1904: 144–5 for date.

[197] Pritchett and Pippin 1956: 182–3; Foxhall 1998b: 35–6.   [198] Humphreys 2010: 86, fn. 11.

[199] Challenging the interpretation of Jordan and Curbera 2008: 143–4.

concerned in the illegal export or re-export of grain from Attica, or in other shady practices.' John Traill tentatively identifies the *akhyreus* named Phileas with Φιλέαν τὸμ μυλωθρόν, Phileas the miller, cursed in *DTA* 68.

Curses against grain processors and sellers fit within a context of anxiety and suspicion about the grain trade and those involved in it across the fourth century in particular. Attica was dependent on grain imports, particularly from the Black Sea region. The first half of the fourth century had seen numerous threats to this supply. The Spartan navy had temporarily cut it off in spring 387, during the Corinthian War, and again in summer 376; there had been widespread shortages, probably due to crop failures, in the late 360s and again in 357/6;[200] further shortages would follow in the 320s. Constant public concern about the supply by the later fourth century is evident from the fact that, by the time the Aristotelian *Athenaion politeia* was composed in the 320s, the grain supply was a regular formal agenda item at the major Assembly meetings held every thirty-five or thirty-six days (*Ath. pol.* 43.4), and from the careful regulation of the trade. Grain sales in Athens and Peiraieus were supervised by designated officials, the *emporiou epimelētai* (import-market supervisors) and *sitophylakes* (grain-inspectors). Among the responsibilities of the *sitophylakes* was to ensure that millers sold barley (*alphita*) at a fair price (*Ath. pol.* 51.3–4). In 386, public anger at rising grain prices, possibly combined with anti-immigrant sentiment, had led to the prosecution of the grain retailers (*sitopōlai*), mostly metics who bought up grain from importers and sold it on (Lys. 22). They were accused of buying more than the legal maximum, profiteering, and, significantly for our purposes, collaborating (συνέστησαν, Lys. 22.21) against importers. Possibly Satyra, Phileas, and the other cereal processors and retailers cursed in this tablet were professionally and socially connected – for example, Phileas might have milled barley for Satyra and sold on the by-products[201] – and the curser feared their individual and collective influence.

These curses suggest the influence of working women, and in particular the influence they gained through their work relationships, whether shaping and spreading community talk through local taverns or affecting grain prices and lawsuits through their commercial and informational networks. They were named, understood, and feared in their capacity as workers, and as workers in relationship with others.

---

[200] Late 360s: [Dem.] 50.6, 17, 61; 357/6: Dem. 20.31–3.   [201] Compare Diog. Laert. 8.168–9.

Women Workers in Relationship

Some dedications also attest to work relationships: joint dedications by colleagues. Between 510 and 500, Euarkhis and Lysias made first-offerings to Athena on the Akropolis individually but together (*IG* I³ 644). Euarkhis is sometimes identified as a man – for example, in the item's label at the Acropolis Museum – but 'Euarkhis' is almost certainly a woman's name.[202] They had a marble statue base inscribed, with cuttings for two statues:

> Λυσίας ἀνέθεκεν Ἀθεναίαι
> ἀπαρχέν. Εὐαρχὶς ἀνέθεκεν
> δεκάτεν Ἀθεναίαι.

> Lysias dedicated an *aparkhē* to Athena. Euarkhis dedicated a *dekatē* to Athena.

The cutting on the viewer's right probably held the 'red shoes *korē*' (Akropolis 683);[203] the cutting on the viewer's left, half the size, held a *korē* half as big. Keesling argues that as the inscription is written and read left-to-right, the *korai* should also be read left-to-right,[204] that is, the smaller *korē* represents Lysias' *aparkhē*, and the larger *korē*, the 'red shoes *korē*', represents Euarkhis' *dekatē*, worth considerably more. Even if the *korai* were purchased with a joint sum rather than paid for individually, the inscription shows that Lysias and Euarkhis conceived of their income separately: Lysias offered a certain amount of his and Euarkhis offered a certain, different, amount of hers. These distinct proportions of distinct incomes were put towards a joint dedication, an interplay between independence and collaboration.[205]

Though there is no explicit indication either way, these may be 'family' dedications as well as 'work' dedications; there need not be a distinction, as families sometimes shared a trade.[206] We may compare a joint *dekatē* dedicated to Phoibos Apollo in Phokis, dedicated by Philon and his children (Φίλον δη-|κάταν ἀνήθ-|ηκη . . . αὐτõ καὶ πα-|ίδον, *FD* 4:187 = *CEG* (1) 345), which Day suggests was 'perhaps the result of a joint venture'.[207] Possibly, as

---

[202] Compare *IG* II² 9593, *FD* 3:54.4; also *SEG* 51:321.

[203] Keesling 2003b: 9. *IG* I³ prints Εὐάρχις (which would be a man's name) rather than Εὐαρχίς (a woman's name), but *LGPN* recognises all four attestations of the name, including this one, as women's names.

[204] Keesling 2003b: 10.

[205] *IG* I³ 700, EM 6383+12780, c. 500–480(?), a joint dedication by a woman named Phryne and a person called Smikythe (possibly but not necessarily the *plyntria* who dedicated *IG* I³ 616) or Smikythos, may also have been a first-offering.

[206] Kin as colleagues: Humphreys 2018: 171–84. [207] Day 2010: 189.

with Melinna, Euarkhis' role as an earner was part of her role(s) as a family
member, but unlike Melinna, she does not spell this out.

A much later inscription shows women operating within a wider group
of colleagues. In the mid fourth century, a group of launderers jointly
dedicated a Pentelic marble slab with a carved relief to the Nymphs and all
the gods (*IG* 11² 2934); it was found at the Panathenaic Stadium.[208]

> οἱ πλυνῆς : Νύμφαις : εὐξάμενοι : ἀνέθεσαν : καὶ θεοῖς πᾶσιν
> Ζωαγόρας : ⟨Ζ⟩ωκύπρου : Ζώκυπρος : Ζωαγόρου : Θάλλος : Λεύκη
> Σωκράτης Πολυκράτους : Ἀπολλοφάνης : Εὐπορίωνος : Σωσίστρατος
> Μάνης : Μυρρίνη : Σωσίας : Σωσιγένης : Μίδας.

The clothes washers, after praying, dedicated [this] to the Nymphs and all
the gods.

Zoagoras son of [Z]okypros, Zokypros son of Zoagoras, Thallos, Leuke
(f.), Sokrates son of Polykrates, Apollophanes son of Euporion, Sosistratos,
Manes, Myrrhine (f.), Sosias, Sosigenes, Midas.

The relief above the inscription shows Hermes with three Nymphs, the
river-god Akheloios, and a seated Pan. The relief below shows an altar
approached by a bearded man with a horse; behind the altar sits a goddess,
while another goddess stands nearby with torches: Demeter and Persephone.
Dedication to Nymphs, who inhabited rivers, makes sense for clothes
washers, as does dedication to Akheloios; Pan and Hermes are associated
with the Nymphs in cult and myth; Demeter and Persephone received cult
on the banks of the River Ilissos, though this connection is more tenuous.
The dedication is a votive, made in response to an answered prayer
(εὐξάμενοι); the identification of the dedicators as οἱ πλυνῆς (the clothes
washers) and the choice of deities make clear that they made their prayer and
offering in relation to their work. Dedications by large groups identified by
occupation are very rare, though there is one parallel from c. 268/7, a statue
with a surviving round Hymettian marble base, dedicated by accountants,
secretaries, and overseers ὑπὸ τοῦ κοινοῦ τῶν ἐργαζ[ομένων – – –], 'on
behalf of the workers' association' (*IG* 11² 2941), all men.

In 2015, Taylor emphasised the lack of distinction between citizen
and non-citizen in the list of names: counter to prevailing fourth-
century epigraphic custom, none of the dedicators' demotics or cities
of origin are mentioned, nor are any identified as enslaved[209] (as in *IG*

---

[208] Staatliche Museen, Berlin, SK 709.

[209] Taylor 2015: 43. Taylor suggests that the commissioners could have identified enslaved people by
the adjective *khrēstos*, but we would not expect a term of praise on a dedication as we might on
a funerary monument. Some curse tablets (e.g. *DTA* 87 and *SGD* 11) qualify names of enslaved

II[2] 2941, where all dedicators are identified by mononym, without even patronymics). The names Zoagoras and Zokypros (presumably father and son) are probably Cypriot, but neither has a toponymic. Further, the names are not organised by gender: Leuke and Myrrhine are not grouped as 'women'; their gender seems to have been unimportant in this context. While some steps of the dedication process (e.g., negotiating with the sculptor) may have been carried out by one or more individuals on behalf of the group, others (e.g., choosing the design, being present at the dedication) may have been more widely collaborative. The inscription also attests to the shared prayer which preceded the dedication (εὐξάμενοι), probably for the shared aim of safety and success at work.

Returning to the relief in 2017, Taylor suggested that Thallos and Leuke were enslaved by Zoagoras and Zokypros, 'given that they follow them on the inscription and have no patronymic',[210] and that Sosistratos and those listed after him were enslaved by Sokrates and Apollophanes. If so, the dedicators *are* listed by legal status: free men first, then enslaved people, according to who kept whom in slavery. (Myrrhine still is listed neither first nor last of the supposed 'group' of people enslaved by Sokrates and Apollophanes, suggesting the relative unimportance of her gender within her (possible) status as enslaved, at least in the act of dedication.) This complicates our understanding of 'collaboration'. Even if the enslavers worked alongside those they kept in slavery, it is harder to understand the dedication as a shared act reflecting shared labour; the dedication and the labour may have been done as a group, but under violent compulsion. Another possibility is that Zoagoras, Zokypros, Sokrates, and Apollophanes owned the business but not its workers, whom rather they employed; this might explain why they alone are given the dignity of patronymics. At the least, we can say that Leuke and Myrrhine worked and worshipped, freely or unfreely, within a mixed-gender, mixed-ethnicity group and were publicly identified as doing so.[211]

Either way, this is an unusual dedication; perhaps the shared religious activity between colleagues of various statuses to which it attests was the

---

 people with *ho oiketēs*, often with the enslaver's name in the genitive; the enslaved workers listed in the Erekhtheion building accounts of 408/7 (*IG* I[3] 476) are identified with their name followed by their enslaver's name in the genitive. Compare fn. 215.

[210] Taylor 2017: 223, fn. 115.

[211] For what seems to be another fourth-century, mixed-gender, mixed-ethnicity dedication to nymphs, see *SEG* 54:318 (= Schörner, Goette, and Hallof 2004: 64–7, NAM 2009), discussed on my pp. 288–9. *SEG* 12:166 (NAM 4465) is a fourth-century group dedication to the Nymphs made by three men with Greek names: Gaifman 2008: 94–6. For group dedications as evidence for social networks, see Taylor 2015b, Taylor 2011c, the latter on women's networks.

exception rather than the norm. However, it and the curse tablets shed light from different angles on the same phenomenon. The dedication attests to joint religious activity between a diverse but united group arising from shared work; the curse tablets represent a different kind of supernatural activity carried out by a sole actor in order to prevent what she or he perceived as malicious collaborative activity between people connected by their work.

A Case Study: Phanostrate

In Chapter 1, we saw how Nikarete's work for Kleidikos' family led to a lasting relationship with them. New epigraphic evidence attests to a similar relationship arising from a woman's work as a midwife and doctor.[212] The mid fourth-century grave *stēlē* of Phanostrate (*IG* 11² 6873, NAM Γ993, Figure 4.9) shows a standing, veiled woman, labelled 'Antiphile', holding hands with a seated woman labelled 'Phanostrate'. Around them are four children, three girls and a baby boy. Beneath the relief, the following epigram:

> μαῖα καὶ ἰατρὸς Φανοστράτη ἐνθάδε κεῖται
> [ο]ὐθενὶ λυπη⟨ρ⟩ά, πᾶσιν δὲ θανοῦσα ποθεινή.

> The midwife and doctor Phanostrate lies here;
> She caused pain to no one, and dead, everyone misses her.

The dead woman's name is inscribed along the top; a break in the stone leaves Φανο- (easily restored from the epigram and label as Φανο[στράτη], with enough space afterwards for an andronymic) and on the line below, Μελ-. Georges Daux restored this as Μελιτέως, genitive of the demotic 'of Melite', assuming it belonged to a genitive patronymic missing on the first line. Rebecca Futo Kennedy proposes instead Μελιταίς (feminine nominative) or Μελιταιέως (masculine genitive), 'from Melite' (modern Malta),[213] arguing that Phanostrate was most likely of metic rather than citizen status.[214] Either is possible.

---

[212] *IG* 11² 6873 + *SEG* 33:214; see also *GE* 53 and *CAT* 11.890 (the latter correcting some of the interpretation of the former).

[213] Daux 1972: 550–4. Kennedy's inspection of the stone found the crossbar of the E uncertain, so she also proposes (and favours) Μιλησία (fem. nom.) or Μιλησίου (masc. gen.), 'from Miletos', noting that Milesians represented the largest group of metics in Attica (Kennedy 2014: 141–3, with fn. 69); Kellogg 2013: 67, fn. 92, finds five Milesians living in Akharnai. When I inspected the stone I found the crossbar secure.

[214] Dallas 1987: 124 also thinks Phanostrate was a metic.

Figure 4.9 Grave *stēlē* of Phanostrate, mid fourth century, Athens, National Archaeological Museum NAM Γ993. © Hellenic Ministry of Culture.

Phanostrate's *stēlē* was found in Akharnai, northern Attica. Stephen Lambert writes, 'among the several possible explanations [for the findspot] is that Phanostrate had married a man from Acharnai, who had since died, and/or that (unusually for a citizen woman) she worked in Acharnai as an independent woman, not cohabiting with any man'.[215] Akharnai was home to a number of Athenians from other demes and to metics: Danielle Kellogg finds over twenty citizens from across fifteen other demes – including Melite – living there in the classical period, and at least twelve

---

[215] Lambert 2018a says 'it cannot be entirely ruled out that she was or (perhaps less unlikely) had been a slave of the man from Melite', but the comparandum he cites for enslaved people's names given with the genitive of their enslaver's name is a list of crew of Athenian triremes (*IG* I³ 1032), not an individual's grave monument. None of the enslaved nurses discussed by Kosmopoulou 2001 is identified in this form. Genitive of former enslaver would be even odder for a metic grave monument. Graves of known metic women tend to give ethnics (e.g. *IG* II² 8440, 9099, 9112). Though these may have been freeborn immigrants (like *IG* II² 7873, with patronymic), I know of no examples of freedwomen (or -men) commemorated with their former enslaver's name in the genitive; none are mentioned by Sawtell 2018: 70. For women moving independently, see Taylor 2011b: 126–7, citing Aristarkhos' female relatives in Xen. *Mem.* 2.7 – but they are moving to live with natal kin.

metics.[216] She hypothesises that they were drawn by 'the dominant cross-roads position of Acharnai in the plain north of Athens', 'economic attractions, in the form of desirable agricultural holdings and the production of charcoal', and for metics, perhaps the residence there of their *prostatai*. As Attica's most populous deme, it offered a midwife and doctor plenty of potential clients.

Scholars variously suggest that Antiphile was Phanostrate's relative,[217] client[218]/'wealthy patroness',[219] assistant,[220] or the wife of Phanostrate's *prostatēs*.[221] Given what Angeliki Kosmopoulou refers to as the 'specificity in the iconography' (the distinctly portrayed children, of different ages and genders), and the fact that the girl in the centre looks towards Antiphile rather than Phanostrate, it seems likeliest that Antiphile was the children's mother, and that Phanostrate helped deliver them and keep them healthy.

In 2017, Jaime Curbera rectified the misreading of an inscribed mid fourth-century dedication to Asklepios (*IG* ii³ 700) which begins with the name Φανοστράτη (previously incorrectly read as Φανόστρατο[ς]). The inscription, on a Hymettian marble statue base from the Asklepieion on the slopes of the Akropolis, reads:

Φανοστράτη [– – –].

Δηλοφάνης ἀνέθηκε Χο[λαργεὺς εἰκόνα τήνδε],/
τῆς αὑτοῦ θυγατρὸς Δ[– ‿ ‿ εὐξαμένης]./
Λυσιμάχηι γὰρ μητρὶ ‿ – ‿ ‿ – ‿ ‿ – ‿
χεῖρα μέγας σωτὴρ – ‿ ‿ – ‿ ‿ –

ἐπὶ Πατ[αίκου ἱερέως].

Phanostrate – – –

Delophanes of Kholargos dedicated this likeness
after/because of the prayer-vow of his daughter D– .[222]
for over(?) her(?) mother Lysimakhe (you extended?)
your hand, great Saviour.[223]

In the priesthood of Pataikos.

---

[216] Kellogg 2013: 67; her prosopographical appendix of Akharnians and her index of monuments do not include Phanostrate because she herself is not identified as Akharnian. Movement within Attica was not always centripetal, as shown by Kellogg here and by Osborne 1991.

[217] Laes 2011: 159. [218] Laes 2011: 159. [219] Kosmopoulou 2001: 300. [220] Lambert 2018a.

[221] Kennedy 2014: 141; likewise Dallas 1987: 124.

[222] In archaic dedicatory epigrams, 'a family member's earlier vow is often expressed in a genitive absolute': Day 2010: 190.

[223] Wilhelm, Engelmann, and Wundsam 1980: 11, no. 7, offer the following restoration: Δηλοφάνης ἀνέθηκε Χο[λαργεὺς εἰκόνα τήνδε] / τῆς αὑτοῦ θυγατρὸς Δ[ωρίδος εὐξαμένης]· / Λυσιμάχηι γὰρ μητρὶ [φίληι, Ἀσκληπιέ, τὴν σήν] / χεῖρα μέγας σωτὴρ [ἐξεφάνης ἐπιθείς].

Curbera suggests that this Phanostrate may have been Delophanes' daughter (in which case the delta of l. 5 would have to initiate something other than a name), or that she was a healer, 'perhaps' (*'fortasse'*) the Phanostrate of the above grave *stēlē*. Pataikos was priest at some point before 343/2,[224] so the chronology fits. Lambert considers the latter identification 'likely' and suggests that 'this dedication of a statue of [Phanostrate] commemorates her successful treatment of Lysimache for a gynaecological problem. Appropriately enough in these circumstances the dedication results from a vow made (probably) by her daughter, D– (l. 3), and is set up by (probably) her husband and D– 's father, Delophanes.'[225] (Alternatively, Lysimakhe was Delophanes' mother, not his wife, and therefore D– 's grandmother, not mother.) We will call D – *Doris*.[226]

If the identification is correct, together the inscriptions allow us to build a picture of the relationships arising from Phanostrate's work. With connections in Akharnai, Kholargos, and either Melite, Athens, or Melite, Malta, Phanostrate earned the gratitude of two families of wealthy clients who sufficiently valued their relationship with her to commemorate it in stone. When Lysimakhe became ill, it was apparently her daughter *Doris* who made a prayer-vow for her healing, but when Lysimakhe was healed, it was *Doris*' father who fulfilled her vow by making the dedication. Lambert's hypothesis that *Doris* made the prayer-vow because it concerned a gynaecological problem is possible but not necessary. A man's making a prayer-vow for gynaecological healing may have been understood as inappropriate male interference in the intimate sphere of female health,[227] or appropriate husbandly concern for a wife's health – and perhaps fertility, a primary concern of fourth-century gynaecology.[228] In any case, *Doris* made the prayer and Delophanes the dedication, presumably because he was the one with the capital to do so (or *Doris* died in the interim). We have an endearing picture of a daughter's love for her mother

---

[224] Aleshire 1989: 126, 70.   [225] Lambert 2018b, based on Curbera in *IG* ii³.

[226] The suggestion of Wilhelm (see fn. 223). An appealing but less likely possibility is 'Delia', a rare name which shares an onomastic stem with Delophanes; a Delia dedicated in the Asklepieion in the third century or before (*IG* ii² 1534.194). The last syllable of the genitive would scan long, so it would not strictly fit, but often licence is taken in epigrams to accommodate names. Though tempting, we cannot securely associate this woman with the one who made the vow to Asklepios.

[227] Compare e.g. Eur. *Hipp.* 273–6.

[228] In Attica, one other man made a dedication to Asklepios on behalf of his wife (ὑπὲρ τῆς γυναικός) in the mid fourth century (*IG* ii² 4372), and another in the early third (*IG* ii³ 1, 898.47); I do not know of Attic women making dedications on behalf of husbands described as such.

and a father's love for his daughter. Which of the three decided that the statue should be of Phanostrate, the woman whose human healing work was associated with the divine healing work of Asklepios? The gesture of Antiphile's daughter towards Phanostrate on her grave *stēlē* suggests that the midwife and doctor had positive relationships with her clients' children as well as her clients themselves.

Phanostrate's work led to her inclusion in a monument highly concerned with kinship; the epigram features two kinship terms (*thygatēr*, daughter, and *mētēr*, mother) *and* the names of everyone involved. Phanostrate's own name, though separated by the arrangement of the text, features alongside the names of the family. Familial inclusion is even more apparent in Phanostrate's grave *stēlē*, where she clasps hands with her client as if the two were kin, surrounded by her client's children as if they were her own. Uniquely to this *stēlē*, the children are at once an index of family inclusion and a representation of Phanostrate's occupation.[229] Similarly, '[o]ὐθενὶ λυπη⟨ρ⟩ά' ('she caused grief/pain to no one') may praise her amiable personality, medical and therapeutic skill, or both.[230] Delophanes' dedication in the sanctuary of Asklepios of a statue of Phanostrate which implicitly praises her work, probably during her lifetime, would have significantly increased her professional and social reputation.[231]

Phanostrate's commemoration by non-relatives suggests she had no living relatives in Attica. Kennedy suggests Phanostrate's father predeceased her;[232] as we have seen, Lambert suggests she was either widowed or single. Her inclusion in the families of Antiphile and Lysimakhe on the monumental level likely reflected her inclusion on the intangible, interpersonal level in her lifetime, which would have mitigated her potential isolation if she had been single. In a similar way, Nikarete's work as a wet nurse during her separation from her husband brought her a kind of inclusion into Kleidikos' family. As classical Attic women typically

---

[229] Kosmopoulou 2001: 300 comments: 'Unlike other gravestones, where children interact with the adults and are part of the composition, the children here serve as "attributes" connoting the domain of Phanostrate's expertise' (she later seems to go back on herself: 'As is the case with other professionals, the deceased is not ... characterized by special attributes'). But the children are part of the composition and do interact with the adults: the baby reaches up to them, and the girl on the right offers something to Phanostrate.

[230] Compare Kosmopoulou 2001: 300.

[231] Taylor 2011c: 715 refutes the suggestion that women's friendships provide little access to status in her discussion of women's joint benefactions in the second-century Aegean; this is another counter-example.

[232] Kennedy 2014: 142–3, but the assertion at Pl. *Tht.* 149b that midwives were necessarily postmenopausal, which Kennedy cites here, is unsubstantiated: Leitao 2012: 234–5.

Figure 4.10 Grave *stēlē* of Melitta, c. 340, London, British Museum BM 1909,0221.1,
c. 340. © The Trustees of the British Museum.

breastfed their own children,[233] Kleinias' mother, Kleidikos' wife, had most
likely died before Nikarete was employed; Nikarete may have become
a mother-figure to Kleinias.

We saw in Chapter 3 that some families erected sepulchral monuments
for enslaved nurses, sometimes showing them clasping hands with their
commemorating enslavers like family members. Others did the same for
paid free nurses.[234] The *stēlē* of the metic nurse Melitta (*IG* II² 7873, BM
1909,0221.1, Figure 4.10, c. 340) describes her as 'Melitta, the daughter of
Apollodoros the *isotelēs*' ([[Μέλιττα]] Ἀπολλοδώρου | ἰσοτελοῦ
θυγάτηρ; the name 'Melitta' was later erased, presumably for reuse).
Isoteleia was a privilege granted to certain metics, exempting them from

---

[233] Lys. 1.10, 12; Ar. *Lys.* 879–81.
[234] For example, EM 8844 = *IG* II² 9112, with Kennedy 2014: 133–4, and EM 10506 = *IG* II² 9079.

the metic tax without granting citizenship. The relief depicts the nurse on a pillowed seat, facing a girl of perhaps twelve. They raise their arms towards each other, though their hands do not touch – perhaps they exchanged an object? The word *titthē* (nurse) is inscribed under the seated woman; the name 'Melitta' appears above the girl, though from the associated epigram (here printed metrically), it must refer to the woman:

ἐνθάδε τὴν χρηστὴν τίτθην κατὰ γαῖα καλύπτ|ει
Ἱπποστράτης· καὶ νῦν ποθεῖ σε.
καὶ ζῶσαν σ' ἐφίλ-|ουν, τίτθη, καὶ νῦν σ' ἔτι τιμῶ
οὖσαν καὶ κατὰ γῆς | καὶ τιμήσω σε ἄχρι ἂν ζῶ·
οἶδα δὲ σοὶ ὅτι καὶ κατὰ γ-|ῆς, εἴπερ χρηστοῖς γέρας ἐστίν,
πρώτει σοὶ τιμ-|αί, τίτθη, παρὰ Φερσεφόνει Πλούτωνί τε κεῖνται.

Here the earth covers over the good nurse
of Hippostrate, and now she misses you.
While you lived, I loved you, nurse, and even now I still honour you,
though you are under the earth, and I will honour you as long as I live;
and I know that for you, even under the earth, if there really is a reward for the
  good,
there are honours for you first, nurse, laid up with Persephone and Plouton.

Paired with the relief, this epigram 'speaks' in the voice of a young child, Hippostrate. Perhaps Hippostrate's father commissioned it on her behalf, aware of his daughter's affection for Melitta. Alternatively, Hippostrate commissioned it as an adult – this may be implicit in the statement that she is honouring her nurse in death – and chose to portray herself at an age when she had been particularly close to her nurse, while emphasising the persistence of her affection and respect for her.

Phanostrate, apparently commemorated by her client Antiphile, and Melitta, commemorated by or on behalf of her former charge Hippostrate, are two of three or four free women in classical Attica commemorated by a woman not related to them. The others are Biote, commemorated by her *hetaira* (friend/companion/girlfriend) Euthylla (*IG* i³ 1295 bis), and possibly Anthemis, commemorated by Herophile (her *hetaira*?) and other *hetairoi* (*IG* i³ 1329), discussed in Chapter 5. We can draw no sweeping conclusions from this tiny group, but it does seem that remunerated work had the potential not only to bring women into contact with more and different people than they would otherwise have encountered but in some cases also enabled them to form close and profound relationships with their clients.

Conclusion

This chapter has drawn out three main themes of remunerated work in women's social lives. First, women's paid work offered a social role complementary to or independent of their kin relationships, which they sometimes articulated in their self-identification to the gods and the community in public dedications. Second, it shaped the dynamics of kin relationships within the household. Third, it gave women the opportunity to form relationships outside their kin group and neighbourhood, and to build networks across Attica and beyond.

Income-generating work offered an alternative site of 'identity-production' to the family and an alternative framework of relationships. Melinna's dedication shows that women might understand their role as earners as an integral part of their role as mothers, developing – or reframing – their traditional role. The account of Aristarkhos' relatives, however, suggests the potential of remunerated work to destabilise or expand traditional roles, particularly in richer households where women's paid work was not the norm. This reframing is suggested by the sepulchral relief of Phanostrate, where the iconography of a dead mother surrounded by her children is reapplied to a dead midwife surrounded by her client and the success stories of her work. Retailers and other women who worked beyond the family home or agricultural plot are portrayed without reference to relatives more often than not; their marital status is rarely apparent. Rather, they sometimes appear in connection to non-relatives in similar lines of work. Women who sold goods in markets or shops must have interacted with the widest range of people of almost any women in Attica. Interactions of economic exchange (entailing mutuality if not equality) with such a number and range of people must have given these women a very different social experience to that of women whose work (paid or unpaid) was primarily in the home or on plots of land worked by more or less the same local people, many of them probably relatives, every day.[235] This accounts for the Aristophanic implication that the nature of the interactions involved in retail work made female retailers notably assertive.

The appearance of female retailers in fourth-century curse tablets which suggest their relationships with a range of other people corroborates and

---

[235] Compare Osborne 1985b: 17–19 on the Attic *agros* (agricultural plot); p. 41 on the possibility that Attica's nucleated settlement pattern, where communities lived in clusters and travelled out to their plots of land, rather than living on isolated farmsteads, allowed for 'greater concentration of and control over the family'; and pp. 47–62 on the Attic preference for holding and working land in or near the hereditary deme.

develops this picture. The cursers cursed these women in their capacity as
earners connected to other earners. It was through their work, and their
working relationships, that they were influential and – to the curser –
threatening. This, with the evidence of Antiphile's and Delophanes' monuments to Phanostrate, attests to the capacity of remunerated work to give
women access to new forms of relationship with new and different people,
and to the emotional power of those relationships. We see again women's
capacity to reshape and replace family relationships and adapt the very
concept of 'family'. Remunerated work reshaped women's social landscapes,
offering alternatives to family- and neighbourhood-based sociality and
integrating women into more areas of the rich social landscape of Attica.

Appendix   Dedications found on the Akropolis which describe themselves as *dekatai* or *aparkhai*

The dedications were all almost certainly to Athena (in this context usually
spelt Athenaia), but not all the dedicators specify this in their dedications.
They are ordered by approximate date and then reference number.

IG i³ 615

Museum inventory no.: EM 6321
Dedicator (as described in inscription): Ergokleia
Type: *aparkhē*
Dedicatee (as described): not specified
Likely date: 525–510
Item: Column with capital of dark (Hymettian?) marble, with incisions
    to attach bronze plinth
Inscription: Ἐργόκλεια ⁝ ἀ[νέθεκε – – – – –] ἀπαρχέν

IG i³ 644

Museum inventory no.: EM 6348 / Akr. 683
Dedicator (as described in inscription): Euarkhis (and Lysias)
Type: *aparkhē* (and *dekatē*)
Dedicatee (as described): Athena
Likely date: 510–500
Item: Upper part of column with Pentelic marble platform on top, with
    hollows for two plinths; right-hand plinth now known to have held
    'red shoes *korē*'

Inscription: Λυσίας ἀνέθεκεν Ἀθεναίαι ἀπαρχέν. Εὐάρχις ἀνέθεκεν δεκάτεν Ἀθεναίαι.

IG I³ 767

Museum inventory no.: Akr. ? (known formerly to have been at the Acropolis Museum in Athens but not found by the editors of *IG* I³)
Dedicator (as described in inscription): Empedia
Type: *dekatē*
Dedicatee (as described): Athena
Likely date: 500–480
Item: Pentelic marble column with hole to support capital
Inscription: Ἐμπεδία δεκάτεν ἀνέθεκεν [τ]ε̑ι Ἀθ[ε]να-|ίαι

IG I³ 547

Museum inventory no.: Akr. 5905
Dedicator (as described in inscription): Lysilla
Type: *aparkhē*
Dedicatee (as described): Athena
Likely date: 500–475
Item: Bronze disc with hole (for statue?)
Inscription: Λύσιλλα ἀπαρχὲν Ἀθεναίαι

IG I³ 794

Museum inventory no.: Akr. 607
Dedicator (as described in inscription): Smikythe the launderer
Type: *dekatē*
Dedicatee (as described): not specified
Likely date: 490–480
Item: Columnar limestone base with hollow for basin
Inscription: Σμικύθε πλύντρια δεκάτεν ἀνέθεκεν

IG I³ 921

Museum inventory no.: EM 6541 + 5503 + 13389
Dedicator (as described in inscription): Kallikrite
Type: *aparkhē*
Dedicatee (as described): Athena
Likely date: 490–480
Item: Pentelic(?) marble basin

Inscription: Καλ(λ)ικρίτε μ' ἀνέθεκεν ἀπα[ρχὲ]ν τἀθ[εναί]αι (hexameter)

IG I³ 536

Museum inventory no.: NAM X. 6944
Dedicator (as described in inscription): Glyke
Type: *dekatē*
Dedicatee (as described): Athena
Likely date: 480
Item: Bronze base with two holes for feet of statue
Inscription: Γλύκε δεκά-|τεν τἀθεναία-|⟨ι⟩

IG I³ 548 bis

Museum inventory no.: Kanellopoulos 724
Dedicator (as described in inscription): Glyke
Type: *dekatē*
Dedicatee (as described): Not specified
Likely date: 480
Item: Bronze mirror-handle
Inscription: Γλύκε ⁝ δεκάτεν ἀνέθεκεν

IG I³ 565

Museum inventory no.: NAM X. 7336
Dedicator (as described in inscription): Kapanis
Type: *dekatē*
Dedicatee (as described): Athena
Likely date: 480
Item: Bronze dish with four nail-holes where two handles were attached
Inscription: Καπανὶς δεκά[τ]εν ἀνέθεκεν τἀθεναίαι

IG I³ 814

Museum inventory no.: AM 6507
Dedicator (as described in inscription): Kallis
Type: *dekatē*
Dedicatee (as described): Athena
Likely date: 480
Item: Pentelic marble column
Inscription: Κάλις δεκάτεν ἀνέθεκεν Ἀθεναίαι

IG I³ 540

Museum inventory no.: NAM X. 6447
Dedicator (as described in inscription): Meleso
Type: *dekatē*
Dedicatee (as described): Athena (perhaps as Promakhos, given the statuette)
Likely date: 480–470
Item: Bronze (once gilded) statuette of Athena Promakhos, on a base which once stood on a marble column
Inscription: Μελεσὸ ἀνέθεκεν | δεκά-|τεν τἀθεναίαι

IG I³ 574

Museum inventory no.: NAM X. 7274
Dedicator (as described in inscription): Smikythe
Type: *dekatē*
Dedicatee (as described): Athena?
Likely date: 475
Item: Fragment of (?)hydria
Inscription: [τἀθεναίαι ἀνέθεκε(?) Σ]μικύθε δεκάτεν

IG I³ 934

Museum inventory no.: EM 6527
Dedicator (as described in inscription): Kallisto, daughter of Naukydes
Type: *aparkhē*
Dedicatee (as described): Athena
Likely date: 480–470
Item: Island marble basin
Inscription: [Καλ]λιστὸ Ναυκύδος θυγ[άτερ τἀθεναίαι μ' ἀνέθεκε]ν ἀπαρχέ[ν]

IG I³ 857

Museum inventory no.: EM 6254
Dedicator (as described in inscription): Mikythe, on behalf of her children and herself
Type: *dekatē*
Dedicatee (as described): Athena
Likely date: 470–450
Item: Pentelic marble column which once supported decoration in low relief

Inscription: See p. 205 (hexameters)

IG 11² 4889

Museum inventory no.: EM 9043
Dedicator (as described in inscription): Kallisto, wife of Sibyrtios
Type: *dekatē*
Dedicatee (as described): Athena (perhaps as Ergane, in whose temple it was found)
Likely date: 400–350
Item: Pentelic marble base
Inscription: [Καλ]λιστὼ [ἀνέ]θηκεν δεκάτην Σιβυρτίο γυνή

IG 11² 4334

Museum inventory no.: EM 8804 (erroneously recorded in *IG* 11² as EM 8004)
Dedicator (as described in inscription): Melinna
Type: *aparkhē*
Dedicatee (as described): Athena Ergane
Likely date: 350–300
Item: Hymettian marble base
Inscription: See p. 209 (hexameters)

CHAPTER 5

Euthylla and Biote
Women's Friendships

This chapter focuses on non-kin relationships characterised primarily by affection: friendships.[1] As discussed in the Introduction to this book, 'friendship' is not a transparent, cross-cultural category and, in the Athenian mind, was not straightforwardly extricable from kinship. However, Attic women did have close, affectionate, mutually supportive relationships with people – predominantly but not exclusively women – who were not understood as kin, and it is these relationships with which this chapter is concerned. The chapter takes two contexts of female friendship as large case studies. First, it argues that neighbours and neighbourhoods were an accessible and even necessary source of friendships for women. Second, it demonstrates the potential of female-dominated religious spaces and occasions for the development of female friendships. Both contexts offered women opportunities to encounter other women, spend time in their company, and construct and define their own spatial and social worlds. The chapter then demonstrates the importance of women's friendships as a source of practical and emotional support, particularly when male relatives failed. Finally, it examines two cases in which women were commemorated by friends rather than kin, one of which provided an opportunity for the commemorating woman to discuss her friendship with and feelings about the commemorated woman. It concludes with a new examination of the language of female friendship, demonstrating its similarities to the verbal language of male friendship and the behavioural language of kinship. The chapter shows that women's personal, affective relationships with non-relatives complemented and sometimes supplanted their kin relationships and constituted a valuable support system.

---

[1] See Taylor 2011c: 716, fn. 5 for the inadequacy and androcentrism of existing scholarship on friendship; she notes some exceptions, particularly in iconography, at fn. 41 (p. 719). Konstan 2018 is not an improvement.

Good Neighbours Become Good Friends

The Place of Neighbours in Imagination and Society

In the 1980s, Robin Osborne made the case for the Attic demes as central structuring forces in the lives of classical Athenian men in particular, arguing for a norm of deme residence and strong social and economic ties to one's deme.[2] By contrast, he argues:

> women do not even belong to demes, they are located more precisely by the demotic of their father and then their husband but in their own right they are residents in settlements whose political status is irrelevant: thus it is that Lysistrate refers to Kalonike at the opening of the *Lysistrata* as ἥ γ' ἐμὴ κωμῆτις (line 5), one who lives in the same village, rather than as one who lives in the same deme.

For women, it may make sense to look at 'units' of sociality and community other than the deme. In the following decade, with more of an emphasis on the socio-legal than the socio-political, David Cohen argued for the importance of the neighbourhood in structuring the life of classical Athenians, particularly women; he focused on the role of the neighbourhood in policing behaviour.[3] Cohen demonstrated that 'the social functions of friends and neighbors made the Athenian *oikos* far less private than some scholars have imagined': friends and neighbours – male and female – had intimate access to each other's homes, families, and lives.[4] He notes that the language in which friends (not specifically neighbours) are described often situates them within the 'private sphere' and sometimes comes close to identifying them with the household, using the term *oikeios* ('intimate', 'part of the family').[5]

Attention to the framing of neighbours in rhetorical and philosophical treatises reveals a similar conceptualisation of neighbours: family relationships are paired with neighbour relationships in ways which place neighbours nearer

---

[2] Osborne 1985b, with quotation from p. 183; see also Osborne 1985a.

[3] Cohen 1991: 47–69, (esp. 47–51), 86–90, 154–6. The importance of neighbours in Athenian thinking is visible in the Poletai records' frequent identification of properties by the names of the neighbours as well as the owners (e.g. *SEG* 32:161.6–7, dated 402/1).

[4] Cohen 1991: 87; for instances of neighbours knowing of and being involved in each other's affairs, he cites Lys. 3.7, Lys. 7.18, 28, Arist. frg. 84, Isae. 3.13–4, Thuc. 2.37, Aeschin. 3.174, [Dem.] 25.88–90, and [Dem.] 53.4, to which add [Dem.] 43.57, 60–1; for the possibility of *moikheia* with a neighbour's wife or daughter, he cites Arist. *NE* 1137a (=5.9); Eur. *El.* 921–4, also cited, does not refer to a neighbour and is almost certainly an interpolation, but add Menander's *Georgos* and *Samia*. More recently, see Gherchanoc 2012: 89–94 for 'neighbourhood sociability in a domestic context' ('une sociabilité de voisinage dans un cadre domestique', p. 89).

[5] Cohen 1991: 78–9. On the term, see Chapter 2, pp. 104–6.

the 'family' end of a conceptual family–stranger spectrum of familiarity. Aristotle pairs the experience of having bad neighbours with the experience of having bad children (*Rhetoric* 1395b); the Athenian in Plato's *Laws* asks Megillos whether he would welcome a housemate or neighbour (*synoikos ē geitōn*) who lacked self-control (3.696b). The implication in both cases is that a neighbour, like a child or housemate, would be a significant presence in one's life, such that obnoxious qualities on their part would be a real nuisance.

Similar phrasing by a Haouchi (Lebanese) woman interviewed by anthropologist Judith Williams helps us imagine the relevance to women of this conceptual positioning. The woman claims that she and her daughters 'are here in the house and we have nothing to do with anyone; we just stay in the house and see our neighbours'.[6] For her, as in the conceptual schemes implicit in Aristotle and Plato, 'neighbours' (with whom the woman admits to interacting) are distinct from 'anyone' (with whom she says she does not interact). She positions them closer to the 'we' of acceptable interaction constituted by herself and her daughters than the 'anyone' of unacceptable interaction. Though women's mobility and opportunities to network were limited by patriarchal social conventions, they barely needed to leave the house to visit close neighbours[7] and would know when the neighbours' menfolk were out and a visit would be possible.[8] Xenophon's Sokrates expects that a man would want to please his neighbour so he could later rely on him for help (*Mem.* 2.2.12) – a connection the Boiotian Hesiod made three or four centuries previously (*Op.* 342–51).[9] The actual or potential provision of neighbourly help is ubiquitous in literature, in scenarios ranging from everyday problems, like needing to relight a child's lamp or borrow a pot, to crises, like break-ins and serious accidents.[10] Again, this would have been particularly relevant for women, who would have been the beneficiaries as well as dispensers of

---

[6] Williams 1968: 76–7, quoted by Cohen 1989: 11, who rightly asks how the neighbours got there.

[7] Akbar 1982: 167 mentions that in pre-1945 Riyadh, which bore certain architectural and cultural similarities to classical Athens, some neighbourhoods had 'a bridge across the street for groups of neighboring women to meet without going outside'. A reconstruction of a residential block in Peiraeus (Figure 5.2), discussed on pp. 279–80, shows that it would be possible for some residents to cross the roof to the next-door house.

[8] Compare Cutileiro 1971: 137 on twentieth-century Vila Velha, Portugal: 'Since women remain in the villages most of the time, whereas men go to work outside, neighborly relations are basically feminine relations.'

[9] Compare Pl. *Leg.* 8.842e–844d.

[10] For example, [Dem.] 47.57, 60–2; Men. *Dys.* 392–31, 590–2, 666–85; *Pk.* 184–5, 262–4; Lys. 1.14; and Men. *Sam.* (see pp. 269–70); cf. also Alcman frg. 123. Compare Cutileiro 1971: 137 on Vila Velha: 'Supervising children's play, borrowing cooking utensils or provisions ... are some of the favors exchanged among poor neighbors.'

things like cooking equipment or ingredients – in Theophrastus' third-century *Characters* (10.13), the author does not say that the miserly man refuses to lend salt, herbs, or a lamp-wick, but that he forbids his wife to do so; she is the one being asked.

Friendships between Female Neighbours in Literature

Visits both developed and defined neighbourly friendships. The speaker of Demosthenes 55, a mid fourth-century lawsuit between two men who owned neighbouring land, briefly mentions the friendship between their widowed mothers:[11]

> τῆς γὰρ μητρὸς τῆς ἐμῆς χρωμένης τῇ τούτων μητρὶ πρὶν τούτους ἐπιχειρῆσαί με συκοφαντεῖν, καὶ πρὸς ἀλλήλας ἀφικνουμένων, οἷον εἰκὸς ἅμα μὲν ἀμφοτέρων οἰκουσῶν ἐν ἀγρῷ καὶ γειτνιωσῶν, ἅμα δὲ τῶν ἀνδρῶν χρωμένων ἀλλήλοις ἕως ἔζων. (§23)

> My mother was friends (*khraomai*) with their mother, before they [the neighbouring woman's sons] tried maliciously to sue me, and they [the women] used to visit one another, as was natural given that they both lived in the countryside and were neighbours, and given that their husbands had been friends (*khraomai*) while they were alive.

This description introduces an episode in which the speaker's mother (*Metrodora*)[12] goes to visit her friend (*Kallikleia*).[13] *Kallikleia* laments (ἀποδυραμένης) that some of their produce has been damaged by flooding and shows *Metrodora* the damage (§24). The speaker is keen to stress that the women's friendship is normal. This is because of the counter-intuitiveness of mothers of opposed litigants being friends, and the need to explain why *Metrodora*, whose second-hand testimony is crucial, had access to his opponents' property. It is not because a friendship between women was in itself unusual: the speaker appeals to a shared understanding among the jurors that women in such circumstances would 'naturally' (οἷον εἰκός) become friends.

The reasons the speaker gives for the friendship are informative. First, both women live in the countryside and are neighbours; the two elements are given in conjunction. The implication is that in a sparsely populated rural setting, one naturally forms relationships with those living and

---

[11] Compare [Dem.] 53.4 (and cf. §16) for similar intimacy between male neighbours.
[12] Because the mother's testimony is a gift to her son's case.
[13] Because she is the mother of Kallikles.

working nearby.[14] Florence Gherchanoc comments, 'geographic proximity and friendship are inseparable and reinforce female solidarity'.[15] Second, the women's husbands were friends. The speaker may mention this to legitimate the women's friendship (his mother's reputation is at stake), though the evidence discussed in this chapter suggests female friendships, particularly with neighbours, did not necessarily need legitimating. Cohen points out that male friends spent time at each other's houses so often and for so long that they probably got to know their friends' female relatives, who could not always keep out of sight and likely helped serve food.[16] This passage shows that friendships between men could lead to friendships between *women* – which could outlive the men who occasioned them. We should be open to the possibility that attestations of male friendships in our sources may mark the existence of unattested female friendships.

A character in Menander's *Samia* describes visits between his father's partner Khrysis and the woman and her daughter (Plangon) who live in the neighbouring house:

φ]ιλανθρώπος δὲ πρὸς τὴν τοῦ πατρὸς
Σαμίαν διέκειθ' ἡ τῆς κόρης μήτηρ, τά τε
πλεῖστ' ἦν παρ' αὐταῖς ἥδε, καὶ πάλιν ποτὲ
αὗται παρ' ἡμιν.   (35–8)

The girl [next door]'s mother was kind (*philanthrōpos*) to my father's Samian [Khrysis], and she [Khrysis] spent a lot of time with them, and they in turn used to spend a lot of time with us.

Khrysis' partner and her neighbour's husband are also friends, but unlike the friendship between *Metrodora* and *Kallikleia*, the women's relationship is not portrayed as derivative of the men's but as independent, arising out of one neighbour's kindness (φιλανθρώπος) to another. This friendship features prominently in the plot.[17] The three women celebrate the Adonia

---

[14] Osborne 1985b: 17–18 argues that the families in the dispute do not in fact live on the adjoining plots of land but are 'members of the same community who own adjacent pieces of land' and that 'the grain that was harmed was not in a house'. He does not mention the women in his discussion; if he is right, it would mean the women went to visit each other not at each other's houses but on their sons' farms, given that the pattern of normal visits seems to include a visit on which *Kallikleia* shows *Metrodora* the grain (§§23–4). Roy 1988 and Langdon 1991 both think this description of the women's relationship testifies against Osborne's overall argument against farmstead residence in Attica.

[15] Gherchanoc 2012: 92: 'Proximité géographique et amitié sont indissociables et renforcent des solidarités féminines.'

[16] Cohen 1991: 87, noting Antiph. 1.14, Lys. 1.22–3 (to which add §28), [Dem.] 53.4; elsewhere he notes Dem. 23.53–6, which implies men's potential sexual access to friends' female relatives.

[17] Lines 39–41; 55–6 with Sommerstein 2013 *ad loc.* 77–8, 84–5, 265–6, 410–11; 407–18.

festival together, with some others. Khrysis helps to nurse and raise Plangon and Moskhion's son in order to conceal his parentage, protecting Plangon and her family from social condemnation at considerable risk to herself.[18] Nikeratos and his wife take Khrysis in after she is thrown out by her partner. Across the course of the play, the women's friendship is revealed to be much stabler than the men's, who at one point brawl with each other (ll. 574–6).[19] This friendship between a citizen-status wife, an unmarried girl, and a metic crossed supposed boundaries of socio-legal status and age.[20] New Comedy plots usually take two next-door houses as their set and focus on the shifting relationships between their inhabitants, often ending in marriages linking the households.[21] We should not assume this makes the neighbour friendships they feature a mere dramatic necessity which over-exaggerates this aspect of Attic social life: friendships between neighbouring women appear incidentally in other New Comedies, Old Comedy, and forensic oratory.

For women, friendships may only have been possible with women living nearby. Robinette Kennedy describes how in the Cretan mountain village of Hatzi in the twentieth century, women 'consider the practicalities involved in carrying on a future friendship, for example, the proximity of a potential friend's house and whether it is in the same neighbourhood', because the community does not consider it 'correct social behaviour to be outside one's neighbourhood for a purpose not recognized by mainstream culture'.[22] Classical Attica, where, as we will see, women probably had

---

[18] Compare Thonemann 2022: 351–4 for a comparable story of two women from different households collaborating to conceal their teenaged children's premarital sex and pregnancy in second- or third-century AD Graeco-Roman Anatolia: 'we can only be struck by the risks which Syntyche chose to run in the name of interfamilial solidarity and friendship' (p. 354).

[19] See Foxhall 1998a: 51, 61 on the volatility of many male friendships.

[20] For example, the assumption of a distinct social 'world of wives' and 'world of maidens' (Sommerstein 2007: 184). As well as the metic–Athenian friendships discussed in this chapter, cf. also the friendship between an enslaved woman and a citizen-status woman (not her enslaver) in Antiph. 1.14.

[21] Compare Cox 2002a, Cox 2002b. Neat Menandrian conclusions may not be realistic, but being neighbours allowed families to get to know each other as a basis for arranging a marriage. Plato's sister Potone was married to their neighbour Eurymedon of Myrrhinous and thus 'consolidated two contiguous landed estates for two generations' (Cox 1988: 386; Cox 1998: 187–8): Diog. Laert. 3.4, 3.42, 4.1; *APF*, no. 8792 xi D. Osborne 1985b: 22 uses Menander's plays as evidence for deme sociality: 'Menander's plays rely on an intense and intimate social life, so the fact that at least three were set in Attic demes [*Heros* in Ptelea, *Sikyonios* in Eleusis, and *Epitrepontes* in an unknown deme] must be an indication that the demes remained close communities down to the last years of the fourth century.' As I argue across this chapter, for women the 'neighbourhood' may have been of more social significance than the deme.

[22] Kennedy 1986: 129.

more freedom of movement within the neighbourhood than beyond it, may have had similar patterns of friendship.

Men might both accept and suspect friendships between neighbouring women. In Lysias 1, the speaker has *Thesmonike* explain away the noise of her lover's entrance in the night by saying that their child's light had gone out, and that she had gone to relight it at the neighbours' house (literally 'from the neighbours', ἐκ τῶν γειτόνων, §14). That she might go to her neighbours' house during the night to relight a lamp presumes a close relationship with them. The speaker's narrative suggests that 'the neighbours excuse' was uncomfortably hard for men to reject, even in suspicious circumstances.[23] Female neighbourly help in *Samia* (here 'real' within the drama rather than invented as an excuse) is also part of a plot to deceive men: the women are hiding the parentage of an illegitimate baby from their respective menfolk. Stories of women using visits to neighbours for assistance as a cover for deceiving men in order to rebel against their sexual control suggests some men felt the irreproachability and potency of women's neighbourly relationships threatened their authority.

The Neighbourhood

As well as the social importance of individual neighbours, literary, archaeological, and comparative anthropological evidence suggests that Athenians had a concept of 'neighbourhoods', social groups broadly mapped onto spatial zones within the city or in villages, and that these neighbourhoods may have been particularly important to women.[24] In Aristophanes' *Lysistrata*, the title character is friends with her older neighbour Kalonike (ll. 5–7). As we have seen, Lysistrate describes Kalonike as *ēmē kōmētis*: 'a woman from my village (*kōmē*)' or 'from my district of town'. The third-century AD grammarian Julius Pollux quotes the line in his description of the parts of the *asty* of Athens – doubtless inflected by his experience of Roman towns – in his thesaurus of Attic words and phrases:

---

[23] Compare Gherchanoc 2012: 92: 'this reality [the inseparability of geographic proximity and friendship among women, and solidarity between female neighbours], exploited by Aristophanes for comic purposes, serves to characterise female perfidiousness'.

[24] Gherchanoc 2012: 92–3 writes of how bonds between female neighbours and friends, drawn on for help and service, particularly in, for example, childbirth (Ar. *Eccl.* 529–30; Eurip. *El.* 1128–30), constitute 'solidarity between women which, within the framework of the house, is exercised around the domains where female knowledge reigns, [and] extends from one *oikos* to another, through the ties woven by neighbourhood (*les liens que tissent le voisinage*) and the movements of these women who, from one house to another, offer their knowledge and know-how.'

[9.35] τὰ δ' ἔνδον ἀγυιαὶ μὲν κατὰ Ξενοφῶντα[25] καὶ καθ' Ὅμηρον[26] ... [36] ταῦτα δὲ καὶ ἄμφοδα ἔστιν εὑρεῖν κεκλημένα οὐ παρ' Ἀριστοφάνει[27] μόνον ... ἀλλὰ καὶ παρ' Ὑπερείδῃ ἐν τῷ περὶ ἀντιδόσεως πρὸς Πασικλέα· "τὴν οἰκίαν τὴν μεγάλην τὴν Χαβρίου καλουμένην καὶ τὸ ἄμφοδον".[28] καλοῖτο δ' ἂν καὶ κῶμαι ταῦτα, ὅθεν καὶ κωμήτας τοὺς γείτονας καὶ κωμήτιδας ὠνόμαζον· Ἀριστοφάνης γοῦν ἐν μὲν Δράμασιν ἢ Κενταύρῳ ἔφη· "ἐν κωμήτισι καπηλοῖς ἐπίχαρτον",[29] ἐν δὲ Λυσιστράτῃ· "πλὴν ἤ γ' ἐμὴ κωμῆτις ... "[30] [37] τοὺς μὲν δὴ γείτονας καὶ προσοίκους καὶ συνοίκους καὶ παροικοῦντας καὶ προσοικοῦντας, τάχα δὲ καὶ παροίκους καὶ ἀγχιθύρους ἐρεῖς, Εὔπολις δὲ ἐν Κόλαξι[31] καὶ συμπαροίκους εἴρηκεν.

The [parts] inside [the walls are called] *aguiai* (streets) in Xenophon and in Homer ... and one also finds them called *amphoda* (streets, or perhaps 'blocks'), not only in Aristophanes ... but also in Hyperides, in the speech about the property exchange with Pasikles: 'the large house called Khabrios' house and the street/block' (*amphodon*). And these may also be called *kōmai* (literally 'villages', so, 'neighbourhoods'), from which they have the word 'villagers' (*kōmētai*) for 'neighbours', and 'female villagers' (*kōmētides*); Aristophanes, at any rate, says in *Dramas* or *Centaur* 'a source of spiteful joy among the neighbourhood tavern-women' (*kōmētides kapēloi*), and in *Lysistrata* 'here is my neighbour' (*kōmētis*) ... Indeed, you say *geitones* (neighbours) and [there follows a list of words for 'neighbours', which all express the idea of living close to one] *prosoikoi* and *synoikoi* and *paroikountes* and *prosoikountes*, and perhaps *paroikoi* and *ankhithyroi* (literally 'near-doors'; compare English 'next-door neighbour'), and Eupolis in *Flatterers* has said '*symparoikoi*'.

The variety of attested terms for 'neighbour' suggests the rich complexity of Attic neighbour relations, which may have been particularly salient to women. *Synoikos* could denote a person who lived in a different apartment within the same tenement-block (*synoikia*); the flax spinner in *Frogs* refers to the women she lives with as *synoikoi* (l. 1342).[32] José Cutiliero's description of neighbour relations in a twentieth-century Portuguese village helps us to imagine another potential set of distinctions between 'types' of neighbour: 'From her doorstep a woman can hear what is said at five or six other doorsteps and see what goes on in front of an even larger number of houses.'[33] The many terms Pollux cites may contain similar, now-lost

---

[25] *Cyrop.* 2.4.3.　　[26] *Il.* 5.642.　　[27] All Aristophanic attestations are now lost.

[28] Fragment 137 Kenyon.　　[29] Fragment 274 Kock.　　[30] Line 5.　　[31] Fragment 189.

[32] See further p. 278.

[33] Cutileiro 1971: 137, quoted by Cohen 1991: 49. Compare Freeman 1970: 86–7 on Valdemoro, Castile, the other way round: 'the physical arrangement of the pueblo is such that even houses which are shielded from the general view at the edges of the nucleus are still within hearing distance, and there is no house which is not within sight of at least two others'.

distinctions between next-door neighbours (*ankhithyroi?*), neighbours within earshot, neighbours within eyeline, and further-off neighbours still near enough to pass daily in the street.

We infer from Lysistrate's reference to Kalonike as *ēmē kōmētis* that *kōmai* were geographical areas which gave their inhabitants a social identity as *kōmētai* (masculine) and *kōmētidai* (feminine).[34] Lysistrate's connection to Kalonike is not that she lives next door but that she comes from the same *kōmē*, which functions as a social coagulant: the two are friends. The Aristophanic phrase ἐν κωμήτισι καπηλοῖς ἐπίχαρτον, 'a source of spiteful joy among the neighbourhood tavern-women', implies a community of women living near each other, not just relations between individual neighbours. It also imagines a common emotional experience among those women, possibly pointing in its original context to an affective relationship between them. Perhaps they are not simply experiencing the same spiteful joy but actively sharing that experience with each other, by joining each other in spiteful mockery or triumphalism.

In the fifth and fourth centuries, γειτόνων, the genitive plural of γείτων, 'neighbour', is used in the sense of 'neighbourhood'. One Aristophanic character refers to ἡ καπηλὶς ἡκ τῶν γειτόνων ('the tavernkeeper (f.) from the neighbours [i.e. neighbourhood]', *Plut.* 435). A fourth-century curse tablet discussed in Chapter 4 uses the same phrase for a male tavernkeeper (τὸν κάπηλον τὸν ἐγ γειτόνων, *DTA* 87.1). In *Lysistrata*, a woman describes how she hosted a party in honour of the goddess Hekate and 'invited [her] friend (*hetaira*, f.) from the neighbourhood' (τὴν ἑταίραν ἐκάλεσ' ἐκ τῶν γειτόνων, l. 701). Demosthenes and Menander push the plural γειτόνων for 'neighbourhood' further, describing plots of land as ἐν γειτόνων, 'among the neighbours', that is, 'in the neighbourhood', as if the genitive plural were a dative, eliding the individuals and the area ([Dem.] 53.10, Men. *Dys.* 25).[35]

The passage in *Lysistrata* about the party (παιγνία) for Hekate offers another picture of community relations in the neighbourhood. Responding

---

[34] Isoc. 7.46 refers to deliberate division of the city into *kōmai*, paralleled with division of the countryside into demes; Arist. *Pol.* 1.1252b sees the *polis* as an organic coagulation of once-separate *kōmai*. Pollux's Aristophanic citations suggest that in fifth-century Athens *kōmai* were informal rather than political entities. The speaker at Ar. *Nub.* 964–5 says that 'in the good old days' boys from the same district (*kōmētai*) used to go together to the harp-teacher; it is not clear how formal this 'catchment area' was.

[35] Osborne 1985b takes a different and more surprising line, arguing that *geitōn* in fact carries no implication of residence, only of ownership of neighbouring land. When people are described as 'neighbours', 'two possible cases [are] envisaged: dwelling close together in a village and farming a piece of land that neighbours another, and these two instances are distinct' cf. fn. 14.

to insults from the Men's Chorus, the Women's Chorus tells the man speaking, ἀπήχθου πᾶσι καὶ τοῖς γείτοσιν ('you are hated by everyone, especially the neighbours (m. pl.)', l. 699). One reason is that the friend invited to the party was not able to come because of a decree the men had imposed. In fact, the 'friend' turns out to be a Boiotian eel – a delicacy in Attica – and the decree a ban on imports. Jeffrey Henderson explains: 'The women liken the Greek world to a neighbourhood disrupted by a trouble-maker: just as the war has disrupted oikos-life, so has it disrupted friendships among oikoi ... The kind of neighbourhood picnic that would be possible in peaceful times cannot be held because of the "feud".'[36] Obliquely, we get a picture of a 'neighbourhood' in which female neighbours have parties at each other's houses (like the Adonia celebration in *Samia*),[37] and occasional enmities develop.

Neighbourhoods in the Asty

Literary evidence for the social importance of neighbours and neighbour-hoods to women is corroborated by archaeological evidence. Lisa Nevett, reconstructing a 'female topography' of Athens, argues that the *asty* was physically and socially composed of lots of small 'neighbourhoods', each of which 'may have lain conceptually between the fully enclosed space of the house and the civic space of the city at large', being outside the house but populated by families intimately known to each other. Nevett points out that Athens, unlike many later, planned Greek cities, was not built on a grid; rather, its street system grew up organically over time. The third-century tourist Heraclides Criticus describes Athens as being κακῶς ἐρρυμοτομημένη διὰ τὴν ἀρχαιότητα ('badly laid out because of its age', 1.1; the word ἐρρυμοτομημένη specifically refers to its division by streets). Because the city's terrain is not flat, road orientation was often determined by gradient, so clusters of houses between the roads had different orientations.[38]

Nevett argues that despite Athenian houses' architectural emphasis on isolating the household from the world outside, the windows and roofs, particularly on slopes, enabled occupants to look down into streets and doorways, across to other roofs, or even into neighbours' courtyards. Aristotelian texts mention regulations against upper storeys of houses

---

projecting into the streets ([Arist.] *Oec.* 1347a, *Ath. pol.* 50.2), which suggests this was a problem. Many classical Attic and other Greek sources, literary and iconographic, depict people looking down from roofs and upper-storey windows.[39] In a Greek letter from first-century Egypt, two women tell their younger sisters, μὴ παῖζε ἐν τῇ αὐλῇ, ἀλλὰ | ἔσω εὐτάκτει, 'don't play in the courtyard, but be well-behaved inside' (*P.Athen.* 60.12–13). Possibly this reflected concern about the girls' skin darkening in the sun; alternatively (or additionally), the architecture of their neighbourhood meant their courtyard was overlooked and was not a private space.[40] Thinness of walls also gave neighbours access to each other's private lives: texts refer to the possibility of digging through walls (Ar. *Thesm.* 484–5, Men. *Phasma* 49–56, Hyp. *Lyc.*), and of listening for neighbours' conversations (Pl. *Resp.* 7.531a). Nevett argues that such interplay between privacy and intimacy, also recognised by Cohen, resulted in 'a fragmentation of the city into separate neighbourhoods within which female residents may have felt relatively safe and may have been likely to encounter, by and large, relatively fewer strangers',[41] allowing women greater freedom of movement and association beyond – but not too far beyond – the home.

Jamel Akbar's description of the architectural and social structure of pre-1945 Riyadh in Saudi Arabia allows us to imagine how women might have understood and experienced their city:[42]

> In the traditional pattern there is a definite hierarchical order in the formation of the alleyways. Main alleyways enclose large blocks of houses which, in turn, are divided into smaller blocks by narrow alleyways that finally lead to closed alleyways. These closed alleyways provide more security for their inhabitants because they exclude nearly all strangers and passers-by. Nowadays, with the increase of social mobility in massive development, the cluster-scale social group and its cultural values are being forgotten. The relationship between man and his community becomes very limited, because upon leaving the dwelling he is transplanted into the town level without an immediate hierarchy of spaces.

Nevett's 'neighbourhoods', imagined like Akbar's 'blocks', may be Aristophanes' and Hyperides' *amphoda* and *kōmai*.

---

[39] Nevett 2011: 579–81, with fn. 16. In women, this was often associated with flirtatiousness, sexual immorality, even prostitution (for which see especially the Thasian *stèle du port* (OR 104) with Graham 1998 and later emendations by Henry 2002). However, in Ar. *Ach.* 262, a man instructs his wife to watch a religious procession from the roof, here appropriate behaviour for women.

[40] I thank Aneurin Ellis-Evans for drawing my attention to this letter.   [41] Nevett 2011: 581.

[42] Compare Khan 1982: 194 on Old Jeddah. See my p. 28 for the comparative use of modern Islamic societies.

Here Nevett follows the prevailing view that classical Athenian houses typically consisted in rooms organised around a central courtyard, and sharply demarcated the 'private' space indoors from the outside world.[43] There is literary evidence for such houses,[44] and some excavated classical-period buildings from Athens and Olynthos have these features.[45] However, Janett Morgan has questioned the assumption that each of these buildings was a single home for a single household. Noting that some have multiple external doors, or internal doors which connect rooms into 'suites' or 'wings', she suggests that multiple 'households' may some-times have occupied what we usually assume to be one 'house'.[46] Residential buildings could also be modified and redivided during the period of their occupation. In such buildings, if there were a courtyard, it would not be private but shared.

In a more recent work, Nevett suggests that 'Building Z' in the Kerameikos may have been used in some phases of its history as a communal dwelling.[47] This large building seems originally to have been built in the late 430s and was then adapted in around 420, adapted again in the late fourth century after a period of disuse, and then again more dramatically in the third century. Its excavators have suggested that it was initially used as a house, and then reconstructed in the fourth century for use as a tavern, inn, textile workshop, and possibly a brothel, though Claire Taylor has questioned the assumptions underlying the brothel interpretation.[48] According to Nevett, in this third,

---

[43] Articulated by e.g. Jameson 1990. The description in Akbar 1982 of the architecture and ideology of pre-1945 Riyadh 'courtyard houses' is strikingly similar.

[44] For example, Ar. *Vesp.* 1212–17 and [Dem.] 47.55, with Morgan 2010: 46; note also Lys. 12.15–16, which suggests a *prothyron* (an entranceway with inner and outer doors, serving as a transitional space between indoors and outdoors).

[45] Morgan 2010: 48, 59, with Plans 1, 2, and 4 on pp. 173–5.

[46] Morgan 2010: 48–50, 65–6. Saliou 1992 offers a detailed study of a first-century AD Greek papyrus from Doura-Europos, Syria (*P.Dura* 19), which records an agreement that two buildings which had in the previous generation been united into one household, jointly inhabited by two brothers, should be divided between the four sons of one of the brothers following his death. Each son, with his household, would inhabit an area of the house newly separated from the other three by (re)constructing dividing walls and blocking up connecting doors, but with a communal entranceway and courtyard. See also Baird 2022 on 'how the life cycles of material houses tend to pivot around human – and less formal – scales of generational time' (p. 412), with pp. 427–8 on *P.Dura* 19. Compare Pudsey 2022 on similar domestic arrangements in the Fayum region of Roman Egypt in the context of kinship structures there, esp. pp. 305–7 (on houses divided between siblings but with some shared areas) and 310–12 (on sharing and leasing of houses and parts of houses between neighbours and non-kin as well as between kin); here divisions agreed on in contracts did not necessarily require physical barriers. Boozer 2019: 82 suggests that archaeologically attested locks on internal doors in buildings in Roman Egypt may suggest occupation by unrelated individuals or groups.

[47] Nevett 2023: 16–17, 80–1.

[48] Knigge 2005, summarised by Ault 2016, though Ault argues for its use as a brothel not only in its third stage but also in its first two stages; see Taylor 2024: 6–10 for problems with this interpretation.

fourth-century phase the building had at least sixteen rooms which could be accessed from at least three different 'circulation spaces', including what seems to have been an open courtyard with a well.[49] Though the building's overall structure resembles that of a 'courtyard house', its size and densely built rooms, together with the large numbers of loom weights found from the first and third phases, and the number of pots for cooking, eating, and drinking, 'suggest the presence of large numbers of individuals', perhaps using the building 'as some kind of apartment complex or establishment renting out rooms'.[50]

In literature, such complexes are called *synoikiai*, 'houses where people live together' (*synoikeō*). These were residential buildings in which units were rented out by different individuals or families.[51] What would relations with 'internal' neighbours have looked like in *synoikiai*? Many references to *synoikiai* simply list them among the assets of rich landowners;[52] others offer more detail. The pseudo-Xenophontic *Constitution of the Athenians* ('Old Oligarch') comments that anyone who owns and leases out a *synoikia* benefits from Athens' policy of judging certain trials involving its allies in the Athenian courts (1.17), apparently because allies coming for trials would need to rent somewhere to stay. Some *synoikiai*, then, were rented short-term by visitors to Athens.

Euktemon in Isaeus 6 owned at least two *synoikiai*, one in Peiraieus and one near the city gate and wine shops of the Kerameikos (§§19, 20). This speech, discussed in Chapter 2, is one of our most detailed sources for life in Attic *synoikiai* but is given by a speaker intent on bringing his opponents into disrepute, which complicates it as a source. According to the speaker, Euktemon's Peiraieus *synoikia* was managed by a freedwoman Euktemon had previously kept in slavery, and functioned partly as a brothel. One enslaved woman, Alke, who was prostituted in the brothel 'for many years', seemingly lived there with her children and freedman partner, in an informal family (§§19–20). Alke was later (freed and?) made manager of the Kerameikos *synoikia*. According to the speaker, Euktemon visited regularly to collect the rent and, in doing so, developed a relationship

---

[49] Nevett 2023: 81; Ault 2016: 83 counts twenty-two rooms and focuses on the central courtyard as a circulation space.

[50] Nevett 2023: 81.

[51] Aeschin. 1.124 speaks of *synoikiai* as occupied by many (πολλοί) renters; Aristophanes' throwaway reference to τὴν Ἱπποκράτους ξυνοικίαν ('Hippokrates' tenement-house', *Thesm.* 273), implies audience familiarity with the property, which may suggest it was large and easily visible. Compare Boozer 2019: 62–6 for residence in a fourth- to seventh-century AD apartment building in Kom el-Dikka, ancient Alexandria.

[52] Dem. 36.6, 36.34, 53.13; [Dem.] 45.28; Isae. 2.27, 5.26–7.

with Alke, eventually moving in with her and her children (§21). The story suggests some *synoikiai* were large enough and home to enough residents to require dedicated, live-in managers; that not all residents were short-term; that residents might be a mixture of enslaved people, metics, and citizens; and that *synoikiai* could be multifunctional, in this case functioning both as a brothel and as home to individuals and families.

In Menander's *Samia*, Khrysis is horrified by the prospect that a nurse (*titthē*) might raise the baby she has been caring for 'in some *synoikia*' (ἐν συνοικίᾳ τινί, ll. 84–5), a place she apparently envisions as grim. Alan Sommerstein notes that tenement-houses 'could be fire-traps and were doubtless often insanitary, a hazard to the health of all and particularly of infants'.[53] As we saw in Chapter 4, Aristophanes' *Frogs* also features a poor woman living and working in a *synoikia*. Her situation is presented as the familiar stuff of daily life (l. 959), which suggests that living in a *synoikia* was nothing strange to the majority of the citizen audience. The mock-Euripidean monody Aeschylus sings in this persona does not easily lend itself to historical inference because of its parodic mix of the supposedly mundane with a high tragic style. The woman calls for help from her *synoikoi* (housemates, l. 1342), one of whom is called Mania (l. 1345). 'Mania' seems to have been a Phrygian name; it was frequently used for fictional enslaved characters,[54] and Aristophanes' choice of it may have been intended to suggest that the imagined *synoikia* was home to enslaved and freedwomen – like the *synoikiai* in Isaeus 6. The singing character's description of how her stolen cockerel 'flew up, flew up into the *aether*' (ἀνέπτατ' ἀνέπτατ' ἐς αἰθέρα, l. 1352), coupled with appeals to mountain deities (Νύμφαι ὀρεσσίγονοι, l. 1344; Ἴδας τέκνα, l. 1356), suggests a two-storey building in which the supposed thief, Glyke, lives upstairs – either in the same *synoikia* as the singer and Mania's or a neighbouring one.[55] Relationships between individual occupants in the imagined *synoikia* or *synoikiai* are sometimes inimical (as with the singer and Glyke), sometimes cooperative (as with the singer and Mania).

Residential buildings might also be shared on a smaller scale. Classical and Hellenistic inscriptions recording leases of property owned by the sanctuaries of Delian Apollo on Delos, Rheneia, and Mykonos sometimes refer to the leasing of parts of properties (floors or individual rooms).[56] Antiphon 1 describes a house whose *hyperōion*

---

[53] Sommerstein 2013 *ad loc*.   [54] Vlassopoulos 2010: 122.
[55] Compare Sommerstein 1996 *ad* 1344 and 1345.   [56] Osborne 1985a: 120–2.

(upper floor, or upper room) was occupied by the householder's friend Philoneos when he visited Athens (§14).[57] In this case, the householder's wife (*Mnesodike*)[58] became friends (*epoiēsato philēn*) with Philoneos' enslaved partner (*Phile*).[59] According to the speaker, Philoneos intended to consign *Phile* to a brothel. The speaker alleges that *Mnesodike*, who was his stepmother, learnt of Philoneos' intention and tricked *Phile* into administering to him and her husband what *Phile* thought was a love potion to win him back and save her, but was in fact poison, which killed both men. Whatever the truth of the story, it makes sense that a woman who sometimes stayed in the upper apartment of a house should befriend the woman who lived downstairs; we might also see this as a friendship between women occasioned by a friendship between men. The speaker unapologetically uses the language of 'friendship' for the relationship between an enslaved woman and a woman of citizen status.

This reconsidered view of classical Athenian domestic architecture acknowledges that 'typical' courtyard houses sharply separating the resident family from the outside world reflected the reality of some but not all Athenians' domestic lives. It does not negate the argument for the 'intermediary' space of neighbourhoods which brought neighbours, particularly neighbouring women, into acceptable contact with each other but complements it, recognising that for some Athenians, neighbours lived much more intimately.[60]

Neighbourhoods outside the Asty

Nevett and Pollux's observations deal only with the *asty*. In contrast to Athens, with its organic growth, multiple hills, and haphazard street layout, stood the grid-planned Peiraieus, which seems to have had artificial neighbourhoods 'built in'. Excavations show that the grid was divided into 'blocks' consisting in two rows of four residential buildings, as in Figures 5.1 and 5.2.

The reconstruction allows us to imagine the nuances of neighbour-networks based on different degrees of 'neighbouringness', which may account for the variety of terms recorded by Pollux. The inhabitants of,

---

[57] Compare also Ar. *Eq.* 1001, where the sausage seller says he has 'an upstairs floor and two apartment buildings' (ὑπερῷον καὶ ξυνοικία δύο) full of oracles, though the scholia suggest '*synoikia*' here may mean 'storeroom'.

[58] Because of the language of justice attributed to her in Antiphon 1.15.

[59] Because she became a friend.   [60] Compare Cohen 1991: 155.

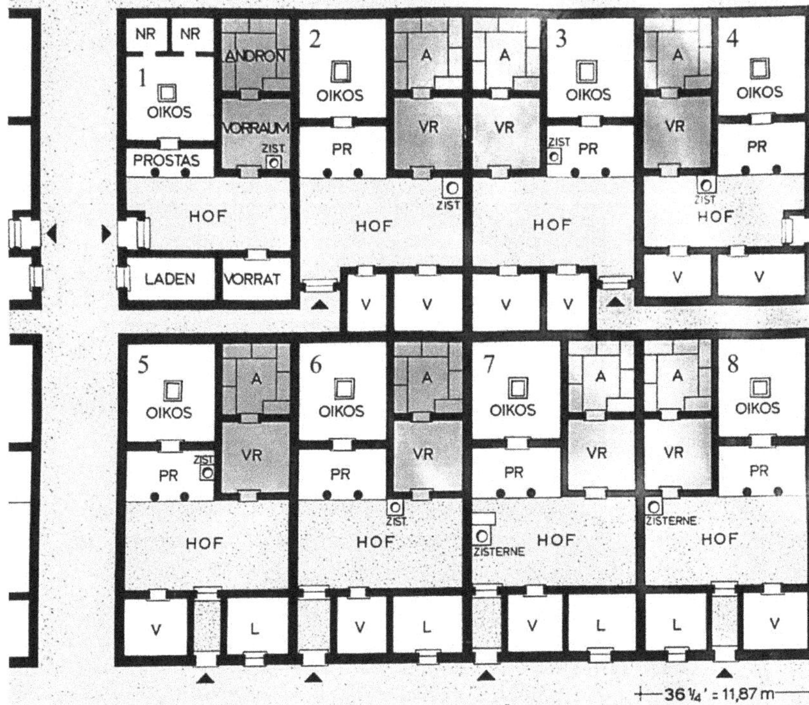

Figure 5.1 Diagram of Peiraieus block, adapted from Hoepfner et al. 1994: 39, fig. 31,
courtesy of Wolfram Hoepfner.

say, House 2 would have had a particularly intimate relationship with the
inhabitants of House 3, possibly being able to cross over to their house by the
roof without needing to use the street. From their upper windows or roofs,
the inhabitants of Houses 1, 3, 5, and 6 would have been able to see the
inhabitants of House 2 entering or leaving their house through the alleyway.
The inhabitants of House 3 would have been able to see into the courtyards
of Houses 1 and 2; the inhabitants of Houses 6 and 7 might have been able to
see into the courtyards of all the other houses in the block.

Archaeological evidence suggests that in the countryside too, homes
tended to be clustered together, either in deme centres or hamlets.[61]
Residence patterns ranged from demes with nucleated – sometimes even
walled – centres, like Rhamnous, to demes where residents lived in small

---

[61] For descriptions of each deme by turn, see Humphreys 2018, vol. 2.

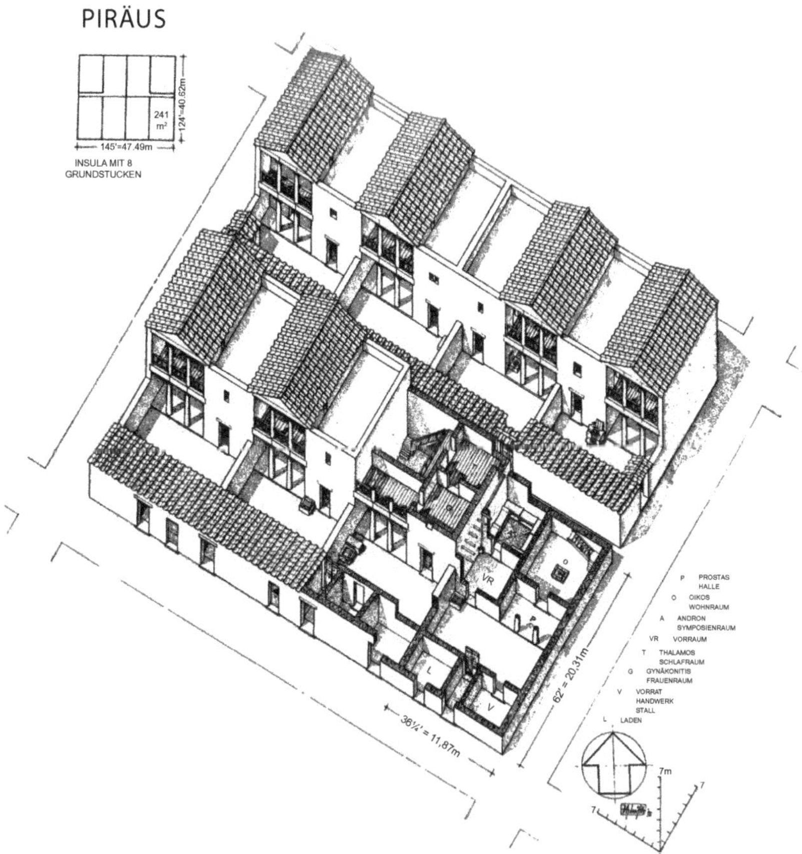

Figure 5.2 Reconstruction of block from Hoepfner 1999: 219, courtesy of
Wolfram Hoepfner

hamlets, like Atene. Experiences of neighbourhood would have differed in
these different settings.[62]

The excavated residential buildings of Halai Aixonides, a deme on the west
coast of Attica, are mostly concentrated in two neighbourhoods and on the
deme's acropolis.[63] The south-eastern settlement cluster occupied the corner
of a triangle formed by three ancient roads. It was intersected by several

[62] Compare Osborne 2011 on how different built environments at Rhamnous and Thorikos reflected
and engendered different attitudes to one's history and community.
[63] Andreou 1994: 195.

narrower streets, dividing the area into 'islands' occupied by groups of houses and sometimes, small sanctuaries.[64] One such island consisted in about six or seven houses bounded by the surrounding roads. As Ioanna Andreou describes it, 'the "islands" of buildings of the south-east neighbourhood form a compact urban ensemble' ('Οι οικοδομικές νησίδες του ΝΑ. συνοικισμού απαρτίζουν ένα συμπαγες πολεοδομικό σύνολο').[65] Again, this allows us to imagine neighbourhood and community identities below the level of the deme – identities which may have had particular significance to women. With the felt privacy and security of Riyadh's old narrow alleyways in mind, we may imagine a familiarity and intimacy between women who lived in this 'compact' area and a degree of freedom of movement within the 'neighbourhood', for which the sanctuaries may have been focal points – as was the shrine of Pan for the Phyle neighbourhood described in Menander's *Dyskolos*, discussed in the next section. By contrast, settlement in the deme of Sounion seems to have been 'extraordinarily spread about'; at least two and 'as many as five agoras may be attested for the deme'.[66] Here, these *agorai* may have formed focal points for neighbourhoods.

Sylvian Fachard has argued that most agricultural land was farmed by residents of towns or hamlets who walked daily to their fields.[67] More isolated farmsteads were the preserve of a few rich landowners, and even these were often situated within a few hundred yards of the nearest road, and within sight of the next farmstead along. This aligns with the literary evidence. The agricultural land owned by the speaker of [Demosthenes] 47, near the Hippodrome by the Ilissos river,[68] was within sight, hearing, and a short walk of multiple neighbouring households and a frequently used road (§§53, 57, 60–1). Similarly, the agricultural plot owned by the speaker of Lysias 7 was surrounded by roads and had neighbours living on both sides; he describes it as 'visible from all angles' (πανταχόθεν κάτοπτον, §28). Menander's *Dyskolos* centres on three neighbouring plots in the northern deme of Phyle on Mount Parnes; Demosthenes 55 features a friendship between two women whose families owned neighbouring land; [Demosthenes] 53, a friendship between two men in the same situation.[69]

---

[64] Andreou 1994: 196, updating Osborne 1985b: 24, 'a very compact residential area, with narrow streets and at least one tiny shrine'.

[65] Andreou 1994: 197.   [66] Osborne 1985b: 34–5.

[67] In 'Rural Attica: Farmsteads, Production, and Agricultural Investment', a paper given at the Hilary 2020 Classical Archaeology Seminar 'The Archaeology of the Ancient Greek Economy' at the University of Oxford, 2 March 2020. Osborne 1985b: 17–18 maintains that there is 'no clear evidence in the literature for anyone who lives and farms out on his own in the country'; Jones 1999: 65–6, following Langdon 1991, disputes this.

[68] §53, with Scafuro 2011: 317, fn. 70; discussed in Chapter 2, pp. 135–41.   [69] [Dem.] 53.4, 16.

As in the *asty*, residential 'clusters' in rural Attica presumably formed social as well as spatial units. In the countryside, however, the difference between neighbourhoods was probably much more geographically obvious: the next neighbourhood might have been miles rather than yards away. This 'clustering' would have allowed for the kind of resource-sharing assumed between rural neighbours in *Dyskolos* where one expects a neighbour to help with agricultural labour (ll. 328–31) or lend a pot (ll. 456–521; also a norm in the city, ll. 590–2).

We saw that one curse tablet against tavern-keepers, *DTA* 87, situated its victims within a neighbourhood, cursing 'the tavern-keeper from the neighbourhood' (l. 1); a tavern 'nearby' (l. 2); 'Kittos the neighbour' (l. 8); and 'Mania, the tavern-keeper (f.) by the spring' (l. 8). This last designation implies the spring was a familiar neighbourhood landmark. Comparative anthropological evidence suggests that in both urban and rural communities, communal water sources would have been central to women's spatial and social experiences of their neighbourhoods. Susan Freeman shows how patterns of water use structured community relations in the Castilian hamlet Valdemoro, where the communally owned public fountain and adjacent washing place were 'the most important physical locus of continual interaction across household lines'. Men came to the fountain each morning and evening to water their livestock; women – even those from houses with private water supplies – made several trips each day, sometimes staying longer to launder clothes.[70] Freeman, Cutiliero (describing Vila Velha in Portugal), and Kennedy (describing Hatzi in Crete) identify shared washing places as important spaces for women's interaction with other women, which Freeman and Cutiliero characterise as 'gossip' and Kennedy as 'visiting a woman friend'.[71] This was evidently true in Attica too: a woman in *Lysistrata* describes a spring as 'crowded and noisy' (ὑπ' ὄχλου καὶ θορύβου); trying to get water she was 'jostled by slave-women' (δούλαισιν ὠστιζομένη, ll. 329–30). As suggested in Chapter 3 (p. 164), this suggests that water sources could serve as meeting-points for enslaved as well as free women. Even enslaved women living further away from Attica's densely populated, multiethnic centre or larger demes might have been able to mitigate their isolation by timing their water-collection trips, as far as possible, to coincide with those of other enslaved women from the neighbourhood.

[70] Freeman 1970: 87–9.
[71] Freeman 1970: 88, Cutileiro 1971: 138–9, Kennedy 1986: 129, quoted by Cohen 1991: 47–8.

Figure 5.3 Attic red-figure *hydria* by the Berlin painter showing women talking at a fountain, c. 500–480, Madrid, Museo Arqueologico Nacional Inv. 11117. Photo: Jose Luis Municio Garcia.

Alexandre Mitchell brings together a number of pots which show women engaged in conversation as they collect water.[72] Two early classical pots show women who have turned away from their pots to chat and failed to notice that the pots have long filled up and are now overflowing.[73] The winged Eros above the head of the woman who has forgotten her pot in a *hydria* by the Berlin Painter (Figure 5.3) may suggest the sexual nature of her thoughts or conversation,[74] or her sexual appeal. Women and girls collecting water were visible and accessible to men, which could be a source of danger or opportunity. In Menander's

---

[72] Mitchell 2015: 174–9.

[73] Figure 5.3 here, and Attic black-figure *lekythos*, c. 510–490, Thebes Archaeological Museum, 6151. Compare Attic black-figure *hydria*, c. 550–515, Oxford, Ashmolean Museum 1910.775: women talking as they collect water.

[74] Sem. 7.90–1 (mid seventh-century Amorgos) praises a woman who οὐδ' ἐν γυναιξὶ ἥδεται καθημένη / ὅκου λέγουσιν ἀφροδισίους λόγους, 'does not enjoy sitting with women in places where they talk about sex'; water sources may have been among these places.

Dyskolos, a girl's trip to collect water from the spring at the local shrine of Pan (ll. 199–201) leads to an encounter with the man who wants to marry her.[75] Judith Williams and Anne Fuller note that girls in Haouch el Harimi and Buarij, Lebanon, used water-collection trips to show themselves off to young men.[76]

For women, a shared water source could have been the social centre of the neighbourhood; in densely populated urban areas, use of the same water source might have defined to which neighbourhood or micro-community a woman belonged. A woman's mental conception of her neighbourhood might have looked quite different from a man's.

Religion and Relation

The religious sphere was also an important context for women's sociality. More significantly, it was a sphere in which women were able to organise themselves and to enact their own social structures. Women's organisation of festivals attests to the existence of close working relationships between women. As Cohen writes, 'historians have failed to explore the social implications of the fact that Athenian women's networks were organized enough to carry out the full range of activities associated with such an undertaking, including election of officials and a governing council, rehearsals, supplies, finances, etc.'.[77] A set of regulations for the celebration of the Thesmophoria at Kholargos from 334/3 attests to this organisation. It stipulates that the *arkhousai*, the two women in charge of the festival, had to give to the priestess various foodstuffs (small amounts of barley, wheat, figs, wine, olive oil, honey, sesame, poppyseeds, at least 200 g of cheese and 200 g of garlic), a torch, and some cash, 'for the festival and for managing the Thesmophoria' (τὰς δὲ ἀρχούσας κοινεῖ ἀμφοτ-|έρας διδόναι τῆς ἱερείας εἰς | τὴν ἑορτὴν καὶ τὴν ἐπιμέλεια-|ν τῶν Θεσμοφορίων ..., *IG* II² 1184, ll. 3–6). *Arkhousai* (l. 3) is the feminine form of *arkhontes*, the title of Athens' political officials (cf. ll. 23–4). The Thesmophoria expenses were charged to the deme (ll. 24–5), which presumably required the two *arkhousai* to keep a record to present to the deme treasurer as well as to source the supplies.[78] A description of the selection process for the two

---

[75] This episode is discussed further on pp. 289–290.
[76] Williams 1968: 77, fn. 19, Fuller 1961: 47, fn. 29, quoted by Cohen 1989: 11–12.
[77] Cohen 1991: 152.
[78] For accountability procedures for women in public religious roles, see Aeschin. 3.18 and Lycurg. 6, cited by Lambert 2020b: 30 with fn. 129, in relation to *IG* I³ 6 (c. 475–450), where the priestess of Demeter at Eleusis is responsible for paying expenses worth 1,600 *drakhmai*. Eddie Jones (pers.

arkhousai for the Thesmophoria at Pithos may imply that the women were selected by lot from a shortlist of appropriate candidates (*prokrinō*), as drawn up by the women of the deme (Isae. 8.19–20, discussed at pp. 310–11).[79] The female-only context created for such festivals and rites was religiously efficacious: for the Thesmophoria, for example, it was essential for the efficacy of the rites that married women, and only married women, celebrated. However, it also created a space in which women could develop and determine their own relationships and hierarchies.

Religious Sites as Women's Spaces

Religious rituals and sites – including spaces other than sanctuaries where religious rites were performed, like homes – helped construct female relationships and community. They provided a space in which interactions between women, often without the presence of men, were acceptable and even necessary. These spaces were, for the duration of women's festivals, controlled by women. As we will see later in this chapter, this meant that women could control which women were allowed to enter, which offered them a means of defining their own and others' social status. It may also have meant that such spaces played a socio-spatial role in constructing community for women: a woman may have defined her 'neighbours' as those she would invite to her house for the Adonia, or her 'village' or 'neighbourhood' as the area within which she regularly visited shrines. These definitions may not have mapped onto men's (informal or administrative) definitions of the same people or spaces.

A mid fourth-century decree from Peiraieus (*IG* 11² 1177) concerning the deme's Thesmophorion (the sanctuary of Demeter Thesmophoros) nicely illustrates the control women might have over certain religious spaces at particular times. The decree forbade anyone from carrying out certain religious activities at the sanctuary without the priestess (ll. 2–7). If someone were to make a sacrifice or a dedication or to gather a *thiasos* (a group of religious worshippers), the priestess had to be present; she had oversight and control over day-to-day religious activities in the sanctuary. However, there were significant exceptions. The rule applied,

comm.) also points out ll. 13–17 on Face B of the 'Hekatompedon decree' (*IG* 1³ 4, from 485/4), where the priestess and (female) temple officials ([τὰς] ḥιερέα[ς] τὰς ἐμ πόλει ⁚ καὶ τ-|ὰς ζακόρος are subject to formal accountability procedures (εὐθύ-|νε[σθαι]) and liable to fines for misconduct. On women's numeracy, see Blok 2018: 22 and Wolicki 2021: 190–1; see also Kapparis 2019: 50 on evidence from oratory for women's knowledge of household finances.

[79] Griffith-Williams 2013 *ad loc.*

[ἀ]λ-
λ’ ἢ ὅταν ἡ ἑορτὴ τῶν Θεσμοφορίων
καὶ Πληροσίαι καὶ Καλαμαίοις κ-
αὶ τὰ Σκίρα καὶ εἴ τινα ἄλλην ἡμέ-
ραν συνέρχονται αἱ γυναῖκες κατὰ τὰ πάτρια·

(ll. 7–12)

except when it is the festival of the Thesmophoria and Plerosia and at the Kalamaia and the Skira and if there is any other day when the women come together in accordance with ancestral custom.

These were all women's religious festivals for Demeter. The Thesmophoria was in Pyanopsion (the fourth month of the year, roughly corresponding to our October/November). The Plerosia (better known as the Proerosia), the festival that preceded the ploughing, was in spring. The Kalamaia, an agricultural festival about which less is known, was probably in summer (*kalamai* were stalks of corn).[80] The Skira was in Skirophorion, the last month of the year, roughly corresponding to our June/July. Evidently they were all marked by women's gatherings at the local Thesmophorion, as were other occasions not specified here. Any such occasion was not subject to the decree's controls on religious activity. The priestess would presumably be present at these women's festivals, which raises the question of what difference the exception made, but the deme clearly felt that these occasions were beyond the purview of this decree. If the first lines of the decree assigned joint responsibility (with the priestess) for enforcing the rule to the (male) demarch, as in Ulrich Köhler's restoration,[81] this may have been a recognition that he could not police what went on in the sanctuary during the women-only festivals.

The women's festivals named in the Peiraieus decree were all annual festivals in the Attic religious calendar, but women could also organise informal, 'off-calendar' religious celebrations. A passage in Aristophanes' *Lysistrata* hints at the popularity and variety of such women's gatherings. At the beginning of the play, Lysistrate complains that she has organised a meeting of women to discuss her plan for a sex strike to end the Peloponnesian War, but no one has come:

---

[80] For the celebration of Proerosia and Kalamaia at the sanctuary of Demeter at Eleusis, see *LSCG* 7 A, ll. 4–7 and *IG* ii² 949, ll. 8–9.

[81] [ἐπιμελεῖσθαι — — — τὸν δήμαρχον]|[μετὰ] τῆς ἱερείας τὸν [ἀεὶ δημαρχ]-|[οῦ]ντα τοῦ θεσμοφορίου, '[the demarch, together with] the priestess – that is, the [demarch in office at any given time], shall have charge of the Thesmophorion', ll. 0–2.

ἀλλ' εἴ τις ἐς Βακχεῖον αὐτὰς ἐκάλεσεν,
ἢ 'ς Πανὸς ἢ 'πὶ Κωλιάδ' εἰς Γενετυλλίδος,[82]
οὐδ' ἂν διελθεῖν ἦν ἂν ὑπὸ τῶν τυμπάνων.
νῦν δ' οὐδεμία πάρεστιν ἐνταυθοῖ γυνή.　　　　　(1–4)

> If someone had invited them to a Bakkhic sanctuary instead, or [a grotto] of Pan, or [the sanctuary] of Genetyllis at Kolias, you wouldn't have been able to move for drums. But now there isn't a single woman here.

The humour here depends on caricature; an historian may approach this by toning down the caricature to something more conservative, but this too is a matter of inference. One way of approaching misogynistic jokes as a feminist historian is to ask, 'if this were more or less true, but not negative, what would it mean?'. The joke here seems to be a stereotyping exaggeration of the premise 'attending gatherings at religious sanctuaries is popular with women'.[83]

In the context of her discussion about the women's meeting she has organised, Lysistrate's comparison to sanctuaries highlights their role as sites for encounters between women. One potential location mentioned for a sacrifice and a celebration is a grotto or sacred cave of Pan, of which Attica had several.[84] The best known is the two-room grotto of Pan at Vari, near the deme Anagyrous. Several inscribed dedications attest to women's worship here, including a fifth-century *skyphos* (wine-cup) dedicated by a woman named Timo (*IG* I^2 794); a fifth- or fourth-century *kratēr* (bowl for mixing wine) dedicated by a woman whose name ended -xene (*IG* I^2 796); and another fifth- or perhaps fourth-century *skyphos* dedicated by a woman who described herself as 'beautiful Mika' (Μίκα καλή ἀνέθηκεν, 'beautiful Mika dedicated (this)', *IG* I^2 797).[85] We also know that women participated in group worship at the cave: two women seem to have participated in the joint dedication here of a Hymettian marble relief showing Pan, Hermes, and two Nymphs, themselves seemingly depicted in a cave. The inscription begins Νύφαις | οἵδ' ἀνέθεσαν ('these people dedicated to the Nymphs', *SEG* 54:318), then lists thirteen names,

---

[82]　Sommerstein 2007's text: 'the manuscripts have "or to Colias or to Genetyllis' shrine" [ἢ 'πὶ Κωλιάδ' ἢ 'ς Γενετυλλίδος], but the only well-known Attic sanctuary of ... the Genetyllides was at the headland of Colias near Phalerum'. Compare Henderson 1990 *ad loc.*, citing for the location Hdt. 8.96 and Paus. 1.1.5; cf. also Ap. *Neaira* 33–4, Plut. *Vit. Sol.* 8.4.

[83]　Compare Men. *Dys.* 260–3.

[84]　Including on the Akropolis; at Eleusis; at Oinoe, near Marathon; and on Mounts Parnes (near Phyle), Pentele, Hymettos (near Anagyrous, modern Vari), and Aigaleos: Camp 2001: 50. Compare Ar. *Thesm.* 978 for women's worship of Pan within the context of the Thesmophoria.

[85]　Schörner, Goette, and Hallof 2004: 96–7.

including the woman's name Soteris ([Σω]τηρίς, l. 14, previously misidentified as a man's name) and a name ending -ov, perhaps the ending of a woman's name ending in the diminutive suffix -ιον (l. 11).[86] The other names, including Lydos, 'the Lydian', and Phryx, 'the Phrygian', suggest a mixed-ethnicity and possibly mixed-status group; some and perhaps all of these dedicators were or had been enslaved. The dedicators would have come to the cave together to worship and make their dedication.

We also learn of women's religious celebrations at shrines of Pan from elsewhere in literature. The three agricultural properties in Menander's *Dyskolos*, set in the deme of Phyle, centre round a shrine of Pan, probably the sacred cave of Pan on Mount Parnes.[87] The shrine is depicted as a place not just for religious actions but also for social interactions, particularly for women. The play is structured around a sacrifice and associated party there, which is organised and attended by a large group of women (γυναῖκές, l. 404; later πολύς τις . . . / ὄχλος, 'a great crowd', ll. 404–5). Women coming individually to worship at the shrine also find themselves meeting others there, including men. The unnamed daughter of the title character is seen by her future husband while she is worshipping at the shrine (ll. 50–2).[88] As mentioned, she later encounters him and his friend outside the shrine, where the two men are chatting; she has come to fetch water from the shrine's spring (ll. 199–201). She says her father will beat her if he catches her outside (ἔπειτα πληγὰς λ[ή]ψομ', ἄν με καταλάβῃ ἔξω, l. 205) and later retreats to her doorway: her next line, φέρε δεῦρο, 'bring it here', l. 212, implies she has moved away from the shrine towards her house.[89] It is not clear whether this threat reflects her father Knemon's violent and misanthropic character or a social norm: male violence against dependants, particularly female dependants, was probably widespread in classical Attica,[90] but it is evident from the play

---

[86] Schörner, Goette, and Hallof 2004: 64–7, with fns. 377 on -ιον and 380 on [Σω]τηρίς. All Attic attestations of this name where the gender is certain (e.g. where the names are associated with gendered participles or kinship terms) are female. Of all 139 attestations of the name in *LGPN* across the Greek world in all periods, 128 are listed as women, 3 as men (accented by the editors as Σωτῆρις based on prosopographical information, though it is not impossible that 1 of these is a metronymic rather than a patronymic; the other 2 are second-/third- and fourth-century AD respectively); and 8 as uncertain. In any case, *LGPN* also sometimes misreads women's names as men's. Compare my p. 235.

[87] The excavation was published by Rhomaios 1905, Rhomaios 1906, and Skias 1918.

[88] See Ar. *Ach.* 253–5 and New Comedy rape plots for examples of religious rites as occasions on which marriageable girls were exposed to male view.

[89] See Llewellyn-Jones 2003: 195–6, 206–7 for depictions on Greek pots of women peering round doors. Despite this caution, her behaviour still attracts scandal (ll. 218–46, 289–92).

[90] See Fisher 1998 and Llewellyn-Jones 2003: 166–9 on male violence against female relatives as a 'punishment' for 'immodesty'.

that Knemon's violence is extreme. Nevertheless, his daughter's frequent trips to the shrine despite her conservative upbringing imply that girls' and women's leaving the house to worship, as well as for water, was generally socially acceptable, even though it exposed them to criticism, gossip, or mockery. Indeed, Pan praises her for it (ll. 36–9).

As well as the shrines to Pan in Vari and Phyle, there was one on the slopes of the Akropolis,[91] which may similarly have facilitated women's social interactions with other women – and men. Later in *Lysistrata* the grotto serves as a meeting place for Myrrhine and her husband (ll. 911–79). Though they are married, their encounter – outside the home, and characterised by flirtatious deferral on Myrrhine's part – is presented like an interaction between illicit lovers.[92]

Lysistrate also mentions gatherings at Kolias, a promontory on the Attic coast a little south of Peiraieus and Halimous, likely modern Hagios Kosmas or Hagios Georgios. The sanctuary had a temple to Aphrodite and also incorporated the shrine of Genetyllis (sometimes Genetyllides, plural), a goddess or goddesses associated with childbirth, primarily if not exclusively worshipped by women.[93] The possibility that women might have travelled to this sanctuary from elsewhere in Attica for a celebration is intriguing, but perhaps the pilgrimage was made only by locals, or very rich women who could afford an enslaved escort; the aristocratic wife in Aristophanes' *Clouds* is a devotee of Aphrodite Kolias and Genetyllis (l. 52). Robert Parker suggests women would likelier have called on deities with shrines closer to home.[94]

The sanctuary of Aphrodite at modern Dafni (Haidari), about seven miles north-west of the *asty* on the Sacred Way to Eleusis, has left epigraphical traces of women's worship. Among the many women's dedications there is an inscribed votive dedicated jointly by Euandria, Phile, and probably another dedicator (*IG* II² 4574):[95]

---

[91] Compare Hdt. 6.105 and Borgeaud 1988: 150–3.

[92] Compare Henderson 1990 *ad* 845. For a rape in this(?) grotto, cf. Eur. *Ion* 10–13. This contextualises the anxieties of Knemon's daughter in *Dyskolos* when she encounters a man at her local shrine of Pan.

[93] See Parker 2005: 432–3.   [94] Parker 2005: 439–40 with fn. 86.

[95] I suspect the third column gave a woman's mononym (on analogy with the names of Euandria and Phile), followed by Ἀφροδίτει, 'to Aphrodite'. Further dedications by individual women (probably of both citizen and metic status) include *IG* II² 4575 (a sculpted vulva, which exhorts passers-by to praise: Φιλουμένη Ἀφρο[δ]ίτε[ι χ]αριζομέ-|νη· ἐπαινεῖτε οἱ παριόντες, 'Philoumene (dedicates this) to please Aphrodite; praise [her; the verb is usually used of praising humans rather than gods, so probably Philoumene rather than Aphrodite], you who pass by'), 4576 (another sculpted vulva), 4579, 4582, and 4584.

Εὐα[ν]δρία ⋮ Ἀφ-   Φίλη Ἀφροδίτει   Π – –
ροδίτει εὐξαμ-   A – –
ένη ἀνέθηκε

Euandria, having made a prayer-vow, dedicated [this] to
   Aphrodite.
Phile, to Aphrodite.
P – – [to?] A[phrodite?]

These women – mother and daughter(s)? sisters? friends? – must have
visited together to make their dedication.

Bakkheia, 'places of Bakkhic/Dionysiac worship', seem to have been less
monumental, but the word is used in inscriptions to designate both organised groups of Bakkhic worshippers, and the places they met.[96] Parker argues
for a cross-cultural pattern of 'certain peripheral spirits, perhaps of foreign
origin' attacking 'people whose position in society is as peripheral as their
own, men without status and, above all, women'.[97] Those afflicted charac-
teristically respond with 'lifelong devotion to the cult of the possessing
spirit', made up of 'the community of past victims' and taking an ecstatic
form. Such cults, Parker argues, 'undoubtedly have a clandestine significance
from which victims of the spirit gain psychological benefit'; they offer
'personal relief for persons shut out from the central morality cults' and
offer to women specifically 'a religious experience, a sphere of interest, and
an identity, each of them opposed to the typical female role'. Parker argues
that maenadism, women's ecstatic worship of Dionysos, whom Greeks
conceived of as 'foreign' despite his long Greek history, fits this pattern.
He writes that the 'social significance of maenadism, a form of behaviour not
originally shared by both sexes but performed by one in defiance of the
other, has tended to be underestimated'. All this is hard to test against the
classical Attic evidence. However, the production of Euripides' *Bacchae* in
405 suggests that maenadism, depicted as involving 'young and old women,
and girls still unmarried' (l. 694), who leave their babies (l. 702) and their
looms and shuttles (ll. 117–19) to gather in the mountains and worship, was
prominent in the Athenian consciousness.

In Plato's *Laws*, the Athenian proposes that men of procreative age
convicted of misbehaviour should not be allowed to attend weddings

---

[96] Henderson 1990 *ad Lys.* 1–2. Parker 2005: 290–2 refers to local sanctuaries of Dionysos which may
have played a role in Dionysiac festivals.

[97] Parker 1983: 246–7, citing, among others, Lewis 1971, chapter 3 and pp. 79–85, Dodds 1951: 77–80,
Pl. *Euthyd.* 277d.

(*gamoi*) or dedication ceremonies for children (τὰς τῶν παίδων ἐπιτελειώσεις),[98] while *women* in the same position should not be allowed to participate in 'women's outings', honours, or attendance at weddings or children's birth(day?) celebrations (τῶν ἐξόδων … τῶν γυναικείων καὶ τιμῶν καὶ τῶν εἰς τοὺς γάμους καὶ γενέθλια τῶν παίδων φοιτήσεων μὴ μετεχέτω, 6.784d). Though the legal code is hypothetical, the imagined prohibitions give us a vivid picture of what women's social lives looked like in Plato's time. 'Women's outings' presumably include excursions to sanctuaries, for celebrations like those described in *Lysistrata* and the women's sacrifice-cum-picnic depicted in Menander's *Dyskolos* and to offer dedications.

Not all such excursions were religious: in Euripides' (fragmentary) *Hypsipyle*, the Nemean women invite Hypsipyle – whom, despite her status as a slave, they address as *phila* ('dear one', 'friend', frg. 752f Nauck, l. 15, and 752g Nauck, l. 33) – to come with them to see the army of the Seven against Thebes mustered on the Nemean plain (frg. 752f, ll. 29–38). Possibly Hypsipyle is a special case because of her 'former life' as a princess, but it is particularly surprising that here an enslaved woman is invited to join the excursion. Similarly, the married women of Khalkis in Euripides' *Iphigenia at Aulis* come out of the city (Χαλκίδα πόλιν ἐμὰν προλιποῦσ[α], l. 168) and to the beach (ἔμολον ἀμφὶ παρακτίαν, l. 164) to see the Greek navy as it sets off for Troy.[99] As with the mustering of the Seven's army on its way to Thebes, this belongs to the realm of the mythical past, but it opens up the intriguing possibility that women in Attica might go out to see, from a distance, the mustered Athenian army or navy before it departed on campaign.[100] Were there women in 'the crowd – practically everyone in the city' (ὁ … ὅμιλος ἅπας ὡς εἰπεῖν ὁ ἐν τῇ πόλει, Thuc. 6.30) who went down to Peiraieus to see off their friends, relatives, and sons on the Sicilian Expedition in 415? Had some of them helped to make the sails?

Sanctuaries and shrines visited by women, and myriad other religious sites across Attica,[101] were or could temporarily and licitly become 'women's spaces', bringing women into each other's company and under

---

[98] The exact nature of these celebrations is unclear, but they seem to have been associated with either the birth or infancy of a child: cf. Walter 1937: 108, who draws a link with the celebration of Khoes. The phrase may also refer to the *amphidromia* and *dekatē*, or ceremonies like them.

[99] We know they are married because they speak of their husbands: ἁμέτεροι πόσεις, l. 176.

[100] We recall Sappho's famous comment, from a different socio-historical context, on the visual beauty of an army in frg. 16 Voigt.

[101] For cult activity across the demes, see Humphreys 2018: 801–8.

female social control. Henderson comments on *Lysistrata* 1–4 (quoted on p. 288) that 'male suspicion that women's religious activities were an excuse for licentious, even immoral, behaviour' is articulated in Euripides' *Bacchae* and a raft of comedies.[102] He notes that these suspicions were directed not only at privately organised celebrations like the ones Lysistrate imagines, or the party for Hekate (ll. 700–1; note *kaleō*, 'invite', in both contexts), but also at the major women's festivals of the *polis* like the Thesmophoria and Skira, where women plot in *Thesmophoriazusae* and *Ecclesiazusae* respectively. Such suspicion arose from the simple fact that women were together and unsupervised on such occasions.

Male authors and characters persistently sexualise women's religious and para-religious activities. We can read through these sexualising accounts to glimpse moments of intimacy between women. There is considerable charm, for example, concealed in Sikos' leering description of enslaved girls dancing together at the celebration for Pan towards the end of *Dyskolos*:

> καί τις βραχεῖσα προσπόλων εὐήλικος προσώπου
> ἄνθος κατεσκιασμένη χορεῖον εἰσέβαινε
> ῥυθμὸν μετ᾽ αἰσχύνης ὁμοῦ μέλλουσα καὶ τρέμουσα·
> ἄλλη δὲ συγκαθῆπτε ταύτῃ χεῖρα κἀχόρευεν.   (950–3)

And one of the attendants, steeped [i.e. drunk], shadowed [with a veil] the youthful flower of her face and began a rhythmic dance, but demurely, hesitating and trembling, and another girl clasped hands with her and danced too.

Dancing together played a part in many female religious celebrations and features on a number of pots. Some of these scenes, like the scene in *Dyskolos*, involve the intimacy of hand-holding. One early example is the shoulder of a *lekythos* attributed to the Amasis painter (c. 550–530), which shows a line of women dancing and holding hands (Figure 5.4). A seated woman on the other side may represent a goddess for whom they dance.[103] The main image on the pot shows women collaborating in textile production, a beautiful depiction of the sharedness of women's lives. Nancy Rabinowitz reads such intimacy as potentially erotic;[104] citing in particular Sappho frg. 94 Voigt, ll. 25–8, where the speaker responds to her (female)

---

[102] Henderson 1990 *ad* Ar. *Lys.* 1–2, citing Eupolis' *Dippers*, Lysippus' and Diocles' *Bacchae*, Autocrates' *Tympanistae*, Pherecrates' *Kitchen* or *All-Night Festival*; cf. Ar. *Lys.* 387–98.
[103] New York, Metropolitan Museum of Art 31.11.10, c. 550–530.   [104] Rabinowitz 2002: 129–30.

Figure 5.4 Detail of shoulder of Attic black-figure *lekythos* attributed to the Amasis painter showing women dancing c. 550–530. New York, Metropolitan Museum of Art 31.11.10. Fletcher Fund, 1931.

lover's grief at leaving her – perhaps for marriage – with memories of dancing together at festivals:

> . . . οὔ]τε τι
> ἶρον οὐδ᾽ ὐ[   ]
> ἔπλετ᾽ ὄππ[οθεν ἄμ]μες ἀπεσκομεν,
> οὐκ ἄλσος [χο]ρός
> [   ]ψόφος

> nor was there any sacred place . . .
> from which we were absent
> no grove . . . dance . . .
> sound

Doubtless there were occasionally elements of homoeroticism in women's dancing, but by no means all intimacy is erotic,[105] and we should avoid 'reading away' deeply felt affectionate friendship. Women might also carry with them fond memories of dancing at festivals with friends.

Religious and Ritual Occasions as a Sphere for Developing and Rekindling Relationships

Arkteia and Thesmophoria

Female-dominated religious sites and occasions offered women protected opportunities to develop and foster relationships with each other across the course of their lives. One of Attica's most important sanctuaries for women

---

[105] Compare Rabinowitz 2002: 115.

was the sanctuary of Artemis at Brauron near the east coast of Attica. The sanctuary at Brauron was the location of the Arkteia, a festival for pre-pubescent Attic girls, who 'served as bears' (*arkteuō*) for Artemis.[106] At some point probably between the ages of six and ten,[107] citizen-status girls travelled out to the sanctuary in eastern Attica and stayed at the sanctuary under the care of the priestess of Artemis Brauronia, where, in the words of the Chorus of Women in Aristophanes' *Lysistrata*, each girl 'shed [her] saffron dress and was a bear' (καταχέουσα τὸν κροκωτὸν ἄρκτος ἦ, l. 645).[108] Being a bear, through ritual play-acting, seems to have allowed girls to access, express, and ultimately leave behind its wildness in preparation for adult womanhood.

Ancient scholiasts differ on whether *every* Attic girl served as a bear or only certain girls who 'represented' all the others.[109] Painted pots found at Brauron show girls running or dancing near altars; most are in short dresses, but some are nude.[110] Scholars have taken different views on the kinds of relationships these rites might have engendered between the girls. Nancy Demand's reading of the Arkteia implies that nude racing between girls at different stages of physical development promoted competitive, potentially threatening relationships between girls.[111] Chryssanthi Papadopoulou offers a bolder suggestion, that the division of the girls into two groups suggested by the sources may point to a situation in which one group of girls danced naked for the other, clothed, watching group, before reversing roles, allowing the dancing group simultaneously to experience a sense of liberation and of peer-induced shame, socialising them into the demands of female adolescence and adult womanhood.[112] Papadopoulou also argues, however, that the overall experience of the rites enabled girls to develop a sense of the power of Artemis and her protection over them as they went on to face the challenges of womanhood, including childbearing. This very vulnerable and powerful experience may have led to strong bonds – perhaps of solidarity, perhaps of anxiety or resentment, perhaps a combination – within the 'cohorts' of girls who took part, but it is hard to know what opportunities they would have had to cultivate those bonds after leaving the sanctuary.

---

[106] The definitive treatment of the Arkteia is Sourvinou-Inwood 1988; more recently, see Demand 1994: 107–14 and Papadopoulou 2015.

[107] As with most aspects of the Arkteia, the age of the participants is unclear from the ancient sources and controversial in modern scholarship: see Sommerstein 2007 *ad* 643–4 and more fully, Sourvinou-Inwood 1971, disputed by Demand 1994: 109–12.

[108] There are problems with the text in this passage: the quotation here is the text of Sommerstein 2007 (645 n.), based on Sourvinou-Inwood 1971.

[109] See e.g. Sommerstein 2007: *ad* 644–5 and Demand 1994: 112.   [110] Kahil 1965.

[111] Demand 1994: 107–14.   [112] Papadopoulou 2015: 147–54.

For married women, the most religiously and socially important festival was the Thesmophoria, in honour of Demeter Thesmophoros. As it was celebrated in local sanctuaries across Attica,[113] the festival was accessible to almost all married Athenian women. The Thesmophoria allowed – even obliged – women to spend three days in each other's company, away from the demands of domestic work or childcare (except for those who brought nursing babies).[114] Although the second day, *Nesteia* ('Fasting'), may have required silence, the festival also involved sexually obscene talk, doubtless an enjoyable bonding experience, as well as ritually important. Parker, who suggests that women 'joked and laughed at festivals such as the Thesmophoria about the embarrassing details of sexuality and about the inadequacies (collective and individual) of their husbands', calls the Thesmophoria 'a festival of female bonding occurring, *inter alia*, through a kind of verbal taboo-breaking licensed by the ritual context'.[115] During the festival, women shared tents, probably in twos: there is a reference in Aristophanes' *Thesmophoriazusae* to a 'tent-companion' or 'tent-buddy' (*syskēnētria*, l. 624). The word is a *hapax*, but one scholiast glosses it with the words *philē* (female friend) and *syndiaitos* (one who lives with another, a companion); tent-sharing was understood in terms of *philia*. Some women would have shared with a relative; others perhaps with a neighbour or friend. During the festival, the women shared a feast paid for – at least in some demes – as a liturgy by those of their husbands whose property rendered them eligible to bear public expenses (Isae. 3.80).

As the festival seems to have been celebrated on the deme level,[116] it would have offered a particular opportunity for women who had married within their demes to reconnect with their mothers and other natal female kin. Foxhall observes that 'some of the most touching accounts we have of women's relationships involve separation and reunification of mothers and daughters'. She cites as an example the *Homeric Hymn to Demeter* which 'set[s] out the aetiological myth behind the ritual of the Thesmophoria, a festival where women usually separated by marriage might be reunited for a brief period in the year'.[117] The poem describes Demeter and her daughter Persephone wild with joy at their reunion, and finding respite in that joy from the grief of separation:

---

[113] Clinton 1996; Parker 2005: 271–2.

[114] Compare Parker 2005: 271: 'The Thesmophoria must have been the most striking interruption of the year in the routine of women's lives . . . Three days away from the wool basket!'

[115] Compare Winkler 1990: 188–209.   [116] See fn. 113.   [117] Foxhall 2012: 193–4.

ἡ δὲ ἰδοῦσα
ἤϊξ' ἠΰτε μαινὰς ὄρος κάτα δάσκιον ὕλης.
Περσεφόνη δ' ἑτέρ[ωθεν ἐπεὶ ἴδεν ὄμματα καλὰ]
μητρὸς ἑῆς κατ' [ἄρ' ἥ γ' ὄχεα προλιποῦσα καὶ ἵππους]
ἆλτο θέει[ν, δειρῇ δέ οἱ ἔμπεσεν ἀμφιχυθεῖσα·]   (385–9)

Ὥς τότε μὲν πρόπαν ἦμαρ ὁμόφρονα θυμὸν ἔχουσαι
πολλὰ μάλ' ἀλλήλων κραδίην καὶ θυμὸν ἴαινον
ἀμφαγαπαζόμεναι, ἀχέων δ' ἀπεπαύετο θυμός.
γηθοσύνας δὲ δέχοντο παρ' ἀλλήλων ἔδιδ[όν τε.]   (434–7)

> And when [Demeter] saw her,
> she rushed [to her], like a maenad rushing down a mountain shaded
>   with trees,
> and Persephone, on the other side, when she saw the lovely eyes
> of her mother, left the chariot and horses and
> leapt down to run to her, and fell on her neck and poured herself around her . . .
>
> So then the whole day, with spirits as one,
> they greatly warmed each other's hearts and spirits,
> hugging each other tightly; their spirits had respite from their griefs
> and they received joy from each other and gave back joy.

Death and Birth

Women's religious and ritual activity, and its shaping role in women's relationships, was not confined to festivals and celebrations. It also shaped ordinary life – and death. Funerary rites, in which women played a central role, could serve to reunite female kin in similar ways to the Thesmophoria.[118] A law quoted by [Demosthenes] implies that even after Solon's restrictions on the number of women involved in funerals, a significant number of female relatives of the dead person would come to that person's house:

> γυναῖκα δὲ μὴ ἐξεῖναι εἰσιέναι εἰς τὰ τοῦ ἀποθανόντος μηδ' ἀκολουθεῖν ἀποθανόντι, ὅταν εἰς τὰ σήματα ἄγηται, ἐντὸς ἑξήκοντ' ἐτῶν γεγονυῖαν, πλὴν ὅσαι ἐντὸς ἀνεψιαδῶν εἰσι· μηδ' εἰς τὰ τοῦ ἀποθανόντος εἰσιέναι, ἐπειδὰν ἐξενεχθῇ ὁ νέκυς, γυναῖκα μηδεμίαν πλὴν ὅσαι ἐντὸς ἀνεψιαδῶν εἰσίν. ([Dem.] 43.62.)

> And a woman who is less than sixty years old should not come into the [home] of the dead person or follow the dead person when he is taken to the tomb, except those who are within [the degree] of cousins' children [i.e. are

---

[118] On the sociality of funeral rites, and their place within other aspects of *oikos* religious practice, see Gherchanoc 2012: 49–65.

the dead person's cousins' children or nearer], nor should any woman go into the [home] of the dead person when the corpse is carried out, except those who are within [the degree of cousins' children].

The various clauses of this law seem to assume a norm of female relatives going into the house of the dead person – in particular at the time of the carrying-out (*ekphora*) but also more generally, to take care of the corpse – and accompanying the corpse to the tomb. We see this played out in Isaeus 6, where the long-estranged wife and daughters of Euktemon, *Ergo*, *Khairestrate*, who was married and probably living separately from her mother, and *Korallion*, who had been married and then widowed (§§6, 29), learned of his death from a third party, came (ἦλθον) to the house where he died, and 'were around the dead person' (περὶ τὸν τετελευτηκότα ἦσαν, §§39–41).

A late fifth-century law from Iulis, Keos (*IG* XII 5, 593), which had close ties to Athens through the fifth and fourth centuries,[119] paints a similar picture:

> ὅπου ἂν θάνηι, ἐ[πὴν ἐ]-
> ξενιχθῆι, μὲ ἰέναι γυναῖκας π[ρὸ]ς τ[ὴν οἰ]-
> κίην ἄλλας ἒ τὰς μιαινομένας· μι[αίνεσθ]-
> [α]ι δὲ μητέρα καὶ γυναῖκα καὶ ἀδε[λφεὰς κ]-
> [α]ὶ θυγατέρας· πρὸς δὲ ταύταις μὲ π[λέον π]-
> [έ]ντε γυναικῶν· παῖδας δὲ τ[ῶν θ]υγ[ατρῶν κ]-
> [ἀ]νεψιῶν· ἄλλον [δ]ὲ μ[ε]δέν[α]. (ll. 23–9)

> Whenever someone dies, when he is carried out, women should not go to the house, other than those who are polluted/pollute themselves; the polluted/those polluting themselves are mother, wife, sisters, and daughters, and in addition to these, not more than five women, and children of the daughters(?)[120] and of cousins, and no one else.

Parker notes that 'as this inner group of the polluted is not determined simply by relationship [not least because of the possibility for five "additional" women, not determined by specific relationships], there was presumably some specific act or duty by which it was defined' – possibly handling the corpse. However, based on the Spartan custom stipulating the pollution of two free people per household on the death of a king, he

---

[119] Member of Delian League: Thuc. 7.57.4; *ATL* 1.306f, 3.197f. Member of Second Athenian League: *IG* II² 404. Under close Attic control: RO 39, 40; cf. Chapter 4, pp. 235–6.

[120] 'Children' and 'of cousins' are secure, but Hoffman's 'of the daughters' fits uneasily: the definite article and the krasis (κἀνεψιῶν) are odd, and one would expect daughters of sisters also to be included: see Bechtel *ad SGDI* 5398.

suggests that 'more probably the reference is to self-defilement of some kind', women's tearing their clothes, hair, or cheeks: '"being polluted" is more like going into mourning than catching a disease'.[121] Parker rightly sees death pollution partly in terms of the emotional and social significance of death, and of beliefs and practices around pollution as a way to mark and cope with change.

This kind of spread of female relatives would rarely have all lived in the same house as the dead person. Rather, those who lived elsewhere would come to the house (ἰέναι . . . π[ρὸ]ς τ[ὴν οἰ-]|κίην, *IG* XII 5, 593, ll. 24–5; cf. ἦλθον, Isae. 6.40) and spend the days around the funeral in close, isolated company with other women they may only have seen on family occasions like deaths, marriages, or births. The close interaction and collaboration of the women at this emotionally heightened time, and their separation from those outside the 'inner group' (basins of water were put outside the polluted house to purify those going out, which also served as a warning to others not to come in)[122] might have strengthened their relationships.

It could also be a fractious time. A number of emotive scenes in fifth-century tragedy speak to questions around burial and commemoration of the dead, and it is striking that questions of who is or should be involved in funerary ritual for relatives constitute major points of contention between kin – and perhaps particularly between female kin – in Attic tragedy, as well as occasionally in oratory. Most famous is the request of Sophocles' Antigone to her sister Ismene to 'share the toil and the task' (ξυμπονήσεις καὶ ξυνεργάσει, *Ant.* 41) of burying their brother, against the edict of their maternal uncle Kreon, together bringing their hands to lift the corpse (εἰ τὸν νεκρὸν ξὺν τῇδε κουφιεῖς χερί, 'Will you lift the corpse with this hand (of mine)?', l. 43). To Ismene's grief, her refusal creates a rift between the sisters. Sophocles' Elektra claims that she is the only one who laments her father (κοὐδεὶς τούτων οἶκτος ἀπ᾽ ἄλλης / ἢ ᾽μοῦ φέρεται, σοῦ, πάτερ, 'and no pity for this [his murder by his wife and her lover] comes to you, father, from any woman but me', *El.* 100–1). However, later in the play his wife (and murderer) Klytaimnestra sends their other surviving daughter, Khrysothemis, to pour libations at his tomb (l. 406). Khrysothemis' sister Elektra persuades her to abandon those offerings and instead give some of her own and Elektra's hair, and Elektra's girdle, which she does (ll. 431–71). Khrysothemis later describes her father's tomb as her and Elektra's concern and no one else's, except their brother's: τῷ γὰρ προσήκει πλήν

---

[121] Parker 1983: 40–1, and 32–48 more generally.
[122] Ar. *Eccl.* 1030–5; Eur. *Alc.* 98–100, cited by Parker 1983: 35.

γ' ἐμοῦ καὶ σοῦ τόδε;, 'whose concern is this [tomb] but mine and yours?' (l. 909).

Women came together at births as well as deaths. A woman in Aristophanes' *Ecclesiazusae*, needing to explain a suspicious absence, claims that she went to help a friend who was in labour (γυνή μέ τις νύκτωρ ἑταίρα καὶ φίλη / μετεπέμψατ' ὠδίνουσα ('a woman – my companion (*hetaira*) and friend (*philē*) – was in labour and sent for me at night', ll. 528–9); evidently this was routine. Various authors, most explicitly a scholiast on Plato's *Theaetetus*, describe how women who assisted at a birth – an event which made those present ritually impure or 'polluted' – were purified at the *amphidromia*, the celebration five or seven days after a child's birth (καθαιρόμεναι τὰς χεῖρας αἱ συναψάμεναι τῆς μαιώσεως, 'those who take have taken part in the delivery purifying their hands', schol. Pl. *Tht.* 160e).[123] The feminine plural participles suggest that multiple women would typically offer support.

Differently, a plot point in Euripides' *Electra* suggests that even if a woman's mother was not in close contact with her daughter, she might still come to visit her for the *dekatē* (tenth-day ceremony) or afterwards. When Elektra wants to lure her mother to her house to kill her, she sends someone to tell her that she gave birth to a male baby ten days ago and that her period of childbirth-pollutedness is over.[124] (Parker convincingly argues that the Greeks probably associated the 'impurity' of the postpartum mother and her newborn baby with the danger of death they both faced in the first week especially: 'Pollution would thus have helped to define and so limit a period of danger and anxiety.')[125] Despite their estrangement and mutual contempt, Elektra is sure her mother will come to visit her.

> Ἠλέκτρα: λεχώ μ' ἀπάγγελλ' οὖσαν ἄρσενος τόκῳ.
> Πρέσβυς: πότερα πάλαι τεκοῦσαν ἢ νεωστὶ δή;
> Ἠλέκτρα: δέχ' ἡλίους, ἐν οἷσιν ἁγνεύει λεχώ.
> Πρέσβυς: καὶ δὴ τί τοῦτο μητρὶ προσβάλλει φόνον;
> Ἠλέκτρα: ἥξει κλύουσα λόχιά μου νοσήματα. (652–6)

---

[123] Others say ten days, which may either represent confusion with the *dekatē*, or a practice of sometimes combining the two. Compare Hesychios *s.v.* ἀμφιδρόμια, Suda *s.v.* ἀμφιδρόμια, Σ. Ar. *Lys.* 757. On the *amphidromia* and *dekatē*, see Gherchanoc 2012: 35–48, Laes 2014: 366–9, and Golden 2015: 20.

[124] Parker 1983: 49–52, however, thinks that contact with a postpartum mother was only a source of pollution for the first three or so days.

[125] Parker 1983: 65.

Elektra: Tell her I have just given birth, that I've had a male child.
Old man: That you gave birth some time ago, or just recently?
Elektra: Ten days ago, the period in which a woman who has given
    birth observes purity laws.
Old man: And how does this get us the slaughter of your mother?
Elektra: She will come, when she hears of my suffering in childbirth.

Again, the circumstances here are those of tragedy – the two are estranged because Klytaimnestra has killed Elektra's father – but the expectation that even an estranged mother (in real life, perhaps estranged by distance or even by a less extreme family quarrel) would come to visit a daughter who had given birth may reflect the expectations of her fifth-century audience.

Apatouria

Even some men's religious practices offered social opportunities to women. The phratry festival of the Apatouria, through predominantly celebrated by men, may also have enabled women to reconnect with relatives and women they had been close to in earlier stages of their lives but from whom marriage had separated them. Though many of the activities of the festival itself (not least the athletics and much of the boozy feasting)[126] were likely restricted to men and boys, elements of the festival suggest that women were present on its peripheries.

The Apatouria was celebrated at phratry centres, so those who lived in or near the *asty* seemingly travelled back to rural villages to which they had family connections for the three-day celebration.[127] This was the time when sacrifices were made on the presentation to the phratry of infant and adolescent boys (the *meion* and the *koureion* respectively),[128] so we may assume the infants' mothers travelled with the boys and their fathers to the villages, probably bringing their unmarried daughters too, even if the women and girls did not attend the sacrifice.

---

[126] See Lambert 1993: 158-61 on the 'riotous', 'orgiastic' character of the festival and on the 'range of pursuits, athletic and intellectual'.

[127] Lambert 1993: 152–61; Humphreys 2018: 580. For travel, see Lambert 1993: 158 and Humphreys 2018: 580 with fn. 2 and 586 with fn. 63. It is important to note a large degree of variation in practice between phratries in all these matters: see e.g. Lambert 1993: 166–7, 173–4, 178, 180–1.

[128] Lambert 1993: 97, 161–78; Humphreys 2018: 580–3. On the fraught question of whether or not little girls were introduced, to which the tentative answer seems to be 'only sometimes, in some phratries, if at all', see Lambert 1993: 178–81. Perhaps the relative informality of the phratries, at least historically, should be stressed here – it is possible that the sole mention of the possibility of introducing a girl, in Isae 3.73, a statement which says the girl in question had no such introduction, could refer to something much more informal than the *meion*, which would then be very difficult to prove or disprove.

The Apatouria was also the occasion for *gamēliai*, wedding feasts given by newly married men to their phratrymen, at which they introduced their new bride to the phratry.[129] The *gamēlia* is described as being 'because/on behalf of (ὑπέρ) the bride' but 'for the phratrymen', τοῖς φράτορσι (e.g. Dem. 57.43, Isae. 3.79). However, given its use as evidence about legitimacy, the fact that Athenians sometimes combined the *gamēlia* with the *gamos* (wedding celebration), and comments in later writers (e.g. the first-century scholar Didymos said that the *gamēlia* was 'the introduction of women to the phratrymen', τὴν εἰς τοῦς φράτορας εἰσαγωγὴν τῶν γυναικῶν),[130] it seems likely – though not certain – that these brides were present for at least part of the festivities, perhaps (especially in the case of combination with the *gamos*) along with other women, not least the new mother-in-law.[131]

Mothers may also have had some involvement in the hair-cutting ritual for adolescents that probably took place on the third day of the Apatouria, Koureotis. The fifth-century AD lexicographer Hesychios describes Koureotis as the day 'on which they dedicate to Artemis the hair cut from the head of children (or boys?)' (ἐν ᾗ τὰς ἀπὸ τῆς κεφαλῆς τῶν παίδων ἀποκειροντες τρίχας Ἀρτέμιδι θύουσιν). Elsewhere he says that it is οἱ μέλλοντες ἐφηβεύειν, 'those about to come of age', who have their hair cut. (There is an etymological link between Koureotis and *keirō*, 'cut [hair]'.)[132] Pausanias says that the practice of cutting off and dedicating a young man's hair to a kourotrophic deity is shared among all the Greeks and has a long history (1.37.3). Even if the boys' mothers were not present at the *koureion* sacrifices, there is evidence for at least one dedication by a mother to mark her son's hair-cutting, which may attest to a role for mothers in this part of the coming-of-age process. Pausanias mentions

---

[129] Compare Chapter 1, pp. 74–5.

[130] *FGrH* 325 Phanodemos F17; see Lambert 1993: 183 with fn. 219; Pollux 8.107 says that on the third day, Koureotis, the *koureion* was sacrificed for males and the *gamēlia* for females, but the verb used in other sources for the *gamēlia* is not 'sacrifice' (θύω) but 'bring in' (εἰσφέρω). If it is possible to separate the error from the apparent sense that the two were somehow equivalent as introductions of new kin to the phratrymen, the evidence is still instructive. Compare Σ Ar. *Ach.* 146, discussed on p. 303, which claims that on Koureotis *kouroi* and *korai* were inscribed as members (τοὺς κούρους καὶ τὰς κόρας ἐγγράφειν εἰς τὰς φρατρίας). Again, there seems to be an error here – girls were not members of phratries in the way boys were – but there might be confusion with the introduction of *brides* at *gamēliai*. On all this see Lambert 1993: 179, fn. 198.

[131] For her role in weddings, see e.g. Oakley and Sinos 1993: 26 and index *s.v.* mother of bridegroom. Cole 1984: 236–7 argues that brides were not present, and that the status of the bride's father, not the bride herself, was at issue.

[132] Hesychios *s.v.* Κουρεῶτις and *s.v.* οἰνιστήρια; Lambert 1993: 163–5 with fns. 117–20; cf. also Plut. *Vit. Thes.* 5.1.

two (undated) statues set up by a woman named Mnesimakhe on the River Kephisos, of which one represented her son cutting his hair for the eponymous kourotrophic river deity : ἀγάλματα δὲ ἐπὶ τῷ ποταμῷ Μνησιμάχης, τὸ δὲ ἕτερον ἀνάθημα κειρομένου οἱ τὴν κόμην τοῦ παιδός ἐστι τῷ Κηφισῷ, 'and at the river are Mnesimakhe's statues, of which one is a dedicatory statue of her son cutting his hair for Kephisos' (1.37.3).[133]

The Apatouria, then, offered some opportunities for female sociality, and in the case of women who had moved to the *asty* or its environs on marriage, the chance to return to the villages in which they had grown up and be reunited for a few days with female relatives and other women they had known as children.[134] They may have worked together to cook the copious amounts of food the men consumed. A scholiast on Aristophanes' *Acharnians* 146, where the phrase 'eat the Apatouria black pudding' (φαγεῖν ἀλλᾶντας ἐξ Ἀπατουρίων) is used as a light-hearted equivalent of 'participate in the Apatouria', explains that the first day of the festival was called Dorpia (from *dorpon*, meal) and involved an evening feast; the second day was called Anarrhysis, from *anarrhyō*, to sacrifice, and involved sacrifices to Zeus Phratrios and to Athena (Phratria); and the third day was called Koureotis, after the registration of *kouroi*, marked by *koureion* sacrifices – and almost certainly, though he does not say it, *meion* sacrifices for infant boys.[135] All these sacrifices would have generated meat to be cooked alongside the other food, presumably by women, girls, and enslaved people. At least some of the meat was taken home to eat ([Dem.] 43.82), where it might have been shared by the women. In Aristophanes' *Thesmophoriazusae*, Euripides' in-law claims women steal the meat from the Apatouria, give it to the women who orchestrate their extra-marital affairs as a bribe or payment, then blame the theft on domestic ferrets (mustelids were kept as mousers): τὰ κρέ' ἐξ Ἀπατουρίων ταῖς μαστροποῖς

---

[133] Walter 1937 implies a phratry context for Xenokrateia's dedication to Kephisos (discussed on pp. 33 and 39), which he understands as a mother's dedication of her son to the god; he suggests potential connections with various phratry activities and celebrations (Walter 1937: 104, 108). Compare Lambert 1993: 309. Blok 2018: 18, fn. 64, notes that the phratry Gleontis had a cult of Kephisos.

[134] See Osborne 1985b on strong family ties to the demes, even by those who also held property elsewhere. On the relationship between deme and phratry locality, see Osborne 1985b: 73–4 and Jones 1999: 212–13. Aristophanes' *Peace* illustrates *men*'s emotive connection to the villages of Attica and the phratric celebrations associated with them, which they missed in their absence (in this case, because of the wartime evacuation of the countryside and its occupation by the Lakedaimonians); see Lambert 1993: 159–61 and Humphreys 2018: 586–9 for the play as strongly associated with the phratry and its celebrations, especially the Apatouria.

[135] Compare Lambert 1993: 153 with fn. 59: the scholiast also says that girls (*korai*) as well as boys (*kouroi*) were registered on Koureotis, which is not otherwise attested: Lambert 1993: 161–2, 185.

διδοῦσαι / ἔπειτα τὴν γαλῆν φαμεν ('we give the meat from the Apatouria to our go-betweens (f.), then say it was the ferret', ll. 558–9). This is a quintessentially Athenian misogynistic joke, combining two of the most frequent complaints against women – that they steal food, and that they have affairs – with the added layer of irony, illustrative of the anxieties about women and legitimacy discussed in Chapter 2, that the Apatouria was a festival for the admission of legitimately born children and so doubly violated by the stealing of the sacrificial meat for the furthering of extra-marital affairs.

Religion and the Expansion of Women's Networks

Earlier in this chapter we saw how relationships between men (in the case of Demosthenes 55, the relationship between two neighbours) might bring women connected to those men into relationships with each other – relationships which sometimes ceased to depend on the men who occasioned them. Bearing in mind the relationship-building qualities of shared religious participation, it is likely that where predominantly male groups involved women in their religious practice, those women formed relationships with each other – and with some of the men.

Again, phratry celebrations may have provided opportunities, including through *orgeōnes*, phratry 'subgroups' which sacrificed together. A fourth-century or early third-century decree of an association of *orgeōnes*, who seem to have been based in the *asty* and in the nearby deme of Xypete (between Peiraieus and Phaleron), includes provisions for women (*SEG* 21:530).[136] In the decree, found on the Areiopagos, the group acts to perpetuate sacrifices for all time for τῶι κοι]-|[ν]ῶι τῶι πρὸς τοῖς Καλλιφάνους καὶ τῶ[ι τοῦ ἥρωος Ἐ]-|χέλου (ll. 3-5), 'the *koinon* near the [property] of Kalliphanes' (presumably somewhere near the findspot?) and the *koinon* (association) 'of the hero Ekhelos', the eponymous hero of a place called Ekhelai, now identified as a site near Phaleron where a number of monuments dedicated to him have been found. The decree nevertheless speaks of a single sanctuary (ἐν τῶι ἱερῶι, l. 7) for the publication of its documents. Sacrifices were to be held on the seventeenth and eighteenth of Hekatombaion (roughly corresponding to our July/ August, the first month of the Attic year, ll. 12–14) and the meat distributed as follows (ll. 17–23):

---

[136] Meritt 1942: 282–7, no. 55, Ferguson and Nock 1944: 73–9, Lambert 1993: 186, Jones 1999: 251–3, favouring a fourth-century date.

[ν]-
[ἐμέτω] δὲ τὰ κρέα τοῖς {οις} ὀργεῶσι τοῖς παροῦσι καὶ τοῖ[ς]
[ὑοῖς τὴν] εἰς ἡμίσεαν καὶ ταῖς γυναιξὶ ταῖς τῶν ὀργεώ[ν]-
[ων, διδ]οὺς ταῖς ἐλευθέραις τὴν ἰσαίαν καὶ ταῖς θυγ[α]-
[τράσι τὴν εἰς ἡμί]σεαν καὶ ἀκολούθωι μιᾶι τὴν εἰς ἡμ[ί]-
[σεαν· παραδιδότω δὲ τ]ῷι ἀνδρὶ τῆς γυναικὸς τὴν με-
[ρίδα.]

> Let him distribute the meat to the *orgeōnes* who are present and up to a half-portion to the sons and to the women of the *orgeōnes*, having given(?) an equal-sized portion to the free women, and to the daughters, up to a half-portion, and to one female attendant, up to a half-portion. And let him hand over the portion of the woman to the man.

The nature of the groups distinguished here is not exactly clear. William Scott Ferguson believed that 'the free women' who are opposed here to 'the daughters' 'comprise wives, widows and spinsters (possibly aunts and married daughters) of the orgeonic families', which seems to me a more convincing reading of ἐλευθέρα than Benjamin Meritt's 'independent', that is, 'women who were orgeones of their own right'.[137] The significance of the 'one female attendant' is also unclear; was this a woman who had a religious role in the sacrifice, or an enslaved woman used for practical tasks entailed by the celebration,[138] or does the stipulation cover enslaved women kept by the orgeonic households – in which case this would be a striking instance of inclusion?[139] In any case, women (possibly including enslaved women) connected to the *orgeōnes* were apportioned meat from the orgeonic sacrifices and so were in some sense included in the group. The stipulation that the women receive their portions *via* the male *orgeōnes* with whom they were associated may mean that the men brought the meat home to them, in which case women's relationships with *each other* through the group would be only symbolic (which is not to say meaningless). Alternatively, this was merely a distribution mechanism, to preserve the distinctness of the relationship between *orgeōnes* proper, and perhaps also to ensure that all the women were legitimately connected to an *orgeōn* – in which case these women, like the *orgeōnes* to whom they were related, might have been present together at the sacrifice, and even have eaten together afterwards. Given that orgeonic religious practice was the

---

[137] Ferguson and Nock 1944: 75 with fn. 18; Meritt 1942: 287 with fn. 28.
[138] Lambert 2020a, n. 3.
[139] Jones 1999: 253 suggests that restriction to one may imply some families kept more than one woman as an enslaved attendant, and therefore that at least some members were reasonably wealthy. Compare the depicted inclusion of the enslaved nurse Pyraikhme in the Anthesteria, p. 189.

main expression of phratry religion beyond the Apatouria, all this would fit with our picture of phratries as particularly concerned with their members' wives and children. But for our purposes, it also suggests the possibility that through orgeonic religion, women might encounter and interact with women from other demes, kin groups, and local communities, in this case on an annual basis. If so, the relatively small size of known orgeonic groups would have facilitated a degree of familiarity.[140] It is never explicitly attested, but women in the same orgeonic groups might also have spent time together when the whole phratry came together at the Apatouria and the men were occupied with male-only phratry feasting.

We also find three women, Hesykhia, Erotis, and Aitherion, named at the end of a list from the Athenian-controlled island of Salamis of fifteen *thiasotai* honouring several men for their behaviour towards the *thiasos*, from the second half of the fourth century or later (*IG* II² 2347, ll. 31–3).[141] It is not clear what relationship, if any, they had with each other or with the male *thiasotai* beyond being fellow-*thiasotai*, but they were apparently active members. Two further documents thought to be lists of *thiasotai*, but where the actual words *thiasos* or *thiasotai* must be reconstructed, also include women. One late fourth-century group with a formal enough structure to have a *tamias* and a *grammateus* mentions at least six individuals, including a Soteris (*IG* II² 2348, l. 7). Soteris is the last fully legible name, with a K – – below her; the fragment is broken off ('*undique truncatum*') so we cannot know how many other names followed, but if the group's conventions followed those of the Salamis group, with women listed last, Soteris and K – – might have been two (among more?) women members – though this is uncertain.

These groups would have facilitated women's relationships not just with other women but also with men beyond the kinship group. Lysias 31, discussed more fully in the next section, criticises a man named Philon for failing in his duties to his (presumably widowed) mother, *Philo*. The speaker claims that because she could not trust her son, *Philo* had to entrust her burial to a man named Antiphanes, 'though she was no relation of his' (οὐδὲν προσήκουσα, §21). Perhaps this is rhetorical distortion, and Antiphanes *was* a relative, but just outside the immediate kin group, or possibly he was connected to her another way. A relationship through her husband's phratry, perhaps mediated through shared membership of a religious phratry subgroup, would be one possible scenario. Traditionally, phratry members had responsibility to each other in certain

---

[140] Jones 1999: 253; Ferguson and Nock 1944: 78.   [141] Jones 1999: 218–19.

contexts where kin were unavailable: Draco's ancient homicide law, a version of which remained in force across the fifth and fourth centuries (*IG* I³ 104), ordained that the phratrymen of a victim of involuntary homicide should decide whether the killer should be allowed within Attica if there were no nearer kin than cousins (probably including cousins once removed: [Dem.] 43.62–3) to make a decision about reconciliation.[142]

Mark Golden notes a possible instance of such a relationship in Menander.[143] In Terence's *Adelphoe*, based partly on Menander's second *Adelphoi*, a widowed *epiklēros* named Sostrata learns that the man pledged to marry her daughter Pamphila, who is pregnant with the man's child, has abducted an enslaved girl. Terrified that her pregnant daughter's expected marriage is now in jeopardy, Sostrata sends the man she keeps in slavery to a man named Hegio for help, because Hegio was 'very important' to her dead husband Simulus and has always looked after her family (*nam is nostro Simulo fuit summus et nos coluit maxume*, l. 352). The surviving, abridged version of Donatus' fourth-century AD commentary on the play says that in Menander, Hegio is introduced as Sostrata's *frater* ('brother') ('*apud Menandrum Sostratae frater indicitur*', 3.2.53.1 Wessner). That sits uneasily with Terence's plot and what we know of Menander's, in which Sostrata is apparently socially isolated, without the support of relatives.[144] Various explanations have been proposed. Golden suggests that Donatus' *frater* was in fact a transliteration of φράτηρ, 'phratryman': Sostrata and Hegio were part of the same phratry. For Golden, this supports a maximalist argument for women's association with phratries; Lambert's more conservative rendition ('Golden's suggestion that, in Menander, Hegio was in fact a fellow phrater of Sostrata (i.e., of her deceased husband?)') seems securer.[145] The apparent representation of a woman as a phratry member, or at least closely connected to her former husband's phratrymen, Lambert writes, 'would not be particularly surprising in this unusual case … of a widowed, unremarried epiklēros, anxious to obtain a proper heir by marrying off her daughter, with no close male relatives on either her own or her husband's side. That she might, in the absence of relatives, turn next to phrateres for help is credible enough.' If Golden's suggestion is correct, this would be a fictional instance of a woman maintaining a relationship initially occasioned through her husband even after his death – and in this case, drawing on that relationship for support in the absence or failure

---

[142] Compare Lambert 1993: 248–9; see also his pp. 239 and 188, fn. 243.
[143] Golden 1985: 11–13, followed by Lambert 1993: 187–8. [144] Rieth and Gaiser 1964: 72–7.
[145] Lambert 1993: 187–8.

of male relatives. The relationship between Antiphanes and *Philo* in Lysias 31 may have worked in a similar way; among other possibilities, Antiphanes may have been a phratryman of *Philo*'s dead husband.

On a more informal level, weddings (*gamoi*), funerals, and some celebrations to mark the birth of children would also have been mixed-sex occasions, though presumably men and women self-segregated at such events to some degree. The funeral at which *Thesmonike*'s supposed relationship with Eratosthenes began (Lysias 1.8) is not the only example.[146] The scholiast on Plato's *Theaetetus* who says that women who assisted at births purified themselves at the *amphidromia* says that the family's wider circle, οἵ τε φίλοι τε καὶ οἰκεῖοι καὶ ἁπλῶς οἱ προσήκοντες, 'the *philoi* and *oikeioi* and the relatives (*prosēkontes*) in general', sent gifts (most commonly octopuses) but, implicitly, did not visit, perhaps in part because it might have exposed them to pollution (schol. Pl. *Tht.* 160e). However, the tenth-day *dekatē* celebration was a bigger affair, when relatives and friends, male and female, would be likely to visit. The verbal phrase used is δεκάτην ἑστιάω, 'host a *dekatē*' or 'host a '*dekatē*-feast' (e.g. Dem. 40.28, 59; compare γάμους ἑστιάω, 'host a wedding-feast/wedding celebration', Isae. 8.18). One Aristophanic man tells of dressing up in a Phrygian wool cloak (χλαῖναν … Φρυγίων ἐρίων, *Birds* 493) to attend one, at which he drank heavily: ἐς δεκάτην γάρ ποτε παιδαρίου κληθεὶς ὑπέπινον ἐν ἄστει, 'I had once been invited to a baby's *dekatē* in the city, and drank too much' (l. 494). As with *gamoi*, litigants sometimes bring forward relatives and friends who were present at *dekatai* celebrations as witnesses in legal cases which turn on a child's identity and legitimacy – necessarily men, as women could not testify in jury courts (Isae. 3.30; Dem. 40.28, 59). Through such occasions, women could expand their networks, even across gendered boundaries.

Religion as a Spatial and Social Structurer

In the *Lysistrata* passage quoted near the beginning of this chapter, Lysistrate speaks of someone 'inviting' (*ekalēsen*, from *kaleō*, l. 1) other women to a religious sanctuary, as the woman hosting a party for Hekate invited (*ekalēs[a]*, l. 701) her friends, perhaps to her home. Unlike the Adonia, typically celebrated on the roofs of private homes, the celebrations

---

[146] Eratosthenes' apparent presence at Euphiletos' mother's funeral sits uneasily with Euphiletos' claim never to have seen the man before he allegedly caught him in bed with *Thesmonike* (§45) – did Eratosthenes know Euphiletos' mother but not her son? Or did he merely see the funerary procession as a passer-by rather than a participant at the funeral?

Lysistrate imagines and the sacrifice Sostratos' mother organises in the deme's *nympheion* in *Dyskolos* were in public places. The organisation of such activities represents a remarkable degree of potential female control over these spaces, if only for a limited amount of time: they could organise their own rites there and populate them with their friends. Sostratos' mother invites a large number of female friends to her sacrifice and post-sacrificial picnic (*Dys.* 404–5),[147] though her son also attends the picnic and invites his own friend (ll. 558–60).

Domestic and public spaces in which women celebrated festivals would in turn have structured women's experiences of space and of local topography – potentially in ways which challenged or offered alternatives to men's conception and use of space. In *Dyskolos*, Sostratos jokes:

μέλλουσα δ' ἡ μήτηρ θεῷ θύειν τινί,
οὐκ οἶδ' ὅτῳ – ποεῖ δὲ τουθ' ὁσημέραι,
περιέρχεται θύουσα τὸν δῆμον κύκλῳ
ἅπαντ[α] ...

(260–3)

My mother's going to make a sacrifice to some god,
I don't know which one – she does this every day,
she goes around the whole deme sacrificing!

The woman's religious practice motivates and legitimises her movement across the deme. In the daily experience of women, the physical space of the deme may not have been delineated by which *oikoi* were eligible to provide men to fill the deme's bouleutic quota, but by its religious sites. How typical was such behaviour? As with celebrations at Kolias, the mobility described for Sostratos' mother may only have been possible for rich women, whose households could spare enslaved workers to escort them.[148]

Women's religious and para-religious celebrations in private homes represented a temporary appropriation of control over domestic space, similar to their temporary appropriation of public sanctuaries, and may even have limited men's freedom in their own homes. The rooftop Adonia celebration Khrysis organises in *Samia* in the absence of her partner and his son Moskhion spreads out (ἐσκεδασμέναι, l. 46) to occupy the whole house. When Moskhion returns unexpectedly, the noise of their celebrations prevents him from sleeping (ll. 43–4) and he becomes a 'spectator' ([ἐγι]νόμην, οἴμοι, θεατής, 'I became – oh dear – a spectator', l. 43), an

---

[147] Compare Humphreys 2018: 385; Burton 1998: 152–3.
[148] Women escorted to festivals by enslaved people: Ar. *Thesm.* 279–94, Men. *Dys.* e.g. ll. 440–1.

outsider in his own home. It seems that practices of segregation in the classical Attic household were premised on keeping unrelated men from mixing with the women inside, primarily by keeping male guests to one room near the entrance; hangings could divide smaller dwellings.[149] However, if the house were full of unrelated women, the men of the household may have felt it proper to avoid mixing with them, and use of space might have become awkward. This would have been particularly true in the small homes of ordinary Athenians. Such awkwardness and inconvenience to men is apparent in Moskhion's account.

The opportunities afforded by religion for women to exercise social control are reflected in male authors' portrayals of women using public women's festivals – particularly the Thesmophoria – to define their own and other women's social identities. As Joan Burton argues, 'in the ancient Greek world, where women were typically denied modes of self-expression like voting in civic elections or serving on juries, women's religious festivals and celebrations also provided important opportunities for women to establish a sense of self-identity and community'.[150]

How did this work in practice? In Isaeus 8, the speaker offers as evidence for his mother *Klearete*'s identity as the legitimate daughter of the citizen Kiron the behaviour of his father ([ἃ] ὁ πατὴρ ἡμῶν ἔπραξε, 'what our father did', §18), namely hosting their *gamos*, inviting relatives and friends, giving a *gamēlia* for her to his phratrymen, and successfully introducing their sons to his phratry. As parallel evidence, the speaker cites the recognition of the married women of the deme ([ἃ] αἱ γυναῖκες αἱ τῶν δημοτῶν περὶ αὐτῆς ἐγίγνωσκον, 'what the wives of the demesmen recognised (*gignōskō*)', §18), which was illustrated by their choosing *Klearete* to copreside as *arkhousa* at the Thesmophoria celebrations of the central Attic deme Pithos:[151]

> αἵ τε γυναῖκες αἱ τῶν δημοτῶν . . . προύκριναν αὐτὴν μετὰ τῆς Διοκλέους γυναικὸς τοῦ Πιθέως ἄρχειν εἰς τὰ Θεσμοφόρια καὶ ποιεῖν τὰ νομιζόμενα μετ' ἐκείνης. (§19)

> The wives of the demesmen . . . chose (*prokrinō*) our mother, together with the wife of Diokles of Pithos, to preside (*arkhō*) at the Thesmophoria and carry out the ceremonies jointly with her.

The speaker avers that the women would not have chosen *Klearete* had she not been a citizen-status wife:

μὴ οἴεσθ' ἄν, εἰ τοιαύτη τις ἦν ἡ μήτηρ ἡμῶν οἵαν οὗτοί φασι … [μή] τὰς τῶν ἄλλων δημοτῶν γυναῖκας αἱρεῖσθαι ἂν αὐτὴν συνιεροποιεῖν τῇ Διοκλέους γυναικὶ καὶ κυρίαν ποιεῖν ἱερῶν, ἀλλ' ἑτέρᾳ ἄν τινι περὶ τούτων ἐπιτρέπειν … (§20)

> Do not imagine that if our mother had been the kind of woman [our opponents] claim … the wives of the other demesmen would have chosen her to celebrate the festival with the wife of Diokles and put her in charge of the rites/sacred objects, and not rather have entrusted this [role] to another woman …

Throughout the fuller passage, predominantly male rituals and processes, mostly on the phratry level and concerned with social recognition of family ties (the *gamēlia* and the young boys' phratry admission, carefully scrutinised by the phratrymen), are paralleled with the women's selection of *Klearete,* at the deme level, to preside at their celebration of the Thesmophoria, which constitutes recognition (*gignōskō*) of her social status. Griffith-Williams points out that the verb *prokrinō* ('choose', but really 'pre-choose') 'implies a system of sortition from pre-selected candidates'; 'the pre-selection in itself would be sufficient proof that her status as a citizen was accepted by the community'.[152]

The scene in *Thesmophoriazusae* where the women celebrating are asked to vouch for each other as part of the hunt for an intruder (ll. 603–18) is an illuminating parallel. Here the intruder is a man, not a woman whose social status excludes her from celebrating, but it is made clear that women were expected to know the identity (and therefore social status) of their fellow celebrants. The Chorus Leader identifies Euripides' in-law, disguised as a woman, as μόνην … ὧνερ οὐ γιγνώσκομεν, 'the only one we don't know' (l. 614). Parker, following Kevin Clinton, argues that the Thesmophoria was 'probably a "diffused" rite, one celebrated at numerous locations (some twenty to thirty?) throughout Attica, in specially designated Thesmophoria or other sanctuaries of Demeter called into service as such'. He suggests that city women, in the likely absence of a 'city Thesmophorion', probably celebrated either in the city Eleusinion or in the Thesmophorion of a city deme, like that at Melite.[153] Though this celebration in the city would have been more anonymous, at smaller-scale, deme-level celebrations, it may well have been that (almost) all the women celebrating knew (almost) all the others. Compare the speaker's statement in Isaeus 6 that most *men* of the

---

[152] Griffith-Williams 2013 *ad loc.*; cf. Whitehead 1986: 114, fn. 147.
[153] Parker 2005: 271, with fn. 8, following Clinton 1996.

deme (as well as phratrymen and relatives) knew a given man's daughters, and his wife, her marital status, and her family identity:

δύο θυγατέρας, καὶ τὴν μητέρα αὐτῶν, ἣν ἔγημεν ὁ Εὐκτήμων, Μειξιάδου Κηφισιῶς θυγατέρα … ἴσασι … τῶν δημοτῶν οἱ πολλοί … (§10)

Most of the demesmen know [Euktemon's] two daughters, and their mother, whom Euktemon married, the daughter of Meixiades of Kephisia …

Male-authored sources recognise that celebrating private or public festivals together was an index of female friendship (Men. *Sam.* 35–8, Lys. 1.20). Women's ability to choose invitees to private religious celebrations constituted an opportunity for them to define their inner social circles, which might transect socio-legal divisions – in other words, to establish social roles and enact social stratifications along axes other than those of the *polis* as a political entity. When the metic Khrysis hosts an Adonia celebration in the house where she lives with her partner (l. 40), she invites her citizen-status female neighbours, because she is fond of them. One of these friends is a married woman, the other an unmarried girl. Khrysis is not only friends with these two but is also integrated into the wider social circle of neighbourhood women, whom she also invites: Moskhion reports that Khrysis and her next-door neighbours celebrated 'with some other women' (μετά τινων / [ἄλλω]ν γυναικῶν, ll. 40–1). Sommerstein comments that like other Menandrian *pallakai*, including Glykera in *Perikeiromene* and Habrotonon in *Epitrepontes*, Khrysis has an 'ability to form a network of support among persons of more assured social status. Nikeratos' wife and daughter treat her as a friend (35–8); so do other women of the neighbourhood (40–1).'[154] That Khrysis is the host presupposes her social acceptance by the women, and even her relatively high social standing among them. Her status as a metic in an informal partnership with a citizen man is not an obstacle here; nor is her history as a *hetaira*.[155]

Similarly, in *Epitrepontes*, the enslaved Habrotonon, engaged to play the harp for citizen-status girls during the night-time dancing at the Tauropolia, describes playing games with them:

πέρυσι, ναί,
Ταυροπο[λίοις· π]αισὶν γὰρ ἔψαλλον κόραις,
αὐτ[ή] θ᾽ [ὁμοῦ συ]νέπαιζον·　　　　　　　　　　(476–8)

---

[154] Sommerstein 2013: 21.
[155] Compare Taylor 2011c: 714–15 on the relative unimportance of 'status homophily' in Greek women's friendships.

> Last year, yes, at the Tauropolia; I was playing the harp for some young girls,
> and I joined in their games myself.

The apparently unforced dancing between enslaved girls at Sostratos'
mother's party for Pan (*Dyskolos* 950–3) may reflect similarly relaxed social
divisions at another religious celebration.

In Euripides' *Electra*, the Argive women invite Elektra to a sacrifice, saying
that 'all the girls are going to go to the sanctuary of Hera' (πᾶσαι δὲ παρ᾽
῾Η-/ραν μέλλουσιν παρθενικαὶ στείχειν, ll. 173–4). Though the sacrifice has
seemingly been organised by the men of the community (καρύσσουσιν
θυσίαν / Ἀργεῖοι᾽, 'the Argives have proclaimed a sacrifice', 172–3), it is the
women who are portrayed as bringing other women the news and encouraging them to come. When Elektra says she is too sad to go and dance, they
double down on their persuasive efforts and even offer to lend her an
outfit:[156]

> ἀλλ᾽ ἴθι,
> καὶ παρ᾽ ἐμοῦ χρῆσαι πολύ-
> πηνα φάρεα δῦναι,
> χρύσεά τε – χαρίσαι – προσθήματ᾽ ἀγλαΐας. (190–3)

> Do come, and borrow closely woven clothes from me to wear, and gold
> accessories to go with the splendid outfit – it would make me happy.

Elektra is in the near-unique position of being in an unconsummated
marriage (ll. 25–49), both a *damar* (wife, l. 35) and a *parthenos* (virgin,
unmarried girl, l. 44). Here, the (presumably) married women (*gynaikes*,
l. 215) invite her to a dance for girls (*parthenikai*, l. 173, unmarried girls; but
then *nymphai*, l. 179, either young wives or soon-to-be married girls), but
we may be supposed to understand that they themselves will also attend: it
is a mixed-status occasion, and the women take care to include a woman of
ambiguous status.

Women could also establish social positions through subtler processes
than choosing whom to invite. We saw in the last chapter how women used
religious dedications to present themselves to their communities. At sanctuaries predominantly frequented by women, we might also see such dedications as ways for women to negotiate their identities and social positions in
relation to other women specifically. Extensive mid fourth-century

---

[156] As Denniston 1939 *ad loc.* notes we also find women lending out special clothes and jewellery for
religious occasions at Ar. *Lys.* 1188–94 (and various other instances); these are women offering to
lend clothes to any woman who wants them for her son or basket-bearing (and therefore necessarily
unmarried) daughter.

catalogues from the sanctuary of Artemis at Brauron attest to women's dedications offered there, and by implication, women's visits to the sanctuary. As well as more typical dedications of precious metals and pottery, along with ivory and horn, Brauron is most famous for women's dedications of textiles.[157] Examples from the records for 348/7–346/5 include a woman named Kallippe who dedicated 'a spiky-bordered short *khitōn*, patterned all over', with 'letters inwoven' (χιθωνίσκο[ς κτεν]-|[ωτ]ὸς περιποίκιλος, Καλλίππη· οὗτος ἔχει γράμ[ματ]-|[α ἐ]νυφασμένα); Thuaine and Malthake, apparently visiting together, who dedicated 'a sea-purple short *khitōn*, patterned all over, in a case' (χιτωνίσκος ἀλουργὸ-|ς ποικίλος ἐμ πλαισίωι, Θυαίν(η) καὶ Μαλθάκη ἀνέθ[η]-|κεν); and Nikoboule, who dedicated 'a new, patterned mantle [with] a design in the middle, of Dionysos pouring a libation, and a woman pouring wine for drinking' ([Νικ]-|οβούλη ἐπίβλη [μ]α ποικίλον καινόν, σημεῖον ἔ[χ]ει [ἐ]-|μ μέσωι, Διόνυσος σπένδων καὶ γυνὴ οἰνοχοοῦσα).[158]

Susan Cole has convincingly argued that the dedications were typically made in thanksgiving for successful childbearing, and that the inventories of dedications displayed at Brauron and at its sister-sanctuary on the Akropolis (the Brauronion) 'reminded the community of the successful performance of public ritual, ... stood to remind the gods of a history of collective ritual [and] symbolised the city's achievement in promoting its rituals, supervising its women, and producing its crop of healthy children'.[159] The clothes themselves and their catalogue descriptions also attest to the skills and to the social and economic status of their dedicators, as would clothes when worn.[160] Some of the dedicated clothes seem to have been displayed on racks (the foundations of which have been found in excavations)[161] or on the cult statues (some entries mention that the garment in question is being worn by a particular statue). Brauron may have been a context of homosocial status display and negotiation between women, as well as a context for women to travel with or encounter for the first time other women who wanted to celebrate their successful childbearing or -rearing.

<hr>

157 On the Brauron inventories, see Linders 1972, Cleland 2005; on Brauron more generally, see Cole 1998.

158 *IG* II[2] 1514.7–8 = 1515.1–2 = Cleland 2005, ll. 7–8; *IG* II[2] 1514.12–14 = 1515.6–7 = Cleland 2005, ll. 12–13; *IG* II[2] 1514.30–2 = 1515.22–4 = 1516.10–11 = Cleland 2005, ll. 30–2.

159 Cole 1998: 41–2, cited by Cleland 2005: 8; similarly Dakoronia and Gounaropoulou 1992: 219–23.

160 Cleland 2005: xii, and see pp. xii–xvi, 8–10, 72–82 on the social meaning of the Brauron clothing catalogues more generally.

161 Kondis 1967: 173–4, with plate 106.

We might also imagine social relations, competitive or affectionate, negotiated at the Thesmophoria through whose tent was pitched next to whose or in the best location; Aristophanes apparently wrote a play called *Women Claiming Tent-Sites*, Σκηνὰς καταλαμβάνουσαι (*P.Oxy.* 2659).[162] Women whose husbands were funding that year's Thesmophoria feast for their local celebration might have used the opportunity to show off their household wealth – to which they, of course, contributed – or their personal taste and skill by the quantity or quality of the food.[163]

Meritxell Ferrer's study of cooking vessels (*pignatte*) from the *akropoleis* of eighth- to sixth-century western Sicily shows how continuity between women's food preparation in a day-to-day domestic context and women's food preparation as part of religious ritual could shape women's perceptions of themselves and of the structures of their communities.[164] In western Sicily, this continuity came about because women made the same porridge, often in the same personally owned, homemade vessels, both at home on a day-to-day basis and for community rituals on the *akropoleis*. Their domestic role took on a new meaning in the ritual context, while everyday domestic food preparation became imbued with memories of ritual food preparation and its meanings, including social meanings: a sense of one's role in community worship; a sense of connection with those sharing food from the same sacrifice or pot; a sense of distinction from others served earlier, later, or differently.

The Haloa, a women's festival celebrated at Eleusis, seems to have involved handling genitalia made out of dough, which were either made at the festival or made at home and brought along. Matt Dillon suggests that women's (collective?) preparation of phallic (and yonic?) dough-shapes for the Haloa, and their shared handling of the shapes, would have been an opportunity for bonding.[165] One might take this further along Ferrer's line: continuity between women's production and shaping of dough for domestic consumption and their production and shaping of dough for the ritual may have meant that a woman shaping dough into loaves alone at home might remember making and touching dough-genitalia with other women as part of the Haloa. This remembering would reinforce her sense of herself as an important part of the ritual life

---

162 Compare Ar. *Pax* 880 with Sommerstein 2005 *ad loc.*
163 Compare Hodkinson 1983: 253–4 on e.g. Xen. *Lak. pol.* 5.3 for how this worked among men at the Spartan *syssition*. For the funding of the Thesmophoria feast, see Isae. 3.80.
164 Ferrer 2017.   165 Dillon 2017: 176–7.

of her community but would also reinforce her intimate, affectionate bonds with other women despite her current separation from them.[166] Strengthening of social ties as part of the ritual did not end with the ritual.

Thesmonike *and* Eratokleia *at the Thesmophoria*

What kinds of social (self-)definitions are at play in Lysias 1.20, where *Thesmonike*, the speaker's wife, and *Eratokleia*, her alleged lover Eratosthenes' mother, are said to have gone to the sanctuary together for the Thesmophoria – if it happened at all? The reported incident is the culmination of *Praxagora*'s confession to Euphiletos about the development of the adulterous relationship between *Thesmonike* and Eratosthenes. In Euphiletos' narrative, *Praxagora* explains how Eratosthenes enlisted her as messenger and persuaded *Thesmonike* to begin an affair, how she got Eratosthenes into the house for encounters with *Thesmonike*, and 'how at the Thesmophoria, when I [Euphiletos] was in the country, [my wife] went to the sanctuary with [Eratosthenes'] mother', (ὡς Θεσμοφορίοις ἐμοῦ ἐν ἀγρῷ ὄντος ᾤχετο εἰς τὸ ἱερὸν μετὰ τῆς μητρὸς τῆς ἐκείνου).[167] The inclusion of the incident serves Euphiletos' argument about the socially disruptive potential of adultery in a number of ways. The Thesmophoria in Attica celebrated and ensured both the fertility of the fields and the fertility of the (married, citizen-status) women.[168] The function of the latter was to produce children to continue the father's line. Adultery, Euphiletos points out (§§32–3), has the potential to corrupt this line; it is directly counter to Thesmophoric values.[169] The festival's celebration by an adulterous woman is bitterly ironic and illustrates that *Thesmonike*'s adultery corrupted not just the *oikos* but also a civic religious festival. There is further irony in this adulterous woman's attending the married women's fertility festival with her adulterous lover's mother.

As we saw in Chapter 2 (pp. 112–3), shared participation in private and public religious rites could be an index of family relationships. The supposed grandsons of Kiron in Isaeus 8 cite as proof (τεκμήρια) of their descent from him that he took them to public festivals and invited them to his house for private festivals (§§15–16). Conversely, the speaker

---

[166] Compare Taylor 2011c: 712–13 on the role in women's friendships of conceptually overcoming separation, based on analysis of Sappho and Erinna.

[167] *Eratokleia*'s marital deme was Oe; Clinton 1996 takes this line to suggest there was a Thesmophorion there. We wonder how much is implied by the phrase ᾤχετο εἰς τὸ ἱερὸν μετά – that they travelled together? That they were mainly in each other's company during the celebration? That they shared a tent?

[168] Compare Parker 2005: 275–83.   [169] Compare Parker 2005: 279.

of Isaeus 1 disputes Kleonymos' intention to make Pherenikos his heir by pointing out Kleonymos' alleged failure to include him in sacrifices to which he invited τοὺς οἰκείους ἄπαντας, 'all his family members (*oikeioi*)' (§31). The speaker of Isaeus 9, arguing against the claim that his half-brother Astyphilos adopted the son of his cousin Kleon, remarks on the strangeness of the fact that Astyphilos did not include Kleon in his sacrifices despite Kleon's being his demesman, cousin, and the father of his proposed adoptive son (§21). He contrasts this with his own father's inclusion of his stepson Astyphilos at rites along with his biological son (§30). To include someone in such celebrations was to treat them as kin.

In Lysias 1, Euphiletos portrays adultery as constructing a kind of rival *oikos*. Adulterous men, he argues, make wives *oikeioterai* to themselves than their husbands: 'closer', but also 'more part of their *oikos*' (§33). An *oikos* consisted in a nexus of relationships, not just the relationship between a wife and husband; so, in the rival, pastiche *oikos* of *Thesmonike*'s adulterous relationship, *Thesmonike* does not just have a relationship with her lover, but also with his mother. This woman is implicitly conceived of as a 'rival mother-in-law' to replace her actual husband's mother-in-law, whose death is implied to be a cause of the affair (§7), ostensibly because it was at her funeral that *Thesmonike* was first seen by Eratosthenes, but perhaps implicitly because a mother-in-law would play a central role in integrating a new wife into the household and maintaining discipline.[170] (Is the μοι of Euphiletos' ἐπειδὴ δέ μοι ἡ μήτηρ ἐτελεύτησε, πάντων τῶν κακῶν ἀποθανοῦσα αἰτία μοι γεγένηται, 'but then my mother died, and her dying was the cause of all the bad things that happened to me', not a possessive but a dative of disadvantage – 'my mother died on me'?) Foxhall, discussing the difference in classical Athenian male thought between rape and *moikheia* (adultery), writes:

> *Moikheia*, at least in the few cases where we have some details, implied a longer-term, larger-scale relationship, with a more active role played by women (and female networks). For example, in [Lysias 1], the wife was said to have been close to (and attended a major religious festival with) the mother of the murdered adulterer, while a slave girl acted as go-between for the lovers. The husband claimed he was finally informed about what was

---

[170] Role of mothers-in-law: Demand 1994: 15–17, Foxhall 1994: 93, 97, 99; cf. Hübner 2013: 141–9, 154–5. Mothers-in-law in the iconography of wedding processions, serving as an index of the bride's transfer into a new household: Oakley and Sinos 1993: 26, and index *s.v.* mother of bridegroom. Compare the biblical story of Ruth, variously dated to the late sixth or mid fifth century, for an ancient Near Eastern account of a woman's very positive relationship with her mother-in-law, which outlasted the man who occasioned it.

going on by a disgruntled ex-lover (female) of the adulterer. And perhaps most significantly, all the trouble with the wife started (so the husband says) when his mother (who lived with the couple) died.[171]

Eratokleia's displacement of Euphiletos' mother as *Thesmonike*'s 'mother-in-law' parallels and develops Eratosthenes' displacement of Euphiletos as her 'husband'. This explains the incident's place at the *culmination* of the account of the developing intimacy (*oikeiotēs*, a theme of the speech, §§6, 33), even after Eratosthenes' 'entrances' (*eisodoi*) both into Euphiletos' house and into *Thesmonike*'s (i.e. Euphiletos'?) body. Worse than the extra-marital sex is the dissolution of *oikos* boundaries entailed by but not limited to sex, as Euphiletos stresses elsewhere (§§32–3). The incident serves a similar argumentative function to the image in Isaeus 6 of Euktemon leaving his wife, daughters, and *oikia* to move into the household of another woman. Like cohabitation, joint festival attendance symbolises the escalation of sexual relationships into family relationships, which are presented as rivalling or replacing pre-existing, socially sanctioned families. That *Thesmonike* and *Eratokleia* are said to have attended the Thesmophoria together – rather than, say, to have spent time at each other's houses, which other men cite as an index of female friendship[172] – may have a social as well as a civic and religious significance.[173] We may assume a norm of going to the sanctuary for the Thesmophoria with the married women of one's household, including one's mother-in-law if she were still alive and still married.[174] In this case, the mention of *Eratokleia*'s going with *Thesmonike* shows her *acting* in the role of mother-in-law rather than merely occupying it by virtue of being Eratosthenes' mother.

This was apparently Euphiletos' reading. What was the social meaning of the event to *Thesmonike* and *Eratokleia*? Possibly the Thesmophoria offered them an opportunity to define their relationship for themselves, even if not for others, by behaving in a more formal capacity as mother- and daughter-in-law, though we must ask what value this 'definition' had if the behaviour which constituted it was socially invisible to other women celebrating, which it presumably was if the report only made it back to Euphiletos through *Praxagora* later. Perhaps they went together simply

---

[171] Foxhall 1994: 97; similarly Foxhall 1996: 151.   [172] Dem. 55.23, Men. *Sam.* 35–8.

[173] Further, shared attendance at the Thesmophoria was public, at least to other women, which may give the account the semblance of provability, though none of the men in the court could have confirmed or denied it, and we assume Euphiletos' witnesses do not include men who claim their wives saw the women together (§29, cf. §24).

[174] It is not clear whether widows attended.

because they enjoyed each other's company, and (*Praxagora* and?) Euphiletos interpreted – or pretended to interpret – the behaviour of friendship as the behaviour of kinship. The Thesmophoria enabled women to spend time with friends as well as female relatives; it may have been normal for unrelated women to attend together as friends, but easy for Euphiletos to imply something more significant. Perhaps what the episode really tells us is about the terms in which men were able to understand or imagine women's expressions of their relationships with other women.

Support Networks

Chapter 1 ('Two Women in Attica') argued for a female strategy of 'diversifying' relationships, which enabled women whose *kyrios* was absent or at odds with them to seek support from other people, usually men. Sometimes these were relations from previous marriages (*Diognete*'s son-in-law); sometimes they were not relations (Nikarete's former employers). Friendships, too, were part of this strategy: women sometimes turned to friends for help, particularly when male protectors failed.

Philo, the widowed mother of Philon in Lysias 31 whom we met in the previous section, is one example. The speech was delivered to the *Boulē* (Council) shortly after the restoration of democracy in 403. Anyone elected by lot as a public official or *Boulē* member had to undergo a scrutiny (*dokimasia*) of his eligibility, which often amounted to a scrutiny of his life and conduct, before taking office. Philon had been elected as a *Boulē* member; in the speech, an existing member objects to his taking up the role. The speaker focuses on Philon's abstention from the *stasis* between oligarchs and democrats in 403, and his alleged exploitation of the people of northern Attica where he was living at the time. He adds that *Philo*'s attitude to him further testifies against him:

> [20] οἷα μὲν οὖν ζῶσα ἡ μήτηρ αὐτοῦ κατηγόρει, παρήσω· ἐξ ὧν δὲ τελευτῶσα τὸν βίον διεπράξατο τεκμαιρομένοις ῥάδιόν ἐστιν ὑμῖν γνῶναι ὁποῖός τις ἦν περὶ αὐτήν. [21] ἐκείνη γὰρ τούτῳ μὲν ἠπίστησεν ἀποθανοῦσαν ἑαυτὴν ἐπιτρέψαι, Ἀντιφάνει δὲ οὐδὲν προσήκουσα πιστεύσασα ἔδωκεν εἰς τὴν ἑαυτῆς ταφὴν τρεῖς μνᾶς ἀργυρίου, παραλιποῦσα τοῦτον ὑὸν ὄντα ἑαυτῆς. ἆρα δῆλον ὅτι εὖ ᾔδει αὐτὸν οὐδὲ διὰ τὸ προσήκειν αὐτῇ τὰ δέοντα ἂν ποιήσαντα;

The sort of thing his mother accused him of while she was alive I shall pass over, but based on the evidence constituted by the actions she took at the end of her life it will be easy for you to judge what sort of a man he was to her. For she did not trust him to take care of her on her death, but she gave three minas of silver to Antiphanes for her burial, though she was no relation of his (*ouden prosēkō*), but she trusted (*pisteuō*) him, passing over [Philon] though he was her own son. Clearly she was well aware that despite her son's relationship to her he would not carry out his obligations.

We should treat with caution the claim that *Philo* was 'no relation' of Antiphanes. The speaker may be exaggerating *Philo*'s lack of family support further to blacken Philon's name, using *prosēkō* in a more restricted sense: perhaps *Philo* was not *immediately* related to Antiphanes but was, say, his mother-in-law (we recall *Diognete*'s support from her son-in-law when let down by her father, an immediate biological relative). If they were genuinely unrelated, was Antiphanes a neighbour? The husband or son of a female friend? A friend of her husband or even of Philon? Given that the relationship involved trust and a favour, we may also term it a friendship.[175]

The speaker implies that Philon abused *Philo* during her lifetime, whether financially (e.g. defrauding her) or in other ways. He also reveals the measures *Philo* took to protect herself. According to the speaker, she made informal accusations against her son, perhaps to her friends. She formed at least one relationship of trust (*pisteuō*) with a man from outside her household or immediate kin, and perhaps from outside her kin group altogether, in order not to become dangerously isolated. Carey notes the possibility that *Philo* made her burial arrangements during the *stasis* of 403, while Philon was in Oropos.[176] For the purposes of my argument, this alters only the reasons for her inability to trust Philon with her burial: he was not there to carry them out and could not be trusted to return to do so. The speaker portrays Philon's absence as a dereliction of duty to the *polis*; it was also a dereliction of duty to his mother.[177]

Like many individuals mentioned in forensic oratory, Antiphanes is not given a demotic or patronymic. The name was extremely common in classical Attica and is attested overwhelmingly for citizens. If Antiphanes was a citizen, in a worst-case scenario he would have been able to take Philon to court for mistreating his parent, but evidently he never had: the speaker would have mentioned it otherwise.[178] By entrusting to Antiphanes

---

[175] Compare Lewis 2002: 183–5 for the possibility of male–female relationships outside of the family.

[176] Carey 1989 *ad loc.*

[177] Criticism of (adoptive) sons for failing to bury parents: Isae. 4.19 and 9.4. Self-exculpation for being abroad and unable to bury a relative: Isae. 9.4. Compare also Xenophon's Sokrates' criticism of his son Lamprokles for behaving harshly and negligently towards his mother; this kind of ingratitude towards one's parents, Sokrates says, is condemned by the *polis* (Xen. *Mem.* 2.2).

[178] At the *dokimasia* for archons, the candidate was asked to prove that he had family tombs in Attica and knew their location, and that he treated his parents well ([Arist.] *Ath. pol.* 55.1–3). These

the arrangements for her burial, the task of a son or husband, *Philo* effectively made him, a man of her own choosing who was not an immediate relative or eligible for *kyrieia* over her, her de facto *kyrios*, because of her friendship with him.

New Comedy also portrays friends assisting women when male protectors fail. As we saw in Chapter 2 ('Bringing People In'), in *Samia* (l. 418) and *Perikeiromene* (ll. 184–5, 262–4), women in long-term but insecure partnerships seek refuge with the women next door when their partners become aggressive or violent; in *Samia*, Khrysis' next-door neighbour continues to advocate for her (l. 421). In *Perikeiromene*, the neighbour's action is characterised as maternal (ll. 242–4). Indeed, this is the role of close kin in *Dyskolos*, where a woman leaves her aggressive husband to live with her son from a former marriage (ll. 13–29), and in Xenophon's *Memorabilia* 2.7, where women go to stay with a male relative when their own menfolk flee, but the Samian Khrysis has no relatives to turn to. Because these short-distance separations are central to their respective plots, the outcomes of problems set up to be resolved in the course of each play, it is hard to assess how representative they are. The women's being next-door neighbours is in part a staging necessity, though we have seen the value to women of relationships with close neighbours. We also saw that the speaker of [Demosthenes] 47, influenced by his wife, took in a vulnerable freedwoman when her quasi-marital partnership ended (in this case because of her partner's death). He was motivated by gratitude for her services as a nurse, a sense of obligation, and the desires of his wife. Though the circumstances are different, Nikeratos' wife felt a similar sense of gratitude and obligation to Khrysis: gratitude for having nursed her grandson, and the obligation conferred by friendship. Perhaps the comic scenarios are not so fantastical.

In Chapter 1 ('Two Women in Attica'), we saw how *Diognete*, whose father Diogeiton had defrauded her children, asked her son-in-law to assemble αὐτῆς τὸν πατέρα καὶ τοὺς φίλους ('her father and friends', Lys. 32.11) – who were men (ἀνδράσι) – so that action could be taken against Diogeiton. First among these 'friends' was her own second husband (§12); the others are referred to as *hoi alloi epitēdeioi* (the other friends/ allies), and then *hoi philoi* (the friends/relations; as we have seen, the meanings of these words are not easily extricable). Apart from the

---

considerations were apparently relevant to *dokimasiai* for other roles but not necessarily asked about explicitly. Aeschin. 1, positioning itself as part of a procedure called the *dokimasia* of public speakers (*rhētores*), is also concerned with mistreatment of parents (§28).

indication in §11 (αὐτῆς … τοὺς φίλους, 'her *philoi*'), the absence of genitives or possessives leaves undistinguished whether the friends are *Diognete*'s, Diogeiton's, or the son-in-law's; they may have been connected to the family as a whole, an effect of the epiklerate. *Diognete* accuses Diogeiton before these relatives and friends of defrauding her children, and they are able to compel him to submit to a scrutiny of his finances, which leads to his prosecution.

[Demosthenes] 25 tells of a metic named Zobia who shielded her former friend or partner, the citizen Aristogeiton, from the Eleven (the officials responsible for guarding prisoners and carrying out certain executions) after he had escaped from prison. Zobia lent him eight *drakhmai* and some clothing (§§56–8). According to the speaker, when Zobia later asked for it back, Aristogeiton beat her and threatened her. The speaker continues, οὐκ ἐπαύεθ' ἡ ἄνθρωπος, ἀλλὰ γυναίου πρᾶγμ' ἐποίει καὶ πρὸς τοὺς γνωρίμους προσιοῦσ' ἐνεκάλει, 'the woman (derogatory) did not give up, but did the thing women do (*gynaiou pragm[a]*) and, going to her acquaintances (*gnōrimoi*), made accusations [against him]' – what *Diognete* and perhaps *Philo* had done. (Aristogeiton apparently retaliated by dragging her to the officials responsible for exacting the metic tax, who could sell her into slavery for non-payment, though as she had in fact paid her tax, she maintained her freedom.)

Zobia, *Diognete*, and perhaps *Philo* used male friends to seek justice; they had few other options. Johnstone considers the potential psychosocial effects of women's having to 'treat the men they knew well as a means to an end', while men could achieve their ends through formal, impersonal relationships, like their relationship to the citizen body and to depersonalised jurors.[179] By way of example, he discusses Neaira's relationships with her friends and lovers, whom she had to persuade to cooperate to contribute money for her freedom (Ap. *Neaira* 30–2) and later play off against each other to keep her property (§§37–47). He shows that these 'were not simply relationships of pleasure or affection (as they were for the men): they were also relationships she had to maintain to control her property'.[180] Johnstone suggests that the necessity for women to instrumentalise their personal relationships with men was 'both a less effective means of pursuing interests than the impersonal relationships open to men, and … one that must have considerably affected these personal relationships'.

---

[179] Johnstone 2003, though Isae. 5.39 describes Dikaiogenes' mother making public accusations against him in a sanctuary.

[180] Johnstone 2003: 270.

Because women had fewer avenues of agency, female friends would not have been able to support *Diognete*, Zobia, and Neaira in the way their male friends had. A side effect of this may have been to remove some of the pressure from friendships between women, though doubtless they had pressures and tensions of their own. For *Metrodora* and *Kallikleia* in Demosthenes 55, the friendship was itself the support, providing company and sympathy. The two friends visited one another (πρὸς ἀλλήλας ἀφικνουμένων, §23). This company was probably particularly important after the deaths of their husbands, which may have resulted in social isolation. They probably supported each other in mourning and adjusting to widowhood. The speaker explains that when his neighbour's property flooded, *Metrodora* went to visit *Kallikleia*, who 'wept … and showed her what had happened' (ἀποδυραμένης … ἐκείνης τὰ συμβάντα καὶ δεικνυούσης, §24). He recounts what *Metrodora* later told him of the damage: 'she said what she had seen and heard from their mother' (ἦ μὴν ὁρᾶν καὶ τῆς τούτων μητρὸς ἀκούειν ἔφη), including how she had seen their soaked barley drying. The speaker is invested in minimising the damage (for which he is being sued) but does not minimise *Kallikleia*'s distress. He mentions that *Metrodora* saw the damage in order to explain how he knew how little damage there was. He must work hard, given that his only evidence is a woman's word: he swears an oath to the court when he adduces this evidence (§24). From the women's point of view, however, we have a distressed woman telling her friend about the flooding she and her sons have suffered, walking with her round the property and showing her what had been damaged and what steps they were taking to counter the damage.[181] Presumably it was a relief and a comfort to *Kallikleia* to be able to express her grief to *Metrodora*. Even if the speaker entirely fabricated the friendship between the women, and *Metrodora*'s visit, in order to fabricate evidence, he considered the neighbourly visit of one widow to another, and their commiseration, easy for the jurors to imagine.

When the speaker introduces the friendship between *Metrodora* and *Kallikleia*, he begins, τῆς … μητρὸς τῆς ἐμῆς χρωμένης τῇ τούτων μητρὶ πρὶν τούτους ἐπιχειρῆσαί με συκοφαντεῖν, 'my mother was friends with [my opponents'] mother, before [my opponents] tried maliciously to sue me' (§23). We infer that the lawsuit brought an end to the women's friendship.[182] Did they come to share their sons' enmity for each other,

---

[181] Compare *BGU* 16.2665, where a first-century Egyptian woman tells her son of flood damage.

[182] Other possibilities are that *Metrodora* continued to be friends with *Kallikleia* but concealed it from her son; or that the speaker pretended to the jury that the friendship had ended because of its

or was their affection for each other undiminished by a dispute from which they detached themselves? If the latter, it must have been painful to have their interaction weaponised in the lawsuit. Humphreys suggests that 'women may … in many cases have had an even more negative attitude towards the law as a means of settling disputes between kin or friends than men did'.[183] She notes this case as 'a rare glimpse of informal communication between women which cuts through the pretensions of male dealings in the public sphere' but also observes that 'friendship between the mothers had not, however, been enough to stop the two sons quarrelling'.[184] If *Metrodora* and *Kallikleia*'s visits to each other ceased after the instigation of the lawsuit, they may have become quite isolated; certainly their respective social circles would have shrunk.

Women's emotional support for each other in a crisis is dramatised in Menander's *Georgos*, where Myrrhine, whose daughter is pregnant by rape, confides in Philinna:

> ἀ]λλ' ὡς πρὸς εὔνουν, ὦ Φίλιννα, τοὺς λόγους
> π]οουμένη σε πάντα τἀμαυτῆς λέγω.
> ἐν τ]οῖσδ' ἐγὼ νῦν εἰμι. (22–4)

I'm speaking to you as a friend (tr. Balme)[185] *or* It's because you're sympathetic I'm talking to you (tr. Arnott),[186] Philinna, and telling you all my [problems]. This is the situation I'm now in.

Not enough survives of *Georgos* to determine the nature of the relationship between Myrrhine and Philinna. Most scholars assume Philinna is Myrrhine's former nurse, partly because she addresses Myrrhine as τέκνον ('child', ll. 25, 84).[187] Eleanor Dickey writes that 'speakers other than parents who use τέκνον are usually in some sense *in loco parentis* for the addressees: tutors, old nurses, friends of their parents, etc.'. She adds, 'τέκνον [was] used outside the family not as the usual way of addressing a given person, but as a way of expressing particular feelings'.[188] Lysistrate's (older?) friend Kalonike calls her τέκνον in Aristophanes (*Lys.* 7).[189] Possibly this is an exception to Dickey's general rule, or

---

inconvenience to his picture of his neighbours' malice towards him. Compare Foxhall 1998a: 63 for a different view.

[183] Humphreys 2018: 258. Contrast Osborne 1985b: 1–6 for an example of men using the law to sort out matters between friends.

[184] Compare *P.Flor.* 3.332 (second-century AD Egypt), where a woman maintains a positive relationship with her sister-in-law despite a dispute with her brother.

[185] Balme 2001.   [186] Arnott 1979.

[187] For example, Gomme and Sandbach 1973 *ad Georgos* 22.   [188] Dickey 1996: 68, 89.

[189] Compare Willi 2003: 187 and 161–2, though note Dickey 1996: 65–6 *contra*. On the potential age difference between Kalonike and Lysistrate, see Henderson 1990 *ad Lys.* 7.

older women's friendships with younger women – if there is such an age discrepancy between Lysistrate and Kalonike – might take on a maternal quality, as in the case of *Thesmonike* and *Eratokleia*.[190] Arnold Gomme and Harry Sandbach, citing this term of address for their suggestion that Philinna is 'probably Myrrhine's old nurse', comment that Philinna 'presumably does not live with [Myrrhine], since she is unacquainted with the family situation. Perhaps . . . she is a freedwoman.'[191] Certainly Philinna is unlikely to be of citizen status. While the enslaved Daos treats Myrrhine with great politeness (e.g. ll. 41–3), he treats Philinna with marked contempt, initially ignoring her (ll. 41–3), then shutting her up with a contemptuous σιώπα, γρᾴδιον ('shut up, crone', l. 54),[192] which Myrrhine does not censure.[193] Gomme and Sandbach adduce this line for their argument too. However, if Philinna is a freedwoman, it does not necessarily follow that it was Myrrhine who had formerly kept her in slavery. Possibly the two are neighbours who have become friends, like the metic Khrysis and the citizen-status wife of Nikeratos in *Samia*, or the enslaved *Phile* and the citizen-status *Mnesodike* in Antiphon 1. Myrrhine calls Philinna *philē* (ll. 33, 87); by comparison, Phaidra in Euripides' *Hippolytus* (performed 428) calls her nurse *maia* (ll. 243, 311) and reserves *philai* for the free women of Troizen (l. 674). Or perhaps Philinna *had* previously been enslaved by Myrrhine, and their relationship has changed quality since the end of Philinna's enslavement into more of a friendship – though we might also see it as a continuation of Myrrhine's emotional dependence on her former nurse, and of her exploitation of Philinna's emotional labour.[194]

---

[190] See pp. 316–9; cf. Men. *Pk.* 242–4 with p. 140.

[191] Gomme and Sandbach compare the nurse in *Samia*, but she lives with her former enslavers; the freed nurse in [Dem.] 47 initially did not.

[192] Arnott 1979 attributes the line to Myrrhine, not Daos, but elsewhere in classical literature (e.g. Aristophanes, Xenophon) the diminutive conveys derision or grim pity, rather than affection, making it very unlikely for Myrrhine. Willi 2003: 187 notes that in Aristophanes, at least, diminutive forms of address including -ίδιον, are 'used affectionately and ingratiatingly by men' but 'not usually used by women'. Compare Gomme and Sandbach 1973 *ad* Men. *Pk.* 389 for another Menandrian diminutive of contempt.

[193] Dickey 1996: 82 writes that 'in Menander γραῦ and γρᾴδιον are addressed only to elderly female servants, generally in orders or rebukes'; she cites this line, but the rule does not easily account for Philinna, who is presumably not *currently* a servant (enslaved or freed) to Myrrhine if she does not live with her. There are few elderly citizen-status women in extant Menander to compare. At p. 212, Dickey observes that 'older women [in Menander] who appear to be free are always addressed by name or with [friendship terms, like τέκνον]', citing only Philinna and Myrrhine (fn. 15). It is not clear whether her inclusion of Philinna is a mistake: though on p. 82 Dickey counts Philinna as a servant, she may be a *free* servant – but γρᾴδιον is not a friendship term.

[194] I thank Dan-el Padilla Peralta for this suggestion.

Whatever the nature of their relationship, its direct portrayal onstage is exceptional in what we have of Menander. The only other sustained onstage interaction between two women in Menander's extant corpus is twenty lines exchanged between Pamphile and Habrotonon in *Epitrepontes* (ll. 857–77), who did not know each other personally before this scene. Other Menandrian female friends (Khrysis, Plangon, and Nikeratos' wife in *Samia*; Myrrhine and Glykera in *Perikeiromene*) are never shown interacting. Indeed, Nikeratos' wife never appears onstage, and Plangon never speaks; it is not clear whether Myrrhine in *Perikeiromene* appeared or spoke. This is in contrast to a number of sympathetic portrayals in tragedy of women providing emotional support to other women in crisis. These include Euripides' *Medea* and *Hippolytus*, in which Medea and Phaidra respectively – both, like Khrysis, newcomers to their city of residence – are supported by a chorus of local women, with whom they are portrayed as having friendly relationships. Although Aristotle's philosophical discussions of friendship imagine only friendships between men, sympathetic relationships between unrelated women were evidently familiar to tragic authors and spectators.

Sociolinguistic analyses of Aristophanic comedy may shed some light on salient features of women's conversation in fifth-century Attica, and therefore on how female friends typically related to one another. Andreas Willi, drawing analogies with the results of a study of the depiction of female speech in androcentric, male-authored Japanese soap operas,[195] argues that a male playwright writing female characters

> operates with an intuitive concept of what women's conversation sounds like, without being able to pin down the exact features that produce the desired effect. For instance, if the author had heard female speakers use conservative morphology a thousand times, he would automatically introduce a larger amount of conservative morphology into his representation, even though he might occasionally give the same forms also to a male speaker and be unable to analyse grammatically what makes his female discourse 'female'.[196]

Sommerstein shows that in Aristophanic comedy, women use obscenities in front of each other but not usually in front of men;[197] this may indicate a norm of fairly relaxed conversation between women.[198] Possibly shared

---

[195] Shibamoto 1987: 40–7.   [196] Willi 2003: 167.
[197] Sommerstein 1995: 78–80; similarly McClure 1995: 205–59; cf. Willi 2003: 188.
[198] One Hatzian woman said that before embarking on a friendship with a woman, she would 'see if she can take a joke' (Kennedy 1986: 129).

experience of ritual obscenity at women's festivals reduced women's inhibitions among themselves even in secular conversation. Willi observes that 'exchange of compliments is a striking feature of the first, women-only, scene in *Lysistrata*. [While] men in Greek comedy do not praise each other for their appearance . . . the women in *Lysistrata* compliment each other in an ordinary conversation.'[199] The compliments also include affectionate scolding: μὴ σκυθρώπαζ' ὦ τέκνον. / οὐ γὰρ πρέπει σοι τοξοποιεῖν τὰς ὀφρῦς, 'Don't make a grumpy face, babe. It doesn't suit you to arch your brows', ll. 7–8.[200] This is too scant a basis for solid inference, but it offers an image of how affectionate relationships between women were built up and maintained.

Women's Friendships in Women's Words

The final friendships in this chapter are those women describe in their own words. A simple tombstone apparently found in the Kerameikos,[201] probably from the late fifth century, commemorates a young woman named Biote (*IG* I³ 1295 bis, EM 8852, Figure 5.5).[202] According to the inscription, it was erected by a woman named Euthylla, who describes herself as Biote's *hetaira* (companion, friend). *Hetaira* is the word that Aristophanes' Praxagora in *Ecclesiazusae* uses of a woman she claims to have helped in childbirth (l. 528), and which the speaker of the Women's Chorus in *Lysistrata* uses of a woman she has invited to her religious celebration (l. 701). Sappho uses the word for the relationship between the goddess Leto and the mythical Niobe: Λάτω καὶ Νιόβα μάλα μὲν φίλαι ἦσαν ἔταιραι, 'Leto and Niobe were very dear friends' (frg. 142 Voigt). She also uses it for the women in her own circle, announcing that she will sing ἐταίραις / ταὶς ἔμαις, 'for my [female] companions' (frg. 160 Voigt). Though the top line of Biote's monument is damaged, we can still read Euthylla telling us that she set it up 'because of faithful and sweet (or "delightful", "pleasant", "enjoyable") friendship/affection/love (*philotēs*)'.[203]

---

[199] Willi 2003: 190 on *Lys.* 79–80, 83, 88–90; cf. 8, 707. Alcman, a man writing songs in late seventh-century Sparta for performance by young women, has the young women effusively praise each other (frgs. 1 and 3).

[200] Compare *P.Brem.* 64.4–9, second-century AD Egypt.   [201] Poland 1893: 192.

[202] *CEG* (1) 97.

[203] See González González 2019: 77–86 for discussion of various interpretations of the epigram, esp. p. 79 for different valences of *philotēs*; the term is predominantly used for the love of friends, but in Homer and Pindar is sometimes used for erotic love.

Figure 5.5 Grave *stēlē* of Biote, late fifth century, Athens, Epigraphic Museum EM
8852. © Hellenic Ministry of Culture/Hellenic Organization of Cultural Resources
Development (H.O.C.RE.D.). Photograph by author.

πισ[τ]ῆς ἡδείας τε χά[ρι]-
ν φιλότητος ἑταίρα /
Εὔθυλλα στήλην τήνδ᾽ ἐ-
πέθηκε τάφωι /
σῶι, Βιότη· μνήμηγ γὰρ
ἀεὶ δακρυτὸν ἔχοσα /
ἡλικίας τῆς σῆς κλαί-
ει ἀποφθιμένης.

For the sake of faithful (*pistos*) and sweet (*hedys*) friendship (*philotēs*), your companion
Euthylla has placed this tombstone on your grave,
Biote, because she tearfully keeps your memory forever,
weeping for your lost youth.

William Poland, who published the inscription, writes: 'It is an extraordinary thing that the stone was erected by a friend, not by a member of the
family of the deceased.' He suggests that Biote 'was not an Athenian, and
perhaps that she was from some rather distant region, living in Athens
without her family' and was perhaps enslaved.[204] But where in Poland's
time, the close of the nineteenth century, there were thirteen Biotes in the
epigraphic record, only one of whom was known to be from Attica, the
record has since expanded to reveal as many as twenty-one Biotes in Attica
alone.[205] At least three were of citizen status.[206] Inscriptions from the third

---

[204] Poland 1893: 197.   [205] *LGPN* II, *s.v.* Βιότη.   [206] *IG* II² 6162, 6567, 6949.

century and later record metic Biotes in Attica from Miletos, Herakleia, and Dardanos.

Two fourth-century Attic inscriptions name Euthyllas. One, from the *agora*, seems to name a Euthylla (the first and last letters are missing) as the daughter of a man whose name is lost, and the wife of a man of the deme Leukonoion, whose name is also lost (*SEG* 19:255). Benjamin Meritt, noting the rarity of the name, suggests this was the Euthylla who commemorated Biote.[207] The plausibility of this appealing identification decreased slightly with the discovery of one or two further fourth-century Euthyllas, in *SEG* 29:207. A Euthylla, daughter of Peisikrates of Kerameikos, is listed beneath a man named Teisikles, son of Teisimakhos of Kerameikos (her husband?) and seemingly above another Euthylla – a daughter named after her?[208] – though only the letters Εὐθυ- are visible. 'Euthylla', therefore, was a name given to citizen-status women.

Euthylla's self-description as Biote's *hetaira* probably rules out Poland's suggestion that she kept Biote in slavery, at least at the time of her death; perhaps she had once, but had since freed her – though it would be surprising for a woman to call herself the *hetaira* of a woman she had once enslaved. If Biote was a metic, her friendship with Euthylla might have been similar to the friendship in the *Samia*: a citizen-status woman forming a close friendship with a metic who lived nearby. Or Biote was of citizen status, a second instance, along with *Philo*, of a citizen-status woman buried by a friend rather than a relative. Two citizens in Isaeus were also apparently buried by non-relatives: Astyphilos, by his *philoi* (friends) and *systratiōtai* (comrades, 9.4), and Nikostratos, by *hoi mēden prosēkontes* ('people who were no relation to him', 4.19); they may have been commemorated by them too. The monument's likely date towards the end of the Peloponnesian War may go some way towards explaining this: the period was marked by elevated mortality and population displacement, leading to widespread dislocation and family breakdown. Perhaps, like *Diognete* with whom this book began, Biote was without husband or brothers, and had to rely on friends – in this case, a female friend.

Another late fifth-century marble *stēlē*, this time from Peiraieus, commemorates Anthemis (*IG* I³ 1329, c. 420–400). The *stēlē* has been lost since its discovery, but according to descriptions, it was probably painted with

---

[207] Meritt 1960: 71.
[208] Compare Humphreys 2018: 271 for girls named after their mothers: *SEG* 18:85, 26:302; possibly *IG* II² 10867.

the figures of two women, labelled 'Herophile' (spelt with a final epsilon) and 'Anthemis'. The elegiac inscription read as follows:

> Ἀνθεμίδος τόδε σῆμα· κύκλωι στεφα-
> νοῦσ⟨ι⟩ν ἑταῖροι / μνημείων ἀρετῆς
> οὕνεκα καὶ φιλίας.

> This is the monument of Anthemis; her companions [m. pl.] encircle [it] with garlands (*stephanō*), as memorials of her excellence (*aretē*) and friendship (*philia*).

As noted in Chapter 2, white-ground *lekythoi*, often used for liquid offerings to the dead and frequently decorated with scenes of funerary ritual, offer numerous depictions of individuals or pairs garlanding or preparing to garland grave monuments with *tainiai* and *stephanoi* (see for example Figure 2.1).[209] Humphreys notes that Xenophon takes the requirement for archonship candidates to be able to say where the tombs of their parents were as implying a duty to *decorate* one's parents' tombs (τῶν γονέων τελευτησάντων τοὺς τάφους … κοσμῇ, Xen. *Mem.* 2.2.13; cf. [Arist.], *Ath. pol.* 55. 2–3);[210] decoration was evidently part of commemoration. On one *lekythos*, a woman places a garland on a monument itself decorated with a relief of another woman, who sits with her hair up, wrapped in a *himation*, looking in a handheld mirror (Figure I.2, in the Introduction). These images, and Anthemis' epigram, illustrate that commemoration involved but was not limited to the provision of a monument. Xenophon's gloss makes clear that even the less monumental elements of this process – decoration with perishable *stephanoi* or *tainiai* – were strongly connected with family membership.

Plenty of funerary epigrams mention a number of mourners who may have had different levels and types of involvement in the commemoration process and different relationships to the dead person. One Arkhestrate, for example, is said to have left great longing to her loved ones, 'especially her husband'; the inscription later mentions the grief she left to her mother, brother, husband, and child (*IG* ii² 7227, mid fourth century). Her husband may have paid the full cost of the funeral and stone but chose to mention on it her other close relatives, who shared in his grief and mourning, or they may have contributed financially too. Almost certainly they contributed to the wider commemoration process by visiting and

---

209 P. 117. See also NAM 1929, Athens, a white-ground *lekythos* showing women preparing grave-offerings including *lekythoi*, *stephanoi*, and *tainiai*, printed in Kurtz 1975, pl. 20.
210 Humphreys 2018: 328.

decorating the tomb. Given that Herophile is named and depicted with the dead Anthemis, she probably had a central role in the commemoration process, though it evidently involved – and announced its involvement of – multiple people: Anthemis' *hetairoi*, who decorated the monument and may have contributed to the cost of the stone as well as the garlands; 'garlanding' may be a metonym for the erection of the monument. Perhaps Herophile was a *hetaira* of Anthemis, to be understood as *pars pro toto* of the *hetairoi*,[211] though another relationship is possible (mother, daughter, sister?). In either case, Anthemis is commemorated by her friends, who assumed a role proper to close relatives.[212] The masculine plural implies that at least some of Anthemis' friends were men – as was the case for *Philo*.

The Language of Female Friendship

Given the uniqueness of Euthylla's epigram as a female voice on female friendship, it is worth comparing it to the language used around female friendship in male-authored literary sources. *Pistis* (trust) features prominently, as in the language of male friendship.[213] David Konstan argues that in classical Athenian thought on friendship, 'to be trustworthy or loyal – *pistos* in Greek – is the quality of a friend; to fall short of it is simply not to be a friend at all ... Trustworthiness and friendship are covariant: the one is the mark of the other'; 'trustworthiness was an attribute or consequence of *philia*; where *philia* obtained, trust was not a separate and distinct value of its own'.[214] In the extremely brief account of *Philo*'s friendship with Antiphanes, *pisteusasa* (from *pisteuō*) is the entirety of the language used for the friendship; the only other descriptor of their relationship is that she was 'not at all related' (*ouden prosēkō*) to him. Only *pisteusasa* allows us to apply the label 'friendship', not an unreasonable application if we follow Konstan. *Pistos* is the first word that Euthylla uses to describe her

---

[211] Clairmont 1970: 156.

[212] By contrast, Calame 1999: 114–15 argues that Anthemis was a *hetaira* in the sexual sense, and that the *hetairoi* were identifying themselves as symposiasts; he too pairs the monument with Biote's, for which a 'sympotic' reading is even unlikelier. For instances of women commemorated by friends in other periods, see Poseidippos AB 53, third century BC, an epitaph for Kalliope, mourned (and commemorated?) by *hetairai*, and *IG* I³ 1205, c. 530, Melissa, buried and commemorated by a woman named Terpo. Humphreys 2018: 105 fn. 19 suggests Terpo was a friend rather than a kin member, but this is uncertain.

[213] Compare Konstan 2018: 61–93; also Foxhall 1998a: 59 on other elements of the language of male friendship, including *eunoia*.

[214] Konstan 2018: 86, 62.

friendship with Biote, and the first word of her epigram for her: she describes their *philotēs* (friendship) as *pistos* (trustworthy, faithful) and *hedys* (pleasant, sweet, enjoyable). In Chapter 2, I suggested that the evaluation of *Piste*, the former nurse in [Dem.] 47, as *pistē*, made her 'the sort of woman' *Hipparkhe* wanted to keep her company and help during her husband's absence, and that this evaluation might have been *Hipparkhe*'s own, or at least shared by her.

The other quality that made *Piste* desirable company for *Hipparkhe* was that she was *eunous*, the assessment Menander's Myrrhine makes of Philinna which prompts her to confide in her (*Georgos* 22), which in turn is an expression of trust. It is because of Philinna's *eunoia* that Myrrhine is able to tell her 'everything of mine', 'all my [problems]' (πάντα τἀμαυτῆς, l. 23), and specifically about the rape and pregnancy of her daughter. The importance for Euthylla, *Philo*, *Hipparkhe*, and Myrrhine of trust in a relationship, which Menander portrays as a willingness to confide, is echoed in Kennedy's accounts of women's friendships in the village of Hatzi, Crete, in the twentieth century, discussed in the Introduction to this book. Patterns of life in Hatzi, and particularly gender relations, in some ways resemble those of classical Attica.[215] Kennedy contextualises the depth and importance of the friendships she describes within a social milieu characterised by sharp gendered segregation of time, space, and work, and by pervasive interpersonal distrust, particularly between men and women.

> Unlike many of their relationships with others, women's friendships provide an environment in which they can feel secure about sharing their real selves and telling their secrets and other personal information. Unlike their marital relationship, in which the partners are largely isolated in separate spheres of activity . . . friendships are based primarily upon the expression of the participant's personal feelings and secrets.[216]

One woman Kennedy interviewed described her relationship with her best friend as follows: 'She comforted me, because I had so many children and so much trouble with them. I needed comforting, and she was a great comfort to me. We were completely open, we never kept anything from each other.'[217] Another said, 'We can be as we truly feel together, having our outside like our inside. Truth and trust . . . If I am upset, I can tell her about it.'[218] Kennedy notes: 'Trustworthiness is more highly valued and more frequently mentioned as a characteristic of an ideal friend than love

---

[215] Compare e.g. Cohen 1991: 59, fn. 104; Foxhall 1998a: 55, fn. 13.   [216] Kennedy 1986: 131.
[217] Kennedy 1986: 130, discussed in the Introduction, p. 32.   [218] Kennedy 1986: 134.

is. Love, according to the women in Hatzi, may grow from trust, but trust is not necessarily a byproduct of love.' The centrality of trustworthiness to friendship in Greek thought is illustrated by an exchange in Euripides' *Electra*. Elektra is explaining to her brother Orestes a secret she and her husband keep from her mother; he gestures to the Chorus of local women and asks, 'so are these women who are listening to what we're saying your *philai* (friends)?' (αἵδ' οὖν φίλαι σοι τούσδ' ἀκούουσιν λόγους;) Yes, she says, 'so they will keep my words and yours well hidden' (ὥστε στέγειν γε τἀμὰ καὶ σ' ἔπη καλῶς, ll. 272–3). It is their trustworthiness that makes them *philai*; that they are *philai* means they can be trusted.

In *Samia*, Nikeratos' wife is *philanthrōpos*, 'kind', to Khrysis (l. 35). Sommerstein calls this 'an appropriate word: Plangon's mother treated Chrysis not as a *hetaira* but as a fellow human being [*anthrōpos*], regularly making her welcome in her home'.[219] The speaker of Demosthenes 55 identifies *Metrodora*'s friendship with *Kallikleia* with the same construction as their respective late husbands' friendship: *khraomai tini*, 'be intimate with someone'.[220] Here and in *Samia*, women's friendships are marked by time spent at each other's houses (Dem. 55.23, Men. *Sam.* 35–8). Women seem frequently to have made small-scale, informal visits to friends' houses.

A red-figure *pyxis* painted c. 440 and now in the Nicholson Collection of the Chau Chak Wing Museum, Sydney (53.06, Figures 5.6 and 5.7), may show such a visit. The image shows six women in various states of veiledness. One is unveiled but wears a headband; she stands in a relaxed but authoritative position, one hand on her hip and the other extended as if in conversation, revealing the patterned *khitōn* underneath her *himation*, and her bare forearm. On either side sit two women, legs casually crossed, veiled in their *himatia*. One, veil pulled across her lower face, looks out to the viewer; Lloyd Llewellyn-Jones suggests that she 'seems to invite us into the closed world of female gossip'.[221] Behind the other stands another veiled woman, looking over her shoulder at the speaking woman and leaning forward as if to listen. To the left of this group is a woman in a *sakkos*, tugging at her *himation* with an exposed forearm. Beside her, a woman in motion looks back at the door as if she has just come in; the artist has attempted to show her hair covered by her *himation* as well as her arms.[222] Llewellyn-Jones proposes that the scene shows a group of women who have come to visit another woman in her home: the standing woman is the host; the others are

---

[219] Sommerstein 2013 *ad loc.*

[220] LSJ *s.v.* χράω C.ivb, 'χρῆσθαί τινι (without φίλῳ) *to be intimate with* a man' (*sic*).

[221] Llewellyn-Jones 2003: 207.

[222] The *himation* over her hair is not visible in the drawing but can be seen in photographs.

Figure 5.6 Drawing of design on Attic red-figure *pyxis*, c. 440, Sydney, Nicholson Collection, Chau Chak Wing Museum, The University of Sydney, NM53.06. Drawing from Llewellyn-Jones 2003: 207, fig. 145, courtesy of Lloyd Llewellyn-Jones.

Figure 5.7 Attic red-figure *pyxis*, c. 440, Sydney, Nicholson Collection, Chau Chak Wing Museum, The University of Sydney, NM53.06.

visitors who veiled themselves to travel to their friend's house and have yet to unveil. There are some problems with this interpretation – if two women have been inside long enough to sit down and make themselves comfortable, why have they not unveiled?[223] – but overall it persuades and fits within a pattern Llewellyn-Jones identifies of painted pots which seem to play at

[223] But cf. Obermeyer 1979: 33–4 for a description of a situation in twentieth-century North Yemen when a man unexpectedly entered a house where some women had removed just the material veiling their faces, but others had removed their veils entirely.

Figure 5.8 Attic red-figure tripod *pyxis*, second half of fifth century, Athens, Archaeological Museum of Kerameikos 2697 © Hellenic Ministry of Culture.

exposing the hidden.[224] Llewellyn-Jones' reading is supported by a *pyxis* from the Kerameikos which shows a woman in a *sakkos* moving away from a door (Figure 5.8, far left). Behind her, closer to the door, is a woman whose *himation* veils her head and lower face. The veiled woman seems just to have come in; the woman in the *sakkos* may be welcoming her into her home. Inside the house is a man with a box, then further round the pot, a winged boy presents a box to seated woman in a *sakkos*, and an unveiled woman feeds or remonstrates with a goose, while another unveiled woman looks back at her – the scene is not straightforwardly realistic. If the Chau Chak Wing *pyxis* does depict a visit, it conveys an image of a large group of friends in conversation; the Kerameikos *pyxis* may show the visit of a woman being welcomed into a house busy with other things.

Visits between friends also appear in comedy. One of Menander's plays, now mostly lost, was entitled *Synaristosai*, 'Women having breakfast/lunch

[224] Llewellyn-Jones 2003: 87–91. Another possibility is that the women are gathered in the wake of a death and some are veiled in mourning.

(*ariston*) together'. A fourth-century AD mosaic from Lesbos labelled '*Synaristosai*, Act One' shows the scene which presumably gave the play its name: three women, one older, eating together.[225] Plautus' adaptation of the play, *Cistellaria*, allows us to make inferences about the original: a young woman has invited her friend and her friend's mother for a meal (in Plautus, and probably Menander, the young women are prostitutes and the older woman a former prostitute, now prostituting her daughter). When a man in Aristophanes' *Ecclesiazusae* finds his wife missing early in the morning, his neighbour suggests that one of her women friends may have invited her over for the morning meal, *ariston* (μῶν ἐπ' ἄριστον γυνὴ / κέκληκεν αὐτὴν τῶν φίλων; ll. 348–9, 'Could some woman have invited her for the morning meal, one of her friends?'; note again *keklēken*, from *kaleō*, 'invite').[226] He does not use the word 'neighbour', which may imply wider social circles and more freedom of movement than we might assume – or simply a recognition that these women's role in the wife's life is primarily defined by her affection for them. In the play, the character Praxagora's excuse for her own absence on the same occasion (the women were in fact plotting a government takeover) is that her 'companion and friend' (again, not specified as a neighbour) was in labour and sent for her to help: γυνή μέ τις νύκτωρ ἑταίρα καὶ φίλη / μετεπέμψατ' ὠδίνουσα ('a woman – my companion (*hetaira*) and friend (*philē*) – was in labour and sent for me at night', ll. 528–9). These visits were tolerated by men, but not without suspicion. Praxagora's husband is deeply suspicious and vindicated by the plot: she is lying. The promotion of the word *gynē* (woman) in lines 348–9 and 528–9 may be an implicit rejection of suspicions that the women had been meeting men for sexual liaisons. Euripides' Andromakhe in *Trojan Women* cites as an example of her extreme virtue that she did *not* have female friends over to talk: ἔσω τε μελάθρων κομψὰ θηλειῶν ἔπη / οὐκ εἰσεφρούμην ('and I did not let the clever words of women into my halls', ll. 651–2).

In Euripides' *Orestes*, which Konstan identifies as 'a proving ground for ancient Greek conceptions of friendship',[227] and which portrays what was perhaps classical Attica's archetypal friendship, that between Orestes and Pylades, Orestes describes his friend as φίλτατον βροτῶν, ἡδεῖαν ὄψιν, πιστός ('dearest of mortals', 'a sweet sight', 'faithful', *Or.* 725–8), phrases

---

[225] Mosaic in the 'House of Menander', Mytilene.

[226] Compare Burton 1998: 150–5 on women eating together, sometimes informally but particularly on religious occasions. For men inviting friends over for meals, see e.g. Lys. 1.22–3 (δεῖπνον) and 3.11 (ἄριστον).

[227] Konstan 2018: 82.

echoed by Euthylla's tribute to her 'faithful and sweet friendship/dearness' (πιστῆς ἡδείας τε … φιλότητος) with Biote. The Chorus later describes Pylades as πιστότατος πάντων … / ἰσάδελφος ἀνήρ ('most faithful of all, a man like a brother', ll. 1114–15). Though this language of quasi-kinship is never explicitly used of female friendship, I have argued that some of the behaviour of female friends (attending the Thesmophoria together, burying and commemorating each other) adopts the 'behavioural language' of kin relationships. But perhaps it is just that our language for and understanding of female friendship in classical Attica is (as yet?) too poor to reveal its own templates, forcing us, in the meantime, to borrow from the neighbouring language of kinship.

Conclusion

This chapter brings out of brief phrases in oratory and comedy a sense of the emotional quality of women's relationships, filled out with epigraphic testimonies. Though the role of the neighbourhood and of religion in fostering women's friendships is already recognised, this chapter has shown how women used these contexts to shape and define their social environments and relationships, making spaces and communities their own. It builds up a 'social picture' from literary evidence of *synoikiai* as buildings which were home to families and to single women, as well as short-term visitors, an exercise Boozer has done from the archaeological evidence from fourth-century AD Alexandria,[228] but which has not yet been done for Attica. It shows the different ways women could use religious activity to enact different social definitions. It demonstrates that women's friendships could transcend boundaries of status and age, outlast the connections which initially occasioned them, and be valuable sources of support, particularly when male protectors failed. Finally, it offers an analysis of the language of women's friendship, a language which emphasises affection and trust.

---

[228] Boozer 2019: 62–6.

Conclusion

Pictures of Women

> Iaia of Kyzikos, who was always single, painted at Rome during the youth of M. Varro [early first century BC], both with the brush and with an engraving tool on ivory; she produced mostly pictures of women, including a portrait at Naples of an old woman on a large canvas, and also a self-portrait, using a mirror.[1]

This description comes from a list of women painters in Pliny the Elder's *Natural History*. Pliny goes on to say that Iaia painted faster than anyone else and was so talented that her works sold for considerably more than those of her male contemporaries. But what of her choice of subject matter: 'mostly pictures of women'? These women included one who, past nubility, was of less interest to the rest of society; Iaia devoted a 'large canvas' to her, giving her great prominence.[2] They also included Iaia herself. Was there a connection between her lifelong singleness and her interest in painting women, or her choice to depict herself?

In scholarship, de-emphasising marital relationships creates more space on the canvas for other women, other relationships, and other aspects of women's lives. When a woman's identification as a wife is not in play — either because she is not married, or because her marital status is not uppermost in a given context — other roles are operative or come to the

---

[1] *Iaia Cyzicena, perpetua virgo, M. Varronis iuventa Romae et penicillo pinxit et cestro in ebore imagines mulierum maxime et Neapoli anum in grandi tabula, suam quoque imaginem ad speculum* (Plin. *HN* 35.40.147).

[2] For old women in Hellenistic and post-Hellenistic sculpture and coroplasty, part of 'the Hellenistic fashion for highly detailed depictions of low-status individuals', see Masséglia 2012 (quotation from p. 415). For 'genre figures' in Hellenistic (and later) art more generally, see Masséglia 2015: 159–265 with 241–65 on old women and nurses. For an ancient perspective on the aesthetic qualities of a statue of an old man, see e.g. Plin. *Ep.* 3.6. Aesthetic interest in artistic depictions of older people does not necessarily reflect widespread aesthetic interest in, or high social esteem of, older people as a social group (though see Chapter 4, fn. 176 on the value of older women in Greek society).

fore. She offers us a different image of herself. A study of ancient women centred around women's engagement with other women, rather than their relationships to men, paints new and different pictures.

Like Iaia of Kyzikos, this book has used a variety of tools to paint pictures of women. By approaching the women it depicts through their relationships, it offers a fresh look at Athenian society in all its richness and complexity. It also offers a more detailed look at the women themselves, many of whom have left more to the historical record than is often assumed.

A gynocentric rereading of our evidence reveals the richness and dynamism of women's lives in classical Attica. Women's social positions and networks were not based solely on given positions in their households and families – much less on marriage – nor were they static. They were shaped by time, circumstance, remunerated and unremunerated work, topography, and religion. More importantly, within (and sometimes against) the confines of patriarchal systems and expectations, women themselves had a remarkable capacity to shape their social positions and networks, by manipulating social structures and defining their relationships. In doing so, they shaped Athenian society and history.

Fluctuation and Variety

By following *Diognete*, Nikarete, and other women through their own distinct lives in the first chapter, we have gained a detailed, diachronic perspective which reveals variations, patterns, and possibilities not visible in more generalist studies. Scholars have tended to emphasise the potential trauma of transitions between girlhood and marriage, and marriage and widowhood, and the potential severance of relationships entailed by those transitions. The stories of *Diognete*, Nikarete, and the other women we met in Chapter 1 show us that despite the potential for trauma and loss in leaving one home for another, women were able to maintain relationships and social circles across changed circumstances and life stages. In particular, some women drew support from relationships established in earlier life stages to help cope with the vicissitudes of later stages.

Many discussions of women's networks conceive of women as having two sets of kin: natal kin and affines. In fact, women could maintain affective relationships with affines from former marriages, and so with multiple sets of affines. Women's relationships arising from marriages were not time-bound to those marriages; they could persist beyond the end of the marriage and beyond the death of the husband who occasioned the connection. Nikarete, whom we met in Chapter 1, was still sufficiently connected to her relatives from her first marriage – after which she had been divorced, remarried, and widowed – that she could elicit support from her former husband's sons with his second wife, who were not even born at the time of her marriage to him. This could also be true for non-kin relationships through marriage: *Metrodora* and *Kallikleia*, whom we met in Chapter 5, got to know each other through the friendship of their husbands but remained friends after their husbands' deaths.

Many of these stories offer new insights into the lives of women who were widowed or separated, often by Athens' near-constant military campaigns across the fifth and fourth centuries. Extrapolated, these become insights into the potential social effects of such death and instability on Attic family life more generally. We see the diversity of family structures in this period, and the ability of women to shape them – despite attempts at strict legal delimitation of family according to patriline which characterise the late archaic and early classical period.

The most important of these delimitations were the Solonic 'family laws' instituted from around 594/3.[3] These were reinforced and supplemented by the Periklean Citizenship Law of 451/0 (reinstated in 403/2 and re-emphasised by the scrutiny of the deme registers in 346/5). Lape has argued that Solon's family laws (provisions for *engyē*, legitimacy, and heirship) 'privilege[d] the conjugal family in new ways by making legitimacy – a status defined with reference to the marriage bond – necessary for family membership and reproduction' and 'redefined the conjugal family as the sole legitimate family form'.[4] (The Periklean Citizenship Law built on and narrowed this definition by making the conjugal family *in which both spouses were Athenian* the sole legitimate family form.) In other words, Solon defined the family more narrowly and increased the importance of monogamous marriage to that definition. The 'pre-Solonic' family was legally more capacious, treating a *pallakē* (informal sexual partner) and her free children as part of the same family unit as a wife or daughter, and allowing *nothoi* (the father's children by a woman other than his wife) full membership of the family, including heirship. Under Solonic laws, informal partners and children not born of the married couple were not part of the family. Solon may

---

[3] On which see Lape 2002.   [4] Lape 2002: 188–9.

even have attempted to eliminate more informal expressions of family relationship between those who did not fit into the newly defined family: Plutarch, following Heraclides Ponticus, relates that Solon released children born of *hetairai* from the obligation to care for their fathers (Plut. *Vit. Sol.* 22.4). Further, Solonic laws systematised *ankhisteia*, privileging the patriline in the definition of wider family relationships. At some point, a further law was passed which severed the legal relationship between an adopted man and his biological father's *oikos* (family group as defined by eligibility to inherit; Isae. 9.2, 10.4), outlawing simultaneous membership of two *oikoi* – at least on a patrilineal conception of the *oikos*. The adoptee retained a relationship to his mother (Isae. 7.24–5).

Though a high-level, legally oriented view of the Attic family suggests that families were 'regularised' from the sixth century, the first two chapters of this book demonstrate that 'irregularities' persisted in the 'post-Solonic' and 'post-Periklean' family. Humphreys argues that 'in the early archaic period . . . powerful men might incorporate immigrants or sons-in-law into their households without formalities'.[5] This book has shown that even in the classical period, women could persuade their husbands to incorporate needy adults or stepchildren into their households without formalities. Family membership could still be sufficiently capacious to allow for men's (behavioural, not biological) 'fathering' of children not recognised as theirs in law. People might still take on familial care duties for those not legally or biologically related to them: Arkhedamos for his wife's son, at her encouragement (Isae. 7.7); Neaira for the former husband of her daughter or partner's daughter (Ap. *Neaira* 55–6). In some cases, women could influence men to adopt those they cared for, making them legally recognised members of the descent group, despite a law which attempted to invalidate such adoptions.

Despite increasing legislation around kinship, and increased social focus on the family – particularly the nuclear family – after the Peloponnesian War and plague, for women in particular kinship was less rigidly defined, less narrow, and yet also less all-encompassing than has been assumed. Women could enact their own definitions of kinship, shape kinship in line with their own affections and priorities, and build non-kin relationships which competed with or displaced legally recognised ones.

---

[5] Humphreys 2018: 93.

The Language of Belonging

In Chapter 2, through the stories of *Apollodora*, Alke, *Epistheneia*, and others, we saw the means by which women manipulated patriarchal-patrilineal kinship structures – for example, their ability to influence men's decisions in the patriarchal, patrilineal process of adoption – but also their use of alternative, non-patrilineal structures, modes, and expressions of kinship: for example, matrilocal residence after the loss of a husband-father. Closer analysis of the language around fostering children and sheltering vulnerable adults with an eye to women's relationships, emotions, and influence shows how women could shape household composition – another instance of the personal and interpersonal approach providing insights not available in statistically based demographic approaches. Drawing new connections between this ability, women's potential influence over adoptions and the societal anxiety this generated, and the prevalence of stories about supposititious children better contextualises and illuminates all three phenomena.

The stories in the later chapters of the book enrich this new understanding of kinship further by showing how some women used the behavioural 'vocabulary' of kinship to 'describe' relationships with non-relatives, for example, by portraying themselves or others in sepulchral reliefs in postures suggestive of kinship with people who were not kin, like Antiphile's portrayal of Phanostrate with Antiphile's children in Chapter 4, or entrusting to non-kin or remoter kin the responsibilities of close kin, like *Philo*'s 'passing over her own son' to appoint Antiphanes, 'no relation of hers', to take care of her burial in Chapter 5. We might also understand these phenomena in terms not of imitation but actuality: these women, in some sense, *made* these people kin by their behaviour towards them.

More generally, the stories in the later chapters have shown how women used various verbal and behavioural vocabularies to delineate their social relationships. They have shed light on women's social competences, especially their ability to 'enact' social definitions. Women could do this through terms of reference and address: publicly identifying someone as one's *hetaira*; referring to someone as *ēmē kōmētis*; perhaps using other social categorisations only obscurely visible to us, like distinguishing between neighbours on different levels of intimacy. They could also do it by deliberately including a person in shared activities in private or public spaces (*kaleō*: Ar. *Lys.* 1, 701; *Eccl.* 349; cf. also perhaps Lys. 1.20); by collectively and formally assigning religious roles in the community (Isae. 8.19–20); and by post-mortem commemoration.

The stories in Chapter 5 show how women used religious ritual and space to define social positions on a personal level ('these women are my close friends') as well as the formal or structural level traditionally emphasised ('only married, citizen-status women are allowed at the Thesmophoria'). Women could define these positions and relationships counter-normatively: citizen-status women and girls might include enslaved girls in dancing and games at festivals; a metic woman might invite a married, citizen-status woman and her unmarried daughter to a celebration of the Adonia; unrelated women of different ages might attend a festival in each other's company. Religious activity could also be a vehicle for female control of public and private space. The role of religious festivals in shaping women's communities and identities is well recognised,[6] but Chapter 5 shows how this worked on a more fine-grained level, illuminating the agency of individual women.

Friendship between women in ancient Greece is beginning to draw more scholarly attention.[7] The stories in Chapter 5 enrich this nascent field of study by offering a new account of the markers of classical Attic female friendship: how it was communicated between women, how it was publicly expressed, how it manifests in the historical record. New readings of oratory and comedy further our understanding of the emotional quality and the importance of women's friendships. These insights into the emotional quality of women's friendships accompany the insights of Chapter 3 into relationships of quite a different tenor: the fraught, ambivalent, sometimes violent intimacy between free and enslaved members of a household, particularly women. Across the book as a whole, we have seen in greater detail *how* women built up relationships and networks, and the role those relationships and networks played in their lives. Both circumstantial and affective factors, including adverse life events like the loss of a husband, could see women expand or consolidate their networks, through second marriage, employment, or revived relationships with natal family. These relationships and networks could cross boundaries of legal status, ethnicity, and gender.

Many of these insights come from women's own self-representations – as earners, worshippers, mothers, friends – and from women's representations of other women who were important to them. Remunerated work

---

[6] For example, Burton 1998; Parker 2005: 270–89.
[7] For example, Taylor 2011c, with fn. 41, printed on p. 719.

could shape female self-portrayal, and so perhaps self-perception. Free women used enslaved women to negotiate and consolidate their positions in their households, marriages, and society; in doing so, they shaped slavery as an institution at the most intimate level. In this context, women's self-positioning more closely followed men's positioning of women than in women's relationships with family, colleagues, and friends. The moral and affective language of female-authored epigraphic texts poses new questions about female self-expression in the classical and pre-classical world.

Women beyond Wifehood

Athenian women are sometimes referred to as 'citizen-wives'. The stories in this book illustrate the frequency and variety of experiences of 'singleness' among women. 'Singleness' as a temporary or permanent state of life has been subject to recent study within the context of Roman Egypt[8] but has not yet been approached in such terms for pre-Christian Greece. The stories of *Diognete* and Nikarete in Chapter 1, of husbandless women providing for themselves and their children through work in Chapter 4, and of women supported by friends amid the failure of male kin in Chapter 5 demonstrate the unhelpful narrowness of the category 'widow' in discussions of Attic women – and most likely in other sociocultural contexts too. Most saliently, married women could find themselves living apart from their husbands for sustained periods of time, not always knowing whether their husbands were even alive. This might lead them to pursue strategies usually associated with widowhood, like working for money.

The construct – scholarly as much as classical – of the 'Athenian wife' as a social category, to be distinguished from, depending on the author's interest, the *hetaira* (or the 'whore'), the metic woman, the unmarried girl, the widow – is evidently inadequate. Over-commitment to the conceptual category of the 'Athenian wife' obscures certain realities and masks certain women and their experiences. Women had important social roles – as friends, neighbours, employees, employers – that had little to do with their roles as wives or members of their *polis* and could be played by married or single women. Marital status and citizen status *could* be bound up, but sometimes in less than obvious ways: Kennedy, for example, draws out how the deaths of male relatives (including husbands) could jeopardise a woman's citizen status; Adele Scafuro does the same

---

[8] Hübner and Laes 2019.

for divorce.[9] To some extent this process is visible in the story of Nikarete, for whom the loss of her second husband exposed her to slander for her work, and loss of her father (and brother?) left her less able to demonstrate her citizen birth. That said, as Nikarete's (and *Klearete's*) story shows, becoming a widow and being married a second time could paradoxically make one's citizen status securer than that of a woman who had been married only once, by increasing the number of male relatives and public occasions to testify to one's status.

Some scholars have claimed that a girl fully became a *gynē* ('woman-wife') only on the birth of her first child.[10] In fact, the social statuses and identities of wifehood and motherhood were not so interdependent. Obviously women could be mothers without being wives: this was true not least for the many women who lost husbands after having children, but also for informally partnered women like Neaira who may have taken on a maternal role in the lives of their partners' children.[11] Though the Periklean Citizenship Law did enshrine and emphasise the identity of married, citizen-status women as actual or potential mothers of citizens, women making dedications on behalf of their children (of whom at least some were presumably of citizen status) generally placed little emphasis on their or their children's citizen status. They mostly do not make reference to a husband-father – an equally essential component in the production of a citizen – and so give no evidence of the children's paternity, paternal deme, or parents' marriage, on which such a status depended.[12] This tells against the assumptions of, for example, Avramidou, who holds that mothers making dedications on behalf of their children (and on a more extreme level, *all* women making dedications, on the Akropolis at least) did so as mothers of citizens (in any case, the dedications she discusses pre-date the Citizenship Law).[13] Melinna's dedication, which focuses on the role

---

[9] Kennedy 2014: 97–8; Scafuro 1994: 163–4.

[10] For example Demand 1994: 17 (citing Lys. 1.6–7, Cole 1984: 234, who does not claim this, and Vernant 1980–1: 404, a stronger argument); more recently, Lee 2015: 212, citing King 1998: 81 (for 84?).

[11] Menander's Khrysis in *Samia* is shown as more maternal than the child's actual mother or maternal grandmother (not least because those women do not appear onstage until the very end and are mute). As well as breastfeeding him, she is seen holding him onstage (ll. 372–3, with Sommerstein 2013: 50–1 on the iconographic evidence) and is distressed by the thought of him being raised away from her (ll. 84–5).

[12] Exceptions include Xenokrateia's dedication (*IG* i³ 987, on which see Blok 2018), particularly if her son Xeniades was adopted by her father. *IG* ii² 4883 and Bingen 1971: 149, no. 1 (unknown dedicatees) give the mother's patronymic and her father's demotic, but do not mention the children's father.

[13] Avramidou 2015.

of her income-generating work in her children's upbringing, offers another view of childrearing, again without a visible husband.

Beyond the *Polis* – and beyond the *Oikos*

Scholars like Josine Blok have worked against the old structuralist dichotomy that the *oikos* was the realm of women and the *polis* the realm of men by illuminating the importance of women to the *polis*. The stories in this book demonstrate some limits on the structuring force of the *oikos*, in various senses, on the lives of women. Many ways of living in classical Attica did not follow the '*oikos* (family) in an *oikia* (household)' model, held up as an ideal by Euphiletos in Lysias 1 where he, his wife, their child, and his mother-in-law live in an *oikidion* in a state of *oikeiotēs megistē* (§§9, 6). These stories give us a better understanding of households with non-traditional compositions, including an awareness of how individuals' emotions and desires (including women's emotions and desires) could shape those compositions. Across the book, we have seen single-parent households, blended families, informal partnerships, fostering and stepparenting, and family and single life in *synoikiai*. All this expands our understanding of Attic social life. The *oikos* as understood in law was a poor reflection of the richness of women's experiences and relationships. Indeed, the categories of *oikos* and *polis*, once central to modern conceptualisations of classical Attica, are not prominent in many of these stories. We may have overestimated, or at least misunderstood, their importance in the lives of Attic women.

Literary sources suggest that women's relationships transcended the limits of the *oikos*, both in its senses of 'household' and 'descent line'. Their networks spanned multiple households, and they were capable of incorporating into their households those who fell outside its legal remit. Women's ability to influence who became part of a household or descent group saw women bring together members of different households to which they belonged – and not always bringing members of former households into their current households. *Apollodora* saw her son from her first marriage brought into her second marital household (Isae. 7). *Epistheneia* saw her brother from her natal household move into her first marital household and ultimately inherit the property, while she continued to reside in her second marital household (Isae. 2). *Philokrateia* saw her brother brought into her marital *oikos* as her husband's adoptive son and her daughter's husband but then ejected from it. This apparently did not sever her relationship with him: she seems to have chosen him to witness a large loan she made (Dem. 41). Despite the strong connection drawn by law between burial ritual and the inheritance of the *oikos* (family property), a number of women erected sepulchral monuments for individuals who were not part of their family or even household, and whose relationships to them (friendship, employer–employee relationship) were not recognised in law.

Women's relationships sometimes resisted the categories imposed by the *polis*. With the Periklean Citizenship Law, the *polis* of Athens – that is, its decision-making body, whose decisions were proposed and ratified by men – restricted its membership to those born of an Athenian mother and father. However, women – like men in formal associations like *eranoi* – enjoyed other memberships based on other criteria: neighbourhoods, based on proximity and contact; economic networks, based on repeated commercial interactions. Attempted redrawings of the social 'map' of Attica, like that of Edward Cohen in *The Athenian Nation* and Paulin Ismard in *La Cité des Réseaux*, are large-scale, covering large areas with little detail, and, in Ismard's case, excluding women almost entirely.[14] The stories in this book provide some of the missing detail, showing how women built up and made use of personal networks. These networks were less often established formal associations than relationships based on personal encounters through kinship links, proximity of residence, and income-generating work and consolidated through sharing space and time at each other's homes, participating together in religious activity, and exchanging emotional and practical support. Further, relatively few women used a *kyrios'* demotic to describe themselves. Indeed, a majority of women used only their own names to describe themselves to their gods and communities. That their legal status and political membership often did not feature in their self-presentations may suggest that that status and membership was less important to their self-perception (and perception by others?) than one might imagine.

Where Now?

What the stories in this book tell us has wide-ranging implications for the writing and teaching of ancient history. On the historical level, they demonstrate the inadequacy of legal and even socio-legal categorisations for understanding the experiences of real people, especially women. Kinship structures were flexible and malleable. Different religious contexts

---

[14] Compare Eidinow 2012: 4.

allowed for different definitions of in- and out-groups. These stories also reveal phenomena for which detailed analysis has so far been restricted mainly to periods which offer more extensive evidence for women's lives, like Roman Egypt or early Christian antiquity:[15] women's advocacy for friends and family; women's care for vulnerable members of the community; women-headed households and other non-conventional household arrangements. These glimpses from classical Athens offer contextual depth to studies of such phenomena which focus on later periods. We have also seen how classical Attica as a slave society operated on a granular, domestic level, and the affective consequences of that operation, which enriches our understanding of the institution of slavery more generally.

On the historiographical level, we have seen anew the value of epigraphy for social history, particularly for the self-representation of less visible groups, as well as the still underexploited potential of pushing familiar sources harder and in different directions. Including more sepulchral, dedicatory, and graffiti inscriptions in syllabi which otherwise implicitly understand and present classical Attic history as the history of its political processes of decision-making and control (decrees, tribute lists, casualty lists, honours conferred by the *dēmos* or by male-dominated associations) – the history of men – could offer a more comprehensive and accurate picture. Conversely, inclusion of curse tablets like the hundred-name lead tablet NAM 14470 in discussions of political and military strategies to safeguard Attica's grain supply allows us not just to understand the potency of women's social and economic connections but also to recognise the potential role of women like Satyra the barley seller in the political and military climate of mid and late fourth-century Attica. As things stand, under-informed assumptions about women lead to false readings of literary and epigraphic texts, and misinformation in public education on ancient women.

This book speaks into some of the scholarly silence identified in the Introduction. It goes some way towards correcting an historic but persistent 'failure to ask' about women's subjectivity. It asks, and begins to answer, questions like 'what were the salient features of women's identities and self-perception?', 'how did women's relationships change as they moved through their lives?', 'whom did women count as family?', 'how did free women relate to enslaved women in their homes?', 'how did income-generating work affect women's relationships?', and 'how did women make friends, and what were their friendships like?'.

---

[15] For example, Bagnall and Cribiore 2006; Cromwell 2019; Hübner 2013.

Like Iaia of Kyzikos, this book paints a series of pictures of women, including some on large canvases, giving more space than is usual to describing individual women, their lives, experiences, and relationships. It also paints a bigger picture of an Attica populated by women shaping a variety of relationships and institutions – kinship and the household, slavery, the economy, social organisation – and, in doing so, shaping history.

References

Acton, P. (2015). 'Industry Structure and Income Opportunities for Households in Classical Athens' in David M. Lewis, Edward M. Harris, and Mark Woolmer (eds.), *The Ancient Greek Economy: Markets, Households and City-States* (Cambridge University Press: Cambridge), 149–65.

Adams, C. D. (ed.) (1905). *Lysias: Selected Speeches,* XII, XVI, XIX, XXII, XXIV, XXV, XXXII, XXXIV (American Book Company: New York).

Akbar, J. A. (1982). 'Courtyard Houses: A Case Study from Riyadh, Saudi Arabia' in Ismail Serageldin, Samir El-Sadek, and Richard R. Herbert (eds.), *The Arab City, Its Character and Islamic Cultural Heritage: Proceedings of a Symposium Held in Medina, Kingdom of Saudi Arabia, 24–29 Rabi* II, *1401* AH, *28 Feb.–5 Mar., 1981* AD (I. Serageldin: Arlington), 162–94.

Akrigg, B. (2019). *Population and Economy in Classical Athens* (Cambridge University Press: Cambridge).

Albrecht, E. (1883). 'Beiträge zur Texteskritik des Isaios', *Hermes,* 18: 362–81.

Aleshire, S. B. (1989). *The Athenian Asklepieion: The People, Their Dedications, and the Inventories* (Gieben: Amsterdam).

Alexiou, M. (1974). *The Ritual Lament in Greek Tradition* (Cambridge University Press: Cambridge).

Andreou, I. (1994). 'Ὁ δῆμος των Αιξωνίδων Αλών' in William D. E. Coulson (ed.), *The Archaeology of Athens and Attica under the Democracy: Proceedings of an International Conference Celebrating 2500 Years since the Birth of Democracy in Greece, Held at the American School of Classical Studies at Athens, December 4–6, 1992* (Oxbow Books: Oxford), 191–210.

Andrewes, A. (1961). 'Philochoros on Phratries', *Journal of Hellenic Studies,* 81: 1–15.

Ardener, E. (1972). 'Belief and the Problem of Women' in Jean Sibyl La Fontaine (ed.), *The Interpretation of Ritual: Essays in Honour of A. I. Richards* (Tavistock: London), 135–58.

Arnott, W. G. (ed.) (1979). *Menander* (Harvard University Press: Cambridge, MA).

Ault, B. A. (2016). 'Building Z in the Athenian Kerameikos: House, Tavern, Inn, Brothel?' in Allison Glazebrook and Barbara Tsakirgis (eds.), *Houses of Ill Repute: The Archaeology of Brothels, Houses, and Taverns in the Greek World* (University of Pennsylvania Press: Philadelphia), 75–102.

Austin, C., and S. D. Olson (eds.) (2004). *Aristophanes: Thesmophoriazusae* (Oxford University Press: Oxford).

Avramidou, A. (2015). 'Women Dedicators on the Athenian Acropolis and their Role in Family Festivals: The Evidence for Maternal Votives between 530–450 BCE', *Cahiers 'Mondes anciens'*, 6: 1–29.

Backler, K. (2022). 'Sisterhood, Affection and Enslavement in Hyperides' *Against Timandrus*', *Classical Quarterly*, 72: 469–86.

Bagnall, R. S., and R. Cribiore (2006). *Women's Letters from Ancient Egypt, 300 BC–AD 800* (University of Michigan Press: Ann Arbor).

Baird, J. A. (2022). 'Houses and Time: Material Memory at Dura-Europos' in Jennifer A. Baird and April Pudsey (eds.), *Housing in the Ancient Mediterranean World: Material and Textual Approaches* (Cambridge University Press: Cambridge), 412–41.

Bal, M. (1988a). *Death and Dissymmetry: The Politics of Coherence in the Book of Judges* (University of Chicago Press: Chicago).

(1988b). 'The Rape of Narrative and the Narrative of Rape: Speech Acts and Body Language in Judges' in Elaine Scarry (ed.), *Literature and the Body: Essays on Populations and Persons* (Johns Hopkins University Press: Baltimore), 1–32.

Balme, M. G. (ed.) (2001). *Menander: The Plays and Fragments* (Oxford University Press: Oxford).

Barker, A. W. (1924). 'The Costume of the Servant on the Grave-Relief of Hegeso', *American Journal of Archaeology*, 28: 290–2.

Bastian, J. A. (2005). 'Whispers in the Archives: Finding the Voices of the Colonized in the Records of the Colonizer' in Margaret Procter, Michael Cook, and Caroline Williams (eds.), *Political Pressure and the Archival Record* (Society of American Archivists: Chicago), 25–43.

Baumbach, M., A. Petrovic, and I. Petrovic (eds.) (2010). *Archaic and Classical Greek Epigram* (Cambridge University Press: Cambridge).

Beazley, J. D. (1938). 'Review of *Corpus Vasorum Antiquorum: United States of America 6 = The Robinson Collection, Baltimore, Md, 2*. By D. M. Robinson, with the assistance of S. E. Freeman. Pp. 38: 57 plates. Cambridge, Mass.: Harvard University Press, 1937', *Journal of Hellenic Studies*, 58: 267–8.

Bérard, C. (1989). 'The Order of Women' in Claude Bérard (ed.), *A City of Images: Iconography and Society in Ancient Greece* (Princeton University Press: Princeton), 89–107.

Bérard, C., and J.-L. Durand (1989). 'Entering the Imagery' in Claude Bérard (ed.), *A City of Images: Iconography and Society in Ancient Greece* (Princeton University Press: Princeton), 23–37.

Bergemann, J. (1997). *Demos und Thanatos: Untersuchungen zum Wertsystem der Polis im Spiegel der Attischen Grabreliefs des 4. Jahrhunderts v. Chr. und zur Funktion der Gleichzeitigen Grabbauten* (Biering & Brinkmann: Munich).

Biezunska-Malowist, I., and M. Malowist (1989). 'L'esclavage antique et moderne', in Marie-Madeleine Mactoux and Evelyne Geny (eds.),

Mélanges Pierre Lévêque, tome 2: Anthropologie et société (Belles Lettres: Paris), 17–31.

Bingen, J. (1971). 'Inscriptions' in H. F. Mussche (ed.), *Thorikos 1968: Rapport préliminaire sur la cinqième campagne de fouilles (Voorlopig Verslag over de Vijfde Opgravingscampagne)* (Comité des fouilles belges en Grèce: Brussels), 149–62.

Bisel, S. C. (1990). 'Anthropologische Untersuchungen' in Wilfried K. Kovacsovics (ed.), *Kerameikos* XII: *Die Eckterrasse an der Gräberstrasse des Kerameikos* (De Gruyter: Berlin), 151–60.

Blok, J. H. (2001). 'Virtual Voices: Toward a Choreography of Women's Speech in Classical Athens' in A. P. M. H. Lardinois and Laura McClure (eds.), *Making Silence Speak: Women's Voices in Greek Literature and Society* (Princeton University Press: Princeton), 96–116.

(2009). 'Perikles' Citizenship Law: A New Perspective', *Historia: Zeitschrift für Alte Geschichte*, 58: 141–70.

(2017). *Citizenship in Classical Athens* (Cambridge University Press: Cambridge).

(2018). 'An Athenian Woman's Competence: The Case of Xenokrateia', *Eugesta*, 8: 1–48.

Blundell, S., and N. S. Rabinowitz (2008). 'Women's Bonds, Women's Pots: Adornment Scenes in Attic Vase-Painting', *Phoenix*, 62: 115–44.

Boccolini, C. S., M. L. Carvalho, and M. I. C. de Oliveira (2012). 'Risk Factors for Cross Nursing in Two Brazilian Cities' in *Anais do* XVI *Congreso Latinoamericano de Nutrición, 2012, Nov 11–16, Havana, Cuba* (Sociedad Latinoamericana de Nutrición: n.p.).

Boehringer, S., and V. Sebillotte Cuchet (eds.) (2013). *Des femmes en action: L'individu et la fonction en Grèce antique* (EHESS. École des hautes études en sciences sociales: Paris).

Boehringer, S., A. Grand-Clément, S. Péré-Noguès, and V. Sebillotte Cuchet (2015). 'Celles qui avaient un nom: Eurykléia ou comment rendre les femmes visibles', *Pallas: Revue d'Études Antiques*, 99: 11–19.

Boozer, A. L. (2019). 'Looking for Singles in the Archaeological Record of Roman Egypt' in Sabine R. Huebner and Christian Laes (eds.), *The Single Life in the Roman and Later Roman World* (Cambridge University Press: Cambridge), 57–84.

Borgeaud, P. (1988). *The Cult of Pan in Ancient Greece* (University of Chicago Press: Chicago).

Bosworth, A. B. (2000). 'The Historical Context of Thucydides' Funeral Oration', *Journal of Hellenic Studies*, 120: 1–16.

Bowman, L. (2019). 'Hidden Figures: The Women who Wrote Epigrams' in Christer Henriksén (ed.), *A Companion to Ancient Epigram* (Wiley Blackwell: Hoboken), 77–92.

Bradeen, D. W. (1974). *The Athenian Agora* XVII. *Inscriptions: The Funerary Monuments* (American School of Classical Studies at Athens: Princeton).

Braudel, F. (1972). *The Mediterranean and the Mediterranean World in the Age of Philip* ii (Collins: London).

Bremmer, J. (1983). 'The Importance of the Maternal Uncle and Grandfather in Archaic and Classical Greece and Early Byzantium', *Zeitschrift für Papyrologie und Epigraphik*, 50: 173–86.

Brock, R. (1994). 'The Labour of Women in Classical Athens', *Classical Quarterly*, 44: 336–46.

Brulé, P. (1992). 'Infanticide et abandon d'enfants: Pratiques grecques et comparaisons anthropologiques', *Dialogues d'histoire ancienne*, 18: 53–90.

—— (2003). *Women of Ancient Greece* (Edinburgh University Press: Edinburgh).

—— (2009). 'L'exposition des enfants en Grèce antique: Une forme d'infanticide', *Enfances & psy*, 44: 19–28.

Burton, J. (1998). 'Women's Commensality in the Ancient Greek World', *Greece & Rome*, 45: 143–65.

Butz, P. A. (2010). *The Art of the Hekatompedon Inscription and the Birth of the Stoikhedon Style* (Brill: Leiden).

Calame, C. (1999). *The Poetics of Eros in Ancient Greece* (Princeton University Press: Princeton, NJ).

Caldwell, J. (2004). 'Fertility Control in the Classical World: Was There an Ancient Fertility Transition?', *Journal of Population Research*, 21: 1–17.

Caley, E. R., and J. F. C. Richards (eds.) (1956). *Theophrastus: On Stones* (Ohio State University: Columbus).

Camp, J. M. (2001). *The Archaeology of Athens* (Yale University Press: New Haven).

Campa, N. T. (2022). 'In Defence of Female Citizenship: Apollodorus, *Against Neaira* 113', *Classical Quarterly*, 72: 487–92.

Caraveli-Chaves, A. (1980). 'Bridge between Worlds: The Greek Women's Lament as Communicative Event', *The Journal of American Folklore*, 93: 129–57.

Carey, C. (ed.) (1989). *Lysias: Selected Speeches* (Cambridge University Press: Cambridge).

Carsten, J. (1995). 'The Substance of Kinship and the Heat of the Hearth: Feeding, Personhood, and Relatedness among Malays in Pulau Langkawi', *American Ethnologist*, 22: 223–41.

—— (1997). *The Heat of the Hearth: The Process of Kinship in a Malay Fishing Community* (Clarendon Press: Oxford).

—— (2000). 'Introduction: Cultures of Relatedness' in Janet Carsten (ed.), *Cultures of Relatedness: New Approaches to the Study of Kinship* (Cambridge University Press: Cambridge), 1–36.

—— (2004). *After Kinship* (Cambridge University Press: Cambridge).

Carsten, J., and S. Hugh-Jones (1995). *About the House: Lévi-Strauss and Beyond* (Cambridge University Press: Cambridge).

Carugati, F. (2019). *Creating a Constitution: Law, Democracy, and Growth in Ancient Athens* (Princeton University Press: Princeton).

Cenerini, F., and F. Rohr Vio (eds.) (2016). *Matronae in domo et in re publica agentes: Spazi e occasioni dell'azione femminile nel mondo romano fra tarda repubblica e primo impero* (University Press Italiane: Trieste).

Chaniotis, A. (2012). 'Listening to Stones: Orality and Emotions in Ancient Inscriptions' in John K. Davies and J. J. Wilkes (eds.), *Epigraphy and the Historical Sciences* (Oxford University Press: Oxford), 299–328.

Chowdhry, P. (1994). *The Veiled Women: Shifting Gender Equations in Rural Haryana, 1880–1990* (Oxford University Press: New Delhi).

Clairmont, C. W. (1970). *Gravestone and Epigram: Greek Memorials from the Archaic and Classical Period* (Verlag Philipp von Zabern: Mainz am Rhein).

Clairmont, C. W., and A. Conze (1993). *Classical Attic Tombstones* (Akanthus: Kilchberg).

Clark, L. (1983). 'Notes on Small Textile Frames Pictured on Greek Vases', *American Journal of Archaeology*, 87: 91–6.

Cleland, L. (2005). *The Brauron Clothing Catalogues: Text, Analysis, Glossary and Translation* (John and Erica Hedges: Oxford).

Clinton, K. (1996). 'The Thesmophorion in Central Athens and the Celebration of the Thesmophoria in Attica' in Robin Hägg (ed.), *The Role of Religion in the Early Greek Polis: Proceedings from the Third International Seminar on Ancient Greek Cult, Organized by the Swedish Institute at Athens, 16–18 October 1992* (Paul Åströms Förlag: Stockholm), 111–25.

(2005). *Eleusis, the Inscriptions on Stone: Documents of the Sanctuary of the Two Goddesses and Public Documents of the Deme, Volume 1A (Text)* (Archaeological Society at Athens: Athens).

(2008). *Eleusis, the Inscriptions on Stone: Documents of the Sanctuary of the Two Goddesses and Public Documents of the Deme, Volume 2 (Commentary)* (Archaeological Society at Athens: Athens).

Coale, A. J., P. G. Demeny, and B. Vaughan (1983). *Regional Model Life Tables and Stable Populations* (Academic Press: New York).

Cohen, A. (2011). 'Picturing Greek Families' in Beryl Rawson (ed.), *A Companion to Families in the Greek and Roman Worlds* (Wiley-Blackwell: Chichester), 465–87.

Cohen, D. (1989). 'Seclusion, Separation, and the Status of Women in Classical Athens', *Greece & Rome*, 36: 3–15.

(1991). *Law, Sexuality, and Society: The Enforcement of Morals in Classical Athens* (Cambridge University Press: Cambridge).

Cohen, E. E. (2000). *The Athenian Nation* (Princeton University Press: Princeton).

(2015). *Athenian Prostitution: The Business of Sex* (Oxford University Press: New York).

Cohn-Haft, L. (1995). 'Divorce in Classical Athens', *Journal of Hellenic Studies*, 115: 1–14.

Cole, S. G. (1984). 'The Social Function of Rituals of Maturation: The Koureion and the Arkteia', *Zeitschrift für Papyrologie und Epigraphik*, 55: 233–44.

(1998). 'Domesticating Artemis' in Sue Blundell and Margaret Williamson (eds.), *The Sacred and the Feminine in Ancient Greece* (Routledge: London), 29–44.

Constantinou, S. (ed.) (2023). *Breastfeeding and Mothering in Antiquity and Early Byzantium* (Routledge: New York).

Conybeare, C. (2025). 'The Autobiographical Turn' in Gavin Kelly and Aaron Pelttari (eds.), *Cambridge History of Later Latin Literature*, vol. 1 (Cambridge University Press: Cambridge), 696–714.

Coo, L. (2013). 'A Tale of Two Sisters: Studies in Sophocles' Tereus', *Transactions of the American Philological Association*, 143: 349–84.

(2020). 'Greek Tragedy and the Theatre of Sisterhood' in P. J. Finglass and Lyndsay Coo (eds.), *Female Characters in Fragmentary Greek Tragedy* (Cambridge University Press: Cambridge), 40–61.

Corbier, M. (ed.) (1999). *Adoption et fosterage* (De Boccard: Paris).

Cox, C. A. (1988a). 'Sibling Relationships in Classical Athens: Brother–Sister Ties', *Journal of Family History*, 13: 377–95.

(1988b). 'Sisters, Daughters, and the Deme of Marriage', *Journal of Hellenic Studies*, 108: 185–8.

(1998). *Household Interests: Property, Marriage Strategies, and Family Dynamics in Ancient Athens* (Princeton University Press: Princeton).

(2002a). 'Crossing Boundaries through Marriage in Menander's *Dyskolos*', *Classical Quarterly*, 52: 391–4.

(2002b). 'Is Sostratus' Family Urban in Menander's "Dyskolos"?', *The Classical Journal*, 97: 351–8.

Cromwell, J. (2019). '"Listen to My Mistreatment": Support Networks for Widows and Divorcées in the Coptic Record' in Sabine R. Hübner and Christian Laes (eds.), *The Single Life in the Roman and Later Roman World* (Cambridge University Press: Cambridge), 320–38.

Cudjoe, R. V. (2010). *The Social and Legal Position of Widows and Orphans in Classical Athens* (Centre for Ancient Greek and Hellenistic Law, Panteion University of Social and Political Sciences: Athens).

Cutileiro, J. P. (1971). *A Portuguese Rural Society* (Clarendon Press: Oxford).

Dakarēs, S., I. Vokotopoulou, and A. P. Christidēs (eds.) (2013). *Τὰ χρηστήρια ἐλάσματα τῆς Δωδώνης τῶν ἀνασκαφῶν Δ. Ευαγγελίδη* (Η εν Αθήναις Αρχαιολογική Εταιρεία: Athens).

Dakoronia, F., and L. Gounaropoulou (1992). 'Artemiskult auf einem neuen Weihrelief aus Achinos bei Lamia', *Mitteilungen des Deutschen Archäologischen Instituts, Athenische Abteilung*, 107: 219–27.

Dallas, C. (1987). 'The Significance of Costume on Classical Attic Grave Stelai: A Statistical Analysis', Doctoral Thesis, University of Oxford.

Darmezin, L. (1999). *Les affranchissements par consécration en Béotie et dans le monde grec hellénistique* (Association pour la Diffusion de la Recherche sur l'Antiquité, ADRA; De Boccard: Nancy; Paris).

Daux, G. (1972). 'Stèles funéraires et épigrammes', *Bulletin de Correspondance Hellénique* 96: 503–66.

Davidson, J. N. (1997). *Courtesans & Fishcakes: The Consuming Passions of Classical Athens* (HarperCollins: London).

Davidson, G. R., D. B. Thompson, and H. A. Thompson (1943). 'Small Objects from the Pnyx: 1', *Hesperia Supplements*, 7: 1–172.

Davies, G. (1994). 'The Language of Gesture in Greek Art: Gender and Status on Grave Stelai', *Apollo*, 140: 6–11.

Davies, J. K. (1971). *Athenian Propertied Families, 600–300 B.C.* (Clarendon Press: Oxford).

Davies, M. (ed.) (2017). *Sophocles: Trachiniae* (Oxford University Press: Oxford).

Day, J. W. (1994). 'Interactive Offerings: Early Greek Dedicatory Epigrams and Ritual', *Harvard Studies in Classical Philology*, 96: 37–74.

—— (2010). *Archaic Greek Epigram and Dedication: Representation and Reperformance* (Cambridge University Press: Cambridge).

Demand, N. H. (1994). *Birth, Death, and Motherhood in Classical Greece* (Johns Hopkins University Press: Baltimore).

Denniston, J. D. (ed.) (1939). *Euripides: Electra* (Clarendon Press: Oxford).

Dettwyler, K. A. (1988). 'More Than Nutrition: Breastfeeding in Urban Mali', *Medical Anthropology Quarterly*, 2: 172–83.

Dickey, E. (1996). *Greek Forms of Address: From Herodotus to Lucian* (Clarendon Press: Oxford).

Dickmann, J.-A. (2011). 'Space and Social Relations in the Roman West' in Beryl Rawson (ed.), *A Companion to Families in the Greek and Roman Worlds* (Wiley-Blackwell: Chichester), 53–72.

—— (2013). 'A "Private" Felter's Workshop in the Casa dei Postumii in Pompeii' in Judit Pásztókai-Szeőke and Margarita Gleba (eds.), *Making Textiles in Pre-Roman and Roman Times: People, Places, Identities* (Oxbow Books: Oxford), 208–27.

Dillon, M. (2002). *Girls and Women in Classical Greek Religion* (Routledge: London).

—— (2017). 'Women's Ritual Competence and Domestic Dough: Celebrating the Thesmophoria, Haloa, and Dionysian Rites in Ancient Attica' in Matthew Dillon, Esther Eidinow and Lisa Maurizio (eds.), *Women's Ritual Competence in the Greco-Roman Mediterranean* (Routledge: London), 165–81.

Dillon, M., E. Eidinow, and L. Maurizio (eds.) (2017). *Women's Ritual Competence in the Greco-Roman Mediterranean* (Routledge: London).

Dodds, E. R. (1951). *The Greeks and the Irrational* (University of California Press: Berkeley).

Dover, K. J. (1968). *Lysias and the* Corpus Lysiacum (University of California Press: Berkeley).

Du Boulay, J. (1974). *Portrait of a Greek Mountain Village* (Clarendon Press: Oxford).

Earnshaw-Brown, L. (2009). 'The Limits of Knowledge, Demography and the Republic' in Arthur Keaveney and Louise Earnshaw-Brown (eds.), *The Italians on the Land: Changing Perspectives on Republican Italy Then and Now* (Cambridge Scholars: Newcastle upon Tyne), 123–36.

Eddy, S. K. (1970). 'The Value of the Cyzecine Stater at Athens in the Fifth Century', *Museum Notes (American Numismatic Society)*, 16: 13–22.

Edwards, M. (ed.) (1999). *Lysias: Five Speeches: Speeches 1, 12, 19, 22, 30* (Bristol Classical Press: Bristol).

Eidinow, E. (2007). *Oracles, Curses, and Risk among the Ancient Greeks* (Oxford University Press: Oxford).

—— (2012). 'Review of Paulin Ismard, La Cité des Réseaux. Athènes et Ses Associations, VIe-Ier siècle av. J.-C', *Kernos*, 25: 351–5.

—— (2018). *Envy, Poison, and Death: Women on Trial in Classical Athens* (Oxford University Press: Oxford).

Eidinow, E., and C. Taylor (2010). 'Lead-Letter Days: Writing, Communication and Crisis in the Ancient Greek World', *Classical Quarterly*, 60: 30–62.

Engels, D. (1984). 'The Use of Historical Demography in Ancient History', *Classical Quarterly*, 34: 386–93.

Esfandiari, G. (2017). 'Where Is My Name? Afghan Women Campaign to Reclaim Their Identities', *RadioFreeEuropeRadioLiberty*. www.rferl.org/a/afghan-women-campaign-to-reclaim-their-identities/28618186.html.

Evans-Pritchard, E. E. (1940). *The Nuer: A Description of the Modes of Livelihood and Political Institutions of a Nilotic People* (Clarendon Press: Oxford).

Exum, J. C. (2016). *Fragmented Women: Feminist (Sub)versions of Biblical Narratives* (Bloomsbury T&T Clark: London).

Ferguson, W. S., and A. D. Nock (1944). 'The Attic Orgeones and the Cult of Heroes', *The Harvard Theological Review*, 37: 62–140.

Ferrari, G., and B. S. Ridgway (1979). *Aspects of Ancient Greece: An Exhibition Organized by the Allentown Art Museum with the Cooperation of Gloria Ferrari Pinney and Brunilde Sismondo Ridgway, Allentown Art Museum, September 16 through December 30, 1979* (Allentown Art Museum: Allentown).

Ferrer, M. (2017). 'The Forgotten Things: Women, Rituals, and Community in Western Sicily (Eighth–Sixth Centuries BCE)' in Matthew Dillon, Esther Eidinow, and Lisa Maurizio (eds.), *Women's Ritual Competence in the Greco-Roman Mediterranean* (Routledge: London), 11–31.

Finley, M. I. (1985). *Ancient History: Evidence and Models* (Chatto & Windus: London).

Fisher, N. R. E. (1998). 'Violence, Masculinity and the Law in Athens' in Lin Foxhall and John Salmon (eds.), *When Men Were Men: Masculinity, Power, and Identity in Classical Antiquity* (Routledge: London), 68–97.

Flemming, R. (2023). 'Biography, Women and Power', *Journal of Roman Studies*, 113: 1–16.

Foley, H. (2003). 'Mothers and Daughters' in Jenifer Neils and John Howard Oakley (eds.), *Coming of Age in Ancient Greece: Images of Childhood from the Classical Past* (Yale University Press in association with the Hood Museum of Art, Dartmouth College, Hanover, New Hampshire: New Haven).

Forsdyke, S. (2012). *Slaves Tell Tales: And Other Episodes in the Politics of Popular Culture in Ancient Greece* (Princeton University Press: Princeton).

Foucault, M. (1983). 'Self Writing', *Corps Écrit*, 5: 3–23.

Foxhall, L. (1989). 'Household, Gender and Property in Classical Athens', *Classical Quarterly*, 39: 22–44.

(1994). 'Pandora Unbound: A Feminist Critique of Foucault's History of Sexuality' in Andrea Cornwall and Nancy Lindisfarne (eds.), *Dislocating Masculinity: Comparative Ethnographies* (Routledge: London), 92–100.

(1996). 'The Law and the Lady: Women and Legal Proceedings in Classical Athens' in Lin Foxhall and A. D. E. Lewis (eds.), *Greek Law in Its Political Setting: Justifications Not Justice* (Clarendon Press: Oxford), 133–52.

(1998a). 'The Politics of Affection: Emotional Attachments in Athenian Society' in Paul Cartledge, Paul Millett, and Sitta von Reden (eds.), *Kosmos: Essays in Order, Conflict and Community in Classical Athens* (Cambridge University Press: Cambridge), 52–67.

(1998b). 'Snapping up the Unconsidered Trifles: The Use of Agricultural Residues in Ancient Greek and Roman Farming', *Environmental Archaeology*, 1: 35–40.

(2011). 'Loom Weights' in Joseph Coleman Carter, A. Prieto, and Jessica Trelogan (eds.), *The Chora of Metaponto 3. Archaeological Field Survey: Bradano to Basento* (University of Texas Press: Austin), 545–7.

(2012). 'Family Time: Temporality, Gender and Materiality in Ancient Greece' in John Marincola, Lloyd Llewellyn-Jones and Calum Maciver (eds.), *Greek Notions of the Past in the Archaic and Classical Eras: History without Historians* (Edinburgh University Press: Edinburgh), 183–206.

(2013). *Studying Gender in Classical Antiquity* (Cambridge University Press: Cambridge).

Freedman, M. (1979). *The Study of Chinese Society: Essays* (Stanford University Press: Stanford).

Freeman, S. T. (1970). *Neighbors: The Social Contract in a Castilian Hamlet* (University of Chicago Press: Chicago).

Friedländer, P., and H. B. Hoffleit (1987). *Epigrammata: Greek Inscriptions in Verse from the Beginnings to the Persian Wars* (Ares: Chicago).

Frier, B. W. (1994). 'Natural Fertility and Family Limitation in Roman Marriage', *Classical Philology*, 89: 318–33.

Frisch, R. E. (1978). 'Population, Food Intake, and Fertility', *Science*, 199: 22–30.

Frullini, S. (2021). 'Politics and Landscape in the Argive Plain after the Battle of Sepeia', *Journal of Hellenic Studies*, 141: 110–35.

Fuentes, M. J. (2016). *Dispossessed Lives: Enslaved Women, Violence, and the Archive* (University of Pennsylvania Press: Philadelphia).

Fuller, A. H. (1961). *Buarij: Portrait of a Lebanese Muslim Village* (Distributed for the Center for Middle Eastern Studies of Harvard University by Harvard University Press: Cambridge, MA).

Gaca, K. L. (2010). 'The Andrapodizing of War Captives in Greek Historical Memory', *Transactions of the American Philological Association*, 140: 117–61.

(2010–1). 'Telling the Girls from the Boys and Children: Interpreting Παῖδες in the Sexual Violence of Populace-Ravaging Ancient Warfare', *Illinois Classical Studies*, 35–6: 85–109.

(2021). 'Controlling Female Slave Sexuality and Men's War-Driven Sexual Desires' in Deborah Kamen and C. W. Marshall (eds.), *Slavery and Sexuality in Classical Antiquity* (University of Wisconsin Press: Madison), 40–65.

Gagarin, M. (2001). 'Women's Voices in Attic Oratory' in André Lardinois and Laura McClure (eds.), *Making Silence Speak: Women's Voices in Greek Literature and Society* (Princeton University Press: Princeton), 161–76.

Gager, J. G. (1992). *Curse Tablets and Binding Spells from the Ancient World* (Oxford University Press: New York).

Gaifman, M. (2008). 'Visualized Rituals and Dedicatory Inscriptions on Votive Offerings to the Nymphs', *Opuscula: Annual of the Swedish Institute at Athens and Rome*, 1: 85–103.

Gallant, T. W. (1991). *Risk and Survival in Ancient Greece: Reconstructing the Rural Domestic Economy* (Polity Press: Cambridge).

Garland, R. (1982). 'A First Catalogue of Attic Peribolos Tombs', *Annual of the British School at Athens*, 77: 125–76.

Gernet, L. (1920). 'La création du testament', *Revue des Études Grecques*, 33: 123–68.

Gherchanoc, F. (2012). *L'Oïkos en fête: Célébrations familiales et sociabilité en Grèce ancienne* (Publications de la Sorbonne: Paris).

Gibson, R. (2012). 'On the Nature of Ancient Letter Collections', *Journal of Roman Studies*, 102: 56–78.

Gilles, G., K. Frank, C. Plastow, and L. Webb (eds.) (2024a). *Female Agency in the Mediterranean World* (Liverpool University Press: Liverpool).

Gilles, G., K. Frank, C. Plastow, and L. Webb (2024b). 'Introduction' in Greg Gilles, Karolina Frank, Christine Plastow, and Lewis Webb (eds.), *Female Agency in the Mediterranean World* (Liverpool University Press: Liverpool), 1–17.

Gilligan, C. (1982). *In a Different Voice: Psychological Theory and Women's Development* (Harvard University Press: Cambridge, MA).

Glazebrook, A. (2011). 'Porneion: Prostitution in Athenian Civic Space' in Allison Glazebrook and Madeleine Mary Henry (eds.), *Greek Prostitutes in the Ancient Mediterranean, 800 BCE–200 CE* (University of Wisconsin Press: Madison), 34–59.

(2022). *Sexual Labor in the Athenian Courts* (University of Texas Press: Austin).

Golden, M. (1981). 'Demography and the Exposure of Girls at Athens', *Phoenix*, 35: 316–31.

(1985). '"Donatus" and Athenian Phratries', *Classical Quarterly*, 35: 9–13.

(2009). 'Oedipal Complexities' in Sabine R. Hübner and David M. Ratzan (eds.), *Growing Up Fatherless in Antiquity* (Cambridge University Press: Cambridge), 41–60.

(2011). 'Slavery and the Greek Family' in K. R. Bradley and Paul Cartledge (eds.), *The Cambridge World History of Slavery* (Cambridge University Press: Cambridge), 134–52.

(2015). *Children and Childhood in Classical Athens*, 2nd ed. (Johns Hopkins University Press: Baltimore).

Gomme, A. W., and F. H. Sandbach (eds.) (1973). *Menander: A Commentary* (Clarendon Press: Oxford).

González González, M. (2019). *Funerary Epigrams of Ancient Greece: Reflections on Literature, Society and Religion* (Bloomsbury: London).

Gordon, R. L. (2016). 'Negotiating the Temple-Script: Women's Narratives among the "Confession-Texts" of Western Asia Minor', *Religion in the Roman Empire*, 2: 227–55.

Gottesman, A. (2014). *Politics and the Street in Democratic Athens* (Cambridge University Press: Cambridge).

Gould, J. (1980). 'Law, Custom and Myth: Aspects of the Social Position of Women in Classical Athens', *Journal of Hellenic Studies*, 100: 38–59.

Graef, B., and E. Langlotz (1909). *Die Antiken Vasen von der Akropolis zu Athen* (De Gruyter: Berlin).

Graham, A. J. (1998). 'The Woman at the Window: Observations on the 'Stēlē from the Harbour' of Thasos', *Journal of Hellenic Studies*, 118: 22–40.

Griffin, J. (2007). 'Desperate Straits and the Tragic Stage' in Patrick Finglass, C. Collard, and N. J. Richardson (eds.), *Hesperos: Studies in Ancient Greek Poetry Presented to M. L. West on His Seventieth Birthday* (Oxford University Press: Oxford), 189–203.

Griffith-Williams, B. (ed.) (2013). *A Commentary on Selected Speeches of Isaios* (Brill: Leiden).

Grossman, J. B. (2013). *Funerary Sculpture* (American School of Classical Studies at Athens: Princeton).

Hansen, M. H. (1988). *Three Studies in Athenian Demography* (Kongelige Danske Videnskabernes Selskab: Copenhagen).

Hardwick, L. (1993). 'Philomel and Pericles: Silence in the Funeral Speech', *Greece & Rome*, 40: 147–62.

Harris, E. M. (2002). 'Workshop, Marketplace and Household: The Nature of Technical Specialization in Classical Athens and its Influence on Economy and Society' in Paul Cartledge, Edward E. Cohen, and Lin Foxhall (eds.), *Money, Labour and Land: Approaches to the Economies of Ancient Greece* (Routledge: London), 67–99.

(2004). 'Notes on a Lead Letter from the Athenian Agora', *Harvard Studies in Classical Philology*, 102: 157–70.

(2014). 'Wife, Household, and Marketplace: The Role of Women in the Economy of Classical Athens' in Umberto Bultrighini and Elisabetta Dimauro (eds.), *Donne che Contano nella Storia Greca* (Carabba: Lanciano), 183–207.

Harrison, A. R. W. (1968). *The Law of Athens: I. The Family and Property* (Clarendon Press: Oxford).

Hartman, S. V. (2019). *Wayward Lives, Beautiful Experiments: Intimate Histories of Social Upheaval* (Serpent's Tail: London).

Harvey, F. D. (2007). '"Help! I'm Dying Here": A Letter from a Slave', *Zeitschrift für Papyrologie und Epigraphik*, 163: 49–50.

Heine Nielsen, T., L. Bjertrup, M. Hansen, L. Rubinstein, and T. Vestergaard (1989). 'Athenian Grave Monuments and Social Class', *Greek, Roman, and Byzantine Studies*, 30: 411.

Henderson, J. (ed.) (1990). *Aristophanes: Lysistrata* (Clarendon Press: Oxford).

Henry, A. (2002). 'Hookers and Lookers: Prostitution and Soliciting in Late Archaic Thasos', *Annual of the British School at Athens*, 97: 217–21.

Hewitt, M. (2023). 'Inscribing Manumission in the Hellenistic World', Doctoral Thesis, University of Oxford.

Hin, S. (2013). *The Demography of Roman Italy: Population Dynamics in an Ancient Conquest Society, 201 BCE–14 CE* (Cambridge University Press: Cambridge).

Hodkinson, S. (1983) 'Social Order and the Conflict of Values in Sparta', *Chiron*, 13: 239–81.

Hoepfner, W. (ed.) (1999). *Geschichte des Wohnens* I (Deutsche Verlags-Anstalt: Stuttgart).

Hoepfner, W., J. Boessneck, S. Dakarēs, and E.-L. Schwandner (1994). *Haus und Stadt im Klassischen Griechenland* (Deutscher Kunstverlag: Munich).

Hoey, T. F. (1979). 'The Date of the "Trachiniae"', *Phoenix*, 33: 210–32.

Horden, P., and N. Purcell (2000). *The Corrupting Sea: A Study of Mediterranean History* (Blackwell: Oxford).

Hornblower, S. (1991). *A Commentary on Thucydides. Volume* I*: Books* I–III (Oxford University Press: Oxford).

Hübner, S. R. (2013). *The Family in Roman Egypt: A Comparative Approach to Intergenerational Solidarity and Conflict* (Cambridge University Press: Cambridge).

Hübner, S. R., and C. Laes (eds.) (2019). *The Single Life in the Roman and Later Roman World* (Cambridge University Press: Cambridge).

Hübner, S. R., and D. M. Ratzan (2009). 'Fatherless Antiquity? Perspectives on "Fatherlessness" in the Ancient Mediterranean' in Sabine R. Hübner and David M. Ratzan (eds.), *Growing Up Fatherless in Antiquity* (Cambridge University Press: Cambridge), 3–28.

Human Rights Watch (2016). 'Boxed In: Women and Saudi Arabia's Male Guardianship System'. www.hrw.org/report/2016/07/17/boxed/women-and-saudi-arabias-male-guardianship-system.

Humphreys, S. C. (1980). 'Family Tombs and Tomb Cult in Ancient Athens: Tradition or Traditionalism?', *Journal of Hellenic Studies*, 100: 96–126.

(1986). 'Kinship Patterns in the Athenian Courts', *Greek, Roman and Byzantine Studies*, 27: 57–91.

(1989). 'Family Quarrels', *Journal of Hellenic Studies*, 109: 182–5.

(2010). 'A Paranoiac Sycophant? The Curse Tablet NM 14470 (D. R. Jordan and J. Curbera, "ZPE" 166, 2008, 135–150)', *Zeitschrift für Papyrologie und Epigraphik*, 172: 85–6.

(2018). *Kinship in Ancient Athens: An Anthropological Analysis* (Oxford University Press: Oxford).

Hunt, P. (2015). 'Trojan Slaves in Classical Athens: Ethnic Identity among Athenian Slaves' in Claire Taylor and Kostas Vlassopoulos (eds.),

Communities and Networks in the Ancient Greek World (Oxford University Press: Oxford), 128–55.

Hunter, R. L. (ed.) (2022). *Greek Epitaphic Poetry: A Selection* (Cambridge University Press: Cambridge).

Hunter, V. J. (1989). 'The Athenian Widow and Her Kin', *Journal of Family History*, 14: 291–311.

(1990). 'Gossip and the Politics of Reputation in Classical Athens', *Phoenix*, 44: 299–325.

(1994). *Policing Athens: Social Control in the Attic Lawsuits, 420–320 B.C.* (Princeton University Press: Princeton).

Ingalls, W. (2001). 'Παιδα Νεαν Μαλιστα: When Did Athenian Girls Really Marry?', *Mouseion: Journal of the Classical Association of Canada*, 1: 17–29.

(2002). 'Demography and Dowries: Perspectives on Female Infanticide in Classical Greece', *Phoenix*, 56: 246–54.

Isager, S. (1981–2). 'The Marriage Pattern in Classical Athens: Men and Women in Isaios', *Classica et Mediaevalia*, 33: 81–96.

Jacobs, H. A. (2015). *Incidents in the Life of a Slave Girl* (Oxford University Press: Oxford). First published 1861.

Jacqmin, C. (2015). 'Des voix de femmes dans la cité grecque archaïque: Le cas des dédicaces athéniennes', *Pallas: Revue d'etudes antiques*, 99: 31–45.

Jameson, M. H. (1990). 'Domestic Space in the Greek City-State' in Susan Kent (ed.), *Domestic Architecture and the Use of Space: An Interdisciplinary Cross-Cultural Study* (Cambridge University Press: Cambridge), 92–113.

Jebb, R. C. (1888). *Selections from the Attic Orators: Antiphon, Andocides, Lysias, Isocrates, Isaeus, Being a Companion Volume to 'The Attic Orators from Antiphon to Isaeus'* (Macmillan: London).

Jim, T. S. F. (2014). *Sharing with the Gods: Aparchai and Dekatai in Ancient Greece* (Oxford University Press: Oxford).

Johnstone, S. (2003). 'Women, Property, and Surveillance in Classical Athens', *Classical Antiquity*, 22: 247–74.

Jones, N. F. (1999). *The Associations of Classical Athens: The Response to Democracy* (Oxford University Press: New York).

Jordan, D. R. (2000). 'A Personal Letter Found in the Athenian Agora', *Hesperia: The Journal of the American School of Classical Studies at Athens*, 69: 91–103.

Jordan, D. R., and J. Curbera (2008). 'A Lead Curse Tablet in the National Archaeological Museum, Athens', *Zeitschrift für Papyrologie und Epigraphik*, 166: 135–50.

Joya, B. (2017). 'Where Is My Name? Afghan Women Fight for Their Own Identity', www.reuters.com/article/world/where-is-my-name-afghan-women-fight-for-their-own-identity-idUSKBN1AC3F6/.

Just, R. (1989). *Women in Athenian Law and Life* (Routledge: London).

Kaczko, S. (2016). *Archaic and Classical Attic Dedicatory Epigrams: An Epigraphic, Literary and Linguistic Commentary* (De Gruyter: Berlin).

Kahil, L. (1965). 'Autour de L'Artemis attique', *Antike Kunst*, 8: 20–33.

Kaibel, G. (ed.). (1878). *Epigrammata Graeca ex Lapidibus Conlecta* (G. Reimer: Berlin).

Kakavoyannis, E. (2001). 'The Silver Ore-Processing Workshops of the Lavrion Region', *Annual of the British School at Athens*, 96: 365–80.

Kamen, D. (2013). *Status in Classical Athens* (Princeton University Press: Princeton).

Kapparis, K. A. (1999). *Apollodoros' Against Neaira: [D. 59]* (De Gruyter: Berlin).
(2019). *Athenian Law and Society* (Routledge: New York).
(2021). *Women in the Law Courts of Classical Athens* (Edinburgh University Press: Edinburgh).

Karanika, A. (2014). *Voices at Work: Women, Performance, and Labor in Ancient Greece* (Johns Hopkins University Press: Baltimore, MD).

Karouzou, S. (1957). Ἐπιτύμβια στήλη τίτθης στό Ἐθνικό Μουσεῖο', *Ἑλληνικά*, 15: 311–23.

Keesling, C. M. (2003a). 'Rereading the Acropolis Dedications' in David R. Jordan and John Traill (eds.), *Lettered Attica: A Day of Attic Epigraphy*. Athens: Canadian Archaeological Institute at Athens, 41–54.
(2003b). *The Votive Statues of the Athenian Acropolis* (Cambridge University Press: Cambridge).
(2005). 'Patrons of Athenian Votive Monuments of the Archaic and Classical Periods: Three Studies', *Hesperia: The Journal of the American School of Classical Studies at Athens*, 74: 395–426.

Kehrberg, I. (1982). 'The Potter-Painter's Wife: Some Additional Thoughts on the Caputi Hydria', *Hephaistos*, 4: 25–35.

Kellogg, D. L. (2013). *Marathon Fighters and Men of Maple: Ancient Acharnai* (Oxford University Press: Oxford).

Kennedy, R. (1986). 'Women's Friendships on Crete: A Psychological Study' in Jill Dubisch (ed.), *Gender and Power in Rural Greece* (Princeton University Press: Princeton), 121–38.

Kennedy, R. F. (2014). *Immigrant Women in Athens: Gender, Ethnicity, and Citizenship in the Classical City* (Routledge: New York).

Keuls, E. C. (1973). 'The Samia of Menander: An Interpretation of Its Plot and Theme', *Zeitschrift für Papyrologie und Epigraphik*, 10: 1–20.
(1985). *The Reign of the Phallus: Sexual Politics in Ancient Athens: An Illustrated History* (Harper & Row: New York).

Khan, S. M. (1982). 'The Influence of Arabian Tradition on the Old City of Jeddah: The Urban Setting' in Ismail Serageldin, Samir El-Sadek and Richard R. Herbert (eds.), *The Arab City, Its Character and Islamic Cultural Heritage: Proceedings of a Symposium Held in Medina, Kingdom of Saudi Arabia, 24–29 Rabi II, 1401 AH, 28 Feb.–5 Mar., 1981 AD* (I. Serageldin: Arlington), 191–7.

King, H. (1998). *Hippocrates' Woman: Reading the Female Body in Ancient Greece* (Routledge: London).

Kirk, A. (2021). *Ancient Greek Lists: Catalogue and Inventory across Genres* (Cambridge University Press: Cambridge).

Knigge, U. (2005). *Der Bau Z* (Hirmer Verlag: Munich).

Kondis, I. D. (1967). Ἄρτεμις Βραυωνία, Ἀρχαιολογικόν Δελτίον, 22: 156–206.

Konstan, D. (2018). *In the Orbit of Love: Affection in Ancient Greece and Rome* (Oxford University Press: New York).

Kosmopoulou, A. (2001). '"Working Women": Female Professionals on Classical Attic Gravestones', *Annual of the British School at Athens*, 96: 281–319.

Krantz, J. Z., and N. S. Kupper (1981). 'Cross-Nursing: Wet-Nursing in a Contemporary Context', *Pediatrics*, 67: 715–17.

Kron, G. (2011). 'The Distribution of Wealth at Athens in Comparative Perspective', *Zeitschrift für Papyrologie und Epigraphik*, 179: 129–38.

Kron, U. (1996). 'Priesthoods, Dedications and Euergetism: What Part Did Religion Play in the Political and Social Status of Greek Women?' in Pontus Hellström and Brita Alroth (eds.), *Religion and Power in the Ancient Greek World: Proceedings of the Uppsala Symposium 1993 (Acta Universitatis Upsaliensis, Boreas, 24)* (Ubsaliensis S. Academiae: Uppsala), 139–82.

Kuenen-Janssens, L. J. T. (1941). 'Some Notes upon the Competence of the Athenian Woman to Conduct a Transaction', *Mnemosyne*, 9: 199–214.

Kurke, L. (1997). 'Inventing the "Hetaira": Sex, Politics, and Discursive Conflicts in Archaic Greece', *Classical Antiquity*, 16: 106–50.

Kurtz, D. C. (1975). *Athenian White Lekythoi: Patterns and Painters* (Clarendon Press: Oxford).

Kwok, C. S., and A. Keenleyside (2015). 'Stable Isotope Evidence for Infant Feeding Practices in the Greek Colony of Apollonia Pontica' in Anastasia Papathanasiou, Michael P. Richards and Sherry C. Fox (eds.), *Archaeodiet in the Greek World: Dietary Reconstruction from Stable Isotope Analysis* (The American School of Classical Studies at Athens: Princeton), 147–70.

Labarre, G. (1998). 'Les métiers du textile en Grèce ancienne', *Topoi. Orient-Occident*, 8: 791–814.

Labarre, G., and M.-T. Le Dinahet (1996). 'Les métiers du textile en Asie Mineure de l'époque hellénistique à l'époque impériale' in Université Lumière-Lyon Institut d'Archéologie et d'Histoire de l'Antiquité Lyon (ed.), *Aspects de l'artisanat du textile dans le monde méditerranéen: Égypte, Grèce, monde romain* (De Boccard: Paris), 49–116.

Lacey, W. K. (1980). 'The Family of Euxitheus (Demosthenes LVII)', *Classical Quarterly*, 30: 57–61.

Laes, C. (2011). 'Midwives in Greek Inscriptions in Hellenistic and Roman Antiquity', *Zeitschrift für Papyrologie und Epigraphik*, 176: 154–62.

(2014). 'Infants between Biological and Social Birth in Antiquity: A Phenomenon of the "Longue Durée"', *Historia: Zeitschrift für Alte Geschichte*, 63: 364–83.

Lagia, A. (2014). 'Health Inequalities in the Classical City: A Biocultural Approach to Socioeconomic Differentials in the Polis of Athens during the Classical, Hellenistic, and Imperial Roman Periods' in Anne-Catherine Gillis (ed.), *Corps, travail et statut social: L'apport de la paléoanthropologie funéraire aux sciences historiques* (Presses Universitaires du Septentrion: Villeneuve-d'Ascq), 95–115.

(2015). 'Diet and the Polis: An Isotopic Study of Diet in Athens and Laurion during the Classical, Hellenistic, and Early Roman Periods' in Anastasia Papathanasiou, Michael P. Richards and Sherry C. Fox (eds.), *Archaeodiet in the Greek World: Dietary Reconstruction from Stable Isotope Analysis* (The American School of Classical Studies at Athens: Princeton), 119–45.

Lamb, W. R. M. (ed.) (1957). *Lysias* (Harvard University Press: Cambridge, MA).

Lambert, H. (2000). 'Sentiment and Substance in North Indian Forms of Relatedness' in Janet Carsten (ed.), *Cultures of Relatedness: New Approaches to the Study of Kinship* (Cambridge University Press: Cambridge), 73–89.

Lambert, S. D. (1993). *The Phratries of Attica* (University of Michigan Press: Ann Arbor).

(2000). 'The Erechtheum Workers of IG II^2 1654', *Zeitschrift für Papyrologie und Epigraphik*, 132: 157–60.

(2018a). 'Attic Inscriptions Online, IG II^2 6873'. www.atticinscriptions.com/ inscription/IGII2/6873.

(2018b). 'Attic Inscriptions Online, IG II^3 4 700'. www.atticinscriptions.com/ inscription/IGII34/700.

(2018c). 'Attic Inscriptions Online, RO 40'. www.atticinscriptions.com/ inscription/RO/40.

(2020a). 'Attic Inscriptions Online, SEG 21.530'. www.atticinscriptions.com/ inscription/IGII2/6873.

(2020b). 'Regulations Concerning the Eleusinian Mysteries', *AIUK (Attic Inscriptions in UK Collections)*, 4.2: 21–35.

Lambert, S. D., and J. D. Morgan (2016). 'The Last Erechtheion Building Accounts', *AIO Papers*, 7: 1–10. www.atticinscriptions.com/papers/aio-papers-7/.

Lamont, J. L. (2023). *In Blood and Ashes: Curse Tablets and Binding Spells in Ancient Greece* (Oxford University Press: New York).

Lang, M. (1976). *The Athenian Agora* xxi. *Graffiti and Dipinti* (American School of Classical Studies at Athens: Princeton).

Langdon, M. K. (1991). 'On the Farm in Classical Attica', *The Classical Journal*, 86: 209–13.

Lape, S. (2002). 'Solon and the Institution of the "Democratic" Family Form', *The Classical Journal*, 98: 117–39.

Lardinois, A. P. M. H. (2001). 'Keening Sappho: Female Speech Genres in Sappho's Poetry' in André P. M. H. Lardinois and Laura McClure (eds.), *Making Silence Speak: Women's Voices in Greek Literature and Society* (Princeton University Press: Princeton), 75–92.

Lardinois, A. P. M. H., and L. McClure (eds.) (2001). *Making Silence Speak: Women's Voices in Greek Literature and Society* (Princeton University Press: Princeton).

Lauffer, S. (1979). *Die Bergwerksklaven von Laureion* (F. Steiner: Wiesbaden).

Lazar, L. (2024). *Athenian Power in the Fifth Century* BC (Oxford University Press: Oxford).

Lee, M. M. (2015). *Body, Dress, and Identity in Ancient Greece* (Cambridge University Press: Cambridge).

Leitao, D. D. (2012). *The Pregnant Male as Myth and Metaphor in Classical Greek Literature* (Cambridge University Press: New York).

Lewis, D. M. (1955). 'Notes on Attic Inscriptions (II): XXIII. Who Was Lysistrata?', *Annual of the British School at Athens*, 50: 1–36.

Lewis, I. M. (1971). *Ecstatic Religion: An Anthropological Study of Spirit Possession and Shamanism* (Penguin: Harmondsworth).

Lewis, S. (1995). 'Barbers' Shops and Perfume Shops: "Symposia Without Wine"' in Anton Powell (ed.), *The Greek World* (Routledge: London), 432–41.

(1998–9). 'Slaves as Viewers and Users of Athenian Pottery', *Hephaistos*, 16–17: 71–90.

(2002). *The Athenian Woman: An Iconographic Handbook* (Routledge: London).

Linders, T. (1972). *Studies in the Treasure Records of Artemis Brauronia Found in Athens* (Svenska Institutet i Athen: Stockholm).

Lissarrague, F. (1989). 'The World of the Warrior' in Claude Bérard (ed.), *A City of Images: Iconography and Society in Ancient Greece* (Princeton University Press: Princeton), 38–51.

(1990). *L'autre guerrier: Archers, peltastes, cavaliers dans l'imagerie attique* (La Découverte, École Française de Rome: Paris).

Liston, M. A. (2012). 'Reading the Bones: Interpreting the Skeletal Evidence for Women's Lives in Ancient Greece' in Sharon L. James and Sheila Dillon (eds.), *A Companion to Women in the Ancient World* (Wiley-Blackwell: Chichester), 125–40.

Llewellyn-Jones, L. (2003). *Aphrodite's Tortoise: The Veiled Woman of Ancient Greece* (Classical Press of Wales: Swansea).

Ma, J. (2013). *Statues and Cities: Honorific Portraits and Civic Identity in the Hellenistic World* (Oxford University Press: Oxford).

(2024). *Polis: A New History of the Ancient Greek City-State from the Early Iron Age to the End of Antiquity* (Princeton University Press: Princeton).

Maas, P. (1934). 'Erinnae in Baucidem Nenia', *Hermes*, 69: 206–9.

Mair, L. (1971). *Marriage* (Penguin: Harmondsworth).

Marchiandi, D. (2011). *I periboli funerari nell'Attica classica: Lo specchio di una 'Borghesia'* (Scuola Archeologica Italiana di Atene/Pandemos: Athens).

Margariti, K. (2016). 'A Mother's Gaze: Death and Orphanhood on Classical Attic Grave Reliefs', *Babesch*, 91: 87–104.

Marshall, C. W. (2013). 'Sex Slaves in New Comedy' in Ben Akrigg and Rob Tordoff (eds.), *Slaves and Slavery in Ancient Greek Comic Drama* (Cambridge University Press: Cambridge), 173–96.

(2017). 'Breastfeeding in Greek Literature and Thought', *Illinois Classical Studies*, 42: 185–201.

Mashal, M. (2017). 'Their Identities Denied, Afghan Women Ask, "Where Is My Name?"'. www.nytimes.com/2017/07/30/world/asia/afghanistan-womens-rights-whereismyname.html.

Masséglia, J. (2012). 'Reasons to be Cheerful? Conflicting Emotions in the Drunken Old Women of Munich and Rome' in Angelos Chaniotis (ed.), *Unveiling Emotions: Sources and Methods for the Study of Emotions in the Greek World* (Franz Steiner Verlag: Stuttgart), 389–412.

  (2013). 'Phrygians in Relief: Trends in Self-Representation' in Peter Thonemann (ed.), *Roman Phrygia: Culture and Society* (Cambridge University Press: Cambridge), 95–123.

  (2015). *Body Language in Hellenistic Art and Society* (Oxford University Press: Oxford).

Maurizio, L. (2017). 'Shared Metres and Meanings: Delphic Oracles and Women's Lament' in Matthew Dillon, Esther Eidinow, and Lisa Maurizio (eds.), *Women's Ritual Competence in the Greco-Roman Mediterranean* (Routledge: London), 97–114.

McClees, H. (1920). *A Study of Women in Attic Inscriptions* (Columbia University Press: New York).

McClure, L. (1995). 'Female Speech and Characterization in Euripides' in Francesco De Martino and Alan H. Sommerstein (eds.), *Lo Spettacolo delle Voci* (Levante: Bari).

  (1999). *Spoken Like a Woman: Speech and Gender in Athenian Drama* (Princeton University Press: Princeton).

McHugh, M. (2019). 'To Reap a Rich Harvest: Experiencing Agricultural Labour in Ancient Greece', *World Archaeology: Rural Archaeologies*, 51: 208–25.

McKinley, R. (1981). 'Cain and Abel on the Malay Peninsula' in Mac Marshall (ed.), *Siblingship in Oceania: Studies in the Meaning of Kin Relations* (University of Michigan Press: Ann Arbor), 335–418.

  (2001). 'The Philosophy of Kinship: A Reply to Schneider's "Critique of the Study of Kinship"' in Richard Feinberg and Martin Ottenheimer (eds.), *The Cultural Analysis of Kinship: The Legacy of David M. Schneider* (University of Illinois Press: Urbana), 131–67.

Meiggs, R. (1982). *Trees and Timber in the Ancient Mediterranean World* (Clarendon Press: Oxford).

Menken, J., J. Trussell, and S. Watkins (1981). 'The Nutrition Fertility Link: An Evaluation of the Evidence', *The Journal of Interdisciplinary History*, 11: 425.

Meritt, B. D. (1942). 'Greek Inscriptions', *Hesperia: The Journal of the American School of Classical Studies at Athens*, 11: 275–98.

  (1960). 'Greek Inscriptions', *Hesperia: The Journal of the American School of Classical Studies at Athens*, 29: 1–77.

Meyer, E. A. (2010). *Metics and the Athenian Phialai-Inscriptions: A Study in Athenian Epigraphy and Law* (Steiner: Stuttgart).

Miller, M. C. (1997). *Athens and Persia in the Fifth Century B.C.: A Study in Cultural Receptivity* (Cambridge University Press: Cambridge).

Mitchell, A. (2015). 'Humour, Women, and Male Anxieties in Ancient Greek Visual Culture' in Anna Foka and Jonas Liliequist (eds.), *Laughter, Humor, and the (Un)making of Gender: Historical and Cultural Perspectives* (Palgrave Macmillan: Basingstoke), 163–90.

Moeller, W. O. (1976). *The Wool Trade of Ancient Pompeii* (Brill: Leiden).

Moore, J. D. (1982). 'Diogeiton's Dioikisis: Persuasive Language in Lysias 32', *Greek, Roman, and Byzantine Studies*, 23: 351–5.

Morgan, J. (2010). *The Classical Greek House* (Bristol Phoenix Press: Exeter).

Mouffe, C. (1995). 'Feminism, Citizenship, and Radical Democratic Politics' in Linda J. Nicholson and Steven Seidman (eds.), *Social Postmodernism: Beyond Identity Politics* (Cambridge University Press: Cambridge).

Neri, C. (2003). *Erinna: Testimonianze e frammenti* (Pàtron: Bologna).

Nevett, L. C. (1994). 'Separation or Seclusion? Towards an Archaeological Approach to Investigating Women in the Greek Household in the Fifth to Third Centuries BC' in Michael Parker Pearson and Colin Richards (eds.), *Architecture and Order: Approaches to Social Space* (Routledge: London), 89–112.

(1995). 'Gender Relations in the Classical Greek Household: The Archaeological Evidence', *Annual of the British School at Athens*, 90: 363–81.

(2010). *Domestic Space in Classical Antiquity* (Cambridge University Press: Cambridge).

(2011). 'Towards a Female Topography of the Ancient Greek City: Case Studies from Late Archaic and Early Classical Athens (c.520–400 BCE)', *Gender & History*, 23: 576–96.

(2023). *Ancient Greek Housing* (Cambridge University Press: Cambridge).

Nielsen, H. S. (1999). 'Quasi-kin, Quasi-adoption and the Roman Family' in Mireille Corbier (ed.), *Adoption et fosterage* (De Boccard: Paris), 249–62.

Nixon, L. (1999). 'Women, Children, and Weaving', in P. P. Betancourt, V. Karageorghis, R. Laffineur, and W.-D. Niemeier (eds.), *Meletemata: Studies in Aegean Archaeology Presented to Malcolm H. Wiener as He Enters His 65th Year* (Université de Liège and University of Texas: Liège and Austin), 561–7.

Noble, J. V. (1966). *The Techniques of Painted Attic Pottery* (Faber & Faber: London).

Nogueira, C. M. R. (2008/9). 'Conhecimento sobre Aleitamento Materno de Parturientes e Prática de Aleitamento Cruzado na Unidade Hospitalar e Maternidade Venâncio Raimundo de Sousa – Horizonte – Ceará', Doctoral Thesis, Fundação Oswaldo Cruz, Escola Nacional de Saúde Pública Sergio Arouca.

NSPCC (2010). 'Siblings in Care: Law and Practice. An NSPCC Factsheet'.

O'Neill, E. G. (1942). 'The Localization of Metrical Word-Types in the Greek Hexameter: Homer, Hesiod, and the Alexandrians', *Yale Classical Studies*, 8: 105–78.

Oakley, J. H. (2000). 'Some 'Other' Members of the Athenian Household: Maids and Their Mistresses in Fifth-century Athenian Art' in Beth Cohen (ed.), *Not *the Classical Ideal: Athens and the Construction of the Other in Greek Art* (Brill: Leiden), 227–47.

Oakley, J. H., and R. H. Sinos (1993). *The Wedding in Ancient Athens* (University of Wisconsin Press: Madison).

Ober, J. (2010). 'Wealthy Hellas', *Transactions of the American Philological Association*, 140: 241–86.

Obermeyer, C. M. (1979). *Changing Veils: Women and Modernisation in North Yemen* (Croom Helm: London).

Ogden, D. (1996). *Greek Bastardy in the Classical and Hellenistic Periods* (Clarendon Press: Oxford).

Oliver, G. J. (2000). 'Athenian Funerary Monuments: Style, Grandeur and Cost' in G. J. Oliver (ed.), *The Epigraphy of Death: Studies in the History and Society of Greece and Rome* (Liverpool University Press: Liverpool), 59–80.

Oliver, J. H., and S. Dow (1935). 'Greek Inscriptions', *Hesperia: The Journal of the American School of Classical Studies at Athens*, 4: 5–90.

Olson, S. D. (2013). 'Slaves and Politics in Early Aristophanic Comedy' in Ben Akrigg and Rob Tordoff (eds.), *Slaves and Slavery in Ancient Greek Comic Drama* (Cambridge University Press: Cambridge), 63–75.

Osborne, R. (1985a). 'Buildings and Residence on the Land in Classical and Hellenistic Greece: The Contribution of Epigraphy', *Annual of the British School at Athens*, 80: 119–28.

(1985b). *Demos: The Discovery of Classical Attika* (Cambridge University Press: Cambridge).

(1991). 'The Potential Mobility of Human Populations', *The Oxford Journal of Archaeology*, 10: 231–52.

(1997). 'Law, the Democratic Citizen and the Representation of Women in Classical Athens', *Past & Present*, 155: 3–33.

(1999). 'Inscribing Performance' in Simon Goldhill and Robin Osborne (eds.), *Performance Culture and Athenian Democracy* (Cambridge University Press: Cambridge), 341–58.

(2011). 'Local Environment, Memory, and the Formation of the Citizen in Classical Attica' in Stephen D. Lambert (ed.), *Sociable Man: Essays on Ancient Greek Social Behaviour in Honour of Nick Fisher* (Classical Press of Wales: Swansea), 25–43.

Page, D. L. (1942). *Greek Literary Papyri* (Harvard University Press: Cambridge, MA).

Papadopoulos, D. (1951). "Ἔθιμα καὶ Δοξασίαι περὶ τοὺς Νεκροὺς τοῦ Χωρίου Σταυρίν', Ἀρχεῖον Πόντου, 16: 179–97.

Papadopoulou, C. (2015). 'A Brief, Phenomenological Reading of the Arkteia' in Zetta Theodoropoulou Polychroniadis, and Doniert Evely (eds.), *AEGIS: Essays in Mediterranean Archaeology: Presented to Matti Egon by the Scholars of the Greek Archaeological Committee UK* (Archaeopress: Oxford), 147–54.

Parker, R. (1983). *Miasma: Pollution and Purification in Early Greek Religion* (Clarendon Press: Oxford).

(2005). *Polytheism and Society at Athens* (Oxford University Press: Oxford).

Parsons, P. (ed.) (1974). *The Oxyrhynchus Papyri*, Vol. 42 (Egypt Exploration Society: London).

Patterson, C. (1981). *Pericles' Citizenship Law of 451–50 B.C.* (Ayer: Salem).

(1985). '"Not Worth the Rearing": The Causes of Infant Exposure in Ancient Greece', *Transactions of the American Philological Association*, 115: 103–23.

(1991). 'Marriage and the Married Woman in Athenian Law' in Sarah B. Pomeroy (ed.), *Women's History and Ancient History* (University of North Carolina Press: Chapel Hill), 48–72.

(1994). 'The Case against Neaira and the Public Ideology of the Athenian Family' in Alan L. Boegehold and Adele C. Scafuro (eds.), *Athenian Identity and Civic Ideology* (Johns Hopkins University Press: Baltimore, MD), 199–216.

Peek, W. (1960). *Griechische Grabgedichte, griechisch und deutsch* (Akademie-Verlag: Berlin).

Pelling, C. (2000). *Literary Texts and the Greek Historian* (Routledge: London).

Petersen, L. H. (1997). 'Divided Consciousness and Female Companionship: Reconstructing Female Subjectivity on Greek Vases', *Arethusa*, 30: 35–74.

Petrova, M. (2019). 'Single as a Lena: The Depiction of Procuresses in Augustan Literature' in Sabine R. Hübner and Christian Laes (eds.), *The Single Life in the Roman and Later Roman World* (Cambridge University Press: Cambridge), 165–78.

Phelan, K. L. (2016). 'A Social and Historical Commentary on Demosthenes' Against Euboulides', Doctoral Thesis, National University of Ireland.

Photos-Jones, E., C. W. Knapp, D. Venieri, G. E. Christidis, C. Elgy, E. Valsami-Jones, I. Gounaki, and N. C. Andriopoulou (2018). 'Greco-Roman Mineral (Litho)therapeutics and Their Relationship to Their Microbiome: The Case of the Red Pigment Miltos', *Journal of Archaeological Science: Reports*, 22: 179–92.

Pittakis, K. (1839). Untitled article in *Εφημερίς Αρχαιολογική*, 17.

Poland, W. (1893). 'A Sepulchral Inscription from Athens', *American Journal of Archaeology and of the History of the Fine Arts*, 8: 191.

Pomeroy, S. B. (ed.) (1994). *Xenophon: Oeconomicus. A Social and Historical Commentary, with a New English Translation* (Clarendon Press: Oxford).

(1997). *Families in Classical and Hellenistic Greece: Representations and Realities* (Clarendon Press: Oxford).

Pratt, L. (2000). 'The Old Women of Ancient Greece and the Homeric Hymn to Demeter', *Transactions of the American Philological Association*, 130: 41–65.

Pritchard, D. (2014). 'The Position of Attic Women in Democratic Athens', *Greece & Rome*, 61: 174–93.

Pritchett, W. K., and A. Pippin (1956). 'The Attic Stelai: Part II', *Hesperia: The Journal of the American School of Classical Studies at Athens*, 25: 178–328.

Pudsey, A. (2022). 'Housing and Community: Structures in Houses and Kinship in Roman Tebtynis' in Jennifer A. Baird and April Pudsey (eds.), *Housing in the Ancient Mediterranean World: Material and Textual Approaches* (Cambridge University Press: Cambridge), 300–21.

Quercia, A., and L. Foxhall (2014). 'Temporality, Materiality and Women's Networks: The Production and Manufacture of Loom Weights in the Greek and Indigenous Communities of Southern Italy' in Katharina Rebay-Salisbury, Ann Brysbaert, and Lin Foxhall (eds.), *Knowledge Networks and Craft Traditions in the Ancient World: Material Crossovers* (Routledge: New York), 66–82.

Rabinowitz, N. S. (1998). 'Slaves with Slaves: Women and Class in Euripidean Tragedy' in Sandra R. Joshel and Sheila Murnaghan (eds.), *Women and Slaves in Greco-Roman Culture: Differential Equations* (Routledge: London), 56–68.

—— (2002). 'Excavating Women's Homoeroticism in Ancient Greece: The Evidence from Attic Vase Painting' in Nancy Sorkin Rabinowitz and Lisa Auanger (eds.), *Among Women: From the Homosocial to the Homoerotic in the Ancient World* (University of Texas Press: Austin), 106–66.

Raubitschek, A. E. (1949). *Dedications from the Athenian Akropolis: A Catalogue of the Inscriptions of the Sixth and Fifth Centuries* B.C. (Archaeological Institute of America: Cambridge, MA).

Renault, M. (1956). *The Last of the Wine* (Longmans, Green: London).

Rhodes, P. J., and R. Osborne (eds.) (2003). *Greek Historical Inscriptions, 404–323* BC (Oxford University Press: Oxford).

Rhomaios, K. (1905). 'Εὑρήματα ἀνασκαφῆς τοῦ ἐπὶ τῆς Παρνήθος ἄντρου', *Εφημερίς Αρχαιολογική*: 99–158.

—— (1906). 'Εὑρήματα ἀνασκαφῆς τοῦ ἐπὶ τῆς Παρνήθος ἄντρου', *Εφημερίς Αρχαιολογική*: 89–116.

Richlin, A. (ed.) (1992). *Pornography and Representation in Greece and Rome* (Oxford University Press: New York).

Richlin, A. (1993). 'The Ethnographic Dilemma and the Dream of a Lost Golden Age' in Nancy Sorkin Rabinowitz and Amy Richlin (eds.), *Feminist Theory and the Classics* (Routledge: New York), 272–303.

Ricl, M. (2009). 'Legal and Social Status of Threptoi and Related Categories in Narrative and Documentary Sources' in David J. Wasserstein, Hannah M. Cotton, Jonathan J. Price, and Robert G. Hoyland (eds.), *From Hellenism to Islam: Cultural and Linguistic Change in the Roman Near East* (Cambridge University Press: Cambridge), 93–114.

Rieth, O., and K. Gaiser (1964). *Die Kunst Menanders in den 'Adelphen' des Terenz* (G. Olms: Hildesheim).

Robinson, D. M. (1937). *Corpus Vasorum Antiquorum: United States of America. The Robinson Collection, Baltimore, Md.* (Harvard University Press: Cambridge, MA).

Roebuck, D. (2001). *Ancient Greek Arbitration* (Arbitration Press, HOLO Books: Oxford).

Rosivach, V. J. (1989). '"Talasiourgoi" and "Paidia" in IG II² 1553–78: A Note on Athenian Social History', *Historia: Zeitschrift für Alte Geschichte*, 38: 365–70.

Ross, L. (1837). 'Inschriften. Ueber Attische Gräbe und Grabschriften' in *Intelligenzblatt der Allgemeinen Literatur-Zeitung*, 5: 689–712.

Roy, J. (1988). 'Demosthenes 55 as Evidence for Isolated Farmsteads in Classical Attica', *Liverpool Classical Monthly*, 13: 57–9.

Rubinstein, L. (1993). *Adoption in iv. Century Athens* (Museum Tusculanum Press: Copenhagen).

(2000). *Litigation and Cooperation: Supporting Speakers in the Courts of Classical Athens* (Verlag: Stuttgart).

(2018). 'Summary Fines in Greek Inscriptions and the Question of "Greek Law"' in Paula Jean Perlman (ed.), *Ancient Greek Law in the 21st Century* (University of Texas Press: Austin), 104–43.

(2021). 'Penalties in Delphic Paramone Clauses: A Gender Perspective' in K. Harter-Uibopuu and W. Reiss (eds.), *Symposion 2019: Vorträge zur Griechischen und Hellenistischen Rechtsgeschichte* (Verlag der Österreichischen Akademie der Wissenschaften: Vienna), 455–79.

Rudhardt, J. (1962). 'La reconnaissance de la paternité, sa nature et sa portée dans la société athénienne: Sur un discours de Démosthène', *Museum Helveticum*, 19: 39–64.

Sahlins, M. (2013). *What Kinship Is – And Is Not* (The University of Chicago Press: Chicago).

Saliou, C. (1992). 'Les quatre fils de Polémocratès (P. Dura 19): Texte et archéologie', *Syria*, 69: 65–100.

Saller, R. P. (1994). *Patriarchy, Property and Death in the Roman Family* (Cambridge University Press: Cambridge).

(1998). 'Symbols of Gender and Status Hierarchies in the Roman Household' in Sandra R. Joshel and Sheila Murnaghan (eds.), *Women and Slaves in Greco-Roman Culture: Differential Equations* (Routledge: London), 85–91.

Sawtell, C. (2018). 'Non-Citizen Commemoration in Fifth and Fourth Century BC Attica', Doctoral Thesis, University of Sheffield.

Scafuro, A. C. (1994). 'Witnessing and False Witnessing: Proving Citizenship and Kin Identity in Fourth-Century Athens' in Alan L. Boegehold and Adele C. Scafuro (eds.), *Athenian Identity and Civic Ideology* (Johns Hopkins University Press: Baltimore).

Scafuro, A. C. (ed.) (2011). *Demosthenes: Speeches 39–49* (University of Texas Press: Austin).

Schaps, D. M. (1977). 'The Woman Least Mentioned: Etiquette and Women's Names', *Classical Quarterly*, 27: 323–30.

(1979). *Economic Rights of Women in Ancient Greece* (Edinburgh University Press: Edinburgh).

Scheidel, W. (1995). 'The Most Silent Women of Greece and Rome: Rural Labour and Women's Life in the Ancient World (1)', *Greece & Rome*, 42: 202–17.

(1996). 'The Most Silent Women of Greece and Rome: Rural Labour and Women's Life in The Ancient World (11)', *Greece & Rome*, 43: 1–10.

(2009). 'The Demographic Background' in Sabine R. Hübner and David M. Ratzan (eds.), *Growing Up Fatherless in Antiquity* (Cambridge University Press: Cambridge), 31–40.

(2010). 'Real Wages in Early Economies: Evidence for Living Standards from 1800 BCE to 1300 CE', *Journal of the Economic and Social History of the Orient*, 53: 425–62.

Schmitz, W. (2012). '"Sklavenfamilien" im archaischen und klassischen Griechenland', in Johannes Deissler and Heinz Heinen (eds.), *Kindersklaven – Sklavenkinder: Schicksale zwischen Zuneigung und Ausbeutung in der Antike und im interkulturellen Vergleich: Beiträge zur Tagung des Akademievorhabens Forschungen zur antiken Sklaverei (Mainz, 14. Oktober 2008)* (Franz Steiner Verlag: Stuttgart), 63–102.

Schneider, D. M. (1968). *American Kinship: A Cultural Account* (Prentice-Hall: Englewood Cliffs).

(1984). *A Critique of the Study of Kinship* (University of Michigan Press: Ann Arbor).

Schömann, G. F. (1830). *Isäus der Redner* (J.B. Metzler: Stuttgart).

(1831). *Isaei Orationes XI cum Aliquot Deperditarum Fragmentis, Recogn. Annotationem Criticam et Comm. Adjecit G.F. Schömann* (Impensis E. Mauritii: Greifswald).

Schörner, G., H. R. Goette, and K. Hallof (2004). *Die Pan-Grotte von Vari* (Philipp von Zabern: Mainz am Rhein).

Schulthess, O. (1886). *Vormundschaft nach attischem Recht* (Mohr: Freiburg).

Schulze, B. (2004). *Die Votivtafeln der Archaischen und Klassischen Zeit von der Athener Akropolis* (Bibliopolis: Möhnesee).

Schulze, H. (1998). *Ammen und Pädagogen: Sklavinnen und Sklaven als Erzieher in der Antiken Kunst und Gesellschaft* (Philipp von Zabern: Mainz am Rhein).

Sebillotte Cuchet, V. (2017) '"Gender studies" et domination masculine: Les citoyennes de l'Athènes classique, un défi pour l'historien des institutions', *Cahiers du Centre Gustave Glotz*, 28: 7–30.

Shear, T. L. (1937). 'The Campaign of 1936', *Hesperia: The Journal of the American School of Classical Studies at Athens*, 6: 333–81.

Shibamoto, J. S. (1987). 'The Womanly Woman: Manipulation of Stereotypical and Nonstereotypical Features of Japanese Female Speech' in Susan Urmston Philips, Susan Steele, and Christine Tanz (eds.), *Language, Gender, and Sex in Comparative Perspective* (Cambridge University Press: Cambridge), 26–49.

Simon, E. (1963). 'Ein Anthesterien-skyphos des Polygnotos', *Antike Kunst*, 6: 6–22.

Skias, A. (1918). Τὸ παρὰ τὴν Φυλὴν ἄντρον τοῦ Πανὸς', Αρχαιολογική Εφημερίς: 1–28.

Skinner, M. B. (1987). *Rescuing Creusa: New Methodological Approaches to Women in Antiquity* (Texas Tech University Press: Lubbock).

Sneed, D. (2021). 'Disability and Infanticide in Ancient Greece', *Hesperia: The Journal of the American School of Classical Studies at Athens*, 90: 747–72.

Snodgrass, A. M. (1989–90). 'The Economics of Dedication at Greek Sanctuaries', *Scienze dell'antichità: Storia, archeologia, antropologia*, 3: 287–94.

Snyder, J. M. (1981). 'The Web of Song: Weaving Imagery in Homer and the Lyric Poets', *The Classical Journal*, 76: 193–6.

Sommerstein, A. H. (ed.) (1983). *Aristophanes: Wasps* (Aris & Phillips: Warminster).

(1994). *Aristophanes: Thesmophoriazusae* (Aris & Phillips: Warminster).

(1996). *Aristophanes: Frogs* (Aris & Phillips: Warminster).

(1998). *Aristophanes: Ecclesiazusae* (Aris & Phillips: Warminster).

(2005). *Aristophanes: Peace* (Aris & Phillips: Warminster).

(2007). *Aristophanes: Lysistrata* (Aris & Phillips: Warminster).

(2009). 'The Naming of Women in Greek and Roman Comedy' in Alan H. Sommerstein (ed.), *Talking about Laughter and Other Studies in Greek Comedy* (Oxford University Press: Oxford), 43–69.

(2013). *Menander: Samia* (Cambridge University Press: Cambridge).

Sosin, J. D. (2015). 'Manumission with "Paramone": Conditional Freedom?', *TAPA*, 145: 325–81.

Sourvinou-Inwood, C. (1971). 'Aristophanes, Lysistrata, 641–647', *Classical Quarterly*, 21: 339–42.

(1988). *Studies in Girls' Transitions: Aspects of the Arkteia and Age Representation in Attic Iconography* (Kardamitsa: Athens).

Sowry, N. (2012). 'Silence, Accessibility, and Reading against the Grain: Examining Voices of the Marginalized in the India Office Records', *InterActions: UCLA Journal of Education and and Information Studies*, 8.2. https://doi.org/10.5070/D482011848.

Spantidaki, S. (2016). *Textile Production in Classical Athens* (Oxbow Books: Oxford).

Spelman, E. V. (1988). *Inessential Woman: Problems of Exclusion in Feminist Thought* (Beacon Press: Boston).

Spivey, N. J. (1991). 'Greek Vases in Etruria' in Tom Rasmussen and Nigel Jonathan Spivey (eds.), *Looking at Greek Vases* (Cambridge University Press: Cambridge), 131–50.

Stafford, C. (2000). 'Chinese Patriliny and the Cycles of yang and laiwang' in Janet Carsten (ed.), *Cultures of Relatedness: New Approaches to the Study of Kinship* (Cambridge University Press: Cambridge), 37–54.

Stanley, L. (1992). *The Auto/biographical I: The Theory and Practice of Feminist Auto/biography* (Manchester University Press: Manchester).

Steiner, A. (2002). 'Private and Public: Links between Symposion and Syssition in Fifth-Century Athens', *Classical Antiquity*, 21.2, 347–90.

Stoler, A. L. (1985). 'Perceptions of Protest: Defining the Dangerous in Colonial Sumatra', *American Ethnologist*, 12.4, 642–58.

Strathern, M. (1988). *The Gender of the Gift: Problems with Women and Problems with Society in Melanesia* (University of California Press: Berkeley).

(1992). *After Nature: English Kinship in the Late Twentieth Century* (Cambridge University Press: Cambridge).

Sutton, R. F. (1992). 'Pornography and Persuasion on Attic Pottery' in Amy Richlin (ed.), *Pornography and Representation in Greece and Rome* (Oxford University Press: New York), 3–35.

(1997–8). 'Nuptial Eros: The Visual Discourse of Marriage in Classical Athens', *The Journal of the Walters Art Gallery*, 55/56: 27–48.

(2004). 'Family Portraits: Recognizing the "Oikos" on Attic Red-Figure Pottery', *Hesperia Supplements*, 33: 327–50.

Taylor, C. (2011a). 'Graffiti and the Epigraphic Habit: Creating Communities and Writing Alternate Histories in Classical Attica' in Jennifer A. Baird and Claire Taylor (eds.), *Ancient Graffiti in Context* (Routledge: New York), 90–109.

(2011b). 'Migration and the Demes of Attica' in Claire Holleran and April Pudsey (eds.), *Demography and the Graeco-Roman World: New Insights and Approaches* (Cambridge University Press: Cambridge).

(2011c). 'Women's Social Networks and Female Friendship in the Ancient Greek City', *Gender & History*, 23: 703–20.

(2015a). 'Graffiti in a House in Attica: Reading, Writing and the Creation of Private Space' in Rebecca Benefiel and Peter Keegan (eds.), *Inscriptions in the Private Sphere in the Greco-Roman World* (Brill: Leiden), 117–34.

(2015b). 'Social Networks and Social Mobility in Fourth-Century Athens' in Claire Taylor and Kostas Vlassopoulos (eds.), *Communities and Networks in the Ancient Greek World* (Oxford University Press: Oxford), 32–59.

(2017). *Poverty, Wealth, and Well-Being: Experiencing Penia in Democratic Athens* (Oxford University Press: Oxford).

(2020). 'Onomastic Patterns of So-Called Hetaira Names in the Greek World', *Mètis: Anthropologie des mondes grecs anciens*, 18: 55–81.

(2024). 'Women, Gender and the Ancient Economy: Towards a Feminist Economic History of the Ancient Greek World', *Journal of Hellenic Studies*, 144: 1–28.

Taylor, C., and K. Vlassopoulos (eds.) (2015). *Communities and Networks in the Ancient Greek World* (Oxford University Press: Oxford).

Tchernetska, N., E. Handley, C. Austin, and L. Horváth (2007). 'New Readings in the Fragment of Hyperides' "Against Timandros" from the Archimedes Palimpsest', *Zeitschrift für Papyrologie und Epigraphik*, 162: 1–4.

Thalmann, W. G. (1998). 'Female Slaves in the Odyssey' in Sandra R. Joshel and Sheila Murnaghan (eds.), *Women and Slaves in Greco-Roman Culture: Differential Equations* (Routledge: London), 22–34.

Thompson, W. E. (1972). 'Athenian Marriage Patterns: Remarriage', *California Studies in Classical Antiquity*, 5: 211–25.

Thonemann, P. (2020). 'Lysimache and Lysistrata', *Journal of Hellenic Studies*, 140: 128–42.

(2022). *The Lives of Ancient Villages: Rural Society in Roman Anatolia* (Cambridge University Press: Cambridge).

Thorley, V. (2008). 'Breasts for Hire and Shared Breastfeeding: Wet Nursing and Cross Feeding in Australia, 1900–2000', *Health and History*, 10: 88–109.

(2009). 'Mothers' Experiences of Sharing Breastfeeding or Breastmilk: Co-feeding in Australia 1978–2008', *Breastfeeding Review*, 17: 9–18.

Todd, S. C. (1993). *The Shape of Athenian Law* (Clarendon Press: Oxford).

Todd, S. C. (ed.) (2000). *Lysias* (University of Texas Press: Austin).

Tsagalis, C. (2008). *Inscribing Sorrow: Fourth-Century Attic Funerary Epigrams* (De Gruyter: Berlin).

Tsakirgis, B. (2016). 'Whole Cloth: Exploring the Question of Self-Sufficiency through the Evidence for Textile Manufacture and Purchase in Greek Houses' in David M. Lewis, Edward M. Harris and Mark Woolmer (eds.), *The Ancient Greek Economy: Markets, Households and City-States* (Cambridge University Press: Cambridge), 166–86.

Tuck, A. (2006). 'Singing the Rug: Patterned Textiles and the Origins of Indo-European Metrical Poetry', *American Journal of Archaeology*, 110: 539–50.

Tueller, M. A. (2008). *Look Who's Talking: Innovations in Voice and Identity in Hellenistic Epigram* (Peeters: Leuven).

Venit, M. (1988). 'The Caputi Hydria and Working Women in Classical Athens', *Classical World*, 81: 265.

Venticinque, P. (2022). 'Bound for Success: Cursing and Commerce in Classical Athens', *Greece & Rome*, 69: 52–71.

Vernant, J.-P. (1980–1). 'Étude comparée des religions antiques', *Annuaire du Collège de France*, 81: 391–405.

Vestergaard, T. (2000). 'Milesian Immigrants in Late Hellenistic and Roman Athens' in Graham J. Oliver (ed.), *The Epigraphy of Death: Studies in the History and Society of Greece and Rome* (Liverpool University Press: Liverpool), 391–405.

Vickers, M. (1985). 'Artful Crafts: The Influence of Metal Work on Athenian Painted Pottery', *Journal of Hellenic Studies*, 105: 108–28.

Vlassopoulos, K. (2007). 'Free Spaces: Identity, Experience and Democracy in Classical Athens', *Classical Quarterly*, 57: 33–52.

(2010). 'Athenian Slave Names and Athenian Social History', *Zeitschrift für Papyrologie und Epigraphik*, 175: 113–44.

(2011). 'Two Images of Ancient Slavery: The "Living Tool" and the Koinônia' in Elisabeth Herrmann-Otto (ed.), *Sklaverei und Zwangsarbeit zwischen Akzeptanz und Widerstand* (Georg Olms Verlag: Hildesheim), 465–75.

(2014). 'Which Comparative Histories for Ancient Historians?', *Synthesis (La Plata)*, 21: 31–47.

(2015). 'Plotting Strategies, Networks, and Communities in Classical Athens: The Evidence of Slave Names' in Claire Taylor and Kostas Vlassopoulos (eds.), *Communities and Networks in the Ancient Greek World* (Oxford University Press: Oxford), 101–27.

Von Seehausen, M. P., M. I. C. de Oliveira, and C. S. Boccolini (2017). 'Fatores associados ao aleitamento cruzado', *Ciencia & Saude Coletiva*, 22: 1673–82.

Von Seehausen, M. P., M. I. C. de Oliveira, C. S. Boccolini, and M. de C. Leal (2017). 'Fatores associados ao aleitamento cruzado em duas cidades do sudeste do Brasil', *Cadernos de Saúde Pública*, 33.4.

Wagner-Hasel, B., and M.-L. Nosch (eds.) (2019).*Gaben, Waren und Tribute. Stoffkreisläufe und antike Textilökonomie. Akten eines Symposiums (9./10. Juni 2016 in Hannover)* (Franz Steiner Verlag: Stuttgart).

Walter, O. (1937). 'Die Reliefs aus dem Heiligtum der Echeliden in Neu-Phaleron', *Αρχαιολογική Εφημερίς*, 100: 97–119.

Watson, J. L. (1982). 'Chinese Kinship Reconsidered: Anthropological Perspectives on Historical Research', *The China Quarterly*, 92: 589–622.

—— (1986). 'Anthropological Overview: The Development of Chinese Descent Groups' in Patricia B. Ebrey and James L. Watson (eds.), *Kinship Organization in Late Imperial China, 1000–1940* (University of California Press: Berkeley), 274–92.

Watson, P. A. (1995). *Ancient Stepmothers: Myth, Misogyny and Reality* (Brill: Leiden).

Weber, M. (1982). *Gesammelte Aufsätze zur Wissenschaftslehre* 5th ed. (J. C. B. Mohr: Tübingen). First published 1922.

Weber, M., E. Shils, and H. A. Finch (1949). *The Methodology of the Social Sciences* (Free Press: New York).

West, M. L. (1977). 'Erinna', *Zeitschrift für Papyrologie und Epigraphik*, 25: 95–119.

—— (1978). *Hesiod: Works and Days* (Clarendon Press: Oxford).

Whitehead, D. (1986). *The Demes of Attica, 508/7–ca. 250 B.C.: A Political and Social Study* (Princeton University Press: Princeton).

—— (1990). 'Abbreviated Athenian Demotics', *Zeitschrift für Papyrologie und Epigraphik*, 81: 105–61.

—— (2009). 'Hypereides' *Timandros*: Observations and Suggestions', *Bulletin of the Institute of Classical Studies*, 52: 135–48.

Wilhelm, A. (1904). 'Über die Zeit einiger Attischer Fluchtafeln', *Jahreshefte des Österreichischen Archäologischen Institutes in Wien*, 7: 105–26.

Wilhelm, A., H. Engelmann, and K. Wundsam (1980). *Griechische Epigramme* (R. Habelt: Bonn).

Willi, A. (2003). *The Languages of Aristophanes: Aspects of Linguistic Variation in Classical Attic Greek* (Oxford University Press: Oxford).

Williams, D. (2009). 'Picturing Potters and Painters' in John Howard Oakley and Olga Palagia (eds.), *Athenian Potters and Painters, Volume* II (Oxbow Books: Oxford), 306–17.

Williams, J. R. (1968). *The Youth of Haouch el Harimi, a Lebanese Village* (Harvard University Press: Cambridge, MA).

Wilson, P. J. (1996). 'Tragic Rhetoric: The Use of Tragedy and the Tragic in the Fourth Century' in Michael S. Silk (ed.), *Tragedy and the Tragic: Greek Theatre and Beyond* (Clarendon Press: Oxford), 310–31.

Winkler, J. J. (1990). *The Constraints of Desire: The Anthropology of Sex and Gender in Ancient Greece* (Routledge: New York).

Wolicki, A. (2021). 'Greek Priestesses and Literacy' in Irene Salvo and Tanja Susanne Scheer (eds.), *Religion and Education in the Ancient Greek World* (Mohr Siebeck: Tübingen), 183–96.

Wrenhaven, K. L. (2009). 'The Identity of the "Wool-Workers" in the Attic Manumissions', *Hesperia: The Journal of the American School of Classical Studies at Athens*, 78: 367–86.

—— (2012). *Reconstructing the Slave: The Image of the Slave in Ancient Greece* (Bristol Classical Press: London).

Wyse, W. (1904). *The Speeches of Isaeus* (Cambridge University Press: Cambridge).

Yee, G. A. (2009). '"Take This Child and Suckle It for Me": Wet Nurses and Resistance in Ancient Israel', *Biblical Theology Bulletin*, 39: 180–9.

Zak, G. (2012). 'Modes of Self-Writing from Antiquity to the Later Middle Ages' in Ralph J. Hexter and David Townsend (eds.), *The Oxford Handbook of Medieval Latin Literature* (Oxford University Press: New York), 485–507.

Zweig, B. (1992). 'The Mute Nude Female Characters in Aristophanes' Plays' in Amy Richlin (ed.), *Pornography and Representation in Greece and Rome* (Oxford University Press: New York), 63–89.

Index Locorum

Aeschylus
  Agamemnon: 175
  Choephori: 118
    759–60 and 896–8: 189
  Eumenides 658–61: 109
Agora Inv. IL 1702: 8
Andocides 1
  48: 120
  124–7: 146–7, 149
Antiphanes
  Akestria: 223
  Frg. 89: 165–7
Antiphon 1: 177, 278–9
Antiphon the Sophist, Frg. 49 Pendrick:
    9
Apollodorus of Karystos, Frg. 30: 223
Apollodorus, *Against Neaira*: 74, 126, 134–5,
    148–9, 176, 195
  29–35: 195, 322
  35 and 46: 62, 192
  37–47: 322
  50–63: 86–7, 110–11, 144–6
Aristophanes
  Acharnians 146 (schol.): 303
  Birds 493–4: 308
  Clouds 41–55: 290
  Ecclesiazusae: 293
    41–51: 3
    241–7: 241
    348–9: 336
    528–9: 300, 327, 336
    1023–5: 40
  Frg. 274 Kock: 246, 271–3
  Frogs
    549–78: 238, 241, 242
    959: 225, 278
    1342–63: 225–6, 272, 278
  Lysistrata: 5, 7
    1–4: 287–93
    5–8: 9, 239, 271, 273, 327
    176–9: 241–2

    329–30: 164, 283
    379: 243
    435–6: 243
    456–60: 241–2
    463–5: 243
    495: 164
    556–64: 239–40
    645: 295
    699–701: 274, 293, 327
    911–79: 290
  Peace 1127–39: 172
  Thesmophoriazusae: 293
    293–4: 70
    340–2: 178
    347–8: 245
    443–58: 196, 238–9
    484–5: 275
    502–16: 179
    558–9: 179, 303–4
    603–18: 70, 311
    624: 296
    898: 37
  Wasps
    235–9: 241
    488–503: 195, 239
    1388–414: 241–3
  Wealth 426–36: 241, 245, 273
  Women Claiming Tent-Sites:
    315
Aristotle
  Nicomachean Ethics
    1159b-1160a: 12
    1161b: 108–9
  Rhetoric 1395b: 267
[Aristotle]
  Athenaion politeia
    26: 12
    43: 248
    50: 275
    51: 248
  Oeconomicus 1347a: 275

Index Feminarum

List of attested classical Attic women discussed.

Aitherion (*IG* 11² 2347; member of *thiasos*
   honouring several benefactors), 306
Alke (Isaeus 6; survivor of sex slavery, partnered
   with a freedman and then her former
   enslaver(?)), 111, 144, 148–55, 176, 177,
   277–8
Ameinokleia (*IG* 1² 1082; daughter of
   Andromenes, commemorated with relief
   showing enslaved girl), 159, 168–70
Ampharete (*IG* 11² 10650; grandmother,
   commemorated with daughter's child),
   59, 121–3
Anthemis (*IG* 1³ 1329; commemorated by
   companions in memory of her excellence
   and friendship), 329–31
Antidike (*IG* 1³ 1409bis; graffitist, carved name at
   Laureion), 37
Antiphile (*IG* 11² 6873, *IG* 11³ 700; client(?) and
   commemorator of Phanostrate), 252–8
Anyta (*DTA* 68; tavern-keeper, named in
   curse), 244
Apollodora (Isaeus 7; mother of Apollodoros
   and *Arkhedike*, persuaded second
   husband to raise child from first
   marriage?), 81, 123–7
Areskousa (*DTA* 68; go-between or 'procuress',
   named in curse), 244
Aristonike (1) (*RA* (1968,1) 157; commemorated
   alongside Bako, Sokrates, with relief
   showing two enslaved women and
   a baby), 183
Aristonike (2) (*SEG* 18:36 B 112–22; daughter of
   Malthake (1) and Attas the pulse-seller(?),
   sister of Plangon and Moskhon), 228,
   232–3
Arkhedike (Isaeus 7; daughter of Arkhedamos and
   Apollodora, close relationship with
   brother Apollodoros, who adopted her
   son), 81, 85, 148, 155–6

Arkhestrate (*IG* 11² 7227; missed by mother,
   brother, child, and especially husband
   after death), 330
Arkhippe (1) (*IG* 11² 6216; commemorated with
   brother, husband, and sister-in-law
   Nikoptoleme), 94
Arkhippe (2) ([Demosthenes] 45; wife of bankers
   Pasion then Phormion, received two
   enslaved women in Pasion's will),
   160, 192
Arkhis (NAM 14470; *laikastria* (prostitute),
   named in curse against network of
   litigants, grain traders, and
   prostitutes), 247
Artemis (1) (*I.Eleusis* 177.64; seller of reeds to
   Eleusinion from Piraeus warehouse),
   233–7
Artemis (2) (*DTA* 69; gilder, wife of Dionysios
   the helmet-maker, named in curse), 238

Bako (*RA* (1968,1) 157; commemorated alongside
   Aristonike and Sokrates, with relief
   showing two enslaved women and
   a baby), 183
Biote (*IG* 1³ 1295bis; *hetaira* of Euthylla), 327–32

Demokleia (*IG* 11² 5479; commemorated with
   brother and husband), 94
Diognete (Lysias 32; separated, widowed,
   remarried, mobilised network to
   prosecute father), 1–2, 4–5, 7–8, 17,
   48–66, 72–7, 81, 192, 321–2
Doris (*IG* 11³ 700; daughter of Delophanes and
   Lysimakhe, for whose health she prayed),
   254–6

Elephantis (*IG* 11² 11254; *himation*-seller), 226–8
Empedia (*IG* 1³ 767; dedicator of marble column
   as *dekatè*), 204, 261

General Index

abuse, 55, 160, 320
    by guardian, 51–5, 57, 65, 81
    financial, 51–5, 57, 65, 81, 320
    sexual, of enslaved women, 170–7
    verbal, 241
        see also violence, male
Adonia, 8, 269, 312–13
adoption, 82–6, 141–57
    as part of 'kinship doubling', 57
    'at the persuasion of a woman', 84, 141–57
    does not sever relationship to mother, 143, 341
    patriarchal and patrilineal, 102, 111, 142–3
    to perpetuate *oikos* and ensure care in old age,
        85, 107, 110–11, 143
    women as gatekeepers, 155–7
affines: *see* relatives, spousal
Afghanistan, 3, 215
age
    agelessness of women on pots, 185
    factor in affection between brothers, 109
    factor in experience of widowhood, 72–3
    friendship between women of different,
        269–70, 325, 336
    older women, 128, 136, 175, 179, 239, 242, 338
        see also care, of elderly; demography
agency
    framework for feminist historiography, 20
    limitations on women's, 25, 129, 323
    of enslaved women, 15, 62, 163–4, 195, 283
    over inscribed objects, 20, 33–43
        see also persuasion; property, women's
        control of
agora
    morality, 163, 214, 226, 239–40
    retail, 225–6, 228, 243
    sociality, 163–4, 243
agriculture, 194–6, 282–3
Akropolis, 198–218, 236–7, 249, 254, 290, 314
alcohol: *see* drinking
America
    antebellum American South, 191
    twentieth-century North America, 24, 131
amphidromia, 152, 292, 300, 308
androcentrism
    of scholarship, 25, 44, 265
    of sources, 4, 44, 48, 230, 326
Anthesteria, 2, 189
anthrōpos, used derogatorily of women, 86,
        153, 179
anxiety
    about absent husbands, 5
    about disruption to *oikos*, 59, 175
    about female sexuality, 103, 157
    about first week postpartum, 300
    about grain supply, 248
    about women's influence over kinship, 103,
        142–3, 157, 304
    at Arkteia, 294–5
    male, 129, 142–3, 157, 177–82, 307
        (*see also* authority, challenges
        to male)
aparkhē: *see* dedication, first-offering
Apatouria, 146, 179, 301–4
Aphrodite, 8, 290–1
Apollo, 113, 249, 278
arbitration, 61–3, 160, 192
Arkteia, 294–5
Artemis, 127, 302
    at Brauron, 186, 200, 294–5, 313–14
Asklepios, 127, 254–6
Athena, 33, 198–218
    Ergane, 198–218
    Parthenos, 1
    Phratria, 303
    Promakhos, 263
    represented on loom weights, 212–13
    suspicious of remarried women, 65
Australia, 130–1
authority
    challenges to male, 63, 73, 178, 231, 271
    in household, 53, 63, 164–7, 173–7, 231
    nurses as figures of, 214